The Broadview Anthology of

SEVENTEENTH-CENTURY
VERSE & PROSE

VOLUME I: VERSE

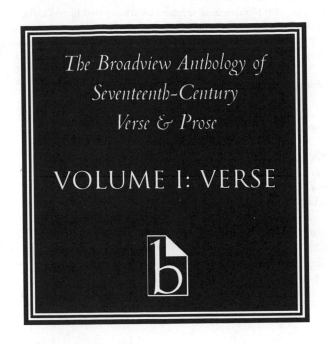

The Broadview Anthology of
Seventeenth-Century
Verse & Prose

VOLUME I: VERSE

EDITED BY

ALAN RUDRUM, JOSEPH BLACK, & HOLLY FAITH NELSON

BROADVIEW ANTHOLOGIES OF ENGLISH LITERATURE

broadview press

Canadian Cataloguing in Publication Data

Main entry under title:
  The Broadview anthology of seventeenth-century verse and prose

(Broadview anthologies of English literature)
Includes bibliographical references and indexes.
Contents: v. 1. Verse — v. 2. Prose.
ISBN 1-55111-462-3 (v. 1)   ISBN 1-55111-463-1 (v. 2)

1. English poetry – Early modern, 1500-1700. 2. English prose literature – Early modern, 1500-1700. I. Rudrum, Alan, 1932- . II. Black, Joseph Laurence, 1962- . III. Nelson, Holly Faith, 1966- . IV. Series.

PR1127.B76 2001   820.8'004   B2001-930370-X

Broadview Press Ltd., is an independent, international publishing house, incorporated in 1985.

North America:
P.O. Box 1243, Peterborough, Ontario, Canada K9J 7H5
3576 California Road, Orchard Park, NY 14127
TEL: (705) 743-8990; FAX: (705) 743-8353;
E-MAIL: customerservice@broadviewpress.com

United Kingdom:
Turpin Distribution Services Ltd.,
Blackhorse Rd., Letchworth, Hertfordshire SG6 1HN
TEL: (1462) 672555; FAX (1462) 480947; E-MAIL: turpin@rsc.org

Australia:
St. Clair Press, P.O. Box 287, Rozelle, NSW 2039
TEL: (02) 818-1942; FAX: (02) 418-1923

www.broadviewpress.com

Broadview Press gratefully acknowledges the financial support of the Book Publishing Industry Development Program, Ministry of Canadian Heritage, Government of Canada.

Cover design by George Kirkpatrick

PRINTED IN CANADA

Copyrights

✑✐✑

Editorial Preface

Regular church-goers have sometimes remarked on an oddity of modern preaching: many sermons are delivered in apparent unawareness of the last two centuries of biblical scholarship and theological discussion. To a less dramatic extent, there has been a similar situation in the resources available to students of seventeenth-century literature. For many years now, no teaching anthology has been available which reflects current scholarship and criticism. As long ago as 1986 I wrote to a major American publisher, drawing attention to this situation. They were not interested, and there the matter rested until several years later a publisher's representative came to my office, and I suggested that his firm might consider the relationship between scholarly discussion and available classroom texts. No longer thinking of compiling such an anthology myself, and unaware that I was talking to Broadview's president, I had no idea what this brief conversation was to lead to.

One more piece of history. On accepting the commission I suggested that, while I take responsibility for male-authored verse, two editors be appointed to take overall responsibility for male-authored prose and for women's writing. The assumption was that both would be senior scholars. However, shortly after Professor David Wootton joined the project he accepted a chair in England with administrative responsibilities, and thereafter lacked time to contribute. He did, however, make a number of useful suggestions for which we are grateful. I eventually suggested that Holly Nelson, then a Ph.D. candidate at Simon Fraser University, should take responsibility for women's writing. Later, Joseph Black, then of the University of Toronto, took responsibility for prose; he also suggested and prepared several verse selections.

Literature used to be taught as *belles-lettres*. Texts were valued for their aesthetic qualities, and studied for the most part with little reference to the historical moment into which they were published. Milton, for example, was taught, and treated in histories of literature, as a pre-Restoration author, though his major poems were published, and almost certainly mainly written, after 1660. The aim of this anthology is certainly not to suggest that readers should forget about aesthetic quality. If we did not enjoy literature, there would be small point in reading it. However, if we feel the need to understand what we enjoy, we may well find ourselves taken out of "literature" and into "life," which is rarely aesthetically shaped. We shall find ourselves thinking of the historical context of what we read, of what the author hoped his or her work might accomplish in the furtherance of a particular project. We shall want to set ourselves at an author's own viewpoint, to learn, so far as we can, of the formative influences that turned the person into the writer. What about their families, their schools or their tutors? Why did Westminster School, for example, produce so many poets? Were the parents or grandparents of a given writer Catholic or Protestant? What did such choices mean to a family's security or hope of prosperity? What sort of influence might family background have at the point when minds had to be made up as political and religious tensions broke into civil war? What social forces operated to bring it about that people of similar religious views found themselves on opposite sides in that conflict? How did censorship, implicit or official, operate through that author's writing lifetime? How did education, personality, impoverishment or the possibility of enrichment combine to lead people into this choice or that? How did the social networks in which given authors lived and wrote influence their work? How was the meaning of texts shaped by the material conditions of their publication and distribution?

This anthology has been compiled in order to suggest the importance of such questions, and to provide some of the materials that students of seventeenth-century literature will need in their own explorations. What James VI/I thought about kingship might not be great literature; set out in his own words, it suggests vividly the atmosphere in which those who sought influence had to operate. Lawrence Clarkson's autobiographical *The Lost Sheep Found* and Thomas Edwards's *Gangraena* might not be the finest examples of the period's prose, but one illustrates the variety of religious choices briefly available, and the other the virulence of anti-tolerationist sentiment that such choices gave rise to in those (and they were the majority) who thought that their way was the only way. These are three examples of works which have not formerly been anthologized along with "canonical" literature. Most of the women's writing, of course, also falls into that category.

Analysis and comparison have been said to be the tools of criticism, and we have tried to make comparison possible, for example by including more than one "country house" poem, more than one poem on Jonson's response to the disastrous reception of *The New Inn*, more than one translation of Horace's "Beatus ille" ode. We have also tried, in headnotes and footnotes, to cross-refer from one such work to another to facilitate such comparisons. Some of our headnotes are longer than is customary. If we seem to be following Samuel Johnson's enjoyment of "the biographical part of literature" it is in the hope that a knowledge of the life will promote interest in and understanding of the work. In the early stages a good deal of thought was given to footnotes, and I liked the suggestion of one correspondent, who shares my view that annotating a poem is perhaps the best way to discipline oneself to a careful reading, that some poems should be printed "blank" and then again with notes. The question had to be faced as to whether detailed annotation is likely to facilitate learning, or to impede it. In the end, habit, custom, and the realization that very few undergraduates are likely to have the time and resources to deal on their own with poets such as Cleveland or Vaughan led me to think that we should annotate as thoroughly as possible. One pitfall of working in this period is that many words were spelled as they are today, and appear in contexts in which today's meanings look plausible, but may not represent the author's intentions: "horrid," "nice," and "conscience" readily spring to mind. When we are reading *Sir Gawain and the Green Knight*, we know that we are on unfamiliar linguistic territory; early modern English, in its apparent similarity to our own language, is more insidious; and we have tried to bear this too in mind when annotating. Of course, experience suggests that full accuracy in editing is difficult.

Numerous queries about our progress, in the last two years or so, suggest that university and college teachers were anxious to see the anthology in print. I am sorry for what must have seemed a slow march to completion. All three of us have experienced periods when work on the anthology had to give way to other priorities. We all hope that the result of our labours will be found at least provisionally satisfactory: a benefit of modern printing technology is the comparative ease with which improvements can be incorporated, and we shall be glad to receive comments and suggestions.

Alan Rudrum
Vancouver, April 23, 2000

A NOTE ON MODERNIZATION

With one or two brief exceptions, our texts are modernized. However, through much of the verse we have retained the italics so frequent in early modern printing; they do not impede understanding, and in fact quite often help us to hear an author's emphases. Most initial capitals have been removed, but we have sometimes introduced them where the early texts did not, to indicate personification.

ACKNOWLEDGEMENTS

This anthology is to a high degree a collective enterprise. At the outset, university teachers were asked, on electronic discussion groups such as Ficino and Milton-L, what they would like to see in an anthology of seventeenth-century verse and prose. So long ago was this, and so fickle the computer, that the following list is likely to be deficient. If so, we shall be glad to hear from those who wrote to us so that we can rectify omissions in the future. The anonymous reviewers who commented on the penultimate draft made a great many useful suggestions. In addition, we should like to thank Sharon Achinstein, Jonquil Bevan, David Boocker, Lisa Celovsky, Anne Coldiron, Tabitha Driver, Joseph Holtgen, Alan Howard, Ana Kothe, John Leonard, Michael Lofaro, Diane McColley, Mark McDayter, the denizens of Ficino and Milton-L, David Northrup, Hugh de Quehen, Sheila Roberts, Peggy Samuels, Paul Stanwood, June Sturrock, Stefano Villani, Germaine Warkentin, John Watkins, Thomas Wheeler, Samuel Wong, David Wootton, and James D. Young. Sharon Alker, Hannah Calder, Jim Daems, and Jasmine McAdam gave valuable help as research assistants. Holly Nelson wishes to thank for proof-reading: Juliet Henderson, Marion Henderson and Russell Nelson. Joseph Black wishes to thank the Northrop Frye Centre (Victoria College, University of Toronto); Trinity College, University of Toronto; the Department of English, University of Edinburgh; the Centre for the History of the Book, University of Edinburgh; the Department of English, University of Tennessee; and the Graduate School, University of Tennessee. Alan Rudrum wishes to thank the staff of Simon Fraser University Library, of the Newberry Library, and of four research libraries which have been happy hunting grounds for many years: the Bodleian Library, Oxford; the British Library; the Clark Library, Los Angeles; and the Henry E. Huntington Library, San Marino, California. Finally, at Broadview Press, it has been a pleasure to work with Don LePan; and Eileen Eckert as proofreader and Kathryn Brownsey as production coordinator have worked miracles of observation, endurance and patience.

In the notes we have used the following abbreviations:

OED	*The Oxford English Dictionary*
OCD	*The Oxford Classical Dictionary*
OCCL	*The Oxford Companion to Classical Literature*
ODCC	*The Oxford Dictionary of the Christian Church*

Contents

A MISCELLANY

INDEXES

Mary Sidney Herbert, Countess of Pembroke
1561 – 1621

Mary Sidney Herbert was born at Tickenhall near Bewdley, Worcestershire. Her parents were Sir Henry Sidney and Mary Dudley, the daughter of the Duke of Northumberland. Sir Henry Sidney held concurrent positions as Lord President of the Council of Wales (1559–86) and Lord Deputy of Ireland (1565–71, 1575–78). Mary was educated at home, where she read in the Church Fathers, the classics, and Latin, French, and Italian language and literature. She may also have studied Hebrew and Greek. She joined the royal household as Maid of Honour to Elizabeth I at the age of fourteen. Less than two years later, she married Henry Herbert, Earl of Pembroke, by whom she had four children. She assumed the role of hostess at Pembroke's Wiltshire estates and their London home, Baynards Castle. She transformed Wilton House into a sanctuary for poets and became one of the foremost patrons of the age. The Countess's father died in May and her mother in August 1586. In the same year, her brother, Sir Philip Sidney, died from injuries sustained in an attack on a Spanish convoy in the Netherlands.

The Countess undertook to complete her brother's paraphrase of the Psalms and assumed responsibility for publishing his works. She made revisions to Sir Philip's versions of Psalms 1–43, and completed the Psalter herself with paraphrases of Psalms 44 through 150.[1] Although the Sidney-Pembroke Psalter was not printed until the nineteenth century, copies circulated in manuscript, and their version was praised by such writers as John Donne, Ben Jonson and George Herbert. Donne wrote, "They tell us why, and teach us how to sing," and Herbert found in them the archetype of devotional poetry. The Countess's agility with metre, stanza forms and rhyme scheme, and her ability to respond to contemporary commentaries on the Psalms have been admired. Her Psalms might aptly be characterized products of creative paraphrase rather than literal translation.[2] The Countess produced three other translations: Philippe de Mornay's *A Discourse of Life and Death*, Robert Garnier's tragedy *Antonius* and Petrarch's *Triumph of Death*, works concerned with pious living, punishment of worldly desire, and preparation for death. As well as editing and publishing her brother's *Arcadia*, the Countess wrote a pastoral dialogue and two dedicatory poems addressed to Elizabeth I and Sir Philip Sidney. After she was widowed in 1601, the Countess resided in Houghton House until her death of smallpox.

☙❧

---

[1] For the complex textual history of these poems, see the apparatus in the edition on which this selection is based: *The Collected Works of Mary Sidney Herbert Countess of Pembroke*, eds. Margaret P. Hannay, Noel J. Kinnamon and Michael G. Brennan, Vol. II (Oxford: Clarendon P, 1998).

[2] Pembroke particularly relied on Théodore de Bèze's Latin commentary on the Psalms, and took as her primary literary model the French-Genevan metrical Psalter, *The Psalms of David*, by Bèze and Clément Marot. Of the English translations of Scripture, she favoured the 1560 Geneva Bible.

The Psalms of David

Psalm 52 Quid Gloriaris? [1]

Tyrant, why swell'st thou thus,
    Of mischief vaunting? [2]
Since help from God to us,
    Is never wanting?

5 Lewd lies the tongue contrives,
    Loud lies it soundeth:
Sharper than sharpest knives
    With lies it woundeth.

Falsehood thy wit approves,
10   All truth rejected:
Thy will all vices loves,
    Virtue neglected.

Not words from cursed thee,
    But gulfs are poured.
15 Gulfs wherein daily be
    Good men devoured.

Think'st thou to bear it so? [3]
    God shall displace thee
God shall thee overthrow,
20   Crush thee, deface thee.

The just shall fearing see
    These fearful chances: [4]
And laughing shoot at thee
    With scornful glances.

25 Lo, lo the wretched wight, [5]
    Who God disdaining,
His mischief made his might,
    His guard his gaining.

I as an olive tree, [6]
30   Still green shall flourish:
God's house the soil shall be
    My roots to nourish.

My trust on his true love
    Truly attending,
35 Shall never thence remove,
    Never see ending.

Thee will I honour still
    Lord, for this justice:
There fix my hopes I will,
40   Where thy saints' trust is.

Thy saints trust in thy name,
    Therein they joy them:
Protected by the same
    Nought can annoy them. [7]
—1823 (ca. 1588–1601)

---

[1] *Psalm 52* Psalm 52 is prefaced in the Geneva Bible: "1 David describeth the arrogant tyranny of his adversary Doeg: who by false surmises caused Ahimél[e]ch with the rest of the Priests to be slain 5 David prophecieth his destruction, 6 And encourageth the faithful to put their confidence in God, whose judgments are most sharp against his adversaries. 9 And finally he rendreth thanks to God for his deliverance. In this Psalm is lively set forth the kingdom of Antichrist." For the story of Doeg, see I Samuel 22.

[2] *vaunting* boasting (*OED* vaunting *vb sb*).

[3] *to bear it* to carry by assault; to carry the day (*OED* bear *v¹ Obs* 3f).

[4] *fearful chances* dreadful events (*OED* fearful *a* I.1; *OED* chance *sb* A.I.2).

[5] *wight* person (*OED* wight 2).

[6] *olive tree* In biblical literature, the olive tree is often an image of providence or abundance.

[7] *nought* nothing (*OED* nought *sb* A.1).

Psalm 58 *Si Vere Utique* [1]

And call ye this to utter what is just,
You that of justice hold the sov'reign throne?
And call ye this to yield, O sons of dust, [2]
    To wronged brethren ev'ry man his own?
        O no: it is your long malicious will [3]
5   Now to the world to make by practice known
        With whose oppression you the balance
          fill,
Just to your selves, indiff'rent else to none.

But what could they, who ev'n in birth declined
10   From truth and right to lies and injuries?
To show the venom of their canc'red mind [4]
    The adder's image scarcely can suffice.
        Nay scarce the aspic may with them
          contend,
On whom the charmer all in vain applies

15   His skillfuls't spells: aye missing of his
          end, [5]
While she self-deaf, and unaffected lies. [6]

Lord crack their teeth, Lord crush these lions' jaws,
    So let them sink as water in the sand:
When deadly bow their aiming fury draws,
20   Shiver the shaft ere past the shooter's hand.
        So make them melt as the dishoused snail
Or as the embryo, whose vital band
        Breaks ere it holds, and formless eyes do fail
To see the sun, though brought to lightful
        land.

25 O let their brood, a brood of springing thorns,
    Be by untimely rooting overthrown
Ere bushes waxed, they push with pricking horns,
    As fruits yet green are off by tempest blown. [7]
        The good with gladness this revenge shall see,
30   And bathe his feet in blood of wicked one.
        While all shall say: "the just rewarded be,
There is a God that carves to each his own."

—1823 (ca. 1588–1601)

---

[1] *Psalm 58* Psalm 58 is prefaced in the Geneva Bible: "1 He [David] describeth the malice of his enemies, the flatterers of Saúl, who both secretly & openly sought his destruction, from whom he appealeth to God's judgment, 10 Showing that the just shall rejoice when they see the punishment of the wicked to the glory of God." In his heading to this Psalm, Bèze describes David's enemies as "a council of the states" gathered by Saul to prosecute David. Calvin labels them "rather a rout of murderers, than a Session of Judges."

[2] *sons of dust* probably an allusion to Genesis 3:14: "And the Lord God said unto the serpent…upon thy belly shalt thou go, and dust shalt thou eat all the days of thy life"; perhaps also an allusion to Genesis 2:7, the story of man's creation from dust, as suggested by Pembroke's editors (Oxford, 1998).

[3] *long malicious will* long in duration, yet only now recognized by their actions.

[4] *canc'red* infected with evil; corrupt (*OED* cankered *ppl.a* 5).

[5] *skillfuls't* most clever (*OED* skilful *a* 4a); *aye missing of his end* always failing to achieve his purpose (*OED* ay,aye *adv* 1a; *OED* end *sb* II.14a).

[6] *she self-deaf* The Geneva notes for Psalm 58:4: "They pass in malice, and subtlety the crafty serpent, which could preserve himself by stopping his ear from the enchanter." The serpent is female in the Psalter, as she is in many medieval and early-modern representations of the Garden of Eden.

[7] *waxed* have grown (*OED* wax *v¹* I.1 *pa.pple*); *horns* pointed or tapering projections (*OED* horn *sb* IV.21).

Psalm 74 *Ut Quid, Deus* [1]

O God, why hast thou thus
   Repulsed, and scattered us?
Shall now thy wrath no limits hold?
   But ever smoke and burn?
5   Till it to ashes turn
The chosen flock of thy dear fold?

Ah! think with milder thought
   On them, whom thou hast bought,
And purchased from endless days:
10   Think of thy birthright lot,
   Of Sion, on whose plot,
Thy sacred house supported stays.

Come Lord, O come with speed,
   This sacrilegious seed
15 Root quickly out, and headlong cast:
   All that thy holy place
   Did late adorn and grace,
Their hateful hands have quite defaced.

Their beastly trumpets roar,
20   Where heavenly notes before
In praises of thy might did flow:
   Within thy temple they
   Their ensigns eft display
The ensigns, which their conquest show. [2]

25 As men with axe on arm
   To some thick forest swarm,
To lop the trees which stately stand:

They to thy temple flock,
   And spoiling, cut and knock
30 The curious works of carving hand.

Thy most most holy seat
   The greedy flames do eat,
And have such ruthless ruins wrought,
   That all thy house is 'rased, [3]
35   So 'rased, and so defaced,
That of that all remaineth nought.

Nay they resolved are,
   We all alike shall fare,
All of one cruel cup shall taste.
40   For not one house doth stand
   Of God in all the land,
But they by fire have laid it waste.

We see the signs no more
   We wont to see before, [4]
45 Nor any now with sp'rit divine
   Amongst us more is found,
   Who can to us expound,
What term these dolours shall define. [5]

How long, O God, how long
50   Wilt thou wink at the wrong
Of thy reviling railing foe?
   Shall he that hates thy name,
   And hated paints with shame, [6]
So do, and do for ever so?

55 Woe us! what is the cause
   Thy hand his help withdraws?

---

[1] *Psalm 74* Psalm 74 is prefaced in the Geneva Bible: "1 The faithful complain of the destruction of the Church & true religion, 2 Under the name of Zión, and the Temple destroyed: 11 And trusting in the might & free mercies of God, 20 By his covenant, 21 They require help & succour for the glory of God's holy Name, for the salvation of his poor afflicted servants, 23 And the confusion of his proud enemies."

[2] *eft* again (*OED* eft *adv* 1); *Their ensigns...the ensigns* Their standard bearers display the banners (*OED* ensign *sb* 7, 5a,b).

[3] *'rased* utterly destroyed (*OED* erase *v* 3).

[4] *the signs* acts of a miraculous nature which demonstrate divine power (*OED* sign *sb* II.10); *wont* used (*OED* wont *pa.pple* A.1).

[5] *Who can....shall define* "Who can to us expound the appointed time for these sorrows to be brought to an end"; or more loosely, "Who can to us expound the boundary of these sorrows" (*OED* term *sb* I.1,II.4; *OED* dolour 2b; *OED* define *v* 1a,2).

[6] *paints* to give a false colouring or complexion to (*OED* paint *v*¹ 5).

That thy right hand far from us keeps?
 Ah let it once arise,
 To plague thine enemies,
60 Which now embosomed idly sleeps.

Thou art my God, I know,
 My King, who long ago
Didst undertake the charge of me:
 And in my hard distress
65 Didst work me such release,
That all the earth did wond'ring see.

Thou by thy might didst make
 That seas in sunder brake,
And dreadful dragons which before
70 In deep or swam or crawled,
 Such mortal strokes appalled, [1]
They floated dead to every shore.

Thou crushed that monster's head
 Whom other monsters dread,
75 And so his fishy flesh didst frame,
 To serve as pleasing food
 To all the ravening brood,
Who had the desert for their dame.

Thou wondrously didst cause
80 Repealing nature's laws
From thirsty flint a fountain flow
 And of the rivers clear,
 The sandy beds appear,
So dry thou mad'st their channels grow.

85 The day arrayed in light,
 The shadow-clothed night,
Were made, and are maintained by thee.
 The sun and sun-like rays,
 The bounds of nights and days,
90 Thy workmanship no less they be.

---

[1] *or swam* either swam; *appalled* enfeebled (*OED* appalled *v* II.6).

To thee the earth doth owe,
 That earth in sea doth grow,
And sea doth earth from drowning spare:
 The summer's corny crown,
95 The winter's frosty gown,
Nought but thy badge, thy livery are.

Thou then still one, the same,
 Think how thy glorious name
These brain-sick men's despite have borne, [2]
100 How abject enemies
 The Lord of highest skies,
With cursed taunting tongues have torn.

Ah! give no hawk the power
 Thy turtle to devour, [3]
105 Which sighs to thee with mourning moans:
 Nor utterly out-rase
 From tables of thy grace
The flock of thy afflicted ones. [4]

But call thy league to mind,
110 For horror all doth blind,
No light doth in the land remain:
 Rape, murder, violence,
 Each outrage, each offence,
Each where doth range, and rage and reign.

115 Enough, enough we mourn:
 Let us no more return
Repulsed with blame and shame from thee:
 But succour us oppressed,
 And give the troubled rest,
120 That of thy praise their songs may be.

Rise God, plead thine own case,
 Forget not what disgrace

---

[2] *despite* contempt (*OED* despite *sb* 1).

[3] *turtle* turtle dove.

[4] *out-rase* erase or efface (*OED* out-rase *v Obs*).

These fools on thee each day bestow:
Forget not with what cries
125   Thy foes against thee rise,
    Which more and more to heaven do grow.
—1823 (ca. 1588–1601)

Psalm 120 Ad Dominum [1]

As to th'Eternal often in anguishes
Erst have I called, never unanswered, [2]
    Again I call, again I calling
    Doubt not again to receive an answer.

5   Lord rid my soul from treasonous eloquence
Of filthy forgers craftily fraudulent:
    And from the tongue where lodged resideth
    Poisoned abuse, ruin of believers.

Thou that reposeth vainly thy confidence
10   In wily wronging, say by thy forgery
    What good to thee? What gain redoundeth? [3]
    What benefit from a tongue deceitful?

Though like an arrow strongly delivered
It deeply pierce, though like to a juniper
15   It coals do cast which quickly fired,
    Flame very hot, very hardly quenching? [4]

Ah God! too long here wander I banished,
Too long abiding barbarous injury:
    With Kedar and with Mesech harboured, [5]
20   How? in a tent, in a houseless harbour.

Too long, alas, too long have I dwelled here
With friendly peace's furious enemies:
    Who when to peace I seek to call them,
    Faster I find to the war they arm them.
—1823 (ca. 1588–1601)

---

[1] *Psalm 120* Psalm 120 is prefaced in the Geneva Bible: "1 The prayer of David being vexed by the false reports of Saul's flatterers. 5 And therefore he lamenteth his long abode among those infidels, 7 Who were given to all kind of wickedness and contention."

[2] *Erst* formerly (*OED* erst *adv* B.5a).

[3] *reposeth* settles (*OED* repose *v*² 1b); *redoundeth* returns (*OED* redound *v* I.4).

[4] *juniper* The coal of juniper wood was fabled to have a wonderful power of remaining glowing (*OED* juniper 1); *very hardly* not easily (*OED* hardly *adv* 6).

[5] *With Kedar…harboured* The exiled Psalmist roams in the remote regions of northern Arabia and Asia Minor.

Michael Drayton
1563 — 1631

Not much is known of Drayton's early life or education; he may have been a page in the household of Sir Henry Goodere, to whom he said he was indebted for "the most part" of his education. There is no record of a university education. If his verse is to be taken as indicative, he loved the same woman for thirty years, but never married. "Since there's no help, come let us kiss and part" is one of the finest love-sonnets in the language, indicating that Drayton learned well from Spenser and from Shakespeare. His early verse is imitative of Spenser's *The Shepheardes Calender* (1579), and much of his verse represents a continuation of the high strain of English patriotism which was fostered in the reign of Elizabeth both by the deliberate propaganda of the ruling elite and by such events as the defeat of the Spanish Armada in 1588. Drayton shared the historical, antiquarian, and topographical enthusiasms which were manifestations of this patriotism; his major poem is the *Poly-Olbion*, the subtitle of which characterizes it as "a description of all the tracts, rivers, mountains, forests and other parts…of Great Britain." He seems to have had a wide acquaintance among his literary contemporaries, and there is a story to the effect that Shakespeare's death was the result of a drinking bout with Drayton and Ben Jonson. Drayton was buried in Westminster Abbey, and the verses on his monument have been ascribed to Ben Jonson.

❧❧❧

To the Virginian Voyage [1]

You brave heroic minds,
   Worthy your country's name,
      That honour still pursue,
      Go, and subdue,
5 Whilst loit'ring hinds [2]
Lurk here at home, with shame.

Britons, you stay too long,
Quickly aboard bestow you,
      And with a merry gale
10   Swell your stretch'd sail,
With vows as strong,
As the winds that blow you.

Your course securely steer,
West and by south forth keep,

15 Rocks, lee shores, nor shoals,
      When Aeolus scowls, [3]
You need not fear,
So absolute the deep. [4]

And cheerfully at sea,
20 Success you still entice,
      To get the pearl and gold,
      And ours to hold,
Virginia,
Earth's only paradise.

25 Where nature hath in store,
Fowl, venison, and fish,
      And the fruitfull'st soil,
      Without your toil,
Three harvests more,
30 All greater then you wish.

---

[1] *Virginian Voyage* An expedition, chartered by James I and organized by English merchants, left England in December 1606 to colonize and settle Virginia.

[2] *hinds* rustics, boors (*OED* hind sb² 3).

[3] *Aeolus* the mythic god of the winds.

[4] *absolute* disengaged, far away from (rocks, lee shores and shoals); see *OED* absolute a.

7

And the ambitious vine
Crowns with his purple mass,
    The Cedar reaching high
    To kiss the sky,
35 The Cypress, pine
And useful Sassafras. [1]

To whose, the golden age
Still nature's laws doth give,
    No other cares that tend,
40   But them to defend
From winter's age,
That long there doth not live.

When as the luscious smell
Of that delicious land,
45   Above the seas that flows,
    The clear wind throws,
Your hearts to swell
Approaching the dear strand.

In kenning of the shore [2]
50 (Thanks to God first given,)
    O you the happy'st men,
    Be frolic then,
Let cannons roar,
Frighting the wide heaven.

55 And in regions far
Such heroes bring ye forth,
    As those from whom we came,
    And plant our name,
Under that star
60 Not known unto our north.

And as there plenty grows
Of laurel everywhere,

    Apollo's sacred tree, [3]
    You it may see,
65 A poet's brows
To crown, that may sing there.

Thy voyages attend,
Industrious Hakluyt, [4]
    Whose reading shall inflame
70   Men to seek fame,
And much commend
To after-times thy wit.
—1606

To the Cambro-Britons,[5] and their Harp, his Ballad of Agincourt [6]

Fair stood the wind for France,
  When we our sails advance,
Nor now to prove our chance,
    Longer will tarry;
5 But putting to the main,
At Caux, the mouth of Seine, [7]
With all his martial train,
    Landed King Harry. [8]

---

[1] *Sassafras* a small tree native to North America which is useful for medicinal purposes (*OED* sassafras 1,2).

[2] *kenning* range of sight (*OED* kenning *vb sb*[1] 4).

[3] *laurel...Apollo's sacred tree* The laurel was the sacred plant of Apollo, god of music. A crown of laurel was used as an emblem of victory or of distinction in poetry (*OED* laurel *sb*[1]2).

[4] *Hakluyt* Richard Hakluyt (ca. 1522–1616), geographer, voluminous writer, promoter of overseas expansion, and one of the patentees of the Virginia voyage.

[5] *Cambro-Britons* Welsh Britons. Cambro is derived from Cambrian, "pertaining to Wales, Welsh" (*OED* Cambrian *a* 1).

[6] *Agincourt* a village in northern France, site of an English victory over the French in 1415, during the Hundred Years War. Names mentioned throughout the poem refer to men fighting on the English side. Of special note are the Duke of York, the King's uncle, who was killed in battle, and the King's brothers, the Duke of Gloucester and the Duke of Clarence.

[7] *the mouth of Seine* Henry's troops invaded France from the estuary of the Seine in August 1415.

[8] *King Harry* Henry V (ruled 1413–1422).

And taking many a fort,
10 Furnish'd in warlike sort,
Marcheth tow'rds Agincourt,
    In happy hour;
Skirmishing day by day,
With those that stopped his way,
15 Where the French Gen'ral lay,
    With all his power.

Which in his height of pride,
King Henry to deride,
His ransom to provide
20   To the King sending.
Which he neglects the while,
As from a nation vile,
Yet with an angry smile,
    Their fall portending.

25 And turning to his men,
Quoth our brave Henry then,
Though they to one be ten,
    Be not amazed.
Yet have we well begun,
30 Battles so bravely won,
Have ever to the sun,
    By fame been raised.

And for my self (quoth he,)
This me full rest shall be,
35 England ne'r mourn for me,
    Nor more esteem me.
Victor I will remain,
Or on this earth lie slain,
Never shall she sustain,
40   Loss to redeem me.

Poiters and Cressy tell, [1]
When most their pride did swell,
Under our swords they fell,

No less our skill is,
45 Then when our grandsire great,
Claiming the regal seat,
By many a warlike feat,
    Lopped the French lilies.

The Duke of York so dread,
50 The eager vaward led; [2]
With the main, Henry sped,
    Amongst his hench-men. [3]
Excester had the rear,
A braver man not there,
55 O Lord, how hot they were,
    On the false French-men!

They now to fight are gone,
Armour on armour shone,
Drum now to drum did groan,
60   To hear, was wonder;
That with cries they make,
The very earth did shake,
Trumpet to trumpet spake,
    Thunder to thunder.

65 Well it thine age became,
O noble Erpingham,
Which didst the signal aim,[4]
    To our hid forces;
When from a meadow by,
70 Like a storm suddenly,
The English archery
    Stuck the French horses,

---

[1] *Poiters and Cressy* sites of English victories earlier in the Hundred Years War. The English defeated the French at Poitiers in 1356 and at the Battle of Crecy in 1346.

[2] *vaward* vanguard, i.e. the foremost division of an army (*OED* vaward and vanguard 1)

[3] *hench-men* squires or pages of honour to a prince or great man. In connection with the English court, the word came to connote a position of honour, and the royal henchmen of the fifteenth and sixteenth centuries were usually young men of rank (*OED* henchman 1b).

[4] *Which* equivalent to who, as in the version of the Lord's Prayer found in the Anglican Book of Common Prayer: "Our Father, which art in heaven."

With Spanish yew so strong,
Arrows a cloth-yard long,
75 That like to serpents stung,
    Piercing the weather;
None from his fellow starts,
But playing manly parts,
And like true English hearts,
80   Stuck close together.

When down their bows they threw,
And forth their bilboes drew, [1]
And on the French they flew,
    Not one was tardy;
85 Arms were from shoulders sent,
Scalps to the teeth were rent,
Down the French peasants went,
    Our men were hardy.

This while our noble King,
90 His broad sword brandishing,
Down the French host did ding, [2]
    As to o'r-whelm it;
And many a deep wound lent,
His arms with blood besprent,
95 And many a cruel dent
    Bruised his helmet.

Gloster, that Duke so good,
Next of the royal blood,
For famous England stood,
100   With his brave brother;
Clarence, in steel so bright,
Though but a maiden knight,
Yet in that furious fight,
    Scarce such another.

105 Warwick in blood did wade,
Oxford the foe invade,

And cruel slaughter made,
    Still as they ran up;
Suffolk his axe did ply,
110 Beaumont and Willoughby
Bare them right doughtily, [3]
    Ferrers and Fanhope,

Upon Saint Crispin's day [4]
Fought was this noble fray,
115 Which fame did not delay,
    To England to carry;
O, when shall English men
With such acts fill a pen,
Or England breed again,
120   Such a King Harry?
—1606

Sonnet 61

Since there's no help, come let us kiss and part,
    Nay, I have done: you get no more of me,
And I am glad, yea glad with all my heart,
That thus so cleanly, I myself can free;
5 Shake hands for ever, cancel all our vows,
And when we meet at any time again,
Be it not seen in either of our brows,
That we one jot of former love retain;
Now at the last gasp, of love's latest breath,
10 When his pulse failing, passion speechless lies,
When faith is kneeling by his bed of death,
And innocence is closing up his eyes,
    Now if thou would'st, when all have given
        him over
    From death to life, thou might'st him yet
        recover.
—1619

---

[1] *bilboes* swords noted for the temper and elasticity of their blades (*OED* bilbo 1a).

[2] *ding* beat, knock, strike with heavy blows (*OED* ding *v2*).

---

[3] *doughtily* valiantly, stoutly (*OED* doughtily *adv*).

[4] *St. Crispin's Day* The day of the battle, October 25th, was St. Crispin's day. Crispin, the patron saint of shoemakers, was an early Christian martyr.

Thomas Campion
1567 – 1620

Thomas Campion was the second child of John Campion and Lucy Trigg, a widow, who had married in 1564, the year of Shakespeare's birth. Shortly after the marriage, John Campion became an official of the Court of Chancery, perhaps paying for the office with his wife's money. He is likely to have resided in the Cursitors' Office in Chancery Lane, and Thomas was baptized in St. Andrew's, Holborn. John Campion died in 1576; his widow left London, and was remarried soon after to Augustine Steward, of a family from which Oliver Cromwell was descended through his mother, Elizabeth Steward. Steward had considerable estates in Hertfordshire. Lucy did not survive long to enjoy her third marriage, however; she died in 1580. Augustine remarried, again to a widow, Anne Sisley, who had a son about Thomas's age. Thomas Campion and Thomas Sisley were then sent off to Peterhouse, at that time one of the most flourishing colleges in Cambridge. Their names appear in the Buttery Books for 1581, and from Augustine Steward's account books we have a detailed record of the money spent on their education, down to the cost of paper and candles and washing and mending their clothing and shoes. At Cambridge Campion acquired a good knowledge of, and reverence for, classical literature; and he became a close friend of Thomas Nashe. Campion left Cambridge in 1584 and was admitted to Gray's Inn, perhaps with the intention of pursuing law or some related profession. Campion did not find the study of law fascinating, and began at this period to write Latin epigrams and English verse. From internal evidence it seems likely that Campion was a member, as a "Gentleman Adventurer," of the expedition of four thousand men levied by the Queen and commanded by the Earl of Essex, which was sent to the assistance of Henri IV, arriving at Dieppe in August 1591. The English soldiers, nominally sent to oppose the Spanish invaders of Brittany, were in fact used to subdue Henri's Catholic subjects. In 1591 Campion's first printed poems

appeared anonymously, and by that time were already appearing in manuscript commonplace books. His first published book, in 1595, was a collection of Latin poems which won him an immediate reputation. His first English book, *A Book of Airs*, was published in 1601; his *Observations in the Art of English Poesy* appeared in the following year. His reputation may be suggested by the fact that he was one of ten poets mentioned as "among the most pregnant wits of these our times" in Camden's *Remains*, 1605; the fact that Sidney, Spenser, Ben Jonson and Shakespeare are listed reminds us that the competition was not feeble. However, after the *Observations* there was a silence of four years, during which time Campion seems to have studied medicine, probably on the Continent; there are no medical allusions in the Latin poems he published in 1595, and a great many in the one published in 1619. In 1613 he published *Songs of Mourning* on the death of Prince Henry, and in the same year three other masques and, probably, his *Two Books of Airs*. One of the masques was for a wedding which became notorious, between Frances Howard and Robert Carr, after the annulment of Frances Howard's marriage. Sir Thomas Overbury, who opposed the match as immoral, was subsequently murdered by the couple. Their intermediaries, who conveyed poison to Overbury, were executed; the couple were imprisoned and subsequently released. History has cleared Campion of any complicity in the murder, and we may enjoy his poems and the *Epithalamium* which Donne wrote for the occasion with a clear conscience. In 1617 appeared the *Third and Fourth Book of Airs*; an undated technical work on music, the *New Way of Making Four Parts in Counter-point*, may also belong to this period. Campion was buried at St. Dunstan's in the West, Fleet Street, and was described in the register as "doctor of Physic." He left his entire estate of £22 to Philip Rosseter, his friend and collaborator in *A Book of Airs*.

⁓⁓⁓

From *A Book of Airs*

VI

Let him that will be free and keep his heart
   from care,
Retir'd alone, remain where no discomforts are.
For when the eye doth view his grief, or hapless
   ear his sorrow hears,
Th' impression still in him abides, and ever in one
   shape appears.

5 Forget thy griefs betimes; long sorrow breeds long
   pain,
For joy far fled from men, will not return again;
O happy is the soul which heaven ordained to live
   in endless peace;
His life is a pleasing dream, and every hour his
   joys increase.

You heavy sprites, that love in severed shades to
   dwell,
10 That nurse despair, and dream of unrelenting hell,
Come sing this happy song, and learn of me the
   art of true content,
Load not your guilty souls with wrong, and
   heaven then will soon relent.
     —1601

X

Follow your Saint, follow with accents sweet;
  Haste you, sad notes, fall at her flying feet:
There, wrapped in cloud of sorrow pity move,
And tell the ravisher of my soul I perish for her
   love.
5 But if she scorns my never-ceasing pain,
Then burst with sighing in her sight and nere
   return again.

All that I sung still to her praise did tend,
Still she was first; still she my songs did end.
Yet she my love and Music both doeth fly,
10 The Music that her Echo is and beauties'
   sympathy;
Then let my Notes pursue her scornful flight:
It shall suffice that they were breath'd and died
   for her delight.
     —1601

From *Two Books of Airs*

XI

Sweet, exclude me not, nor be divided
  From him that ere long must bed thee:
All thy maiden doubts Law hath decided;
  Sure we are, and I must wed thee.
5   Presume then yet a little more:
      Here's the way, bar not the door.

Tenants, to fulfil their landlord's pleasure,
  Pay their rent before the quarter:
'Tis my case, if you it rightly measure;
10   Put me not then off with laughter.
    Consider then a little more:
      Here's the way to all my store.

Why were doors in love's despite devised?
  Are not laws enough restraining?
15 Women are most apt to be surprised
  Sleeping, or sleep wisely feigning.
    Then grace me yet a little more:
      Here's the way, bar not the door.
     —1613

XIII [1]

As by the streams of *Babylon*
Far from our native soil we sat,
Sweet *Sion*, thee we thought upon,
And ev'ry thought a tear begat.

5 Aloft the trees, that spring up there,
Our silent harps we pensive hung:
Said they that captived us, Let's hear
Some song, which you in *Sion* sung.

Is then the song of our God fit
10 To be profaned in foreign land?
O *Salem*, thee when I forget,
Forget his skill may my right hand!

Fast to the roof cleave may my tongue,
If mindless I of thee be found:
15 Or if, when all my joys are sung,
Jerusalem be not the ground.

Remember, Lord, how *Edom's* race
Cried in *Jerusalem's* sad day,
Hurl down her walls, her towers deface,
20 And, stone by stone, all level lay.

Cursed *Babel's* seed! for *Salem's* sake
Just ruin yet for thee remains!
Blest shall they be thy babes that take
And 'gainst the stones dash out their brains.
—1613

From *The Third Book of Airs*

XI

If Love loves truth, then women do not love;
Their passions all are but dissembled shows;

Now kind and free of favour if they prove,
Their kindness straight a tempest overthrows.
5 Then as a seaman the poor lover fares;
The storm drowns him ere he can drown his
cares.

But why accuse I women that deceive?
Blame then the foxes for their subtle wile:
They first from Nature did their craft receive:
10 It is a woman's nature to beguile.
Yet some, I grant, in loving steadfast grow;
But such by use are made, not nature, so.

O why had Nature power at once to frame
Deceit and Beauty, traitors both to Love?
15 O would Deceit had died when Beauty came
With her divineness ev'ry heart to move!
Yet do we rather wish, what ere befall,
To have fair women false than none at all.
—1617

From *The Fourth Book of Airs*

VII

There is a garden in her face,
Where roses and white lilies grow;
A heav'nly paradise is that place,
Wherein all pleasant fruits do flow.
5 There cherries grow, which none may buy
Till cherry ripe themselves do cry.

Those cherries fairly do enclose
Of orient pearl a double row;
Which when her lovely laughter shows,
10 They look like rose-buds filled with snow.
Yet them nor peer nor prince can buy,
Till cherry ripe themselves do cry.

Her eyes like angels watch them still;
Her brows like bended bows do stand,

---

[1] This is a rendering of the famous Psalm 137, which begins, in the Book of Common Prayer version, "By the waters of Babylon we sat down and wept: when we remembered thee, O Sion."

15 Threat'ning with piercing frowns to kill
All that attempt with eye or hand
  Those sacred cherries to come nigh,

  Till cherry ripe themselves do cry.
 —1617

Henry Wotton
1568 – 1639

Henry Wotton was educated at Winchester School and New College, Oxford. He entered the Middle Temple, where he became, and was to remain, a close friend of Donne. In 1595 he became secretary to the Earl of Essex, gathering foreign intelligence. He was not implicated in the conspiracy against Elizabeth which resulted in the execution of Essex for treason in 1601. Wotton was knighted, as were a good many others, when James I came to the throne; but Wotton's knighthood was perhaps more than a royal money-raising device, as he was certainly a man of great ability. He was appointed ambassador to Venice. His epigram, that an ambassador was an honest man sent to lie abroad for the good of his country, is one of the better puns of the time. After his ambassadorship in Venice, Wotton was engaged in diplomatic missions to Germany and Holland; between 1604 and 1624 he spent most of his time abroad. From 1624 until his death Wotton was Provost of Eton; the letter of introduction he supplied to Milton before his travels to Europe helped Milton to meet well-known Italian scholars and writers. His *Elements of Architecture* was published in 1624. His poems were published after his death in the volume *Reliquiae Wottonianae*, 1651.

ↄ⳹ↄ

On his Mistress, the Queen of Bohemia

You meaner beauties of the night,
  That poorly satisfy our eyes,
More by your number, than your light,
You common people of the skies;
5   What are you when the sun shall rise?

You curious chanters of the wood,
That warble forth Dame Natures lays,
Thinking your voices understood;
By your weak accents; what's your praise
10   When Philomel her voice shall raise? [1]

You violets, that first appear,
By your pure purple mantles known,
Like the proud virgins of the year,
As if the spring were all your own;
15   What are you when the rose is blown?

So, when my Mistress shall be seen
In form and beauty of her mind,
By virtue first, then choice a Queen,
Tell me, if she were not design'd
20   Th' eclipse and glory of her kind?
—1651

The Character of a Happy Life

How happy is he born and taught,
  That serveth not another's will?
Whose armor is his honest thought,
And simple Truth his utmost skill?

5 Whose passions not his masters are,
Whose soul is still prepared for death,
Untied unto the world by care
Of public fame or private breath.

Who envies none that Chance doth raise,
10 Nor Vice hath ever understood,
How deepest wounds are given by praise,
Nor rules of state, but rules of good.

---

[1] *Philomel* the nightingale.

15

But fill your lamps with oil of burning zeal,
That to your faith he may his truth reveal. [1]

15 Let all your robes be purple scarlet white,
Those perfect colours purest virtue wore, [2]
Come decked with lilies that did so delight
To be preferred in beauty, far before
Wise Solomon in all his glory dight:
20 Whose royal robes did no such pleasure yield,
As did the beauteous lily of the field. [3]

Adorn your temples with fair Daphne's crown
The never changing laurel, always green; [4]
Let constant hope all worldly pleasures drown,
25 In wise Minerva's paths be always seen;
Or with bright Cynthia, though fair Venus
frown: [5]
With hyssop cross the posts of every door,
Where sin would riot, making virtue poor. [6]

And let the Muses your companions be,
30 Those sacred sisters that on Pallas wait; [7]
Whose virtues with the purest minds agree,
Whose godly labours do avoid the bait
Of worldly pleasure, living always free
From sword, from violence, and from ill report,
35 To these nine worthies all fair minds resort. [8]

Anoint your hair with Aaron's precious oil, [9]
And bring your palms of vict'ry in your hands,
To overcome all thoughts that would defile
The earthly circuit of your soul's fair lands;
40 Let no dim shadows your clear eyes beguile:
Sweet odours, myrrh, gum, aloes, frankincense,
Present that King who died for your offence.

Behold, bright Titan's shining chariot stays,
All decked with flowers of the freshest hue, [10]
45 Attended on by Age, Hours, Nights, and Days, [11]
Which alters not your beauty, but gives you
Much more, and crowns you with eternal praise:
This golden chariot wherein you must ride,
Let simple doves, and subtle serpents guide.

50 Come swifter than the motion of the sun,
To be transfigured with our loving Lord,

[1] ll.8–14 as the wise virgins did in preparation for the arrival of the bridegroom (Matthew 25:1–13).

[2] *Let all…virtue wore* "The robes that Christ wore before his death" (original marginalia).

[3] *Come decked…the field* "And why take ye thought for raiment? Consider the lilies of the field, how they grow; they toil not, neither do they spin: And yet I say unto you, That even Solomon in all his glory was not arrayed like one of these" (Matthew 6:28–29); *dight* clothed (*OED* dight *v* III.10).

[4] *Daphne's crown* "In token of constancy" (original marginalia); Daphne fled from the unwanted sexual advances of Apollo and was turned into a laurel tree in response to her prayer for assistance.

[5] *Minerva* the goddess of wisdom; *Cynthia* the goddess of the moon and chastity; *Venus* the goddess of love, beauty and fertility.

[6] *hyssop* emended from *Esop*, as proposed by John Ulreich (Lanyer discussion list). Ulreich's argument is that the allusion appears to be to the Hebraic ritual of using twigs of the hyssop plant in purifying ceremonies: "Then Moses called for all the elders of Israel, and said unto them, Draw out and take you a lamb according to your families, and kill the passover. And ye shall take a bunch of hyssop, and dip it in the blood that is in the basin, and strike the lintel and the two side posts with the blood that is in the basin" (Exodus 12:21–22).

[7] *Muses* The Nine Muses are the Greek deities who preside over music, poetry, the arts and sciences; *Pallas* Pallas Athena, the virgin warrior and goddess of wisdom. In Samuel Daniel's court masque *Vision of Twelve Goddesses* (presented Jan. 8, 1604), Queen Anne chose the part of Pallas.

[8] *nine* here, the Nine Muses.

[9] *Aaron's precious oil* Chosen for official priesthood, Aaron was anointed with holy oil by Moses (Leviticus 8:12); only he could enter into the Holy of Holies on the Day of Atonement to make a sacrifice for the sins of the Israelites.

[10] *Titan* a name for the sun-god, Sol, or for the sun personified.

[11] *Age…Days* personifications of the forces which created and represented time.

Let glory end what grace in you begun, [1]
Of heav'nly riches make your greatest hoard,
In Christ all honour, wealth, and beauty's won:
    By whose perfections you appear more fair
55   Than Phoebus, if he seven times brighter
        were. [2]

God's holy angels will direct your doves,
And bring your serpents to the fields of rest,
Where he doth stay that purchased all your loves
60 In bloody torments, when he died oppressed,
There shall you find him in those pleasant groves
    Of sweet Elysium, by the well of life, [3]
        Whose crystal springs do purge from worldly
        strife.

Thus may you fly from dull and sensual earth,
65 Whereof at first your bodies formed were,
That new regen'rate in a second birth, [4]
Your blessed souls may live without all fear,
Being immortal, subject to no death:
    But in the eye of heaven so highly placed,
70   That others by your virtues may be graced.

Where worthy ladies I will leave you all,
Desiring you to grace this little book;
Yet some of you methinks I hear to call
Me by my name, and bid me better look,
75 Lest unawares I in an error fall:
    In general terms, to place you with the rest,
    Whom fame commends to be the very best.

Tis true, I must confess (O noble fame)
There are a number honoured by thee,

80 Of which, some few thou didst recite by name,
And willed my Muse they should remembered be;
Wishing some would their glorious trophies frame:
    Which if I should presume to undertake,
    My tired hand for very fear would quake.

85 Only by name I will bid some of those,
That in true honour's seat have long been placed,
Yea even such as thou hast chiefly chose,
By whom my Muse may be the better graced;
Therefore, unwilling longer time to lose,
90   I will invite some ladies that I know,
    But chiefly those as thou hast graced so.
—1611

The Author's Dream to the Lady Mary, the Countess Dowager of Pembroke [5]

Me thought I passed through th' Idalian
    groves,
And asked the Graces, if they could direct
Me to a lady whom Minerva chose,
To live with her in height of all respect. [6]

5 Yet looking back into my thoughts again,
The eye of reason did behold her there
Fast tied unto them in a golden chain,
They stood, but she was set in honor's chair. [7]

And nine fair virgins sat upon the ground,
10 With harps and viols in their lily hands; [8]

---

[1] *Let glory* emended from "Lest" etc., accepting John Ulreich's suggestion (Lanyer discussion list). The meaning is "Allow your glorification to complete what grace has begun in you."

[2] *Phoebus* Apollo, the Sun-god; the sun personified.

[3] *Elysium* the state or abode of the blessed after death, (fig.) a place or state of perfect happiness.

[4] *second birth* spiritual birth; see John 3:3 and I Peter 1:23.

[5] *The Author's Dream* The dream vision as a form of patronage poetry dates back to medieval times; *Lady Mary...Pembroke* A brief biography of Mary Sidney Herbert (1561–1621), Countess of Pembroke, introduces a selection of her Psalms in this volume.

[6] *Idalian* groves in Cyprus where Aphrodite was worshipped; *the Graces* the sister-goddesses who bestow beauty and charm.

[7] *she* Lady Mary, the Countess Dowager of Pembroke.

[8] *nine fair virgins* the Nine Muses.

Whose harmony had all my senses drowned,
But that before mine eyes an object stands,

Whose beauty shined like Titan's clearest rays,
She blew a brazen trumpet, which did sound
15 Through all the world that worthy lady's praise, [1]
And by eternal fame I saw her crowned.

Yet studying, if I were awake, or no,
God Morphy came and took me by the hand,
And willed me not from slumber's bower to go,
20 Till I the sum of all did understand. [2]

When presently the welkin that before
Looked bright and clear, methought, was
      overcast, [3]
And dusky clouds, with boist'rous wind's great
      store,
Foretold of violent storms which could not last.

25 And gazing up into the troubled sky,
Methought a chariot did from thence descend,
Where one did sit replete with majesty,
Drawn by four fiery dragons, which did bend

Their course where this most noble lady sat,
30 Whom all these virgins with due reverence
Did entertain, according to that state
Which did belong unto her excellence.

When bright Bellona, so they did her call,
Whom these fair nymphs so humbly did receive,
35 A manly maid which was both fair and tall,
Her borrowed charret by a spring did leave. [4]

With spear, and shield, and currat on her breast, [5]
And on her head a helmet wondrous bright,
With myrtle bays, and olive branches dressed,
40 Wherein methought I took no small delight.

To see how all the Graces sought grace here,
And in what meek, yet princely sort she came;
How this most noble lady did embrace her,
And all humours unto hers did frame. [6]

45 Now fair Dictina by the break of day,
With all her damsels round about her came, [7]
Ranging the woods to hunt, yet made a stay,
When harkening to the pleasing sound of fame;

Her ivory bow and silver shafts she gave
50 Unto the fairest nymph of all her train;
And wondering who it was that in so grave,
Yet gallant fashion did her beauty stain:

She decked herself with all the borrowed light
That Phoebus would afford from his fair face,
55 And made her virgins to appear so bright,
That all the hills and vales received grace.

Then pressing where this beauteous troop did
      stand,
They all received her most willingly,
And unto her the lady gave her hand,
60 That she should keep with them continually.

Aurora rising from her rosy bed,
First blushed, then wept, to see fair Phoebe
      graced, [8]

---

[1] *brazen* brass (*OED* brazen *a* 1a).

[2] *Morphy* "The god of dreams" (original marginalia). Morpheus, one of the sons of Sleep, sent visions of human forms.

[3] *welkin* the sky (*OED* welkin 2).

[4] *Bellona* "Goddess of war and wisdom" (original marginalia); *charret* in classical and biblical use, a war-chariot (*OED* charet *Obs*).

[5] *currat* a piece of armour for the body (*OED* cuirass 1).

[6] *And all humours unto hers did frame* This line is out of rhythm; probably a monosyllabic word was dropped before "humours."

[7] *Dictina* "The moon" (original marginalia).

[8] *Aurora* "The morning" (original marginalia); the Roman goddess of the dawn; *Phoebe* the goddess of the moon, or the moon personified.

And unto Lady May these words she said,
"Come, let us go, we will not be out-faced."

65 "I will unto Apollo's waggoner, [1]
A[nd] bid him bring his master presently,
That his bright beams may all her beauty mar,
Gracing us with the lustre of his eye."

"Come, come, sweet May, and fill their laps with
    flowers,
70 And I will give a greater light than she:
So all these ladies' favours shall be ours,
None shall be more esteemed than we shall be."

Thus did Aurora dim fair Phoebus' light,
And was received in bright Cynthia's place,
75 While Flora all with fragrant flowers dight,
Pressed to show the beauty of her face. [2]

Though these, methought, were very pleasing
    sights,
Yet now these worthies did agree to go,
Unto a place full of all rare delights,
80 A place that yet Minerva did not know.

That sacred spring where art and nature strived
Which should remain as sov'reign of the place;
Whose ancient quarrel being new revived,
Added fresh beauty, gave far greater grace.

85 To which as umpires now these ladies go,
Judging with pleasure their delightful case;
Whose ravished senses made them quickly know,
'Twould be offensive either to displace.

And therefore willed they should forever dwell,
90 In perfect unity by this matchless spring:

Since 'twas impossible either should excel,
Or her fair fellow in subjection bring.

But here in equal sov'reignty to live,
Equal in state, equal in dignity,
95 That unto others they might comfort give,
Rejoicing all with their sweet unity.

And now methought I long to hear her name,
Whom wise Minerva honoured so much,
She whom I saw was crowned by noble fame,
100 Whom envy sought to sting, yet could not touch.

Methought the meagre elf did seek by ways
To come unto her, but it would not be;
Her venom purified by virtue's rays,
She pined and starved like an anatomy: [3]

105 While beauteous Pallas with this lady fair,
Attended by these nymphs of noble fame,
Beheld those woods, those groves, those bowers rare,
By which Pergusa, for so hight the name

Of that fair spring, his dwelling place and
    ground; [4]
110 And through those fields with sundry flowers clad,
Of sev'ral colours, to adorn the ground,
And please the senses ev'n of the most sad:

He trailed along the woods in wanton wise,
With sweet delight to entertain them all;
115 Inviting them to sit and to devise
On holy hymns; at last to mind they call

Those rare sweet songs which Israel's king did
    frame

---

[1] *Apollo* the god of the sun; the patron of music and poetry.

[2] *Flora* the goddess of flowers.

[3] *anatomy* an emaciated creature (*OED* anatomy I.6).

[4] *hight* called (*OED* hight *v*[1] *arch*).

Unto the Father of Eternity; [1]
Before his holy wisdom took the name
120 Of great Messiah, Lord of unity.

Those holy sonnets they did all agree,
With this most lovely lady here to sing;
That by her noble breast's sweet harmony,
Their music might in ears of angels ring.

125 While saints like swans about this silver brook
Should hallelujah sing continually,
Writing her praises in th'eternal book
Of endless honour, true fame's memory.

Thus I in sleep the heavenliest music heard,
130 That ever earthly ears did entertain;
And durst not wake, for fear to be debarred
Of what my senses sought still to retain.

Yet sleeping, prayed dull slumber to unfold
Her noble name, who was of all admired;
135 When presently in drowsy terms he told
Not only that, but more than I desired.

This nymph, quoth he, great Pembroke hight by
        name,
Sister to valiant Sidney, whose clear light
Gives light to all that tread true paths of fame,
140 Who in the globe of heav'n doth shine so bright; [2]

That being dead, his fame doth him survive,
Still living in the hearts of worthy men;
Pale death is dead, but he remains alive,
Whose dying wounds restored him life again.

145 And this fair earthly goddess which you see,
Bellona and her virgins do attend;
In virtuous studies of divinity,
Her precious time continually doth spend.

So that a sister well she may be deemed,
150 To him that lived and died so nobly;
And far before him is to be esteemed
For virtue, wisdom, learning, dignity.

Whose beauteous soul hath gained a double life,
Both here on earth, and in the heav'ns above,
155 Till dissolution end all worldly strife:
Her blessed spirit remains, of holy love,

Directing all by her immortal light,
In this huge sea of sorrows, griefs, and fears;
With contemplation of God's powerful might,
160 She fills the eyes, the hearts, the tongues, the ears

Of after-coming ages, which shall read
Her love, her zeal, her faith, and piety;
The fair impression of whose worthy deed,
Seals her pure soul unto the Deity.

165 That both in heav'n and earth it may remain,
Crowned with her maker's glory and his love;
And this did Father Slumber tell with pain,
Whose dulness scarce could suffer him to move.

When I awaking left him and his bower,
170 Much grieved that I could no longer stay;
Senseless was sleep, not to admit me power,
As I had spent the night to spend the day: [3]

Then had god Morphy showed the end of all,
And what my heart desired, mine eyes had seen;

---

[1] *Those rare…did frame* "The Psalms written newly by the Countess Dowager of Pembroke" (original marginalia); *Israel's King* King David, the Psalmist.

[2] *great Pembroke* Mary Sidney Herbert, the Countess Dowager of Pembroke; she was the sister of Sir Philip Sidney; *valiant Sidney* A courtier in the court of Queen Elizabeth I, Sidney (1554–1586) became a model for the heroic poet after he was fatally injured in an attack on a Spanish convoy in the Low Countries.

[3] *Senseless…the day* Sleep was powerless to allow her to spend the day as she had the night.

175 For as I waked methought I heard one call
For that bright charet lent by Jove's fair queen. [1]

But thou, base cunning thief, that robs our sp'rits
Of half that span of life which years doth give;
And yet no praise unto thy self it merits,
180 To make a seeming death in those that live. [2]

Yea wickedly thou doest consent to death,
Within thy restful bed to rob our souls;
In slumber's bower thou steal'st away our breath,
Yet none there is that thy base stealths controls.

185 If poor and sickly creatures would embrace thee,
Or they to whom thou giv'st a taste of pleasure,
Thou fliest as if Actaeon's hounds did chase thee, [3]
Or that to stay with them thou hadst no leisure.

But though thou hast deprived me of delight,
190 By stealing from me ere I was aware;
I know I shall enjoy the selfsame sight,
Thou hast no power my waking sprites to bar. [4]

For to this lady now I will repair,
Presenting her the fruits of idle hours;
195 Though many books she writes that are more rare,
Yet there is honey in the meanest flowers: [5]

Which is both wholesome, and delights the taste:
Though sugar be more finer, higher prized,

Yet is the painful bee no whit disgraced,
200 Nor her fair wax, or honey more despised. [6]

And though that learned damsel and the rest,
Have in a higher style her trophy framed;
Yet these unlearned lines being my best,
Of her great wisdom can no whit be blamed.

205 And therefore, first I here present my dream,
And next, invite her honour to my feast, [7]
For my clear reason sees her by that stream,
Where her rare virtues daily are increased.

So craving pardon for this bold attempt,
210 I here present my mirror to her view, [8]
Whose noble virtues cannot be exempt,
My glass being steel, declares them to be true. [9]

And madam, if you will vouchsafe that grace,
To grace those flowers that springs from virtue's
    ground;
215 Though your fair mind on worthier works is
    placed,
On works that are more deep, and more
    profound;

Yet is it no disparagement to you,
To see your Saviour in a shepherd's weed, [10]
Unworthily presented in your view,
220 Whose worthiness will grace each line you read.

---

[1] *Jove's fair queen* Juno, the goddess of marriage and childbirth, was the wife of Jove, the god of the sky.

[2] *And yet...that live* "To sleep" (original marginalia).

[3] *Actaeon's hounds...chase thee* A keen hunter, Actaeon came upon Diana bathing; she transformed him into a stag and he was killed by his own hounds.

[4] *sprites* spirits.

[5] *rare* of uncommon excellence or merit (*OED* rare *a*[1] 6).

[6] *painful* diligent, labouring (*OED* painful *a* 4).

[7] *my feast* Lanyer's poem on Christ's passion that follows the patronage poems.

[8] *mirror* not only that which gives a faithful reflection, but also that which exhibits something to be imitated (*OED* mirror 4a,5a).

[9] *My glass...true* A mirror made of polished steel was believed to provide a "truthful" reflection.

[10] *weed* garment (*OED* weed *sb*[2] 1); Christ is figured as a good shepherd throughout the New Testament (John 10:11,14; Hebrews 13:20; I Peter 5:4).

315 This story; that whole worlds with books would fill,
In these few lines, will put me out of breath,
To run so swiftly up this mighty hill,
I may behold it with the eye of faith;
     But to present this pure unspotted Lamb, [1]
320 I must confess, I far unworthy am.

Yet if he please t'illuminate my spirit,
And give me wisdom from his holy hill,
That I may write part of his glorious merit,
If he vouchsafe to guide my hand and quill,
325 To show his death, by which we do inherit
Those endless joys that all our hearts do fill;
     Then will I tell of that sad black faced night,
     Whose mourning mantle covered heavenly
          light.

That very night our Saviour was betrayed, [2]
330 Oh night! exceeding all the nights of sorrow,
When our most blessed Lord, although dismayed,
Yet would not he one minute's respite borrow,
But to Mount Olives went, though sore afraid,
To welcome night, and entertain the morrow; [3]
335   And as he oft unto that place did go,
     So did he now, to meet his long nursed woe.

.   .   .   .

What could thy innocency now expect,
450 When all the sins that ever were committed,
Were laid to thee, whom no man could detect? [4]

Yet far thou wert of man from being pitied,
The judge so just could yield thee no respect,
Nor would one jot of penance be remitted;
455   But greater horror to thy soul must rise,
     Than heart can think, or any wit devise.

Now draws the hour of thy affliction near,
And ugly death present himself before thee;
Thou now must leave those friends thou held'st
          so dear,
460 Yea those disciples, who did most adore thee;
Yet in thy countenance doth no wrath appear,
Although betrayed to those that did abhor thee:
     Thou did'st vouchsafe to visit them again,
     Who had no apprehension of thy pain. [5]

465 Their eyes were heavy, and their hearts asleep,
Nor knew they well what answer then to make
          thee;
Yet thou as Watchman, had'st a care to keep
Those few from sin, that shortly would forsake
          thee;
But now thou bidst them henceforth rest and
          sleep,
470 Thy hour is come, and they at hand to take thee:
     The Son of God to sinners made a prey,
     Oh hateful hour! oh blest! oh cursed day!

Lo here thy great humility was found,
Being King of heaven, and Monarch of the earth,
475 Yet well content to have thy glory drowned,
By being counted of so mean a birth;
Grace, love, and mercy did so much abound,
Thou entertainedst the cross, even to the death: [6]
     And nam'dst thyself, the Son of Man to be,
480   To purge our pride by thy humility.

---

[1] *unspotted lamb* Referred to as the Lamb of God throughout the
New Testament, Jesus is symbolically associated with the sacrificial
lamb of the Old Testament (e.g. John 1:29–30; I Peter 1:19; Revelation 5:6).

[2] *That very night…was betrayed* "Here begins the Passion of Christ"
(original marginalia).

[3] *But to…morrow* On the Mount of Olives, Jesus prayed that he
might escape his role as sacrificial lamb, but he resolved to do as God
wished: "And he went a little farther, and fell on his face, and prayed,
saying, O my Father, if it be possible, let this cup pass from me:
nevertheless not as I will, but as thou wilt" (Matthew 26:39).

[4] *detect* expose (as guilty of sin) (*OED* detect *v* 2a).

[5] *vouchsafe* show a gracious readiness (*OED* vouchsafe *v* II.6).

[6] *entertainedst* took upon yourself (*OED* entertain *v* 16).

But now thy friends whom thou didst call to go,
Heavy spectators of thy hapless case,
See thy betrayer, whom too well they know,
One of the twelve, now object of disgrace,
485   A trothless traitor, and a mortal foe, [1]
With feigned kindness seeks thee to embrace;
     And gives a kiss, whereby he may deceive thee,
     That in the hands of sinners he might leave
       thee. [2]

Now muster forth with swords, with staves, with
     bills,
490   High priests and scribes, and elders of the land,
Seeking by force to have their wicked wills,
Which thou didst never purpose to withstand; [3]
Now thou mak'st haste unto the worst of ills,
And who they seek, thou gently dost demand;
495   This didst thou Lord, t'amaze these fools the
      more,
     T'inquire of that, thou knew'st so well before.

When lo these monsters did not shame to tell,
His name they sought, and found, yet could not
     know
Jesus of Nazareth, at whose feet they fell,
500   When heavenly wisdom did descend so low
To speak to them: they knew they did not well,
Their great amazement made them backward go:
     Nay, though he said unto them, I am he,
     They could not know him, whom their eyes
      did see. [4]

505 How blind were they could not discern the light!
   How dull! if not to understand the truth,
   How weak! if meekness overcame their might;
   How stony hearted, if not moved to ruth: [5]
   How void of pity, and how full of spite,
510 'Gainst him that was the lord of light and truth:
     Here insolent boldness checked by love and
      grace,
     Retires, and falls before our Maker's face.

For when he spake to this accursed crew,
And mildly made them know that it was he:
515 Presents himself, that they might take a view;
And what they doubted they might clearly see;
Nay more, to reassure that it was true,
He said: "I say unto you, I am he."
     If him they sought, he's willing to obey,
520   Only desires the rest might go their way.

Thus with a heart prepared to endure
The greatest wrongs impiety could devise,
He was content to stoop unto their lure,
Although his greatness might do otherwise:
525 Here grace was seizèd on with hands impure,
And virtue now must be suppressed by vice.
     Pure innocency made a prey to sin,
     Thus did his torments and our joys begin.

Here fair obedience shined in his breast,
530 And did suppress all fear of future pain;
Love was his leader unto this unrest,
Whil'st righteousness doth carry up his train;
Mercy made way to make us highly blest,
When patience beat down sorrow, fear and pain:
535   Justice sat looking with an angry brow,
     On blessed misery appearing now.

---

[1] *trothless* faithless, disloyal (*OED* trothless *a* 1).

[2] *See thy…leave thee* Judas Iscariot, paid thirty pieces of silver by the chief priests to lead the Roman soldiers to Jesus, identified Jesus by kissing him (Matthew 26:14–16,49).

[3] *staves* sticks of wood, used as weapons (*OED* stave *sb*[1] I); *bills* concave axe-like weapons (*OED* bill *sb*[1]2a); *purpose* intend (*OED* purpose *v* II.6).

[4] ll. 496–504 "Jesus therefore, knowing all things that should come upon him, went forth, and said unto them, Whom seek ye? They answered him, Jesus of Nazareth. Jesus saith unto them, I am he. And Judas also, which betrayed him, stood with them. As soon then as he

had said unto them, I am he, they went backward, and fell to the ground" (John 18:4–6).

[5] *ruth* pity (*OED* ruth 1).

More glorious than all the conquerors
That ever lived within this earthly round,
More powerful than all kings, or governors
540 That ever yet within this world were found;
More valiant than the greatest soldiers
That ever fought, to have their glory crowned:
    For which of them, that ever yet took breath,
    Sought t'endure the doom of heaven and
        earth? [1]

.   .   .   .   .   .

745 Now Pontius Pilate is to judge the cause
Of faultless Jesus, who before him stands; [2]
Who neither hath offended prince, nor laws,
Although he now be brought in woeful bands:
O noble governor, make thou yet a pause,
750 Do not in innocent blood imbrue thy hands;
    But hear the words of thy most worthy wife,
    Who sends to thee, to beg her Saviour's life. [3]

Let barb'rous cruelty far depart from thee,
And in true justice take affliction's part;
755 Open thine eyes, that thou the truth may'st see,
Do not the thing that goes against thy heart,
Condemn not him that must thy Saviour be;
But view his holy life, his good desert.
    Let not us women glory in men's fall,
760   Who had power given to over-rule us all.

Till now your indiscretion sets us free,
And makes our former fault much less appear; [4]

Our mother Eve, who tasted of the tree,
Giving to Adam what she held most dear,
765 Was simply good, and had no power to see,
The after-coming harm did not appear:
    The subtle serpent that our sex betrayed,
    Before our fall so sure a plot had laid. [5]

That undiscerning ignorance perceived
770 No guile, or craft that was by him intended;
For had she known, of what we were bereaved,
To his request she had not condescended.
But she (poor soul) by cunning was deceived,
No hurt therein her harmless heart intended:
775   For she alleged God's word, which he denies,
    That they should die, but even as gods, be
      wise.

But surely Adam cannot be excused,
Her fault though great, yet he was most to blame;
What weakness offered, strength might have refused,
780 Being lord of all, the greater was his shame:
Although the serpent's craft had her abused,
God's holy word ought all his actions frame,
    For he was lord and king of all the earth,
    Before poor Eve had either life or breath. [6]

785 Who being framed by God's eternal hand,
The perfect'st man that ever breathed on earth;
And from God's mouth received that strait command,
The breach whereof he knew was present death:
Yea having power to rule both sea and land,
790 Yet with one apple won to lose that breath
    Which God had breathed in his beauteous face,
    Bringing us all in danger and disgrace.

And then to lay the fault on Patience' back,
That we (poor women) must endure it all;
795 We know right well he did discretion lack,

---

[1] *doom* last judgement (*OED* doom *sb* 2).

[2] *Pontius Pilate* fifth Roman governor of Judea, Samaria, and Idumaea, who ruled 26–36 C.E. According to Jewish historians, he demonstrated anti-Jewish prejudice and brutality; *cause* case.

[3] *But hear...worthy wife* "When he was set down on the judgment seat, his wife sent unto him, saying, Have thou nothing to do with that just man: for I have suffered many things this day in a dream because of him" (Matthew 27:19).

[4] *Til now...us free* "Eve's apology" (original marginalia); *our former fault* Eve's disobedience to God in eating the fruit from the tree of knowledge of good and evil and in giving that fruit to Adam (Genesis 3).

[5] *subtle* cunning (*OED* subtle *a* 10).

[6] *For he was...or breath* Genesis 2:7–23.

Being not persuaded thereunto at all;
If Eve did err, it was for knowledge sake,
The fruit being fair persuaded him to fall:
    No subtle Serpent's falsehood did betray him,
800   If he would eat it, who had power to stay
        him? [1]

Not Eve, whose fault was only too much love,
Which made her give this present to her dear,
That what she tasted, he likewise might prove, [2]
Whereby his knowledge might become more clear;
805 He never sought her weakness to reprove,
With those sharp words, which he of God did
       hear:
    Yet men will boast of knowledge, which he took
    From Eve's fair hand, as from a learned book.

If any evil did in her remain,
810 Being made of him, he was the ground of all;
If one of many worlds could lay a stain
Upon our sex, and work so great a fall
To wretched man, by Satan's subtle train; [3]
What will so foul a fault amongst you all?
815   Her weakness did the serpent's words obey;
    But you in malice God's dear son betray.

Whom, if unjustly you condemn to die,
Her sin was small, to what you do commit;
All mortal sins that do for vengeance cry,
820 Are not to be compared unto it:
If many worlds would altogether try,
By all their sins the wrath of God to get;
    This sin of yours, surmounts them all as far
    As doth the sun, another little star.

825 Then let us have our liberty again,
And challenge to yourselves no sov'reignty; [4]
You came not in the world without our pain,
Make that a bar against your cruelty;
Your fault being greater, why should you disdain
830 Our being your equals, free from tyranny?
    If one weak woman simply did offend,
    This sin of yours, hath no excuse, nor end.

To which (poor souls) we never gave consent,
Witness thy wife (O Pilate) speaks for all;
835 Who did but dream, and yet a message sent,
That thou should'st have nothing to do at all
With that just man; which, if thy heart relent,
Why wilt thou be a reprobate with Saul? [5]
    To seek the death of him that is so good,
840   For thy soul's health to shed his dearest blood.

    .   .   .   .   .   .

945 And now this long expected hour draws near,
When blessed saints with angels do condole; [6]
His holy march, soft pace, and heavy cheer,
In humble sort to yield his glorious soul,
By his deserts the foulest sins to clear;
950 And in th'eternal book of heaven to enrol
    A satisfaction till the general doom, [7]
    Of all sins past, and all that are to come.

They that had seen this pitiful procession,
From Pilate's palace to Mount Calvary, [8]
955 Might think he answered for some great transgression,
Being in such odious sort condemned to die;

---

[1] *stay him* stop him (*OED* stay *v*[1] I.2a).

[2] *prove* test (*OED* prove *v* B.I.1a).

[3] *train* treachery (*OED* train *sb*[2] 1).

[4] *challenge to* claim for (*OED* challenge *v* 6b).

[5] *Saul* the first Israelite king who conspired to kill his successor, David, a "man after God's own heart" (I Samuel 22–23); or Saul, renamed Paul after his conversion, who, in killing Christians, persecuted Christ (Acts 9:4–5;22:4–8).

[6] *And now...draws near* "Christ going to death" (original marginalia).

[7] *general doom* day of judgment; the apocalypse (*OED* doom *sb* 7).

[8] *Mount Calvary* the site of Jesus's crucifixion.

He plainly showed that his own profession
Was virtue, patience, grace, love, piety:
    And how by suffering he could conquer more
960   Than all the kings that ever lived before.

First went the crier with open mouth proclaiming
The heavy sentence of iniquity,
The hangman next, by his base office claiming
His right in hell, where sinners never die,
965 Carrying the nails, the people still blaspheming
Their maker, using all impiety;
    The thieves attending him on either side,
    The serjeants watching, while the women
      cried. [1]

Thrice happy women that obtained such grace
970 From him whose worth the world could not contain;
Immediately to turn about his face,
As not rememb'ring his great grief and pain,
To comfort you, whose tears poured forth apace
On Flora's banks, like showers of April's rain:
975   Your cries enforced mercy, grace, and love
    From him, whom greatest princes could not
      move:

To speak one word, nor once to lift his eyes
Unto proud Pilate, no nor Herod, king;
By all the questions that they could devise,
980 Could make him answer to no manner of thing; [2]
Yet these poor women, by their piteous cries
Did move their Lord, their Lover, and their King,
    To take compassion, turn about, and speak

To them whose hearts were ready now to
    break. [3]

985 Most blessed daughters of Jerusalem,
Who found such favour in your Saviour's sight,
To turn his face when you did pity him;
Your tearful eyes, beheld his eyes more bright;
Your faith and love unto such grace did climb,
990 To have reflection from this heav'nly light:
    Your eagles' eyes did gaze against this sun,
    Your hearts did think, he dead, the world were
      done.

When spiteful men with torments did oppress
Th'afflicted body of this innocent dove,
995 Poor women seeing how much they did transgress,
By tears, by sighs, by cries entreat, may prove,
What may be done among the thickest press,
They labour still these tyrants' hearts to move;
    In pity and compassion to forbear
1000   Their whipping, spurning, tearing of his hair.

But all in vain, their malice hath no end,
Their hearts more hard than flint, or marble stone;
Now to his grief, his greatness they attend,
When he (God knows) had rather be alone;
1005 They are his guard, yet seek all means to offend:
    Well may he grieve, well may he sigh and groan,
      Under the burden of a heavy cross,
      He faintly goes to make their gain his loss.

        ·   ·   ·   ·   ·   ·

—1611

---

[1] *while the women cried* "The tears of the daughters of Jerusalem" (original marginalia).

[2] *To speak…of thing* "And when he [Jesus] was accused of the chief priests and elders, he answered nothing. Then said Pilate unto him, Hearest thou not how many things they witness against thee? And he answered him to never a word; insomuch that the governor marvelled greatly" (Matthew 27:12–14).

---

[3] ll. 981–1000 In Luke 23:27–31, Jesus addresses the daughters of Jerusalem and foretells monumental disasters.

The Description of Cooke-ham [1]

Farewell (sweet Cooke-ham) where I first
    obtained
Grace from that grace where perfect grace
    remained; [2]
And where the Muses gave their full consent,
I should have power the virtuous to content:
5 Where princely palace willed me to indite,
The sacred story of the soul's delight. [3]
Farewell (sweet place) where virtue then did rest,
And all delights did harbour in her breast:
Never shall my sad eyes again behold
10 Those pleasures which my thoughts did then
    unfold:
Yet you (great lady) mistress of that place,
From whose desires did spring this work of
    grace; [4]
Vouchsafe to think upon those pleasures past,
As fleeting worldly joys that could not last:
15 Or, as dim shadows of celestial pleasures,
Which are desired above all earthly treasures.
Oh how (methought) against you thither came,
Each part did seem some new delight to frame!
The house received all ornaments to grace it,
20 And would endure no foulness to deface it.
The walks put on their summer liveries,
And all things else did hold like similes:
The trees with leaves, with fruits, with flowers clad,
Embraced each other, seeming to be glad,

25 Turning themselves to beauteous canopies,
To shade the bright sun from your brighter eyes:
The crystal streams with silver spangles graced,
While by the glorious sun they were embraced:
The little birds in chirping notes did sing,
30 To entertain both you and that sweet spring.
And Philomela with her sundry lays, [5]
Both you and that delightful place did praise.
Oh how methought each plant, each flower, each
    tree
Set forth their beauties then to welcome thee:
35 The very hills right humbly did descend,
When you to tread upon them did intend.
And as you set your feet, they still did rise,
Glad that they could receive so rich a prize.
The gentle winds did take delight to be
40 Among those woods that were so graced by thee.
And in sad murmur uttered pleasing sound,
That pleasure in that place might more abound:
The swelling banks delivered all their pride,
When such a Phoenix once they had espied. [6]
45 Each arbor, bank, each seat, each stately tree,
Thought themselves honoured in supporting thee.
The pretty birds would oft come to attend thee,
Yet fly away for fear they should offend thee:
The little creatures in the burrow by
50 Would come abroad to sport them in your eye;
Yet fearful of the bow in your fair hand,
Would run away when you did make a stand.
Now let me come unto that stately tree,
Wherein such goodly prospects you did see;
55 That oak that did in height his fellows pass,
As much as lofty trees, low growing grass:
Much like a comely cedar straight and tall,
Whose beauteous stature far exceeded all:
How often did you visit this fair tree,

---

[1] *The Description of Cooke-ham* Written in honour of Margaret Clifford, Countess Dowager of Cumberland, this poem describes the crown manor of Cookeham leased by the Countess's brother, Lord William Russell of Thornhaugh.

[2] *Grace from...grace remained* Lanyer's pun on "grace" reflects multiple denotations of the word: (1) favourable qualities; (2) the condition of being favoured; (3) the source of divine grace or its recipient; (4) a courtesy title given to those who hold particular titles (*OED* grace *sb* I.1; II.7; 11a,d; 16b).

[3] *indite* compose (*OED* indite *v* 3).

[4] *this work of grace* this poem.

[5] *Philomela* the nightingale.

[6] *Phoenix* A mythical bird that lives five or six hundred years; it then burns itself on a funeral pyre of twigs only to emerge from its ashes with renewed youth. The point of the reference here is the uniqueness of the Phoenix.

60 Which seeming joyful in receiving thee,
Would like a palm tree spread his arms abroad,
Desirous that you there should make abode:
Whose fair green leaves much like a comely veil,
Defended Phoebus when he would assail: [1]

65 Whose pleasing boughs did yield a cool fresh air,
Joying his happiness when you were there.
Where being seated, you might plainly see,
Hills, vales, and woods, as if on bended knee
They had appeared, your honour to salute,

70 Or to prefer some strange unlooked for suit: [2]
All interlaced with brooks and crystal springs,
A prospect fit to please the eyes of kings:
And thirteen shires appeared all in your sight,
Europe could not afford much more delight.

75 What was there then but gave you all content,
While you the time in meditation spent,
Of their Creator's power, which there you saw,
In all his creatures held a perfect law;
And in their beauties did you plain descry,

80 His beauty, wisdom, grace, love, majesty.
In these sweet woods how often did you walk,
With Christ and his Apostles there to talk;
Placing his holy writ in some fair tree,
To meditate what you therein did see:

85 With Moses you did mount his holy hill,
To know his pleasure, and perform his will. [3]
With lovely David you did often sing,
His holy hymns to heaven's eternal King. [4]
And in sweet music did your soul delight,

90 To sound his praises, morning, noon, and night.
With blessed Joseph you did often feed
Your pined brethren, when they stood in need. [5]

And that sweet lady sprung from Clifford's race,
Of noble Bedford's blood, fair stream of grace;

95 To honourable Dorset now espoused,
In whose fair breast true virtue then was housed: [6]
Oh what delight did my weak spirits find
In those pure parts of her well framed mind:
And yet it grieves me that I cannot be

100 Near unto her, whose virtues did agree
With those fair ornaments of outward beauty,
Which did enforce from all both love and duty.
Unconstant fortune, thou art most to blame,
Who casts us down into so low a frame:

105 Where our great friends we cannot daily see,
So great a difference is there in degree. [7]
Many are placed in those orbs of state,
Parters in honour, so ordained by fate; [8]
Nearer in show, yet farther off in love,

110 In which, the lowest always are above.
But whither am I carried in conceit?
My wit too weak to conster of the great. [9]
Why not? although we are but born of earth,
We may behold the heavens, despising death;

115 And loving heaven that is so far above,
May in the end vouchsafe us entire love.
Therefore sweet memory do thou retain
Those pleasures past, which will not turn again:
Remember beauteous Dorset's former sports, [10]

120 So far from being touched by ill reports;
Wherein myself did always bear a part,
While reverend love presented my true heart:

---

[1] *Defended Phoebus* protected her from the sun.

[2] *prefer* proffer (*OED* prefer *v* II.4); *suit* petition (*OED* suit *sb* 11).

[3] *Moses* Moses spoke with God on Mount Sinai and received the law and commandments (Exodus 24–33).

[4] *David* the Psalmist.

[5] *Joseph* Joseph gave provisions to his brothers though they had sold him into slavery and informed their father that he was dead (Genesis 37:26–36; 50:15–21).

[6] *stream* emended from "steam"; *And that sweet…espoused* an allusion to Lady Anne Clifford, the daughter of George Clifford, third Earl of Cumberland, and Margaret Russell, Countess of Cumberland. She is "of noble Bedford's blood" because her mother was the daughter of Francis Russell, third Earl of Bedford. On Feb. 25, 1609, Lady Anne married Richard Sackville, third Earl of Dorset.

[7] *great* of eminent rank or place; noble (*OED* great *a* A.III.12a).

[8] *Parters in honour* divided as a result of rank.

[9] *to conster of* to expound on (*OED* construe *v* 8,6)

[10] *former sports* e.g. masques, dancing, horseback riding and shuttlecock.

Those recreations let me bear in mind,
Which her sweet youth and noble thoughts did
    find:
125 Whereof deprived, I evermore must grieve,
Hating blind fortune, careless to relieve.
And you sweet Cooke-ham, whom these ladies
    leave,
I now must tell the grief you did conceive
At their departure; when they went away,
130 How everything retained a sad dismay:
Nay long before, when once an inkling came,
Methought each thing did unto sorrow frame:
The trees that were so glorious in our view,
Forsook both flowers and fruit, when once they
    knew
135 Of your depart, their very leaves did wither,
Changing their colours as they grew together.
But when they saw this had no power to stay you,
They often wept, though speechless, could not
    pray you;
Letting their tears in your fair bosoms fall,
140 As if they said, "Why will ye leave us all?"
This being vain, they cast their leaves away,
Hoping that pity would have made you stay:
Their frozen tops like Age's hoary hairs,
Shows their disasters, languishing in fears:
145 A swarthy rivelled ryne all overspread,
Their dying bodies half alive, half dead. [1]
But your occasions called you so away,
That nothing there had power to make you stay:
Yet did I see a noble grateful mind,
150 Requiting each according to their kind, [2]
Forgetting not to turn and take your leave
Of these sad creatures, powerless to receive
Your favour when with grief you did depart,
Placing their former pleasures in your heart;
155 Giving great charge to noble memory,
There to preserve their love continually:

But specially the love of that fair tree,
That first and last you did vouchsafe to see:
In which it pleased you oft to take the air,
160 With noble Dorset, then a virgin fair:
Where many a learned book was read and scanned
To this fair tree, taking me by the hand,
You did repeat the pleasures which had past,
Seeming to grieve they could no longer last.
165 And with a chaste, yet loving kiss took leave,
Of which sweet kiss I did it soon bereave:
Scorning a senseless creature should possess
So rare a favour, so great happiness.
No other kiss it could receive from me,
170 For fear to give back what it took of thee:
So I ungrateful creature did deceive it,
Of that which you vouchsafed in love to leave it.
And though it oft had giv'n me much content,
Yet this great wrong I never could repent:
175 But of the happiest made it most forlorn,
To show that nothing's free from fortune's scorn,
While all the rest with this most beauteous tree,
Made their sad consort sorrow's harmony.
The flowers that on the banks and walks did grow,
180 Crept in the ground, the grass did weep for woe.
The winds and waters seemed to chide together,
Because you went away they know not whither:
And those sweet brooks that ran so fair and clear,
With grief and trouble wrinkled did appear.
185 Those pretty birds that wonted were to sing,
Now neither sing, nor chirp, nor use their wing;
But with their tender feet on some bare spray,
Warble forth sorrow, and their own dismay.
Faire Philomela leaves her mournful ditty,
190 Drowned in dead sleep, yet can procure no pity:
Each arbour, bank, each seat, each stately tree,
Looks bare and desolate now for want of thee; [3]
Turning green tresses into frosty grey,
While in cold grief they wither all away.
195 The sun grew weak, his beams no comfort gave,

---

[1] *rivelled ryne*   wrinkled or shrivelled bark (*OED* rivelled *a* 1c,2; rind).

[2] *Requiting*   rewarding (*OED* requite *v* 1).

[3] *want*   lack (*OED* want *sb²* 2a).

SONGS AND SONNETS

The Apparition

When by thy scorn, O murdress, I am dead,
 And that thou thinkst thee free
From all solicitation from me,
Then shall my ghost come to thy bed,
5 And thee, fain'd vestal, in worse arms shall see; [1]
Then thy sick taper will begin to wink,
And he, whose thou art then, being tir'd before,
Will, if thou stir, or pinch to wake him, think
 Thou call'st for more,
10 And in false sleep will from thee shrink,
And then poor aspen wretch, neglected thou [2]
Bath'd in a cold quicksilver sweat wilt lie [3]
 A verier ghost than I,
What I will say, I will not tell thee now,
15 Lest that preserve thee; and since my love is spent,
I'had rather thou shouldst painfully repent,
Than by my threatnings rest still innocent.
 —1633

The Flea

Mark but this flea, and mark in this,
 How little that which thou deny'st me is;
Me it suck'd first, and now sucks thee, [4]
And in this flea, our two bloods mingled be;
5 Thou know'st that this cannot be said
A sin, nor shame, nor loss of maidenhead,
 Yet this enjoys before it woo,

And pamper'd swells with one blood made of
 two,
And this, alas, is more than we would do. [5]

10 Oh stay, three lives in one flea spare,
Where we almost, nay more than married are.
This flea is you and I, and this
Our marriage bed, and marriage temple is;
Though parents grudge, and you, w'are met,
15 And cloistered in these living walls of jet.
 Though use make you apt to kill me,
 Let not to that, self murder added be,
 And sacrilege, three sins in killing three.

Cruel and sudden, hast thou since
20 Purpled thy nail, in blood of innocence?
Wherein could this flea guilty be,
Except in that drop which it sucked from thee?
Yet thou triumph'st, and say'st that thou
Find'st not thy self, nor me the weaker now;
25 'Tis true, then learn how false, fears be;
 Just so much honor, when thou yield'st to me,
 Will waste, as this flea's death took life from
 thee.
 —1633

The Good-Morrow

I wonder by my troth, what thou, and I
 Did, till we lov'd? were we not wean'd till then?
But suck'd on country pleasures, childishly?
Or snorted we in the seven sleepers' den? [6]
5 T'was so; But this, all pleasures fancies be
If ever any beauty I did see,

---

[1] *vestal*   virgin, a chaste woman (*OED* vestal *sb* 2).

[2] *aspen*   tremulous, quivering, quaking, timorous (*OED* aspen *a* 2).

[3] *quicksilver*   pertaining to quicksilver, the metal mercury, so called for its liquid mobile form at ordinary temperatures (*OED* quicksilver *a* 3, *sb* 1).

[4] "one world" in the 1633 edition.

[5] In Aristotelian physiology coition was thought to be a mingling of bloods.

[6] *seven sleepers*   The seven sleepers of Ephesus were the heroes of a Christian legend. Having been walled up alive in a cave during the persecution of Christians by the Roman emperor Decius, they slept for 187 years.

Which I desir'd, and got, t'was but a dream of
    thee.

And now good morrow to our waking souls,
Which watch not one another out of fear;
10 For love, all love of other sights controls,
And makes one little room, an every where.
Let sea-discoverers to new worlds have gone,
Let maps to others, worlds on worlds have shown,
Let us possess our world, each hath one, and is
15   one. [1]

My face in thine eye, thine in mine appears,
And true plain hearts do in the faces rest,
Where can we find two better hemispheres
Without sharp North, without declining West?
20 What ever dies, was not mixed equally; [2]
If our two loves be one, or, thou and I
Love so alike, that none do slacken, none can die.
    —1633

Love's Alchemy

Some that have deeper digged love's mine than I,
Say, where his centric happiness doth lie: [3]
    I have lov'd, and got, and told, [4]
But should I love, get, tell, till I were old,
5 I should not find that hidden mystery;
    Oh, 'tis imposture all:
And as no chymic yet th'elixir got, [5]
    But glorifies his pregnant pot,

If by the way to him befall
10 Some odoriferous thing, or medicinal, [6]
    So, lovers dream a rich and long delight,
    But get a winter-seeming summer's night.

Our ease, our thrift, our honour, and our day,
Shall we, for this vain bubble's shadow pay?
15   Ends love in this, that my man, [7]
Can be as happy as I can; if he can
Endure the short scorn of a bridegroom's play?
    That loving wretch that swears,
'Tis not the bodies marry, but the minds,
20   Which he in her angelic finds,
    Would swear as justly, that he hears,
In that day's rude hoarse minstralsy, the spheres. [8]
  Hope not for mind in women; at their best
Sweetness and wit they are but *mummy*,
    possessed. [9]
    —1633

The Indifferent

I can love both fair and brown,
Her whom abundance melts, and her whom
    want betrays
Her who loves loneness best, and her who masks
    and plays,
Her whom the country formed, and whom the
    town,

---

[1] *our world* "one world" in 1633. I agree with Helen Gardner, though without her characteristic certainty, that "our world" is the better reading; the question of which is the more meaningful is worth a good deal of consideration.

[2] *What ever dies, was not mixed equally* in reference to the theory that disease originated from unbalanced elements in the body.

[3] *centric* central.

[4] *told* counted (*OED* tell *v* II 10).

[5] *chymic* chemist.

[6] *Some odoriferous thing…medicinal* The search for the elixir of life or the philosopher's stone was expected to have such byproducts; their presence was often cited by the alchemist as signalling likely success in the quest.

[7] *my man* my servant.

[8] *rude hoarse minstralsy* Seventeenth-century wedding days typically included music and bawdy humour.

[9] *mummy* i.e. as preserved flesh; the word was also used to refer to a medicine made from the substance of mummies (*OED* mummy); *possessed* possessed by a spirit; possessed sexually; owned (*OED* possess *v* 4, 3b,2).

5   Her who believes, and her who tries, [1]
Her who still weeps with spongy eyes,
And her who is dry cork, and never cries;
I can love her, and her, and you and you,
I can love any, so she be not true.

10   Will no other vice content you?
Will it not serve your turn to do, as did your
    mothers?
Have you old vices spent, and now would find
    out others?
Or doth a fear, that men are true, torment you?
Oh we are not, be not you so,
15   Let me, and do you, twenty know.
Rob me, but bind me not, and let me go.
Must I, who came to travail thorough you, [2]
Grow your fixed subject, because you are true?

Venus heard me sigh this song,
20   And by Love's sweetest part, variety, she swore,
She heard not this till now; and that it should be
    so no more.
She went, examined, and returned ere long,
And said, "Alas, some two or three
Poor heretics in love there be,
25   Which think to stablish dangerous constancy.
But I have told them, 'Since you will be true,
You shall be true to them, who are false to you.'"
—1633

The Anniversary

All Kings, and all their favorites,
All glory of honors, beauties, wits,

The Sun itself, which makes times, as they pass,
Is elder by a year, now, than it was
5   When thou and I first one another saw:
All other things, to their destruction draw,
    Only our love hath no decay;
This, no tomorrow hath, nor yesterday,
Running it never runs from us away,
10   But truly keeps his first, last, everlasting day.

    Two graves must hide thine and my corse, [3]
    If one might, death were no divorce,
Alas, as well as other princes, we,
(Who prince enough in one another be,)
15   Must leave at last in death, these eyes, and ears,
Oft fed with true oaths, and with sweet salt tears;
    But souls where nothing dwells but love
(All other thoughts being inmates) then shall
    prove [4]
This, or a love increased there above,
20   When bodies to their graves, souls from their
    graves remove.

    And then we shall be throughly blest,
    But we no more, than all the rest,
Here upon earth, we'are Kings, and none but we
Can be such Kings, nor of such subjects be;
25   Who is so safe as we? where none can do
Treason to us, except one of us two.
    True and false fears let us refrain,
Let us love nobly, and live, and add again
Years and years unto years, till we attain
30   To write threescore: this is the second of our
    reign.
—1633

---

[1] *Her who believes, and her who tries* the woman who believes a lover's vows, and the one who puts them to the test.

[2] *travail* trouble, hardship (*OED sb*[1] travail); to journey (*OED* travail *v* II 5); *travel* in 1635 and subsequent editions. The word may be understood both as a noun and, with "to," as the infinitive of the verb. The possibilities of word-play are intriguing, but the primary meaning is that the speaker entered into a relationship, intending to pass through it and on to another.

---

[3] *corse* corpse (*OED* corse *sb* 2).

[4] *inmates* foreigners, strangers (*OED* inmate *sb* 1b).

The Sun Rising

Busy old fool, unruly Sun,
  Why dost thou thus,
Through windows, and through curtains call on us?
Must to thy motions lovers' seasons run?
5   Saucy pedantic wretch, go chide
      Late school boys and sour prentices, [1]
    Go tell Court-huntsmen, that the King will ride,
    Call country ants to harvest offices; [2]
Love, all alike, no season knows, nor clime, [3]
10 Nor hours, days, months, which are the rags of
    time.

    Thy beams, so reverend, and strong
      Why shouldst thou think?
I could eclipse and cloud them with a wink,
But that I would not lose her sight so long:
15   If her eyes have not blinded thine,
      Look, and tomorrow late, tell me,
    Whether both the Indias of spice and mine [4]
    Be where thou leftst them, or lie here with me.
Ask for those Kings whom thou saw'st yesterday,
20 And thou shalt hear, all here in one bed lay.

    She'is all States, and all Princes, I,
      Nothing else is.
Princes do but play us, compar'd to this,
All honor's mimic; all wealth alchemy;[5]
25   Thou sun art half as happy'as we,
      In that the world's contracted thus.
    Thine age asks ease, and since thy duties be
    To warm the world, that's done in warming us.

Shine here to us, and thou art everywhere;
30 This bed thy center is, these walls, thy sphere.
    —1633

The Canonization

For Godsake hold your tongue, and let me love,
  Or chide my palsy, or my gout,
My five gray hairs, or ruin'd fortune flout, [6]
    With wealth your state, your mind with arts
      improve,
5   Take you a course, get you a place,
      Observe his honour, or his grace,
Or the King's real, or his stamped face [7]
    Contemplate, what you will, approve,
    So you will let me love.

10 Alas, alas, who's injur'd by my love?
    What merchant's ships have my sighs drown'd?
Who says my tears have overflow'd his ground?
    When did my colds a forward spring remove?
      When did the heats which my veins fill
15   Add one more to the plaguy bill? [8]
Soldiers find wars, and lawyers find out still
    Litigious men, which quarrels move,
    Though she and I do love.

Call us what you will, we are made such by love;
20   Call her one, me another fly,
We'are tapers too, and at our own cost die,
    And we in us find the Eagle and the Dove,

---

[1] *sour prentices*   peevish, discontented apprentices (*OED* sour *a* 5).

[2] *harvest offices*   the duties of harvest time.

[3] *clime*   climate (*OED* clime 1) or region (*OED* clime 2).

[4] *the Indias of spice and mine*   the East and West Indies; Donne wrote in a letter of 1624 "Eastward…is the way to the land of Perfumes and Spices…Westward…is the way to the land of Gold, and of Mines."

[5] *alchemy*   glittering dross, refuse, rubbish (*OED* alchemy 4).

---

[6] *palsy…gout / …five grey hairs*   Nowadays it might be said to a young person seen smoking, "You are too old to do that." Donne is suggesting that his interlocutor might make a similar objection to his throwing away his health and worldly prospects on a love affair.

[7] *his stamped face*   the king's face stamped on coins.

[8] *plaguy bill*   the official list of the deaths caused by the plague in any district (*OED sb* plague 4c).

The Phoenix riddle hath more wit [1]
   By us, we two being one, are it.
25 So, to one neutral thing both sexes fit,
   We die and rise the same, and prove
   Mysterious by this love. [2]

We can die by it, if not live by love,
   And if unfit for tombs and hearse
30 Our legend be, it will be fit for verse;
   And if no piece of chronicle we prove, [3]
     We'll build in sonnets pretty rooms;
     As well a well wrought urn becomes
The greatest ashes, as half-acre tombs,
35   And by these hymns, all shall approve
     Us *canonized* for love. [4]

And thus invoke us: "You whom reverend love
   Made one another's hermitage;
You, to whom love was peace, that now is rage,
40   Who did the whole world's soul contract, and
     drove
     Into the glasses of your eyes [5]
     So made such mirrors, and such spies,
That they did all to you epitomize,
   Countries, towns, courts: Beg from above
45   A pattern of your love."
—1633

Confined Love

Some man unworthy to be possessor
   Of old or new love, himself being false or
     weak,
Thought his pain and shame would be lesser,
If on womankind he might his anger wreak,
5   And thence a law did grow,
     One should but one man know;
     But are other creatures so? [6]

   Are sun, moon, or stars by law forbidden,
To smile where they list, or lend away their light?
10   Are birds divorc'd, or are they chidden
If they leave their mate, or lie abroad a night?
     Beasts do no jointures lose [7]
     Though they new lovers choose,
     But we are made worse than those.

   Who e'r rigged fair ship to lie in harbours,
15 And not to seek new lands, or not to deal withal?
   Or built fair houses, set trees, and arbours,
Only to lock up, or else to let them fall?
     Good is not good, unless
20   A thousand it possess,
     But doth waste with greediness. [8]
—1633

---

[1] *The Phoenix riddle* The phoenix is a mythical bird which burns itself to ashes every five hundred years, and emerges renewed from the fire (*OED* phoenix 1).

[2] *die* often used to refer to sexual climax.

[3] *legend* the life of a saint; *chronicle* the life of a king or great man.

[4] *canonized* i.e. they will be universally recognized as saints.

[5] *contract* Helen Gardner preferred *extract,* which has manuscript authority and yields an alchemical metaphor. Donne was at least as addicted to kinetic words as he was to alchemical ones; and the reader who "traces the leading thought throughout the whole" (Coleridge on this poem) may understand why *contract* is the better reading.

---

[6] Helen Gardner suggests that this poem is spoken by a woman, and notes a speech in Ovid's *Metaphorphoses* (320–355) in which Myrrha expresses regret that human laws forbid what nature does nothing to prohibit: "other animals mate as they will, nor is it thought base for a heifer to endure her sire, nor for his own offspring to be a horse's mate....Happy they who have such privilege! Human civilization has made spiteful laws; and what nature allows, the jealous laws forbid..." (trans. J.F. Miller, 1916).

[7] *jointures* payments made to widows, which cease upon re-marriage (*OED* jointure 2).

[8] *waste with greediness* wastes away as a result of the greed of its possessor, who keeps even what he cannot use.

Air and Angels

Twice or thrice had I loved thee,
   Before I knew thy face or name;
So in a voice, so in a shapeless flame,
Angels affect us oft, and worship'd be,
5   Still when, to where thou wert, I came
Some lovely glorious nothing I did see,
   But since, my soul, whose child love is,
Takes limbs of flesh, and else could nothing do,
   More subtle than the parent is,
10 Love must not be, but take a body too,
     And therefore what thou wert, and who
       I did Love ask, and now
That it assume thy body, I allow,
And fix itself in thy lip, eye, and brow.

15 Whilst thus to ballast love, I thought,
And so more steadily to have gone,
With wares which would sink admiration,
I saw, I had love's pinnace overfraught,
     Ev'ry thy hair for love to work upon
20 Is much too much, some fitter must be sought;
     For, nor in nothing, nor in things
Extreme, and scattring bright, can love inhere;
   Then as an Angel, face, and wings
Of air, not pure as it, yet pure doth wear, [1]
25   So thy love may be my love's sphere;
       Just such disparity
As is twixt Air and Angel's purity,
T'wixt women's love, and men's will ever be.
     —1633

---

[1] *face, and wings / Of air* Angels were thought to achieve visibility by assuming a body of air.

Twicknam Garden [2]

Blasted with sighs, and surrounded with tears,
   Hither I come to seek the spring,
   And at mine eyes, and at mine ears,
Receive such balms, as else cure everything,
5   But O, self traitor, I do bring
The spider love, which transubstantiates all, [3]
   And can convert manna to gall, [4]
And that this place may thoroughly be thought
   True Paradise, I have the serpent brought. [5]

10 'Twere wholesomer for me, that winter did
     Benight the glory of this place, [6]
   And that a grave frost did forbid
These trees to laugh and mock me to my face;
     But that I may not this disgrace
15 Endure, nor leave this garden, Love let me
     Some senseless piece of this place be;
Make me a mandrake, so I may grow here, [7]
     Or a stone fountain weeping out my year.

Hither with crystal vials, lovers come,
20   And take my tears, which are love's wine,
   And try your mistress' tears at home,
For all are false, that taste not just like mine;
     Alas, hearts do not in eyes shine,

---

[2] *Twicknam Garden* the residence of Lucy, Countess of Bedford, Donne's patron.

[3] *transubstantiates* transforms, transmutes (*OED* transubstantiate *v*). The word was used most commonly to refer to the Roman Catholic belief that the sacramental bread and wine are transformed into the body and blood of Christ.

[4] *manna* food sent by God to the Israelites during their exodus from Egypt (Exodus 16:4–35); *gall* a bitter substance. Jesus, during his crucifixion, asked for wine, and was given wine mixed with gall. After tasting it he refused to drink (Matthew 27:34).

[5] *the serpent* Genesis 3:1–15.

[6] *Benight* darken, cloud (*OED* benight *v* 2).

[7] *mandrake* a plant, whose forked root is thought to resemble the human form. It was fabled to utter a deadly shriek when plucked up from the ground (*OED* mandrake 1).

Nor can you more judge woman's thoughts by
    tears,
25   Then by her shadow, what she wears.
O perverse sex, where none is true but she,
    Who's therefore true, because her truth kills me.
    —1633

A Valediction: of Weeping

Let me pour forth
    My tears before thy face, whil'st I stay
    here,
For thy face coins them, and thy stamp they bear,
And by this mintage they are something worth,
5   For thus they be
    Pregnant of thee,
Fruits of much grief they are, emblems of more,
When a tear falls, that thou falls which it bore,
So thou and I are nothing then, when on a diverse
    shore.

10   On a round ball
A workman that hath copies by, can lay
An Europe, Afric, and an Asia,
And quickly make that, which was nothing, *All*,
    So doth each tear,
15   Which thee doth wear,
A globe, yea world by that impression grow,
Till thy tears mixed with mine do overflow
This world, by waters sent from thee, my heaven
    dissolved so.

    O more than Moon,
20 Draw not up seas to drown me in thy sphere,
Weep me not dead, in thine arms, but forbear
To teach the sea, what it may do too soon,
    Let not the wind
    Example find,
25 To do me more harm, than it purposeth,
Since thou and I sigh one another's breath,

Who e'r sighs most, is cruellest, and hastes the
    other's death.
—1633

The Ecstasy

Where, like a pillow on a bed,
    A pregnant bank swell'd up, to rest
The violet's reclining head,
    Sat we two, one another's best;

5   Our hands were firmly cemented
    With a fast balm, which thence did spring,
Our eye-beams twisted, and did thread
    Our eyes, upon one double string;

So to entergraft our hands, as yet
10   Was all our means to make us one,
And pictures in our eyes to get
    Was all our propagation. [1]

As 'twixt two equal armies, Fate
    Suspends uncertain victory,
15 Our souls, (which to advance their state,
    Were gone out,) hung 'twixt her, and me.

And whil'st our souls negotiate there,
    We like sepulchral statues lay;
All day, the same our postures were,
20   And we said nothing, all the day.

If any, so by love refin'd,
    That he soul's language understood,
And by good love were grown all mind,
    Within convenient distance stood,

25 He (though he knew not which soul spake,
    Because both meant, both spake the same)

---

[1] *pictures in our eyes* reflections of each other; "seeing babies" is the idiomatic expression of Donne's thought in these two lines.

Might thence a new concoction take, [1]
    And part far purer than he came.

This Ecstasy doth unperplex
30   (We said) and tell us what we love,
We see by this, it was not sex,
    We see, we saw not what did move:

But as all several souls contain
    Mixture of things, they know not what,
35 Love, these mixed souls, doth mix again,
    And makes both one, each this and that.

A single violet transplant,
    The strength, the colour, and the size,
(All which before was poor, and scant,)
40   Redoubles still, and multiplies.

When love, with one another so
    Interinanimates two souls,
That abler soul, which thence doth flow,
    Defects of loneliness controls.

45 We then, who are this new soul, know,
    Of what we are compos'd, and made,
For, th'atomies of which we grow,
    Are souls, whom no change can invade.

But O alas, so long, so far
50   Our bodies why do we forbear?
They are ours, though not we, we are
    The intelligences, they the sphere. [2]

We owe them thanks, because they thus,
    Did us, to us, at first convey,

55 Yielded their forces, sense, to us,
    Nor are dross to us, but allay. [3]

On man heaven's influence works not so,
    But that it first imprints the air,
So soul into the soul may flow,
60   Though it to body first repair.

As our blood labours to beget
    Spirits, as like souls as it can, [4]
Because such fingers need to knit
    That subtle knot, which makes us man: [5]

65 So must pure lovers' souls descend
    T'affections, and to faculties,
Which sense may reach and apprehend,
    Else a great Prince in prison lies.

To our bodies turn we then, that so
70   Weak men on love reveal'd may look;
Love's mysteries in souls do grow,
    But yet the body is his book.

And if some lover, such as we,
    Have heard this dialogue of one,
75 Let him still mark us, he shall see
    Small change, when we'are to bodies gone.
    —1633

---

[1] *concoction* bringing to a state of perfection (*OED* concoction 2).

[2] *The intelligences* The celestial spheres were thought to be moved by incorporeal "intelligences."

[3] *dross* the scum or extraneous matter thrown off from metals in the process of melting (*OED* dross *sb* 1); *allay* alloy, a mixture of metals (*OED* alloy *sb* 5).

[4] *Spirits* In contemporary thought "spirit" was thought to mediate between body and soul.

[5] *subtle* finely woven; see the etymology under *OED* subtle *a*.

Farewell to Love [1]

W hilst yet to prove, [2]
I thought there was some deity in love,
So did I reverence, and gave
Worship, as atheists at their dying hour
5 Call, what they cannot name, an unknown power,
As ignorantly did I crave:
Thus when
Things not yet known are coveted by men,
Our desires give them fashion, and so [3]
10 As they wax lesser, fall, as they size, grow. [4]

But, from late fair
His highness sitting in a golden chair, [5]
Is not less cared for after three days
By children, than the thing which lovers so
15 Blindly admire, and with such worship woo;
Being had, enjoying it decays: [6]
And thence,
What before pleased them all, takes but one sense, [7]
And that so lamely, as it leaves behind
20 A kind of sorrowing dullness to the mind.

Ah cannot we,
As well as cocks and lions jocund be, [8]
After such pleasures, unless wise
Nature decreed (since each such act, they say,
25 Diminisheth the length of life a day) [9]
This; as she would man should despise
The sport, [10]
Because that other curse of being short, [11]
And only for a minute made to be
30 Eager, desires to raise posterity. [12]

Since so, my mind [13]
Shall not desire what no man else can find,
I'll no more dote and run
To pursue things which had endamaged me.
35 And when I come where moving beauties be, [14]
As men do when the summer's sun
Grows great,
Though I admire their greatness, shun their heat;
Each place can afford shadows. If all fail,
40 'Tis but applying worm-seed to the tail. [15]
—1635

---

[1] A.J. Smith observes that "Petrarch renounced his love of Laura for the love of God at one stage in the moral turmoil of his self-destructive obsession with a fellow-creature" and that "an abrupt dismissal of love became a customary Petrarchan move," referring to Sidney's sonnet which begins "Leave me O love which reachest but to dust, / And thou my mind aspire to higher things."

[2] *Whilst yet to prove* subject to a testing process (*OED* prove 1).

[3] *fashion* characteristic form (*OED* fashion *sb* 1).

[4] *size* increase in size (*OED* size *v* 5b).

[5] *from late fair...golden chair* At the large annual fair held in the churchyard of St. Bartholomew's, Smithfield (Bartholomew Fair) images in gingerbread of foreign monarchs or of the Pope, designed for the consumption of children, were commonly sold.

[6] *Being had, enjoying it decays* This is the same thought as in Shakespeare's sonnet beginning "The expense of spirit in a waste of shame/ Is lust in action." Once sexual enjoyment has been achieved, it ceases to be interesting.

[7] *pleased them all* that is, pleased all the senses; *takes* is attractive to.

[8] *cocks and lions* It was believed that these creatures were distinguished by their ability to resist "dullness" after orgasm.

[9] *Diminisheth the length of life a day* According to Aristotle sexual activity shortens life; Christianity linked this claim to the alleged sinfulness of such activity.

[10] *as she would* as Nature would [have it that].

[11] *curse of being short* the shortness of human life (resulting from the original sin in the Garden) as well as the shortness of the detumescent male organ.

[12] *to raise posterity* to raise children (i.e. it is a curse resulting from the Fall that we desire to perpetuate our mortal selves through having offspring; but that desire results in our killing ourselves through sex; hence Nature, in order to prolong our lives, may have instilled in us a sense of disillusionment about sex).

[13] *Since so* since this is so.

[14] *moving* "affecting" (*OED* moving *a* 2b) as well as "in motion."

[15] *worm-seed* a strong anaphrodisiac; *the tail* the penis.

A Valediction: forbidding Mourning

As virtuous men pass mildly away,
   And whisper to their souls, to go,
Whilst some of their sad friends do say,
   The breath goes now, and some say, no:

5 So let us melt, and make no noise,
   No tear-floods, nor sigh-tempests move,
T'were profanation of our joys,
   To tell the laity our love.

Moving of th'earth brings harms and fears,
10   Men reckon what it did and meant, [1]
But trepidation of the spheres, [2]
   Though greater far, is innocent.

Dull sublunary lovers' love [3]
   (Whose soul is sense) cannot admit
15 Absence, because it doth remove
   Those things which elemented it.

But we by a love, so much refined,
That our selves know not what it is,
Inter-assured of the mind,
20 Care less, eyes, lips, and hands to miss.

Our two souls therefore, which are one,
Though I must go, endure not yet
A breach, but an expansion,
Like gold to airy thinness beat.

25 If they be two, they are two so
As stiff twin compasses are two,

Thy soul the fixed foot, makes no show
To move, but doth, if th'other do.

And though it in the centre sit,
30 Yet when the other far doth roam,
It leans, and hearkens after it,
And grows erect, as that comes home.

Such wilt thou be to me, who must
Like th'other foot, obliquely run;
35 Thy firmness makes my circle just,
And makes me end, where I begun.
—1633

A Nocturnal upon S. Lucy's Day being the shortest day [4]

'Tis the year's midnight, and it is the day's,
   Lucy's, who scarce seven hours herself unmasks,
   The Sun is spent, and now his flasks [5]
   Send forth light squibs, no constant rays; [6]
5   The world's whole sap is sunk:
The general balm th'hydroptic earth hath drunk, [7]
Whither, as to the bed's-feet, life is shrunk,
Dead and interred, yet all these seem to laugh,
Compar'd with me, who am their Epitaph.

10 Study me then, you who shall lovers be
At the next world, that is, at the next Spring:
   For I am every dead thing,
      In whom love wrought new Alchemy.
         For his art did express

---

[1] *Moving of th'earth...did and meant* In contrasting the damage caused by earthquakes and the harmlessness of the trepidation of the spheres, Donne is preparing for the contrast between his love and that of "dull sublunary lovers."

[2] *trepidation* vibration, oscillation (*OED* trepidation 2).

[3] *sublunary* inferior, subordinate (*OED* sublunary *a* 2).

[4] *Nocturnal* night-piece (*OED* nocturnal *sb* B1).

[5] *flasks* used to hold gunpowder (*OED* flask *sb²* 2); the reference is probably to the stars, believed to store light from the sun. See *Paradise Lost* 7:346–369.

[6] *squibs* explosive devices used as missiles or means of attack (*OED* squib *sb* 2a).

[7] *hydroptic* (an erroneous formation from hydropsy) insatiably thirsty (*OED* hydropic *a* 2). In one of his letters Donne wrote of having "an hydroptique immoderate desire of humane learning and languages."

15　A quintessence even from nothingness,
From dull privations, and lean emptiness:
He ruin'd me, and I am re-begot
Of absence, darkness, death; things which are not.

All others, from all things, draw all that's good,
20　Life, soul, form, spirit, whence they being have,
I, by love's limbeck, am the grave [1]
Of all, that's nothing. Oft a flood
Have we two wept, and so
Drowned the whole world, us two; oft did we
25　grow
To be two Chaosses, when we did show
Care to ought else; and often absences
Withdrew our souls, and made us carcasses.

But I am by her death, (which word wrongs her)
30　Of the first nothing, the elixir grown; [2]
Were I a man, that I were one,
I needs must know; I should prefer,
If I were any beast,
Some ends, some means; yea plants, yea stones
detest,
35　And love; all, all some properties invest;
If I an ordinary nothing were,
As shadow, a light, and body must be here.

But I am none; nor will my Sun renew.
You lovers, for whose sake, the lesser Sun
40　At this time to the Goat is run
To fetch new lust, and give it you,
Enjoy your summer all;
Since she enjoys her long night's festival,
Let me prepare towards her, and let me call
45　This hour her vigil, and her eve, since this
Both the year's, and the day's deep midnight is.
　　—1633

---

[1]　*limbeck*　an apparatus used in distilling (*OED* alembic 1).

[2]　*elixir*　a preparation thought to change metals into gold (*OED* elixir *sb* 1). Elixir also means the quintessence or soul of a thing, its kernel or secret principle (*OED* elixir *sb* 3b).

The Relic

When my grave is broke up again
Some second guest to entertain
(For graves have learn'd that woman-head
To be to more than one a bed) [3]
5　And he that digs it, spies
A bracelet of bright hair about the bone,
Will he not let us alone,
And think that there a loving couple lies,
Who thought that this device might be some way
10　To make their souls, at the last busy day,
Meet at this grave, and make a little stay? [4]

If this fall in a time, or land,
Where mis-devotion doth command, [5]
Then, he that digs us up, will bring
15　Us, to the Bishop, and the King,
To make us relics; then
Thou shalt be a Mary Magdalen, [6] and I
A something else thereby;
All women shall adore us, and some men;
20　And since at such time, miracles are sought, [7]
I would have that age by this paper taught
What miracles we harmless lovers wrought. [8]

First, we lov'd well and faithfully,
Yet knew not what we lov'd, nor why,
25　Difference of sex no more we knew,

---

[3]　*woman-head*　womanliness (with a play on "maidenhead").

[4]　*this device*　the inclusion of a lock of hair in the grave. At the Resurrection souls are supposed to be scattered; the suggestion here is that the lock of hair might help them find each other.

[5]　*mis-devotion*　i.e. devotion to relics.

[6]　*Mary Magdalen*　Mary Magdalen was usually represented in art with bright, golden hair.

[7]　*miracles are sought*　i.e. verification of miracles is sought for in relics.

[8]　*this paper*　this poem.

Than our guardian angels do, [1]
   Coming and going, we,
Perchance might kiss, but not between those
   meals.
   Our hands ne'r touched the seals,
30 Which nature, injur'd by late law, sets free:[2]
These miracles we did; but now alas,
All measure, and all language, I should pass,
Should I tell what a miracle she was.[3]

—1633

ELEGIES

Elegy VI

Oh, let me not serve so, as those men serve
   Whom honours' smokes at once fatten and
     sterve; [4]
Poorly enrich't with great men's words or looks;
Nor so write my name in thy loving books
5 As those idolatrous flatterers, which still
Their Prince's styles with many realms fulfill
Whence they no tribute have, and where no sway. [5]
Such services I offer as shall pay
Themselves, I hate dead names: Oh then let me
10 Favorite in ordinary, or no favorite be.

---

[1] *Difference of sex…guardian angels do* The love of angels is spiritual and has no sexual component.

[2] *the seals, / Which nature, injur'd by late law, sets free* In the original condition of free created nature, there were no restrictions on love; to conform to law requires "miracles".

[3] *I should pass* exceed (*OED* pass v B III 37).

[4] *honours' smokes* the smoke of honours, that fatten a name through added titles but which are essentially empty (making the "dead names" of l. 9); *sterve* starve; the original spelling is retained to indicate the rhyme created by contemporary pronunciation.

[5] *Their Prince's styles* Flatterers swell the royal "style" or title with the names of realms over which the Prince does not in fact rule; Donne may be glancing at English monarchs, who continued to be styled the rulers of France long after England lost its last foothold on the continent in 1558.

When my soul was in her own body sheath'd,
Nor yet by oaths betroth'd, nor kisses breath'd
Into my Purgatory, faithless thee,
Thy heart seem'd wax, and steel thy constancy.
15 So, careless flowers strowed on the water's face,
The curled whirlpools suck, smack, and embrace,
Yet drown them; so, the taper's beamy eye
Amorously twinkling, beckons the giddy fly,
Yet burns his wings; and such the devil is,
20 Scarce visiting them, who are entirely his.
When I behold a stream, which, from the spring,
Doth with doubtful melodious murmuring,
Or in a speechless slumber, calmly ride
Her wedded channel's bosom, and then chide
25 And bend her brows, and swell if any bough
Do but stoop down, to kiss her upmost brow:
Yet, if her often gnawing kisses win
The traitorous bank to gape, and let her in,
She rusheth violently, and doth divorce
30 Her from her native, and her long-kept course,
And roars, and braves it, and in gallant scorn,
In flattering eddies promising return,
She flouts the channel, who thenceforth is dry;
Then say I: that is she, and this am I.
35 Yet let not thy deep bitterness beget [6]
Careless despair in me, for that will whet
My mind to scorn; and Oh, love dull'd with pain
Was ne'er so wise, nor well arm'd as disdain.
Then with new eyes I shall survey thee, and spy
40 Death in thy cheeks, and darkness in thine eye.
Though hope bred faith and love; thus taught, I
   shall
As nations do from Rome, from thy love fall. [7]
My hate shall outgrow thine, and utterly
I will renounce thy dalliance: and when I

---

[6] *bitterness* cruelty, severity.

[7] *As nations do from Rome* that is, as nations that become Protestant "fall" from the Roman Catholic church.

45 Am the recusant, in that resolute state, [1]
What hurts it me to be excommunicate?
—1633

Elegy VII

Nature's lay idiot, I taught thee to love, [2]
And in that sophistry, oh, thou dost prove [3]
Too subtle: Fool, thou didst not understand
The mystic language of the eye nor hand:
5 Nor couldst thou judge the difference of the air
Of sighs, and say, this lies, this sounds despair:
Nor by the eyes' water call a malady
Desperately hot, or changing feverously.
I had not taught thee then, the alphabet
10 Of flowers, how they devisefully being set
And bound up, might with speechless secrecy
Deliver errands mutely, and mutually.
Remember since all thy words used to be
To every suitor; *Ay, if my friends agree.*
15 Since, household charms, thy husband's name to
    teach,
Were all the love tricks, that thy wit could reach; [4]
And since, an hour's discourse could scarce have
    made
One answer in thee, and that ill arrayed
In broken proverbs, and torn sentences.
20 Thou art not by so many duties his,
That from the world's common having sever'd
    thee,
Inlaid thee, neither to be seen, nor see,
As mine: who have with amorous delicacies
Refin'd thee into a blissful paradise.
25 Thy graces and good words my creatures be;

---

1 *recusant* generally, one who refuses to acknowledge authority, but in this period a Catholic who refused to attend the parish church.

2 *lay* uninstructed, unlearned (*OED* lay *a* 3a).

3 *sophistry* cunning, craft (*OED* sophistry *sb* 3).

4 *household charms...name to teach* rituals thought to reveal the name of a young woman's future husband.

I planted knowledge and life's tree in thee, [5]
Which oh, shall strangers taste? Must I alas
Frame and enamel plate, and drink in glass?
Chafe wax for others' seals? break a colt's force [6]
30 And leave him then, being made a ready horse?
—1633

Elegy VIII
The Comparison

As the sweet sweat of roses in a still, [7]
As that which from chaf'd musk cat's pores
    doth trill,
As the almighty balm of th'early East,
Such are the sweat drops of my mistress' breast,
5 And on her neck her skin such lustre sets,
They seem no sweat drops, but pearl carcanets. [8]
Rank sweaty froth thy mistress' brow defiles,
Like spermatic issue of ripe menstruous boils,
Or like that scum, which, by need's lawless law
10 Enforc'd, Sanserra's starved men did draw [9]
From parboiled shoes, and boots, and all the rest
Which were with any sovereign fatness blest,
And like vile lying stones in saffroned tin, [10]
Or warts, or weals, they hang upon her skin.
15 Round as the world's her head, on every side,
Like to the fatal ball which fell on Ide, [11]
Or that whereof God had such jealousy,

---

5 *knowledge and life's tree* See Genesis 2:9.

6 *Chafe* warm, heat (*OED* chafe *v* 1).

7 *still* an apparatus for distillation (*OED* still *sb¹*).

8 *carcanets* ornamental collars or necklaces (*OED* carcanet 1).

9 *Sanserra's starved men* In 1573 the Protestants of Sancerre were besieged by Catholics for nine months, enduring starvation for much of that period.

10 *lying stones in saffroned tin* fake stones in a fake setting of gilded tin (A.J.Smith).

11 *fatal ball which fell on Ide* the golden apple of discord which Paris was asked to award to the most beautiful of three powerful goddesses. His choice led to the Trojan wars.

As, for the ravishing thereof we die.
Thy head is like a rough-hewn statue of jet,
20 Where marks for eyes, nose, mouth, are yet scarce
    set;
Like the first Chaos, or flat seeming face
Of Cynthia, where th'earth's shadows her
    embrace. [1]
Like Proserpine's white beauty-keeping chest, [2]
Or Jove's best fortune's urn, is her fair breast. [3]
25 Thine's like worm eaten trunks, cloth'd in seal's
    skin,
Or grave, that's dust without, and stink within.
And like that slender stalk, at whose end stands
The woodbine quivering, are her arms and hands,
Like rough-bark'd elmboughs, or the russet skin
30 Of men late scourg'd for madness, or for sin,
Like sun-parch'd quarters on the city gate, [4]
Such is thy tann'd skin's lamentable state.
And like a bunch of ragged carrots stand
The short swoll'n fingers of thy gouty hand
35 Then like the Chymic's masculine equal fire, [5]
Which in the Limbeck's warm womb doth inspire
Into th'earth's worthless part a soul of gold,
Such cherishing heat her best lov'd part doth hold.
Thine's like the dread mouth of a fired gun,
40 Or like hot liquid metals newly run
Into clay moulds, or like to that Ætna [6]
Where round about the grass is burnt away.
Are not your kisses then as filthy, and more,

As a worm sucking an invenom'd sore?
45 Doth not thy fearful hand in feeling quake,
As one which gath'ring flowers, still fears a snake?
Is not your last act harsh, and violent,
As when a plough a stony ground doth rent?
So kiss good turtles, so devoutly nice [7]
50 Are priests in handling reverent sacrifice,
And such in searching wounds the surgeon is
As we, when we embrace, or touch, or kiss.
Leave her, and I will leave comparing thus,
She, and comparisons are odious.
—1633

Elegy IX
The Autumnal

No *spring*, nor *summer* beauty hath such grace,
    As I have seen in one *autumnal* face, [8]
Young beauties force your love, and that's a rape,
    This doth but counsel, yet you cannot scape.
5 If 'twere a shame to love, here 'twere no shame,
    Affection here takes reverence's name.
Were her first years the Golden Age; that's true,
    But now she's gold oft tried, and ever new. [9]
That was her torrid and inflaming time,
10   This is her tolerable tropic clime.
Fair eyes, who asks more heat than comes from
    hence,
    He in a fever wishes pestilence.
Call not these wrinkles, graves; if graves they were,
    They were Love's graves; for else he is no where.
15 Yet lies not Love dead here, but here doth sit

---

[1] *Cynthia* the moon.

[2] *Proserpine's white beauty-keeping chest* In Apuleius's *Golden Ass*
Psyche is ordered to take a box into the depths of hell and to beg from
Proserpina (Persephone) a little beauty for Venus.

[3] *Jove's best fortune urn* The two urns of Jove contained good fortune
and bad fortune (*Iliad* 24:527).

[4] *quarters* the four parts each containing a limb of a human body
similarly divided, as was commonly done in the case of those executed
for treason (*OED* quarter *sb* 2b).

[5] *Chymic* alchemist (*OED* chemic *sb* B1).

[6] *Ætna* a volcanic mountain near the east coast of Sicily, claimed to
be the smithy of Vulcan.

[7] *turtles* turtle doves.

[8] It was common for Renaissance authors to extol mature beauty; in
his essay *Of Beauty* Bacon writes *pulchrorum autumnus pulcher* (the
autumn of beautiful persons is beautiful).

[9] *Golden Age; that's true, / But now she's gold oft tried, and ever new* The
Golden Age was the age of innocence, like her early years; but now she
has been tried by experience and, like gold, has retained her virtue.

20   They love them for that, by which they are not
      they?
   Makes virtue woman? Must I cool my blood
   Till I both be, and find one wise and good?
   May barren angels love so. Bit if we
   Make love to woman, virtue is not she:
25   As beauty is not nor wealth. He that strays thus
   From her to hers, is more adulterous [1]
   Than if he took her maid. Search every sphere
   And firmament, our *Cupid* is not there. [2]
   He's an infernal god and under ground
30   With *Pluto* dwells, where gold and fire abound. [3]
   Men to such gods, their sacrificing coals
   Did not on altars lay, but pits and holes. [4]
   Although we see celestial bodies move
   Above the earth, the earth we till and love:
35   So we her airs contemplate, words and heart,
   And virtues; but we love the centric part. [5]
      Nor is the soul more worthy, or more fit
   For love than this, as infinite as it. [6]
   But in attaining this desired place
40   How much they stray, that set out at the face!
   The hair a forest is of ambushes,
   Of springes, snares, fetters and manacles: [7]
   The brow becalms us when 'tis smooth and plain,
   And when 'tis wrinkled, shipwrecks us again.
45   Smooth, 'tis a Paradise, where we would have
   Immortal stay, and wrinkled 'tis our grave.

---

[1] *From her to hers* from the unified essence of the woman to individual qualities attributed to her (but which may not truly belong to her).

[2] *Search every sphere...Cupid is not there* i.e. no constellation or planet is named after this god.

[3] *Pluto* the god of the underworld, also known as Hades. (N.B. The planet Pluto was not discovered and named until the twentieth century.)

[4] *pits and holes* Offerings to such pagan gods as these were to be thrown into trenches in the earth.

[5] *centric* earth, the centre of the universe.

[6] *than this* this part (i.e. the "centric part") of the body.

[7] *springes* snares; see *OED* springe *sb.*

The nose, like to the first meridian, runs
Not 'twixt an east and west, but 'twixt two suns;
It leaves a cheek, a rosy hemisphere
50   On either side, and then directs us where
   Upon the Islands Fortunate we fall, [8]
   Not faint *Canary*, but *ambrosial*,
   Her swelling lips; To which when we are come,
   We anchor there, and think ourselves at home,
55   For they seem all: there sirens' songs, and there
   Wise Delphic oracles do fill the ear;
   There in a creek where chosen pearls do swell,
   The Remora, her cleaving tongue doth dwell. [9]
   These, and the glorious promontory, her chin
60   O'er past; and the strait *Hellespont* between [10]
   The *Sestos* and *Abydos* of her breasts,
   (Not of two lovers, but two loves the nests)
   Succeeds a boundless sea, but yet thine eye
   Some Island moles may scattered there descry;
65   And sailing towards her *India*, in that way [11]
   Shall at her fair Atlantic navel stay;
   Though thence the current be thy pilot made,
   Yet ere thou be where thou wouldst be embayed,
   Thou shalt upon another forest set,
70   Where many shipwreck, and no further get.
   When thou art there, consider what this chase
   Mispent by thy beginning at the face.
      Rather set out below; practise my art,
   Some symmetry the foot hath with that part
75   Which thou dost seek, and is thy map for that
   Lovely enough to stop, but not stay at:

---

[8] *Islands Fortunate* The first (or Greenwich) meridian, dividing the earth into eastern and western hemispheres, was thought to pass through the Canary Islands, also then known as the Fortunate Islands. The Canary Islands also produced light wine, contrasted here with the stronger ambrosia of the gods.

[9] *Remora* a fish, believed to be able to stop the progress of any ship by attaching itself to it and sucking.

[10] *Hellespont* The strait of Hellespont separated the cities of Sestos and Abydos (homes respectively of the lovers Hero and Leander).

[11] *India* a conventional short form for the East Indies, thought of as the source of fabulous wealth.

Least subject to disguise and change it is; [1]
Men say the Devil never can change his.
It is the emblem that hath figured
80 Firmness; 'tis the first part that comes to bed. [2]
Civility, we see refin'd the kiss
Which at the face begun, transplanted is
Since to the hand, since to the imperial knee, [3]
Now at the papal foot delights to be: [4]
85 If kings think that the nearer way, and do [5]
Rise from the foot, lovers may do so too.
For as free spheres move faster far than can [6]
Birds, whom the air resists, so may that man
Which goes this empty and etherial way,
90 Than if at beauties' elements he stay.
Rich Nature hath in women wisely made
Two purses, and their mouths aversely laid: [7]
They then, which to the lower tribute owe,
That way which that exchequer looks, must go: [8]
95 He which doth not, his error is as great,
As who by clyster gave the stomach meat. [9]
—1654, 1669

---

[1] *Least subject to disguise*   The Devil was said to be unable to disguise his cloven foot.

[2] *Firmness*   Helen Gardner notes that theological authorities saw the foot as "an emblem of *firmitas* or *soliditas*."

[3] *Since*   then (*OED* since *n* 1).

[4] *papal foot*   One kissed the foot of the Pope to demonstrate complete subservience to him.

[5] *nearer way*   readiest way [to demonstrate their devotion to the Pope].

[6] *spheres*   heavenly bodies (*OED* sphere *sb* 2).

[7] *Two purses*   the mouth and the vagina. As Helen Gardner observes, the phrase "pursing of the lips" draws on the analogy between the way purse-strings draw tight the opening to a purse and the way in which human lips may be tightened.

[8] *They then....exchequer looks, must go*   i.e. [They] which owe to the lower of the two mouths an offering of submission (or a tax) must go to that exchequer (or treasury).

[9] *Clyster*   enema (*OED* clyster).

Satire III

Kind pity chokes my spleen; brave scorn
        forbids [10]
Those tears to issue which swell my eye-lids;
I must not laugh, nor weep sins, and be wise,
Can railing then cure these worn maladies?
5 Is not our mistress fair Religion,
As worthy of all our soul's devotion,
As virtue was to the first blinded age? [11]
Are not heaven's joys as valiant to assuage
Lusts, as earth's honour was to them? Alas,
10 As we do them in means, shall they surpass
Us in the end, and shall thy father's spirit
Meet blind philosophers in heaven, whose merit
Of strict life may be imputed faith, and hear
Thee, whom he taught so easy ways and near
15 To follow, damn'd? O if thou dar'st, fear this.
This fear great courage, and high valour is;
Dar'st thou aid mutinous Dutch, and dar'st thou
        lay [12]
Thee in ships wooden sepulchers, a prey
To leaders rage, to storms, to shot, to dearth?
20 Dar'st thou dive seas, and dungeons of the earth?
Hast thou more courageous fire to thaw the ice
Of frozen North discoveries? and thrice
Colder than salamanders, like divine
Children in th'oven, fires of Spain, and the line, [13]

---

[10] *spleen*   the seat of melancholy or morose feelings (*OED* spleen *sb* 1b).

[11] *first blinded age*   the age before Christianity was thought to be without the light of the gospel.

[12] *mutinous Dutch*   The Dutch were engaged in an ongoing dispute against Spanish rule.

[13] *divine / Children in th'oven*   Shadrach, Meshach, and Abednego were three young men thrown in a fire for refusing to worship a golden statue built by King Nebuchadnezzar. An angel appeared in the midst of the flames and allowed the three men to stay unharmed (Daniel 3: 1–97).

25 Whose countries' limbecks to our bodies be, [1]
Canst thou for gain bear? and must every he
Which cries not, Goddess, to thy Mistress, draw,
Or eat thy poisonous words? courage of straw!
O desperate coward, wilt thou seem bold, and
30 To thy foes and his (who made thee to stand
Sentinel in his world's garrison) thus yield,
And for the forbidden wars, leave th'appointed
    field?
Know thy foes; the foul devil, whom thou
Striv'st to please: for hate, not love, would allow
35 Thee fain, his whole Realm to be quit; and as [2]
The world's all parts wither away and pass,
So the world's self, thy other lov'd foe, is
In her decrepit wane, and thou loving this,
Dost love a withered and worn strumpet; last,
40 Flesh (itself's death) and joys which flesh can taste,
Thou lovest; and thy fair goodly soul, which doth
Give this flesh power to taste joy, thou dost loath;
    Seek true religion. O where? Mirreus [3]
Thinking her unhous'd here, and fled from us,
45 Seeks her at Rome, there, because he doth know
That she was there a thousand years ago,
He loves her rags so, as we here obey
The statecloth where the Prince sat yesterday, [4]
Crants to such brave loves will not be enthrall'd,
50 But loves her only, who at Geneva is call'd [5]
Religion, plain, simple, sullen, young,
Contemptuous, yet unhandsome. As among
Lecherous humors, there is one that judges

No wenches wholesome, but coarse country
    drudges.
55 Graius stays still at home here, and because
Some Preachers, vile ambitious bauds, and laws
Still new like fashions, bid him think that she
Which dwells with us, is only perfect, he
Embraceth her, whom his godfathers will
60 Tender to him, being tender, as wards still
Take such wives as their guardians offer, or
Pay values. Careless Phrygius doth abhor [6]
All, because all cannot be good, as one
Knowing some women whores, dares marry none.
65 Graccus loves all as one, and thinks that so
As women do in divers countries go
In divers habits, yet are still one kind;
So doth, so is religion; and this blind-
Ness too much light breeds; but unmoved thou
70 Of force must one, and forc'd but one allow;
And the right; ask thy father which is she,
Let him ask his; though truth and falsehood be
Near twins, yet truth a little elder is;
Be busy to seek her, believe me this,
75 He's not of none, nor worst, that seeks the best.
To adore, or scorn an image, or protest, [7]
May all be bad; doubt wisely, in strange way
To stand inquiring right, is not to stray;
To sleep, or run wrong, is: on a huge hill,
80 Cragg'd, and steep, Truth stands, and he that will
Reach her, about must, and about must go;
And what the hill's suddenness resists, win so;
Yet strive so, that before age, death's twilight,
Thy soul rest, for none can work in that night.
85 To will, implies delay, therefore now do.
Hard deeds, the bodies' pains; hard knowledge too
The mind's endeavours reach, and mysteries
Are like the sun, dazzling, yet plain to all eyes;

---

[1] *limbecks* alembics, apparatus used in distilling (*OED* alembic 1).

[2] *his whole Realm to be quit* to have access to his whole realm in exchange for your soul. Quit, in this phrase, has the sense of being in exchange for something (*OED v* quit 11c).

[3] *Mirreus…Crants…Graius…Phrygius…Graccus* The five imaginary individuals presented by Donne represent various different sects of Christianity.

[4] *as we here obey…statecloth where the Prince sat yesterday* the royal canopy, still a symbol of respect even when the Prince is absent.

[5] *Geneva* Calvinism originated in Geneva.

[6] *Pay values* Wards who refused to marry their guardian's choice had to pay values or fines.

[7] *protest* protest against the Catholic church, ie. to convert to Protestantism.

Keep the truth which thou hast found; men do
    not stand
90 In so ill case here, that God hath with his hand
Sign'd King's blank-charters to kill whom they
    hate, [1]
Nor are they vicars, but hangmen to fate. [2]
Fool and wretch, wilt thou let thy soul be tied
To man's laws, by which she shall not be tried
95 At the last day? Will it then boot thee [3]
To say a Philip, or a Gregory,
A Harry, or a Martin taught thee this? [4]
Is not this excuse for mere contraries,
Equally strong? cannot both sides say so?
100 That thou mayest rightly obey power, her bounds
    know;
Those past, her nature, and name is chang'd; to
    be
Then humble to her is idolatry;
As streams are, Power is; those blest flowers that
    dwell
At the rough stream's calm head, thrive and do well,
105 But having left their roots, and themselves given
To the stream's tyrannous rage, alas are driven
Through mills, and rocks, and woods, and at last,
    almost
Consum'd in going, in the sea are lost:
So perish souls, which more choose men's unjust
110 Power from God claim'd, than God himself to
    trust.
—1633

Holy Sonnets

VI

This is my play's last scene, here heavens
    appoint
My pilgrimage's last mile; and my race
Idly, yet quickly run, hath this last pace,
My span's last inch, my minute's latest point, [5]
5 And gluttonous death, will instantly unjoint
My body, and soul, and I shall sleep a space,
But my ever-waking part shall see that face, [6]
Whose fear already shakes my every joint:
Then, as my soul, to heaven her first seat, takes
    flight, [7]
10 And earth born body, in the earth shall dwell,
So, fall my sins, that all may have their right,
To where they are bred, and would press me, to
    hell.
Impute me righteous, thus purg'd of evil, [8]
For thus I leave the world, the flesh, and devil.
—1633

VII

At the round earth's imagined corners, blow
Your trumpets, angels, and arise, arise
From death, you numberless infinities
Of souls, and to your scattered bodies go,
All whom the flood did, and fire shall o'erthrow,
5 All whom war, dearth, age, agues, tyrannies,
Despair, law, chance, hath slain, and you whose eyes
Shall behold God and never taste death's woe.[9]
But let them sleep, Lord, and me mourn a space,
For if above all these my sins abound,

---

[1] *blank-charters* documents given to agents of the Crown with power to fill them in as they pleased (*OED a* blank 10).

[2] *vicars* earthly representatives of God or Christ (*OED* vicar 1).

[3] *boot* profit (*OED sb¹* boot 3).

[4] *Philip* Philip II, the Catholic Ruler of Spain; *Gregory* one of several Pope Gregories; *Harry* Henry VIII who brought Protestantism to England; *Martin* Martin Luther.

[5] *span* life span.

[6] *that face* God's face.

[7] *seat* residence, abode (*OED sb* seat III).

[8] *Impute* Protestant teaching held that Christ's grace is imputed, or attributed, to Christians.

[9] See Luke 9:27.

10 'Tis late to ask abundance of thy grace
When we are there; here on this lowly ground,
Teach me how to repent; for that's as good
As if thou hadst sealed my pardon with thy blood.
—1633

IX

If poisonous minerals, and if that tree,
Whose fruit threw death on else immortal us,
If lecherous goats, if serpents envious
Cannot be damn'd; alas; why should I be
5 Why should intent or reason, born in me,
Make sins, else equal, in me more heinous
And mercy being easy, and glorious
To God, in his stern wrath, why threatens he?
But who am I, that dare dispute with thee
10 O God? Oh! of thine only worthy blood
And my tears, make a heavenly Lethean flood [1]
And drown in it my sins' black memory;
That thou remember them, some claim as debt,
I think it mercy, if thou wilt forget.
—1633

X

Death be not proud, though some have called
thee
Mighty and dreadful, for, thou are not so,
For, those, whom thou think'st, thou dost
overthrow,
Die not, poor death, nor yet canst thou kill me;
5 From rest and sleep, which but thy pictures be,
Much pleasure, then from thee, much more must
flow,
And soonest our best men with thee do go,
Rest of their bones, and soul's delivery.
Thou art slave to Fate, chance, kings, and
desperate men,
10 And dost with poison, war, and sickness dwell,
And poppy, or charms can make us sleep as well
And better then thy stroke; why swell'st thou then?

---

[1] *Lethean* causing oblivion or forgetfulness (*OED* lethean *a*).

One short sleep past, we wake eternally,
And death shall be no more, Death, thou shalt die.
—1633

XI

Spit in my face ye Jews, and pierce my side,
Buffet, and scoff, scourge, and crucify me,
For I have sinn'd, and sinn'd, and only he,
Who could do no iniquity, hath died:
5 But by my death can not be satisfied
My sins, which pass the Jews' impiety:
They kill'd once an inglorious man, but I
Crucify him daily, being now glorified; [2]
Oh let me then, his strange love still admire:
10 Kings pardon, but he bore our punishment.
And *Jacob* came cloth'd in vile harsh attire
But to supplant, and with gainful intent: [3]
God cloth'd himself in vile man's flesh, that so
He might be weak enough to suffer woe.
—1633

XII

Why are we by all creatures waited on?
Why do the prodigal elements supply [4]
Life and food to me, being more pure than I,
Simple, and further from corruption?
5 Why brook'st thou, ignorant horse, subjection?
Why dost thou bull, and boar so sillily
Dissemble weakness, and by one man's stroke
die, [5]
Whose whole kind, you might swallow and feed
upon?
Weaker I am, woe is me, and worse then you,
10 You have not sinn'd nor need be timorous,

---

[2] *Crucify him daily* Hebrews 6:6.

[3] *Jacob came cloth'd...to supplant* Jacob, in order to steal his elder brother's blessing from his blind father Isaac, dressed in animal skins so that he would feel hairy like his brother (Genesis 27:1–38).

[4] *prodigal* wastefully lavish (*OED* prodigal *a* 2).

[5] *Dissemble weakness* that is, disguise their real nature so as to appear weak (*OED* dissemble *v¹* 1).

But wonder at a greater wonder, for to us
Created nature doth these things subdue,
But their Creator, whom sin, nor nature tied,
For us, his creatures, and his foes, hath died.
—1633

XIII

What if this present were the world's last
 night?
Mark in my heart, O Soul, where thou dost dwell,
The picture of Christ crucified, and tell
Whether that countenance can thee affright,
5 Tears in his eyes quench the amazing light,
Blood fills his frowns, which from his pierc'd
  head fell,
And can that tongue adjudge thee unto hell,
Which pray'd forgiveness for his foes' fierce spite?
No, no; but as in my idolatry
10 I said to all my profane mistresses,
Beauty, of pity, foulness only is
A sign of rigour: so I say to thee
To wicked spirits are horrid shapes assign'd,
This beauteous form assures a piteous mind.
—1633

XIV

Batter my heart, three person'd God; for you [1]
 As yet but knock, breathe, shine, and seek to
  mend;
That I may rise, and stand, o'erthrow me, and
  bend
Your force, to break, blow, burn and make me
  new.
5 I, like an usurped town, to another due,
Labour to admit you, but oh, to no end,
Reason your viceroy in me, me should defend,
But is captiv'd, and proves weak or untrue, [2]
Yet dearly I love you, and would be lov'd fain,
10 But am betroth'd unto your enemy,

---

[1] *three person'd God* that is, Father, Son and Holy Ghost.

[2] *viceroy* Reason, God's viceroy in man, is vitiated by the Fall.

Divorce me, untie, or break that knot again,
Take me to you, imprison me, for I
Except you enthral me, never shall be free,
Nor ever chaste, except you ravish me.
—1633

XV

I am a little world made cunningly
 Of elements, and an angelic sprite, [3]
But black sin hath betrayed to endless night
My world's both parts, and (oh) both parts must
  die.
5 You which beyond that heaven which was most
  high
Have found new spheres, and of new lands can
  write
Pour new seas in mine eyes, that so I might
Drown my world with my weeping earnestly,
Or wash it if it must be drown'd no more:
10 But oh it must be burnt; alas the fire
Of lust and envy have burnt it heretofore,
And made it fouler; let their flames retire,
And burn me O Lord, with a fiery zeal
Of thee and thy house, which doth in eating heal. [4]
—1635

Holy Sonnets
from the Westmoreland MS [5]

XVII

Since she whom I lov'd hath paid her last debt
 To Nature, and to hers, and my good is dead,
And her soul early into heaven ravished,
Wholly on heavenly things my mind is set.
5 Here the admiring her my mind did whet
To seek thee God; so streams do shew the head;

---

[3] *sprite* spirit (*OED* sprite *sb* [1])

[4] *a fiery zeal / Of thee and thy house* For the zeal of thine house hath eaten me up (Psalm 69:9).

[5] This and the following two sonnets from the Westmoreland Manuscript were not printed until the nineteenth century.

But though I have found thee, and thou my thirst
    hast fed,
A holy thirsty dropsy melts me yet. [1]
But why should I beg more love, when as thou
10 Dost woo my soul for hers; offring all thine:
And dost not only fear lest I allow
My love to saints and angels, things divine,
But in thy tender jealousy dost doubt
Least the world, flesh, yea Devil put thee out.
—1894

XVIII

Show me dear Christ, thy spouse, so bright and
    clear. [2]
What! is it she, which on the other shore [3]
Goes richly painted? or which robbed and tore
Laments and mourns in Germany and here?
5 Sleeps she a thousand, then peeps up one year?
Is she self truth and errs? now new, now
    outwore? [4]
Doth she, and did she, and shall she evermore
On one, on seven, or on no hill appear? [5]
Dwells she with us, or like adventuring knights
10 First travail we to seek and then make love?
Betray kind husband thy spouse to our sights,
And let mine amorous soul court thy mild dove, [6]
Who is most true, and pleasing to thee, then
When she is embrac'd and open to most men.
—1894

---

[1] *dropsy* an insatiable thirst or craving (*OED* dropsy *sb* 2).

[2] *thy spouse* the Church (Revelation 21:2). Christ is the bridegroom.

[3] *she, which… / Goes richly painted* the Roman Catholic Church, contrasted with the Protestant church in Germany and England.

[4] *Is she self truth and errs?* The Church, as Christ's representative on earth, should be Truth (see John 14:6); but the conflicting claims of the competing branches of Christianity cannot all be true.

[5] *On one, on seven, or on no hill appear* The one hill may be a dual reference, to Mount Moriah, where Solomon built his temple, and St. Paul's, on Ludgate Hill; Rome is built on seven hills, Geneva on none.

[6] *dove* The turtle-dove symbolized marital fidelity; the Church is supposed to be filled with the holy spirit, also symbolized by the dove (Matthew 3:16 and other places).

XIX

Oh, to vex me, contraries meet in one:
    Inconstancy unnaturally hath begot
A constant habit; that when I would not
I change in vows, and in devotion.
5 As humorous is my contrition
As my profane love, and as soon forgot:
As riddlingly distempered, cold and hot, [7]
As praying, as mute; as infinite, as none.
I durst not view heaven yesterday; and today
10 In prayers, and flattering speeches I court God:
Tomorrow I quake with true fear of his rod.
So my devout fits come and go away
Like a fantastic ague: save that here
Those are my best days, when I shake with fear.[8]
—1894

Good Friday, 1613. Riding Westward

Let man's soul be a sphere, and then, in this,
    The intelligence that moves, devotion is, [9]
And as the other spheres, by being grown
Subject to foreign motions, lose their own, [10]
5 And being by others hurried every day,
Scarce in a year their natural form obey:
Pleasure or business, so, our souls admit
For their first mover, and are whirled by it. [11]
Hence is't, that I am carried towards the West
10 This day, when my soul's form bends towards the
    East.
There I should see a sun, by rising set,

---

[7] *distempered* disordered condition of the body or mind (*OED sb¹* distempered 4).

[8] *ague* fit of shaking or shivering (*OED* ague 3).

[9] *Let man's soul…devotion is* The soul is (or should be) moved by devotion as the spheres are moved by intelligences.

[10] *foreign motions* Cosmologists of the time thought that the spheres were deflected from their natural orbit by various cosmic forces.

[11] *first mover* in reference to the Primum Mobile (first moving thing), supposed to revolve round the earth from east to west in twenty-four hours, carrying the other spheres with it (*OED* Primum Mobile).

And by that setting endless day beget;
But that Christ on this Cross, did rise and fall,
Sin had eternally benighted all. [1]
15 Yet dare I almost be glad, I do not see
That spectacle of too much weight for me.
Who sees God's face, that is self life, must die;
What a death were it then to see God die?
It made his own Lieutenant Nature shrink,
20 It made his footstool crack, and the Sun wink. [2]
Could I behold those hands which span the poles,
And tune all spheres at once pierc'd with those
    holes?
Could I behold that endless height which is
Zenith to us, and to our Antipodes, [3]
25 Humbled below us? or that blood which is
The seat of all our souls, if not of his,
Made dirt of dust, or that flesh which was worn
By God, for his apparel, ragg'd, and torn?
If on these things I durst not look, durst I
30 Upon his miserable mother cast mine eye,
Who was God's partner here, and furnish'd thus
Half of that sacrifice, which ransom'd us?
Though these things, as I ride, be from mine eye,
They are present yet unto my memory,
35 For that looks towards them; and thou look'st
    towards me,
O Saviour, as thou hang'st upon the tree;
I turn my back to thee, but to receive
Corrections, till thy mercies bid thee leave.
O think me worth thine anger, punish me,
40 Burn off my rusts, and my deformity,
Restore thine image, so much, by thy grace,
That thou may'st know me, and I'll turn my face.
—1633

---

[1] *benighted* involved in moral darkness (*OED* benight *v* 2b).

[2] *his footstool crack, and the Sun wink* The earth is held to be God's footstool (Isaiah 66:1); there was an earthquake at the crucifixion (Matthew 27:51) and also an eclipse of the sun (Matthew 27:45).

[3] *Zenith* the highest point of the celestial sphere as viewed from any particular place (*OED* zenith 1); *Antipodes* places on the earth directly opposite to each other (*OED* antipodes *sb* 3).

A Hymn to Christ, at the Author's last going into Germany [4]

In what torn ship soever I embark,
That ship shall be my emblem of thy Ark;
What sea soever swallow me, that flood
Shall be to me an emblem of thy blood;
5 Though thou with clouds of anger do disguise
Thy face, yet through that mask I know those
    eyes,
    Which, though they turn away sometimes,
        They never will despise.

I sacrifice this island unto thee,
10 And all whom I lov'd there, and who lov'd me;
When I have put our seas twixt them and me,
Put thou thy sea betwixt my sins and thee. [5]
As the tree's sap doth seek the root below
In winter, in my winter now I go,
15   Where none but thee, th'eternal root
        Of true love I may know.

Nor thou nor thy religion dost control,
The amorousness of an harmonious soul,
But thou would'st have that love thyself: as thou
20 Art jealous, Lord, so I am jealous now,
Thou lov'st not, till from loving more, thou free
My soul: Who ever gives, takes liberty:
    O, if thou car'st not whom I love
        Alas, thou lov'st not me.

25 Seal then this bill of my divorce to all,
On whom those fainter beams of love did fall;
Marry those loves, which in youth scattered be
On fame, wit, hopes (false mistresses) to thee.
Churches are best for prayer, that have least light:
30 To see God only, I go out of sight:

---

[4] Donne was in Germany from May 1619 to January 1620, as chaplain to the Earl of Doncaster's mission.

[5] *Put thou thy sea betwixt my sins and thee* that is, the sea of Christ's blood.

And to scape stormy days, I choose
    An everlasting night.
—1633

A Hymn to God my God,
in my sickness

Since I am coming to that holy room,
    Where, with thy choir of saints for evermore,
I shall be made thy music; as I come
    I tune the instrument here at the door,
5   And what I must do then, think here before.

Whilst my physicians by their love are grown
    Cosmographers, and I their map, who lie
Flat on this bed, that by them may be shown
    That this is my southwest discovery
10   *Per fretum febris*, by these straits to die, [1]

I joy, that in these straits, I see my West;
    For, though their currents yield return to none,
What shall my West hurt me? As West and East
    In all flat maps (and I am one) are one,
15   So death doth touch the Resurrection.

Is the Pacific Sea my home? Or are
    The Eastern riches? Is Jerusalem?
Anyan, and Magellan, and Gibraltar, [2]
    All straits, and none but straits are ways to them
20   Whether where Japhet dwelt, or Cham, or Sem.[3]

We think that Paradise and Calvary,
    Christ's cross, and Adam's tree, stood in one
       place; [4]

Look Lord, and find both Adams met in me; [5]
    As the first Adam's sweat surrounds my face
25   May the last Adam's blood my soul embrace.

So, in his purple wrapp'd receive me Lord,
    By these his thorns give me his other crown; [6]
And as to others' souls I preach'd thy word,
    Be this my text, my sermon to mine own,
30   Therefore that he may raise the Lord throws
       down. [7]
—1635

A Hymn to God the Father

I

Wilt thou forgive that sin where I begun, [8]
    Which was my sin, though it were done
       before?
Wilt thou forgive that sin, through which I run,
    And do run still: though still I do deplore?
5   When thou hast done, thou hast not done,
        For, I have more.

II

Wilt thou forgive that sin which I have won
    Others to sin? and, made my sin their door?
Wilt thou forgive that sin which I did shun
10   A year, or two: but wallowed in, a score?
       When thou hast done, thou has not done,
        For I have more.

---

[1] *Per fretum febris* a pun, since "fretum" can mean both "strait" and "raging heat": through the strait (or raging heat) of fever.

[2] *Anyan, and Magellan, and Gibraltar* all straits; in relation to the first, it is not clear to which of the various possibilities Donne refers.

[3] *Japhet dwelt, or Cham, or Sem* The three sons of Noah divided the earth among them; Japhet took Europe, Ham Africa, and Shem Asia.

[4] *Christ's cross, and Adam's tree...one place* in reference to the tradition that Golgotha, the site of the crucifixion, occupied the same place as the Garden of Eden.

[5] *both Adams* Christ is the second Adam, who overcame the consequences of the sin of the first.

[6] *his other crown* the crown of eternal life.

[7] *Therefore that he may raise the Lord throws down* perhaps based on Psalm 145:14, "The Lord upholdeth all that fall, and raiseth up all those that be bowed down."

[8] *that sin where I begun* in reference to "original sin": "Behold, I was shapen in wickedness, and in sin hath my mother conceived me" (Psalm 51:5).

III

I have a sin of fear, that when I have spun
    My last thread, I shall perish on the shore;
But swear by thy self, that at my death thy son
    Shall shine as he shines now, and heretofore; [1]

And, having done that, Thou hast done,
    I fear no more.

—1633

---

[1] *thy son / Shall shine as he shines now* The symbolic equation of
Christ and the Sun originates in Malachi 4:2: "But unto you that fear
my name shall the Sun of Righteousness arise with healing in his
wings."

Ben Jonson
1572/3 – 1637

Ben Jonson was born, by his own account, a month after the death of his father. Two years later, his mother married a bricklayer, who seems to have taken care of his stepson's education. After a period at a private school, he was educated at Westminster School, then probably the most famous school in England, under the headship of William Camden. Camden may himself have paid for Jonson's tuition at Westminster, and Jonson showed himself grateful in a poem which begins "Camden, most reverend head, to whom I owe / All that I am in arts, all that I know." The great teacher and his great pupil became friends after the completion of Jonson's formal education. Jonson was married in 1594 to Anne Lewis, whom he described to Drummond as "a shrew, yet honest." There were several children of this marriage, and probably others outside it. In 1597 he was mentioned in Henslowe's diary as an actor, and in 1598 was indicted for killing a fellow actor, Gabriel Spencer, in a duel. He pleaded self-defence, was given benefit of clergy, branded on the thumb, and his goods confiscated. While in prison he converted to Catholicism, and is said to have continued in that religion for twelve years. In 1605 he and his co-authors were imprisoned for libel in *Eastward Ho!* In the following year he and his wife appeared before the Consistory Court on charges of recusancy. In 1612–13 he was in France as tutor to Sir Walter Raleigh's son. In 1618–19 he travelled on foot to Scotland, where he was a guest of Drummond of Hawthornden, who recorded his conversation. Jonson's *Works* were published in folio in 1616; between then and his death he received a variety of honours and suffered from a variety of ailments. He was buried in Westminster Abbey.

Jonson was a major playwright, whose satirical comedies and tragedies are still read and staged. "Clerimont's Song" and "A Vision of Beauty" come from his plays. The reign of King James created a context in which Jonson's talent throve. Often commissioned to writes masques and plays for the court, he was well-respected both by the aristocracy and by other artists, and became financially comfortable. Jonson was also an astute literary critic, who recognized the genius of his contemporary Shakespeare. Jonson was treated less well after the accession of Charles, however, and his health suffered. His masques and plays ceased to enjoy success, and although no particular occasion is known, no doubt this prompted "An Ode. To Himself." He was far from alone in the world, however. Acquainted with most of the celebrated men of his age, Jonson was at the centre of a group of young poets calling themselves the "Sons of Ben." He enjoyed close relationships with several aristocratic families, including the Sidneys and the Countess of Bedford, celebrated in "To Penshurst" and "On Lucy, Countess of Bedford." Jonson was also connected with leading literary and academic men, including Camden, his master at Westminster School, Donne, Chapman, Fletcher, Selden, and Shakespeare.

❧❧❧

To the Reader

Pray thee take care, that tak'st my book in hand,
To read it well; that is, to understand.
—1616

To Alchemists

If all you boast of your great art be true,
Sure, willing poverty lives most in you.
—1616

On Something that Walks Somewhere

At court I met it, in clothes brave enough
  To be a courtier, and looks grave enough
To seem a statesman. As I near it came,
  It made me a great face; I asked the name;
5 A lord, it cried, buried in flesh and blood,
  And such from whom let no man hope least good,
For I will do none; and as little ill,
  For I will dare none. Good lord, walk dead still.
—1616

To William Camden [1]

Camden, most reverend head, to whom I owe
  All that I am in arts, all that I know,
(How nothing's that?) to whom my country owes
  The great renown and name wherewith she goes;
5 Than thee the age sees not that thing more grave,
  More high, more holy, that she more would crave.
What name, what skill, what faith hast thou in
    things!
  What sight in searching the most ántique springs!
What weight, and what authority in thy speech!
10 Man scarce can make that doubt, but thou canst
    teach.
Pardon free truth, and let thy modesty,
  Which conquers all, be once overcome by thee.
Many of thine this better could than I;
  But for their powers, accept my piety.
—1616

On My First Daughter [2]

Here lies, to each her parents' ruth,
  Mary, the daughter of their youth;
Yet, all heaven's gifts being heaven's due,
It makes the father less to rue.
5 At six months' end she parted hence
With safety of her innocence; [3]
Whose soul heaven's Queen (whose name she bears),
In comfort of her mother's tears,
Hath placed amongst her virgin train;
10 Where, while that severed doth remain, [4]
This grave partakes the fleshly birth; [5]
Which cover lightly, gentle earth.
—1616

On My First Son [6]

Farewell, thou child of my right hand, and joy; [7]
  My sin was too much hope of thee, loved boy.
Seven years thou wert lent to me, and I thee pay,
  Exacted by thy fate, on the just day.
5 Oh, could I lose all father now! For why [8]
  Will man lament the state he should envy?
To have so soon 'scaped world's and flesh's rage,
  And, if no other misery, yet age?
Rest in soft peace, and, asked, say here doth lie
10 Ben Jonson his best piece of poetry;
For whose sake, henceforth, all his vows be such,
  As what he loves may never like too much.
—1616

---

[2] Mary Jonson, probably born after 1598, died at 6 months.

[3] *With safety of* without damage to (*OED* safety 1c).

[4] *that* the soul, disassociated from the body.

[5] *while that…fleshly birth* i.e. until the Resurrection, the grave has its share of the body.

[6] Jonson's son Benjamin died in 1611.

[7] "Benjamin," the name of Jacob's youngest son (Genesis 35:18), means son of the right hand; sitting to the right has been traditionally associated with honour (*OED* 2c).

[8] *lose all father* that is, all parental sentiment.

---

[1] Camden (1551–1623), Jonson's master at Westminster School; the publication of his *Britannia* (1586) made Camden the most celebrated antiquary of the era (see l. 4).

On Lucy, Countess of Bedford [1]

This morning, timely rapt with holy fire, [2]
  I thought to form unto my zealous muse
What kind of creature I could most desire
  To honour, serve and love, as poets use.
5 I meant to make her fair, and free, and wise, [3]
  Of greatest blood, and yet more good than great;
I meant the day-star should not brighter rise, [4]
  Nor lend like influence from his lucent seat. [5]
I meant she should be courteous, facile, sweet, [6]
10 Hating that solemn vice of greatness, pride;
I meant each softest virtue there should meet,
  Fit in that softer bosom to reside.
Only a learnèd and a manly soul
  I purposed her, that should, with even powers, [7]
15 The rock, the spindle and the shears control
  Of destiny, and spin her own free hours. [8]
Such when I meant to feign and wished to see,
  My muse bade, *Bedford* write, and that was she.
  —1616

To Sir Henry Savile [9]

If, my religion safe, I durst embrace
  That stranger doctrine of Pythagoras, [10]
I should believe the soul of Tacitus [11]
  In thee, most weighty Savile, lived to us:
5 So hast thou rendered him in all his bounds
  And all his numbers, both of sense and sounds. [12]
But when I read that special piece, restored,
  Where Nero falls and Galba is adored,
To thine own proper I ascribe then more, [13]
10 And gratulate the breach I grieved before: [14]
Which fate, it seems, caused in the history
  Only to boast thy merit in supply.
Oh, wouldst thou add like hand to all the rest!
  Or (better work!) were thy glad country blest
15 To have her story woven in thy thread,
  Minerva's loom was never richer spread. [15]
For who can master those great parts like thee,
  That liv'st from hope, from fear, from faction free;
That hast thy breast so clear of present crimes
20 Thou need'st not shrink at voice of after-times;
Whose knowledge claimeth at the helm to stand,
  But wisely thrusts not forth a forward hand,
No more than Sallust in the Roman state. [16]
  As, then, his cause, his glory emulate.
25 Although to write be lesser than to do,

---

1 remembered as a patron of poets.

2 *timely*   early and/or opportunely (*OED* timely *adv* 1,2).

3 *free*   Several meanings are apposite: not in bondage to sin (*OED* free *a* 1b); of gentle birth (free *a* 3); magnanimous (free *a* 4a).

4 *the day-star*   either the morning star (*OED* day-star 1), or the sun (*OED* day-star 2).

5 *lucent*   luminous, shining (*OED* lucent *a* 1b).

6 *facile*   affable, gentle (*OED* facile *a* 4a,c).

7 *even*   steady, even-tempered (*OED* even *a* 8); equal to the task of controlling destiny (see *OED* even *a* 13a).

8 The rock, spindle, and shears in the Hesiodic theology are symbolic of the three Fates: with her distaff (or rock), Clotho chooses the moment of our birth, Lachesis weaves the tapestry of events of our lives, and Atropos severs the thread (*OCD*).

---

9 Sir Henry Savile (1549-1622), Warden of Merton College, Oxford, and later Provost of Eton.

10 *That stranger doctrine*   Pythagoras taught the transmigration of souls, whereby after death each soul enters another body, still cognizant of its past life (*OCD*).

11 Savile translated the *Histories* of Tacitus in 1591.

12 *numbers*   parts, categories (*OED* number *sb* 7c).

13 *proper*   special or intrinsic attribute (*OED* proper C *sb* or quasi-*sb* 3).

14 *gratulate*   celebrate, rejoice over (*OED* gratulate *v* 2).

15 *Minerva*   the Roman goddess of handicrafts, especially of weaving.

16 Sallust, after fighting with Julius Caesar in the African campaign, withdrew from the military life to write history.

It is the next deed, and a great one too.
We need a man that knows the several graces
    Of history, and how to apt their places: [1]
Where brevity, where splendour, and where height,
30 Where sweetness is required, and where weight;
We need a man can speak of the intents,
    The counsels, actions, orders and events
Of state, and censure them; we need his pen [2]
    Can write the things, the causes, and the men.
35 But most we need his faith (and all have you)
    That dares nor write things false, nor hide things
        true.
—1616

To Sir Thomas Roe [3]

Thou hast begun well, Roe, which stand well
    too,
    And I know nothing more thou hast to do.
He that is round within himself, and straight,
    Need seek no other strength, no other height;
5   Fortune upon him breaks herself, if ill,
    And what would hurt his virtue makes it still.
That thou at once, then, nobly may'st defend
    With thine own course the judgement of thy
        friend,
Be always to thy gathered self the same,
10   And study conscience, more than thou wouldst
        fame.
Though both be good, the latter yet is worst,
    And ever is ill-got without the first.
—1616

To the Same

That thou hast kept thy love, increased thy will,
    Bettered thy trust to letters; that, thy skill;

Hast taught thyself worthy thy pen to tread,
    And that to write things worthy to be read:
5   How much of great example wert thou, Roe,
    If time to facts, as unto men, would owe?
But much it now avails what's done, of whom:
    The self-same deeds, as diversely they come
From place, or fortune, are made high or low,
10   And even the praiser's judgement suffers so.
Well, though thy name less than our great ones
        be,
    Thy fact is more: let truth encourage thee.
—1616

Inviting a Friend to Supper

Tonight, grave sir, both my poor house and I
    Do equally desire your company;
Not that we think us worthy such a guest,
    But that your worth will dignify our feast
5   With those that come; whose grace may make that
        seem
    Something, which else could hope for no esteem.
It is the fair acceptance, sir, creates
    The entertainment perfect, not the cates. [4]
Yet shall you have, to rectify your palate,
10   An olive, capers, or some better salad
Ushering the mutton; with a short-legged hen,
    If we can get her, full of eggs, and then
Lemons, and wine for sauce; to these, a coney [5]
    Is not to be despaired of, for our money;
15 And though fowl now be scarce, yet there are clerks,
    The sky not falling, think we may have larks.
I'll tell you of more, and lie, so you will come:
    Of partridge, pheasant, woodcock, of which some
May yet be there; and godwit, if we can;
20   Knat, rail and ruff, too. Howsoe'er, my man [6]
Shall read a piece of Virgil, Tacitus,

---

[1] *to apt*   to adapt to, to make suitable for (*OED* apt *v* 1).

[2] *censure*   offer an opinion of (*OED* censure *v* 1).

[3] Roe (1581–1644), diplomat and explorer.

[4] *cates*   victuals, often choice and delicate (*OED*).

[5] *coney*   rabbit (*OED* coney *sb* 1a).

[6] *godwit...knat, rail and ruff*   commonly eaten birds.

Livy, or of some better book to us,
Of which we'll speak our minds, amidst our meat;
And I'll profess no verses to repeat;
25 To this, if aught appear which I not know of,
That will the pastry, not my paper, show of.
Digestive cheese and fruit there sure will be;
But that which most doth take my muse and me
Is a pure cup of rich Canary wine, [1]
30 Which is the Mermaid's now, but shall be
mine; [2]
Of which had Horace or Anacreon tasted, [3]
Their lives, as do their lines, till now had lasted.
Tobacco, nectar, or the Thespian spring [4]
Are all but Luther's beer to this I sing. [5]
35 Of this we will sup free, but moderately;
And we will have no Poley or Parrot by; [6]
Nor shall our cups make any guilty men,
But at our parting we will be as when
We innocently met. No simple word
40 That shall be uttered at our mirthful board
Shall make us sad next morning, or affright
The liberty that we'll enjoy tonight.
—1616

To Penshurst [7]

Thou art not, Penshurst, built to envious show
Of touch or marble, nor canst boast a row [8]
Of polished pillars, or a roof of gold;

Thou hast no lantern whereof tales are told, [9]
5 Or stair, or courts; but stand'st an ancient pile,[10]
And these grudged at, art reverenced the while.
Thou joy'st in better marks, of soil, of air, [11]
Of wood, of water; therein thou art fair.
Thou hast thy walks for health as well as sport:
10 Thy Mount, to which the dryads do resort, [12]
Where Pan and Bacchus their high feasts have
made,[13]
Beneath the broad beech and the chestnut
shade;
That taller tree, which of a nut was set
At his great birth, where all the muses met. [14]
15 There, in the writhèd bark, are cut the names
Of many a sylvan taken with his flames;
And thence the ruddy satyrs oft provoke [15]
The lighter fauns to reach thy lady's oak.
Thy copse, too, named of Gamage, thou hast there,
20 That never fails to serve thee seasoned deer [16]
When thou wouldst feast or exercise thy friends.
The lower land, that to the river bends,
Thy sheep, thy bullocks, kine and calves do feed;
The middle grounds thy mares and horses breed.
25 Each bank doth yield thee conies, and the tops, [17]
Fertile of wood, Ashour and Sidney's copse,

---

[1] Light, sweet wine from the Canary Islands (*OED* canary *sb* 2).

[2] The Mermaid was a tavern in Cheapside.

[3] *Horace or Anacreon* celebrated classical poets, both of whom wrote in praise of wine.

[4] Created when Bellerophon's horse struck the ground with its hoof, the Thespian Spring lies above the Grove of the Muses and below Mount Helicon. It is sacred to the Muses (*OCD*).

[5] *Luther's beer* continental beer, less strong than English ale.

[6] Poley and Parrot were both spies.

[7] Penshurst, in Kent, had been the home of the Sidneys since 1552.

[8] *touch* black stone (*OED* touch *sb* 6).

[9] *lantern* glass turret (*OED* lantern *sb* 4).

[10] *an ancient pile* Penshurst was built about 1340; *pile* may refer to a small castle or stronghold (*OED* pile *sb* [2]) or simply to a lofty mass of buildings (*OED* pile *sb* [3] 4).

[11] *marks* distinctive features (*OED* mark *sb* 1 10b).

[12] *dryads* wood-nymphs (*OED*).

[13] Pan, a Greek god of the pastoral world, half man and half goat, was connected with both shepherds and hunting. Bacchus was the god of (among other things) wine, intoxication and ritual madness (*OCD*).

[14] *his great birth* Sir Philip Sidney's.

[15] *sylvan* woodlander (*OED* sylvan *sb* 1b); *satyrs* woodland gods, part human, part beast (*OED* satyr 1a).

[16] *seasoned* flavoured, spiced (*OED* seasoned *ppl.a* 2); of an appropriate age (*OED* seasoned *ppl.a* 3a); acclimatized, tame (*OED* seasoned *ppl.a* 3c).

[17] *conies* rabbits (*OED*); *tops* the highest points (*OED* top *sb*[1] 3a).

To crown thy open table, doth provide
    The purpled pheasant with the speckled side;
The painted partridge lies in every field,
30   And for thy mess is willing to be killed. [1]
And if the high-swoll'n Medway fail thy dish, [2]
    Thou hast thy ponds that pay thee tribute fish:
Fat, agèd carps, that run into thy net;
    And pikes, now weary their own kind to eat,
35 As loath the second draught or cast to stay,
    Officiously, at first, themselves betray; [3]
Bright eels, that emulate them, and leap on land
    Before the fisher, or into his hand.
Then hath thy orchard fruit, thy garden flowers,
40   Fresh as the air and new as are the hours:
The early cherry, with the later plum,
    Fig, grape and quince, each in his time doth
      come;
The blushing apricot and woolly peach
    Hang on thy walls, that every child may reach.
45 And though thy walls be of the country stone,
    They're reared with no man's ruin, no man's
      groan;
There's none that dwell about them wish them
      down,
    But all come in, the farmer and the clown,
And no one empty-handed, to salute
50   Thy lord and lady, though they have no suit. [4]
Some bring a capon, some a rural cake, [5]
    Some nuts, some apples; some that think they
      make
The better cheeses, bring 'em; or else send
    By their ripe daughters, whom they would
      commend
55 This way to husbands; and whose baskets bear

    An emblem of themselves, in plum or pear. [6]
But what can this (more than express their love)
    Add to thy free provisions, far above [7]
The need of such? whose liberal board doth flow
60   With all that hospitality doth know!
Where comes no guest but is allowed to eat
    Without his fear, and of thy lord's own meat;
Where the same beer and bread and self-same wine
    That is his lordship's shall be also mine;
65 And I not fain to sit, as some this day [8]
    At great men's tables, and yet dine away.
Here no man tells my cups, nor, standing by, [9]
    A waiter, doth my gluttony envy,
But gives me what I call, and lets me eat;
70   He knows below he shall find plenty of meat,
Thy tables hoard not up for the next day.
    Nor, when I take my lodging, need I pray
For fire or lights or livery: all is there, [10]
    As if thou then wert mine, or I reigned here;
75 There's nothing I can wish, for which I stay.
    That found King James, when, hunting late
      this way
With his brave son, the Prince, they saw thy fires
    Shine bright on every hearth as the desires
Of thy Penates had been set on flame [11]
80   To entertain them; or the country came
With all their zeal to warm their welcome here.
    What (great, I will not say, but) sudden cheer [12]
Didst thou then make 'em! and what praise was
      heaped
    On thy good lady then! who therein reaped
85 The just reward of her high housewifery:

---

[1] *mess* meal (*OED* mess *sb* 1a).

[2] *Medway* a river close by Penshurst.

[3] *Officiously* obligingly, courteously (*OED* officiously *adv* 1); dutifully (*OED* officiously *adv* 2).

[4] *suit* supplication (*OED* suit *sb* 11a).

[5] *capon* a castrated cock (*OED* capon *sb* 1).

[6] *an emblem* of the sexual maturity of the daughters.

[7] *free* liberal, abundant (*OED* free *a* 22c).

[8] *fain* necessitated, obliged (*OED* fain *a* 2b).

[9] *tells* counts (*OED* tell *v* 21).

[10] *livery* provisions, often clothing (*OED* livery *sb* 1b).

[11] *Penates* in Roman mythology, guardian gods of household and state, worshipped indoors (*OED*).

[12] *sudden* speedy (*OED* sudden *a* 3a).

To have her linen, plate, and all things nigh
When she was far; and not a room but dressed
   As if it had expected such a guest!
These, Penshurst, are thy praise, and yet not all.
90   Thy lady's noble, fruitful, chaste withal;
His children thy great lord may call his own,
   A fortune in this age but rarely known.
They are and have been taught religion; thence
   Their gentler spirits have sucked innocence.
95 Each morn and even they are taught to pray
   With the whole household, and may every day
Read in their virtuous parents' noble parts
   The mysteries of manners, arms and arts.
Now, Penshurst, they that will proportion thee [1]
100   With other edifices, when they see
Those proud, ambitious heaps, and nothing else,
   May say, their lords have built, but thy lord
     dwells.
—1616

To Heaven

Good and great God, can I not think of thee,
  But it must straight my melancholy be?
Is it interpreted in me disease
   That, laden with my sins, I seek for ease?
5 Oh, be thou witness, that the reins dost know, [2]
   And hearts of all, if I be sad for show;
And judge me after, if I dare pretend
   To aught but grace, or aim at other end.
As thou art all, so be thou all to me,
10   First, midst, and last; converted one and three;
My faith, my hope, my love; and in this state,
   My judge, my witness, and my advocate.
Where have I been this while exiled from thee?
   And whither rapt, now thou but stoop'st to me?
15 Dwell, dwell here still: Oh, being everywhere,

How can I doubt to find thee ever here?
I know my state, both full of shame and scorn,
   Conceived in sin, and unto labour born,
Standing with fear, and must with horror fall,
20   And destined unto judgement, after all.
I feel my griefs too, and there scarce is ground
   Upon my flesh to inflict another wound.
Yet dare I not complain, or wish for death
   With holy Paul, [3] lest it be thought the breath
25 Of discontent; or that these prayers be
   For weariness of life, not love of thee.
—1616

Song
To Celia [4]

Come, my Celia, let us prove, [5]
  While we may, the sports of love;
Time will not be ours for ever;
He at length our good will sever.
5 Spend not then his gifts in vain.
Suns that set may rise again;
But if once we lose this light,
'Tis with us perpetual night.
Why should we defer our joys?
10 Fame and rumour are but toys.
Cannot we delude the eyes
Of a few poor household spies?
Or his easier ears beguile,
So removèd by our wile?
15 'Tis no sin love's fruit to steal,
But the sweet theft to reveal:

---

[1] *proportion* compare (*OED* proportion *v* 6).

[2] *reins* the kidneys or loins, but figuratively the passions, thought to be seated in these parts of the body.

[3] See Romans 7:24.

[4] This poem is based on Catullus v (*Vivamus, mea Lesbia, atque amemus*), one of the most frequently translated of the poems of Catullus. See also Herrick's "Corinna's Going A Maying," line 68 and note.

[5] *prove* Several meanings apply: to show authenticity (*OED* prove *v* 7a); to make trial of (*OED* prove *v* 2); to learn through experience (*OED* prove *v* 3).

To be taken, to be seen,
These have crimes accounted been.
—1616

Her Triumph [1]

See the chariot at hand here of Love,
Wherein my lady rideth!
Each that draws is a swan or a dove,
    And well the car Love guideth.
5   As she goes, all hearts do duty
        Unto her beauty;
And enamoured, do wish, so they might
        But enjoy such a sight,
    That they still were to run by her side,
10 Through swords, through seas, whither she would
        ride. [2]

Do but look on her eyes, they do light
    All that Love's world compriseth!
Do but look on her hair, it is bright
    As Love's star when it riseth! [3]
15 Do but mark, her forehead's smoother
        Than words that soothe her!
And from her arched brows, such a grace
        Sheds itself through the face,
    As alone there triumphs to the life
20 All the gain, all the good, of the elements' strife.

Have you seen but a bright lily grow,
    Before rude hands have touched it?
Have you marked but the fall o' the snow,
    Before the soil hath smutched it? [4]
25 Have you felt the wool o' the beaver?
        Or swan's down ever?

Or have smelled o' the bud o' the briar?
        Or the nard i' the fire? [5]
        Or have tasted the bag o' the bee?
30 O so white! O so soft! O so sweet is she!
—1640

An Epistle to Master John Selden [6]

I know to whom I write. Here, I am sure,
Though I am short, I cannot be obscure; [7]
Less shall I for the art or dressing care,
Truth and the graces best when naked are.
5   Your book, my Selden, I have read, and much
Was trusted, that you thought my judgement such
To ask it; though in most of works it be
A penance, where a man may not be free,
Rather than office, when it doth or may
10 Chance that the friend's affection proves allay [8]
Unto the censure. Yours all need doth fly
Of this so vicious humanity.
Than which there is not unto study a more
Pernicious enemy; we see before
15 A many of books, even good judgements wound
Themselves through favouring what is there not
        found.
But I on yours far otherwise shall do,
Not fly the crime, but the suspicion too;
Though I confess (as every muse hath erred,
20 And mine not least) I have too oft preferred
Men past their terms, and praised some names too
        much; [9]
But 'twas with purpose to have made them such.

---

[1]   This section comes fourth in "A Celebration of Charis in Ten Lyric Pieces."

[2]   *whither* wherever (*OED* whither *adv* 4).

[3]   *Love's star* the planet Venus.

[4]   *smutched* blackened (*OED* smutched *ppl.a* 1).

[5]   *nard* aromatic balsam used in the ancient world (*OED* nard *sb* 1).

[6]   Drummond reported that Jonson described Selden as "the law-book of the judges of England, the bravest man in all languages." This poem was prefixed to Selden's *Titles of Honour* (1614); in its preface, Selden testifies to Jonson's learning.

[7]   *short* brief. Horace had warned that brevity could lead to obscurity.

[8]   *allay* a tempering (*OED* allay *sb*[1] 8), or check (*OED* allay *sb*[1] 9). Friendship makes it difficult to criticise freely.

[9]   *terms* limits, i.e. true capacities (*OED* term *sb* 1a).

Since being deceived, I turn a sharper eye
Upon myself, and ask to whom, and why,
25 And what I write? And vex it many days
Before men get a verse, much less a praise;
So that my reader is assured I now
Mean what I speak, and still will keep that vow.
Stand forth my object, then, you that have been
30 Ever at home, yet have all countries seen;
And like a compass keeping one foot still
Upon your centre, do your circle fill
Of general knowledge; watched men, manners too,
Heard what times past have said, seen what ours do.
35 Which grace shall I make love to first: your skill,
Or faith in things? Or is't your wealth and will
To instruct and teach, or your unwearied pain
Of gathering, bounty in pouring out again?
What fables have you vexed, what truth redeemed,
40 Antiquities searched, opinions disesteemed,
Impostures branded, and authorities urged!
What blots and errors have you watched and purged
Records and authors of! How rectified
Times, manners, customs! Innovations spied!
45 Sought out the fountains, sources, creeks, paths,
      ways,
And noted the beginnings and decays!
Where is that nominal mark, or real rite,[1]
Form, art, or ensign that hath 'scaped your sight?[2]
How are traditions there examined, how
50 Conjectures retrieved! And a story now
And then of times, besides the bare conduct
Of what it tells us, weaved in to instruct!
I wondered at the richness, but am lost
To see the workmanship so exceed the cost;[3]
55 To mark the excellent seasoning of your style,
And manly elocution, not one while

With horror rough, then rioting with wit:
But to the subject still the colours fit[4]
In sharpness of all search, wisdom of choice,
60 Newness of sense, antiquity of voice!
      I yield, I yield, the matter of your praise
Flows in upon me, and I cannot raise
A bank against it. Nothing but the round
Large clasp of nature such a wit can bound.
65 Monarch in letters! 'mongst thy titles shown
Of others' honours, thus enjoy thine own.
I first salute thee so, and gratulate,
With that thy style, thy keeping of thy state,
In offering this thy work to no great name
70 That would, perhaps, have praised and thanked
      the same,
But naught beyond. He thou hast given it to,[5]
Thy learnèd chamber-fellow, knows to do
It true respects. He will not only love,
Embrace, and cherish, but he can approve[6]
75 And estimate thy pains, as having wrought
In the same mines of knowledge, and thence brought
Humanity enough to be a friend,
And strength to be a champion and defend
Thy gift 'gainst envy. O how I do count
80 Among my comings-in, and see it mount,[7]
The gain of your two friendships! Hayward and
Selden: two names that so much understand;
On whom I could take up, and ne'er abuse[8]
The credit, what would furnish a tenth muse!
85 But here's no time, nor place, my wealth to tell;
You both are modest: so am I. Farewell.
—1640

---

[1] *nominal mark, or real rite* ceremonial titles. "Real" is a variant spelling of "royal" (*OED*). These terms are Selden's own from *Titles of Honour*.

[2] *ensign* symbol of dignity or office (*OED* ensign *sb* 4).

[3] *cost* quality (i.e. of the events Selden wrote about) (*OED* cost *sb* [1] 2).

[4] *still* always (*OED* still *adv* 3a); *colours* of rhetoric (*OED* colour *sb* [1] 13).

[5] *He thou hast given it to* Edward Hayward of the Inner Temple.

[6] *approve* corroborate, attest to (*OED* approve *v* [1] 2).

[7] *comings-in* gains, income.

[8] *take up* borrow from (*OED* take-up *v* 93c); believe without question (*OED* take-up *v* 93h).

An Epistle Answering to One that Asked to be Sealed of the Tribe of Ben [1]

Men that are safe and sure in all they do
    Care not what trials they are put unto;
They meet the fire, the test, as martyrs would,
    And though opinion stamp them not, are gold.
5 I could say more of such, but that I fly
    To speak myself out too ambitiously,
And showing so weak an act to vulgar eyes,
    Put conscience and my right to compromise.
Let those that merely talk, and never think,
10   That live in the wild anarchy of drink,
Subject to quarrel only, or else such
    As make it their proficiency how much
They have glutted in and lechered out that week,
    That never yet did friend or friendship seek
15 But for a sealing: let these men protest.
    Or the other on their borders, that will jest
On all souls that are absent, even the dead,
    Like flies or worms which man's corrupt parts fed:
That to speak well, think it above all sin,
20   Of any company but that they are in;
Call every night to supper in these fits,
    And are received for the covey of wits;
That censure all the town, and all the affairs,
    And know whose ignorance is more than theirs;
25 Let these men have their ways, and take their times
    To vent their libels, and to issue rhymes:
I have no portion in them, nor their deal
    Of news they get to strew out the long meal.
I study other friendships, and more one
30   Than these can ever be; or else wish none.
What is't to me whether the French design

Be, or be not, to get the Valtelline? [2]
    Or the States' ships sent forth belike to meet [3]
    Some hopes of Spain in their West Indian Fleet?
35 Whether the dispensation yet be sent, [4]
    Or that the match from Spain was ever meant?
I wish all well, and pray high heaven conspire
    My prince's safety and my king's desire;
But if, for honour, we must draw the sword,
40   And force back that which will not be restored,
I have a body yet that spirit draws
    To live, or fall, a carcass in the cause.
So far without inquiry what the States,
    Brunsfield, and Mansfield,[5] do this year, my fates
45 Shall carry me at call; and I'll be well,
    Though I do neither hear these news, nor tell
Of Spain or France; or were not pricked down one
    Of the late mystery of reception,
Although my fame to his not underhears, [6]
50   That guides the motions and directs the bears.
But that's a blow, by which in time I may
    Lose all my credit with my Christmas clay
And animated porcelain of the court;
    Aye, and for this neglect, the coarser sort
55 Of earthen jars there may molest me too:
    Well, with mine own frail pitcher, what to do
I have decreed; keep it from waves and press,
    Lest it be jostled, cracked, made naught, or less;
Live to that point I will, for which I am man,

---

[1] *Tribe of Ben* a biblical phrase (Revelation 7:8), here applied to Jonson's followers or poetic "sons."

[2] *Valtelline* a valley in Lombardy, fought over by France and Spain throughout the 1620s.

[3] *States'* Dutch.

[4] *dispensation* papal permission for (the Protestant) Prince Charles (later Charles I) to marry the Spanish Infanta (the "match from Spain" in the line following).

[5] *Brunsfield, and Mansfield* referring generally to military events on the continent; Brunsfield is unidentified, Mansfield commanded the forces of Frederick, Elector Palatine.

[6] *his* designer and architect Inigo Jones, Jonson's collaborator and rival, who was helping plan the reception for the Spanish Infanta.

60 And dwell as in my centre as I can,
Still looking to, and ever loving, heaven;
    With reverence using all the gifts thence given.
'Mongst which, if I have any friendships sent,
    Such as are square, well-tagged, and permanent,
Not built with canvas, paper, and false lights,
65   As are the glorious scenes at the great sights,
And that there be no fevery heats, nor colds,
    Oily expansions, or shrunk dirty folds,
But all so clear and led by reason's flame,
    As but to stumble in her sight were shame;
70 These I will honour, love, embrace, and serve,
    And free it from all question to preserve.
So short you read my character, and theirs
    I would call mine, to which not many stairs
Are asked to climb. First give me faith, who know
75   Myself a little. I will take you so,
As you have writ yourself. Now stand, and then,
    Sir, you are sealèd of the tribe of Ben.
    —(1623) 1640

An Ode. To Himself

Where dost thou careless lie,
    Buried in ease and sloth?
Knowledge that sleeps doth die;
And this security,
5   It is the common moth
That eats on wits and arts, and [oft] destroys
    them both.

Are all the Aonian springs
    Dried up? Lies Thespia waste? [1]
Doth Clarius' harp want strings, [2]
10 That not a nymph now sings?
    Or droop they, as disgraced

To see their seats and bowers by chattering pies
    defaced? [3]

    If hence thy silence be,
        As 'tis too just a cause,
15   Let this thought quicken thee:
    Minds that are great and free,
        Should not on fortune pause;
'Tis crown enough to virtue still, her own
applause.

20   What though the greedy fry
        Be taken with false baits
    Of worded balladry,
    And think it poesy?
        They die with their conceits,
25 And only piteous scorn upon their folly waits.

    Then take in hand thy lyre,
        Strike in thy proper strain;
    With Japhet's line, aspire [4]
    Sol's chariot for new fire
30   To give the world again; [5]
Who aided him, will thee, the issue of Jove's brain. [6]

    And since our dainty age
        Cannot endure reproof,
    Make not thyself a page
35   To that strumpet, the stage;
        But sing high and aloof,

---

[1] *Aonian springs* sacred to the Muses; *Thespia* a town at the foot of Mount Helicon, also sacred to the Muses.

[2] *Clarius* Apollo, sun god, patron of music and poetry, as worshipped in Claros, in Ionia.

[3] *pies* magpies, applied figuratively to cunning or saucy people (*OED* pie *sb* [1] 2).

[4] *Japhet* for the biblical reference see Genesis 9:26-27. Jonson is thinking of Prometheus; see Horace, Odes I.iii.25-28; *aspire* ascend (*OED* aspire *v* 8).

[5] Prometheus stole fire from the gods and brought it to humankind.

[6] *issue of Jove's brain* Minerva, or Athena, who sprang from the head of Zeus, was goddess of crafts and battle. She also represented intelligence. Jonson may want his audience to recall her role as mythological helper of male heroes.

Safe from the wolf's black jaw, and the dull ass's
   hoof.
—1640

To the Immortal Memory and Friendship of that Noble Pair, Sir Lucius Cary and Sir H. Morison [1]

The Turn

Brave infant of Saguntum, clear
Thy coming forth in that great year
When the prodigious Hannibal did crown
His rage with razing your immortal town.
5 Thou, looking then about,
Ere thou wert half got out,
Wise child, didst hastily return,
And mad'st thy mother's womb thine urn. [2]
How summed a circle didst thou leave mankind
10 Of deepest lore, could we the centre find!

The Counter-Turn

Did wiser nature draw thee back
From out the horror of that sack?
Where shame, faith, honour, and regard of right
Lay trampled on; the deeds of death and night
15 Urged, hurried forth, and hurled
Upon the affrighted world:
Sword, fire, and famine with fell fury met,
And all on utmost ruin set;
As, could they but life's miseries foresee,
20 No doubt all infants would return like thee.

The Stand

For what is life, if measured by the space,
Not by the act?
Or maskèd man, if valued by his face
Above his fact?
25 Here's one outlived his peers
And told forth fourscore years;
He vexèd time, and busied the whole state;
Troubled both foes and friends,
But ever to no ends:
30 What did this stirrer, but die late?
How well at twenty had he fallen or stood!
For three of his fourscore he did no good.

The Turn

He entered well by virtuous parts,
Got up and thrived with honest arts;
35 He purchased friends and fame and honours then,
And had his noble name advanced with men;
But weary of that flight,
He stooped in all men's sight
To sordid flatteries, acts of strife,
40 And sunk in that dead sea of life
So deep, as he did then death's waters sup,
But that the cork of title buoyed him up.

The Counter-Turn

Alas, but Morison fell young!
He never fell: thou fall'st, my tongue.
45 He stood, a soldier to the last right end,
A perfect patriot, and a noble friend;
But most, a virtuous son.
All offices were done
By him so ample, full, and round,
50 In weight, in measure, number, sound,
As, though his age imperfect might appear,
His life was of humanity the sphere.

The Stand

Go now, and tell out days summed up with fears,
And make them years;

---

[1] Cary (?1610–1643), second Viscount Falkland, famed for his learning and for the intellectual circle associated with his estate Great Tew. Sir Henry Morison (1608–1629), Cary's brother-in-law, died probably of smallpox. Jonson's celebration of their friendship is the first sustained attempt in English to imitate the tripartite structure of the Pindaric ode.

[2] *infant of Saguntum* according to Pliny (*Natural History*, Vii.iii), an infant born in Saguntum (in Spain) while Hannibal was sacking the town immediately returned to its mother's womb.

55 Produce thy mass of miseries on the stage,
To swell thine age;
Repeat of things a throng,
To show thou hast been long,
Not lived; for life doth her great actions spell
60 By what was done and wrought
In season, and so brought
To light: her measures are, how well
Each syllabe answered, and was formed, how fair;
These make the lines of life, and that's her air.

The Turn

65 It is not growing like a tree
In bulk, doth make man better be;
Or standing long an oak, three hundred year,
To fall a log at last, dry, bald, and sere:
A lily of a day
70 Is fairer far, in May,
Although it fall and die that night;
It was the plant and flower of light.
In small proportions we just beauty see,
And in short measures life may perfect be.

The Counter-Turn

75 Call, noble Lucius, then for wine,
And let thy looks with gladness shine;
Accept this garland, plant it on thy head;
And think, nay know, thy Morison's not dead.
He leaped the present age,
80 Possessed with holy rage
To see that bright eternal day,
Of which we priests and poets say
Such truths, as we expect for happy men;
And there he lives with memory, and Ben

The Stand

85 Jonson, who sung this of him, ere he went
Himself to rest,
Or taste a part of that full joy he meant
To have expressed

In this bright asterism: [1]
90 Where it were friendship's schism
(Were not his Lucius long with us to tarry)
To separate these twi-
Lights, the Dioscuri; [2]
And keep the one half from his Harry.
95 But fate doth so alternate the design,
Whilst that in heaven, this light on earth must
    shine.

The Turn

And shine as you exalted are;
Two names of friendship, but one star:
Of hearts the union. And those not by chance
100 Made, or indentured, or leased out to advance
The profits for a time.
No pleasures vain did chime,
Of rhymes, or riots, at your feasts,
Orgies of drink, or feigned protests:
105 But simple love of greatness, and of good;
That knits brave minds and manners, more than
    blood.

The Counter-Turn

This made you first to know the why
You liked; then after, to apply
That liking; and approach so one the t'other,
110 Till either grew a portion of the other:
Each stylèd, by his end,
The copy of his friend.
You lived to be the great surnames
And titles by which all made claims
115 Unto the virtue. Nothing perfect done
But as a Cary, or a Morison.

The Stand

And such a force the fair example had,
As they that saw

---

[1] *asterism* constellation.

[2] *Dioscuri* Castor and Pollux, the twins set among the stars to form
the constellation Gemini.

The good and durst not practise it, were glad
120 That such a law
Was left yet to mankind;
Where they might read and find
Friendship in deed was written, not in words;
And with the heart, not pen,
125 Of two so early men
Whose lines her rolls were, and records.
Who, ere the first down bloomèd on the chin,
Had sowed these fruits, and got the harvest in.
—1640 (1629?)

[Horace, Epode ii]
The Praises of a Country Life [1]

Happy is he, that from all business clear
As the old race of mankind were,
With his own oxen tills his sire's left lands,
And is not in the usurer's bands;
5 Nor, soldier-like, started with rough alarms,
Nor dreads the sea's enragèd harms;
But flees the bar and courts, with the proud boards
And waiting-chambers of great lords.
The poplar tall he then doth marrying twine
10 With the grown issue of the vine;
And with his hook lops off the fruitless race,
And sets more happy in the place;
Or in the bending vale beholds afar
The lowing herds there grazing are;
15 Or the pressed honey in pure pots doth keep
Of earth, and shears the tender sheep;
Or when that autumn through the fields lifts round
His head, with mellow apples crowned,
How, plucking pears his own hand grafted had,
20 And purple-matching grapes, he's glad!
With which, Priapus, he may thank thy hands,

And, Silvane, thine, that kept'st his lands. [2]
Then, now beneath some ancient oak he may,
Now in the rooted grass, him lay,
25 Whilst from the higher banks do slide the floods;
The soft birds quarrel in the woods,
The fountains murmur as the streams do creep,
And all invite to easy sleep.
Then when the thundering Jove his snow and showers
30 Are gathering by the wintry hours,
Or hence, or thence, he drives with many a hound
Wild boars into his toils pitched round;
Or strains on his small fork his subtle nets
For the eating thrush, or pitfalls sets;
35 And snares the fearful hare and new-come crane,
And 'counts them sweet rewards so ta'en.
Who, amongst these delights, would not forget
Love's cares so evil, and so great?
But if, to boot with these, a chaste wife, meet
40 For household aid and children sweet,
Such as the Sabines'; or a sun-burnt blowze,
Some lusty, quick Apulian's spouse, [3]
To deck the hallowed hearth with old wood fired
Against the husband comes home tired;
45 That penning the glad flock in hurdles by,
Their swelling udders doth draw dry;
And from the sweet tub wine of this year takes,
And unbought viands ready makes:
Not Locrine oysters I could then more prize,
50 Nor turbot, nor bright golden-eyes; [4]
If with bright floods, the winter troubled much,
Into our seas send any such,

---

[1] Drummond writes that Jonson read this poem to him "and admired it." This may be regarded as an example of "self-esteem, founded on just and right" (Milton), for this is a fine translation, imitating the form of the original to the extent of having the same number of lines. Horace's second epode has been frequently translated.

---

[2] *Priapus* Greek and Roman god of fertility and hence of gardens, vineyards, etc. *Silvane* Silvanus, the Roman god of forests and agriculture.

[3] The Sabines were ancient Italians, inhabiting the central Apennines, whose wives had a reputation for modesty, constancy, and thrift; *blowze* a sunburnt female, often of the working or rustic class (*OED*). The Apulians lived in southern Italy.

[4] The Romans especially prized oysters of the Lucrine Lake; *turbot* European coastal fish, much-esteemed as food; *golden-eyes* probably another species of fish, although also a species of sea-duck (*OED*).

The Ionian godwit, nor the Guinea-hen[1]
   Could not go down my belly then
55 More sweet than olives that new-gathered be
   From fattest branches of the tree;
Or the herb sorrel that loves meadows still,
   Or mallows, loosing body's ill;[2]
Or at the feast of bounds, the lamb then slain,
60   Or kid forced from the wolf again.[3]
Among these cates how glad the sight doth come[4]
   Of the fed flocks approaching home!
To view the weary oxen draw, with bare
   And fainting necks, the turnèd share!
65 The wealthy household swarm of bondmen met,
   And 'bout the steaming chimney set!
These thoughts when usurer Alfius, now about
   To turn mere farmer, had spoke out,
'Gainst the ides his moneys he gets in with pain
70   At the calends, puts all out again.[5]
—1640

On The New Inn
Ode. To Himself[6]

Come, leave the loathèd stage,
   And the more loathsome age,
Where pride and impudence, in faction knit,
   Usurp the chair of wit:
5 Indicting and arraigning every day
   Something they call a play.

   Let their fastidious, vain
      Commission of the brain
   Run on and rage, sweat, censure, and condemn:
10 They were not made for thee, less thou for them.

   Say that thou pour'st them wheat,
      And they will acorns eat:
   'Twere simple fury still thyself to waste
      On such as have no taste:
15 To offer them a surfeit of pure bread
      Whose appetites are dead.
   No, give them grains their fill,
      Husks, draff to drink and swill;[7]
   If they love lees, and leave the lusty wine,
20 Envy them not, their palate's with the swine.

   No doubt some mouldy tale
      Like *Pericles*, and stale
   As the shrieve's crusts, and nasty as his fish-
      Scraps out of every dish,[8]
25 Thrown forth, and raked into the common tub,
      May keep up the play club:
   There sweepings do as well
      As the best-ordered meal.
   For who the relish of these guests will fit
30 Needs set them but the alms-basket of wit.

   And much good d't you then:
      Brave plush and velvet men
   Can feed on orts; and safe in your stage-clothes
      Dare quit, upon your oaths,
35 The stagers and the stage-wrights too (your peers)
      Or larding your large ears
   With their foul comic socks,
      Wrought upon twenty blocks:

---

[1] *Ionian godwit...Guinea-hen*   edible birds (*OED*).

[2] *sorrel...mallows*   edible herbs.

[3] *feast of bounds*   in honour of Terminus, god of boundaries. Meat was eaten at this feast. The wolf was thought to take the best of the flock.

[4] *cates*   delicacies (*OED*).

[5] *ides* and *calends*   days upon which debts and interest came due. The poem ends sardonically; in spite of his praise of the country life, Alfius will continue to practise usury in the town.

[6] *The New Inn*   a play by Jonson, hissed off the stage in 1629; Jonson published this ode with the play in 1631.

---

[7] *draff*   dregs.

[8] *Pericles*   by Shakespeare, first printed in 1609; *shrieve's*   sheriff's; referring to the food, often leftovers, collected to feed impoverished prisoners.

Which, if they're torn and turned and patched
   enough,
40   The gamesters share your guilt, and you their stuff.

     Leave things so prostitute,
     And take the Alcaic lute,
Or thine own Horace, or Anacreon's lyre;
     Warm thee by Pindar's fire: [1]
45   And though thy nerves be shrunk and blood be
   cold
     Ere years have made thee old,
     Strike that disdainful heat
     Throughout, to their defeat:
As curious fools, and envious of thy strain,
50   May, blushing, wear no palsy's in thy brain.

     But when they hear thee sing
     The glories of thy king,
His zeal to God, and his just awe o'er men:
     They may, blood-shaken, then
55   Feel such a flesh-quake to possess their powers,
     As they shall cry: Like ours
     In sound of peace or wars
     No harp e'er hit the stars,
In tuning forth the acts of his sweet reign:
60   And raising Charles's chariot 'bove his Wain. [2]
     —1631

To the Memory of My Beloved, The Author, Mr William Shakespeare, And What He Hath Left Us [3]

To draw no envy, Shakespeare, on thy name,
  Am I thus ample to thy book and fame; [4]
While I confess thy writings to be such
    As neither man nor muse can praise too much:
5 'Tis true, and all men's suffrage. But these ways
    Were not the paths I meant unto thy praise:
For silliest ignorance on these may light,
    Which, when it sounds at best, but echoes right;
Or blind affection, which doth ne'er advance
10   The truth, but gropes, and urgeth all by chance;
Or crafty malice might pretend this praise,
    And think to ruin where it seemed to raise.
These are as some infamous bawd or whore
    Should praise a matron: what could hurt her
    more?
15 But thou art proof against them, and indeed
    Above the ill fortune of them, or the need.
I therefore will begin. Soul of the age!
    The applause, delight, the wonder of our stage!
My Shakespeare, rise: I will not lodge thee by
20   Chaucer or Spenser, or bid Beaumont lie
A little further, to make thee a room;
    Thou art a monument without a tomb, [5]
And art alive still while thy book doth live,
    And we have wits to read, and praise to give.
25 That I not mix thee so, my brain excuses:
    I mean with great, but disproportioned, muses;
For if I thought my judgement were of years [6]
    I should commit thee surely with thy peers:

---

[3] This poem was printed with the Droeshout portrait in the First Folio.

[4] *ample* large or excellent enough to satisfy demands (*OED* ample *a* 4a); treating matters at full length (*OED* ample *a* 5).

[5] *a monument without a tomb* recalling the famous opening of Horace, *Odes* III. 30.

[6] *of years* probably, of appropriate maturity.

---

[1] *Alcaic…Pindar's fire* return to classical genres, as represented by such renowned lyric poets as Alcaeus, Horace, Pindar, and Anacreon.

[2] *Charles…his Wain* the Big Dipper; named for Charlemagne ("wain" is a chariot), but referring here to King Charles.

And tell how far thou didst our Lyly outshine,
30   Or sporting Kyd, or Marlowe's mighty line.
And though thou hadst small Latin, and less Greek,
     From thence to honour thee I would not seek
For names, but call forth thundering Aeschylus,
     Euripides, and Sophocles to us,
35 Pacuvius, Accius, him of Cordova dead, [1]
     To life again, to hear thy buskin tread
And shake a stage; or, when thy socks were on, [2]
     Leave thee alone for the comparison
Of all that insolent Greece or haughty Rome
40   Sent forth, or since did from their ashes come.
Triumph, my Britain, thou hast one to show
     To whom all scenes of Europe homage owe.
He was not of an age, but for all time!
     And all the muses still were in their prime
45 When like Apollo he came forth to warm
     Our ears, or like a Mercury to charm! [3]
Nature herself was proud of his designs,
     And joyed to wear the dressing of his lines,
Which were so richly spun and woven so fit
50   As, since, she will vouchsafe no other wit.
The merry Greek, tart Aristophanes,
     Neat Terence, witty Plautus, now not please, [4]
But antiquated and deserted lie
     As they were not of nature's family.
55 Yet must I not give nature all: thy art,
     My gentle Shakespeare, must enjoy a part.
For though the poet's matter nature be,
     His art doth give the fashion. And that he [5]
Who casts to write a living line must sweat [6]

60   (Such as thine are) and strike the second heat
Upon the muses' anvil: turn the same
     (And himself with it) that he thinks to frame;
Or for the laurel he may gain a scorn: [7]
     For a good poet's made, as well as born;
65 And such wert thou. Look how the father's face
     Lives in his issue: even so, the race [8]
Of Shakespeare's mind and manners brightly shines
     In his well-turnèd and true-filèd lines:
In each of which he seems to shake a lance,
70   As brandished at the eyes of ignorance.
Sweet swan of Avon! What a sight it were
     To see thee in our waters yet appear,
And make those flights upon the banks of Thames
     That so did take Eliza, and our James!
75 But stay, I see thee in the hemisphere
     Advanced, and made a constellation there!
Shine forth, thou star of poets, and with rage
     Or influence chide or cheer the drooping stage;
Which, since thy flight from hence, hath
          mourned like night,
80   And despairs day, but for thy volume's light.
—1623

Clerimont's Song [9]

Still to be neat, still to be dressed,
As you were going to a feast;
Still to be powdered, still perfumed:
Lady, it is to be presumed,
5 Though art's hid causes are not found,
All is not sweet, all is not sound.

Give me a look, give me a face,
That makes simplicity a grace;
Robes loosely flowing, hair as free:

---

[1] Aeschylus, Euripides and Sophocles were Athenian tragedians; Pacuvius and Accius were Latin tragic poets; *him of Cordova* Seneca.

[2] *buskin* boot worn by actors in Athenian tragedy; *socks* low shoes or slippers worn by comic actors (*OED* sock *sb*[1] 3).

[3] *Apollo* god of poetry; *Mercury* god of eloquence.

[4] Aristophanes and Plautus were both Greek comic playwrights; Terence was a Roman stage-poet. *Neat* well-spoken, eloquent (*OED* neat *a* 8a).

[5] *fashion* shape, style (*OED* fashion *sb* 2b,3a).

[6] *casts* determines, aspires (*OED* cast *v* 44a).

[7] *laurel* symbol of poetic glory.

[8] *race* offspring (*OED* race *sb*[2] 1); onward movement (*OED* race *sb*[1] 5a); liveliness (*OED* race *sb*[2] 10b).

[9] From *Epicoene, or the Silent Woman*.

10 Such sweet neglect more taketh me
Than all the adulteries of art:
They strike mine eyes, but not my heart.
—1616

A Vision of Beauty [1]

It was a beauty that I saw
So pure, so perfect, as the frame
Of all the universe was lame;

To that one figure, could I draw,
5 Or give least line of it a law!

A skein of silk without a knot!
A fair march made without a halt!
A curious form without a fault!
A printed book without a blot!
10 All beauty, and without a spot!
—1631

---

[1] From *The New Inn*.

Richard Corbett
1582 – 1635

Corbett was the only son of Vincent Corbett, a nurseryman of Ewell, Surrey. He was educated at Westminster School and then at Broadgates Hall, which later became Pembroke College, Oxford. He received his B.A. in 1602, his M.A. in 1605, and then took holy orders. In 1612, as Junior Proctor of the university, Corbett gave a funeral oration on the death of Prince Henry. After Corbett had served for some years as the vicar of Cassington, James I made him one of the royal chaplains. In 1617 he was admitted B.D. at Oxford, and in 1620 appointed Dean of Christ Church. In 1621 an embarrassing incident occurred which became a source of much amusement to Corbett's contemporaries. During a sermon before the King at Woodstock, Corbett became preoccupied by a ring that the King had given him and completely forgot his sermon. Corbett was made Bishop of Oxford in 1628 and Bishop of Norwich in 1632. He married Alice Hutton, a vicar's daughter, by whom he had two children. Aubrey's version is that "he married Alice Hutton, whom 'twas said that he begot. She was a very beautiful woman, and so was her mother." Aubrey's life of Corbett, reflecting the wit, humour, conviviality and love of fun we find in the verse, is highly entertaining, though not perhaps edifying. This is perhaps as it should be, since throughout his life Corbett expressed dislike of puritan theology and would not tolerate practices he perceived as puritan. He wrote in a wide variety of genres, including satires, epigrams, epistles, and elegies. His works were first published in 1647.

❦❦❦

Upon an Unhandsome Gentlewoman, who made Love unto him

Have I renounc't my faith, or basely sold
Salvation, and my loyalty for gold?
Have I some foreign practice undertook
By poison, shot, sharp-knife, or sharper book
5 To kill my King? have I betrayed the state
To fire and fury, or some newer fate,
Which learned murderers, those grand destinies,
The Jesuits, have nurs'd? if all of these [1]
I guilty am, proceed; I am content
10 That Mallet take me for my punishment. [2]

For never sin was of so high a rate,
But one night's hell with her might expiate.
Although the law with Garnet, and the rest, [3]
Dealt far more mildly; hanging's but a jest
15 To this immortal torture. Had she been then
In Mary's torrid days engend'red, when [4]
Cruelty was witty, and invention free
Did live by blood, and thrive by cruelty,
She would have been more horrid engines far
20 Then fire or famine, racks, and halters are.
Whether her wit, form, talk, smile, tire I name,
Each is a stock of tyranny, and shame;
But for her breath, spectators come not nigh,
That lays about; God bless the company.
25 The man, in a bear's skin baited to death,

---

[1] *Jesuits* members of the Society of Jesus, a Roman Catholic order. Several Jesuits were suspected of involvement in the Gunpowder Plot of 1605, an unsuccessful attempt to blow up the houses of Parliament and kill James I and his heir.

[2] *Mallet* Mrs. Mallet, the widow of the servant of the Vice Chancellor, who had apparently made unwelcome amorous approaches to Corbett. Some of the manuscripts of this poem are entitled *Mr. Corbett on Mrs Mallet; an ill favoured creature that would need be in love with the Author.*

[3] *Garnet* Henry Garnet (1555–1606), the Superior of the English Jesuits, was implicated in the Gunpowder Plot and executed along with its primary instigators.

[4] *Mary* During the reign of Mary Tudor (1553–1558), there was intense persecution of Protestants.

Would choose the dogs much rather then her
    breath;
One kiss of hers, and eighteen words alone
Put down the Spanish Inquisition.
Thrice happy we (quoth I thinking thereon,)
30 That see no days of persecution;
For were it free to kill, this grisly elf
Would martyrs make in compass of herself;
And were she not prevented by our prayer,
By this time she corrupted had the air.
35   And am I innocent? and is it true,
That thing (which poet Pliny never knew,
Nor Africk, Nile, nor ever Hackluyt's eyes [1]
Descried in all his East, West-voyages;
That thing, which poets were afraid to feign,
40 For fear her shadow should infect their brain;
This spouse of Antichrist, and his alone, [2]
She's dressed so like the Whore of Babylon;) [3]
Should dote on me? as if they did contrive,
The Devil and she, to damn a man alive.
45 Why doth not Welcome rather purchase her, [4]
And bear about this rare familiar?
Six market days, a wake, and a fair too't,
Would save his charges, and the ale to boot.
No tiger's like her; she feeds upon a man
50 Worse than a tigress or a leopard can.
    Let me go pray, and think upon some spell,
At once to bid the Devil and her farewell.
—1647

A Proper New Ballad Entitled
The Fairies Farewell:
Or God-a-Mercy Will

Farewell, rewards & Fairies,
    Good housewives now may say;
For now foul sluts in dairies
    Do fare as well as they;
5 And though they sweep their hearths no less
    Then maids were wont to do,
Yet who of late for cleanliness
    Finds six-pence in her shoe?

Lament, lament, old abbeys,
10   The Fairies lost command:
They did but change priests' babies, [5]
    But some have changed your land;
And all your children sprung from thence
    Are now grown puritans: [6]
15 Who live as changelings ever since
    For love of your demains. [7]

At morning and at evening both
    You merry were and glad,
So little care of sleep or sloth
20   These pretty ladies had.
When Tom came home from labour,
    Or Ciss to milking rose,
Then merrily, merrily went their tabor, [8]
    And nimbly went their toes .

---

[1] *Hackluyt* Richard Hakluyt (ca. 1522–1616), an English geographer and voluminous writer who promoted overseas expansion.

[2] *Antichrist* sometimes used to denote the title of a great personal opponent of Christ and his kingdom, expected by the early church to appear before the end of the world (*OED* antiChrist 2). At other times, used more generally to refer to an enemy of Christ (*OED* antiChrist 1). See I John 2:18–22.

[3] *Whore of Babylon* See Revelation 17:1–18:24, especially 17:4.

[4] *Welcome* J.A.W. Bennett and H.R. Trevor-Roper speculate that this may be the name of an itinerant showman (*The Poems of Richard Corbett*, Oxford: Clarendon Press, 1955).

[5] *change priest's babies* According to legend, fairies would steal human infants, leaving their own in their place.

[6] *puritans* English Protestants who regarded the Reformation of Elizabeth I as incomplete and called for further "purification" of the English Church from what they considered to be unscriptural and corrupt forms and ceremonies (*OED* puritan sb1).

[7] *demains* domains (*OED* demain(e)).

[8] *tabor* the earlier name of the drum. In later use, a small drum, used chiefly as accompaniment to the pipe or trumpet (*OED* tabor sb¹).

25 Witness those rings and roundelays [1]
 Of theirs, which yet remain,
Were footed in Queen Mary's days
 On many a grassy plain;
But, since of late Elizabeth,
30 And later James, came in, [2]
They never danc'd on any heath
 As when the time hath been.

By which we note the Fairies
 Were of the old profession; [3]
35 Their songs were *Ave Marias,*
 Their dances were procession.
But now, alas, they all are dead,
 Or gone beyond the seas,
Or farther for religion fled,
40 Or else they take their ease.

A tell-tale in their company
 They never could endure,
And who so kept not secretly
 Their mirth, was punished sure.
45 It was a just and Christian deed
 To pinch such black and blue.
O, how the Commonwealth doth need
 Such justices as you!

Now they have left our quarters
50 A register they have,
Who looketh to their charters,
 A man both wise and grave;
An hundred of their merry pranks
 By one that I could name

55 Are kept in store, conn twenty thanks [4]
 To William for the same. [5]

I marvel who his cloak would turn
 When Puck had led him round, [6]
Or where those walking fires would burn, [7]
60 Where Cureton would be found;
How Broker would appear to be,
 For whom this age doth mourn;
But that their spirits live in thee,
 In thee, old William Chourne. [8]

65 To William Chourne of Staffordshire
 Give laud and praises due,
Who every meal can mend your cheer
 With tales both old and true.
To William all give audience,
70 And pray ye for his noddle, [9]
For all the Fairies' evidence
 Were lost, if that were addle. [10]
—1647

The Distracted Puritan

Am I mad, o noble Festus, [11]
 When zeal and godly knowledge
Have put me in hope
To deal with the Pope,
5 As well as the best in the College?

[1] *roundelays* fairy circles or rings (*OED* roundelay 3b, this place cited).

[2] *Elizabeth…James* in reference to the Protestantism of Elizabeth (1558–1603) and James (1603–1625).

[3] *the old profession* Roman Catholic.

[4] *conn* offer. To conn thanks is to express thanks (*OED* conn *v*[1]4).

[5] *William* the servant of Corbett's friend Dr. Leonard Hutton.

[6] *Puck* the name of a fancied mischievous goblin or sprite, also known as Robin Goodfellow and Hobgoblin (*OED sb*[1]).

[7] *walking fires* will o' the wisps.

[8] *Cureton…Broker* Bennett and Trevor-Roper speculate that Cureton and Broker were Staffordshire worthies whose spirits Chourne could conjure up.

[9] *noddle* head (*OED sb*[1]2b).

[10] *addle* muddled, confused, unsound (*OED* addle *a* 2).

[11] *Festus* See Acts 24–26, especially 26:24.

Boldly I preach, hate a cross, hate a surplice,
    Miters, copes, and rochets: [1]
Come hear me pray nine times a day,
    And fill your heads with crotchets. [2]

10 In the house of pure Emmanuel [3]
I had my education;
Where my friends surmise
I dazzled my eyes,
With the light of Revelation. [4]
15   Boldly I preach, &c.

They bound me like a bedlam, [5]
They lashed my four poor quarters;
Whilst this I endure
Faith makes me sure
20 To be one of Foxe's martyrs. [6]
    Boldly I preach, &c.

These injuries I suffer
Through Anti-Christs' invasions.
Take of this chain,
25 Neither Rome nor Spain
Can resist my strong persuasions:
    Boldly I preach, &c.

Of the beast's ten horns (God bless us) [7]
I have knocked off three already.
30 If they let me alone,
I'll leave him none;
But they say I am too heady.
    Boldly I preach, &c.

When I sacked the Seven-Hilled city, [8]
35 I met the great red dragon: [9]
I kept him aloof
With the armor of proof,
Though here I have never a rag on.
    Boldly I preach, &c.

40 With a fiery sword and target
There fought I with this monster:
But the sons of pride
My zeal deride,
And all my deeds misconster. [10]
45   Boldly I preach, &c.

I unhorsed the whore of Babel
With a lance of inspirations:
I made her stink,
And spill her drink
50 In the cup of abominations. [11]
    Boldly I preach, &c.

I have seen two in a vision,
With a flying book between them: [12]
I have been in despair

---

[1] *Miters* head dress forming part of the insignia of a bishop in the Western Church (*OED* mitre *sb*[1]2b); *copes* a vestment resembling a long cloak, worn by ecclesiastics in procession (*OED* cope *sb*[1]2); *rochets* a vestment of linen, usually worn by bishops and abbots (*OED* rochet [1]2).

[2] *crotchets* whimsical fancies, perverse conceits (*OED* crotchet *sb*[1]9).

[3] *Emmanuel* Emmanuel College, Cambridge was strongly Calvinist and Puritan.

[4] *Revelation* the final book of the New Testament; a book of prophecy.

[5] *bedlam* one fit for a lunatic asylum; a madman (*OED* Bedlam 5).

[6] *Foxe's martyrs* John Foxe's *Acts and Monuments* (1563), commonly known as *The Book of Martyrs*, a history of Protestant martyrs from the fourteenth to the sixteenth centuries, was one of the most widely read books of the early modern period.

[7] *beast's ten horns* See Revelation 13.

[8] *Seven-Hilled City* Rome. See Revelation 17: 9.

[9] *red dragon* a symbol of Satan. See Revelation 12: 3, 4.

[10] *misconster* misconstrue.

[11] *cup of abominations* See Revelation 17:1–18:24, especially 17:4.

[12] *two in a vision, / with a flying book between them* Bennett and Trevor Roper refer to *The worldes warning of an Alarum from sinne by the vision of 2 dragons seene fighting in the ayre neere Gaunte* (registered 6 Feb. 1609).

55 Five times a year,
And cured by reading Greenham. [1]
   Boldly I preach, &c.

I observ'd in Perkins' tables [2]
The black lines of damnation:
60 Those crooked veins
So stuck in my brains,
That I fear'd my reprobation.
   Boldly I preach, &c.

In the holy tongue of Chanaan [3]
65 I plac'd my chiefest pleasure:
Till I pricked my foot
With an Hebrew root,

That I bled beyond all measure.
   Boldly I preach, &c.

70 I appear'd before the Archbishop,
And all the high Commission: [4]
I gave him no grace,
But told him to his face
That he favour'd superstition.
75   Boldly I preach, hate a cross, hate a surplice,
     Miters, copes, and rochets:
   Come hear me pray nine time a day,
     And fill your heads with crotchets.
—1647

[1] *Greenham* Richard Greenham (1535?–1594?), a Puritan theologian who published works on comforting an afflicted mind.

[2] *Perkin's tables* William Perkins (1558–1602), a Puritan systematic theologian; one of his works includes a table illustrating the causes of salvation and damnation.

[3] *the holy tongue of Chanaan* the Hebrew language.

[4] *high Commission* a court of ecclesiastical jurisdiction, founded under Elizabeth I, which gave the crown power to commission persons to try various offences against the ecclesiastical establishment, and to crush any resistance to the supremacy of the crown in these matters. Abolished in 1641 (*OED* commission *sb*[1]7).

Edward, Lord Herbert of Cherbury
1582 — 1648

George Herbert's brother led an active, varied and studious life; he was a historian and a colourful autobiographer, and has a place in the history of philosophy. In George Herbert, Donne's influence expressed itself in religious verse; in Edward Her-bert's in secular love poetry. As a young man Herbert travelled a good deal, and held some diplomatic appointments. In the Civil War he made an accommodation with Parliament in order to save his library.

⁊⁊⁊

An Ode upon a Question moved, Whether Love should continue for ever?

Having interr'd her infant-birth,
  The wat'ry ground that late did mourn,
  Was strew'd with flow'rs for the return
Of the wish'd bridegroom of the earth.

5 The well accorded birds did sing
    Their hymns unto the pleasant time,
    And in a sweet consorted chime
Did welcome in the cheerful spring.

To which, soft whistles of the wind,
10   And warbling murmurs of a brook,
    And varied notes of leaves that shook,
An harmony of parts did bind.

While doubling joy unto each other,
    All in so rare consent was shown,
15   No happiness that came alone,
Nor pleasure that was not another.

When with a love none can express,
    That mutually happy pair,
    Melander and Celinda fair,
20 The season with their loves did bless.

Walking thus towards a pleasant grove,
    Which did, it seem'd, in new delight
    The pleasures of the time unite,
To give a triumph to their love,

25 They stay'd at last, and on the grass
    Reposed so, as o'r his breast
    She bow'd her gracious head to rest,
Such a weight as no burden was.

While over either's compass'd waist
30   Their folded arms were so compos'd,
    As if in straightest bonds enclos'd,
They suffer'd for joys they did taste.

Long their fixed eyes to Heaven bent,
    Unchanged, they did never move,
35   As if so great and pure a love
No glass but it could represent.

When with a sweet, though troubled look,
    She first brake silence, saying, Dear friend,
    O that our love might take no end,
40 Or never had beginning took!

I speak not this with a false heart,
    (Wherewith his hand she gently strain'd)
    Or that would change a love maintain'd
With so much faith on either part.

45 Nay, I protest, though death with his
    Worst counsel should divide us here,

His terrors could not make me fear,
To come where you lov'd presence is.

Only if love's fire with the breath
50   Of life be kindled, I doubt,
    With our last air 'twill be breath'd out,
And quenched with the cold of death.

That if affection be a line,
    Which is clos'd up in our last hour;
55   Oh how 'twould grieve me, any pow'r
Could force so dear a love as mine!

She scarce had done, when his shut eyes
    An inward joy did represent,
    To hear Celinda thus intent
60 To a love he so much did prize.

Then with a look, it seem'd, denied
    All earthly pow'rs but hers, yet so,
    As if to her breath he did owe
This borrowed life, he thus replied;

65 O you, wherein, they say, souls rest,
    Till they descend pure heavenly fires,
    Shall lustful and corrupt desires
With your immortal seed be blest?

And shall our love, so far beyond
70   That low and dying appetite,
    And which so chaste desires unite,
Not hold in an eternal bond?

Is it, because we should decline,
    And wholly from our thoughts exclude
75   Objects that may the sense delude,
And study only the divine?

No sure, for if none can ascend
    Ev'n to the visible degree

    Of things created, how should we
80 The invisible comprehend?

Or rather since that pow'r expressed
    His greatness in his works alone,
    B'ing here best in his creatures known,
Why is he not lov'd in them best?

85 But is't not true, which you pretend,
    That since our love and knowledge here,
    Only as parts of life appear,
So they with it should take their end.

O no, belov'd, I am most sure,
90   Those virtuous habits we acquire,
    As being with the soul entire,
Must with it evermore endure.

For if when sins and vice reside,
    We find so foul a guilt remain,
95   As never dying in his stain,
Still punish'd in the soul doth bide,

Much more that true and real joy,
    Which in a virtuous love is found,
    Must be more solid in its ground,
100 Then fate or death can e'r destroy.

Else should our souls in vain elect,
    And vainer yet were Heaven's laws,
    When to an everlasting cause
They gave a perishing effect.

105 Nor here on earth then, nor above,
    Our good affection can impair,
    For where God doth admit the fair,
Think you that he excludeth love?

These eyes again then, eyes shall see,
110   And hands again these hands enfold,

And all chaste pleasures can be told
Shall with us everlasting be.

For if no use of sense remain
   When bodies once this life forsake,
115   Or they could no delight partake,
Why should they ever rise again?

And if every imperfect mind
   Make love the end of knowledge here,
   How perfect will our love be, where
120 All imperfection is refin'd?

Let then no doubt, Celinda, touch,
   Much less your fairest mind invade,
   Were not our souls immortal made,
Our equal loves can make them such.

125 So when one wing can make no way,
   Two joinèd can themselves dilate,

   So can two persons propagate,
When singly either would decay.

So when from hence we shall be gone,
130   And be no more, nor you, nor I,
   As one another's mystery,
Each shall be both, yet both but one.

This said, in her up-lifted face,
   Her eyes which did that beauty crown,
135   Were like two stars, that having faln down,
Look up again to find their place:

Which such a moveless silent peace
   Did seize on their becalmed sense,
   One would have thought some influence
140 Their ravish'd spirits did possess.
   —1665

Lady Mary Wroth

ca. 1587 – ca. 1651-53

The poet and romance writer Lady Mary Wroth was the eldest child of Sir Robert Sidney, first Earl of Leicester, and Lady Barbara Gamage. Her father was the younger brother of Sir Philip Sidney. As a child, Wroth often accompanied her mother to the Continent to visit her father, then governor of Flushing in the Netherlands, returning home to the Penshurst estate. In a letter to her father, the estate manager Rowland Whyte wrote of Wroth's education: "God bless her, she is very forward in her learning, writing, and other exercises she is put to, as dancing and the virginals." Wroth's writings suggest that she was widely read in English and Continental romances and pastorals, and in English drama and poetry. In 1604, she married Sir Robert Wroth, who had been knighted by James I the previous year. Her husband's friendship with the King positioned Wroth within Queen Anne's circle of friends, and she participated in Jonson's court masque, *The Masque of Blackness* (1605).

During her marriage, Wroth was both patron and poet. The former role may explain why her work, circulated in manuscript, was praised by Ben Jonson and William Drummond. In February, 1614 her first son, James, was born, and the following month her husband died. Wroth was left greatly indebted, as her jointure of £1,200 was insufficient to reduce the £23,000 debt left her by her husband.

Though the estate reverted to Sir Robert's uncle on the death of her son in 1616, she struggled for the remainder of her life to settle her husband's debts. Although Wroth never remarried, a manuscript history of the Herbert-Pembroke family records that she bore two illegitimate children by her first cousin, William Herbert, Earl of Pembroke.

In 1621, Wroth published her prose romance, *The Countess of Montgomery's Urania*. As the work alluded to contemporary court scandals, it evoked criticism. In a letter to the Duke of Buckingham, Wroth insisted that her work had not only been published without her permission but that it had been misconstrued: "the strange constructions which are made of my book [were] contrary to my imagination, and as far from my meaning as is possible for truth to be from conjecture"(December 15, 1621). She immediately withdrew *Urania* from circulation. *Pamphilia to Amphilanthus*, a sonnet sequence interspersed with songs, was appended to *Urania*. It was the first sonnet sequence published by a woman in England. Wroth revived the genre of the sonnet sequence to examine the theatre of female desire against the backdrop of the inconstant masculine "other." Wroth wrote, but did not publish, a pastoral play, *Love's Victory*, and died leaving unfinished a sequel to *Urania*.

 espe

Pamphilia to Amphilanthus [1]

A SONNET SEQUENCE [2]

I

When night's black mantle could most darkness prove,

And sleep, death's image, did my senses hire [3]
From knowledge of myself, then thoughts did
    move
Swifter than those most swiftness need
    require:

---

[1] *Pamphilia and Amphilanthus* the female and male protagonists of Wroth's *Urania*, to which these sonnets are appended. Pamphilia means "all-loving," while Amphilanthus signifies "the lover of two."

[2] The sequence and numbering of the songs and sonnets are based on that in Josephine A. Roberts's edition *The Poems of Lady Mary Wroth* (Baton Rouge: Louisiana State U P, 1983).

[3] *hire* engage (*OED* hire *v* 1a).

5 In sleep, a chariot drawn by winged desire [1]
　　I saw: where sat bright Venus, Queen of Love,
　　And at her feet her son, still adding fire
　　To burning hearts, which she did hold above, [2]

But one heart flaming more than all the rest
10　　The goddess held, and put it to my breast, [3]
　　"Dear son, now shut," said she, "thus must we win;"

He her obeyed, and martyred my poor heart.
　　I, waking, hoped as dreams it would depart
　　Yet since: O me: a lover I have been.

8

Love, leave to urge, thou know'st thou hast the hand; [4]
　　'Tis cowardice, to strive where none resist:
　　Pray thee leave off, I yield unto thy band; [5]
　　Do not thus, still, in thine own power persist,

5 Behold I yield: let forces be dismissed;
　　I am thy subject, conquered, bound to stand,
　　Never thy foe, but did thy claim assist
　　Seeking thy due of those who did withstand;

But now, it seems, thou would'st I should thee love;
10　　I do confess, 'twas thy will made me choose;
　　And thy fair shows made me a lover prove
　　When I my freedom did, for pain refuse.

Yet this, Sir God, your boyship I despise; [6]
Your charms I obey, but love not want of eyes. [7]

13

Cloyed with the torments of a tedious night
　　I wish for day; which come, I hope for joy: [8]
　　When cross I find new tortures to destroy
　　My woe-killed heart, first hurt by mischief's might, [9]

5 Then cry for night, and once more day takes flight
　　And brightness gone; what rest should here enjoy
　　Usurped is; Hate will her force employ;
　　Night cannot grief entomb though black as spite.

My thoughts are sad; her face as sad doth seem: [10]
10　　My pains are long; her hours tedious are:
　　My grief is great, and endless is my care:
　　Her face, her force, and all of woe's esteem:

Then welcome night, and farewell flatt'ring day
Which all hopes breed, and yet our joys delay.

15

Dear famish not what you yourself gave food;
　　Destroy not what your glory is to save;
　　Kill not that soul to which you spirit gave;
　　In pity, not disdain, your triumph stood;

5 An easy thing it is to shed the blood
　　Of one who, at your will, yields to the grave;
　　But more you may true worth by mercy crave

---

[1] *a chariot…winged desire* Venus's chariot was often represented as drawn by doves.

[2] *her son* Cupid.

[3] *But one heart…goddess held* On the title page of *Urania*, Venus holds a flaming heart.

[4] *hand* upper hand (advantage).

[5] *band* custody, imprisonment (*OED* band *sb*[1] I.1b).

---

[6] *Sir God* Pamphilia's mocking address to Cupid echos Astrophil's ("sir fool") in Sidney's *Astrophil and Stella* (53.7).

[7] *want* lack (*OED* want *sb* 2).

[8] *Cloyed* burdened (*OED* cloyed *ppl.a*).

[9] *cross* ill-tempered, out of humour (*OED* cross *a* 5b).

[10] *her face* Night's face.

When you preserve, not spoil, but nourish
   good;

Your sight is all the food I do desire;
10   Then sacrifice me not in hidden fire,
    Or stop the breath which did your praises
      move: [1]

Think but how easy 'tis a sight to give;
    Nay ev'n desert; since by it I do live, [2]
    I but chameleon-like would live, and love. [3]

16

Am I thus conquered? Have I lost the powers
  That to withstand, which joys to ruin me? [4]
  Must I be still while it my strength devours
  And captive leads me prisoner, bound, unfree?

5 Love first shall leave men's fant'sies to them free,
    Desire shall quench love's flames, spring hate
      sweet showers,
    Love shall loose all his darts, have sight, and see
    His shame, and wishings hinder happy hours; [5]

Why should we not Love's purblind charms resist?
    Must we be servile, doing what he list? [6]
10   No, seek some host to harbour thee: I fly

Thy babish tricks, and freedom do profess;
    But O my hurt, makes my lost heart confess
    I love, and must: So farewell liberty.

22

Come darkest night, becoming sorrow best;
  Light; leave thy light; fit for a lightsome soul; [7]
  Darkness doth truly suit with me oppressed
  Whom absence' power doth from mirth
    control:

5 The very trees with hanging heads condole
    Sweet summer's parting, and of leaves distressed
    In dying colours make a grief-full role;
    So much (alas) to sorrow are they pressed.

Thus of dead leaves her farewell carpet's made:
10   Their fall, their branches, all their mournings
      prove;
    With leafless, naked bodies, whose hues vade
    From hopeful green, to wither in their love, [8]

If trees and leaves, for absence, mourners be
No marvel that I grieve, who like want see.

25

Like to the Indians, scorched with the sun, [9]
  The sun which they do as their god adore
  So am I used by Love, for ever more
  I worship him, less favours have I won,

5 Better are they who thus to blackness run,
    And so can only whiteness' want deplore [10]
    Than I who pale and white am with grief's store,
    Nor can have hope, but to see hopes undone;

---

[1] *move* utter (*OED* move *v* I.4).

[2] *desert* deserved (*OED* desert *sb¹* 3).

[3] *chameleon-like* From their inanimate appearance, and power of existing for long periods without food, chameleons were formerly supposed to live on air (*OED* chameleon 1).

[4] *Have I lost...ruin me* Have I lost the power to withstand love ("That") which takes joy in ruining me?

[5] *wishings* longings (*OED* wishing *vbl.sb*).

[6] *list* desires (*OED* list *v¹* 1b).

---

[7] *lightsome soul* a soul not weighed down by care, pain or sorrow (*OED* lightsome *a¹* 2).

[8] *vade* fade (*OED* vade *v¹ Obs.*1).

[9] *Like to the Indians...* In Ben Jonson's *Masque of Blackness* (1605) Wroth performed the role of one of the beautiful daughters of Niger who came to England to gain white skin from James I, the Sun-King.

[10] *whiteness' want deplore* grieve the lack of whiteness.

Besides their sacrifice received's in sight
10   Of their chose saint: mine hid as worthless rite;
    Grant me to see where I my offerings give,

Then let me wear the mark of Cupid's might
    In heart as they in skin of Phoebus' light [1]
    Not ceasing off'rings to Love while I live.

26

When everyone to pleasing pastime hies, [2]
    Some hunt, some hawk, some play, while
        some delight [3]
    In sweet discourse, and music shows joy's
        might
    Yet I my thoughts do far above these prize.

5 The joy which I take, is that free from eyes
    I sit, and wonder at this daylike night
    So to dispose themselves, as void of right; [4]
    And leave true pleasure for poor vanities;

When others hunt, my thoughts I have in chase;
10   If hawk, my mind at wished end doth fly,
    Discourse, I with my spirit talk, and cry
    While others, music choose as greatest grace.

O God, say I, can these fond pleasures move?
Or music be but in sweet thoughts of love?

39

Take heed mine eyes, how you your looks do cast
    Lest they betray my heart's most secret thought;
    Be true unto yourselves for nothing's bought

More dear than doubt which brings a lover's
    fast.

5 Catch you all watching eyes, ere they be past,
    Or take yours fixed where your best love hath
        sought
    The pride of your desires; let them be taught
    Their faults for shame, they could no truer
        last;

Then look, and look with joy for conquest won
10   Of those that searched your hurt in double kind;
    So you kept safe, let them themselves look blind
    Watch, gaze, and mark, till they to madness
        run,

While you, mine eyes, enjoy full sight of love
Contented that such happinesses move.

40

False hope which feeds but to destroy, and spill
    What it first breeds; unnatural to the birth
    Of thine own womb; conceiving but to kill, [5]
    And plenty gives to make the greater dearth,

5 So tyrants do who falsely ruling earth
    Outwardly grace them, and with profits fill [6]
    Advance those who appointed are to death
    To make their greater fall to please their will.

Thus shadow they their wicked vile intent
10   Colouring evil with a show of good
    While in fair shows their malice so is spent;
    Hope kills the heart, and tyrants shed the
        blood.

For hope deluding brings us to the pride
Of our desires the farther down to slide.

---

[1] *Phoebus' light* sunlight.

[2] *hies* hastens (*OED* hie *v* 2).

[3] *play* play cards, dice or another specified diversion.

[4] *eyes* the gaze of others; *and wonder…void of right* and wonder at the blindness of those who participate in such activities, conducting themselves as if deprived of reason or a sense of that which is morally due (*OED* void *a* A.II.13b; *OED* right *sb*[1] I.5,3).

[5] *spill* destroy by depriving of life (*OED* spill *v* I.1a); *unnatural…kill* an image of miscarriage.

[6] *grace* show favour to; confer honour upon (*OED* grace *v* 2,5).

48

If ever Love had force in human breast?
  If ever he could move in pensive heart?
    Or if that he such power could but impart
    To breed those flames whose heat brings joy's
      unrest.

5 Then look on me; I am to these addressed,
  I, am the soul that feels the greatest smart;
    I, am that heartless trunk of heart's depart. [1]
    And I, that one, by love, and grief oppressed.

None ever felt the truth of Love's great miss
10   Of eyes, till I deprived was of bliss;
    For had he seen, he must have pity showed;

I should not have been made this stage of woe
  Where sad disasters have their open show
    O no, more pity he had sure bestowed.
                  Pamphilia. [2]

Song 74

Love, a child, is ever crying,
  Please him, and he straight is flying,
    Give him, he the more is craving
    Never satisfied with having;

5 His desires have no measure,
  Endless folly is his treasure,
    What he promiseth he breaketh
    Trust not one word that he speaketh;

He vows nothing but false matter,
10   And to cozen you he'll flatter, [3]
    Let him gain the hand he'll leave you,
    And still glory to deceive you;

He will triumph in your wailing,
  And yet cause be of your failing:
15   These his virtues are, and slighter
    Are his gifts, his favours lighter,

Feathers are as firm in staying
  Wolves no fiercer in their preying.
    As a child then leave him crying
20   Nor seek him so given to flying.

A Crown of Sonnets Dedicated to Love [4]

77

In this strange labyrinth how shall I turn?
  Ways are on all sides while the way I miss: [5]
    If to the right hand, there, in love I burn;
    Let me go forward, therein danger is;

5 If to the left, suspicion hinders bliss,
  Let me turn back, shame cries I ought return
    Nor faint though crosses with my fortunes
      kiss; [6]
    Stand still is harder, although sure to mourn.

Thus let me take the right, or left hand way;
10   Go forward, or stand still, or back retire;
    I must these doubts endure without allay
    Or help, but travail find for my best hire; [7]

Yet that which most my troubled sense doth move
Is to leave all, and take the thread of Love. [8]

---

[1] *depart* departure (*OED* depart *sb Obs* 1).

[2] *Pamphilia.* This concludes the first section of sonnets.

[3] *cozen* defraud by deceit (*OED* cozen *v* 1).

---

[4] *A Crown of Sonnets* sonnets 77–90; the corona (crown) is an Italian poetic form in which the last line of each of the sonnets is used as the first line of the succeeding sonnet.

[5] *ways* paths (*OED* way *sb*[1] I.1); *the way* the correct path.

[6] *crosses* troubles, adversity (*OED* cross *sb* B.I.10b).

[7] *allay* abatement (*OED* allay *sb*[1] II.8); *travail* "travel" in the 1621 text; labour or toil, esp. of a painful or oppressive nature (*OED* travail *sb*[1] I.1); *hire* reward (*OED* hire *sb* 3).

[8] *thread of love* an allusion to the thread given by Ariadne to Theseus to lead him out of the Labyrinth which enclosed the Minotaur.

78

Is to leave all, and take the thread of Love
Which line straight leads unto the soul's
    content
    Where choice delights with pleasure's wings
      do move,
    And idle phant'sy never room had lent,

5   When chaste thoughts guide us then our minds
      are bent
    To take that good which ills from us remove,
    Light of true love, brings fruit which none
      repent
    But constant lovers seek, and wish to prove; [1]

Love is the shining star of blessing's light;
    The fervent fire of zeal, the root of peace,
    The lasting lamp fed with the oil of right;
    Image of faith, and womb for joy's increase. [2]

Love is true virtue, and his ends delight;
His flames are joys, his bands true lovers' might.

79

His flames are joys, his bands true lovers' might,
    No stain is there but pure, as purest white,
    Where no cloud can appear to dim his light,
    Nor spot defile, but shame will soon requite,

5   Here are affections, tried by Love's just might
    As gold by fire, and black discerned by white,
    Error by truth, and darkness known by light,
    Where faith is valued for Love to requite,

Please him, and serve him, glory in his might,
10   And firm he'll be, as innocency white,

Clear as th'air, warm as sun beams, as day
    light,
Just as truth, constant as fate, joyed to requite,

Then Love obey, strive to observe his might,
And be in his brave court a glorious light.

80

And be in his brave court a glorious light,
    Shine in the eyes of faith, and constancy,
    Maintain the fires of love still burning bright
    Not slightly sparkling but light flaming be

5   Never to slack till earth no stars can see,
    Till sun, and moon do leave to us dark night,
    And second chaos once again do free
    Us, and the world from all division's spite, [3]

Till then, affections which his followers are
10   Govern our hearts, and prove his powers gain
    To taste this pleasing sting seek with all care
    For happy smarting is it with small pain,

Such as although, it pierce your tender heart
And burn, yet burning you will love the smart.

81

And burn, yet burning you will love the smart,
    When you shall feel the weight of true desire,
    So pleasing, as you would not wish your part
    Of burden should be missing from that fire;

5   But faithful and unfeignèd heat aspire
    Which sin abolisheth, and doth impart
    Salves to all fear, with virtues which inspire
    Souls with divine love, which shows his chaste
      art,

---

[1] *prove* experience (*OED* prove *v.* B.I.3).

[2] *Love is...joy's increase* Biblical echoes resound in this stanza. See
Matthew 2:7, 3:10–11; Isaiah 53:2,5; I Kings 17:14,16; II Kings 4:
1–7; Matthew 25:1–13; Luke 1:44.

[3] *second chaos* In Neoplatonic theory, matter reverts to chaos at the
world's end.

And guide he is to joyings; open eyes
10   He hath to happiness, and best can learn
     Us means how to deserve, this he descries,
     Who blind yet doth our hidenest thoughts
          discern. [1]

Thus we may gain since living in blest love
He may our prophet, and our tutor prove. [2]

82

He may our prophet, and our tutor prove
In whom alone we do this power find,
     To join two hearts as in one frame to move;
     Two bodies, but one soul to rule the mind; [3]

5   Eyes which must care to one dear object bind
     Ears to each other's speech as if above
     All else they sweet and learned were; this kind
     Content of lovers witnesseth true love,

It doth enrich the wits, and make you see
10   That in yourself, which you knew not before,
     Forcing you to admire such gifts should be
     Hid from your knowledge, yet in you the
          store;

Millions of these adorn the throne of Love,
How blest be they then, who his favours prove. [4]

83

How blest be they then, who his favours prove
A life whereof the birth is just desire,
     Breeding sweet flame which hearts invite to
          move
     In these loved eyes which kindle Cupid's fire,

And nurse his longings with his thoughts entire,
5   Fixed on the heat of wishes formed by love,
     Yet whereas fire destroys this doth aspire, [5]
     Increase, and foster all delights above;

Love will a painter make you, such, as you
10   Shall able be to draw your only dear
     More lively, perfect, lasting, and more true [6]
     Than rarest workman, and to you more near,

These be the least, then all must needs confess
He that shuns love doth love himself the less.

84

He that shuns love doth love himself the less
And cursèd he whose spirit not admires
     The worth of love, where endless blessedness
     Reigns, and commands, maintained by
          heav'nly fires

5   Made of virtue, joined by truth, blown by desires
     Strength'ned by worth, renewed by carefulness
     Flaming in never changing thoughts, briars
     Of jealousy shall here miss welcomeness;

Nor coldly pass in the pursuits of love
10   Like one long frozen in a sea of ice,
     And yet but chastely let your passions move
     No thought from virtuous love your minds
          entice.

Never to other ends your phant'sies place
But where they may return with honour's grace.

85

But where they may return with honour's grace
Where Venus' follies can no harbour win

---

[1] *he* Cupid.

[2] *prophet* "profit" in the Folger manuscript.

[3] *two hearts…one soul* The Neoplatonic ideal of love was a single soul in two bodies.

[4] *prove* experience (*OED* prove *v. trans.* B.I.3).

---

[5] *aspire* "respire" in the Folger manuscript; rise, mount up (*OED* aspire *v.* III.5).

[6] *true* accurately (*OED* true *adv.* C.3a).

But chased are as worthless of the face
Or style of Love who hath lascivious been.

5 Our hearts are subject to her son; where sin
    Never did dwell, or rest one minute's space;
    What faults he hath, in her, did still begin,
    And from her breast he sucked his fleeting
        pace,

If lust be counted love 'tis falsely named
10   By wickedness a fairer gloss to set
    Upon that vice, which else makes men
        ashamed
    In the own phrase to warrant, but beget

This child for love, who ought like monster born
Be from the Court of Love, and Reason torn. [1]

86

Be from the Court of Love, and Reason torn
For Love in Reason now doth put his trust,
Desert, and liking are together born [2]
Children of Love, and Reason parents just,

5 Reason adviser is, Love ruler must
    Be of the State which crown he long hath
        worn
    Yet so as neither will in least mistrust
    The government where no fear is of scorn,

Then reverence both their mights thus made of
        one,
10   But wantonness, and all those errors shun
    Which wrongers be, impostures, and alone
    Maintainers of all follies ill began;

Fruit of a sour, and unwholesome ground
Unprofitably pleasing, and unsound. [3]

87

Unprofitably pleasing, and unsound
When heaven gave liberty to frail dull earth
To bring forth plenty that in ills abound
Which ripest yet do bring a certain dearth. [4]

5 A timeless, and unseasonable birth
    Planted in ill, in worse time springing found,
    Which hemlock-like might feed a sick-wit's
        mirth
    Where unruled vapours swim in endless
        round, [5]

Then joy we not in what we ought to shun
10   Where shady pleasures show, but true born
        fires
    Are quite quenched out, or by poor ashes won
    Awhile to keep those cool, and wan desires.

O no let Love his glory have and might
Be given to him who triumphs in his right.

88

Be given to him who triumphs in his right
Nor vading be, but like those blossoms fair [6]
Which fall for good, and lose their colours
    bright
Yet die not, but with fruit their loss repair

---

[1] *gloss* interpretation (*OED* gloss *sb*[1] 1); *which else...for love* "which otherwise makes men ashamed in the same word to authenticate lust as the child of love."

[2] *Desert* merit (*OED* desert *sb*[1] 1b).

[3] *sour* cold and wet (*OED* sour *a*).

[4] *When heaven...forth plenty* Genesis 1:11–12.

[5] *hemlock-like* Hemlock yields a deadly poison; it was used medicinally as a powerful sedative (*OED* hemlock *sb* 1a); *vapours* exhalations in the organs of the body which cause nervous disorders (*OED* vapour *sb* 3a,b).

[6] *vading* "fading" in the 1621 edition; decaying, perishing (*OED* vade *v.*[1] *Obs.*).

5 So may love make you pale with loving care
    When sweet enjoying shall restore that light
    More clear in beauty than we can compare
    If not to Venus in her chosen night,

And who so give themselves in this dear kind
10   These happinesses shall attend them still
    To be supplied with joys, enriched in mind
    With treasures of content, and pleasures fill,

Thus Love to be divine doth here appear
Free from all fogs but shining fair, and clear.

89

Free from all fogs but shining fair, and clear
    Wise in all good, and innocent in ill
    Where holy friendship is esteemed dear
    With truth in love, and justice in our will,

5 In Love these titles only have their fill
    Of happy life maintainer, and the mere
    Defence of right, the punisher of skill,
    And fraud; from whence directions doth
        appear, [1]

To thee then lord commander of all hearts,
10   Ruler of our affections kind, and just
    Great King of Love, my soul from feignèd
        smarts
    Or thought of change I offer to your trust

This crown, my self, and all that I have more
Except my heart which you bestowed before.

90

Except my heart which you bestowed before,
    And for a sign of conquest gave away

As worthless to be kept in your choice store
Yet one more spotless with you doth not stay.

5 The tribute which my heart doth truly pay
    Is faith untouched, pure thoughts discharge
        the score [2]
    Of debts for me, where Constancy bears sway,
    And rules as Lord, unharmed by envies sore,

Yet other mischiefs fail not to attend,
10   As enemies to you, my foes must be;
    Cursed Jealousy doth all her forces bend
    To my undoing; thus my harms I see.

So though in Love I fervently do burn,
In this strange labyrinth how shall I turn?

103

My muse, now happy, lay thy self to rest,
    Sleep in the quiet of a faithful love,
    Write you no more, but let these fant'sies move
    Some other hearts, wake not to new unrest,

5 But if you study, be those thoughts addressed [3]
    To truth, which shall eternal goodness prove;
    Enjoying of true joy, the most, and best,
    The endless gain which never will remove;

Leave the discourse of Venus and her son
10   To young beginners, and their brains inspire
    With stories of great love, and from that fire
    Get heat to write the fortunes they have won,

And thus leave off, what's past shows you can love,
Now let your constancy your honour prove.
                                        Pamphilia.

—1621

---

[1] *mere* absolute, perfect (*OED* mere *a*[2] A.4); *skill* guile (*OED* skill *sb*[1] II.4a).

[2] *score* account (*OED* score *sb* II.10,11).

[3] *study* meditate (*OED* study *v* I.2a).

William Browne
?1590 – ?1645

Browne was the second son of Thomas Browne of Tavistock. William appears to have received his initial schooling at the grammar school in his native town before proceeding to Exeter College, Oxford. After leaving Oxford, without a degree, Browne continued his education at the Inns of Court. He married the daughter of Sir Thomas Eversfield of Den, near Horsham, and dedicated an epitaph to her after her death. Both sons of the marriage died in their infancy. In 1624 Browne returned to Exeter College, where he served as tutor to the Hon. Robert Dormer, and where he received the degree of Master of Arts in 1625. One source suggests that Browne then joined the household of the Herberts at Wilton, where he became wealthy and eventually purchased an estate. Our last record of Browne is of a letter sent from Dorking in 1640 to an acquaintance, and we do not know when or where he died.

Browne's first publication was an elegy on Prince Henry, published in 1613, the year after the prince's death. A line in his verse collection *Britannia's Pastorals* (1613) suggests that he also had written the first book of this work before he reached twenty years of age. The second book of the *Pastorals* was published in 1616, and the third book was not published in the poet's lifetime. The first two books include commendatory verses by a number of respected poets and dramatists including Ben Jonson and Michael Drayton. The second book is dedicated to William, Earl of Pembroke. In 1614 a number of Browne's eclogues were published in a work entitled *The Shepherd's Pipe*. This was followed by the *Inner Temple Masque*, a work on Ulysses and Circe. Browne also wrote a number of sonnets, epigrams and epitaphs.

❧❧❧

On the Countess Dowager of Pembroke

Underneath this sable hearse
Lies the subject of all verse:
Sidney's sister, Pembroke's mother: [1]
Death, ere thou hast slain another,
5 Fair, and learn'd, and good as she,
Time shall throw a dart at thee.

Marble piles let no man raise
To her name, for after days;
Some kind woman born as she,
10 Reading this, like Niobe [2]
Shall turn marble, and become
Both her mourner and her tomb.
—1616

---

[1] *Sidney's sister, Pembroke's mother* Mary Sidney, Sir Philip Sidney's sister, was the mother of William, Earl of Pembroke, Browne's patron.

[2] *Niobe* mythic mother of six sons and six daughters who boasted of her equality to Leto, the Titaness, who had only two children, Apollo and Artemis. Apollo and Artemis killed Niobe's children, and Niobe, wearied with shedding tears, turned into stone (*OCD*).

To the King and Queen, Upon Their Unhappy Distances [1]

Woe, woe to them, who (by a ball of strife)
Do, and have parted here a Man and Wife:
CHARLES the best husband, while MARIA strives
To be, and is, the very best of Wives:
5 Like streams, you are divorc'd; but 'twill come, when
Those eyes of mine shall see you mix again.
Thus speaks the *Oak,* here; C. and M. shall meet, [2]
Treading on *Amber,* with their silver-feet:
Nor wil't be long, ere this accomplish'd be;
10 The words found true, C. M. remember me.
—1648

Delight In Disorder [3]

A sweet disorder in the dress
Kindles in clothes a wantonness:
A lawn about the shoulders thrown
Into a fine distraction:
5 An erring lace, which here and there
Enthralls the crimson stomacher: [4]
A cuff neglectful, and thereby
Ribbands to flow confusedly:
A winning wave (deserving note)
10 In the tempestuous petticoat:
A careless shoe-string, in whose tie
I see a wild civility:

Do more bewitch me, than when Art
Is too precise in every part. [5]
—1648

Duty to Tyrants

Good princes must be pray'd for: for the bad
They must be borne with, and in rev'rence had.
Do they first pill thee, next, pluck off thy skin? [6]
Good children kiss the rods, that punish sin.
5 Touch not the Tyrant; let the Gods alone
To strike him dead, that but usurps a Throne.
—1648

To Dianeme

Sweet, be not proud of those two eyes,
Which star-like sparkle in their skies:
Nor be you proud, that you can see
All hearts your captives; yours, yet free:
5 Be you not proud of that rich hair,
Which wantons with the love-sick air:
When as that *Ruby,* which you wear,
Sunk from the tip of your soft ear,
Will last to be a precious Stone,
10 When all your world of Beauty's gone.
—1648

Corinna's Going A Maying

Get up, get up for shame, the blooming morn
Upon her wings presents the god unshorn. [7]
See how *Aurora* throws her fair [8]

---

[1] Charles I and Henrietta Maria were frequently apart after the outbreak of the Civil War. The title may refer sardonically to that of a speech in Parliament of July 1642, concerning "the present unhappy Distance between His Majesty and the Parliament."

[2] *the Oak* There was an oracle of Zeus in a grove of oaks at Dodona.

[3] Compare Ben Jonson's "Still to be neat."

[4] *stomacher* "an ornamental covering…(often covered with jewels) worn by women under the lacing of the bodice" (*OED* stomacher [1] 3).

---

[5] *precise* The word is an anti-Puritan statement in itself; see *OED* precise and precision.

[6] *pill* There may be a pun; the verb could mean either to flay or to pillage; see *OED* pill *v*[1].

[7] *the god unshorn* Apollo, the sun-god.

[8] *Aurora* Roman goddess of the dawn.

Fresh-quilted colours through the air:
5 Get up, sweet-Slug-a-bed, and see
The dew-bespangling herb and tree.
Each flower has wept, and bow'd toward the east,
Above an hour since; yet you not drest,
Nay! not so much as out of bed!
10 When all the Birds have Matins said, [1]
And sung their thankful Hymns: 'tis sin,
Nay, profanation to keep in,
When as a thousand Virgins on this day,
Spring, sooner then the Lark, to fetch in May.

15 Rise; and put on your Foliage, and be seen
To come forth, like the spring-time, fresh and green;
And sweet as *Flora*. Take no care
For jewels for your gown, or hair:
Fear not; the leaves will strew
20 Gems in abundance upon you:
Besides, the childhood of the Day has kept,
Against you come, some *Orient Pearls* unwept: [2]
Come, and receive them while the light
Hangs on the dew-locks of the night:
25 And *Titan* on the eastern hill [3]
Retires himself, or else stands still
Till you come forth. Wash, dress, be brief in praying:
Few beads are best, when once we go a Maying.

Come, my *Corinna*, come; and coming, mark
30 How each field turns a street; each street a park
Made green, and trimm'd with trees: see how
Devotion gives each house a bough,
Or Branch: Each Porch, each door, ere this,
An Ark a Tabernacle is
35 Made up of white-thorn neatly interwove;
As if here were those cooler shades of love.

Can such delights be in the street,
And open fields, and we not see't?
Come, we'll abroad; and let's obey
40 The Proclamation made for May:
And sin no more, as we have done, by staying;
But my *Corinna,* come, let's go a Maying.

There's not a budding boy, or girl, this day,
But is got up, and gone to bring in May.
45 A deal of youth, ere this, is come
Back, and with *White-thorn* laden home.
Some have dispatched their cakes and cream,
Before that we have left to dream:
And some have wept, and woo'd, and plighted troth,
50 And chose their Priest, ere we can cast off sloth:
Many a green-gown has been given; [4]
Many a kiss, both odd and even:
Many a glance too has been sent
From out the eye, Love's Firmament:
55 Many a jest told of the keys betraying
This night, and locks picked, yet w'are not a
Maying.

Come, let us go, while we are in our prime;
And take the harmless folly of the time.
We shall grow old apace, and die
60 Before we know our liberty.
Our life is short; and our days run
As fast away as does the Sun:
And as a vapour, or a drop of rain
Once lost, can ne'r be found again:
65 So when or you or I are made
A fable, song, or fleeting shade;
All love, all liking, all delight
Lies drown'd with us in endless night. [5]

---

[1] *Matins* has had various meanings through the centuries; Herrick is thinking of the order for public morning service in the Book of Common Prayer.

[2] *Orient Pearls* commonly used in the period to refer to especially valuable pearls; Herrick is referring to the dew.

[3] *Titan* a name for the sun-god.

---

[4] *green-gown* to give a woman a green gown was to roll her in the grass; often a euphemism. See *OED* green A I 1g.

[5] *So when...endless night* one of the more famous expressions of a famous sentiment. Compare Catullus v and Jonson's rendering in "Come my Celia, let us prove / While we may, the sports of love."

Then while time serves, and we are but decaying;
70 Come, my *Corinna,* come, let's go a Maying.
—1648

To live merrily,
and to trust to Good Verses.

Now is the time for mirth,
Nor cheek, or tongue be dumb:
For with the flow'ry earth,
The golden pomp is come. [1]

5 The golden pomp is come;
For now each tree does wear
(Made of her pap and gum)
Rich beads of *amber* here.

Now reigns the *Rose,* and now
10 *Th'Arabian Dew* besmears
My uncontrolled brow,
And my retorted hairs. [2]

Homer, this health to thee,
In sack of such a kind, [3]
15 That it would make thee see,
Though thou wert ne'er so blind.

Next, Virgil, I'll call forth,
To pledge this second health
In wine, whose each cup's worth
20 An Indian Common-wealth.

A goblet next I'll drink
To Ovid; and suppose,

Made he the pledge, he'd think
The world had all one Nose. [4]

25 Then this immensive cup
Of aromatic wine,
Catullus, I quaff up
To that terse Muse *of* thine.

Wild I am now with heat;
30 *O Bacchus!* cool thy rays!
Or frantic I shall ease
Thy *Thyrse,* and bite the bays.[5]

Round, round, the roof does run;
And being ravished thus,
35 Come, I will drink a Tun
To my *Propertius.*[6]

Now, to *Tibullus,* next,
This flood I drink to thee:[7]
But stay; I see a text,
40 That this presents to me.

Behold, *Tibullus* lies
Here burnt, whose small return
Of ashes, scarce suffice
45 To fill a little Urn.

---

[1] *The golden pomp is come* The golden procession is coming; the line is a translation of Ovid, *Amores* 3:2, 44 (*aurea pompa venit*).

[2] *retorted* twisted or bent backward (*OED* retorted *ppl a 2*, this place cited).

[3] *sack* white wine (*OED* sack *sb* [3]).

---

[4] *Ovid* Publius Ovidius Naso (43 B.C.E.–17? C.E.), Roman poet; *one Nose* Herrick is playing on Ovid's surname, which means "large-nosed." The idea is that the wine is so rich that Ovid, smelling it, would think that he was using everybody's nose.

[5] *Thyrse* i.e. thyrsus, "a staff or spear tipped with an ornament like a pine-cone, and sometimes wreathed with ivy or vine-branches; borne by Dionysus (Bacchus) or his votaries"(*OED* thyrsus); *bays* the leaves or sprigs of the bay-laurel, woven into a wreath (*OED* bay *sb* [1] 3).

[6] *Propertius* the Roman poet Sextus Propertius, born between 54 and 48 B.C.E., died between 16 B.C.E. and 2 C.E. He was a friend of Ovid; both were love poets (*OCD*).

[7] *Tibullus* Albius Tibullus, 48?–19 B.C.E., described by Quintilian as terse and elegant. His principal topics are love and longing for a country life (*OCD*).

Trust to good verses then;
They only will aspire,
When pyramids, as men,
Are lost, i'th'funeral fire.

50 And when all bodies meet
In *Lethe* to be drowned;[1]
Then only numbers sweet,
With endless life are crowned.[2]
—1648

To the Virgins, To make much of Time

1

Gather ye Rose-buds while ye may,
Old Time is still a flying:
And this same flower that smiles today,
Tomorrow will be dying.

2

5 The glorious Lamp of Heaven, the Sun,
The higher he's a getting;
The sooner will his race be run,
And nearer he's to setting.

3

That Age is best, which is the first,
10 When Youth and Blood are warmer;
But being spent, the worse, and worst
Times, still succeed the former.

4

Then be not coy, but use your time;
And while ye may, go marry:
15 For having lost but once your prime,
You may for ever tarry.
—1648

[1] *Lethe* a river in Hades, whose waters produced forgetfulness.

[2] *numbers* metrical periods or feet, hence lines, verses (*OED* number *sb* 18b).

The Hock-cart, or Harvest home:[3]

*To the Right Honourahle, Mildmay,
Earle of Westmorland.*[4]

Come sons of Summer, by whose toil,
We are the lords of wine and oil:
By whose tough labours, and rough hands,
We rip up first, then reap our lands.
5 Crowned with the ears of corn, now come,
And, to the pipe, sing harvest home.
Come forth, my Lord, and see the cart
Dressed up with all the country art.
See, here a *Maukin,* there a sheet,[5]
10 As spotless pure, as it is sweet:
The horses, mares, and frisking fillies,
(Clad, all, in linen, white as lilies.)
The harvest swains, and wenches bound
For joy, to see the *Hock-cart* crowned.
15 About the cart, hear, how the rout
Of rural younglings raise the shout;
Pressing before, some coming after,
Those with a shout, and these with laughter.
Some bless the cart; some kiss the sheaves;
20 Some prank them up with oaken leaves:
Some cross the fill-horse; some with great
Devotion, stroke the home-borne wheat:[6]
While other rustics, less attent
To prayers, than to merriment,
25 Run after with their breeches rent.
Well, on, brave boys, to your lord's hearth,
Glitt'ring with fire; where, for your mirth,
Ye shall see first the large and chief
Foundation of your feast, fat beef:

[3] *The Hock-cart* the cart or wagon which carried home the last load of the harvest (*OED*).

[4] *Mildmay, Earle of Westmorland* Mildmay Fane was Herrick's friend and patron. He was the author of *Otia Sacra* (The sacred fruits of leisure), 1648.

[5] *Maukin* probably, a female country servant; see *OED* malkin.

[6] *cross the fill-horse* bestride the shaft-horse; see *OED* cross *v* 5c.

30   With upper stories, mutton, veal
     And bacon, (which makes full the meal)
     With sev'ral dishes standing by,
     As here a custard, there a pie,
     And here all tempting frumenty. [1]
35   And for to make the merry cheer,
     If smirking wine be wanting here,
     There's that, which drowns all care, stout beer;
     Which freely drink to your Lord's health,
         Then to the plough, (the common-wealth)
40   Next to your flails, your fans, your fats;[2]
     Then to the maids with wheaten hats:
     To the rough sickle, and crook'd scythe,
     Drink frolic boys, till all be blithe.
     Feed, and grow fat; and as ye eat,
45   Be mindfull, that the lab'ring neat
     (As you) may have their fill of meat. [3]
     And know, besides, ye must revoke
         The patient ox unto the yoke, [4]
         And all go back unto the plough
50   And harrow, (though they're hanged up now.)
     And, you must know, your lord's word's true,
     Feed him ye must, whose food fills you.
     And that this pleasure is like rain,
     Not sent ye for to drown your pain,
55   But for to make it spring again.
         —1648

To Anthea, who may command him anything

1

Bid me to live, and I will live
     Thy Protestant to be: [5]
Or bid me love, and I will give
     A loving heart to thee.

2

5   A heart as soft, a heart as kind,
     A heart as sound and free,
As in the whole world thou canst find,
     That heart I'll give to thee.

3

Bid that heart stay, and it will stay,
10   To honour thy Decree:
Or bid it languish quite away,
     And't shall do so for thee.

4

Bid me to weep, and I will weep,
     While I have eyes to see:
15   And having none, yet I will keep
     A heart to weep for thee.

5

Bid me despair, and I'll despair,
     Under that *Cypress* tree:
Or bid me die, and I will dare
20   E'en Death, to die for thee.

---

[1] *frumenty*   a dish made of hulled wheat boiled in milk, and seasoned with sugar, cinnamon etc. (*OED* frumenty). When I was a boy in Nottinghamshire it was still part of harvest-home, and pronounced frummety; according to Joseph Wright's *The English Dialect Dictionary*, this was common across several counties.

[2] *fats*   vessels of large size for liquids, vats (*OED* fat *sb* [1] 2).

[3] *neat*   cattle (*OED* neat *sb* 2).

[4] *revoke*   call or summon back (*OED* revoke *v* 3b, this place cited).

---

[5] *Protestant*   As *OED* points out, "in reference to the Church of England, the use has varied with time and circumstances." It is not unusual for Herrick to use an intriguingly enigmatic word in an otherwise clear poem. As L.C. Martin pointed out, the poem may have been influenced by a passage on "Symptoms of Love" in Burton's *Anatomy of Melancholy*. In that passage we find "Hear some of their own…Protestations."

6

Thou art my life, my love, my heart,
  The very eyes of me:
And hast command of every part,
  To live and die for thee.
—1648

To Meadows

1

Ye have been fresh and green,
  Ye have been filled with flowers:
And ye the Walks have been
  Where Maids have spent their hours.

2

5   You have beheld, how they
      With *Wicker Arks* did come
  To kiss, and bear away
      The richer Cowslips home.

3

Y'ave heard them sweetly sing,
10   And seen them in a Round:
  Each Virgin, like a Spring,
      With honey-suckles crown'd.

4

But now, we see, none here,
  Whose silv'ry feet did tread,
15 And with dishevelled hair,
  Adorned this smoother mead.

5

Like unthrifts, having spent,
  Your stock, and needy grown,
Y'are left here to lament
20   Your poor estates, alone.
—1648

Upon Prudence Baldwin her sickness [1]

Prue, my dearest Maid, is sick,
  Almost to be lunatic:
Æsculapius! come and bring
Means for her recovering;
5 And a gallant cock shall be
Offered up by her, to thee.
—1648

On himself

Here down my wearied limbs I'll lay;
  My Pilgrim's staff; my weed of gray: [2]
My Palmer's hat; my Scallop's shell;
My Cross; my Cord; and all farewell.
5 For having now my journey done,
(Just at the setting of the Sun)
Here I have found a chamber fit,
(God and good friends be thanked for it)
Where if I can a lodger be
10 A little while from tramplers free;
At my up-rising next, I shall,
If not requite, yet thank ye all.
Mean while, the *Holy-Rood* hence fright
The fouler Fiend, and evil Spright,
15 From scaring you or yours this night.
—1648

Casualties

Good things, that come of course, far less do
  please,
Then those, which come by sweet contingencies.
—1648

---

[1] Prudence Baldwin outlived Herrick, and was buried in January, 1678.

[2] *weed* garment (*OED* weed *sb*²). The items mentioned are all appurtenances of the pilgrim.

Here, here the Slaves and Pris'ners be
20   From Shackles free:
And weeping Widows long opprest
            Do here find rest.
The wronged Client ends his Laws
            Here, and his Cause.
25 Here those long suits of Chancery lie
            Quiet, or die:
And all Star-chamber-Bills do cease,
            Or hold their peace.
Here needs no Court for our Request, [1]
30   Where all are best;
All wise; all equal; and all just
            Alike i'th'dust.
Nor need we here to fear the frown
            Of Court, or Crown.
35 *Where Fortune bears no sway o're things,*
            There all are Kings.
In this securer place we'll keep,
            As lull'd asleep;
Or for a little time we'll lie,
40   As robes laid by;
To be another day re-worn,
            Turn'd, but not torn:
Or like old testaments engrossed, [2]
            Locked up, not lost:
45 And for a while lie here conceal'd,
            To be revealed
Next, at that great Platonic year, [3]
            And then meet here.
      —1648

---

[1] The Court of Requests was for the relief of persons petitioning the King (*OED* request II.8).

[2] *testaments engrossed*   wills written out in legal form (*OED* engross *v* I,1).

[3] *that great Platonic year*   Some ancient astronomers believed that every thirty thousand years or so the heavenly bodies would return to their original relative positions. Milton in the "Ode on the Morning of Christ's Nativity," stanza 12, imagines this occurring at the time of Christ's birth; Herrick, in this poem, as elsewhere, imagines it occurring at the Day of Judgement. See *OED* platonic A 3b.

His Prayer to Ben. Jonson.

When I a Verse shall make,
   Know I have prayed thee,
For old *Religion's* sake,
   Saint *Ben* to aid me.

5 Make the way smooth for me,
When I, thy *Herrick*,
Honouring thee, on my knee
Offer my *Lyric*.

Candles I'll give to thee,
10   And a new Altar;
   And thou Saint *Ben*, shalt be
Writ in my *Psalter*.
—1648

An Ode for him.

Ah *Ben!*
Say how, or when
Shall we thy guests
Meet at those *lyric* feasts,
5 Made at the *Sun*,
The Dog, the triple *Tun?* [4]
Where we such clusters had, [5]
As made us nobly wild, not mad;
And yet each Verse of thine
10 Out-did the meat, out-did the frolic wine.
—1648

My Ben

Or come again:
   Or send to us,
Thy wit's great over-plus;

---

[4] *the Sun, / The Dog, the triple Tun*   London taverns.

[5] *clusters*   clusters of grapes, that is, wine.

But teach us yet
5 Wisely to husband it;
Lest we that Talent spend:
And having once brought to an end
That precious stock; the store
Of such a wit the world should have no more.
—1648

The bad season makes the Poet sad.

Dull to my self, and almost dead to these
  My many fresh and fragrant mistresses:
Lost to all music now; since every thing
Puts on the semblance here of sorrowing.
5 Sick is the Land to'th'heart; and doth endure
More dangerous faintings by her desp'rate cure.
But if that golden Age would come again,
And Charles here rule, as he before did reign;
If smooth and unperplexed the seasons were,
10 As when the sweet Maria lived here:
I should delight to have my curls half drowned
In Tyrian dews, and head with roses crowned.[1]
And once more yet (ere I am laid out dead)
Knock at a star with my exalted head.
—1648

His return to London.

FROM the dull confines of the drooping West,
  To see the day spring from the pregnant East,
Ravished in spirit, I come, nay more, I fly
To thee, blest place of *my* Nativity!
5 Thus, thus with hallowed foot I touch the ground,
  With thousand blessings by thy Fortune crowned.
O fruitfull Genius! that bestowest here
An everlasting plenty, year by year
O Place! O People! Manners! framed to please
10 All *Nations, Customs, Kindreds, Languages!*
I am a free-born *Roman;* suffer then,

That I amongst you live a Citizen.
London my home is: though by hard fate sent
  Into a long and irksome banishment;
15 Yet since called back; henceforward let me be,
  O native countrey, repossessed by thee!
For, rather then I'll to the West return,
I'll beg of thee first here to have mine Urn.
Weak I am grown, and must in short time fall;
20 Give thou my sacred relics burial.
—1648

His Grange, Or Private Wealth

Though Clock,
To tell how night draws hence, I've none,
    A Cock,
I have, to sing how day draws on.
5   I have
A maid (my *Prew*) by good luck sent,
    To save
That little, Fates me gave or lent.
    A Hen
10 I keep, which creaking day by day,
    Tells when
She goes her long white egg to lay.
    A goose
I have, which, with a jealous ear,
15   Lets loose
Her tongue, to tell what danger's near.
    A Lamb
I keep (tame) with my morsels fed,
    Whose Dam
20 An Orphan left him (lately dead.)
    A Cat
I keep, that plays about my House,
    Grown fat,
With eating many a miching Mouse.[2]
25   To these

---

[1] *Tyrian dews* wine (made from purple grapes); see *OED* Tyrian *a* b.

[2] *miching* pilfering.

A *Trasy* I do keep, whereby [1]
   I please
The more my rural privacy:
   Which are
30 But toys, to give my heart some ease:
   Where care
None is, slight things do lightly please.
  —1648

Upon Julia's Clothes.

WHEN as in silks my *Julia* goes,
 Then, then (me thinks) how sweetly flows
That liquefaction of her clothes.

Next, when I cast mine eyes and see
5 That brave Vibration each way free;
O how that glittering taketh me!
  —1648

A Thanksgiving to God, for his House

Lord, Thou hast given me a cell
   Wherein to dwell;
A little house, whose humble Roof
   Is weather-proof;
5 Under the spars of which I lie
   Both soft, and dry;
Where Thou my chamber for to ward
   Hast set a Guard
Of harmless thoughts, to watch and keep
10   Me, while I sleep.
Low is my porch, as is my Fate,
   Both void of state;
And yet the threshold of my door
   Is worn by'th poor,
15 Who thither come, and freely get
   Good words, or meat:
Like as my Parlour, so my Hall

   And Kitchen's small:
A little Buttery, and therein
20   A little bin,
Which keeps my little loaf of bread
   Unchipped, unflead: [2]
Some brittle sticks of Thorn or Briar
   Make me a fire,
25 Close by whose living coal I sit,
   And glow like it.
Lord, I confess too, when I dine,
   The Pulse is Thine, [3]
And all those other bits, that be
30   There plac'd by Thee;
The Worts, the Purslane, and the mess [4]
   Of Water-cress,
Which of thy kindness Thou hast sent;
   And my content
35 Makes those, and my beloved Beet,
   To be more sweet.
'Tis thou that crown'st my glittering Hearth
   With guiltless mirth;
And giv'st me wassail bowls to drink, [5]
40   Spic'd to the brink.
Lord, 'tis thy plenty-dropping hand,
   That soils my land;
And giv'st me, for my bushel sown,
   Twice ten for one:
45 Thou mak'st my teeming Hen to lay
   Her egg each day:
Besides my healthful Ewes to bear
   Me twins each year:
The while the conduits of my Kine [6]

---

[1] *Trasy* Herrick's spaniel.

[2] *unflead* not flayed or skinned (*OED*, this place cited).

[3] *Pulse* the edible seeds of such plants as peas, beans, lentils, etc. (*OED* pulse *sb²*).

[4] *Wort* a plant, herb or vegetable used for food or medicine, or any plant of the cabbage kind (*OED* wort *sb* ¹ 1, 2); *Purslane* a herb used in salads.

[5] *wassail bowls* bowls from which healths were drunk, or the liquor contained in the bowl (*OED*).

[6] *Kine* an archaic plural of cow.

50   Run Cream, (for Wine.)
All these, and better Thou dost send
    Me, to this end,
That I should render, for my part,
    A thankful heart;
55 Which, fir'd with incense, I resign,
    As wholly Thine;
But the acceptance, that must be,
    My Christ, by Thee.

—1648

His Litany, to the Holy Spirit

1

In the hour of my distress,
When temptations me oppress,
And when I my sins confess,
    Sweet Spirit comfort me!

2

5 When I lie within my bed,
Sick in heart, and sick in head,
And with doubts discomforted,
    Sweet Spirit, comfort me!

3

When the house doth sigh and weep,
10 And the world is drown'd in sleep,
Yet mine eyes the watch do keep;
    Sweet Spirit comfort me!

4

When the artless Doctor sees
No one hope, but of his Fees,
15 And his skill runs on the lees; [1]
    Sweet Spirit comfort me!

5

When his Potion and his Pill,
His, or none, or little skill,

Meet for nothing, but to kill;
20   Sweet Spirit comfort me!

6

When the passing-bell doth toll,
And the Furies in a shoal
Come to fright a parting soul;
    Sweet Spirit comfort me!

7

25 When the tapers now burn blew
And the comforters are few,
And that number more than true;
    Sweet Spirit comfort me!

8

When the Priest his last hath prayed,
30 And I nod to what is said,
'Cause my speech is now decayed;
    Sweet Spirit comfort me!

9

When (God knows) I'm tossed about,
Either with despair, or doubt;
35 Yet before the glass be out,
    Sweet Spirit comfort me!

10

When the Tempter me pursu'th
With the sins of all my youth,
And half damns me with untruth;
40   Sweet Spirit comfort me!

11

When the flames and hellish cries
Fright mine ears, and fright mine eyes,
And all terrors me surprise;
    Sweet Spirit comfort me!

---

[1] *lees* dregs (*OED* lee *sb²*).

12

45 When the Judgment is reveal'd,
And that open'd which was seal'd,

When to Thee I have appeal'd;
    Sweet Spirit comfort me!
—1648

Francis Quarles
1592 – 1644

Quarles was born in Essex, and educated at Christ's College, Cambridge and Lincoln's Inn. He was cupbearer to the Princess Elizabeth ("Elizabeth of Bohemia") at her wedding to the Elector Palatine in 1613, and went to Germany in her retinue. He returned to England in 1620. In 1626 he became secretary to James Ussher, Archbishop of Armagh, who famously worked out a biblical chronology showing that the world was created in 4004 B.C.E., a chronology which can still be found in books published in the nineteenth century. He returned to England in 1633, and in 1635 published the work for which he is best remembered, the *Emblems, Divine and Moral*. This work was extraordinarily popular, and it is frequently said that Quarles was the best-selling British author of the century. Horace Walpole was to remark that Milton "had to wait until the world had done admiring Quarles." There is some irony in Quarles's reputation among his contemporaries; he was much admired by Puritans, but most of the engravings in his volume are copied or adapted from Jesuit emblem books. Quarles himself was an ardent Royalist and disliker of Puritan views.

The European vogue for emblems began with the *Emblematum liber* of Andrea Alciati, and the form was very popular for two hundred years. It typically consisted of a "word" or motto, a woodcut or engraving illustrating the motto, and an *explicatio* or unfolding of the idea expressed in the motto and the illustration. Often the emblem was bilingual or multilingual and so emblem books, in their origin learned, came to be used as language textbooks. Quarles was the most important of English emblem writers.

❧❧❧

Emblem III
(from Book III)

PSALM 17:5
Stay my steps in thy paths, that my feet do not slide.

Whene'er the old exchange of profit rings
    Her silver saints-bell of uncertain gains,
My merchant-soul can stretch both legs and wings;   5
How can I run, and take unwearied pains!
    The charms of profit are so strong that I,
    Who wanted legs to go, finds wings to fly.

—1635/43

Emblem VII
(from Book III)

JOB 13:24
Wherefore hidest thou thy face, and holdest me for thine enemy?

Wherefore hidest thou thy face, & holdest mee for thine Enemy. Iob: 13.24
w.s.sc:

Without that *Light* what light remains in me?
5 Thou art my *Life*, my *Way*, my *Light*; in thee
I live, I move, and by thy beams I see.[1]

Thou art my *Life*; If thou but turn away,
My life 's a thousand deaths: thou art my *Way*:
Without thee, Lord, I travel not but stray.

10 My *Light* thou art; without thy glorious sight,
Mine eyes are darkened with perpetual night.
My God, thou art my *Way*, my *Life*, my *Light*.

Thou art my *Way*; I wander, if thou fly:
Thou art my *Light*; if hid, how blind am I!
15 Thou art my *Life*; if thou withdraw, I die.

Mine eyes are blind and dark, I cannot see;
To whom, or whether should my darkness flee,
But to the *Light*? And who 's that *Light* but thee?

My path is lost; my wand'ring steps do stray;
20 I cannot safely go, nor safely stay;
Whom should I seek but thee, my *Path*, my *Way*?

O, I am dead: to whom shall I, poor I,
Repair? to whom shall my sad ashes fly
But *Life*? And where is *Life* but in thine eye?

25 And yet thou turn'st away thy face, and fly'st me;
And yet I sue for grace, and thou deny'st me;
Speak, art thou angry, Lord, or onely try'st me?

Unscreen those heav'nly lamps, or tell me why
Thou shad'st thy face; perhaps thou think'st, no eye
30 Can view those flames, and not drop down and
die.

Why dost thou shade thy lovely face? O why
Doth that eclipsing hand so long deny
The Sun-shine of my soul-enliv'ning eye?

---

[1] *Thou art my Life, my Way, my Light* "Jesus saith unto him, I am the way and the truth, and the life: no man cometh unto the Father, but by me" (John 14:6). For *Light*, see John 1:1–14.

If that be all, shine forth, and draw thee nigher;
Let me behold and die; for my desire
Is *Phœnix*-like to perish in that fire.

35 Death-conquer'd *Laz'rus* was redeem'd by thee;[1]
If I am dead, Lord, set death's pris'ner free;
Am I more spent, or stink I worse then he?[2]

If my puffed light be out, give leave to tine [3]
My flameless snuff at that bright *Lamp* of thine;
O what's thy *Light* the less for lighting mine?

40 If I have lost my *Path*, great Shepherd, say,
Shall I still wander in a doubtful way?
Lord, shall a Lamb of *Isr'el's* sheepfold stray?

Thou art the Pilgrim's *Path*; the blind man's *Eye*;
The dead man's *Life*; on thee my hopes rely;
45 If thou remove, I err; I grope; I die.

Disclose thy sun-beams; close thy wings, and stay;
See, see how I am blind, and dead, and stray,
O thou, that art my *Light*, my *Life* my *Way*.

S. AUGUST. SOLILOQU. CAP. I.
*Why dost thou hide thy face? Happily thou wilt
say, none can see thy face and live: Ah Lord, let me
die, that I may see thee; let me see thee, that I may die:
I would not live, but die. That I may see Christ, I
desire death; That I may live with Christ, I despise
life.*

ANSELM. MED. CAP. 5.
*O excellent hiding, which is become my perfection!
My God, Thou hidest thy treasure, to kindle my desire;*

---

[1] *Death-conquer'd Laz'rus* For the story of the raising of Lazarus from the dead, see John 11.

[2] *or stink I worse than he?* "Jesus said, Take ye away the stone. Martha, the sister of him that was dead, saith unto him, Lord, by this time he stinketh, for he hath been dead four days" (John 11:39).

[3] *to tine* to ignite, to kindle (OED tind *v*). The verb also occurs in Henry Vaughan's "Cock-Crowing."

*Thou hidest thy pearl, to inflame the seeker; Thou
delayest to give, that Thou may'st teach me to
importune; seem'st not to hear, to make me persevere.*

EPIG. 7.
*If Heav'n's all-quickning eyes vouchsafe to shine
Upon our souls, we slight; If not, we whine:
Our Equinoctiall hearts can never lie
Secure beneath the Tropicks of that eye.*
—1635/1643

Epigram III
(from Book IV)

PSALM 17:5
Stay my steps in thy paths, that my feet do not slide.

*Stay my stepps in thy Pathes that
my feet do not slide. Ps. 17. 5.*
W. M. Sc:

1

When ere the old Exchange of profit rings
    Her silver Saint's-bell of uncertain gains,[1]
My merchant soul can stretch both legs and wings;
    How I can run, and take unwearied pains!
        The charms of profit are so strong, that I
        Who wanted legs to go find wings to fly.

2

If time-beguiling Pleasure but advance
    Her lustful trump, and blow her bold alarms,
O how my sportful soul can frisk and dance,
    And hug that Siren in her twined arms!
        The sprightly voice of sinew-strength'ning
        pleasure
        Can lend my bedrid soul both legs and
        leisure.

3

If blazing Honour chance to fill my veins
    With flatt'ring warmth, and flash of Courtly
    fire,
My soul can take a pleasure in her pains;
    My lofty strutting steps disdain to tire;
    My antic knees can turn upon the hinges
    Of Compliment, and screw a thousand
    cringes.[2]

4

But when I come to Thee, my God, that art
    The royal mine of everlasting treasure,
The real Honour of my better part,
    And living Fountain of eternal pleasure,
        How nerveless are my limbs! how faint and
        slow!
        I have nor wings to fly, nor legs to go.

5

So when the streams of swift-foot Rhene convey
    Her upland riches to the Belgick shore;
The idle vessel slides the wat'ry lay,
    Without the blast, or tug, of wind, or oar;
        Her slipp'ry keel divides the silver foam
        With ease; so facile is the way from home.

6

But when the home-bound vessel turns her sails
    Against the breast of the resisting stream,
O then she slugs; nor sail, nor oar prevails;
    The stream is sturdy, and her tides extreme:
        Each stroke is loss, and ev'ry tug is vain:
        A boat-length's purchase is a league of
        pain.

7

Great All in All, that art my rest, my home;
    My way is tedious, and my steps are slow:
Reach forth thy helpful hand, or bid me come:
    I am thy child, O teach thy child to go:
        Conjoin thy sweet commands to my desire
        And I will venture, though I fall or tire.

S. August. Ser. 15. de Verb. Apost.

Be always displeased at what thou art, if thou desirest to attain to what thou art not: For where thou hast pleased thy self, there thou abidest: But if thou sayest, I have enough, thou perishest: Always add, always walk, always proceed; neither stand still, nor go back, nor deviate: He that standeth still, proceedeth not; He goest back, that continueth not; He deviateth, that revolteth; He goeth better that creepeth in his way, then he that runneth out of his way.[3]

Epig. 3.
Fear not, my soul, to lose for want of cunning;
Weep not; Heav'n is not always got by running:

---

[1] *Exchange of profit* The Stock Exchange as we know it today did not then exist, but there are several relevant entries under *OED* exchange *sb.*

[2] *antic* grotesque, absurd (*OED* antic *a*).

---

[3] *He deviateth, that revolteth* He turns away, who goes back (to the place he came from); see *OED* revolt *v* I 4.

Thy thoughts are swift, although thy legs be slow;
True love will creep, not having strength to go.
—1635/1643

Eclogue VIII [1]

Anarchus   Canonicus

ANARCHUS

Graze on, my sheep; and let your souls defy
The food of common shepherds; Come not
    nigh
The Babylonish *pastures* of this nation;[2]
They are all heathenish, all abomination:
5 Their pastors are profane, and they have trod
The steps of *Belial*, not the ways of God.[3]
You are a chosen, a peculiar crew,
That blessed handful, that selected few
That shall have entrance; set apart and gifted
10 For holy exercises, cleans'd and sifted,
Like flour from bran, and separated from the
    coats
Of the unsanctified, like sheep from goats.
But who comes here? My lambs, why graze ye
    thus?
Why stand ye frighted? 'Tis *Canonicus*.

CANONICUS

15 God-morrow, swain; God keep thee from the
    sorrow
Of a sad day; What speechless? Swain, [4]
    God-morrow!
What, shepherd, not a word to entertain
The wishes of a friend? God-morrow, swain!
Not yet? What mean these silent common-places
20 Of strange aspects? what mean these antic faces?
I fear, his costive words, too great for vent.[5]
Stick in his throat; how like a Jack-a-lent
He stands, for boys to spend their shrovetide
    throws.
Or like a puppet, made to frighten crows![6]

ANARCHUS

25   Thou art a limb of Satan; and thy throat
A sink of poison; thy canonical coat
Is nothing but a liv'ry of the Beast;[7]
Thy language is profane, and I detest
Thy sinful greetings, and that heath'nish fashion
30 Of this your Antichristian salutation;
In brief, God keep me from the greater sorrow
Of thee; and from the curse of thy God-morrow

CANONICUS

How now, *Anarchus?* Has thy hungry zeal
Devoured all thy manners at a meal?

---

[1] An eclogue may be any short poem, but the word was mostly used, as here, of a pastoral dialogue, as in Virgil's *Bucolics*. The participants in this dialogue represent Lawlessness and Order ("canonical" means that which is in conformity with ecclesiastical edict or canon law).

[2] *Babylonish pastures* with the implication that the order which Canonicus represents is really a captivity, as the people of Israel were taken in captivity to Babylon. Every English reader would have known this piece of biblical history and the famous Psalm 137, which begins "By the waters of Babylon we sat down and wept: when we remembered thee, O Sion."

[3] *Belial* In various Old Testament passages, "sons of Belial" refers to dissolute and worthless people.

[4] *God-morrow* a contraction of the phrase, God give you good morrow; equivalent to our greeting "Good morning." See *OED* good morrow; *Swain* here, equivalent to "shepherd"; see *OED* swain *sb* 4.

[5] *costive* constipated (*OED* costive *a*).

[6] *Jack-a-lent* a figure of a man, set up to be pelted; an ancient form of the sport of "Aunt Sally," practised during Lent; figuratively, a butt for every one to throw at (*OED* Jack-a-Lent); *shrovetide* the period comprising Quinquagesima Sunday and the two following days. The first element of the word relates to the custom of confession and being "shriven" at the beginning of Lent. Not only were Jack-a-lents pelted; cockerels were tied up and pelted at this season; see *OED* shrovetide. Cruelty to animals has been practised in many countries in connection with various points of the Christian year.

[7] *the Beast* in reference to the Revelation to John, the last book of the New Testament. The two beasts of that book are said to refer to the Roman empire and to the cult established to further its aims, that of emperor worship and its priestcraft. Anarchus would be thinking of contemporary equivalents: the Roman Catholic church, Charles I and Archbishop Laud, who were thought to be crypto-Catholics.

35 No scraps remain? Or has th' unfruitful year
Made charity so scarce, and love so dear,
That none's allowed, upon the slight occasions
Of interview, or civil salutation?
Is thy store hoarded up? or is it spent?
40 Will thou vent none? or hath thou none to vent?
The curse of my God-morrow? 'Tis most true.
God's blessing proves a curse to such as you.

ANARCHUS

To such as we? Go, save your breath, to blow
Your vain cathedral bagpipes; and bestow [1]
45 Your trivial pray'rs on those that cannot pray
Without their spectacles; that cannot say
Their unregarded prayers, unless they hold
The *Let'ny*, or the charms of *Sorrocold* [2]
Before their purblind eyes; that disinherit
50 Their souls of freedom, and renounce the Spirit;
Perchance, your idle prayers may find an ear
With them; Go spend your vain God-morrows
there.

CANONICUS

Art thou thy self, *Anarchus?* Is thy heart
Acquainted with that tongue, that does impart
55 This brain-sick language? Could thy passion lend
No slighter subject, for thy breath to spend

Her aspine venom at, but that, alone, [3]
That shuts and opens the Eternal Throne
Of the Eternal God? Is prayer become
60 So poor a guest, to be denied a room
In thy opinion? To be scorn'd, contemn'd,
Like school-boys' themes, whose errors have
condemn'd
The guilty truant to the master's rod?
Can that displease thee, that delights thy God?

ANARCHUS

65 Thou child of wrath, and firebrand of Hell,
Flows wholesome water from a tainted well?
Or can those prayers be pleasing, that proceed
Form unregen'rate breasts? Can a foul weed
Delight the smell? or ugly shapes, the view?
70 I say, your prayers are all profane, like you;
They'r like that heatn'nish ruff of thine, that
perks [4]
Upon thy stiff-necked collar, pranked with ferks
Of studied wit, starched with strong lines, and put
75 In a set form, of th' antichristian cut. [5]

CANONICUS

75 Consult with reason, Shepherd, and advise;
Call home thy senses; and cast back thine eyes
On former days; No doubt, but there were they
That liv'd as sanctimonious, that could pray.
Lift up as holy hands, and did inherit
80 As great a share, and freedom of the Spirit,

As you; and these could count it no disgrace
To their profession, in a public place,
To use set forms; did not their wisdoms do
What you contemn, nay more, prescribe it too,
85 (Yet neither quench'd, nor wrong'd the sacred
    motion
Of the prompt Spirit), as helps to dull devotion?
Nay, more; has not th' unanimous consent
Of all reformed Churches (to prevent
Confused babbling, and to disenorm[1]
90 Prepost'rous service) bred us to a form
Of Common Prayer; prayers so divinely penn'd,
That human eloquence does even contend
With heavenly majesty, whilst both conspire
To kindle zeal, and so inflame desire?

ANARCHUS
95 The Book of Common Prayer? what tell'st thou me
Of that? My soul defies both that and thee:
Thou art *Baal's* Priest; and that vain book's no more
Then a mere relic of the Roman whore:[2]
Methinks a Christian tongue should be asham'd
100 To name such trash; I spit to hear it nam'd:
Tell me of Common Prayers? The midnight yelp
Of *Bal* my bandog is as great a help[3]
To raise devotion in a Christian's breast,
As that; the very language of the Beast;
105 That old worn Mass-book of the new Edition;
That Romish rabble, full of Superstition;
That paper Idol; that enchanting Spell;
That printed Image, sent from Rome, from Hell;

That broad-fac'd owl, upon a carved perch;
110 That *Bel* and *Dragon* of the English Church.[4]

CANONICUS
Be not too lavish, Shepherd; half this stuff
Will make a coat, to prove thee fool enough:
Hold, hold: thy brain-sick language does bewray
The self-same spirit, whether rail or pray:
115 For fools that rave, and rage, not knowing, why,
A scourge is far more fit, then a reply:
But say, *Anarchus*, (If it be not treason
Against discretion, to demand a reason
From frantic tongues), resolve me, Shepherd, why
120 This book is grown so odious in thine eye?

ANARCHUS
Because it is an idol, whereunto
You bend you idle knees, as papists do
To their lewd Images.

CANONICUS
    Ay, but we pray
Not to, but by it;

ANARCHUS
    Just so, Papists say:
125 Say, in what place th' Apostles ever did
Command *Set Form?*

CANONICUS
    Where was *Set Form* forbid?
What text commanded you to exercise
Your function over tables? Or baptise
In basins? What Apostle taught your tongue
130 To gibe at bishops? Or to vex and wrong
Your Mother Church? Who taught yee to oppose

---

[1] *disenorm* to free from irregularity; to make conformable to a norm or standard. This place is the only one cited in *OED*.

[2] *the Roman whore* the Roman Catholic church, associated by Protestants with the Whore of Babylon in Revelation 17.

[3] *bandog* a dog tied up either to guard a house or because of its ferocity; the word was proverbially associated with irrationality of speech (*OED* bandog).

[4] *Bel and Dragon* symbols of heathenism. The stories of Bel and the dragon are additions to the Book of Daniel, in the Apocrypha; the point of the tales was to ridicule idolatry and to discredit heathen priestcraft.

Your rulers? Or to whimper in the nose?[1]
But since you call for recedents, (although
'Tis more then our safe practice need to show)
135 Read, to what blessing that blest saint commends
The holy Church, saluted at the ends
Of all his sweet Epistles; Or if these
Suffice not, may your greater wisdoms please
To step into the Law, and read th' express
140 Commanded form, wherein the priest must bless
The parting people; Can thy brazen brow[2]
Deny all this? What refuge have yee now?
Y' are gone by Law and Gospel; They both us'd
Set Form; What Scripture now must be abus'd?

ANARCHUS

145 Well, if the Lord be pleased to allow
Set *form* to Prophets, are they set to you?
Or have ye so much boldness to compare
A *Prelate*'s prattling, to a *Prophet's* pray'r?

CANONICUS

O, that some equal hearer now were by
150 To laugh his treble share, as well as I:
Examples are demanded; which, being given,
We must not follow: Giddybrains! bereaven
Of common sense! Where heaven does make no
   mention,
You style it with the term of man's invention:
155 Where heaven commandeth, and is pleas'd to
   hallow
With blest examples, there we must not follow.

ANARCHUS

So heaven (by blest examples) did enjoin,
Your bended knees to worship Bread, and Wine?

CANONICUS

When your cross-gartered knees fall down before
160 Your parlour-table, what do you adore?

ANARCHUS

So heaven commands, by conjuring words to
   bring
Vow'd hands together, with a hallow'd *ring*

CANONICUS

'Tis true; your fiery zeals cannot abide
Long circumstance; your doctrine's, *Up and Ride*.

ANARCHUS

165 So heaven commmanded, that religious praise
Be given to Saints, and worship to their days?

CANONICUS

Whom you contemn, because they did not preach
Those doctrines, that your western parlours
   teach.

ANARCHUS

So heaven commanded *Bishops*, and the rest
170 Of that lewd *rank*, rank members of the *Beast?*

CANONICUS

Ay, heaven commanded such, and gave them
   power
To scourge, and check such ill-pac'd *beasts* as you
   are:

ANARCHUS

So heaven commanded, that the *high
Commission*
Should plague poor Christians, like the
   Inquisition? [3]

---

[1] *to whimper in the nose* one of many contemporary references to the
vocal affectations of Puritan preachers.

[2] *th'express / Commanded form* Quarles's marginal note refers to
Numbers 6:23, in which God prescribes a form of prayer for the
Israelites.

[3] *high Commission* The Court of High Commission, abolished in
1641, was founded under Elizabeth to give the crown power to
commission persons to try offences against the ecclesiastical establishment, and to crush any resistance to the crown in these matters (*OED*
commission *sb*[1] 7).

CANONICUS

175 Your plagues are what your own behaviours urge;
None, but the guilty, rail against the *scourge.*

ANARCHUS

So heaven commands your prayers, that
buried dust
Of *whores* and *thieves* should triumph with the
just?[1]

CANONICUS

Man may not censure by external view;
180 Forbear; we, sometimes, pray for some of you.

ANARCHUS

So heaven commands your *paintings, pipes,*
and *copes,*
Us'd in your Churches, and ordain'd by *Popes?*

CANONICUS

Where Popish hands hath rais'd in every town
A parish church, shall we pull churches down?
185 But come, *Anarchus* let us leave to play
At childish *Pushpin*; Come, let not the day
Be lost in *trifles*, to a fruitless end;
Let 's fall to hotter service, and contend
By more substantial argument, whose weight
190 May vindicate the truth from light conceit;
Let 's try a *Syllogism*; (Art infuses
Spirit into the children of the *Muses*)
Whereby, stout error shall be forc'd to yield,
And Truth shall sit sole Mistress of the Field.

ANARCHUS

195 Art me no arts; That which the Sp'rit infuses
Shall edge my tongue: What tell'st thou me of
Muses.
Those pagan *gods*; the authors of your schisms?

P'sh! tell me not of arts, and *silisismes:*
I care not for your quirks, and new devices
200 Of studied wit: We use to play our prizes.
With common weapons; and, with downright
knocks,
We beat down sin, and error, like an *Ox*
And cut the throat of heath'nish pop'ry too,
Like *calves*, prepar'd for slaughter; so we do
205 We rash in sunder *heresy*, like an ell
Of *sarc'net*, then convey it down to hell:[2]
We take just measure of a Christian's heart,
By th' yard of judgement; then, by dextrous art.
We cut out doctrines, and from notch to notch
210 We fit our holy *stuff*, (we do not botch
Like you; but make it jump, that it be neither
Too wide nor straight) then stitch it up together,
And make a Robe of *Sanctity*, to fit
The child of Grace; we meddle not with wit;
215 These be the means that overthrow our schisms,
And build Religion, without sigilismes.

CANONICUS

A rare device! But tell me, wert thou made
A butcher, or a tailor by thy trade?
I look'd for scholarship; but it appears,
220 Hoods make no monks, nor beards,
philosophers.

ANARCHUS

Surely, I was, at first, by occupation,[3]
A merchant tailor, till that lewder fashion
Of Spanish cassocks grew into request;
When having left that calling, I professed
225 To chandler, where I was enforc'd to vent
That hellish smoke, whose most unsavory scent
Perfum'd my garments so, that I began

---

[1] *buried dust / Of whores and thieves* Arminian doctrine, favoured by Charles I and Archbishop Laud, meant that in principle everybody was potentially saved from damnation; Calvinist doctrine was that only "the elect" were to be saved, and all others doomed to hell.

[2] *an ell / Of sarc'net* The English ell was 45 inches; sarsanet or sarcenet was a fine and soft silk material (*OED* sarsanet).

[3] *by occupation* The puritan belief that learning was not necessary to a preacher was frequently mocked, as were the "mechanic" trades practised by some Puritan preachers.

To be conceiv'd an unregenerate man:
Which called me from that course of life, to trade
230 In tape and inkle; ere I year'd and day'd
This new employment, O a strange mischance
O'er threw my dealings, which did disadvance
My mean estate; and whereupon, I fled
To *Amsterdam*; where being trencher-fed
235 By holy *Brethren,* liv'd in great respect,
Sr Rev'rence, footing stockings for th' Elect
Surely the savour of the Brethren's feet,
Perfum'd with comings in, is very sweet:
There, twice six months I had not led my life
240 But I became an husband to an wife,
The widow of an *Elder;* in whose stead,
I was, (though I could neither write, nor read)
Accounted worthy (though I say 't) and able
To preach the *gospel* at our *holy table.*

CANONICUS

245 But say, what strange mischance was that, did move thee
To flee thy native soil? What mischief drove thee?
What dire disaster urg'd thy skilful hand
To find employment in a foreign Land?

ANARCHUS

Surely, I was, when that mischance befell,
250 But poor in purse, and was constrain'd to sell
Cadice and *inkle*; now because my trade[1]
Requir'd an help, I entertain'd a Maid;
An able Christian; (though I say't) begot
Of holy Parents; (though the nuptial knot
255 Of ceremonious marriage never tied
Their joined hands) *She was a sanctified*
And undefiled vessel; she would pray,
When others slept; and work when others play:
She was of exc'lent knowledge; and, indeed,
260 She could expound, and preach too, for a need:
She was my servant, and set up my trade

With her own hands; her skilful fingers made
The *tape* and *inkle*, where withal she stor'd
My thriving shop; whereby, I did afford
265 My Brethren better pennyworths; nay, more,
She had a gift, (was all the City o'er
Well known) in making puddings, whose mere view
Would make a proselyte, and convert a Jew;
270 Whose new religion would proclaim our hogs
As clean and holy as their Synagogues;
These would she bear from house to house, and sell
To holy Brethren, who would please her well;
For under that pretence, she oft repeated
275 Some close-preached sermon; oftentimes entreated
Of holy Discipline; sometimes gave warning
Of some rare Lecture held next Thursday morning
I know not how, (frail flesh and blood ye know
Can do no more than flesh and blood can do)
280 But to be short, she would so often fig
From place to place, that she was grown too big
To be conceal'd from wicked neighb'ring eyes;
T' avoid the scandal, I thought good t'arise,
And flee to *Amsterdam*, till I could gather,
285 By information, the reputed Father.

CANONICUS

285 A wholesome hist'ry! able to transform
Abus'd Religion's sunshine to a storm
Of direful thunderbolts, to overthrow
All Christian rulers, that dare longer owe
Confusion to the varlets, and not grind them
290 To dust, and send them to the place design'd them
Had'st thou that impudence, that brazen face,
In the fag end of thy unsav'ry, base,
Triobular trades (foul beast;) nay, piping hot[2]
From thy close strumpet, thus to soil, and blot
295 The beauty of Religion, and to wrong
The Gospel's name with thy illiterate tongue?

---

[1] *Cadice* cotton wool (*OED* caddis, caddice); *inkle* a kind of linen tape (*OED* inkle *sb*).

[2] *triobular* worth three obols, that is, base, petty, contemptible; compare twopenny-halfpenny (*OED* triobolar).

ANARCHUS

Were not th' Apostles fishers, and not fly
Their trades, and preach'd the word as well as I?

CANONICUS

Avoid, presumptuous varlet; urge no more
300 My tired patience; Go, seek out thy whore,
Thy fit compere, and exercise thy trade
Upon her ruin'd stockings, much decayed
With long pursuit, and trudging all about
To find the father of her bastard out;
305 Whils't I remove my zenith, and go hence,[1]
To wail this fruitless hour's misexpence,
And pray to heaven, that heaven would please to keep
Such goats still separated from my sheep.
—1638/1643

_____

[1] *remove my zenith*   that is, move to a different place.

Henry King
1592 — 1669

Henry King was born into a family of churchmen who had been eminent for more than a century. His father had been a chaplain to Queen Elizabeth, was Bishop of London under James, and a friend of John Donne. Henry was educated at Westminster School, where he was an exact contemporary of George Herbert. Part of his education would have consisted of turning Greek and Latin verse into English verse; beyond this, Westminster was unlike other schools in having pupils write English verse as an exercise. The school was a great nursery for poets: Jonson, Herbert, Cowley, Dryden, Randolph, Strode, Corbet all studied there, and the list is not exhaustive.

Henry King married Anne Berkeley, of an ancient and famous family, higher in social rank than King's; at her death more than one writer commented on her modesty in the choice of a husband. King's feelings for her may be guessed at from the "Exequy," one of the greatest elegies in our language, and from another poem, "St. Valentine's Day," probably written more than twenty years after her death.

Though King, like his father, was much esteemed as a preacher, his rewards within the Church were to be short-lived; he was consecrated as Bishop of Chichester on February 6, 1642, the day after the bishops had been deprived of their seats in the House of Lords. An Act abolishing episcopacy was passed in the following year. In December of 1642 Chichester was taken by the Parliamentary forces under Sir William Waller, and King lost his ecclesiastical revenues. During the Interregnum, when it was feared that the Anglican church might die out, King was included in a plan, in the event not acted upon, to go to Charles II's court-in-exile and consecrate as bishops some of the divines who were with Charles. At the Restoration, King was restored to his bishopric and lived quietly in Chichester until his death three years later. His not being given further preferment has been explained by reference to Hyde's anger at his failure, as bishops died off, to consecrate successors in order to re-vivify the church, one of whose defining characteristics was episcopacy. For King to have done so would of course have been contrary to law. The story of how close the Church of England came to dying out, and of how it was kept alive, to flourish after the Restoration, is well told by R.S. Bosher in *The Making of the Restoration Settlement.*

❧❧❧

An Exequy to his Matchless never to be forgotten Friend [1]

Accept, thou shrine of my dead saint!
Instead of Dirges this Complaint; [2]

And, for sweet flowers to crown thy hearse,
Receive a strew of weeping verse
5   From thy griev'd friend; whom thou might'st see
Quite melted into tears for thee.
    Dear Loss! since thy untimely fate
My task hath been to meditate
On thee, on thee: thou art the book,
10 The library whereon I look
Though almost blind. For thee (lov'd clay!)
I languish out, not live the day,

---

[1] *Exequy OED* glosses the word as "funeral rites" and remarks that "an alleged sense 'a funeral ode' has been wrongly inferred from the title of this poem." *Friend* The word was commonly applied to a spouse at the time. Anne King died in January 1624.

[2] *Dirges* The word could refer to songs sung at a funeral, but in view of the opposition set up in the line, King may have had in mind the more formal sense: *Dirge* was originally *Dirige* (Direct), taken from Psalm 5:8 which was the first word of the Antiphon at Matins in the

Office of the Dead; *Complaint* in the early sense of "utterance of grief" (*OED* Complaint 1,2).

Using no other exercise
But what I practise with mine eyes.
15 By which wet glasses I find out
How lazily Time creeps about
To one that mourns: this, only this
My exercise and bus'ness is:
So I compute the weary hours
20 With sighs dissolved into showers.
    Nor wonder if my time go thus
Backward and most preposterous; [1]
Thou hast benighted me. Thy set
This eve of blackness did beget,
25 Who wast my day, (though overcast
Before thou hadst thy noon-tide past)
And I remember must in tears,
Thou scarce hadst seen so many years
As day tells hours. By thy clear Sun
30 My love and fortune first did run;
But thou wilt never more appear
Folded within my hemisphere:
Since both thy light and motion
Like a fled star is fall'n and gone;
35 And 'twixt me and my soul's dear wish
The Earth now interposed is,
Which such a strange eclipse doth make
As ne're was read in almanac.
    I could allow thee for a time
40 To darken me and my sad clime,
Were it a month, a year, or ten,
I would thy exile live till then;
And all that space my mirth adjourn,
So thou wouldst promise to return,
45 And putting off thy ashy shroud
At length disperse this sorrow's cloud.
    But woe is me! the longest date
Too narrow is to calculate
These empty hopes. Never shall I
50 Be so much blest, as to descry
A glimpse of thee, till that day come

Which shall the Earth to cinders doom,
And a fierce fever must calcine
The body of this world, like thine,
55 (My little world!) That fit of fire
Once off, our bodies shall aspire
To our souls' bliss: then we shall rise,
And view our selves with clearer eyes
In that calm region, where no night
60 Can hide us from each other's sight.
    Mean time, thou hast her Earth: much good
May my harm do thee. Since it stood
With Heaven's will I might not call
Her longer mine; I give thee all
65 My short liv'd right and interest
In her, whom living I lov'd best:
With a most free and bounteous grief,
I give thee what I could not keep.
Be kind to her: and prithee look
70 Thou write into thy Doomsday book
Each parcel of this rarity,
Which in thy casket shrin'd doth lie:
See that thou make thy reck'ning straight,
And yield her back again by weight;
75 For thou must audit on thy trust
Each grain and atom of this dust:
As thou wilt answer Him, that lent,
Not gave thee, my dear monument. [2]
    So close the ground, and 'bout her shade
80 Black curtains draw, my bride is lay'd.
    Sleep on (my love!) in thy cold bed
Never to be disquieted.
My last good-night! Thou wilt not wake
Till I thy fate shall overtake:
85 Till age, or grief, or sickness must
Marry my body to that dust
It so much loves; and fill the room
My heart keeps empty in thy tomb.
Stay for me there: I will not fail

---

[1] *preposterous* from the Latin *praeposterus*, reversed (*prae* before, *posterus* after).

---

[2] *monument* apparently used in a sense (tenderly ironical) unknown to *OED*. He needs no memorial or reminder; as he cannot forget her, she herself is a monument.

To meet thee in that hollow vale.
And think not much of my delay;
I am already on the way,
And follow thee with all the speed
Desire can make, or sorrows breed.
95 Each minute is a short degree
And e'ry hour a step towards thee.
At night when I betake to rest,
Next morn I rise nearer my west
Of life, almost by eight hours' sail,
100 Than when Sleep breath'd his drowsy gale.
    Thus from the sun my bottom steers, [1]
And my day's compass downward bears.
Nor labour I to stem the tide, [2]
Through which to thee I swiftly glide.
105   'Tis true; with shame and grief I yield
Thou, like the Van, first took'st the field, [3]
And gotten hast the victory
In thus adventuring to die
Before me; whose more years might crave
110 A just precedence in the grave.
But hark! My pulse, like a soft drum
Beats my approach, tells thee I come;
And, slow howe'r my marches be,
I shall at last sit down by thee.
115   The thought of this bids me go on,
And wait my dissolution
With hope and comfort. Dear! (forgive
The crime) I am content to live
Divided, with but half a heart,
120 Till we shall meet and never part.
    —1657 (1624)

Upon the Death of my ever Desired Friend
Dr Donne Dean of Paul's [4]

To have lived eminent, in a degree
Beyond our loftiest flights, that is, like thee;
Or t'have had too much merit, is not safe;
For such excesses find no epitaph.
5 At common graves we have poetic eyes
Can melt themselves in easy elegies;
Each quill can drop his tributary verse,
And pin it, with the hatchments, to the hearse: [5]
But at thine, poem, or inscription
10 (Rich soul of wit and language!) we have none.
Indeed a silence does that tomb befit,
Where is no herald left to blazon it.
Widowed Invention justly doth forbear
To come abroad, knowing thou art not here,
15 Late her great patron, whose prerogative
Maintained and clothed her SO, as none alive
Must now presume to keep her at thy rate,
Though he the Indies for her dower estate.
Or else that awful fire, which once did burn
20 In thy clear brain, now fall'n into thy urn
Lives there to fright rude Empirics from thence, [6]
Which might profane thee by their ignorance.
Who ever writes of thee, and in a style
Unworthy such a theme, does but revile
25 Thy precious dust, and wake a learned spirit
Which may revenge his rapes upon thy merit.
For all a low-pitched fant'sy can devise
Will prove, at best, but hallowed injuries.
Thou, like the dying swan, didst lately sing

---

[1] *bottom* ship, vessel (*OED* bottom 7).

[2] *stem the tide* The verb can mean to check the tide, or to labour against it (*OED* stem v² 2 and v⁴).

[3] *Van* the foremost division of a military…force when advancing (*OED* van *sb* ² 1).

---

[4] This poem was printed several times before Henry King's collected poems were published in 1657, for example in *Poems by J.D. with Elegies on the Author's Death*, 1633, where it is the first elegy.

[5] *hatchments* the armorial bearings of a deceased person (*OED* hatchment ¹).

[6] *Empirics* charlatans (*OED* empiric *sb* 2b).

30 Thy mournfull dirge in audience of the King; [1]
When pale looks, and faint accents of thy breath
Presented so to life, that piece of death,
That it was feared and prophesied by all,
Thou thither camst to preach thy funeral.
35 O! hadst thou in an elegiac knell
Rung out unto the world thine own farewell,
And in thy high victorious numbers beat
The solemn measure of thy grieved retreat;
Thou mightst the poet's service now have missed
40 As well, as then thou didst prevent the priest,
And never to the world beholden bee
So much as for an epitaph for thee.
    I doe not like the office. Nor is't fit
Thou, who didst lend our age such sums of wit,
45 Shouldst now re-borrow from her bankrupt mine
That ore to bury thee, which once was thine.
Rather still leave us in thy debt; and know
(Exalted soul!) more glory tis to owe
Unto thy hearse, what we can never pay,
50 Then with embased coin those rites defray.
    Commit we then thee to thyself: Nor blame
Our drooping loves, which thus to thy own fame
Leave thee executor. Since, but thy own,
No pen could do thee justice, nor bays crown
Thy vast desert; save that, wee nothing can
Depute to be thy ashes' guardian.

So jewellers no art, or metal trust
To form the diamond, but the diamond's dust.
—1632

Sic Vita [2]

Like to the falling of a star;
    Or as the flights of eagles are;
 Or like the fresh spring's gaudy hue;
Or silver drops of morning dew;
5 Or like a wind that chafes the flood;
Or bubbles which on water stood;
Even such is Man, whose borrowed light
Is straight called in, and paid to Night.

The wind blows out, the bubble dies;
10 The spring entombed in autumn lies:
The dew dries up; the star is shot:
The flight is past: And Man forgot.
—1640

---

[1] *in audience of the King*   an allusion to Donne's sermon *Death's Duel*, preached before the King; its title-page says "his last sermon, and called by his Majesty's household The Doctor's Own Funeral Sermon."

[2] *Sic Vita* Such is life. This poem was first printed in *Poems by Francis Beaumont,* 1640, according to Margaret Crum, *The Poems of Henry King* (Oxford: Clarendon P, 1965), p. 254.

George Herbert
1593 – 1633

George Herbert was born into a wealthy and aristocratic family, his eldest brother being Lord Herbert of Cherbury. His mother, Magdalen Herbert, a friend of Donne's, was probably one of the major influences in his decision to become a priest of the English Church, another being his friend Nicholas Ferrar, the founder of a religious community at Little Gidding. Herbert was educated first privately, then at Westminster School, then at Cambridge, where he had a brilliant career, and coming to the notice of King James in his capacity as the university's Public Orator. As the fifth son, he needed to make his own way in the world, and at first had hopes of preferment at Court, but the death of his patrons, the Duke of Richmond and the Marquess of Hamilton, and of James himself, brought those hopes to an end. His rectorship at Bemerton, though it only lasted three years, is one of the legends of early Anglicanism, thanks to Izaak Walton's description of it in his life of Herbert. He is said to have married his wife, Jane Danvers, on three days' acquaintance, having often heard her praised by her father, who desired the match. Herbert was a good linguist and musician and a "poet's poet," whose verse is often experimental and technically original.

෨෨෨

The Altar

A broken ALTAR, Lord thy servant rears,
Made of a heart, and cemented with tears:[1]
  Whose parts are as thy hand did frame;
  No workman's tool hath touched the same.[2]
5   A HEART alone
        Is such a stone,
        As nothing but
        Thy pow'r doth cut.
        Wherefore each part
10   Of my hard heart
        Meets in this frame,
        To praise thy name.
  That, if I chance to hold my peace,
  These stones to praise thee may not cease.[3]
15 O let thy blessed SACRIFICE be mine,
And sanctify this ALTAR to be thine.
—1633

---

[1] *made of a heart*   See II Corinthians 3:3.

[2] *No workman's tool*   See Exodus 20:25.

[3] *These stones to praise thee*   See Luke 19:40.

Redemption

Having been tenant long to a rich Lord,
  Not thriving, I resolved to be bold,
  And make a suit unto him, to afford
A new small-rented lease, and cancel th'old.[4]
5 In heaven at his manor I him sought:
  They told me there, that he was lately gone
  About some land, which he had dearly bought
Long since on earth, to take possession.
I straight returned, and knowing his great birth,
10   Sought him accordingly in great resorts;
  In cities, theatres, gardens, parks, and courts:
At length I heard a ragged noise and mirth
  Of thieves and murderers: there I him espied,
  Who straight, *Your suit is granted*, said, and died.
—1633

---

[4] *new…old*   figuratively, Christ's New Testament covenant of grace, which "cancelled" the Old Testament covenant of law.

Easter Wings [1]

Lord, who createdst man in wealth and store,
  Though foolishly he lost the same,
    Decaying more and more,
      Till he became
5   Most poor:
        With thee
      O let me rise
    As larks, harmoniously,
  And sing this day thy victories:
10 Then shall the fall further the flight in me. [2]

My tender age in sorrow did begin:
  And still with sicknesses and shame
    Thou didst so punish sin,
      That I became
15   Most thin.
        With thee
      Let me combine,
    And feel this day thy victory:
  For, if I imp my wing on thine, [3]
20 Affliction shall advance the flight in me.
—1633

Affliction (I)

When first thou didst entice to thee my heart,
    I thought the service brave: [4]
So many joys I writ down for my part,
    Besides what I might have

5 Out of my stock of natural delights,
  Augmented with thy gracious benefits.

I looked on thy furniture so fine,
      And made it fine to me:
Thy glorious household-stuff did me entwine,
10   And 'tice me unto thee.
Such stars I counted mine: both heav'n and earth
Paid me my wages in a world of mirth.

What pleasures could I want, whose King I served,
      Where joys my fellows were?
15 Thus argued into hopes, my thoughts reserved
      No place for grief or fear.
Therefore my sudden soul caught at the place, [5]
And made her youth and fierceness seek thy face.

At first thou gav'st me milk and sweetnesses;
20   I had my wish and way:
My days were strawed with flow'rs and
    happiness; [6]
        There was no month but May.
But with my years sorrow did twist and grow,
And made a party unawares for woe.

25 My flesh began unto my soul in pain, [7]
      Sicknesses cleave my bones;
Consuming agues dwell in every vein, [8]
      And tune my breath to groans.
Sorrow was all my soul; I scarce believed,
30 Till grief did tell me roundly, that I lived. [9]

---

[1] printed vertically in the 1633 edition, but left horizontal (as here) in both manuscript versions.

[2] *fall* referring to the "fortunate fall" (*felix culpa*), the belief that Adam and Eve's disobedience could be considered fortunate in that it occasioned the Incarnation and the possibility of redemption.

[3] *imp* from falconry: to engraft a damaged wing with feathers to restore or improve flight (*OED* imp *v* 4).

[4] *service* a situation or place as servant; the serving of a certain master or household (*OED* service *sb* 3a, b); *brave* fine, splendid (*OED* brave *a* 2,3).

---

[5] *sudden* quick to perform, prompt (*OED* sudden *a* 4).

[6] *strawed* strewn.

[7] The likeliest meaning is "My flesh began to remonstrate with my soul." The content of the flesh's complaint is given in the next three lines, in which the verbs are in the present tense.

[8] *agues* acute or violent fevers (*OED* ague 1).

[9] *roundly* plainly, bluntly (*OED* roundly *adv* 3).

When I got health, thou took'st away my life,
     And more; for my friends die: [1]
My mirth and edge was lost; a blunted knife
     Was of more use than I.
35 Thus thin and lean without a fence or friend, [2]
I was blown through with every storm and wind.

Whereas my birth and spirit rather took
     The way that takes the town;
Thou didst betray me to a ling'ring book,
40   And wrap me in a gown.
I was entangled in the world of strife,
Before I had the power to change my life.

Yet, for I threatened oft the siege to raise,
     Not simp'ring all mine age,
45 Thou often didst with Academic praise
     Melt and dissolve my rage.
I took thy sweetened pill, till I came where
I could not go away, nor persevere.

Yet lest perchance I should too happy be
50   In my unhappiness,
Turning my purge to food, thou throwest me
     Into more sicknesses.
Thus doth thy power cross-bias me, not making
Thine own gift good, yet me from my ways
     taking. [3]

55 Now I am here, what thou wilt do with me
     None of my books will show:
I read, and sigh, and wish I were a tree;
     For sure then I should grow
To fruit or shade: at least some bird would trust
60 Her household to me, and I should be just.

Yet, though thou troublest me, I must be meek;
     In weakness must be stout.
Well, I will change the service, and go seek
     Some other master out.
65 Ah my dear God! though I am clean forgot,
Let me not love thee, if I love thee not.
—1633

Prayer (I)

Prayer the Church's banquet, Angels' age,
  God's breath in man returning to his birth,
    The soul in paraphrase, heart in pilgrimage,
  The Christian plummet sounding heav'n and
    earth; [4]
5 Engine against th' Almighty, sinner's tower, [5]
  Reversed thunder, Christ-side-piercing spear, [6]
    The six-days world transposing in an hour, [7]
A kind of tune, which all things hear and fear;
Softness, and peace, and joy, and love, and bliss,
10   Exalted Manna, gladness of the best, [8]
    Heaven in ordinary, man well dressed,
The milky way, the bird of Paradise,
  Church-bells beyond the stars heard, the
    soul's blood,
  The land of spices; something understood.
—1633

---

[1] *my friends die* The reference is not necessarily to intimate friends, but rather to well-disposed men of power who could have furthered Herbert's worldly ambitions.

[2] *fence* means or method of defence (*OED* fence *sb* 3).

[3] *cross-bias* to counter, to run contrary to (*OED*).

---

[4] *plummet* a piece of lead or other metal attached to a line, and used for sounding or measuring the depth of water (*OED* plummet *sb* 2).

[5] *Engine* a machine or instrument used in warfare (*OED* engine *sb* 5a); *tower* a moveable structure used to attack a fortified place (*OED* tower *sb* 5a). The implied metaphor is of a siege against God, by which man will break into heaven. Compare Henry Vaughan's "I threaten heaven" in "Disorder and Frailty."

[6] *spear* See John 19:34.

[7] *six-days world* contrasting the six days it took to create the world with what prayer can accomplish in an hour.

[8] During their forty-year journey through the wilderness, after fleeing from Egypt, the Israelites were given manna to eat (Exodus 16:4).

Jordan (I) [1]

Who says that fictions only and false hair
    Become a verse? Is there in truth no beauty?
Is all good structure in a winding stair?
May no lines pass, except they do their duty
5   Not to a true, but painted chair?

Is it no verse, except enchanted groves
And sudden arbours shadow coarse-spun lines?
Must purling streams refresh a lover's loves?
Must all be veiled,[2] while he that reads, divines,
10   Catching the sense at two removes?

Shepherds are honest people; let them sing: [3]
Riddle who list, for me, and pull for prime: [4]
I envy no man's nightingale or spring
Nor let them punish me with loss of rhyme
15   Who plainly say, *My God, My King.*
—1633

The H. Scriptures I

Oh Book! infinite sweetness! let my heart
    Suck ev'ry letter, and a honey gain,
    Precious for any grief in any part;
To clear the breast, to mollify all pain.
5 Thou art all health, health thriving till it make
      A full eternity: thou art a mass
      Of strange delights, where we may wish and
        take.

Ladies, look here; this is the thankful glass,
10 That mends the looker's eyes: this is the well
    That washes what it shows. Who can endear
    Thy praise too much? thou art heav'n's Lidger
      here, [5]
Working against the states of death and hell.
    Thou art joy's handsel:[6] heav'n lies flat in thee,
15   Subject to ev'ry mounter's bended knee.
—1633

The H. Scriptures II

Oh that I knew how all thy lights combine,
    And the configurations of their glory!
    Seeing not only how each verse doth shine,
But all the constellations of the story.
5 This verse marks that, and both do make a motion
    Unto a third, that ten leaves off doth lie:
    Then as dispersed herbs do watch a potion,
These three make up some Christian's destiny: [7]
Such are thy secrets, which my life makes good,
10   And comments on thee: for in ev'ry thing
    Thy words do find me out, and parallels bring,
And in another make me understood.
    Stars are poor books, and oftentimes do miss:
    This book of stars lights to eternal bliss.
—1633

Church-monuments

While that my soul repairs to her devotion,
    Here I entomb my flesh, that it betimes [8]
May take acquaintance of this heap of dust;

---

[1] *Jordan* the river in which Christ was baptized. The resonances are complex, but in effect Herbert here explores the baptism of his art. Inspired by the Jordan and the Christian story it represents (rather than by the springs of the muses and poetic traditions inspired by classical models), Herbert's poetry employs the techniques of secular art, but its subject is transformed.

[2] *Must all be veiled* referring to allegorical poetry.

[3] *Shepherds...sing* referring to pastoral poetry.

[4] *Riddle who list* let whomever wishes pose riddles; *pull for prime* draw for a winning hand in the card game primero (*OED* prime *sb*[2] 6).

[5] *Lidger* ledger or lieger; a resident ambassador (*OED* ledger *sb* 6).

[6] *handsel* here, a token of what is to come (*OED* handsel 3).

[7] *Then as...destiny* a play on an affinity between "leaves" of plants and books: the general sense is that scattered biblical texts may combine into saving knowledge just as various herbs "watch" for opportunities to combine into medicine.

[8] *betimes* in good time, while there is yet time (*OED* betimes *adv* 3).

To which the blast of death's incessant motion,
5   Fed with the exhalation of our crimes,
Drives all at last. Therefore I gladly trust

My body to this school, that it may learn
To spell his elements, and find his birth [1]
Written in dusty heraldry and lines;
10   Which dissolution sure doth best discern, [2]
Comparing dust with dust, and earth with earth.
These laugh at jet and marble put for signs, [3]

To sever the good fellowship of dust,
And spoil the meeting. What shall point out them, [4]
15   When they shall bow, and kneel, and fall down flat
To kiss those heaps, which now they have in trust?
Dear flesh, while I do pray, learn here thy stem
And true descent; that when thou shalt grow fat, [5]

And wanton in thy cravings, thou mayst know,
20   That flesh is but the glass, which holds the dust [6]
That measures all our time; which also shall
Be crumbled into dust. Mark here below [7]
How tame these ashes are, how free from lust,
That thou mayst fit thy self against thy fall.
—1633

---

[1] The change from "it" to "his" in connection with the body is not especially surprising: "his" continued to be used as a neuter possessive until late in the century; *elements* punning on the elements of which the body is made and the content of learning in an "elementary" school, i.e. the letters of the alphabet; hence, the rudiments of learning (*OED* element *sb pl* IV 14).

[2] *discern* reveal.

[3] *jet* black marble (*OED* jet *sb* 2).

[4] *them* the tombstones and monuments, which will in time themselves fall down.

[5] *thy stem / And true descent* Words from the liturgy for Ash Wednesday are relevant: "Remember, o man, that thou art dust, and unto dust thou shalt return" (based on Genesis 2:7).

[6] *glass* hourglass.

[7] *which also shall / Be crumbled into dust* time, like flesh, will also come to an end; see Psalm 102:25–26 and Hebrews 1:11–12.

The Windows

Lord, how can man preach thy eternal word?
   He is a brittle crazy glass:
Yet in thy temple thou dost him afford
   This glorious and transcendent place,
5   To be a window, through thy grace.

But when thou dost anneal in glass thy story, [8]
   Making thy life to shine within
The holy Preacher's; then the light and glory
   More rev'rend grows, and more doth win:
10   Which else shows wat'rish, bleak, and thin.

Doctrine and life, colours and light, in one
   When they combine and mingle, bring
A strong regard and awe: but speech alone
   Doth vanish like a flaring thing,
15   And in the ear, not conscience ring.
—1633

---

[8] *anneal* to fix colours painted on glass by heating it.

Denial

When my devotions could not pierce
            Thy silent ears;
Then was my heart broken, as was my verse:
      My breast was full of fears
5   And disorder:

My bent thoughts, like a brittle bow,
            Did fly asunder:
Each took his way; some would to pleasures go,
      Some to the wars and thunder
10   Of alarms.

As good go anywhere, they say,
            As to benumb
Both knees and heart, in crying night and day,

Come, come, my God, O come,
                        But no hearing.

15

O that thou shouldst give dust a tongue
                    To cry to thee,
And then not hear it crying! all day long
                   My heart was in my knee,
                        But no hearing.

20

Therefore my soul lay out of sight,
                      Untuned, unstrung:
My feeble spirit, unable to look right,
                  Like a nipped blossom, hung
                      Discontented.

25

O cheer and tune my heartless breast,
                     Defer no time;
That so thy favours granting my request,
                They and my mind may chime,
                      And mend my rhyme.

30
—1633

Vanity (I)

The fleet Astronomer can bore,
    And thread the spheres with his
        quick-piercing mind: [1]
He views their stations, walks from door to door,
    Surveys, as if he had designed

5 To make a purchase there: he sees their dances, [2]
        And knoweth long before
Both their full-eyed aspects, and secret glances. [3]

The nimble Diver with his side
Cuts through the working waves, that he may fetch

10 His dearly earned pearl, which God did hide
        On purpose from the ventrous wretch; [4]
That he might save his life, and also hers,
        Who with excessive pride
Her own destruction and his danger wears. [5]

15   The subtle Chymick can devest
And strip the creature naked, till he find
The callow principles within their nest: [6]
        There he imparts to them his mind, [7]
Admitted to their bed-chamber, before

20   They appear trim and dressed
To ordinary suitors at the door.

        What hath not man sought out and found,
But his dear God? who yet his glorious law
Embosoms in us, mellowing the ground
        With showers and frosts, with love and awe,
So that we need not say, Where's this command?
        Poor man, thou searchest round
To find out *death*, but missest *life* at hand. [8]
—1633

---

[1] *spheres* The universe was conceived as a series of concentric spheres.

[2] *their dances* The cosmic dance, like the ladder and the chain, was one of the categories used in "the Elizabethan world picture."

[3] Herbert deploys the vocabulary of astronomy ("aspect") to suggest a sexuality in the enterprise of the astronomer.

[4] Mention of the pearl helps to tie together the first and second stanzas, since we may think of the astronomer as metaphorically threading a necklace.

[5] *Her own destruction* because Pride is one of the seven deadly sins; her destruction is spiritual, the danger of the pearl-diver physical.

[6] *Chymick* alchemist. "Subtle" was the name of the principal character in Ben Jonson's *The Alchemist*; the word implied acumen and treachery as well as an established association with alchemy, regarded by many as a morally questionable enterprise.

[7] *imparts to them his mind* The metaphor is of the alchemist wooing the principles of nature; the phrase was used of a suitor (see the last line of the stanza) making his affections known to their object.

[8] This poem has been characterized, by Helen Vendler, as a "fearful repudiation of intellectual enquiry." It is not that; but its final stanza might be understood in relation to a saying of Sir Philip Sidney, in the *Apologie for Poetrie*, that "the ending end of all earthly learning being virtuous action, those skills that most serve to bring forth that, have a most just title to be princes over all the rest."

Virtue

Sweet day, so cool, so calm, so bright,
The bridal of the earth and sky:
The dew shall weep thy fall to night;
        For thou must die.

5 Sweet rose, whose hue angry and brave
Bids the rash gazer wipe his eye:
Thy root is ever in its grave,
        And thou must die.

Sweet spring, full of sweet days and roses,
10 A box where sweets compacted lie; [1]
My music shows ye have your closes, [2]
        And all must die.

Only a sweet and virtuous soul,
Like seasoned timber, never gives;
15 But though the whole world turn to coal,
        Then chiefly lives.

—1633

The Pearl. Matth. 13:45

I know the ways of Learning; both the head
And pipes that feed the press, and make it run; [3]
What reason hath from nature borrowed,
Or of itself, like a good housewife, spun
5 In laws and policy; what the stars conspire,
What willing nature speaks, what forced by fire; [4]
Both th'old discoveries, and the new-found seas,
The stock and surplus, cause and history:

10 All these stand open, or I have the keys:
        Yet I love thee.

I know the ways of Honour, what maintains
The quick returns of courtesy and wit:
In vies of favours whether party gains,
When glory swells the heart, and moldeth it
15 To all expressions both of hand and eye,
Which on the world a true-love-knot may tie,
And bear the bundle, whereso'er it goes.
How many drams of spirit there must be
To sell my life unto my friends or foes:
20   Yet I love thee.

I know the ways of Pleasure, the sweet strains,
The lullings and the relishes of it;
The propositions of hot blood and brains;
What mirth and music mean; what love and wit
25 Have done these twenty hundred years, and more:
I know the projects of unbridled store:
My stuff is flesh, not brass; my senses live,
And grumble oft, that they have more in me
Than he that curbs them, being but one to five:
30   Yet I love thee.

I know all these, and have them in my hand:
Therefore not seeled, but with open eyes
I fly to thee, and fully understand
Both the main sale, and the commodities; [5]
35 And at what rate and price I have thy love
With all the circumstances that may move:
Yet through these labyrinths, not my groveling wit,
But thy silk twist let down from heav'n to me,
Did both conduct and teach me, how by it
40   To climb to thee.

—1633

---

[1] *sweets* sweet scents or perfumes (*OED* sweet *sb* 7).

[2] *closes* with a play on the musical meaning of "close," a cadence or concluding phrase (*OED* close *sb²* 2).

[3] *the head / And pipes that feed the press* See Zechariah 4:12–14, where the olive press is an emblem of divine inspiration; Herbert here links the olive and printing presses.

[4] *what forced by fire* in scientific (alchemical) experiments.

[5] *seeled* to seel was a term in falconry for sewing up the eyelids of a hawk or other bird (*OED* seel *v²* 1).

Man

My God, I heard this day,
  That none doth build a stately
      habitation,
But he that means to dwell therein.
What house more stately hath there been,
5 Or can be, than is Man? to whose creation
      All things are in decay.

    For Man is ev'ry thing,
And more: He is a tree, yet bears more fruit;
  A beast, yet is, or should be more:
10   Reason and speech we only bring. [1]
Parrots may thank us, if they are not mute,
    They go upon the score. [2]

    Man is all symmetry,
Full of proportions, one limb to another,
15   And all to all the world besides:
    Each part may call the furthest, brother:
For head with foot hath private amity,
    And both with moons and tides. [3]

    Nothing hath got so far,
20 But Man hath caught and kept it, as his prey.
  His eyes dismount the highest star:
  He is in little all the sphere.

Herbs gladly cure our flesh; because that they
    Find their acquaintance there. [4]

25   For us the winds do blow,
The earth doth rest, heav'n move, and fountains flow.
    Nothing we see, but means our good,
    As our delight, or as our treasure:
The whole is, either our cupboard of food,
30   Or cabinet of pleasure.

    The stars have us to bed;
Night draws the curtain, which the sun withdraws;
    Music and light attend our head.
    All things unto our flesh are kind
35 In their descent and being; to our mind
    In their ascent and cause.

    Each thing is full of duty:
Waters united are our navigation;
    Distinguished, our habitation; [5]
40   Below, our drink; above, our meat; [6]
Both are our cleanliness. Hath one such beauty?
    Then how are all things neat? [7]

    More servants wait on Man,
Than he'll take notice of: in ev'ry path
    He treads down that which doth befriend him,
45   When sickness makes him pale and wan. [8]
Oh mighty love! Man is one world, and hath
    Another to attend him.

---

[1] Herbert argues that a human is more than a microcosm, or little world; he is that, and he is more. Donne wrote that "the Philosopher draws man into too narrow a table, when he says he is *Microcosmos*, an Abridgement of the world in little: *Nazianzen* gives him but his due, when he calls him *Mundum Magnum*, a world to which all the rest of the world is but subordinate" (*XXVI Sermons*, xxv.370, quoted by Hutchinson).

[2] *They go upon the score* They are indebted to man; see *OED* score *sb* 10.

[3] a reference to the idea that different parts of the body are affected by the movements of the heavenly bodies.

---

[4] a reference to the idea that each medicinal herb has an affinity with a particular part of the body; the root of the mandrake, for example, was thought to resemble a human form and accordingly to promote conception when eaten by women.

[5] See Genesis 1:9–10.

[6] *above, our meat* The rain makes the earth fertile to bring forth our food; *meat* is used in its general sense.

[7] If the element of water has so many uses, then the others may also be supposed to be suitable for the service of human beings.

[8] We walk unthinkingly on the herbs which cure our ailments.

Since then, my God, thou hast
50 So brave a Palace built; O dwell in it,
That it may dwell with thee at last!
Till then, afford us so much wit;
That, as the world serves us, we may serve thee,
And both thy servants be.
—1633

Life

I made a posy, while the day ran by:
Here will I smell my remnant out, and tie
My life within this band.
But time did beckon to the flowers, and they
5 By noon most cunningly did steal away,
And withered in my hand.

My hand was next to them, and then my heart:
I took, without more thinking, in good part
Time's gentle admonition:
10 Who did so sweetly death's sad taste convey,
Making my mind to smell my fatal day;
Yet sug'ring the suspicion.

Farewell dear flowers, sweetly your time ye spent,
Fit, while ye lived, for smell or ornament,
15 And after death for cures.
I follow straight without complaints or grief,
Since if my scent be good, I care not, if
It be as short as yours.
—1633

Jordan (II)

When first my lines of heav'nly joys made
mention,
Such was their lustre, they did so excel,
That I sought out quaint words, and trim
invention;
My thoughts began to burnish, sprout, and swell,

5 Curling with metaphors a plain intention,
Decking the sense, as if it were to sell.

Thousands of notions in my brain did run,
Off'ring their service, if I were not sped:
I often blotted what I had begun;
10 This was not quick enough, and that was dead.
Nothing could seem too rich to clothe the sun,
Much less those joys which trample on his head.

As flames do work and wind, when they ascend,
So did I weave myself into the sense.
15 But while I bustled, I might hear a friend
Whisper, *How wide is all this long pretence!*
There is in love a sweetness ready penned:
Copy out only that, and save expense.
—1633

The Quip

The merry world did on a day
With his train-bands and mates agree
To meet together, where I lay, [1]
And all in sport to jeer at me.

5 First, Beauty crept into a rose,
Which when I plucked not, Sir, said she,
Tell me, I pray, Whose hands are those?
But thou shalt answer, Lord, for me.

Then Money came, and chinking still,
10 What tune is this, poor man? said he:
I heard in music you had skill.
But thou shalt answer, Lord, for me.

Then came brave Glory puffing by
In silks that whistled, who but he?
15 He scarce allowed me half an eye.
But thou shalt answer, Lord, for me.

---

[1] *train-bands* trained bands; London's citizen militia.

Then came quick Wit-and-Conversation,
And he would needs a comfort be,
And, to be short, make an oration.[1]
20 *But thou shalt answer, Lord, for me.*

Yet when the hour of thy design
To answer these fine things shall come;
Speak not at large; say, I am thine:
And then they have their answer home.
—1633

Providence [2]

O Sacred Providence, who from end to end
Strongly and sweetly movest, shall I write,
And not of thee, through whom my fingers bend
To hold my quill? shall they not do thee right?

5 Of all the creatures both in sea and land
Only to Man thou hast made known thy ways,
And put the pen alone into his hand,
And made him Secretary of thy praise.

Beasts fain would sing; birds ditty to their notes;
10 Trees would be tuning on their native lute
To thy renown: but all their hands and throats
Are brought to Man, while they are lame and mute.

Man is the world's high Priest: he doth present
The sacrifice for all; while they below
15 Unto the service mutter an assent,
Such as springs use that fall, and winds that blow. [3]

He that to praise and laud thee doth refrain,
Doth not refrain unto himself alone,
But robs a thousand who would praise thee fain,
20 And doth commit a world of sin in one.

The beasts say, Eat me: but, if beasts must teach,
The tongue is yours to eat, but mine to praise.
The trees say, Pull me: but the hand you stretch,
Is mine to write, as it is yours to raise. [4]

25 Wherefore, most sacred Spirit, I here present
For me and all my fellows praise to thee: [5]
And just it is that I should pay the rent,
Because the benefit accrues to me.

We all acknowledge both thy power and love
30 To be exact, transcendent, and divine;
Who dost so strongly and so sweetly move,
While all things have their will, yet none but thine.

For either thy command or thy permission
Lay hands on all: they are thy right and left.
35 The first puts on with speed and expedition;
The other curbs sin's stealing pace and theft.

Nothing escapes them both; all must appear,
And be disposed, and dressed, and tuned by thee,
Who sweetly temper'st all. If we could hear
40 Thy skill and art, what music would it be! [6]

Thou art in small things great, not small in any:
Thy even praise can neither rise, not fall.
Thou art in all things one, in each thing many:
For thou art infinite in one and all.

[1] *oration* Herbert had been Public Orator at Cambridge.

[2] This poem has many echoes of Psalm 104, of which the heading in the Authorized Version is *A meditation upon the majesty and providence of God.*

[3] One of the differences between Herbert and Vaughan is that the latter thought of the creatures as able to praise God for themselves, without Man as intermediary. Hutchinson quotes a relevant passage from Henry More's *Antidote to Atheism*: "One singular end of man's creation is that he may be a *Priest* in this magnificent *Termple* of the *Universe*, and send up Prayers and praises to the great Creator of all things in behalf of the rest of the Creatures."

[4] For a similarly anthropocentric version of humanity's relation to the non-human world, see Donne's Holy Sonnet 12, which begins "Why are we by all creatures waited on?"

[5] Herbert is addressing the Holy Spirit, third Person of the Trinity.

[6] *temper'st* In this context, it seems likely that Herbert has in mind the musical sense, to bring into harmony.

45 Tempests are calm to thee; they know thy hand,
   And hold it fast, as children do their fathers',
   Which cry and follow. Thou hast made poor sand
      Check the proud sea, ev'n when it swells and
         gathers.

   Thy cupboard serves the world: the meat is set,
50 Where all may reach: no beast but knows his feed.
   Birds teach us hawking; fishes have their net:
      The great prey on the less, they on some weed.

   Nothing engendered doth prevent his meat: [1]
   Flies have their table spread, ere they appear.
55 Some creatures have in winter what to eat;
      Others do sleep, and envy not their cheer.

   How finely dost thou times and seasons spin,
   And make a twist checkered with night and day! [2]
   Which as it lengthens winds, and winds us in,
60   As bowls go on, but turning all the way. [3]

   Each creature hath a wisdom for his good.
   The pigeons feed their tender off-spring, crying,
   When they are callow; but withdraw their food
      When they are fledge, that need may teach them
         flying.

65 Bees work for man; and yet they never bruise
   Their master's flower, but leave it, having done,
   As fair as ever, and as fit to use;
      So both the flower doth stay, and honey run.

   Sheep eat the grass, and dung the ground for more:
70 Trees after bearing drop their leaves for soil:

   Springs vent their streams, and by expense get store:
   Clouds cool by heat, and baths by cooling boil.

   Who hath the virtue to express the rare
   And curious virtues both of herbs and stones?
75 Is there an herb for that? O that thy care
      Would show a root, that gives expressions!

   And if a herb hath power, what have the stars?
   A rose, besides his beauty, is a cure. [4]
   Doubtless our plagues and plenty, peace and wars
80 Are there much surer than our art is sure.

   Thou hast hid metals: man may take them thence;
   But at his peril: when he digs the place,
   He makes a grave; as if the thing had sense,
      And threatened man, that he should fill the space. [5]

85 Ev'n poisons praise thee. Should a thing be lost?
   Should creatures want for want of heed their due?
   Since where are poisons, antidotes are most:
      The help stands close, and keeps the fear in view.

   The sea, which seems to stop the traveller,
90 Is by a ship the speedier passage made.
   The winds, who think they rule the mariner,
      Are ruled by him, and taught to serve his trade.

   And as thy house is full, so I adore
   Thy curious art in marshalling thy goods.
95 The hills with health abound; the vales with store;
      The South with marble; North with furs and
         woods.

   Hard things are glorious; easy things good cheap.
   The common all men have; that which is rare

---

[1] *prevent* come, appear, or act before (*OED* prevent *v* 1c). No
creature appears before there is food for it. This sense of "prevent"
came down through the centuries in the Collect for Easter Day in the
Book of Common Prayer, where we read of God's "special grace
preventing us" and putting "into our minds good desires."

[2] *twist* the twisting of threads into a cord (*OED* twist sb [1] II).

[3] In lawn bowling, players roll a ball weighted on one side to make
the ball move in a curved path.

---

[4] Oil of roses was used to mitigate the smart of wounds.

[5] Mining was thought to be a morally dubious activity from early
times; compare Milton's reference to "treasures better hid" in *Paradise
Lost* 1: 688.

Men therefore seek to have, and care to keep.
100 The healthy frosts with summer- fruits compare.

Light without wind is glass: warm without weight
Is wool and fur: cool without closeness, shade:
Speed without pains, a horse: tall without height,
A servile hawk: low without loss, a spade.

105 All countries have enough to serve their need:
If they seek fine things, thou dost make them run
For their offence; and then dost turn their speed
To be commerce and trade from sun to sun. [1]

Nothing wears clothes, but Man; nothing doth
    need
110 But he to wear them. Nothing useth fire,
But Man alone, to show his heav'nly breed:
And only he hath fuel in desire.

When th' earth was dry, thou mad'st a sea of wet:
When that lay gathered, thou didst broach the
    mountains:
115 When yet some places could no moisture get,
The winds grew gard'ners, and the clouds good
    fountains.

Rain, do not hurt my flowers; but gently speed
Your honey drops: press not to smell them here:
When they are ripe, their odour will ascend,
120 And at your lodging with their thanks appear.

How harsh are thorns to pears! and yet they make
A better hedge, and need less reparation. [2]
How smooth are silks compared with a stake,
Or with a stone! yet make no good foundation.

125 Sometimes thou dost divide thy gifts to man,
Sometimes unite. The Indian nut alone [3]
Is clothing, meat and trencher, drink and can, [4]
Boat, cable, sail and needle, all in one.

Most herbs that grow in brooks, are hot and dry.
130 Cold fruits warm kernels help, against the wind. [5]
The lemon's juice and rind cure mutually.
The whey of milk doth loose, the milk doth bind.

Thy creatures leap not, but express a feast, [6]
Where all the guests sit close, and nothing wants.
135 Frogs marry fish and flesh; bats, bird and beast;
Sponges, non-sense and sense; mines, th' earth
    and plants.

To show thou art not bound, as if thy lot
Were worse than ours, sometimes thou shiftest
    hands.
Most things move th' under-jaw; the Crocodile not.
140 Most things sleep lying; th' Elephant leans or
    stands. [7]

----

[3] *Indian nut* coconut.

[4] *trencher* "Until the fifteenth century and sometimes afterwards meat was served on to large trimmed squares of coarse bread…which served as a plate and mopped up the gravy. They were called *trenchers*, and as they were joined and replaced by wooden plates the name was retained" (Jacqueline Fearn, *Domestic Bygones*).

[5] This line can be read three ways; Grosart and Palmer thought of *cold fruits* as a genitive (the warm kernels of the cold fruits); Hutchinson as the object of *help*. I am reading it as the subject of *warm* and of *help*, and have supplied a comma after *help*. The sense is that the fruits, though cold, insulate the kernels and keep them warm in spite of the wind.

[6] This line expresses two related ideas, the fact that nature is gradual, with every rung of the ladder of being occupied; and the idea of nature's bounty, or plenitude.

[7] Hutchinson remarks that the supposed fact that the elephant does not lie down at night was a common illustration in mediaeval preaching; Sir Thomas Browne casts doubt on the idea in *Pseudodoxia Epidemica*.

----

[1] In the fourth chapter of *A Priest to the Temple*, Herbert wrote, in effect, that God disposed matters so that no one country bears all things, in order that commerce might flourish.

[2] *to* compared to.

But who hath praise enough? nay, who hath any?
None can express thy works, but he that knows
    them:
And none can know thy works, which are so many,
And so complete, but only he that owes them. [1]

145 All things that are, though they have sev'ral ways,
Yet in their being join with one advice
To honour thee: and so I give thee praise
In all my other hymns, but in this twice.

Each thing that is, although in use and name
150 It go for one, hath many ways in store
To honour thee; and so each hymn thy fame
Extolleth many ways, yet this one more.
—1633

Paradise

I bless thee, Lord, because I GROW
  Among thy trees, which in a ROW
To thee both fruit and order OW.

5 What open force, or hidden CHARM
Can blast my fruit, or bring me HARM,
While the inclosure is thine ARM?

Inclose me still for fear I START.
Be to me rather sharp and TART,
Than let me want thy hand and ART.

10 When thou dost greater judgements SPARE,
And with thy knife but prune and PARE,
Ev'n fruitful trees more fruitful ARE.

Such sharpness shows the sweetest FREND:
Such cuttings rather heal than REND:
15 And such beginnings touch their END.
—1633

[1] *owes* owns (*OED* owe *v* B I).

The Pilgrimage [2]

I travelled on, seeing the hill, where lay
    My expectation.
A long it was and weary way.
  The gloomy cave of Desperation
5 I left on th' one and on the other side
    The rock of Pride.

And so I came to Fancy's meadow strowed
    With many a flower:
Fain would I here have made abode,
10   But I was quickened by my hour.
So to Care's copse I came, and there got through
    With much ado.

That led me to the wild of Passion, which
    Some call the wold; [3]
15 A wasted place, but sometimes rich.
  Here I was robbed of all my gold,
Save one good Angel, which a friend had tied
    Close to my side. [4]

At length I got unto the gladsome hill, [5]
20   Where lay my hope,
Where lay my heart; and climbing still,
  When I had gained the brow and top,
A lake of brackish waters on the ground
    Was all I found.

[2] This poem may have led Henry Vaughan, a great admirer of Herbert, to write his more complex account of spiritual pilgrimage, "Regeneration."

[3] *wold* a piece of open country, a plain; in later use chiefly, an elevated tract of open country or moorland (*OED* wold 3). Hutchinson points out that the hilly tracts of Lincolnshire, which Herbert had visited, were so called.

[4] *Angel* an old English gold coin (*OED* angel *sb* III.6); it had on it the device of St. Michael, guardian angel of the British Isles; there is also a pun on the sense of guardian angel.

[5] *Gladsome* cheering, pleasant (*OED* gladsome *a* 1).

25 With that abashed and struck with many a sting
Of swarming fears,
I fell, and cried, Alas my King!
Can both the way and end be tears?
Yet taking heart I rose, and then perceived
30 I was deceived:

My hill was further: so I flung away,
Yet heard a cry
Just as I went, *None goes that way*
And lives: If that be all, said I,
35 After so foul a journey death is fair,
And but a chair. [1]

—1633

The Collar

I struck the board, and cried, No more.
I will abroad.
What? shall I ever sigh and pine?
My lines and life are free; free as the road,
5 Loose as the wind, as large as store. [2]
Shall I be still in suit?
Have I no harvest but a thorn
To let me blood, and not restore
What I have lost with cordial fruit?
10 Sure there was wine
Before my sighs did dry it: there was corn
Before my tears did drown it. [3]
Is the year only lost to me?
Have I no bays to crown it?
15 No flowers, no garlands gay? all blasted?
All wasted?
Not so, my heart: but there is fruit,
And thou hast hands.

Recover all thy sigh-blown age
20 On double pleasures: leave thy cold dispute
Of what is fit, and not. Forsake thy cage,
Thy rope of sands,
Which petty thoughts have made, and made to thee
Good cable, to enforce and draw,
25 And be thy law,
While thou didst wink and wouldst not see.
Away; take heed:
I will abroad.
Call in thy death's head there: tie up thy fears. [4]
30 He that forbears
To suit and serve his need,
Deserves his load.
But as I raved and grew more fierce and wild
At every word,
35 Me thoughts I heard one calling, *Child*:
And I replied, *My Lord*.

—1633

The Pulley [5]

When God at first made man,
Having a glass of blessings standing by;
Let us (said he) pour on him all we can:
Let the world's riches, which dispersed lie,
5 Contract into a span.

So strength first made a way;
Then beauty flowed, then wisdom, honour,
pleasure:
When almost all was out, God made a stay,
Perceiving that alone of all his treasure
10 Rest in the bottom lay.

[1] *And but a chair* as comfortable as a sedan chair, an enclosed chair or covered vehicle for one person, carried on poles by two men (*OED* chair *sb* 10).

[2] *store* plenty, abundance (*OED* store *sb* 4b).

[3] *corn* grain.

[4] The death's head, or skull, was a common emblem during the Renaissance, a reminder of the fragility and shortness of earthly life and the inevitability of death and the life hereafter.

[5] This poem reworks a version of the classical story of Pandora's box, in which hope remained at the bottom of her box after the divine blessings it had contained escaped when she opened it.

For if I should (said he)
Bestow this jewel also on my creature,
He would adore my gifts instead of me,
And rest in Nature, not the God of Nature:
15   So both should losers be.

        Yet let him keep the rest,
But keep them with repining restlessness:
Let him be rich and weary, that at least,
If goodness lead him not, yet weariness
20   May toss him to my breast.
        —1633

The Flower

How fresh, O Lord, how sweet and
        clean
Are thy returns! ev'n as the flowers in
        spring;
To which, besides their own demean, [1]
The late-past frosts tributes of pleasure bring.
5   Grief melts away
            Like snow in May,
    As if there were no such cold thing.

    Who would have thought my shrivelled
        heart
Could have recovered greenness? It was gone
10   Quite under ground; as flowers depart
To see their mother-root, when they have blown;
            Where they together
            All the hard weather,
    Dead to the world, keep house unknown.

15   These are thy wonders, Lord of power,
Killing and quick'ning, bringing down to hell
        And up to heaven in an hour;
Making a chiming of a passing-bell.
            We say amiss,

20   This or that is:
    Thy word is all, if we could spell.

    O that I once past changing were,
Fast in thy Paradise, where no flower can wither!
        Many a spring I shoot up fair,
25 Off'ring at heav'n, growing and groaning thither:
            Nor doth my flower
            Want a spring shower,
    My sins and I joining together.

    But while I grow in a straight line,
30 Still upwards bent, as if heav'n were mine own,
        Thy anger comes, and I decline:
What frost to that? what pole is not the zone,
            Where all things burn,
            When thou dost turn,
35   And the least frown of thine is shown?

    And now in age I bud again,
After so many deaths I live and write;
        I once more smell the dew and rain,
And relish versing: O my only light,
40   It cannot be
            That I am he
    On whom thy tempests fell all night.

    These are thy wonders, Lord of love,
To make us see we are but flowers that glide: [2]
45   Which when we once can find and prove,
Thou hast a garden for us, where to bide.
            Who would be more, [3]
            Swelling through store,
    Forfeit their Paradise by their pride.
        —1633

---

[1] *demean* demeanour.

[2] *glide*   to pass from one place to another (*OED* glide *v* 4).

[3] *who would*   those who would be more.

Aaron

Holiness on the head,
  Light and perfections on the breast,
Harmonious bells below, raising the dead
  To lead them unto life and rest:
5   Thus are true Aarons drest. [1]

  Profaneness in my head,
  Defects and darkness in my breast,
A noise of passions ringing me for dead
  Unto a place where is no rest:
10   Poor priest thus am I drest.

  Only another head
  I have, another heart and breast,
Another music, making live not dead,
  Without whom I could have no rest:
15   In him I am well drest.

  Christ is my only head,
  My alone only heart and breast,
My only music, striking me ev'n dead;
  That to the old man I may rest, [2]
20   And be in him new drest.

  So holy in my head,
  Perfect and light in my dear breast,
My doctrine tuned by Christ, (who is not dead
  But lives in me while I do rest)
25   Come people; Aaron's drest.
—1633

The Elixir

Teach me, my God and King,
  In all things thee to see,
And what I do in any thing,
  To do it as for thee:

5 Not rudely, as a beast,
  To run into an action;
But still to make thee prepossessed,
  And give it his perfection.

  A man that looks on glass,
10 On it may stay his eye;
Or if he pleaseth, through it pass,
  And then the heav'n espy.

  All may of thee partake:
  Nothing can be so mean, [3]
15 Which with his tincture (for thy sake)
  Will not grow bright and clean. [4]

  A servant with this clause
  Makes drudgery divine:
Who sweeps a room, as for thy laws,
20 Makes that and th' action fine. [5]

  This is the famous stone
  That turneth all to gold: [6]
For that which God doth touch and own
  Cannot for less be told.
—1633

---

[1] *true Aarons* Aaron, the brother of Moses, was the first priest; for the description of his garments, see Exodus 28:2–43.

[2] *old man* the "old man" of sin, before the believer is "new dressed" in the imputed righteousness of Christ.

---

[3] *mean* shabby (*OED* mean *a* 3d).

[4] *tincture* the action of dyeing, staining, or colouring (tincture *OED sb*3). The "tincture" is Christ's blood, shed for sinners. The Old and New Testaments contain many references to the cleansing power of sacrificially let blood. See Exodus 30:10, Leviticus 1, Psalm 51, Hebrews 13:12, Revelation 7:14.

[5] See Colossians 3:23: "And whatsoever ye do, do it heartily, as to the Lord, and not unto men."

[6] *famous stone* the fabled "philosopher's stone."

Love (III)

Love bade me welcome: yet my soul drew back,
    Guilty of dust and sin.
But quick-eyed Love, observing me grow slack
    From my first entrance in,
5 Drew nearer to me, sweetly questioning,
    If I lacked any thing.

A guest, I answered, worthy to be here:
    Love said, You shall be he.
I the unkind, ungrateful? Ah my dear,
10   I cannot look on thee.
Love took my hand, and smiling did reply,
    Who made the eyes but I?

Truth Lord, but I have marred them: let my shame
15   Go where it doth deserve.
And know you not, says Love, who bore the blame?
    My dear, then I will serve.
You must sit down, says Love, and taste my meat:
20   So I did sit and eat.
  —1633

L'Envoy [1]

King of Glory, King of Peace,
  With the one make war to cease;
With the other bless thy sheep,
Thee to love, in thee to sleep.
5 Let not sin devour thy fold,
Bragging that thy blood is cold,
That thy death is also dead,
While his conquests daily spread;
That thy flesh hath lost his food,
10 And thy cross is common wood.
Choke him, let him say no more,
But reserve his breath in store,
Till thy conquests and his fall
Make his sighs to use it all,
15 And then bargain with the wind
To discharge what is behind.

    Blessed be God alone,
    Thrice blessed three in one.
  —1633

---

[1] *L'Envoy* to send forth a poem; hence, the concluding part of a poetical composition; the author's parting words (*OED* envoy *sb¹* 1).

Thomas Carew
1594/5 – 1640

Thomas Carew was the son of Matthew Carew, a notable lawyer, and his wife Alice Ryvers, whose father and grandfather had been Lord Mayors of London. Nothing is known of Carew's boyhood and early education. He went up to Merton College, Oxford, at the age of thirteen. That college may have been chosen because its Warden, Henry Savile, was a kinsman by marriage. Savile is notable for having expressed a preference for "the plodding student," saying that if he wanted wits he would "go to Newgate" (a London prison). Carew took his B.A. in 1611, and then studied law at the Middle Temple. His period of study there may have been cut short by serious financial losses his father suffered. He became secretary to Sir Dudley Carleton, ambassador to Venice. This position enabled him to spend a considerable time in Italy, and his work indicates a close knowledge of Italian poetry and philosophy. However, he was eventually dismissed, to his father's rage and despair, for writing a satire on his employer and his wife. In 1619 he became secretary to Sir Edward (later Lord) Herbert of Cherbury, and, along with a hundred or so other persons, accompanied Herbert on his embassy to Paris. There is only one reference to Carew in Herbert's autobiography; he is described as "that excellent wit." While in Paris Carew may have met Giambattista Marino, upon whose "fantastic" Italian lyrics he modelled some of his own poems. The Earl of Clarendon mentions Carew as one of the notable wits with whom he was acquainted, in the period 1625–1632 (others in this circle included Ben Jonson, John Selden, Charles Cotton, Sir Kenelm Digby, and Thomas May). Clarendon writes of Carew that he was "a Person of a pleasant and facetious Wit, and made many Poems (especially in the amorous Way) which for the Sharpness of the Fancy, and the Elegancy of the Languge, in which that Fancy was spread, were at least equal, if not superior, to any of that Time." Carew's "A Rapture" is almost certainly one of the poems "in the amorous Way" here mentioned, though it circulated only in manuscript until its publication in 1640; it is echoed in an anonymous tragedy, *Nero*, printed in 1624. In 1630 Carew was appointed to the Court position of "gentleman of the Privy Chamber" and to the post of Sewer in Ordinary to the king. This title, from the Latin verb assidere, to sit, originally signified one who superintended the arrangement of the table, the seating of guests, and the tasting and serving of dishes. By Carew's time it seems to have been applied to one who assisted at ceremonies. Carew's masque *Coelum Britannicum*, with a set designed by Inigo Jones, was performed by the King and his gentleman in 1634. Carew for the most part distanced himself from the political stresses of the 1630s, but he was in the expedition which Charles I led against Scotland in 1639 in the first Bishops' War, as we learn from his poem "To my friend G.N. from Wrest." This campaign may have hastened his death; contemporary accounts confirm the "raging storms" and "cold nights...by the banks of Tweed" mentioned in the poem; the spring of 1639 was abnormally cold, and the expedition was badly supplied. This poem seems to have been completed very shortly before Carew's death in March 1640.

❧❧❧

A deposition from Love

I was foretold, your rebel sex,
  Nor love, nor pity knew;
And with what scorn, you use to vex
  Poor hearts, that humbly sue;
5 Yet I believed, to crown our pain,
  Could we the fortress win,
The happy lover sure should gain
  A Paradise within:

I thought love's plagues, like dragons sate,
10   Only to fright us at the gate.

But I did enter, and enjoy,
What happy lovers prove;
For I could kiss, and sport, and toy,
And taste those sweets of love;
15   Which had they but a lasting state,
Or if in *Celia's* breast,
The force of love might not abate,
Jove were too mean a guest.
But now her breach of faith, far more
20   Afflicts, than did her scorn before.

Hard fate! to have been once possessed
As victor, of a heart,
Achieved with labour, and unrest,
25   And then forced to depart.
If the stout foe will not resign,
When I besiege a town,
I lose, but what was never mine;
But he that is cast down
30   From enjoyed beauty, feels a woe,
Only deposed kings can know.
—1640

Disdain returned.

He that loves a rosy cheek,
    Or a coral lip admires,
Or from star-like eyes doth seek
    Fuel to maintain his fires;
5   As old *Time* makes these decay,
So his flames must waste away.

But a smooth, and steadfast mind,
    Gentle thoughts, and calm desires,
Hearts, with equal love combined,
10   Kindle never dying fires.

Where these are not, I despise
Lovely cheeks, or lips, or eyes.

No tears, *Celia,* now shall win,
    My resolved heart, to return;
15   I have searched thy soul within,
    And find nought, but pride, and scorn;
I have learned thy arts, and now
    Can disdain as much as thou.
Some power, in my revenge convey
20   That love to her, I cast away.
—1640

To Saxham [1]

Though frost, and snow, locked from mine
    eyes
That beauty which without door lies;
Thy gardens, orchards, walks, that so
I might not all thy pleasures know;
5   Yet (Saxham) thou within thy gate,
Art of thy self so delicate;
So full of native sweets, that bless
Thy roof with inward happiness;
As neither from, nor to thy store
10   Winter takes ought, or Spring adds more.
The cold and frozen air had sterved
Much poor, if not by thee preserved; [2]
Whose prayers have made thy table blest
With plenty, far above the rest.
15   The season hardly did afford
Course cates unto thy neighbour's board,
Yet thou hadst dainties, as the sky
Had only been thy Volary; [3]

---

[1] Little Saxham was the home of Sir John Crofts, whose son John
accompanied Carew on the embassy of Lord Herbert of Cherbury.
Carew had close relations with the family, as a number of poems attest.
Compare Jonson's *To Penshurst.*

[2] *sterved*   killed by the cold.

[3] *Volary*   a large bird-cage or aviary (*OED* volary).

Or else the birds, fearing the snow
20 Might to another deluge grow:
The pheasant, partridge, and the lark,
Flew to thy house, as to the Ark.
The willing ox, of himself came
Home to the slaughter, with the lamb,
25 And every beast did thither bring
Himself, to be an offering.
The scaley herd, more pleasure took,
Bathed in thy dish, than in the brook:
Water, earth, air, did all conspire,
30 To pay their tributes to thy fire,
Whose cherishing flames themselves divide
Through every room, where they deride
The night, and cold abroad; whilst they
Like suns within, keep endless day.
35 Those cheerful beams send forth their light,
To all that wander in the night,
And seem to beckon from aloof,
The weary pilgrim to thy roof;
Where if refreshed, he will away,
40 He's fairly welcome, or if stay
Far more, which he shall hearty find,
Both from the master, and the hind.
The strangers welcome, each man there
Stamped on his cheerful brow, doth wear;
45 Nor doth this welcome, or his cheer
Grow less, 'cause he stays longer here.
There's none observes (much less repines)
How often this man sups or dines.
Thou hast no porter at the door
50 T'examine, or keep back the poor;
Nor locks, nor bolts; thy gates have been
Made only to let strangers in;
Untaught to shut, they do not fear
To stand wide open all the year;
55 Careless who enters, for they know,
Thou never didst deserve a foe;
And as for thieves, thy bounty's such,
They cannot steal, thou giv'st so much.
—1640

A Rapture

I will enjoy thee now my Celia, come
And fly with me to love's Elysium: [1]
The giant, Honour, that keeps cowards out,
Is but a masker, and the servile rout
5 Of baser subjects only, bend in vain
To the vast idol, whilst the nobler train
Of valiant lovers, daily sail between
The huge Colossus' legs, and pass unseen [2]
Unto the blissful shore; be bold, and wise,
10 And we shall enter, the grim Swiss denies
Only tame fools a passage, that not know
He is but form, and only frights in show [3]
The duller eyes that look from far; draw near,
And thou shalt scorn, what we were wont to fear.
15 We shall see how the stalking pageant goes
With borrowed legs, a heavy load to those
That made, and bear him; not as we once thought
The seed of gods, but a weak model wrought
By greedy men, that seek to enclose the common,
20 And within private arms impale free woman.
   Come then, and mounted on the wings of love
We'll cut the flitting air, and soar above
The monster's head, and in the noblest seats
Of those blest shades, quench, and renew our
      heats.
25 There, shall the Queen of Love, and Innocence,
Beauty and Nature, banish all offence
From our close ivy twines, there I'll behold
Thy bared snow, and thy unbraided gold.
There, my enfranchised hand, on every side

---

[1] *Elysium*   abode or state of the blessed after death in Greek mythology (*OED* Elysium).

[2] *Colossus*   a statue or image of the human form of very large dimensions; the most famous in the ancient world being the bronze statue of Apollo at Rhodes, one of the seven wonders of the world, reputed to have stood astride the entrance to the Rhodian harbour (*OED* Colossus).

[3] *the grim Swiss*   in allusion to the Swiss guardsmen at the Vatican, and other places in early modern Europe.

30 Shall o'er thy naked polished ivory slide.
No curtain there, though of transparent lawn,
Shall be before thy virgin-treasure drawn;
But the rich mine, to the enquiring eye
Exposed, shall ready still for mintage lie,
35 And we will coin young Cupids. There, a bed
Of roses, and fresh myrtles, shall be spread
Under the cooler shade of cypress groves:
Our pillows, of the down of Venus' doves,
Whereon our panting limbs we'll gently lay
40 In the faint respites of our active play;
That so our slumbers, may in dreams have leisure,
To tell the nimble fancy our past pleasure;
And so our souls that cannot be embraced,
Shall the embraces of our bodies taste.
45 Meanwhile the bubbling stream shall court the
    shore,
Th'enamoured chirping wood-choir shall adore
In varied tunes the deity of love;
The gentle blasts of western winds, shall move
The trembling leaves, and through their close
    bow's breath
50 Still music, whilst we rest our selves beneath
Their dancing shade; till a soft murmur, sent
From souls entranced in amorous languishment
Rouse us, and shoot into our veins fresh fire,
Till we, in their sweet ecstasy expire.
55   Then, as the empty bee, that lately bore,
Into the common treasure, all her store,
Flies 'bout the painted field with nimble wing,
Deflowring the fresh virgins of the spring;
So will I rifle all the sweets, that dwell
60 In my delicious paradise, and swell
My bag with honey, drawn forth by the power
Of fervent kisses, from each spicy flower.
I'll seize the rose-buds in their perfumed bed,
The violet knots, like curious mazes spread
65 O'er all the garden, taste the ripned cherry,
The warm, firm apple, tipped with coral berry:
Then will I visit, with a wandring kiss,
The vale of lilies, and the bower of bliss:

And where the beauteous region doth divide
70 Into two milky ways, my lips shall slide
Down those smooth allies, wearing as I go
A tract for lovers on the printed snow;
Thence climbing o'er the swelling Appenine,
Retire into thy grove of eglantine;
75 Where I will all those ravished sweets distill
Through love's alembic, and with chymic skill
From the mixed mass, one sovereign balm derive,
Then bring that great elixir to thy hive.
    Now in more subtle wreathes I will entwine
80 My sinewy thighs, my legs and arms with thine;
Thou like a sea of milk shalt lie displayed,
Whilst I the smooth, calm ocean, invade
With such a tempest, as when Jove of old
Fell down on Danae in a storm of gold: [1]
85 Yet my tall pine, shall in the Cyprian strait
Ride safe at anchor, and unlade her freight: [2]
My rudder, with thy bold hand, like a tried,
And skillful pilot, thou shalt steer, and guide
My bark into love's channel, where it shall
90 Dance, as the bounding waves do rise or fall:
Then shall thy circling arms, embrace and clip [3]
My willing body, and thy balmy lip
Bathe me in juice of kisses, whose perfume
Like a religious incense shall consume,
95 And send up holy vapours, to those powers
That bless our loves, and crown our sportful
    hours,
That with such halcyon calmness, fix our souls
In steadfast peace, as no affright controls.
There, no rude sounds shake us with sudden
    starts,
100 No jealous ears, when we unrip our hearts
Suck our discourse in, no observing spies
This blush, that glance traduce; no envious eyes

---

[1] *as when Jove of old / Fell down on Danae* The shower of gold was one of Jove's many disguises; see *OCD* Perseus.

[2] *the Cyprian strait* Cyprus was in ancient times famous for the worship of Aphrodite or Venus.

[3] *clip* hug or embrace (*OED* clip *v* [1]).

Watch our close meetings, nor are we betrayed
To rivals, by the bribed chamber-maid.
105 No wedlock bonds unwreathe our twisted loves;
We seek no midnight arbor, no dark groves
To hide our kisses, there, the hated name
Of husband, wife, lust, modest, chaste, or shame,
Are vain and empty words, whose very sound
110 Was never heard in the Elysian ground.
All things are lawful there, that may delight
Nature, or unrestrained appetite;
Like, and enjoy, to will, and act, is one,
We only sin when love's rites are not done.
115   The Roman Lucrece there, reads the divine
Lectures of love's great master, Aretine,
And knows as well as Lais, how to move
Her pliant body in the act of love. [1]
To quench the burning ravisher, she hurls
120 Her limbs into a thousand winding curls,
And studies artful postures, such as be
Carved on the bark of every neighbouring tree
By learned hands, that so adorned the rind
Of those fair plants, which as they lay entwined,
125 Have fanned their glowing fires. The Grecian
        dame, [2]
That in her endless web, toiled for a name
As fruitless as her work, doth there display
Her self before the youth of Ithaca,
And th'amorous sport of gamesome nights prefer,
130 Before dull dreams of the lost traveller.
Daphne hath broke her bark, and that swift foot,
Which th'angry Gods had fastened with a root
To the fixed earth, doth now unfettered run,

To meet th'embraces of the youthful sun: [3]
135 She hangs upon him, like his Delphic lyre,
Her kisses blow the old, and breath new fire:
Full of her god, she sings inspired lays,
Sweet odes of love, such as deserve the bays,
Which she her self was. Next her, Laura lies
140 In Petrarch's learned arms, drying those eyes
That did in such sweet smooth-paced numbers
        flow,
As made the world enamoured of his woe.
These, and ten thousand beauties more, that
        died
Slave to the tyrant, now enlarged, deride
145 His cancelled laws, and for their time misspent,
Pay into love's exchequer double rent.
        Come then my Celia, we'll no more forbear
To taste our joys, struck with a panic fear,
But will depose from his imperious sway
150 This proud usurper and walk free, as they
With necks unyoked; nor is it just that he
Should fetter your soft sex with chastity,
Which nature made unapt for abstinence;
When yet this false impostor can dispense
155 With humane justice, and with sacred right,
And maugre both their laws command me fight [4]
With rivals, or with emulous loves, that dare
Equal with thine, their mistress' eyes, or hair:
If thou complain of wrong, and call my sword
160 To carve out thy revenge, upon that word
He bids me fight and kill, or else he brands
With marks of infamy my coward hands,
And yet religion bids from blood-shed fly,
And damns me for that act. Then tell me why
165 This goblin Honour which the world adores,
Should make men atheists, and not women
        whores.
—1640

---

[1] *The Roman Lucrece* a model of chastity; but "*Aretine's Lucretia* sold her maidenhead a thousand times before she was twenty years old" (Burton, *Anatomy of Melancholy*, Part III, Sect. II, Mem. I, Subs. II). Pietro Aretino was a famous Italian poet of eroticism, author of *Sonnetti Lussuriosi*, 1523. Jonson refers to him both in *Volpone* and *The Alchemist*; *Lais* a famous courtesan of Corinth.

[2] *The Grecian dame* Penelope, the wife of Odysseus.

[3] *Daphne hath broke her bark* Daphne was loved by Apollo, but she would have none of him; when he chased her, she prayed for help, and was turned into a laurel tree.

[4] *maugre* in spite of (*OED* maugre B 1).

To Ben Jonson

*Upon occasion of his Ode of defiance
annexed to his Play of the New Inn.*

Tis true (dear *Ben:*) thy just chastizing hand
Hath fixed upon the sotted Age a brand
To their swol'n pride, and empty
    scribbling due,
It can nor judge, nor write, and yet 'tis true
5 Thy comic Muse from the exalted line
Touched by thy *Alchemist*, doth since decline
From that her zenith, and foretells a red
And blushing evening, when she goes to bed,
Yet such, as shall out-shine the glimmering light
10 With which all stars shall gild the following night.
Nor think it much (since all thy eaglets may
Endure the sunny trial) if we say
This hath the stronger wing, or that doth shine
Tricked up in fairer plumes, since all are thine;
15 Who hath his flock of cackling geese compared
With thy tuned choir of swans? or else who dared
To call thy births deformed? but if thou bind
By city-custom, or by *gavel-kind,* [1]
In equal shares thy love on all thy race,
20 We may distinguish of their sex, and place,
Though one hand form them, & though one
    brain strike
Souls into all, they are not all alike.
Why should the follies then of this dull age
Draw from thy pen such an immodest rage
25 As seems to blast thy (else-immortal) bays,
When thine own tongue proclaims thy itch of
    praise?
Such thirst will argue drouth. No, let be hurled
Upon thy works, by the detracting world,
What malice can suggest; let the rout say;
30 The running sands, that (ere thou make a play)

Count the slow minutes, might a *Goodwin* frame [2]
To swallow when th'hast done thy ship-wreck's
    name.
Let them the dear expense of oil upbraid
Sucked by thy watchfull lamp, that hath betrayed
35 To theft the blood of martyred authors, spilt
Into thy ink, whilst thou growest pale with guilt.
Repine not at the taper's thrifty waste,
That sleeks thy terser poems, nor is haste
Praise, but excuse; and if thou overcome
40 A knotty writer, bring the booty home;
Nor think it theft, if the rich spoils so torn
From conquered authors, be as trophies worn.
Let others glut on the extorted praise
Of vulgar breath, trust thou to after days
45 Thy laboured works shall live, when Time
    devours
Th'abortive off-spring of their hasty hours.
Thou art not of their rank, the quarrel lies
Within thine own verge, then let this suffice,
The wiser world doth greater thee confess
50 Than all men else, than thy self only less.
—1640

An Elegy Upon the Death
of the Dean of Pauls, Dr. John Donne [3]

Can we not force from widowed poetry,
  Now thou art dead (great Donne) one elegy
To crown thy hearse? Why yet dare we not trust
Though with unkneaded dough-baked prose thy
    dust,
5 Such as the uncisored churchman from the flower
Of fading rhetoric, short lived as his hour, [4]
Dry as the sand that measures it, should lay

---

[1] *gavel-kind* a form of inheritance in which intestate property was
divided equally among sons.

[2] *Goodwin* the Goodwin sands, a famous navigational hazard.

[3] Donne had died on March 31, 1631; references by other poets
suggest that Carew's poem was written some time before its publication. It is interesting as literary criticism and as a basis for the discussion of Donne's work.

[4] *uncisored* unscissored, that is, with uncut hair.

Upon thy ashes, on the funeral day? [1]
Have we no voice, no tune? Didst thou dispense
10 Through all our language, both the words and
 sense?
'Tis a sad truth; The pulpit may her plain,
And sober Christian precepts still retain,
Doctrines it may, and wholesome uses frame,
Grave homilies, and lectures, but the flame
15 Of thy brave soul, (that shot such heat and light,
As burnt our earth, and made our darkness bright,
Committed holy rapes upon our will,
Did through the eye the melting heart distill;
And the deep knowledge of dark truths so teach,
20 As sense might judge, what fancy could not
 reach;)
Must be desir'd for ever. So the fire,
That fills with spirit and heat the Delphic choir,
Which kindled first by thy Promethean breath,
Glow'd here a while, lies quench't now in thy
 death;
25 The muses' garden with pedantic weeds
O'rspread, was purg'd by thee; the lazy seeds
Of servile imitation thrown away;
And fresh invention planted, thou didst pay
The debts of our penurious bankrupt age;
30 Licentious thefts, that make poetic rage
A mimic fury, when our souls must be
Possessed, or with Anacreon's ecstasy,
Or Pindar's, not their own; the subtle cheat
Of sly exchanges, and the juggling feat
35 Of two-edg'd words, or whatsoever wrong
By ours was done the Greek, or Latin tongue,
Thou hast redeemed, and opened us a mine
Of rich and pregnant fancy, drawn a line
Of masculine expression, which had good
40 Old Orpheus seen, or all the ancient brood
Our superstitious fools admire, and hold
Their lead more precious, than thy burnished
 gold,
Thou hadst been their exchequer, and no more

They each in other's dust, had raked for ore.
45 Thou shalt yield no precedence, but of time,
And the blind fate of language, whose tuned
 chime
More charms the outward sense; yet thou mayst
 claim
From so great disadvantage greater fame,
Since to the awe of thy imperious wit
50 Our stubborn language bends, made only fit
With her tough-thick-ribbed hoops to gird about
Thy giant fancy, which had proved too stout
For their soft melting phrases. As in time
They had the start, so did they cull the prime
55 Buds of invention many a hundred year,
And left the rifled fields, besides the fear
To touch their harvest, yet from those bare lands
Of what is purely thine, thy only hands
(And that thy smallest work) have gleaned more
60 Than all those times, and tongues could reap
 before;
 But thou art gone, and thy strict laws will be
Too hard for libertines in poetry.
They will repeal the goodly exiled train
Of gods and goddesses, which in thy just reign
65 Were banished nobler poems, now, with these
The silenced tales o'th' Metamorphoses
Shall stuff their lines, and swell the windy page, [2]
Till verse refined by thee, in this last age
Turn ballad rhyme, or those old idols be
70 Adored again, with new apostasy;
 Oh, pardon me, that break with untuned
 verse
The reverend silence that attends thy hearse,
Whose awful solemn murmurs were to thee
More than these faint lines, a loud elegy,
75 That did proclaim in a dumb eloquence
The death of all the arts, whose influence
Grown feeble, in these panting numbers lies
Gasping short winded accents, and so dies:

[1] *the sand that measures it*   the sand of the hourglass.

[2] *Metamorphoses* Ovid's *Metamorphoses* had been the inspiration for
a good many Elizabethan poems.

Whiter than the silver swan
    That swims in Po;
If at any time they move her
Every step begets a lover.

25   All this but the casket is
    Which contains
Such a jewel, as the miss

    Breeds endless pains;
That's her mind, and they that know it
30 May admire, but cannot show it.
    —1651

James Shirley
1596 – 1666

James Shirley was born in St. Mary Woolchurch, London. He was educated at Merchant Taylor's School from 1608–1612 and then spent a few years at St. John's College, Oxford, before proceeding to Catharine Hall, Cambridge, where he received his B.A. He published his earliest known poem, *Eccho, or the Unfortunate Lovers,* in 1618. After taking orders Shirley moved to St. Albans in Hertfordshire where, from 1623–5, he held the mastership at the grammar school. In 1618 Shirley married Elizabeth Gilmet, by whom he had several children. Sometime during this period, although exactly when is unclear, Shirley converted to Catholicism. Around 1625, the year of the accession of Charles I, Shirley left the scholarly life and went to London where he became a playwright. His first play, *Love Tricks, with Complements*, was licensed in 1625–6, and was the first of many successful plays. Shirley became a respected dramatist, and won the favour of a variety of persons of rank. In 1636, the London theatres were closed because of plague, and Shirley went to Ireland, where he remained for four years, writing for the Irish theatre. Upon his return to London in 1640, he became the chief playwright for the King's Men at Blackfriars. In September 1642, as civil war was breaking out, Shirley left London and joined his patron, the Earl of Newcastle, in the wars. In 1644, after the Parliamentary victory at the Battle of Marston Moor, Shirley returned to London, where a number of his friends helped him to become re-established. In 1646 he published a volume of verse and also composed commendatory verses for the works of various other writers. Although he resumed school teaching, primarily at Whitefriars, he continued to publish both poems and plays. His final publications were in 1659. In 1666, James Shirley and his second wife, Frances, were driven from their home by the great fire of London. Both died shortly thereafter.

◦ↄ◦

"The glories of our blood and state"

The glories of our blood and state,
  Are shadows, not substantial things,
There is no armour against fate,
  Death lays his icy hand on kings,
5   Scepter and crown,
      Must tumble down,
And in the dust be equal made,
With the poor crooked scythe and spade.

Some men with swords may reap the field,
10   And plant fresh laurels where they kill, [1]
But their strong nerves at last must yield,
  They tame but one another still;
      Early or late,
      They stoop to fate,
15 And must give up their murmuring breath,
When they pale captives creep to death.

The garlands wither on your brow,
  Then boast no more your mighty deeds,
Upon Death's purple altar now,
20   See where the victor-victim bleeds,
      Your heads must come,
      To the cold tomb,
Only the actions of the just
Smell sweet, and blossom in their dust.
  —1646

---

[1] *laurels* a crown of laurel is used as an emblem of victory (*OED* laurel).

Rachel Speght
ca. 1597 – post 1621

Rachel Speght, the poet and polemical pamphleteer, was the daughter of James Speght, a Calvinist minister and rector of the London churches of St. Mary Magdalene, Milk Street (1592–1637) and St. Clement, Eastcheap (1611–1637). Her mother's identity is unknown. James Speght wrote *A brief demonstration, who have, and of the certainty of their salvation, that have the Spirit of Christ* (1613), and an epiphany sermon, *The Day-spring of Comfort* (1615). Speght's writings reveal that she had received some instruction in rhetoric and logic, a thorough knowledge of Scripture, a facility in Latin, and a familiarity with a wide range of authoritative classical and Christian texts.

In her first publication, *A Muzzle for Melastomus, the Cynical Baiter of, and foul mouthed Barker against Eve's Sex* (1617), Speght defends the nature and worth of women in response to Joseph Swetnam's notorious anti-feminist pamphlet, the *Arraignment of Lewd, Idle, Froward and Unconstant Women* (1615).[1] Of the three direct refutations of Swetnam's treatise, Speght's was the first and the only one published under the author's own name.[2] In 1621, the year of her marriage to William Procter, Speght published *Mortality's Memorandum with a Dream Prefixed*. The title poem of *Mortality's Memorandum* is an extended meditation on death, while the prefixed dream is an allegorical dream vision. In "The Dream" Speght allegorizes the female struggle to acquire knowledge, progressing from ignorance to enlightenment. "The Dream" may be read as a counter-myth to the Edenic tragedy in which female knowledge is inextricably bound up with sin and death. Nothing is known of Speght's life after her marriage.

❧❧❧

The Dream

from *Mortality's Memorandum,*
with a Dream Prefixed

When splendent Sol, which riseth in the East,
Returning thence took harbour in the West;
When Phoebe laid her head in Titan's lap,
And creatures sensitive made haste to rest;[1]
5 When sky which erst looked like to azure blue,
Left colour bright, and put on sable hue.

Then did Morpheus close my drowsy eyes,
And stood as porter at my senses' door,

Diurnal cares excluding from my mind;
10 Including rest, (the salve for labours sore.)[2]
Night's greatest part in quiet sleep I spent,
But nothing in this world is permanent.

For ere Aurora spread her glittering beams,
Or did with robes of light herself invest,
15 My mental quiet sleep did interdict,
By entertaining a nocturnal guest.[3]
A dream which did my mind and sense possess,
With more than I by pen can well express.

At the appointment of supernal power,
20 By instrumental means me thought I came
Into a place most pleasant to the eye,

---

[1] *Phoebe...Titan's lap* Phoebe is emended from Phoebus. Titan, an older god who existed before the Olympians, is often used in poetry for Hyperion, the Sun, and Phoebe for Artemis, the Moon; hence, the moon lays her head on the sun's lap. Lewalski suggests this line refers to the Titans cast out of heaven and immured in Tartarus, beneath the earth, rendering the line: the Titaness Phoebe (brightness) sleeps with her Titan mate in Tartarean darkness (Oxford, 1996).

[2] *Morpheus* one of the sons of Sleep who sends visions of human forms.

[3] *Aurora* goddess of the dawn; *interdict* prohibit (*OED* interdict *v* 1).

Which for the beauty some did Cosmus name, [1]
Where stranger-like on everything I gazed,
But wanting wisdom was as one amazed. [2]

25 Upon a sudden, as I gazing stood,
Thought came to me, and asked me of my state,
Inquiring what I was, and what I would,
And why I seemed as one disconsolate:
To whose demand, I thus again replied,
30 I, as a stranger in this place abide.

The haven of my voyage is remote,
I have not yet attained my journey's end;
Yet know I not, nor can I give a guess,
How short a time I in this place shall spend.
35 For that high power, which sent me to this place,
Doth only know the period of my race. [3]

The reason of my sadness at this time,
Is 'cause I feel myself not very well,
Unto you I shall much obliged be,
40 If for my grief a remedy you'll tell.
Quoth she, if you your malady will show,
My best advice I'll willingly bestow.

My grief, quoth I, is called Ignorance,
Which makes me differ little from a brute:
45 For animals are led by nature's lore,
Their seeming science is but custom's fruit; [4]
When they are hurt they have a sense of pain;
But want the sense to cure themselves again.

And ever since this grief did me oppress,
50 Instinct of nature is my chiefest guide;
I feel disease, yet know not what I ail,

I find a sore, but can no salve provide;
I hungry am, yet cannot seek for food;
Because I know not what is bad or good.

55 And sometimes when I seek the golden mean,
My weakness makes me fail of mine intent, [5]
That suddenly I fall into extremes,
Nor can I see a mischief to prevent; [6]
But feel the pain when I the peril find,
60 Because my malady doth make me blind.

What is without the compass of my brain, [7]
My sickness makes me say it cannot be;
What I conceive not, cannot come to pass;
Because for it I can no reason see.
65 I measure all men's feet by mine own shoe,
And count all well, which I appoint or do.

The pestilent effects of my disease
Exceed report, their number is so great;
The evils, which through it I do incur,
70 Are more than I am able to repeat.
Wherefore, good Thought, I sue to thee again,
To tell me how my cure I may obtain.

Quoth she, I wish I could prescribe your help;
Your state I pity much, and do bewail;
75 But for my part, though I am much employed,
Yet in my judgment I do often fail.
And therefore I'll commend unto your trial
Experience, of whom take no denial.

For she can best direct you, what is meet
80 To work your cure, and satisfy your mind;
I thanked her for her love, and took my leave,
Demanding where I might Experience find.

---

[1] *supernal* heavenly (*OED* supernal *a* A1); *Cosmus* perhaps an allusion to "cosmos," the world or universe as an ordered harmonious system, so called by Pythagoras.

[2] *wanting* lacking (*OED* wanting *vbl sb*).

[3] *period* duration (*OED* period *sb* II.5).

[4] *science* knowledge (*OED* science 1).

[5] *golden mean* the Aristotelian ideal of moderation in all things.

[6] *see…prevent* foresee misfortune to prevent it (*OED* mischief *sb* 1a).

[7] *without* outside (*OED* without *adv* A.I.3).

She told me if I did abroad inquire,
'Twas likely Age could answer my desire.

85 I sought, I found, she asked me what I would;
Quoth I, your best direction I implore:
For I am troubled with an irksome grief,
Which when I named, quoth she declare no more:
For I can tell as much, as you can say,
90 And for your cure I'll help you what I may.

The only medicine for your malady,
By which, and nothing else your help is wrought,
Is Knowledge, of the which there is two sorts,
The one is good, the other bad and nought;
95 The former sort by labour is attained,
The latter may without much toil be gained.

But 'tis the good, which must effect your cure,
I prayed her then, that she would further show,
Where I might have it, that I will, quoth she,
100 In Erudition's garden it does grow:
And in compassion of your woeful case,
Industry shall conduct you to the place.

Dissuasion hearing her assign my help,
(And seeing that consent I did detect)
105 Did many remoraes to me propose, [1]
As dullness, and my memory's defect;
The difficulty of attaining lore,
My time, and sex, with many others more.

Which when I heard, my mind was much perplexed,
110 And as a horse new come into the field,
Who with a Harquebus at first doth start, [2]
So did this shot make me recoil and yield.
But of my fear when some did notice take,
In my behalf, they this reply did make.

115 First quoth Desire, Dissuasion, hold thy peace,
These oppositions come not from above:
Quoth Truth, they cannot spring from reason's root,
And therefore now thou shalt no victor prove.
No, quoth Industry, be assured [of] this,
120 Her friends shall make thee of thy purpose miss.

For with my sickle I will cut away
All obstacles, that in her way can grow,
And by the issue of her own attempt,
I'll make thee *labor omnia vincet* know. [3]
125 Quoth Truth, and sith her sex thou do'st object, [4]
Thy folly I by reason will detect.

Both man and woman of three parts consist,
Which Paul doth body, soul, and spirit call: [5]
And from the soul three faculties arise,
130 The mind, the will, the power; then wherefore shall
A woman have her intellect in vain,
Or not endeavour knowledge to attain.

The talent, God doth give, must be employed, [6]
His own with vantage he must have again: [7]
135 All parts and faculties were made for use; [8]
The God of Knowledge nothing gave in vain.
'Twas Mary's choice our Saviour did approve,
Because that she the better part did love. [9]

---

[1] *remoraes* obstacles (*OED* remora 2).

[2] *Harquebus* an early type of portable gun (*OED* harquebus *sb* 1).

[3] *issue of her own attempt* product of her own endeavours (*OED* issue *sb* III.8a; *OED* attempt *v* I.1a); *labor omnia vincet* labour will conquer all things; an allusion to Virgil's *Georgics* 1.145. Compare to Virgil's "omnia vincit amor" (love conquers all) (*Eclogue* 10.69).

[4] *sith* since (*OED* sith *conj* C2).

[5] *Which Paul...and spirit call:* "I Thess. 5:3" (original marginalia).

[6] *The talent...be employed* "Luke 19:23" (original marginalia). In Luke's version of the parable of the talents, a wealthy man distributes money (talents) to his servants before going on a trip. Those who make a profit through trading are rewarded on his return, while the one who laid the money aside out of fear is berated and his money taken.

[7] *vantage* profit (*OED* vantage *sb* 1a).

[8] *All parts...made for use* "I Sam. 2:3" (original marginalia).

[9] *'Twas Mary's...part did love* "Luke 10:42" (original marginalia). Augustine believed that in Martha and Mary were figured the life temporal and the life eternal (*Sermons* 104.4), while later theologians

Cleobulina, and Demophila,
140 With Telesilla, as historians tell,
(Whose fame doth live, though they have long been
    dead)
Did all of them in poetry excel.
A Roman matron that Cornelia hight
An eloquent and learned style did write. [1]

145 Hypatia in astronomy had skill,
Aspatia was in rhetoric so expert,
As that Duke Pericles of her did learn;
Areta did devote herself to art:
And by consent (which shows she was no fool)
150 She did succeed her father in his school. [2]

And many others here I could produce,
Who were in Science counted excellent;
But these examples which I have rehearsed,
To show thy error are sufficient.
155 Thus having said, she turned her speech to me,
That in my purpose I might constant be.

My friend, quoth she, regard not vulgar talk;
For dung-hill cocks at precious stones will spurn,
And swine-like natures prize nor crystal streams,

160 Contemned mire, and mud will serve their turn. [3]
Good purpose seldom oppositions want:
But constant minds Dissuasion cannot daunt.

Shall every blast disturb the sailor's peace?
Or boughs and bushes travellers affright?
165 True valour doth not start at every noise;
Small combats must instruct for greater fight.
Disdain to be with every dart dismayed;
'Tis childish to be suddenly afraid.

If thou didst know the pleasure of the place,
170 Where Knowledge grows, and where thou mayst it
    gain;
Or rather knew the virtue of the plant
Thou would'st not grudge at any cost, or pain,
Thou canst bestow, to purchase for thy cure
This plant, by which of help thou shalt be sure.

175 Let not Dissuasion alter thy intent;
'Tis sin to nip good motions in the head; [4]
Take courage, and be constant in thy course,
Though irksome be the path, which thou must tread.
Sick folks drink bitter medicines to be well,
180 And to enjoy the nut men crack the shell.

When Truth had ended what she meant to say,
Desire did move me to obey her will,
Whereto consenting I did soon proceed,
Her counsel, and my purpose to fulfill;
185 And by the help of Industry my friend,
I quickly did attain my journey's end.

Where being come, Instruction's pleasant air
Refreshed my senses, which were almost dead,
And fragrant flowers of sage and fruitful plants,

---

identified Martha with the active life, Mary the contemplative.

[1] *Cleobulina...did write* Cleobuline (sixth century B.C.E.) and her father Cleobulus of Lindos co-authored a collection of riddles. Damophyle (seventh century B.C.E.), the lyric poet of Pamphilia, composed erotic poems and hymns to Artemis. Telesilla (fifth century B.C.E.), the Argive poetess, wrote hymns to Apollo and Artemis. She was renowned for arming the women of Argos against Spartan invaders. Cornelia (second century C.E.), the daughter of P. Scipio Africanus and mother of the two Gracchi tribunes, was a Roman letter writer whose epistles, admired by Cicero, were accounted models of style; *hight* called (*OED* hight *v¹* B.II.5).

[2] *Hypatia...in his school* Hypatia (fifth century B.C.E.) was an Alexandrian mathematician, astronomer and philosopher. Aspatia (fifth century B.C.E.), a philosopher who conversed with Socrates, was the mistress of the Athenian statesman Pericles, to whom she taught rhetoric. Areta (fifth century B.C.E.), an Athenian philosopher, was educated by her father Aristippus, the founder of the Cyrenian school of philosophy, and succeeded him as head of the school.

[3] *For dung-hill...their turn* Compare Syrus Publilius's "A cock has great influence on his own dung-hill" (first century B.C.E., Maxim 357) and John Heywood's "Every cock is proud of his own dunghill" (*Proverbs*, 1546, I.2); *contemned* despised (*OED* contemned *ppl.a*).

[4] *motions* inward promptings (*OED* motion *sb* 9a).

190 Did send sweet savours up into my head;
And taste of science appetite did move,
To augment Theory of things above.

There did the harmony of those sweet birds,
(Which higher soar with Contemplation's wings,
195 Then barely with a superficial view,
Denote the value of created things.)
Yield such delight as made me to implore,
That I might reap this pleasure more and more.

And as I walked wand'ring with Desire,
200 To gather that, for which I thither came;
(Which by the help of Industry I found)
I met my old acquaintance, Truth by name;
Whom I requested briefly to declare,
The virtue of that plant I found so rare.

205 Quoth she, by it God's image man doth bear, [1]
Without it he is but a human shape,
Worse than the Devil; for he knoweth much;
Without it who can any ill escape?
By virtue of it evils are withstood;
210 The mind without it is not counted good. [2]

Who wanteth Knowledge is a scripture fool, [3]
Against the ignorant the prophets pray;
And Hosea threatens judgment unto those,
Whom want of Knowledge made to run astray. [4]
215 Without it thou no practic good canst show,
More than by hap, as blind men hit a crow. [5]

True Knowledge is the window of the soul,
Through which her objects she doth speculate; [6]
It is the mother of faith, hope, and love;
220 Without it who can virtue estimate?
By it, in grace thou shalt desire to grow;
'Tis life eternal God and Christ to know. [7]

Great Alexander made so great account,
Of Knowledge, that he oftentimes would say,
225 That he to Aristotle was more bound
For Knowledge, upon which Death could not prey,
Than to his father Philip for his life,
Which was uncertain, irksome, full of strife. [8]

This true report put edge unto Desire,
230 Who did incite me to increase my store,
And told me 'twas a lawful avarice,
To covet Knowledge daily more and more.
This counsel I did willingly obey,
Till some occurrence called me away.

235 And made me rest content with that I had,
Which was but little, as effect does show;
And quenched hope for gaining any more,
For I my time must other-ways bestow.
I therefore to that place returned again,
240 From whence I came, and where I must remain.

---

[1] *Quoth she…does bear* "Col. 3:10" (original marginalia).

[2] *The mind…counted good* "Prov. 19:2" (original marginalia).

[3] *who wanteth…scripture fool* One who lacks knowledge is a fool according to Scripture; "Every prudent man dealeth with knowledge: but a fool layeth open his folly" (Proverbs 13:16).

[4] *And Hosea…run astray* Hosea 4:1–6.

[5] *by hap* by chance (*OED* hap *sb*[1] 4b).

[6] *True knowledge…the soul* a transformation of the commonplace metaphor of the eyes as windows of the soul: "These lovely lamps, these windows of the soul" (Du Bartas, *Divine Weeks and Works*, 1578, Sixth Day); "the windows of mine eyes" (Shakespeare, *King Richard III*, V.iii.17); *speculate* observe, view (*OED* speculate *v* 1).

[7] *'Tis life….Christ to know* "John 17:3" (original marginalia).

[8] *Great Alexander…of strife* Alexander the Great of Macedonia (356–323 B.C.E.), son of Philip II, was tutored by Aristotle. While his political inheritance led, in the final year of his life, to misgovernment and disloyalty, Aristotle's legacy to Alexander, according to Plutarch, was a death-defying knowledge.

But by the way I saw a full fed beast,
Which roared like some monster, or a devil, [1]
And on Eve's sex he foamed filthy froth,
As if that he had had the falling evil;[2]
245 To whom I went to free them from mishaps,
And with a muzzle sought to bind his chaps. [3]

But, as it seems, my mood out-run my might,
Which when a self-conceited creature saw,
She passed her censure on my weak exploit,
250 And gave the beast a harder bone to gnaw;
Haman she hangs, 'tis past he cannot shun it;
For Ester in the Pretertense hath done it. [4]

And yet her enterprise had some defect,
The monster surely was not hanged quite:
255 For as the child of Prudence did conceive,
His throat not stopped, he still had power to bite.
She therefore gave to Cerberus a sop,
Which is of force his beastly breath to stop. [5]

But yet if he do swallow down that bit,
260 She other-ways hath bound him to the peace;
And like an artist takes away the cause,
That the effect by consequence may cease.
This frantic dog, whose rage did women wrong,

Hath Constance wormed to make him hold his
    tongue. [6]

265 Thus leaving them I passed on my way,
But ere that I had little further gone,
I saw a fierce insatiable foe,
Depopulating countries, sparing none;
Without respect of age, sex, or degree,
270 It did devour, and could not daunted be.

Some feared this foe, some loved it as a friend;
For though none could the force of it withstand,
Yet some by it were sent to Tophet's flames, [7]
But others led to heavenly Canaan land. [8]
275 On some it seized with a gentle power,
And others furiously it did devour.

The name of this impartial foe was Death
Whose rigour whil'st I furiously did view,
Upon a sudden, ere I was aware;
280 With piercing dart my mother dear it slew;
Which when I saw it made me so to weep,
That tears and sobs did rouse me from my sleep.

But, when I waked, I found my dream was true;
For Death had ta'en my mother's breath away,
285 Though of her life it could not her bereave,
Sith she in glory lives with Christ for aye; [9]
Which makes me glad, and thankful for her bliss,
Though still bewail her absence, whom I miss.

---

[1] *full fed beast* Joseph Swetnam, the author of *The Arraignment of Lewd, Idle, Froward and Unconstant Women* (1617).

[2] *falling evil* epilepsy.

[3] *And with…bind his chaps* an allusion to *A Muzzle for Melastomus* (1617); *chaps* jaws (*OED* chap *sb*[2] 2).

[4] *Ester in the Pretertense* "Ester Sowernam" (punning on "Swe[e]tnam"), author of *Ester hath hang'd Haman* (1617), wrote that though Speght claimed "to defend women" in *A Muzzle*, she did "rather charge and condemn women." Speght uses "pretertense" (the Latin past tense) to expose Sowernam's self-conceit in claiming to have killed off Swetnam. See Esther 3–7 for the biblical story of Esther and Haman.

[5] *For as…to stop* Constantia Munda's *The Worming of a Mad Dog; Or, a Sop for Cerberus the Jailor of Hell* (1617) is dedicated to her mother, "Lady Prudentia Munda." Cerberus, the three-headed dog who guarded Hades, prevented Aeneas's entry until the Sibyl threw the dog a drugged morsel which put him to sleep (*Aeneid*, Book 6).

[6] *wormed* extracted the "worm" or lytta (a small tendon) from the dog's tongue to safeguard against madness (*OED* worm *v* II.3).

[7] *Tophet's* Hell's. Tophet is a place near Gehenna where the Jews made a human sacrifice to strange gods (Jeremiah 19:4). Later used as a place for the deposit of refuse, Tophet became symbolic of the torments of hell.

[8] *Canaan land* the promised land, which, in a New Testament context, refers to heaven.

[9] *aye* ever (*OED* aye *adv* 1a).

A sudden sorrow piercing to the quick,
290 Speedy encounters fortitude doth try;
Unarmed men receive the deepest wound,
Expected perils time doth lenify; [1]
Her sudden loss hath cut my feeble heart,
So deep, that daily I endure the smart.

295 The root is killed, how can the boughs but fade?
But sith that Death this cruel deed hath done,
I'll blaze the nature of this mortal foe, [2]

And show how it to tyrannize begun.
The sequel then with judgment view aright, [3]
300 The profit may and will the pains requite.

Esto Memor Mortis [4]
—1621

---

[1] *lenify* assuage (*OED* lenify *v* 2).

[2] *blaze* proclaim (*OED* blaze *v²* 2).

[3] *The sequel* "Mortality's Memorandum."

[4] *Esto Memor Mortis* Thou shalt be mindful of death.

Thomas Randolph
1605 – 1635

Randolph was born on June 15, 1605, at Newnham-cum-Badby, near Daventry, in Northamptonshire. His parents were William Randolph and Elizabeth, the daughter of Thomas Smith. William Randolph, according to Aubrey, "was very wild in his youth," and as a result was left one groat by his father. This was in effect disinheritance: the word "groat" was used to symbolize a very small sum, as in the title "A Groatsworth of Wit." Randolph's father, left to make his own way in the world, became a land-surveyor and steward to Sir George Goring in Sussex and to Lord Zouch in Northamptonshire. He resided at Little Houghton in Northamptonshire, which probably accounts for Randolph's acquaintance with Anthony Stafford. Randolph, like other poets represented in this anthology, was educated at Westminster School; he is said to have been very precocious at writing verse during his time there. From Westminster he went to Trinity College, Cambridge, in 1624, taking his B.A. in 1628. He was a favourite son of the college—a letter exists which indicates that the Bishop of Bath and Wells, then the Master of Trinity, thought very highly of him; in 1632 he took his M.A. degree and became a college Fellow. He probably made the acquaintance of Ben Jonson in London during a period when the University was closed due to plague; various anecdotes suggest that Jonson adopted him as one of his "sons." In March 1632 his play, *The Jealous Lovers,* was acted before the King and Queen at Trinity College; another play, *Amyntas,* was, according to the quarto volume published in 1638, "acted before the King and Queen at *White-hall*." According to Anthony à Wood it was "indulging himself too much with the liberal conversation of his admirers (a thing incident to poets)" which "brought him, untimely to his end." Wood was notoriously malicious, but evidence from people well-disposed to Randolph suggests that his health, never robust, may have been undermined by excessive drinking. He died at the Staffords' house at Blatherwycke. A volume, *Poems, with The Muses Looking-glass and Amyntas,* was published three years after his death by his brother Robert; it is regarded as a carefully supervised publication. At his death Randolph's work was praised, perhaps excessively; in our time he has been too much ignored. His poems draw upon extensive knowledge of classical literature, and in that sense may be thought conventional; but there is enough enjoyment in reading him to suggest that he might have matured into a poet of considerable achievement.

❧❧❧

The Second Epode of Horace Translated [1]

Happy the man which, far from city care
    (Such as ancient mortals were),
With his own oxen ploughs his father's land,
    Free from usurer's griping hand.
5 The soldier's trumpets never break his sleep,
    Nor angry seas that raging keep;
He shuns the wrangling hall, nor foot doth set
    On the proud thresholds of the great.

His life is this (O life almost divine!)
10   To marry elms unto the vine;
To prune unfruitful branches, and for them
    To graft a bough of happier stem.
Or else within the low-couched valleys views
    His well-clothed flocks of bleating ewes.
15 Sometimes his honey he in pots doth keep:
    Sometimes he shears his fleecy sheep.
And when his fruits with autumn ripened be
    Gathers his apples from the tree.
And joys to taste the pears himself did plant,

---
[1] Compare Ben Jonson's rendering of the same poem by Horace.

20 And grapes that nought of purple want.
Under an oak sometimes he lays his head,
  Making the tender grass his bed.
Meanwhile the streams along their banks do float,
  And birds do chaunt with warbling throat;
25 And gentle springs a gentle murmur keep,
  To lull him to a quiet sleep.
When winter comes, and th' air doth chiller grow,
  Threat'ning showers and shivering snow,
Either with hounds he hunts the tusked swine,
30 That foe unto the corn and vine;
Or lays his nets, or limes the unctuous bush
  To catch the blackbird, or the thrush.
Sometimes the hare he courses, and one way
  Makes both a pleasure and a prey.
35 But if with him a modest wife doth meet,
  To guide his house and children sweet,
Such as the *Sabine* or *Apulian* wife,
  Something brown, but chaste of life;
Such as will make a good warm fire to burn
40 Against her wearied mate's return,
And shutting in her stalls her fruitful neat,[1]
  Will milk the kine's distended teat:
Fetching her husband of her self-brewed beer,
  And other wholesome country cheer.
45 Sup him with bread and cheese, pudding or pie,
  Such dainties as they do not buy:
Give me but these, and I shall never care
  Where all the *Lucrine* oysters are:
These wholesome country dainties shall to me
50 Sweet as *tench* or *sturgeon* be.
Had I but these, I well could be without
  The *carp*, the *salmon*, or the *trout*:
Nor should the *Phoenix'* self so much delight
  My not ambitious appetite,
55 As should an apple snatched from mine own trees,
  Or honey of my labouring bees.
My cattle's udders should afford me food,
  My sheep my cloth, my ground my wood.

Sometimes a lamb, snatched from the wolf, shall be
60 A banquet for my friend and me:
Sometimes a calf, ta'en from her lowing cow,
  Or tender issue of the sow.
Our gardens sallets yield, mallows to keep
  Loose bodies, lettuce for to sleep.
65 The cackling hen an egg for breakfast lays,
  And duck that in our water plays.
The goose for us her tender plumes hath bred,
  To lay us on a softer bed.
Our blankets are not dyed with orphans' tears,
70 Our pillows are not stuffed with cares.
To walk on our own ground a stomach gets
  The best of sauce to tart our meats.
In midst of such a feast 'tis joy to come
  And see the well-fed lambs at home.
75 'Tis pleasure to behold th' inversed plow,
  The languid necks of oxen bow.
And view th' industrious servants, that will sweat
  Both at labour and at meat.
Lord, grant me but enough; I ask no more
80 *Than will serve mine, and help the poor.*
—1638

An Elegy upon the Lady Venetia Digby [2]

*D*eath, who'ld not change prerogatives with thee,
That dost such rapes, yet may'st not question'd be?
Here cease thy wanton lust, be satisfied:
Hope not a second, and so fair a bride.
5 Where was her *Mars*, whose valiant arms did hold
This *Venus* once, that thou durst be so bold
By thy too nimble theft? I know 'twas fear,
Lest he should come, that would have rescued her.
Monster confess, didst thou not blushing stand,
10 And thy pale cheek turn red to touch her hand?
Did she not lightning-like strike sudden heat

[1] *neat* cattle.

[2] Lady Venetia Digby was a famous beauty; see the selection from Aubrey's *Brief Lives*.

Through thy cold limbs, and thaw thy frost to
    sweat?
Well, since thou hast her, use her gently, *Death*,
And in requital of such precious breath,
15 Watch sentinel to guard her; do not see
The worms thy rivals, for the gods will be.
Remember *Paris*, for whose pettier sin
The *Trojan* gates let the stout *Grecians* in.
So, when time ceases (whose unthrifty hand
20 Has now almost consumed his stock of sand),
Myriads of angels shall in armies come,
And fetch (proud ravisher) their *Helen* home.
And to revenge this rape, thy other store
Thou shalt resign too, and shalt steal no more.
25 Till then, fair ladies (for you now are fair,
But till her death I feared your just despair),
Fetch all the spices that *Arabia* yields,
Distil the choicest flowers of the fields:
And when in one their best perfections meet,
30 Embalm her corse, that she may make them sweet,
Whilst for an epitaph upon her stone
I cannot write, but I must weep her one.

Epitaph

Beauty itself lies here, in whom alone
Each part enjoyed the same perfection.
35 In some the eyes we praise, in some the hair:
In her the lips, in her the cheeks are fair:
That nymph's fine feet, her hands we beauteous
    call:
But in this form we praise no part, but all.
The ages past have many beauties shown,
40 And I more plenty in our time have known.
But in the age to come I look for none;
Nature despairs, because her pattern's gone.
—1638

Upon his Picture

When age hath made me what I am not now:
    And every wrinkle tells me where the plow
Of time hath furrowed; when an ice shall flow
Through every vein, and all my head be snow:
5 When death displays his coldness in my cheek,
And I myself in my own picture seek,
Not finding what I am, but what I was;
In doubt which to believe, this or my glass;
Yet though I alter, this remains the same
10 As it was drawn: retains the primitive frame
And first complexion; here will still be seen
Blood on the cheek, and down upon the chin.
Here the smooth brow will stay, the lively eye,
The ruddy lip, and hair of youthful dye.
15 Behold what frailty we in man may see,
Whose shadow is less given to change than he.
—1638

An Ode to Master Anthony Stafford, to hasten him into the Country[1]

Come, spur away,
    I have no patience for a longer stay.
      But must go down,
And leave the chargeable noise of this great town.
5   I will the country see,
      Where old simplicity,
      Though hid in grey,
      Doth look more gay
Than foppery in plush and scarlet clad.
10   Farewell, you city wits, that are
      Almost at civil war;
'Tis time that I grow wise, when all the world
    grows mad.

---

[1] Anthony Stafford was the youngest son of John Stafford of Blatherwycke in Northamptonshire.

More of my days
I will not spend to gain an idiot's praise;
15   Or to make sport
For some slight puisne of the Inns-of-Court.
        Then, worthy *Stafford*, say,
        How shall we spend the day?
        With what delights
20   Shorten the nights?
When from this tumult we are got secure,
    Where mirth with all her freedom goes,
    Yet shall not finger lose;
Where every word is thought, and every thought
    is pure.

25   There from the tree
We'll cherries pluck, and pick the strawberry.
        And every day
Go see the wholesome country girls make hay,
        Whose brown hath lovelier grace,
30   Than any painted face,
        That I do know
        Hyde Park can show.
Where I had rather gain a kiss than meet
    (Though some of them in greater state
35   Might court my life with plate)
The beauties of the *Cheap*, and wives of *Lombard
    Street*.

        But think upon
Some other pleasures: these to me are none,
        Why do I prate
40   Of women, that are things against my fate?
        I never mean to wed
        That torture to my bed.
        My Muse is she
        My love shall be.
45   Let clowns get wealth and heirs; when I am gone,
        And the great bugbear, grisly death,
        Shall take this idle breath,
If I a poem leave, that poem is my son.

        Of this no more;
50   We'll rather taste the bright *Pomona's* store.
        No fruit shall 'scape
Our palates, from the damson to the grape.
        Then (full) we'll seek a shade,
        And hear what music's made;
55   How Philomel
        Her tale doth tell,
And how the other birds do fill the choir:
    The thrush and blackbird lend their throats
    Warbling melodious notes;
60   We will all sports enjoy which others but desire.

        Ours is the sky,
Whereat what fowl we please our hawk shall fly;
        Nor will we spare
To hunt the crafty fox, or timorous hare;
65   But let our hounds run loose
        In any ground they'll choose,
        The buck shall fall,
        The stag, and all:
Our pleasures must from their own warrants be.
70   For to my *Muse*, if not to me,
        I'm sure all game is free;
Heaven, earth, all are but parts of her great
    royalty.

        And when we mean
To taste of *Bacchus'* blessings now and then,
75   And drink by stealth
A cup or two to noble *Barkley's* health,[1]
        I'll take my pipe and try
        The *Phrygian* melody;[2]
        Which he that hears,
80   Lets through his ears
A madness to distemper all the brain.
        Then I another pipe will take

---

[1] *Barkley*   George Berkeley. See the notes to Suckling's *A Sessions of
the Poets*.

[2] *The Phrygian melody*   warlike music (see OED Phrygian *a*).

And *Doric* music make,
To civilize with graver notes our wits again.[1]
—1638

An Answer to Master Ben. Jonson's Ode to persuade him not to leave the Stage [2]

Ben do not leave the stage,
'Cause 'tis a loathsome age;
For Pride and Impudence will grow too bold
When they shall hear it told
5   They frighted thee. Stand high, as is thy cause;
Their hiss is thy applause.
More just were thy disdain,
Had they approved thy vein.
So thou for them and they for thee were born,
10   They to incense, and thou as much to scorn.

Wilt thou engross thy store
Of wheat, and pour no more
Because their bacon-brains have such a taste
As more delight in mast?[3]
15   No; set 'em forth a board of dainties full,
As thy best Muse can cull;
While they the while do pine
And thirst 'midst all their wine.
What greater plague can hell itself devise,
20   Than to be willing thus to tantalise?

Thou canst not find them stuff
That will be bad enough
To please their palates; let 'em thine refuse
For some *Pie-Corner* muse.[4]

25   She is too fair an hostess, 'twere a sin
For them to like thine *Inn*.
'Twas made to entertain
Guests of a nobler strain,
Yet if they will have any of thy store,
30   Give 'em some scraps, and send them from thy
door.

And let those things in plush,
Till they be taught to blush,
Like what they will, and more contented be
With what *Broome* swept from thee.[5]
35   I know thy worth, and that thy lofty strains
Write not to clothes but brains.
But thy great spleen doth rise,
'Cause moles will have no eyes;
This only in my *Ben* I faulty find;
40   He's angry, they'll not see him that are blind.

Why should the scene be mute,
'Cause thou canst touch a lute,
And string thy *Horace*? let each Muse of nine
Claim thee, and say "Thou art mine."
45   'Twere fond to let all other flames expire
To sit by *Pindar's* fire:
For by so strange neglect,
I should myself suspect
The palsy were as well, thy brains disease;
50   If they could shake thy Muse which way they
please.

And though thou well canst sing
The glories of thy king,
And on the wings of verse his chariot bear
To heaven, and fix it there;
55   Yet let thy Muse as well some raptures raise
To please him as to praise,
I would not have thee choose

---

[1] *Doric*   musical mode, often considered solemn and grave.

[2] See Carew's "To Ben. Jonson."

[3] *mast*   a collective name for the fruit of the beech, oak, chestnut, and other forest trees, especially as food for swine (*OED* mast *sb*[2]).

[4] *Pie-Corner*   was in West Smithfield, and was named from one or more cook-shops there; it was the place from which verses on contemporary events were issued.

---

[5] *what Broome swept from thee*   Within three weeks of the failure of Jonson's *The New Inn*, a play by his servant Richard Brome, *The Love-Sick Maid*, was staged at the same theatre and was very successful.

Only a treble Muse;
But have this envious, ignorant Age to know:
60 Thou that canst sing so high, canst reach as low.
—1638

On the Death of a Nightingale

Go, solitary wood, and henceforth be
Acquainted with no other harmony,
Than the pies' chattering, or the shrieking note
Of boding owls and fatal raven's throat.
5 Thy sweetest chanter's dead, that warbled forth
Lays, that might tempests calm, and still the north,
And call down angels from their glorious sphere
To hear her songs, and learn new anthems there.
That soul is fled, and to *Elysium* gone;
10 Thou a poor desert left. Go then and run,
Beg there to stand a grove, and if she please
To sing again beneath thy shadowy trees;
The souls of happy lovers crowned with blisses
Shall flock about thee, and keep time with kisses.
—1638

A Pastoral Courtship

Behold these woods, and mark, my *sweet*,
How all the boughs together meet!
The *cedar* his fair arms displays,
And mixes branches with the *bays*!
5 The lofty *pine* deigns to descend,
And sturdy *oaks* do gently bend.
One with another subtly weaves
Into one loom their various leaves,
As all ambitious were to be
10 Mine and my *Phyllis'* canopy.
Let's enter, and discourse our loves;
These are, my dear, no tell-tale groves!
There dwell no pies nor parrots there,
To prate again the words they hear,
15 Nor babbling Echo, that will tell

The neighbouring hills one syllable.
Being enter'd, let's together lie,
Twin'd like the *Zodiac's Gemini*!
How soon the flowers do sweeter smell,
20 And all with emulation swell
To be thy pillow! These for thee
Were meant a bed, and thou for me,
And I may with as just esteem
Press thee, as thou mayst lie on them.
25 And why so coy? What dost thou fear?
There lurks no speckled serpent here.
No venomous snake makes this his road,
No canker, nor the loathsome toad.
And yon poor spider on the tree
30 Thy spinster will, no poisoner be,
There is no frog to leap, and fright
Thee from my arms, and break delight;
Nor snail that o'er thy coat shall trace,
And leave behind a slimy lace.
35 This is the hallowed shrine of love;
No wasp nor hornet haunts this grove,
Nor pismire to make pimples rise, [1]
Upon thy smooth and ivory thighs.
No danger in these shades doth lie,
40 Nothing that wears a sting, but I;
And in it doth no venom dwell,
Although perchance it make thee swell.
Being set, let's sport awhile, my fair,
I will tie love-knots in thy hair.
45 See, *Zephyrus* through the leaves doth stray,
And has free liberty to play,
And braids thy locks; and shall I find
Less favour than a saucy wind?
Now let me sit, and fix mine eyes,
50 On thee, that art my Paradise.
Thou art my all; my spring remains
In the fair violets of thy veins;
And that you are my summer's day,
Ripe cherries in thy lips display.

---

[1] *pismire* ant.

55 And when for autumn I would seek,
'Tis in the apples of thy cheek.
But that which only moves my smart,
Is to see winter in thy heart.
Strange, when at once in one appear
60 All the four seasons of the year!
I'll clasp that neck, where should be set
A rich and orient carcanet. [1]
But swains are poor; admit of, then,
More natural chains—the arms of men.
65 Come, let me touch those breasts, that swell
Like two fair mountains, and may well
Be styled the *Alps*, but that I swear
The snow has less of whiteness there.
But stay (my love), a fault I spy;
70 Why are those two fair mountains dry?
Which if they run, no *Muse* would please
To taste of any spring but these.
And *Ganymede* employed should be
To fetch his *Jove nectar* from thee.
75 Thou shalt be nurse, fair *Venus* swears
To the next Cupid that she bears.
Were it not then discreetly done
To ope one spring to let two run?
Fie, fie! this belly, beauty's mint,
80 Blushes to see no coin stamp'd in't.
Employ it then; for, though it be
Our wealth, it is your royalty;
And beauty will have current grace
That bears the image of your face.
85 How to the touch the ivory thighs
Veil gently, and again do rise,
As pliable to impression,
As virgin wax, or *Parian* stone
Dissolv'd to softness, plump and full,
90 More white and soft than *Cotswold wool*,
Or cotton from the *Indian* tree,
Or pretty silkworm's huswifery.
These on two marble pillars raised,

Make me in doubt which should be praised,
95 They or their columns, most: but when
I view those feet, which I have seen
So nimbly trip it o'er the lawns,
That all the *satyrs* and the *fauns*
Have stood amazed, when they would pass
100 Over the leys, and not a grass
Would feel the weight; nor rush, nor bent
Drooping betray which way you went.
O, then I felt my hot desires
Burn more, and flame with double fires.
105 Come, let those thighs, those legs, those feet
With mine in thousand windings meet,
And woven in more subtle twines
Than woodbine, ivy, or the vines.
For when Love sees us circling thus,
110 He'll like no arbour more than us.
Now let us kiss. Would you be gone?
Manners at least allows me one.
Blush you at this? pretty one, stay,
And I will take that kiss away.
115 Thus with a second, and that too
A third wipes off; so will we go
To numbers that the stars outrun,
And all the atoms in the sun.
For though we kiss till *Phœbus'* ray
120 Sink in the sea, and kissing stay,
Till his bright beams return again,
There can of all but one remain:
And if for one good manners call,
In one, good manners, grant me all.
125 Are kisses all? they but forerun
Another duty to be done.
What would you of that minstrel say
That tunes his pipes and will not play?
Say what are blossoms in their prime,
130 That ripen not in harvest-time?
Or what are buds, that ne'er disclose
The longed-for sweetness of the rose?
So kisses to a lover's guest
Are invitations, not the feast.

---

[1] *carcanet* jewelled necklace or collar.

135 See everything that we espy
Is fruitful, saving you and I:
View all the fields, survey the bowers,
The buds, the blossoms, and the flowers,
And say if they so rich could be
140 In barren, base virginity.
Earth's not so coy as you are now,
But willingly admits the plow.
For how had man or beast been fed,
If she had kept her maidenhead?
145 *Cœlia*, once coy as are the rest,
Hugs now a babe on either breast,
And *Chloris*, since a man she took,
Has less of greenness in her look.
Our ewes have eaned, and every dam [1]
150 Gives suck unto her tender lamb.
As by these groves we walked along,
Some birds were feeding of their young.
Some on their eggs did brooding sit,
Sad that they had not hatched them yet.
155 Those that were slower than the rest
Were busy building of the nest.
You only will not pay the fine
You vowed and owe to *Valentine*.
As you were angling in the brook
160 With silken line and silver hook,
Through crystal streams you might descry
How vast and numberless a fry
The fish had spawned, that all along
The banks were crowded with the throng.
165 And shall fair *Venus* more command
By water than she does by land?
The *Phœnix* chaste, yet when she dies,
Herself with her own ashes lies.

But let thy love more wisely thrive,
170 And do the act while th' art alive.
'Tis time we left our childish love,
That trades for toys, and now approve
Our abler skill; they are not wise
Look babies only in the eyes.
175 That smoth'red smile show'd what you meant,
And modest silence gives consent.
That which we now prepare, will be
Best done in silent secrecy.
Come, do not weep, what is't you fear?
180 Lest some should know what we do here.
See, not a flower you pressed is dead,
But re-erects his bended head;
That whoso'er shall pass this way
Knows not by these where *Phyllis* lay.
185 And in your forehead there is none
Can read the act that we have done.

Phyllis
Poor credulous and simple maid,
By what strange wiles art thou betrayed!
A treasure thou hast lost to-day
190 For which thou canst no ransom pay.
How black am I transformed with sin!
How strange a guilt gnaws me within!
Grief will convert this red to pale;
When every wake and Whitsun-ale
195 Shall talk my shame! break, break sad heart!
There is no medicine for my smart,
No herb nor balm can cure my sorrow,
Unless you meet again to-morrow.
—1638

---

[1] *eaned* sometimes yeaned: brought forth lambs (*OED*).

William Habington
1605 – 1654

William Habington was born in Worcestershire. His family was Catholic, and he was educated in France in the expectation that he would become a priest. In 1626 he returned to England. He married Lucy Herbert, the "Castara" after whom a volume of his poems (1634) was named, and lived quietly, accepting the disabilities placed upon him by reason of his Catholicism. His poems celebrate a chaste (which is not to say a celibate) love, and so are distinguished both from strictly "Platonic" love poems and those addressed to "profane mistresses." *Castara* was reissued in an enlarged edition in 1635 and again in 1640, with a section of religious verse. The love poems of Henry Vaughan's first volume, the *Poems* of 1646, show some indebtedness to *Castara*. In addition to his poems, Habington published a play, *The Queen of Aragon* (1640) and some historical writing.

ೲೲ

Nox nocti indicat Scientiam [1]

When I survey the bright
    Celestial sphere:
So rich with jewels hung, that night
Doth like an Æthiop bride appear. [2]

5   My soul her wings doth spread
    And heaven-ward flies,
Th' Almighty's mysteries to read
In the large volumes of the skies.

For the bright firmament
    Shoots forth no flame
10 So silent, but is eloquent
In speaking the Creator's name.

No unregarded star
    Contracts its light
15 Into so small a character,
Remov'd far from our human sight:

But if we steadfast look,
    We shall discern
In it as in some holy book,
20 How man may heavenly knowledge learn.

It tells the Conqueror,
    That far-stretched power
Which his proud dangers traffic for,
Is but the triumph of an hour.

25 That from the farthest North,
    Some Nation may
Yet undiscovered issue forth,
And o'er his new got conquest sway.

Some Nation yet shut in
30   With hills of ice
May be let out to scourge his sin
'Till they shall equal him in vice.

And then they likewise shall
    Their ruin have,
35 For as your selves your empires fall,
And every kingdom hath a grave.

Thus those celestial fires,
    Though seeming mute

---

[1] "Night unto night showeth knowledge" (Psalm 19:2).

[2] *an Æthiop bride* Compare Shakespeare, *Romeo and Juliet* I.v.47–48: "It seems she hangs upon the cheek of night / Like a rich jewel in an Ethiope's ear."

The fallacy of our desires
40 And all the pride of life confute.

For they have watched since first
  The World had birth:

And found sin in itself accursed,
And nothing permanent on earth.
—1634

Edmund Waller
1606 – 1687

Waller was born in 1606 in Coleshill, Hertford-shire, the eldest son of Robert and Anne Waller. He was educated at High Wycombe and, after his father's death in 1616, at Eton and Cambridge, which he appears to have left without a degree. In 1622 he was admitted to Lincoln's Inn. Some sources contend that he first sat in Parliament at the age of sixteen, although it appears more likely that it would have been in 1624, when Amersham, which was his first constituency, recovered its right to return members. In 1631, Waller, who had been left a considerable inheritance by his own father, married Anne Banks, a substantial heiress, and went to live in Beaconsfield where his wife died in 1634 giving birth to their second child. Shortly thereafter

Waller became part of a company of literary men, the "Club," who encouraged his literary efforts. His first publications, in 1633 and 1645, were followed by three editions of his collected verse in 1645. During the Civil War Waller participated in a plot to secure London for the King. When the plot was discovered Waller was imprisoned, declared incapable of sitting in Parliament, fined, and banished from England. Shortly before leaving for France, Waller married Mary Bracey of Oxfordshire. In November 1651 Waller was pardoned and returned to England. In 1661 he was restored to Parliament and served until 1687, when he died at his home in Beaconsfield.

❧❧❧

On a Girdle

That which her slender waist confined,
  Shall now my joyful temples bind;
No monarch but would give his crown,
His arms might do what this has done.

5   It was my heaven's extremist sphere,
The pale which held that lovely deer. [1]
My joy, my grief, my hope, my love,
Did all within this circle move!

    A narrow compass! and yet there
10 Dwelt all that's good, and all that's fair;
Give me but what this riband bound, [2]
Take all the rest the sun goes round.
—1645

---

[1] *pale* fence or enclosing barrier or line of any material (*OED* pale *sb*[1]2).

[2] *riband* ribbon (*OED* riband *sb*1).

Go, Lovely Rose!

Go, lovely rose!
  Tell her that wastes her time and me
That now she knows,
When I resemble her to thee,
5 How sweet and fair she seems to be.

Tell her that's young,
And shuns to have her graces spied,
That hadst thou sprung
In deserts, where no men abide,
10 Thou must have uncommended died.

Small is the worth
Of beauty from the light retired;
Bid her come forth,
Suffer herself to be desired,
15 And not blush so to be admired.

Then die! that she
The common fate of all things rare

May read in thee;
How small a part of time they share
20 That are so wondrous sweet and fair!
—1645

Upon His Majesty's Repairing of Paul's [1]

That shipwrecked vessel which th' Apostle bore, [2]
Scarce suffered more upon Melita's shore,
Than did his temple in the sea of time,
(Our nation's glory, and our nation's crime) [3]
5 When the first monarch of this happy isle, [4]
Moved with the ruin of so brave a pile,
This work of cost and piety begun,
To be accomplished by his glorious son,
Who all that came within the ample thought
10 Of his wise sire has to perfection brought;
He, like *Amphion*, makes those quarries leap
Into fair figures from a confused heap: [5]
For in his art of regiment is found
A power like that of harmony in sound. [6]

15 Those antique minstrels sure were *Charles*-like
kings, [7]
Cities their lutes, and subjects' hearts their strings,
On which with so divine a hand they strook, [8]
Consent of motion from their breath they took
So all our minds with his conspire to grace
20 The Gentiles' great apostle, and deface
Those state-obscuring sheds, that like a chain
Seemed to confine and fetter him again; [9]
Which the glad saint shakes off at his command,
As once the viper from his sacred hand: [10]
25 So joys the aged oak, when we divide
The creeping ivy from his injured side.

Ambition rather would affect the fame
Of some new structure, to have borne her name;
Two distant virtues in one act we find,
30 The modesty and greatness of his mind;
Which not content to be above the rage,
And injury of all-impairing age,
In its own worth secure, doth higher climb,
And things half swallowed from the jaws of Time
35 Reduce ; an earnest of his grand design,
To frame no new church, but the old refine: [11]
Which, spouse-like, may with comely grace
command
More than by force of argument or hand.
For doubtful reason few can apprehend,
40 And war brings ruin where it should amend;

[1] There is evidence that this poem was in manuscript circulation before its publication. For historical context see Margaret Whinney and Oliver Millar, *English Art 1625–1714* (Oxford: Clarendon P, 1957), 29–32, where the point is made (p. 30) that "the work on St. Paul's contributed materially to public discontent, and so ultimately to rebellion." See also David Norbrook, *Writing the English Republic* (Cambridge: CUP, 1999), 74–78.

[2] *th' Apostle* St. Paul. See Acts 27–28. Melita is the modern Malta.

[3] *glory* St. Paul's was regarded as the most imposing building in Europe; *crime* presumably because it had been allowed to fall into decay.

[4] *the first monarch of this happy isle* James I, formerly James VI of Scotland, as the first King of England to rule over a "united kingdom."

[5] *Amphion* the son of Zeus and Antiope; legendary builder of Thebes. The stones moved into their places in response to his lyre (*OCD*). It seems likely that Marvell had this couplet in mind in the opening of *Upon Appleton House*, with its sardonic comment on the megalomaniac "foreign architect / That unto caves the quarries drew." Inigo Jones may not have been a foreign architect but he was certainly influenced by foreign practices.

[6] *regiment* rule or government, especially royal or magisterial authority (*OED* regiment *sb* 1). Milton, who was no admirer of Charles I, may have remembered this couplet, on the consonance

between architecture and music, when he described the building of Pandemonium: "as in an Organ from one blast of wind / To many a row of Pipes the sound-board breathes" (*Paradise Lost*, 1.709–10).

[7] *antique minstrels* Amphion, Orpheus and so on.

[8] *strook* struck.

[9] *state-obscuring sheds* Whinney and Millar (30) write that "difficulties connected with the pulling down of houses abutting on the cathedral were swept aside." "The inhabitants of the houses opposed these changes, which they saw as an exploitation of royal power to override the liberties of the city" (Norbrook, 77).

[10] *As once the viper from his sacred hand* Acts 28:1–6.

[11] *Reduce* in its Latinate sense of "bring back, restore."

But beauty, with a bloodless conquest, finds
A welcome sovereignty in rudest minds.

Not aught which *Sheba's* wond'ring queen
    beheld
Amongst the works of Solomon, excelled [1]
His ships, and building; emblems of a heart
45 His ships, and building; emblems of a heart
Large both in magnanimity and art.
While the propitious heavens this work attend,
Long-wanted showers they forget to send;
As if they meant to make it understood
50 Of more importance than our vital food.

The Sun, which riseth to salute the choir,
Already finished, setting shall admire
How private bounty could so far extend;
55 The King built all, but *Charles* the *western* end. [2]
So proud a fabric to devotion given,
At once it threatneth and obliges heaven.

Laomedon, that had the gods in pay,
Neptune, with him that rules the sacred day, [3]
60 Could no such structure raise: Troy walled so high,
Th'Atrides might as well have forced the sky. [4]

Glad, though amazed, are our neighbour kings,
To see such power employed in peaceful things;
They list not urge it to the dreadful field;
65 The task is easier to destroy, than build.

---

[1] *Sheba's wond'ring queen* See I Kings 10 and II Chronicles 9 for the Queen of Sheba's visit to King Solomon.

[2] *The King built all* etc. The entire reconstruction took place under the King's commission; Charles paid privately for the portico at the western end. Under Cromwell the portico was converted into shops for seamstresses.

[3] *Laomedon* the father of Priam; he refused to pay Poseidon for his work in building the walls of Troy; this led eventually to the city's downfall.

[4] *Th'Atrides* Agamemnon and Menelaus, sons of Atreus. The meaning is that if Troy had been walled as well as the cathedral was, they could no more have conquered Troy than they could have conquered the sky.

...*Sic gratia regum*
  Pieriis tentata modis....—Horace [5]
—1645

On St. James's Park, As Lately Improved by His Majesty

Of the first paradise there's nothing found;
  Plants set by heaven are vanished, and the
    ground;
Yet the description lasts: who knows the fate
Of lines that shall this paradise relate?
5   Instead of rivers rolling by the side
Of Eden's garden, here flows in the tide;
The sea, which always served his empire, now
Pays tribute to our prince's pleasure too.
Of famous cities we the founders know;
10 But rivers, old as seas to which they go,
Are nature's bounty; 'tis of more renown
To make a river than to build a town.
    For future shade, young trees upon the banks
Of the new stream appear in even ranks;
15 The voice of Orpheus, or Amphion's hand, [6]
In better order could not make them stand;
May they increase as fast, and spread their boughs,
As the high fame of their great owner grows!
May he live long enough to see them all
20 Dark shadows cast, and as his palace tall!
Methinks I see the love that shall be made,
The lovers walking in that amorous shade;
The gallants dancing by the river's side;
They bathe in summer, and in winter slide.
25 Methinks I hear the music in the boats,
And the loud echo which returns the notes;
While overhead a flock of new-sprung fowl

---

[5] *Sic gratia regum* etc. "Thus the favour of the kings was sought in Pierian measures" (adapted from Horace, *Ars Poetica*, 404–405). Pieria was the birthplace of the Muses.

[6] *Orpheus* a figure of Greek myth whose singing was said to attract even the trees, wild beasts and stones (*OCD*); *Amphion* a son of Zeus known for his musical abilities (*OCD*).

John Milton
1608 – 1674

Milton was born in London; his parents were John Milton and Sarah Jeffrey. John Milton senior was disinherited by his Catholic father when, as a student at Christ Church, Oxford, he became a Protestant. John Milton senior was a successful scrivener and a good amateur musician. He encouraged his son in his studies, engaging Thomas Young, who later became master of Jesus College, Cambridge, as his tutor. Not later than 1620, Milton went to St. Paul's school, where he learned Latin, Greek, French, Italian and some Hebrew, besides reading widely in English literature. Like Cowley, he was an enthusiastic reader of Spenser's *Faerie Queene*, and later wrote that he dared be known to think Spenser a better teacher than Scotus or Aquinas. Milton became a member of Christ's College, Cambridge, in 1625. Letters to Thomas Young and to his school friends Alexander Gill and Charles Diodati survive from this period, as well as some academic exercises. Milton abandoned any intention of ordination he might have had because he disliked Anglicanism as it developed under Archbishop Laud. From 1632 to 1638 he lived in his father's house in Horton, Buckinghamshire, undertaking a self-administered course of private postgraduate study, punctuated by trips to London to buy books and for private lessons in mathematics and music. The poems of this period, culminating in "Lycidas," would in themselves be sufficient to ensure that he would be remembered. From April 1638 to July 1639 Milton travelled in Europe, with a letter of introduction from Sir Henry Wotton, then Provost of Eton, which helped him to meet well-known scholars and writers, especially in Florence. On hearing of the outbreak of the Scottish troubles, he decided to return to England, lest, as he said, he should be travelling abroad while his countrymen were fighting for liberty. He did not exactly hurry, however, and spent time in Florence and Venice on the way back.

Soon after his return to England Milton undertook the education of two nephews, Edward and John Phillips, whose father had died, and in 1643 took on more pupils. His treatise *Of Education* probably reflects his own practice as a tutor. Milton aligned himself with the attacks upon episcopal church government initiated by the Long Parliament, and wrote his pamphlets on church government. This was the beginning of an involvement with the political life of his country which continued until his death, though necessarily in a more subdued and coded manner after the Restoration. In May 1643 Milton married Mary Powell, the third of eleven children of a Royalist family, then aged seventeen. After a short time Mary went back to her parents on a visit, from which she did not return; it is possible that she found life with Milton dull, that she was distressed by the beatings he administered to his pupils, and that the marriage was not consummated. Milton then published some pamphlets advocating easier access to divorce on grounds of incompatibility, which rendered him notorious in his own time, and make very good reading in ours. The divorce tracts were followed by *Areopagitica*, an argument against censorship. Milton by this time had become disenchanted with the Presbyterians, seeing their system of church government as just as autocratic as Laudian Anglicanism had been. Perhaps because of the defeat of the Royalist cause, Mary Powell or her family decided that she should return to Milton, and after she had begged his pardon, he took her back. She died in 1652, after giving birth to four children. Milton's first book of collected verse was published in 1645, and may have been prompted by the desire to vindicate himself as a person of high culture after the attacks upon him prompted by his writings on divorce. In 1647, after the death of his father, Milton gave up teaching in order, probably, to find more time for writing. The execution of Charles I occasioned more political prose; Milton's justification for the execution, *The Tenure of Kings and Magistrates*, appeared in February 1649. He was then invited to be Latin Secretary to the Council of State, Latin then being the common language of diplomatic correspondence. He also acted as a polemicist for the new regime. *Eikonoklastes* (the image-breaker) appeared in October 1649, as a reply to *Eikon basilike* (the image of a king), which had been published in February of that year. *Eikon basilike*, purporting to have been written by Charles I during his final imprisonment, was a highly successful piece of Royalist propaganda, very frequently reprinted in the years following the execution of Charles. During his work for the Commonwealth, Milton became blind, his duties accordingly became less onerous, and he had a succession of assistants, one of whom was Andrew Marvell. Milton's second marriage, to Catharine Woodcock, took place in November 1656; a daughter was born in October 1657; mother and child both died in the following February. Milton continued as Latin Secretary almost until the Restoration, and even when it

appeared inevitable was still publishing, courageously, against a return to monarchical government. After going into hiding for some time, Milton was arrested and imprisoned. His release was probably brought about by the intercession of friends, among them notably Andrew Marvell. In February 1663 he married Elizabeth Minshull, some thirty years his junior. It is probable, from his relationships and from internal evidence, that in his later years he was sympathetic to Quakerism. *Paradise Lost* was published in 1667, and *Paradise Regained* and *Samson Agonistes*, in the same volume, in 1671. They have been interpreted as representing Milton's withdrawal from the political realm into detached religious meditation; more recently their political significance has been acknowledged.

For Milton see also Aubrey, *Brief Lives*.

On the Morning of Christ's Nativity [1]

I

This is the month, and this the happy morn
Wherein the son of heaven's eternal king,
Of wedded maid, and virgin mother born,
Our great redemption from above did bring;
For so the holy sages once did sing,
     That he our deadly forfeit should release,
And with his father work us a perpetual peace. [2]

II

That glorious form, that light unsufferable,
And that far-beaming blaze of majesty,
Wherewith he wont at heaven's high council-table,
To sit the midst of trinal unity,
He laid aside; and here with us to be,
     Forsook the courts of everlasting day,
And chose with us a darksome house of mortal
     clay.

III

Say heavenly muse, shall not thy sacred vein
Afford a present to the infant God?
Hast thou no verse, no hymn, or solemn strain,
To welcome him to this his new abode,
Now while the heaven by the sun's team untrod, [3]
     Hath took no print of the approaching light,
And all the spangled host keep watch in
     squadrons bright?

IV

See how from far upon the eastern road
The star-led wizards haste with odours sweet, [4]
O run, prevent them with thy humble ode,

---

[1] In his sixth Latin elegy, Milton says that he began this poem before dawn on Christmas Day, 1629. It was printed first in 1645 and in 1673.

[2] *holy sages* Hebrew prophets. See for example the verse made famous by Handel's *Messiah*, Isaiah 9:6: "For unto us a child is born, unto us a son is given"; *our deadly forfeit* the consequences of "original sin" to which all human beings, as descendants of Adam and Eve, were thought to be liable.

[3] *the sun's team* the horses of the sun's chariot.

[4] *star-led wizards* the Magi. See Matthew 2:1–12.

25 And lay it lowly at his blessèd feet; [1]
Have thou the honour first thy Lord to greet,
   And join thy voice unto the angel choir,
From out his secret altar touched with hallowed
   fire. [2]

The Hymn

I

30 It was the winter wild,
While the heaven-born child
   All meanly wrapped in the rude manger lies;
Nature in awe to him
Had doffed her gaudy trim,
   With her great master so to sympathize: [3]
35 It was no season then for her
To wanton with the sun her lusty paramour.

II

Only with speeches fair
She woos the gentle air
   To hide her guilty front with innocent snow,
40 And on her naked shame,
Pollute with sinful blame, [4]
   The saintly veil of maiden white to throw,
Confounded, that her maker's eyes
Should look so near upon her foul deformities.

III

45 But he her fears to cease,
Sent down the meek-eyed Peace; [5]

She crowned with olive green, came softly
   sliding
Down through the turning sphere
His ready harbinger, [6]
50   With turtle wing the amorous clouds dividing,
And waving wide her myrtle wand,
She strikes a universal peace through sea and land.

IV

No war, or battle's sound
Was heard the world around:
55   The idle spear and shield were high up hung,
The hookèd chariot stood
Unstained with hostile blood, [7]
   The trumpet spake not to the armèd throng,
And kings sat still with awful eye,
60 As if they surely knew their sov'reign Lord was
   by. [8]

V

But peaceful was the night
Wherein the prince of light
   His reign of peace upon the earth began:
The winds with wonder whist,
65 Smoothly the waters kissed, [9]
   Whispering new joys to the mild ocean,
Who now hath quite forgot to rave,

---

[1] *prevent* go before, anticipate. Compare the Collect for Easter Day in *BCP*, with its reference to God's special grace preventing us and putting into our minds good desires.

[2] *touched with hallowed fire* See Isaiah 6:1–8.

[3] *sympathize* be in accord with; the accord between natural and human events is common in literature of the ancient world.

[4] *her guilty front...her naked shame...sinful blame* Nature "fell" along with mankind; see *Paradise Lost* 10: 649f.

[5] *Peace* The "peace of Augustus" prevailed throughout the Roman empire at the time of Christ's birth. The idea that this period of peace was especially ordained by God for the reception of Christ into the

---

world became common after the fifth century C.E. It was thought of as fulfilling the sayings of the Hebrew prophets concerning the Messiah. In Dante's *Paradiso* 6: 55–57, Milton could have found a juxtaposition of the idea of peace on earth with that of the harmony of the heavens similar to that he makes in this poem. In the *Convivio* Book 4, chapter 5, Dante introduces the same idea at greater length, and makes more explicit reference to the harmony of the planets at Christ's birth.

[6] *harbinger* forerunner (*OED* harbinger sb 3).

[7] *hookèd* armed with scythes.

[8] *awful* filled with awe, reverential.

[9] *whist* hushed, still.

While birds of calm sit brooding on the charmèd
    wave. [1]

VI

The stars with deep amaze
70 Stand fixed in steadfast gaze,
    Bending one way their precious influence,
And will not take their flight,
For all the morning light,
    Or Lucifer that often warned them thence; [2]
75 But in their glimmering orbs did glow, [3]
Until their Lord himself bespake, and bid them go.

VII

And though the shady gloom
Had given day her room,
    The sun himself withheld his wonted speed, [4]
80 And hid his head for shame,
As his inferior flame,
    The new enlightened world no more should
        need;
He saw a greater sun appear
Than his bright throne, or burning axle-tree could
    bear. [5]

VIII

85 The shepherds on the lawn,
Or ere the point of dawn,

Sat simply chatting in a rustic row;
Full little thought they then,
That the mighty Pan
90   Was kindly come to live with them below, [6]
Perhaps their loves, or else their sheep,
Was all that did their silly thoughts so busy
    keep. [7]

IX

When such music sweet
Their hearts and ears did greet,
95   As never was by mortal finger strook,
Divinely-warbled voice
Answering the stringèd noise,
    As all their souls in blissful rapture took:
The air such pleasure loath to lose,
100 With thousand echoes still prolongs each heav'nly
    close.

X

Nature that heard such sound
Beneath the hollow round
    Of Cynthia's seat, the airy region thrilling,
Now was almost won
105 To think her part was done,
    And that her reign had here its last fulfilling;
She knew such harmony alone
Could hold all heav'n and earth in happier
    union.

XI

At last surrounds their sight
110 A globe of circular light,
    That with long beams the shamefaced night
        arrayed,
The helmèd cherubim

---

[1] *birds of calm* According to ancient fable, the halcyon, or kingfisher, bred about the time of the winter solstice in a nest floating on the sea, and charmed the wind and waves so that the sea was specially calm during this period. See *OED* halcyon.

[2] *Lucifer* the morning star, Venus.

[3] *orbs* the concentric hollow spheres of the Ptolemaic astronomy, in which the planets and stars are carried around the earth.

[4] *The Sun himself withheld his wonted speed* The winter solstice is one of two times in the year when the sun reaches its farthest point from the Equator and appears to stand still before its return. Milton is concerned in this poem with the idea of Christ's birth as marking a turning-point in time.

[5] *a greater Sun* The pun on Sun-Son originates in Malachi 4:2: "But unto you that fear my name shall the Sun of righteousness arise with healing in his wings"; *burning axle-tree* the axle of the Sun's chariot.

---

[6] *Pan* in ancient Greece, the god of shepherds; in the Renaissance a symbol of Christ; *kindly* both in the modern sense and "as one of their kind," in reference to the fact that in the Incarnation God became human.

[7] *silly* simple, unsophisticated, rustic (*OED* simple *a* 3).

And sworded seraphim, [1]
  Are seen in glittering ranks with wings
      displayed,
115 Harping in loud and solemn choir,
With unexpressive notes to heav'n's new-born
      heir. [2]

XII

Such music (as 'tis said)
Before was never made,
  But when of old the songs of morning sung,
120 While the creator great
His constellations set,
  And the well-balanced world on hinges hung,
And cast the dark foundations deep,
And bid the welt'ring waves their oozy channel
      keep. [3]

XIII

125 Ring out, ye crystal spheres,
Once bless our human ears
  (If ye have power to touch our senses so),
And let your silver chime
Move in melodious time;
  And let the base of heaven's deep organ blow,
130

And with your ninefold harmony
Make up full consort to the angelic symphony. [4]

XIV

For if such holy song
Enwrap our fancy long,
135   Time will run back, and fetch the age of gold,
And speckled vanity
Will sicken soon and die,
  And lep'rous sin will melt from earthly mould,
And hell itself will pass away,
140 And leave her dolorous mansions to the peering
      day.

XV

Yea Truth, and Justice then
Will down return to men,
  Orbed in a rainbow; and like glories wearing
Mercy will sit between,
145 Throned in celestial sheen, [5]
  With radiant feet the tissued clouds down
      steering,
And heaven as at some festival,
Will open wide the gates of her high palace hall.

XVI

Bust wisest fate says no,
150 This must not yet be so,
  The babe lies yet in smiling infancy, [6]

---

[1] *cherubim...seraphim* the second and first highest respectively of the nine orders of angels, described by the pseudo-Dionysius in the fifteenth chapter of his *Celestial Hierarchy*. A readable account of his writings (very influential throughout the Middle Ages and as late as the Renaissance) is Frederick Copleston's *A History of Philosophy* (New York: Doubleday 1962), vol 2, part 1, ch. 9.

[2] *unexpressive* inexpressible: one of Shakespeare's coinages.

[3] Dante writes in the *Convivio* Book 4, chapter 5, that since the heavens began to revolve, that is, since the Creation, they had never been in a better disposition than when Christ descended to earth, who made them and governs them; and, he adds, mathematicians are able to prove this by their arts. In terms of the poem, this would mean that the music of the spheres had never been so beautiful since the Fall; it was like a new creation.

[4] *And with your ninefold harmony* etc. The nine orders of angels parallel the nine celestial spheres of Ptolemaic astronomy. The idea of a harmony between the singing of the angels and the music of the spheres may have been suggested by Dante, *Purgatorio* 30: 91–93.

[5] *Truth, Justice, Mercy.* "Mercy and truth are met together; righteousness and peace have kissed each other" (Psalm 85:10). John Leonard points out that the "righteousness" of the Authorized Version is *justitia* in the Vulgate, and that a mediaeval tradition makes Truth, Justice, and Mercy three of the four daughters of God, the other being Peace, which is also a preoccupation of this poem. See John Leonard, ed., *John Milton: The Complete Poems* (London: Penguin Books, 1998). Subsequent references to Leonard's notes will be indicated by "(JL)".

[6] *smiling infancy* Jesus can smile, but not yet speak (Latin *infans* unspeaking). Lancelot Andrewes plays on *logos* (word) and *infans* in a sermon for Christmas 1618: "An infant: *Verbum infans*: the *Word*

That on the bitter cross
Must redeem our loss;
   So both himself and us to glorify:
155 Yet first to those ychained in sleep, [1]
The wakeful trump of doom must thunder
   through the deep. [2]

XVII

With such a horrid clang
As on Mount Sinai rang [3]
   While the red fire, and smould'ring clouds out
   brake:
160 The agèd earth aghast
With terror of that blast,
   Shall from the surface to the centre shake;
When at the world's last session,
The dreadful judge in middle air shall spread his
   throne. [4]

XVIII

165 And then at last our bliss
Full and perfect is,
   But now begins; for from this happy day [5]

Th'old dragon underground [6]
In straiter limits bound,
170   Not half so far casts his usurpèd sway,
And wroth to see his kingdom fail,
Swinges the scaly horror of his folded tail. [7]

XIX

The oracles are dumb,
No voice or hideous hum
175   Runs through the archèd roof in words
   deceiving. [8]
Apollo from his shrine
Can no more divine,
   With hollow shriek the steep of Delphos
   leaving. [9]

in the second part of this poem, for example Apollo, Baalim, Moloch, Ashtaroth. We may see the "Nativity Ode" as a meditation on a Christian festival about which many of Milton's fellow-Puritans had deep reservations. They argued that it was a heathen festival (quite apart from Mithraism, December 25 had been a religious festival in Britain long before the introduction of Christianity), and in 1644 an Act of Parliament was passed forbidding any merriment or religious services on that day. It is, then, significant that Milton did not omit this poem, written in 1629, from the volume he published in 1645, but rather gave it pride of place as the first poem in that volume. His message might be thought of as "What we Puritans hate most is idolatry; at Christmas what we celebrate is the *overthrow* of idolatry."

[6] *Th'old dragon underground* Satan. See Revelation 20:2. In the thirty-fourth canto of the *Inferno* Satan is depicted as crucified upside down at the centre of the earth. For Milton's account of Satan being thrown out of heaven, see *Paradise Lost* 1:44–49.

[7] *Swinges* lashes. The "g" is soft as in "hinges" (JL).

[8] *words deceiving* The Delphic oracle was ambiguous, and so often led astray those who consulted it.

[9] There is a tradition that at the birth of Christ, a priest of Apollo, who was sacrificing near Delphi, suddenly stopped, and declared that the son of a god was at that moment born whose power would equal that of Apollo. This stanza is beautifully illustrated by William Blake, who shows the spirit of Apollo leaping from the statue and diving into the sea with a movement that is the perfect visual rendering of a "hollow shriek." There are similar traditions about the oracles being struck dumb (XIX); about the statue of Apollo sweating or weeping (XXI); about the infant Christ's expulsion of the false gods of Egypt (XXIII–XXV). The historians Josephus and Tacitus both relate how one day the doors of the inner shrine of the temple were thrown open, and "a voice of more than mortal tone was heard to cry that the gods

without a word, the *aeternall Word* not able to speak a word." T.S. Eliot had the misfortune to misquote this passage while writing of how Andrewes impresses himself on the memory. See Alan Rudrum, "T.S. Eliot on Lancelot Andrewes's 'word within a word'," *ANQ: A Quarterly Journal of Short Articles, Notes, and Reviews*, Vol. 9, No. 4 (Fall 1996), 43-44.

[1] *ychained in sleep* that is, the dead.

[2] *trump of doom* signalling the Day of Judgement.

[3] *As on Mount Sinai rang* Exodus 19:16–18.

[4] *middle air* See Matthew 24:30. The clouds occupied the second of the three regions of the air.

[5] From this point through stanza XXVI Milton's theme is the defeat of the pagan gods at the coming of Christ. The cult of the sun-god Mithras spread through the Roman empire and was popular for two centuries after the birth of Christ; his festival was held at the winter solstice, December 25 in the Roman calendar. It was not until after Mithraism had declined in importance that December 25 was fixed as the date of Christmas. Certain of the early Christians disagreed with this date, and accused those in favour of it of sun-worship. The defence was that Christ was "the true Sun." Some of the false sun-gods feature

No nightly trance, or breathèd spell,
180 Inspires the pale-eyed priest from the prophetic
      cell. [1]

                    XX

The lonely mountains o'er,
And the resounding shore,
      A voice of weeping heard, and loud lament;
From haunted spring, and dale
185 Edged with poplar pale,
      The parting genius is with sighing sent,
With flower-inwoven tresses torn
The nymphs in twilight shade of tangled thickets
      mourn.

                    XXI

In consecrated earth,
190 And on the holy hearth,
      The lars, and lemures moan with midnight
          plaint, [2]
In urns, and altars round,
A drear and dying sound
      Affrights the flamens at their service quaint; [3]
195 And the chill marble seems to sweat,
While each peculiar power forgoes his wonted
      seat.

                    XXII

Peor, and Baalim,
Forsake their temples dim, [4]

With that twice battered god of Palestine, [5]
200 And moonèd Ashtaroth,
Heaven's queen and mother both, [6]
      Now sits not girt with tapers' holy shine,
The Libyc Hammon shrinks his horn, [7]
In vain the Tyrian maids their wounded
      Thammuz mourn. [8]

                    XXIII

205 And sullen Moloch fled,
Hath left in shadows dread,
      His burning idol all of blackest hue
In vain with cymbals' ring,
They call the grisly king,
210   In dismal dance about the furnace blue; [9]
The brutish gods of Nile as fast,
Isis and Orus, and the dog Anubis haste.

                    XXIV

Nor is Osiris seen
In Memphian grove, or green,
215   Trampling the unshowered grass with lowings
          loud: [10]
Nor can he be at rest
Within his sacred chest,

---

[5] *that twice battered god of Palestine* Dagon. His idol was thrown down twice when the ark of the Covenant was set beside it; see I Samuel 5:1–5.

[6] *Ashtaroth* the Phoenician moon-goddess. Milton uses the plural form. To Roman Catholics Mary was the "queen of Heaven," and, not for the last time, Milton is being satirical at their expense.

[7] *The Libyc Hammon shrinks his horn* Ammon was a Libyan god depicted as a ram.

[8] *Thammuz* a beautiful youth loved by Astarte and killed by a boar.

[9] *Moloch* an Ammonite fire-god. Children were sacrificed to him while their cries were drowned by the noise of cymbals. See Leviticus 18:21: "And thou shalt not let any of thy seed pass through the fire to Molech"; II Kings 23:10: "that no man might make his son or his daughter to pass through the fire to Molech"; Jeremiah 32:35: "And they built the high places of Baal…to cause their sons and daughters to pass through the fire unto Molech."

[10] *Osiris…with lowings loud* Osiris was worshipped in the form of a bull.

---

were departing. At the same instant there was a mighty stir, as of departure." With the second part of this poem, compare the virtuoso passage on the false gods in *Paradise Lost* 1: 300–522.

[1] *cell* the innermost part of the temple, where the god's idol stood.

[2] *lars, and lemures* The lares were Roman household gods, the lemures Roman spirits of the dead.

[3] *flamens* an order of Roman priests.

[4] *Peor, and Baalim* Baal-Peor, a Canaanite sun-god (Numbers 25:3–5); Baalim is the plural of Baal, referring to such gods as Baal-Zebub and Baal-Perith.

Nought but profoundest hell can be his shroud,
In vain with timbrelled anthems dark
220 The sable-stolèd sorcerers bear his worshipped
    ark. [1]

XXV

He feels from Judah's land
The dreaded infant's hand, [2]
    The rays of Bethlehem blind his dusky eyn; [3]
Nor all the gods beside,
225 Longer dare abide,
    Not Typhon huge ending in snaky twine: [4]
Our babe to show his Godhead true,
Can in his swaddling bands control the damnèd
    crew. [5]

XXVI

So when the sun in bed,
230 Curtained with cloudy red,
    Pillows his chin upon an orient wave,
The flocking shadows pale,

Troop to th' infernal jail,
    Each fettered ghost slips to his several grave, [6]
235 And the yellow-skirted fays,
Fly after the night-steeds, leaving their moon-
    loved maze. [7]

XXVII

But see the virgin blest,
Hath laid her babe to rest.
    Time is our tedious song should here have
      ending:
240 Heav'n's youngest teemèd star,
Hath fixed her polished car, [8]
    Her sleeping Lord with handmaid lamp
      attending:
And all about the courtly stable,
Bright-harnessed angels sit in order serviceable.
—1645

L'Allegro [9]

Hence loathèd Melancholy
Of Cerberus, and blackest Midnight born, [10]

---

[1] *Nor…ark* Set tricked his brother Osiris into entering a chest, which Set cast adrift on the Nile. Isis (Osiris's wife) recovered the chest, but Set dismembered Osiris's body and scattered the pieces over the earth. Isis then gathered the pieces and restored life to the body (JL). Milton makes use of this in a wonderful passage in *Areopagitica*: "Truth indeed came once into the world with her divine Master, and was a perfect shape most glorious to look on: but when he ascended, and his Apostles after him were laid asleep, then strait arose a wicked race of deceivers, who as that story goes of the *Egyptian Typhon* with his conspirators, how they dealt with the good *Osiris*, took the virgin Truth, hewed her lovely form into a thousand pieces, and scattered them to the four winds. From that time ever since, the sad friends of Truth, such as durst appear, imitating the careful search that *Isis* made for the mangled body of *Osiris*, went up and down gathering limb by limb still as they could find them."

[2] *from Judah's land* "And the land of Judah shall be a terror unto Egypt" (Isaiah 19:17).

[3] *eyn* an archaic plural: eyes.

[4] *Typhon* The Egyptian god Set was conflated with the Greek Typhon, a hundred-headed serpent.

[5] *Our babe…crew* in allusion to the infant Hercules, who strangled two snakes sent by Juno to kill him in his cradle. Hercules was a common "type" of Christ (JL).

[6] *Troop…grave* Compare *A Midsummer Night's Dream* 3.2.382–83: "ghosts wandering here and there / Troop home to churchyards" (JL).

[7] *Night-steeds* the horses which draw the chariot of Night. Compare the cry of Marlowe's Faustus: "O lente, lente currite, noctis equi" (slowly, slowly run, horses of the night), ironically adapted from Ovid, *Amores* I.13.40.

[8] *Heav'n's youngest teemèd star* Theologians had debated whether the star of Matthew 2:2 was a new creation (JL); *fixed* "the star, which they saw in the east, went before them, till it came and stood over the place where the young child was" (Matthew 2:9); *polished car* gleaming chariot.

[9] The title means "the cheerful man." Milton probably thought of this and the next poem as being like contrasting movements in a musical composition. Musical directions (*Allegro* being a common one) are usually given in Italian.

[10] *loathèd Melancholy* not to be equated with the "divinest Melancholy" of *Il Penseroso*. For clues as to the relationship between them see "melancholy" and its close relatives in *OED*. The Galenist theory (influential among medical men of the day) was that melancholy was bad; the Aristotelian (influential among literary men) was that it could

Rain influence, and judge the prize
Of wit, or arms, while both contend
To win her grace, whom all commend.
125 There let Hymen oft appear
In saffron robe, with taper clear, [1]
And pomp, and feast, and revelry,
With masque, and antique pageantry,
Such sights as youthful poets dream
130 On summer eves by haunted stream.
Then to the well-trod stage anon,
If Jonson's learnèd sock be on, [2]
Or sweetest Shakespeare, fancy's child,
Warble his native wood-notes wild,
135 And ever against eating cares,
Lap me in soft Lydian airs, [3]
Married to immortal verse
Such as the meeting soul may pierce
In notes, with many a winding bout
140 Of linkèd sweetness long drawn out,
With wanton heed, and giddy cunning,
The melting voice through mazes running;
Untwisting all the chains that tie
The hidden soul of harmony.
145 That Orpheus self may heave his head
From golden slumber on a bed
Of heaped Elysian flowers, and hear
Such strains as would have won the ear
Of Pluto, to have quite set free
150 His half-regained Eurydice. [4]

These delights, if thou canst give,
Mirth with thee, I mean to live.
—1645

Il Penseroso [5]

Hence vain deluding joys,
The brood of folly without father bred,
How little you bestead, [6]
  Or fill the fixèd mind with all your toys; [7]
5 Dwell in some idle brain,
  And fancies fond with gaudy shapes possess,
As thick and numberless
  As the gay motes that people the sunbeams,
Or likest hovering dreams
10 The fickle pensioners of Morpheus' train. [8]
But hail thou goddess, sage and holy,
Hail divinest Melancholy,
Whose saintly visage is too bright
To hit the sense of human sight;
15 And therefore to our weaker view,
O'erlaid with black staid wisdom's hue.
Black, but such as in esteem,
Prince Memnon's sister might beseem, [9]
Or that starred Ethiop queen that strove
20 To set her beauty's praise above
The sea-nymphs, and their powers offended. [10]
Yet thou art higher far descended,
Thee bright-haired Vesta long of yore,

---

[1] *Hymen* the god of marriage.

[2] *Jonson's learnèd sock* in reference to the low-heeled shoe of actors in Greek comedy, and so to Jonson as a noted writer of comedies.

[3] *Lydian airs* Plato condemned the Lydian mode of music as being morally lax, and preferred the Dorian mode; others saw it as relaxing and pleasant. Milton is ironic on the subject in *Areopagitica*: "No music must be heard, no song be set or sung, but what is grave and *Dorick*." Horace, at the end of an ode to Augustus (*Odes* 4:15), is also complimentary about Lydian music.

[4] *That Orpheus…Eurydice* Orpheus sought his dead wife in Hades; Proserpine and Pluto permitted her to return on condition that Orpheus did not look back at her; he did so, and lost her again. See *Il Penseroso* 105–108; *Elysian flowers* Orpheus was reunited with

---

Eurydice in Elysium after his death.

[5] The title means "the thoughtful man."

[6] *bestead* help or relieve (*OED* bestead *v*[1]).

[7] *toys* idle fancies (*OED* toy *sb* 4).

[8] *Morpheus* the god of dreams.

[9] *Memnon* a black Ethiopian king who fought for Troy, described by Homer as the handsomest of men. Later writers gave him a beautiful sister, Himera (JL).

[10] *starred Ethiop queen* Cassiopeia, wife of the Ethiopian king Cephalus, was changed into a constellation because she claimed to be more beautiful than the Nereids (JL).

To solitary Saturn bore; [1]
25 His daughter she (in Saturn's reign,
Such mixture was not held a stain) [2]
Oft in glimmering bowers, and glades
He met her, and in secret shades
Of woody Ida's inmost grove, [3]
30 While yet there was no fear of Jove. [4]
Come pensive nun, devout and pure,
Sober, steadfast, and demure,
All in a robe of darkest grain,
Flowing with majestic train,
35 And sable stole of cypress lawn,
Over thy decent shoulders drawn.
Come, but keep thy wonted state,
With even step, and musing gait,
And looks commercing with the skies,
40 Thy rapt soul sitting in thine eyes:
There held in holy passion still,
Forget thyself to marble, till
With a sad leaden downward cast,
Thou fix them on the earth as fast.
45 And join with thee calm Peace, and Quiet,
Spare Fast, that oft with gods doth diet,
And hears the muses in a ring,
Ay round about Jove's altar sing.
And add to these retired Leisure,
50 That in trim gardens takes his pleasure;
But first, and chiefest, with thee bring,
Him that yon soars on golden wing,
Guiding the fiery-wheelèd throne, [5]

The cherub Contemplation, [6]
55 And the mute Silence hist along,
'Less Philomel will deign a song,
In her sweetest, saddest plight,
Smoothing the rugged brow of night, [7]
While Cynthia checks her dragon yoke,
60 Gently o'er th' accustomed oak; [8]
Sweet bird that shunn'st the noise of folly,
Most musical, most melancholy!
Thee chauntress oft the woods among,
I woo to hear thy even-song;
65 And missing thee, I walk unseen
On the dry smooth-shaven green,
To behold the wandering moon,
Riding near her highest noon,
Like one that had been led astray
70 Through the heaven's wide pathless way;
And oft, as if her head she bowed,
Stooping through a fleecy cloud.
Oft on a plat of rising ground,
I hear the far-off curfew sound,
75 Over some wide-watered shore,
Swinging slow with sullen roar;
Or if the air will not permit,
Some still removèd place will fit,
Where glowing embers through the room
80 Teach light to counterfeit a gloom,
Far from all resort of mirth,
Save the cricket on the hearth,
Or the bellman's drowsy charm,
To bless the doors from nightly harm: [9]
85 Or let my lamp at midnight hour,
Be seen in some high lonely tower,

---

[1] *Vesta* Saturn's daughter, the Roman goddess of the hearth and household.

[2] *Such mixture was not held a stain* Incest was not considered to be sinful.

[3] *woody Ida's inmost grove* Saturn reigned on Mount Ida in Crete.

[4] *While yet there was no fear of Jove* Jove ended the Golden Age by usurping Saturn's throne. See *Paradise Lost* 1:512–516.

[5] *the fiery-wheelèd throne* as in Ezekiel's vision of God's chariot.

---

[6] *The cherub Contemplation* In pseudo-Dionysius, *Celestial Hierarchy* 7.1.31–37 the cherubim are described as having the "faculty of seeing God, and of contemplating the beauty of the Supreme Being."

[7] *Philomel* turned into a nightingale after being raped by Tereus. See Ovid, *Metamorphoses* 6:438ff.

[8] *Cynthia* goddess of the moon.

[9] *bellman* the night-watchman who called the hours.

Where I may oft outwatch the Bear, [1]
With thrice great Hermes, or unsphere [2]
The spirit of Plato to unfold
90 What worlds, or what vast regions hold
The immortal mind that hath forsook
Her mansion in this fleshly nook:
And of those daemons that are found
In fire, air, flood, or underground,
95 Whose power hath a true consent
With planet, or with element.
Sometime let gorgeous Tragedy
In sceptred pall come sweeping by,
Presenting Thebes, or Pelops' line,
100 Or the tale of Troy divine. [3]
Or what (though rare) of later age,
Ennobled hath the buskined stage. [4]
But, O sad virgin, that thy power
Might raise Musaeus from his bower, [5]
105 Or bid the soul of Orpheus sing
Such notes as warbled to the string,
Drew iron tears down Pluto's cheek,
And made hell grant what love did seek.
Or call up him that left half-told
110 The story of Cambuscan bold, [6]
Of Camball, and of Algarsife,
And who had Canace to wife,

That owned the virtuous ring and glass,
And of the wondrous horse of brass,
115 On which the Tartar king did ride;
And if aught else, great bards beside,
In sage and solemn tunes have sung,
Of tourneys and of trophies hung;
Of forest, and enchantments drear,
120 Where more is meant than meets the ear.
Thus Night oft see me in thy pale career,
Till civil-suited Morn appear,
Not tricked and frounced as she was wont,
With the Attic boy to hunt, [7]
125 But kerchiefed in a comely cloud,
While rocking winds are piping loud,
Or ushered with a shower still,
When the gust hath blown his fill,
Ending on the rustling leaves,
130 With minute drops from off the eaves. [8]
And when the sun begins to fling
His flaring beams, me goddess bring
To archèd walks of twilight groves,
And shadows brown that Sylvan loves
135 Of pine, or monumental oak, [9]
Where the rude axe with heavèd stroke,
Was never heard the nymphs to daunt,
Or fright them from their hallowed haunt.
There in close covert by some brook,
140 Where no profaner eye may look,
Hide me from day's garish eye,

---

[1] *outwatch the Bear* keep awake all night (Ursa Major never sets).

[2] *thrice great Hermes* Hermes Trismegistus, the supposed author of the hermetic books, once thought to have been a very ancient source of wisdom. Though by Milton's time they had been shown to have been composed in the first three centuries C.E., they were still widely read and highly esteemed; *unsphere* that is, to summon Plato from the celestial sphere which, according to Neoplatonic philosophy, his soul would inhabit after his death.

[3] *Thebes* the city of Oedipus; *Pelops' line* The descendants of Pelops appear in various Greek tragedies; *the tale of Troy* the scene of tragedies by Sophocles and Euripides.

[4] *buskined* in reference to the high boots of the Greek tragic actor; compare the reference to "sock" in *L'Allegro* 132.

[5] *Musaeus* a mythical Greek poet and priest said to have been the son or pupil of Orpheus (JL).

[6] *him* Chaucer, whose *Squire's Tale* is unfinished.

---

[7] *the Attic boy* Cephalus, an Athenian prince and hunter loved by Aurora (JL). See Ovid, *Metamorphoses*, 7:690–865.

[8] *minute drops* John Leonard remarks that most editors adopt Warton's 1791 note: "drops falling at intervals of a minute," comments that Warton was presumably thinking of minute guns or bells, fired or tolled at intervals of a minute as a sign of mourning, and points out that neither existed in Milton's time. He glosses *minute* as meaning "small," as does another recent editor, Roy Flannagan (*The Riverside Milton*, New York: Houghton Mifflin, 1998, 76). I am inclined to agree with Warton. Minute guns or bells may not have existed in Milton's time, but minute-watches (on the dials of which minutes were marked) did.

[9] *Sylvan* Silvanus, Roman god of the woods.

While the bee with honied thigh,
That at her flowery work doth sing,
And the waters murmuring
145 With such consort as they keep,
Entice the dewy-feathered Sleep;
And let some strange mysterious dream,
Wave at his wings in airy stream,
Of lively portraiture displayed,
150 Softly on my eyelids laid.
And as I wake, sweet music breathe
Above, about, or underneath,
Sent by some spirit to mortals good,
Or th' unseen genius of the wood.
155 But let my due feet never fail,
To walk the studious cloister's pale, [1]
And love the high embowèd roof,
With antique pillars' massy proof,
And storied windows richly dight,
160 Casting a dim religious light. [2]
There let the pealing organ blow,
To the full-voiced choir below,
In service high, and anthems clear,
As may with sweetness, through mine ear,
165 Dissolve me into ecstasies,
And bring all heaven before mine eyes.
And may at last my weary age
Find out the peaceful hermitage,
The hairy gown and mossy cell,
170 Where I may sit and rightly spell,
Of every star that heaven doth shew,
And every herb that sips the dew;
Till old experience do attain
To something like prophetic strain.
175 These pleasures Melancholy give,
And I with thee will choose to live.
—1645

---

[1] *pale* enclosure.

[2] *storied* illustrating scenes from biblical history.

Lycidas

In this monody the author bewails a learned friend, unfortunately drowned in his passage from Chester on the Irish Seas, 1637. And by occasion foretells the ruin of our corrupted clergy then in their height. [3]

Yet once more, O ye laurels, and once more
Ye myrtles brown, with ivy never sere,
I come to pluck your berries harsh and crude,
And with forced fingers rude,
5 Shatter your leaves before the mellowing year.
Bitter constraint, and sad occasion dear,
Compels me to disturb your season due:
For Lycidas is dead, dead ere his prime,
Young Lycidas, and hath not left his peer: [4]
10 Who would not sing for Lycidas? he knew
Himself to sing, and build the lofty rhyme.
He must not float upon his watery bier
Unwept, and welter to the parching wind,
Without the meed of some melodious tear.
15   Begin then, sisters of the sacred well,
That from beneath the seat of Jove doth spring, [5]
Begin, and somewhat loudly sweep the string.
Hence with denial vain, and coy excuse,
So may some gentle muse
20 With lucky words favour my destined urn, [6]
And as he passes turn,
And bid fair peace be to my sable shroud.
For we were nursed upon the self-same hill,
Fed the same flock; by fountain, shade, and rill. [7]

---

[3] This headnote was added in 1645; it would have been highly impolitic in 1638, when the poem was first published.

[4] *dead ere his prime* Edward King was twenty-five years old when he was drowned.

[5] *sisters of the sacred well* the Muses.

[6] *lucky words* fortunate, well-chosen, felicitous.

[7] *the self-same hill* Cambridge, where Milton and King were students, is not conspicuously hilly; this is pastoral's way of saying that they studied in the same place. Critics have sometimes "interpreted" this section in terms of Cambridge undergraduate life in the early modern period. The point of pastoral here, however, is to link Milton's and

Together both, ere the high lawns appeared
Under the opening eyelids of the morn,
We drove afield, and both together heard
What time the grey-fly winds her sultry horn,
Battening our flocks with the fresh dews of night, [1]
Oft till the star that rose, at evening, bright
Toward heaven's descent had sloped his westering
    wheel.
Meanwhile the rural ditties were not mute,
Tempered to the oaten flute,
Rough satyrs danced, and fauns with cloven heel,
From the glad sound would not be absent long,
And old Damoetas loved to hear our song. [2]
    But O the heavy change, now thou art gone,
Now thou art gone, and never must return!
Thee shepherd, thee the woods, and desert caves,
With wild thyme and the gadding vine
    o'ergrown, [3]
And all their echoes mourn.
The willows, and the hazel copses green,
Shall now no more be seen,
Fanning their joyous leaves to thy soft lays.
As killing as the canker to the rose,
Or taint-worm to the weanling herds that graze,
Or frost to flowers, that their gay wardrobe wear,
When first the whitethorn blows;
Such, Lycidas, thy loss to shepherd's ear.
    Where were ye nymphs when the remorseless
    deep
Closed o'er the head of your loved Lycidas?
For neither were ye playing on the steep,

25, 30, 35, 40, 45, 50

Where your old bards, the famous Druids lie, [4]
Nor on the shaggy top of Mona high, [5]
Nor yet where Deva spreads her wizard stream: [6]
Ay me, I fondly dream!
Had ye been there…for what could that have
    done?
What could the muse herself that Orpheus bore, [7]
The muse herself, for her enchanting son
Whom universal nature did lament, [8]
When by the rout that made the hideous roar, [9]
His gory visage down the stream was sent,
Down the swift Hebrus to the Lesbian shore.
    Alas! What boots it with uncessant care
To tend the homely slighted shepherd's trade,
And strictly meditate the thankless muse,
Were it not better done as others use,
To sport with Amaryllis in the shade,
Or with the tangles of Neaera's hair? [10]
Fame is the spur that the clear spirit doth raise
(That last infirmity of noble mind)
To scorn delights, and live laborious days;
But the fair guerdon when we hope to find,
And think to burst out into sudden blaze, [11]

55, 60, 65, 70

King's educational experience to an ancient poetic tradition, and to elevate it by placing it within the European tradition of education and culture. See Alan Rudrum, *Milton: Comus and Shorter Poems* (London: Macmillan, 1967), 63–64.

[1] *Battening* fattening; see *OED* batten *v*[1]. Compare Virgil, Eclogue 8:15: "Scarce had night's cool shade left the sky, what time the dew on the tender grass is sweetest to the flock" (Loeb).

[2] *Damoetas* a conventional pastoral name. Milton may have had a particular tutor in mind.

[3] *gadding* straggling.

[4] *Druids* were both priests and poets, and so have particular relevance to Edward King.

[5] *shaggy* top of Mona. Mona (Anglesey) was not wooded in Milton's time, but Drayton remarks that it had once been dark with sacred oaks (*Poly-Olbion* 9:452–459).

[6] *where Deva spreads her wizard stream* The river Dee was credited with powers of divination (*Poly-Olbion* 10:186–210). Drayton used the adjective "wizard" of another river, the Weaver.

[7] *the muse herself that Orpheus bore* Calliope.

[8] *enchanting* The word is used in a strict sense, in relation to the magical powers of Orpheus.

[9] *the rout that made the hideous roar* Orpheus was torn to pieces by the Maenads, female followers of Bacchus.

[10] *To sport…hair?* Amaryllis and Neaera are conventional names for shepherdesses or nymphs in pastoral verse.

[11] *guerdon* reward or recompense (*OED* guerdon *sb*). The apparently noble but ultimately futile aspiration to fame is expressed in terms of that courtly chivalry ("spurs," "guerdon") which Milton was later to reject in the prologue to Book IX of *Paradise Lost*.

75 Comes the blind Fury with th' abhorrèd shears,
And slits the thin-spun life. But not the praise, [1]
Phoebus replied, and touched my trembling ears;
Fame is no plant that grows on mortal soil,
Nor in the glistering foil
80 Set off to the world, nor in broad rumour lies,
But lives and spreads aloft by those pure eyes,
And perfect witness of all-judging Jove;
As he pronounces lastly on each deed,
Of so much fame in heaven expect thy meed. [2]
85 O fountain Arethuse, and thou honoured flood,
Smooth-sliding Mincius, crowned with vocal
reeds, [3]
That strain I heard was of a higher mood: [4]
But now my oat proceeds, [5]
And listens to the herald of the sea [6]
90 That came in Neptune's plea, [7]
He asked the waves, and asked the felon winds,

What hard mishap hath doomed this gentle swain?
And questioned every gust of rugged wings
That blows from off each beakèd promontory;
95 They knew not of his story,
And sage Hippotades their answer brings,
That not a blast was from his dungeon strayed, [8]
The air was calm, and on the level brine,
Sleek Panope with all her sisters played. [9]
100 It was that fatal and perfidious bark
Built in th' eclipse, and rigged with curses dark,
That sunk so low that sacred head of thine.
Next Camus, reverend sire, went footing slow,
His mantle hairy, and his bonnet sedge, [10]
105 Inwrought with figures dim, and on the edge
Like to that sanguine flower inscribed with woe. [11]
Ah! who hath reft (quoth he) my dearest pledge?
Last came, and last did go,
The pilot of the Galilean lake,
110 Two massy keys he bore of metals twain
(The golden opes, the iron shuts amain), [12]
He shook his mitred locks, and stern bespake,
How well could I have spared for thee, young swain,
Enow of such as for their bellies' sake,
115 Creep and intrude, and climb into the fold?

[1] *the blind Fury* Milton's attention to mythological detail is remarkable. Conventionally, it was the Fates, not the Furies, who cut the thread of life. The Fates were inexorable, but also impartial and just; the Furies on the other hand were spirits of vengeance, seeking out a particular person.

[2] *Phoebus, Jove* It used to be argued, on the basis of these pagan names, that this is a passage of false consolation, to be superseded by the Christian consolation of the poem's close. This argument ignores the common practice of Milton and many other Renaissance poets. Phoebus Apollo, the god of poetry, was frequently equated with Christ; and one only has to go to the first line of *A Mask* for another example of Milton using "Jove" for "God."

[3] *Arethuse, and…Mincius* The fountain-nymph Arethusa fled from the river-god Alpheus and reappeared in Sicily as a spring welling up near the sea; this is one of the poem's resurrection-images, all of which, appropriately to an elegy for a man who was drowned, are related to water. Mincius is an Italian river mentioned ("honoured") by Virgil (*Georgics* 3:14–15). Together, they represent Greek and Roman pastoral poetry.

[4] *That strain I heard was of a higher mood* This refers back to the end of the previous section, placing it higher than the inspiration of the pastoral poets, who lived in pagan times.

[5] *oat* the oaten flute of pastoral.

[6] *the herald of the sea* Triton, Neptune's son.

[7] *in Neptune's plea* in view of the lines which follow, to gather evidence for Neptune's court. See *OED* plea *sb* I.

[8] *Hippotades* the ruler of the winds, more familiar by his name of Aeolus.

[9] *Panope* one of the fifty Nereids (sea-nymphs) who calmed the seas.

[10] *Camus, reverend sire* the river Cam, "reverend" because Cambridge was already an ancient university in the seventeenth century. Camus is not a pagan god, and so the passage provides a subtle transition to the explicit Christianity of the last spirit of the waters: St. Peter, the "pilot of the Galilean lake." Neptune, Camus and the pilot of the Galilean lake form a progression: Nature, Culture, Religion. See Rudrum, *Comus and Shorter Poems*, 71–72.

[11] *that sanguine flower inscribed with woe* the hyacinth, supposed to have sprung from the blood of a youth accidentally killed by Apollo during a game of quoits. It is supposed to be marked with the letters *aiai*, the Greek exclamation expressing grief.

[12] *Two massy keys* "thou art Peter, and upon this rock I will build my church, and the gates of hell shall not prevail against it. And I will give unto thee the keys of the kingdom of heaven: and whatsoever thou shalt bind on earth shall be bound in heaven; and whatsoever thou shalt loose on earth shall be loosed in heaven" (Matthew 16:18–19).

Of other care they little reckoning make,
Than how to scramble at the shearers' feast,
And shove away the worthy bidden guest.
Blind mouths! that scarce themselves know how
    to hold
120 A sheep-hook, or have learned aught else the least
That to the faithful herdman's art belongs! [1]
What recks it them? What need they? They are sped;
And when they list, their lean and flashy songs
Grate on their scrannel pipes of wretched straw,
125 The hungry sheep look up, and are not fed,
But swoll'n with wind, and the rank mist they draw,
Rot inwardly, and foul contagion spread:
Besides what the grim wolf with privy paw [2]
Daily devours apace, and nothing said,
130 But that two-handed engine at the door,
Stands ready to smite once, and smite no more. [3]
    Return Alpheus, the dread voice is past,
That shrunk thy streams; return Sicilian muse, [4]
And call the vales, and bid them hither cast
135 Their bells, and flowrets of a thousand hues.
Ye valleys low where the mild whispers use,

Of shades and wanton winds, and gushing brooks,
On whose fresh lap the swart star sparely looks,
Throw hither all your quaint enamelled eyes,
140 That on the green turf suck the honied showers,
And purple all the ground with vernal flowers.
Bring the rathe primrose that forsaken dies,
The tufted crow-toe, and pale jessamine,
The white pink, and the pansy freaked with jet,
145 The glowing violet,
The musk-rose, and the well-attired woodbine,
With cowslips wan that hang the pensive head,
And every flower that sad embroidery wears:
Bid amaranthus all his beauty shed,
150 And daffodillies fill their cups with tears,
To strew the laureate hearse where Lycid lies. [5]
For so to interpose a little ease,
Let our frail thoughts dally with false surmise
(Ay me!) Whilst thee the shores, and sounding
    seas [6]
155 Wash far away, where'er thy bones are hurled,
Whether beyond the stormy Hebrides
Where thou perhaps under the whelming tide
Visit'st the bottom of the monstrous world;
Or whether thou to our moist vows denied,
160 Sleep'st by the fable of Bellerus old, [7]

---

[1] *Blind mouths* John Ruskin drew attention to the force of this in the first lecture of *Sesame and Lilies*, pointing out that a bishop means one who sees and a pastor is one who feeds, and commenting "The most unbishoply character a man can have is to be blind. The most unpastoral is, instead of feeding, to want to be fed—to be a Mouth."

[2] *the grim wolf with privy paw* the Roman Catholic church, operating in England in secret to undo the Reformation. This was Milton's (and a good many others') view of what was happening in the 1630s; Archbishop Laud and other Anglican clerics were thought to be crypto-Catholics.

[3] *that two-handed engine at the door* a famous crux. Innumerable solutions have been offered, ranging from the Houses of Parliament to the "Jack o'th'Clock" which adorned several churches in Milton's day. The last two lines of this section of the poem may be vague, but they suggest, with adequate clarity and force, the terror and finality of God's avenging justice.

[4] *Return Alpheus...return Sicilian muse* The transition to the third section is achieved in a manner similar to that from the first to the second, in a modulation back to pagan pastoralism. Alpheus is the god of one of the rivers of Arcadia. The Sicilian muse refers to pastoral poetry, the Sicilian Theocritus being traditionally regarded as the father of pastoral poets.

---

[5] The passage which ends here draws upon one of the conventions of pastoral verse, the passage of the flowers. These are flowers that seem to mourn, but the feeling is different from that in the opening section: the passage has more colour than the "brown" myrtles and the "never-sere" ivy. In its gentleness, and delicacy of colour, the passage conveys consolation as much as lament; but it is a false consolation, as the poet recognizes in the close, because Lycidas is not lying on a "laureate hearse"; he died too soon to win poetic laurels, and his body is in the ocean, beyond the reach of his mourners.

[6] *with false surmise / (Ay me!)* Early modern texts tended to be punctuated for sound, for example to indicate pauses, rather than "grammatically." If we are modernizing at all, the original period after "surmise" has to be deleted. I have indicated the pause that it intended by bracketing (Ay me!). The point is that the period after "surmise" yields a syntax in which the "angel" who is asked to "look homeward" must logically be Lycidas rather than Michael.

[7] *fable of Bellerus old* the fabled abode of Bellerus; the latter is a giant or hero invented by Milton in accordance with "Bellerium," the Latin name for Land's End in Cornwall.

Where the great vision of the guarded mount
Looks toward Namancos and Bayona's hold; [1]
Look homeward angel now, and melt with ruth. [2]
And, O ye dolphins, waft the hapless youth. [3]
165   Weep no more, woeful shepherds weep no more,
For Lycidas your sorrow is not dead,
Sunk though he be beneath the watery floor,
So sinks the day-star in the ocean bed,
And yet anon repairs his drooping head,
170 And tricks his beams, and with new spangled ore,
Flames in the forehead of the morning sky: [4]
So Lycidas sunk low, but mounted high,
Through the dear might of him that walked the
    waves, [5]
Where other groves, and other streams along,
175 With nectar pure his oozy locks he laves,
And hears the unexpressive nuptial song,
In the blest kingdoms meek of joy and love. [6]
There entertain him all the saints above,
In solemn troops, and sweet societies
180 That sing, and singing in their glory move,
And wipe the tears for ever from his eyes.
Now Lycidas the shepherds weep no more;

Henceforth thou art the genius of the shore, [7]
In thy large recompense, and shalt be good
185 To all that wander in that perilous flood.
    Thus sang the uncouth swain to th' oaks and
        rills,
While the still morn went out with sandals grey,
He touched the tender stops of various quills,
With eager thought warbling his Doric lay: [8]
190 And now the sun had stretched out all the hills,
And now was dropped into the western bay;
At last he rose, and twitched his mantle blue: [9]
Tomorrow to fresh woods, and pastures new. [10]
—1638, 1645

Sonnet 7 [11]

How soon hath Time the subtle thief of youth,
Stol'n on his wing my three and twenti'th year!
My hasting days fly on with full career,
But my late spring no bud or blossom shew'th. [12]
5 Perhaps my semblance might deceive the truth,
That I to manhood am arriv'd so near, [13]

---

[1] *the great vision of the guarded mount* St. Michael, the guardian angel who was said to have appeared to fishermen on St. Michael's Mount in Cornwall in 495 C.E.; *Namancos and Bayona's hold* a region in north-west Spain and a Spanish fortress respectively.

[2] *Look homeward angel now, and melt with ruth* because the Catholic threat, since the defeat of the Armada in 1588 and the failure of the Gunpowder Plot in 1604, is no longer from Spain but within England itself. In this context we may dismiss the notion that the angel's home is in heaven; there is no reason why he should "melt with ruth" when looking in that particular direction. The relevant consideration is Michael's status as guardian angel of England.

[3] *waft* convey safely to land (*OED* waft v¹2). Dolphins are friendly to humans, and were thought to perform this service both to the living and the dead.

[4] *the day-star* perhaps Lucifer, the morning star; more likely the sun. Both were symbols of resurrection.

[5] *him that walked the waves* Jesus. See Matthew 14:22–33.

[6] *unexpressive* inexpressible; *nuptial song* the marriage song of the Lamb (Revelation 19:1–9).

---

[7] *genius of the shore* that is, the *genius loci*, the guardian spirit of that place.

[8] *eager thought* in contrast to the reluctance expressed in the beginning of the poem; *Doric lay* The pastoral poets Theocritus, Moschus and Bion wrote in the Doric dialect.

[9] *blue* the colour of hope.

[10] *fresh woods, and pastures new* echoing Phineas Fletcher, *The Purple Island* (1633), 6:77: "Tomorrow shall ye feast in pastures new."

[11] The date when this sonnet was written is important to its interpretation. Was it December 9, 1631, Milton's twenty-third birthday, or December 9, 1632, when Milton had ceased being twenty-three? The second of these possibilities has been widely accepted.

[12] *bud or blossom* a common metaphor for poetry. Compare the title of Cowley's first volume, *Poetical Blossoms*.

[13] *deceive the truth* that is, misrepresent it.

And inward ripeness doth much less appear,
That some more timely-happy spirits indu'th. [1]
Yet be it less or more, or soon or slow,
    It shall be still in strictest measure ev' n, [2]
    To that same lot, however mean, or high,
Toward which Time leads me, and the will of
    Heav'n; [3]
    All is, if I have grace to use it so,
    As ever in my great task-master's eye.

—1645

Sonnet 12
On the detraction which followed
upon my writing certain treatises [4]

I did but prompt the age to quit their clogs [5]
  By the known rules of ancient liberty, [6]

When straight a barbarous noise environs me
Of owls and cuckoos, asses, apes and dogs. [7]
As when those hinds that were transformed to frogs
Railed at Latona's twin-born progeny
Which after held the sun and moon in fee. [8]
But this is got by casting pearl to hogs; [9]
That bawl for freedom in their senseless mood,
And still revolt when truth would set them free. [10]

been so impudent as to set his name to it and dedicate it to your-selves."

[5] *quit their clogs* rid themselves of encumbrances. A "clog" was a heavy piece of wood attached to a prisoner's leg or neck to prevent escape (*OED* clog *sb* 2).

[6] *known rules of ancient liberty* the Mosaic law; also the natural law of right reason, which Milton believed to be of "more antiquity" than "marriage itself." (JL)

[7] *owls and cuckoos, asses, apes and dogs* Owls represent ignorance, cuckoos ingratitude, asses obstinate stupidity, apes empty mockery and dogs quarrelsomeness.

[8] *Latona's twin-born progeny* When Latona, with her new-born twins, Apollo and Diana, fled from the wrath of Juno, she came to Lycia and, being thirsty, wished to drink from a lake of clear water. Some countrymen who were there stopped her; when she pleaded with them, they added threats and abusive language. As a punishment, Latona changed them into frogs (Ovid, *Metamorphoses*, 6:331f), (E. A. J. Honigmann, ed., *Milton's sonnets*, London: Macmillan, 1966, 118). In a Christian interpretation of this story, Latona is said to represent "faith or the Scripture, which from the beginning were pregnant with Phoebus and Diana, that is with Christ and the Blessed Virgin." Alexander Ross published in 1653 a work called *Mystogogus Poeticus*; here it is asserted that "Our Saviour Christ is the true Apollo"; and that "God's Church is the true Diana" (Rudrum, *Comus and Shorter Poems*, 90). The reference to Latona and her twins imply that Milton's writings on divorce are a true interpretation of the gospels.

[9] *casting pearl to hogs* See Matthew 7:6. These pearls were conventionally interpreted as "the mysteries of the gospel," and the swine as "profane men, who despise and care nothing about the gospel" (Rudrum, *Comus and Shorter Poems*, 91).

[10] *revolt* draw back from a course of action, return to one's allegiance (*OED* revolt *v* 2b). Milton's Presbyterian detractors "revolt" by sliding back into conservative traditions. Milton also plays on the other sense of "revolt" to imply that the Presbyterians are rebels against Truth. He employs the same pun in his prose, always at the Presbyterians' expense (JL).

[1] *timely-happy* forward, precocious; *indu'th* the inward ripeness that inheres in some more timely-happy spirits; see *OED* endue *v* 9 b, this place cited. There has been a good deal of discussion about which of his contemporaries Milton might have had in mind. One candidate is Thomas Randolph, a Cambridge contemporary who had had a play acted before the King and Queen in 1632. Given the wide acceptance of the later date of composition, Cowley, ten years younger than Milton, is a strong contender for another place. *Poetical Blossoms* has a date of 1633 on the title-page, but its entry in the Stationers' Registers is dated October 24, 1632; it was common for the stationers to give books printed in the last month or two of the year the date of the following year, rather as nowadays "2000 model year" vehicles are available during the second half of the preceding year.

[2] *It* referring back to "inward ripeness."

[3] *Yet be it…will of Heav'n* Whatever the degree of ripeness, whether it comes early or late, it will be equal to, proportionate with, the "lot" towards which the poet is being led by time and the will of heaven. The last two lines of the poem register Milton's own responsibility in the matter.

[4] This title is from the Trinity Manuscript, where it covers this and another sonnet ("A book was writ of late called *Tetrachordon*"). The two sonnets are a response to the attacks upon Milton after he published his divorce tracts. The Presbyterians had been Milton's allies against the bishops, but they were hostile to the divorce tracts. In a sermon preached before both houses of Parliament in August 1644, Herbert Palmer spoke of the disadvantages of religious toleration, and mentioned a new theory of divorce "of which a wicked book is abroad and uncensured, though deserving to be burnt, whose Author hath

Licence they mean when they cry liberty; [1]
For who loves that, must first be wise and good;
  But from that mark how far they rove we see
  For all this waste of wealth, and loss of blood. [2]
—1673

Sonnet 18
On the Late Massacre in Piedmont [3]

Avenge O Lord thy slaughtered saints, whose
   bones
  Lie scattered on the Alpine mountains cold,
  Even them who kept thy truth so pure of old
When all our fathers worshipped stocks and
   stones, [4]
5 Forget not: in thy book record their groans
  Who were thy sheep and in their ancient fold

Slain by the bloody Piedmontese that rolled
  Mother with infant down the rocks. Their moans
The vales redoubled to the hills, and they
  To heaven. Their martyred blood and ashes sow [5]
O'er all the Italian fields where still doth sway
The triple tyrant: that from these may grow [6]
  A hundredfold, who having learnt thy way
Early may fly the Babylonian woe. [7]
—1673

Sonnet 19 [8]

When I consider how my light is spent,
  Ere half my days, in this dark world and
   wide, [9]
And that one talent which is death to hide, [10]
Lodged with me useless, though my soul more
   bent
5 To serve therewith my maker, and present
  My true account, lest he returning chide,
  Doth God exact day-labour, light denied,
  I fondly ask; but patience to prevent
That murmur, soon replies, God doth not need
10   Either man's work or his own gifts, who best

---

[1] *Licence*   probably in reference to the Licensing Order of June 14, 1643; Milton is identifying Truth with freedom of speech and publication; in his prose Milton wrote that "Liberty hath a sharp and double edge, fit only to be handled by just and virtuous men"; and that "none can love freedom heartily, but good men; the rest love not freedom, but licence" (Honigmann, 120).

[2] *For all*   in spite of. Milton is not condemning the Civil War. He is blaming the Presbyterians for making it futile.

[3] The massacre to which this poem refers was one of the most atrocious episodes in the religious conflicts of the seventeenth century. The Waldenses, who practised a simple form of Christianity, took their name from their founder Pierre Valdes. They were excommunicated in 1215. Driven out of the cities and fertile regions, they lived in the Alpine mountains of France and Italy. On the Italian side they lived in the territory of the Duke of Savoy, who made a treaty with them in 1561. In 1655 his successor sent an army to enforce the terms of that treaty. The result was a massacre in which seventeen hundred Waldensians died. Cromwell responded energetically, and refrained from sending an army only because the Duke made peace in August 1655, and accepted the principle of toleration. Milton as Latin Secretary wrote to the Duke of Savoy and other heads of state. Much publicity was given to this episode in England; the language of the poem echoes that in various newsletters: see Honigmann's edition for details.

[4] *who kept thy truth so pure of old*   Protestants of Milton's time thought the sect was even older than it actually was, and that it retained apostolic purity (JL); *stocks and stones*   that is, idols made of wood and stones: "[Israel] defiled the land, and committed adultery with stones and with stocks" (Jeremiah 3:9).

[5] *Their martyred blood and ashes sow*   in reference to the saying that the blood of the martyrs is the seed of the church.

[6] *triple tyrant*   the Pope, with his three-tiered crown.

[7] *the Babylonian woe*   Puritans regarded the Roman Catholic church as the Babylon of the Apocalypse, whose doom is foretold; see Revelation 17 and 18.

[8] The date of this sonnet is not certainly known. Milton's eyesight had been failing since 1644; he became completely blind in 1652.

[9] *Ere half my days*   This has been subject to a good deal of discussion. If Milton had been referring to the biblical "three score years and ten," the sonnet must be dated considerably earlier than the time at which he became completely blind. Some scholars think he may have reckoned his own life-span in relation to his father, who lived to be eighty-four; others that he was referring to an "immemorial popular belief" that man lives for a hundred years. See the interesting discussion in Honigmann, 172–174.

[10] *that one talent which is death to hide*   See Matthew 25:14f. Milton is referring to his literary talent.

Bear his mild yoke, they serve him best, his
    state [1]
Is kingly. Thousands at his bidding speed
    And post o'er land and ocean without rest: [2]
    They also serve who only stand and wait. [3]
—1673

On the New Forcers of Conscience under the Long Parliament [4]

Because you have thrown off your prelate lord, [5]
And with stiff vows renounced his liturgy [6]
To seize the widowed whore plurality
    From them whose sin ye envied, not abhorred, [7]
5 Dare ye for this adjure the civil sword
    To force our consciences that Christ set free,
    And ride us with a classic hierarchy [8]

Taught ye by mere A.S. and Rutherford? [9]
Men whose life, learning, faith and pure intent
10 Would have been held in high esteem with Paul
    Must now be named and printed heretics
By shallow Edwards and Scotch What-d'ye-call: [10]
    But we do hope to find out all your tricks,
    Your plots and packing worse than those of
        Trent, [11]
15   That so the Parliament
May with their wholesome and preventive shears
Clip your phylacteries, though balk your ears, [12]
      And succour our just fears
When they shall read this clearly in your charge,
20 New Presbyter is but old Priest writ large. [13]
—1673

---

[1] *his mild yoke* "Take my yoke upon you, and learn of me...For my yoke is easy, and my burden is light" (Matthew 11: 29–30).

[2] *Thousands at his bidding speed* Milton is referring to the angels, as God's "messengers."

[3] *stand and wait* "Wait on the Lord" is a frequent biblical phrase; see Psalm 27:14 for example.

[4] Honigmann (198) remarks that the most likely date of composition is early in 1646, since two of the Presbyterians referred to attacked Milton in print at about this time. This is a "tailed sonnet," such as was used by Italian poets for humorous or satirical sonnets. The form was not familiar in English.

[5] *thrown off your prelate lord* The "Ordinance for the abolition of archbishops, bishops etc" came out on October 9, 1646; but there had been a series of measures before that, and the Lords and Commons had resolved as early as 1643 that the hierarchical government of the church was evil and would be taken away. There is a probable pun on Archbishop Laud's name; see Honigmann, 197.

[6] *with stiff vows renounced his liturgy* William Prynne, in *Canterburies Doome*, 1646, remarks that the bill of attainder against Laud was passed "the very same hour they voted down the liturgy" (Honigmann, 197).

[7] *widowed whore plurality* The Presbyterians had railed against pluralism, the practice of receiving income from two or more benefices simultaneously, but were quick to adopt the practice themselves.

[8] *classic hierarchy* The "classis" or presbytery was a body of elders which acted as a disciplinary court in the Presbyterian system.

[9] *A.S. and Rutherford* Adam Stuart was a Scot who lived in London and wrote against the Independents; Samuel Rutherford, Professor of Divinity at St. Andrews, sat in the Assembly of Divines as one of the Scottish Commissioners.

[10] *shallow Edwards* Thomas Edwards, who had attacked Milton as a "divorcer" in *Gangraena*, 1646; *Scotch What-d'ye-call* not certainly identified; but Robert Baillie was a Scottish Commissioner who "expressed himself with bitterness against the Independents." Earlier commentators thought that George Gillespie, another Scottish Commissioner, was Milton's target; he was hostile to religious toleration, wrote of sectaries as heretics, and supported the Presbyterian campaign for the right to excommunicate. See Honigmann, 201.

[11] *Trent* Honigmann (202) remarks that the intrigues at the Council of Trent (1545–1563) had become notorious. The Westminster Assembly was partly a political arena for Presbyterians and Independents.

[12] *phylacteries* small boxes containing quotations from the Mosaic law which were worn on the forehead by pious Jews. Their display was treated in the gospel (Matthew 23:5) as a byword for hypocrisy; *balk your ears* stop short of cutting off their ears (a punishment of the time). The Trinity Manuscript had "crop ye as close as marginal P-'s ears," clearly a reference to William Prynne ("marginal" because he was famed for crowding his margins, in his many books, with citations of authorities). Prynne's ears were cropped twice, in 1634 and in 1637.

[13] *New Presbyter is but old Priest writ large* Milton is making a political point out of a philological one; etymologically, "priest" is a contraction of "presbyter."

Sonnet 15
On the Lord General Fairfax
at the Siege of Colchester[1]

Fairfax, whose name in arms through Europe
    rings[2]
  Filling each mouth with envy, or with praise,
  And all her jealous monarchs with amaze,
  And rumours loud, that daunt remotest kings,
5 Thy firm unshaken virtue ever brings
  Victory home, though new rebellions raise
  Their Hydra heads, and the false North displays
  Her broken league, to imp their serpent
    wings,[3]
O yet a nobler task awaits thy hand;
10   For what can war, but endless war still breed,
  Till truth, and right from violence be freed,
And public faith cleared from the shameful brand
  Of public fraud. In vain doth valour bleed[4]

---

[1] This sonnet, from the Trinity Manuscript, was composed in July or August 1648. Perhaps thought unpublishable in 1673 because of its republican tendencies, it was published in 1694 by Edward Phillips. For full historical background see Honigman, 138–144.

[2] *whose name in arms through Europe rings* Fairfax had been a very successful commander for Parliament and was made Commander in Chief of the New Model Army in January 1645. In 1648 several Royalist risings initiated the Second Civil War. Fairfax laid siege to Colchester, which fell on August 27. Fairfax disapproved of the execution of Charles I; his wife, masked, called out from the gallery at Charles's trial, "Oliver Cromwell is a traitor" (C.V. Wedgewood, *A Coffin for King Charles*, New York: Time Incorporated, 1966, 143–144). See Marvell, *Upon Appleton House.*

[3] *Hydra heads* The Hydra was a many-headed serpent; when one head was severed, two more grew in its place; it was slain by Hercules; *false North…broken league* The Scots (who had been Parliament's allies) invaded England in support of the King on July 8, 1648. The invasion violated the Solemn League and Covenant; *imp their serpent wings* engraft feathers so as to improve powers of flight (JL).

[4] *Public Faith* See the note on stanza 10 of Lovelace's *To Lucasta. From Prison*. Honigmann remarks that in Milton's day the phrase was widely used to refer to a form of National Debt incurred by the Parliament; it was also used to fob off the army whose pay was in arrears; *public fraud* Milton was said to have "lent most of his Personal Estate upon the Publick Faith" (Honigmann, 142) and may have been motivated here by a strong sense of personal injury.

While avarice, and rapine share the land.
—1694

Samson Agonistes[5]

OF THAT SORT OF DRAMATIC POEM
WHICH IS CALLED TRAGEDY

Tragedy, as it was anciently composed, hath been ever held the gravest, moralest, and most profitable of all other poems: therefore said by Aristotle to be of power by raising pity and fear, or terror, to purge the mind of those and such-like passions, that is to temper and reduce them to just measure with a kind of delight, stirred up by reading or seeing those passions well imitated.[6] Nor is nature wanting in her own effects to make good his assertion: for so in physic things of melancholic hue and quality are used against melancholy, sour against sour, salt to remove salt humours. Hence philosophers and other gravest writers, as Cicero, Plutarch and others, frequently cite out of tragic poets, both to adorn and illustrate their discourse. The Apostle Paul himself thought it not unworthy to insert a verse of Euripides into the text of Holy Scripture, I Cor. xv.33, and Paraeus commenting on the Revelation, divides the whole book as a tragedy, into acts distinguished each by a chorus of heavenly harpings and song between.[7] Heretofore men in highest dignity have laboured not a little to be thought able

---

Misappropriation of public funds was a charge often brought by Royalists; in this case the Independents and Army-chiefs alleged it of Parliamentarians.

[5] The date of composition has been much discussed. I have always regarded it as a post-Restoration work, and consider this to be now established with moral certitude. See Blair Worden, "Milton, Samson Agonistes, and the Restoration" in *Culture and Society in the Stuart Restoration*, ed. Gerald MacLean (Cambridge: Cambridge U P, 1995), 111–136.

[6] *Aristotle* writes of tragic catharsis in *Poetics* 6.

[7] *Paraeus* David Paraeus (1548–1622) a Calvinist theologian and biblical commentator.

to compose a tragedy. Of that honour Dionysius the elder was no less ambitious, than before of his attaining to the tyranny. [1]Augustus Caesar also had begun his Ajax, but unable to please his own judgement with what he had begun, left it unfinished. Seneca the philosopher is by some thought the author of those tragedies (at least the best of them) that go under that name.[2] Gregory Nazianzen a Father of the church, thought it not unbeseeming the sanctity of his person to write a tragedy, which he entitled, *Christ Suffering*.[3] This is mentioned to vindicate tragedy from the small esteem, or rather infamy, which in the account of many it undergoes at this day with other common interludes; happening through the poet's error of intermixing comic stuff with tragic sadness and gravity; or introducing trivial and vulgar persons, which by all judicious hath been counted absurd; and brought in without discretion, corruptly to gratify the people. And though ancient tragedy use no prologue, yet using sometimes, in case of self-defence, or explanation, that which Martial calls an epistle;[4] in behalf of this tragedy coming forth after the ancient manner, much different from what among us passes for best, thus much beforehand may be epistled; that chorus is here introduced after the Greek manner, not ancient only but modern, and still in use among the Italians. In the modelling therefore of this poem,

with good reason, the ancients and Italians are rather followed, as of much more authority and fame. The measure of verse used in the chorus is of all sorts, called by the Greeks monostrophic, or rather apolelymenon,[5] without regard had to strophe, antistrophe or epode, which were a kind of stanzas framed only for the music, then used with the chorus that sung; not essential to the poem, and therefore not material; or being divided into stanzas or pauses, they may be called alleostropha.[6] Division into act and scene referring chiefly to the stage (to which this work never was intended) is here omitted. It suffices if the whole drama be found not produced beyond the fifth act.

Of the style and uniformity, and that commonly called the plot, whether intricate or explicit, which is nothing indeed but such economy, or disposition of the fable as may stand best with verisimilitude and decorum; they only will best judge who are not unacquainted with Aeschylus, Sophocles, and Euripides, the three tragic poets unequalled yet by any, and the best rule to all who endeavour to write tragedy. The circumscription of time wherein the whole drama begins and ends, is according to ancient rule, and best example, within the space of twenty-four hours.

THE ARGUMENT

Samson made captive, blind, and now in the prison at Gaza, there to labour as in a common workhouse, on a festival day, in the general cessation from labour, comes forth into the open air, to a place nigh, somewhat retired there to sit a while and bemoan his condition. Where he happens at length to be visited by certain friends and equals of his tribe, which make the Chorus, who seek to comfort him what they can; then by his old father Manoa,

---

[1] *Dionysius the elder* Dionysius I of Syracuse (ca. 430–367 B.C.E.).

[2] *Seneca the philosopher is by some thought the author of those tragedies* in fact the same person, but this was not established in Milton's day. Lucius Annaeus Seneca (4 B.C.E.–65 C.E.) was influential in the Renaissance in both capacities.

[3] *Gregory Nazianzen* Bishop of Constantinople (329–389).

[4] *Martial* Martial noted that tragedies and comedies may need epistles since "they cannot speak for themselves" (JL). What this means may be suggested by the following: "Samson Agonistes, the major poem of Milton's we must try to understand without the promptings of a narrative voice, might be held to exemplify the postmodern view that 'meanings are undecidable'" (Alan Rudrum, "Discerning the Spirit in *Samson Agonistes*: the Dalila Episode," in *"All in All": Unity, Diversity and Miltonic Perspective*, eds. Charles W. Durham and Kristin A. Pruitt, London: Associated U P, 1999, 245).

[5] *monostrophic* repeating one stanzaic arrangement; *apolelymenon* Greek: "freed" from the obligation to repeat stanzaic patterns (JL).

[6] *alleostropha* of irregular strophes or stanzas.

who endeavours the like, and withal tells him his purpose to procure his liberty by ransom; lastly, that this feast was proclaimed by the Philistines as a day of thanksgiving for their deliverance from the hands of Samson, which yet more troubles him. Manoa then departs to prosecute his endeavour with the Philistian lords for Samson's redemption; who in the meanwhile is visited by other persons; and lastly by a public officer to require his coming to the feast before the lords and people, to play or show his strength in their presence; he at first refuses, dismissing the public officer with absolute denial to come; at length persuaded inwardly that this was from God, he yields to go along with him, who came now the second time with great threatenings to fetch him; the Chorus yet remaining on the place, Manoa returns full of joyful hope, to procure ere long his son's deliverance: in the midst of which discourse an Hebrew comes in haste confusedly at first; and afterward more distinctly relating the catastrophe, what Samson had done to the Philistines, and by accident to himself; wherewith the tragedy ends.

THE PERSONS

Samson
Manoa, the father of Samson
Dalila his wife
Harapha of Gath
Public Officer
Messenger
Chorus of Danites

The Scene before the Prison in Gaza

Sam. A little onward lend thy guiding hand
To these dark steps, a little further on;
For yonder bank hath choice of sun or shade,
There I am wont to sit, when any chance

5   Relieves me from my task of servile toil,
Daily in the common prison else enjoined me,
Where I a prisoner chained, scarce freely draw
The air imprisoned also, close and damp,
Unwholesome draught: but here I feel amends,
10 The breath of heaven fresh blowing, pure and
      sweet,
With day-spring born; here leave me to respire. [1]
This day a solemn feast the people hold
To Dagon their sea-idol, and forbid [2]
Laborious works, unwillingly this rest
15 Their superstition yields me; hence with leave
Retiring from the popular noise, I seek
This unfrequented place to find some ease,
Ease to the body some, none to the mind
From restless thoughts, that like a deadly swarm
20 Of hornets armed, no sooner found alone,
But rush upon me thronging, and present
Times past, what once I was, and what am now.
O wherefore was my birth from heaven foretold
Twice by an angel, who at last in sight
25 Of both my parents all in flames ascended
From off the altar, where an offering burned,
As in a fiery column charioting
His godlike presence, and from some great act
Or benefit revealed to Abraham's race? [3]
30 Why was my breeding ordered and prescribed
As of a person separate to God,
Designed for great exploits; if I must die

---

[1] *With day-spring born* There has been much discussion as to whether *Samson Agonistes* is a drama of regeneration, or whether Samson is a failed hero, contrasted with the true heroism of Jesus in *Paradise Regained*. For those able to hear biblical echoes, this is an early clue. Compare Luke 1:78–79: "Through the tender mercy of our God, whereby the dayspring from on high hath visited us, to give light to them that sit in darkness and in the shadow of death, and to guide our feet into the way of peace."

[2] *Dagon their sea-idol* the principal god of the Philistines, described at *Paradise Lost* 1.462–63 as a "sea-monster, upward man / And downward fish."

[3] *O wherefore was my birth from heaven foretold* Judges 13:3–5; 13:10–23. In annotating I shall assume that the reader will be familiar with the biblical Samson story in Judges 13–16.

Betrayed, captived, and both my eyes put out,
Made of my enemies the scorn and gaze;
35 To grind in brazen fetters under task
With this heaven-gifted strength? O glorious
    strength
Put to the labour of a beast, debased
Lower than bond-slave! Promise was that I
Should Israel from Philistian yoke deliver;
40 Ask for this great deliverer now, and find him
Eyeless in Gaza at the mill with slaves,
Himself in bonds under Philistian yoke;
Yet stay, let me not rashly call in doubt
Divine prediction; what if all foretold
45 Had been fulfilled but through mine own default,
Whom have I to complain of but myself?
Who this high gift of strength committed to me,
In what part lodged, how easily bereft me,
Under the seal of silence could not keep,
50 But weakly to a woman must reveal it,
O'ercome with importunity and tears.
O impotence of mind, in body strong!
But what is strength without a double share
Of wisdom, vast, unwieldy, burdensome,
55 Proudly secure, yet liable to fall
By weakest subtleties, not made to rule,
But to subserve where wisdom bears command.
God, when he gave me strength, to show withal
How slight the gift was, hung it in my hair.
60 But peace, I must not quarrel with the will
Of highest dispensation, which herein
Haply had ends above my reach to know:
Suffices that to me strength is my bane,
And proves the source of all my miseries;
65 So many, and so huge, that each apart
Would ask a life to wail, but chief of all,
O loss of sight, of thee I most complain!
Blind among enemies, O worse than chains,
Dungeon, or beggary, or decrepit age!
70 Light the prime work of God to me is extinct,
And all her various objects of delight
Annulled, which might in part my grief have eased,

Inferior to the vilest now become
Of man or worm; the vilest here excel me,
75 They creep, yet see, I dark in light exposed
To daily fraud, contempt, abuse and wrong,
Within doors, or without, still as a fool,
In power of others, never in my own;
Scarce half I seem to live, dead more than half.
80 O dark, dark, dark, amid the blaze of noon,
Irrecoverably dark, total eclipse
Without all hope of day!
O first-created beam, and thou great word,
Let there be light, and light was over all;
85 Why am I thus bereaved thy prime decree?
The sun to me is dark
And silent as the moon,
When she deserts the night
Hid in her vacant interlunar cave. [1]
90 Since light so necessary is to life,
And almost life itself, if it be true
That light is in the soul,
She all in every part; why was the sight
To such a tender ball as the eye confined?
95 So obvious and so easy to be quenched,
And not as feeling through all parts diffused,
That she might look at will through every pore?
Then had I not been thus exiled from light;
As in the land of darkness yet in light,
100 To live a life half dead, a living death,
And buried; but O yet more miserable!
Myself, my sepulchre, a moving grave,
Buried, yet not exempt
By privilege of death and burial
105 From worst of other evils, pains and wrongs,
But made hereby obnoxious more
To all the miseries of life, [2]

---

[1] *silent as the moon…her vacant interlunar cave* The sense, applied to the moon, of "not shining" is first recorded in 1646 (*OED* silent *a* 5a); "vacant" means "at leisure"; the ancients supposed that the moon rested in a cave during the interlunar period between old and new moons (JL).

[2] *obnoxious* exposed, liable, exposed to (*OED* obnoxious 1a).

Life in captivity
Among inhuman foes.
110 But who are these? for with joint pace I hear
The tread of many feet steering this way;
Perhaps my enemies who come to stare
At my affliction, and perhaps to insult,
Their daily practice to afflict me more.

115 *Chor.* This, this is he; softly awhile,
Let us not break in upon him;
O change beyond report, thought, or belief!
See how he lies at random, carelessly diffused, [1]
With languished head unpropped,
120 As one past hope, abandoned,
And by himself given over;
In slavish habit, ill-fitted weeds
O'er-worn and soiled;
Or do my eyes misrepresent? Can this be he,
125 That heroic, that renowned,
Irresistible Samson? whom unarmed
No strength of man, or fiercest wild beast could
    withstand;
Who tore the lion, as the lion tears the kid,
Ran on embattled armies clad in iron,
130 And weaponless himself,
Made arms ridiculous, useless the forgery
Of brazen shield and spear, the hammered
    cuirass, [2]
Chalybean-tempered steel, and frock of mail
Adamantean proof; [3]
135 But safest he who stood aloof,
When insupportably his foot advanced,
In scorn of their proud arms and warlike tools,

Spurned them to death by troops. The bold
    Ascalonite
Fled from his lion ramp, old warriors turned
140 Their plated backs under his heel; [4]
Or grovelling soiled their crested helmets in the
    dust.
Then with what trivial weapon came to hand,
The jaw of a dead ass, his sword of bone,
A thousand foreskins fell, the flower of Palestine
145 In Ramath-lehi famous to this day: [5]
Then by main force pulled up, and on his
    shoulders bore
The gates of Azza; post, and massy bar
Up to the hill by Hebron, seat of giants old,
No journey of a sabbath-day, and loaded so; [6]
150 Like whom the Gentiles feign to bear up heaven. [7]
Which shall I first bewail,
Thy bondage or lost sight,
Prison within prison
Inseparably dark?
155 Thou art become (O worst imprisonment!)
The dungeon of thyself; thy soul
(Which men enjoying sight oft without cause
    complain)
Imprisoned now indeed,
In real darkness of the body dwells,
160 Shut up from outward light
To incorporate with gloomy night;
For inward light alas
Puts forth no visual beam.
O mirror of our fickle state,
165 Since man on earth unparalleled!
The rarer thy example stands,
By how much from the top of wondrous glory,

---

[1] *diffused* spread out (*OED* diffuse *v* 3, this place cited).

[2] *cuirass* breastplate. In this passage as in the prologue to *Paradise Lost* 9 Milton suggests his disdain of mediaeval "chivalry" and the "heroism" of warfare.

[3] *Chalybean-tempered steel* The Chalybes were a Black Sea tribe famous for their forging of iron; *Adamantean proof* armour capable of resisting adamant, a mythical substance of impenetrable hardness (JL).

[4] *Ascalonite* Ascalon was one of five Philistine cities.

[5] *A thousand foreskins fell* The Jews were circumcised, the Philistines were not.

[6] *journey of a sabbath-day* Jewish law restricted travel on the sabbath to about three quarters of a mile. Samson carried the massive gates from Gaza to Hebron—about forty miles (JL).

[7] *whom the Gentiles feign to bear up heaven* Atlas.

Strongest of mortal men,
To lowest pitch of abject fortune thou art fallen.
170 For him I reckon not in high estate
Whom long descent of birth
Or the sphere of fortune raises;
But thee whose strength, while virtue was her mate,
Might have subdued the earth,
175 Universally crowned with highest praises.

Sam. I hear the sound of words, their sense the air
Dissolves unjointed ere it reach my ear.

Chor. He speaks, let us draw nigh. Matchless in
    might,
The glory late of Israel, now the grief;
180 We come thy friends and neighbours not unknown
From Eshtaol and Zora's fruitful vale
To visit or bewail thee, or if better,
Counsel or consolation we may bring,
Salve to thy sores, apt words have power to suage
185 The tumours of a troubled mind,
And are as balm to festered wounds.

Sam. Your coming, friends, revives me, for I learn
Now of my own experience, not by talk,
How counterfeit a coin they are who friends
190 Bear in their superscription (of the most
I would be understood), in prosperous days
They swarm, but in adverse withdraw their head
Not to be found, though sought. Ye see, O friends,
How many evils have enclosed me round;
195 Yet that which was the worst now least afflicts me,
Blindness, for had I sight, confused with shame,
How could I once look up, or heave the head,
Who like a foolish pilot have shipwrecked
My vessel trusted to me from above,
200 Gloriously rigged; and for a word, a tear,
Fool, have divulged the secret gift of God
To a deceitful woman: tell me friends,
Am I not sung and proverbed for a fool
In every street, do they not say, how well

205 Are come upon him his deserts? yet why?
Immeasurable strength they might behold
In me, of wisdom nothing more than mean;
This with the other should, at least, have paired,
These two proportioned ill drove me transverse.

210 *Chor.* Tax not divine disposal, wisest men
Have erred, and by bad women been deceived;
And shall again, pretend they ne'er so wise.
Deject not then so overmuch thyself,
Who hast of sorrow thy full load besides;
215 Yet truth to say, I oft have heard men wonder
Why thou shouldst wed Philistian women rather
Than of thine own tribe fairer, or as fair,
At least of thy own nation, and as noble.

Sam. The first I saw at Timna, and she pleased
220 Me, not my parents, that I sought to wed,
The daughter of an infidel: they knew not
That what I motioned was of God; I knew
From intimate impulse, and therefore urged
The marriage on; that by occasion hence
225 I might begin Israel's deliverance, [1]
The work to which I was divinely called;
She proving false, the next I took to wife
(O that I never had! fond wish too late)
Was in the vale of Sorec, Dalila,
230 That specious monster, my accomplished snare.
I thought it lawful from my former act, [2]
And the same end; still watching to oppress
Israel's oppressors: of what now I suffer

---

[1] *I knew / From intimate impulse* For the understanding of such "intimate impulses" in Puritan thinking, see Blair Worden's essay, mentioned above; also Geoffrey F. Nuttall, *The Holy Spirit in Puritan Faith and Experience* (Chicago: U of Chicago P, reprinted 1992).

[2] *I thought it lawful from my former act* "Here Samson marks the distinction between the inner voice and the promptings of the devices and desires of our own hearts…he made the mistake of acting by analogy. He had no 'intimate impulse' but thought it lawful from his former act. In the first instance there was an apparent violation of God's law, in the second a real one" (Rudrum, *Discerning the Spirit*, 253).

She was not the prime cause, but I myself,
235 Who vanquished with a peal of words (O
    weakness!)
Gave up my fort of silence to a woman.

Chor. In seeking just occasion to provoke
The Philistine, thy country's enemy,
Thou never wast remiss, I bear thee witness:
240 Yet Israel still serves with all his sons.

Sam. That fault I take not on me, but transfer
On Israel's governors, and heads of tribes,
Who seeing those great acts which God had done
Singly by me against their conquerors
245 Acknowledged not, or not at all considered
Deliverance offered: I on the other side
Used no ambition to commend my deeds,
The deeds themselves, though mute, spoke loud
    the doer;
But they persisted deaf, and would not seem
250 To count them things worth notice, till at length
Their lords the Philistines with gathered powers
Entered Judea seeking me, who then
Safe to the rock of Etham was retired,
Not flying, but forecasting in what place
255 To set upon them, what advantaged best;
Meanwhile the men of Judah to prevent
The harass of their land, beset me round;
I willingly on some conditions came
Into their hands, and they as gladly yield me
260 To the uncircumcised a welcome prey,
Bound with two cords; but cords to me were
    threads
Touched with the flame: on their whole host I flew
Unarmed, and with a trivial weapon felled
Their choicest youth; they only lived who fled.
265 Had Judah that day joined, or one whole tribe,
They had by this possessed the towers of Gath,
And lorded over them whom now they serve;

But what more oft in nations grown corrupt, [1]
And by their vices brought to servitude,
270 Than to love bondage more than liberty,
Bondage with ease than strenuous liberty;
And to despise, or envy, or suspect
Whom God hath of his special favour raised
As their deliverer; if he aught begin,
275 How frequent to desert him, and at last
To heap ingratitude on worthiest deeds?

Chor. Thy words to my remembrance bring
How Succoth and the fort of Penuel
Their great deliverer contemned,
280 The matchless Gideon in pursuit
Of Madian and her vanquished kings; [2]
And how ingrateful Ephraim
Had dealt with Jephtha, who by argument,
Not worse than by his shield and spear
285 Defended Israel from the Ammonite,
Had not his prowess quelled their pride
In that sore battle when so many died
Without reprieve adjudged to death,
For want of well pronouncing *shibboleth.* [3]

290 *Sam.* Of such examples add me to the roll,
Me easily indeed mine may neglect,
But God's proposed deliverance not so.

Chor. Just are the ways of God,
And justifiable to men;
295 Unless there be who think not God at all,
If any be, they walk obscure;
For of such doctrine never was there school,
But the heart of the fool,
And no man therein doctor but himself. [4]

---

[1] *But what more oft in nations grown corrupt* etc.   This passage has
obvious relevance to England's restoration of Charles II to the throne.

[2] *Gideon*   See Judges 8:5–9.

[3] *Ephraim*   See Judges 11:12–33, 12:1–6.

[4] *the heart of the fool*   "The fool hath said in his heart, There is no
God" (Psalm 14:1).

300   Yet more there be who doubt his ways not just,
As to his own edicts, found contradicting,
Then give the reins to wandering thought,
Regardless of his glory's diminution;
Till by their own perplexities involved
305 They ravel more, still less resolved,
But never find self-satisfying solution.
     As if they would confine the interminable,
And tie him to his own prescript,
Who made our laws to bind us, not himself,
310 And hath full right to exempt
Whom so it pleases him by choice
From national obstriction, without taint [1]
Of sin, or legal debt;
For with his own laws he can best dispense.
315   He would not else who never wanted means,
Nor in respect of the enemy just cause
To set his people free,
Have prompted this heroic Nazarite,
Against his vow of strictest purity,
320 To seek in marriage that fallacious bride,
Unclean, unchaste.
     Down reason then, at least vain reasonings
        down,
Though reason here aver
That moral verdict quits her of unclean:
325 Unchaste was subsequent, her stain not his. [2]
     But see here comes thy reverend sire
With careful step, locks white as down,
Old Manoa: advise
Forthwith how thou ought'st to receive him.

330 *Sam.* Ay me, another inward grief awaked,
With mention of that name renews the assault.

Man. Brethren and men of Dan, for such ye seem,
Though in this uncouth place; if old respect, [3]
As I suppose, towards your once gloried friend,
335 My son now captive, hither hath informed
Your younger feet, while mine cast back with age
Came lagging after; say if he be here.

Chor. As signal now in low dejected state,
As erst in highest, behold him where he lies.

340 *Man.* O miserable change! is this the man,
That invincible Samson, far renowned,
The dread of Israel's foes, who with a strength
Equivalent to angel's walked their streets,
None offering fight; who single combatant
345 Duelled their armies ranked in proud array,
Himself an army, now unequal match
To save himself against a coward armed
At one spear's length. O ever-failing trust
In mortal strength! and O what not in man
350 Deceivable and vain! Nay what thing good
Prayed for, but often proves our woe, our bane?
I prayed for children, and thought barrenness
In wedlock a reproach; I gained a son,
And such a son as all men hailed me happy;
355 Who would be now a father in my stead?
O wherefore did God grant me my request,
And as a blessing with such pomp adorned?
Why are his gifts desirable, to tempt
Our earnest prayers, then given with solemn hand
360 As graces, draw a scorpion's tail behind?
For this did the angel twice descend? for this
Ordained thy nurture holy, as of a plant;
Select, and sacred, glorious for awhile,
The miracle of men: then in an hour
365 Ensnared, assaulted, overcome, led bound,

---

[1] *obstriction* legal obligation, in this case prohibiting marriage with Gentiles. This is a crucial paragraph. The Hebrew Scriptures implicitly make much of God's freedom by showing him working in ways that strict Israelites would have found unorthodox. It is precisely the perceived freedom of God, his not being bound by his own prescripts, which endows his human worshippers with freedom. Dagon, on the other hand, is an idol, because, his will being coterminous with that of the priests and elders of Israel, he has no transcendence. See Rudrum, *Discerning the Spirit*, 248f.

[2] *Unchaste was subsequent* Samson's first wife became unchaste when she was "given to his companion" (Judges 14:20) (JL).

[3] *uncouth* unfamiliar (*OED* uncouth *a* 2).

Thy foes' derision, captive, poor, and blind
Into a dungeon thrust, to work with slaves?
Alas methinks whom God hath chosen once
To worthiest deeds, if he through frailty err,
370 He should not so o'erwhelm, and as a thrall
Subject him to so foul indignities,
Be it but for honour's sake of former deeds.

Sam. Appoint not heavenly disposition, father, [1]
Nothing of all these evils hath befall'n me
375 But justly; I myself have brought them on,
Sole author I, sole cause: if aught seem vile,
As vile hath been my folly, who have profaned
The mystery of God given me under pledge
Of vow, and have betrayed it to a woman,
380 A Canaanite, my faithless enemy.
This well I knew, nor was at all surprised,
But warned by oft experience: did not she
Of Timna first betray me, and reveal
The secret wrested from me in her height
385 Of nuptial love professed, carrying it straight
To them who had corrupted her, my spies,
And rivals? In this other was there found
More faith? who also in her prime of love,
Spousal embraces, vitiated with gold,
390 Though offered only, by the scent conceived
Her spurious first-born; treason against me?
Thrice she assayed with flattering prayers and
    sighs,
And amorous reproaches to win from me
My capital secret, in what part my strength
395 Lay stored, in what part summed, that she might
    know: [2]
Thrice I deluded her, and turned to sport
Her importunity, each time perceiving
How openly, and with what impudence
She purposed to betray me, and (which was worse
400 Than undissembled hate) with what contempt

She sought to make me traitor to myself;
Yet the fourth time, when mustering all her wiles,
With blandished parleys, feminine assaults,
Tongue-batteries, she surceased not day nor night
405 To storm me over-watched, and wearied out.
At times when men seek most repose and rest,
I yielded, and unlocked her all my heart,
Who with a grain of manhood well resolved
Might easily have shook off all her snares:
410 But foul effeminacy held me yoked
Her bond-slave; O indignity, O blot
To honour and religion! servile mind
Rewarded well with servile punishment!
The base degree to which I now am fall'n,
415 These rags, this grinding, is not yet so base
As was my former servitude, ignoble,
Unmanly, ignominious, infamous,
True slavery, and that blindness worse than this,
That saw not how degenerately I served.

420 *Man.* I cannot praise thy marriage-choices, son,
Rather approved them not; but thou didst plead
Divine impulsion prompting how thou might'st
Find some occasion to infest our foes. [3]
I state not that; this I am sure; our foes
425 Found soon occasion thereby to make thee
Their captive, and their triumph; thou the sooner
Temptation found'st, or over-potent charms
To violate the sacred trust of silence
Deposited within thee; which to have kept
430 Tacit, was in thy power; true; and thou bear'st
Enough, and more the burden of that fault;
Bitterly hast thou paid, and still art paying
That rigid score. A worse thing yet remains,
This day the Philistines a popular feast
435 Here celebrate in Gaza, and proclaim

---

[1] *Appoint* both "blame" and "prescribe" (*OED* appoint *v* 8, 18).

[2] *capital* a pun (the word being derived from the Latin for "head");
it was Samson's chief secret, it was in his head, and it was on his head.

---

[3] *thou didst plead / Divine impulsion* Manoa is inaccurate here.
Samson only claimed divine impulsion for the first marriage. Manoa
(like a number of modern commentators) is suggesting that Samson
was unreliable in interpreting "divine motions" (or "the inner voice");
Samson had no such doubts.

Great pomp, and sacrifice, and praises loud
To Dagon, as their god who hath delivered
Thee Samson bound and blind into their hands,
Them out of thine, who slew'st them many a slain.
440 So Dagon shall be magnified, and God,
Besides whom is no god, compared with idols,
Disglorified, blasphemed, and had in scorn
By the idolatrous rout amidst their wine;
Which to have come to pass by means of thee,
445 Samson, of all thy sufferings think the heaviest,
Of all reproach the most with shame that ever
Could have befall'n thee and thy father's house.

Sam. Father, I do acknowledge and confess
That I this honour, I this pomp have brought
450 To Dagon, and advanced his praises high
Among the heathen round; to God have brought
Dishonour, obloquy, and oped the mouths
Of idolists, and atheists; have brought scandal
To Israel, diffidence of God, and doubt
455 In feeble hearts, propense enough before
To waver, or fall off and join with idols;
Which is my chief affliction, shame and sorrow,
The anguish of my soul, that suffers not
Mine eye to harbour sleep, or thoughts to rest.
460 This only hope relieves me, that the strife
With me hath end; all the contest is now
'Twixt God and Dagon; Dagon hath presumed,
Me overthrown, to enter lists with God,
His deity comparing and preferring
465 Before the God of Abraham. He, be sure,
Will not connive, or linger, thus provoked,
But will arise and his great name assert:
Dagon must stoop, and shall ere long receive
Such a discomfit, as shall quite despoil him
470 Of all these boasted trophies won on me,
And with confusion blank his worshippers.

Man. With cause this hope relieves thee, and these words
I as a prophecy receive: for God,

Nothing more certain, will not long defer
475 To vindicate the glory of his name
Against all competition, nor will long
Endure it, doubtful whether God be Lord,
Or Dagon. But for thee what shall be done?
Thou must not in the meanwhile here forgot
480 Lie in this miserable loathsome plight
Neglected. I already have made way
To some Philistian lords, with whom to treat
About thy ransom: well they may by this
Have satisfied their utmost of revenge
485 By pains and slaveries, worse than death inflicted
On thee, who now no more canst do them harm.

Sam. Spare that proposal, father, spare the trouble
Of that solicitation; let me here,
As I deserve, pay on my punishment;
490 And expiate, if possible, my crime,
Shameful garrulity. To have revealed
Secrets of men, the secrets of a friend,
How heinous had the fact been, how deserving
Contempt, and scorn of all, to be excluded
495 All friendship, and avoided as a blab,
The mark of fool set on his front!
But I God's counsel have not kept, his holy secret
Presumptuously have published, impiously,
Weakly at least, and shamefully: a sin
500 That Gentiles in their parables condemn
To their abyss and horrid pains confined.

Man. Be penitent and for thy fault contrite,
But act not in thy own affliction, son,
Repent the sin, but if the punishment
505 Thou canst avoid, self-preservation bids;
Or the execution leave to high disposal,
And let another hand, not thine, exact
Thy penal forfeit from thyself; perhaps
God will relent, and quit thee all his debt;
510 Who evermore approves and more accepts
(Best pleased with humble and filial submission)
Him who imploring mercy sues for life,

Than who self-rigorous chooses death as due;
Which argues over-just, and self-displeased
515   For self-offence, more than for God offended.
Reject not then what offered means, who knows
But God hath set before us, to return thee
Home to thy country and his sacred house,
Where thou may'st bring thy off'rings, to avert
520   His further ire, with prayers and vows renewed.

Sam. His pardon I implore; but as for life,
To what end should I seek it? when in strength
All mortals I excelled, and great in hopes
With youthful courage and magnanimous thoughts
525   Of birth from heaven foretold and high exploits,
Full of divine instinct, after some proof
Of acts indeed heroic, far beyond
The sons of Anak, famous now and blazed, [1]
Fearless of danger, like a petty god
530   I walked about admired of all and dreaded
On hostile ground, none daring my affront.
Then swoll'n with pride into the snare I fell
Of fair fallacious looks, venereal trains,
Softened with pleasure and voluptuous life;
535   At length to lay my head and hallowed pledge
Of all my strength in the lascivious lap
Of a deceitful concubine who shore me
Like a tame wether, all my precious fleece, [2]
Then turned me out ridiculous, despoiled,
540   Shaven, and disarmed among my enemies.

Chor. Desire of wine and all delicious drinks,
Which many a famous warrior overturns,
Thou couldst repress, nor did the dancing ruby
Sparkling, out-poured, the flavour, or the smell,
545   Or taste that cheers the heart of gods and men,
Allure thee from the cool crystalline stream. [3]

Sam. Wherever fountain or fresh current flowed
Against the eastern ray, translucent, pure
With touch ethereal of heaven's fiery rod
550   I drank, from the clear milky juice allaying
Thirst, and refreshed; nor envied them the grape
Whose heads that turbulent liquor fills with
    fumes.

Chor. O madness, to think use of strongest wines
And strongest drinks our chief support of health,
555   When God with these forbidden made choice to rear
His mighty champion, strong above compare,
Whose drink was only from the liquid brook.

Sam. But what availed this temperance, not complete
Against another object more enticing?
560   What boots it at one gate to make defence,
And at another to let in the foe
Effeminately vanquished? by which means, [4]
Now blind, disheartened, shamed, dishonoured,
    quelled,
To what can I be useful, wherein serve
565   My nation, and the work from heaven imposed, [5]
But to sit idle on the household hearth,
A burdenous drone; to visitants a gaze,
Or pitied object, these redundant locks [6]
Robustious to no purpose clustering down,
570   Vain monument of strength; till length of years
And sedentary numbness craze my limbs
To a contemptible old age obscure.

---

[1] *sons of Anak*   giants. See Numbers 13:33.

[2] *wether*   a castrated ram.

[3] *Desire of wine*   This passage reflects the fact that as a Nazarite Samson had to "separate himself from wine and strong drink" (Numbers 6:3).

[4] *Effeminately* through degrading passion for a woman (*OED* effeminately *adv* 2, this place cited, as sole instance).

[5] *To what can I be useful* "a merely rhetorical question. Samson, in his terms, the terms of a champion, can no longer be useful. He has quietly admitted as much (460). But resignation to God's terms is not resignation to Manoa's. The vision of uselessness conjured up by Manoa's proposal wrings from Samson a cry that tells us, the readers, that he still wants to be useful. Born and raised a hero, he can think only in heroic terms" (Alan Rudrum, *Samson Agonistes*, London: Macmillan, 1969, 37).

[6] *redundant* abounding to excess (*OED* redundant *a* 2, where this is remarked as the first instance of the usage in modern English).

Here rather let me drudge and earn my bread,
Till vermin or the draff of servile food
575 Consume me, and oft-invocated death
Hasten the welcome end of all my pains.

Man. Wilt thou then serve the Philistines with
    that gift
Which was expressly given thee to annoy them?
Better at home lie bed-rid, not only idle,
580 Inglorious, unemployed, with age outworn.
But God who caused a fountain at thy prayer
From the dry ground to spring, thy thirst to allay
After the brunt of battle, can as easy
Cause light again within thy eyes to spring,
585 Wherewith to serve him better than thou hast;
And I persuade me so; why else this strength
Miraculous yet remaining in those locks?
His might continues in thee not for naught,
Nor shall his wondrous gifts be frustrate thus.

590 *Sam.* All otherwise to me my thoughts portend,
That these dark orbs no more shall treat with light,
Nor the other light of life continue long,
But yield to double darkness nigh at hand:
So much I feel my genial spirits droop,
595 My hopes all flat, nature within me seems
In all her functions weary of herself;
My race of glory run, and race of shame,
And I shall shortly be with them that rest.

Man. Believe not these suggestions, which proceed
600 From anguish of the mind and humours black, [1]
That mingle with thy fancy. I however
Must not omit a father's timely care
To prosecute the means of thy deliverance
By ransom or how else: meanwhile be calm,
605 And healing words from these thy friends admit.

Sam. O that torment should not be confined
To the body's wounds and sores
With maladies innumerable
In heart, head, breast, and reins; [2]
610 But must secret passage find
To the inmost mind,
There exercise all his fierce accidents,
And on her purest spirits prey,
As on entrails, joints, and limbs,
615 With answerable pains, but more intense,
Though void of corporal sense.
    My griefs not only pain me
As a lingering disease,
But finding no redress, ferment and rage,
620 Nor less than wounds immedicable
Rankle, and fester, and gangrene,
To black mortification.
Thoughts my tormentors armed with deadly stings
Mangle my apprehensive tenderest parts,
625 Exasperate, exulcerate, and raise
Dire inflammation which no cooling herb
Or med'cinal liquor can assuage,
Nor breath of vernal air from snowy alp.
Sleep hath forsook and given me o'er
630 To death's benumbing opium as my only cure.
Thence faintings, swoonings of despair,
And sense of heaven's desertion.
    I was his nursling once and choice delight,
His destined from the womb,
635 Promised by heavenly message twice descending.
Under his special eye
Abstemious I grew up and thrived amain;
He led me on to mightiest deeds
Above the nerve of mortal arm
640 Against the uncircumcised, our enemies.
But now hath cast me off as never known,
And to those cruel enemies,

---

[1] *humours black* in the "Four humours" psychology of the period, melancholy, deriving from "black bile."

[2] *reins* kidneys.

Whom I by his appointment had provoked,
Left me all helpless with the irreparable loss
645   Of sight, reserved alive to be repeated
The subject of their cruelty, or scorn.
Nor am I in the list of them that hope;
Hopeless are all my evils, all remediless;
This one prayer yet remains, might I be heard,
650   No long petition, speedy death,
The close of all my miseries, and the balm.

Chor. Many are the sayings of the wise
In ancient and in modern books enrolled;
Extolling patience as the truest fortitude; [1]
655   And to the bearing well of all calamities,
All chances incident to man's frail life
Consolatories writ
With studied argument, and much persuasion
     sought
Lenient of grief and anxious thought,
660   But with the afflicted in his pangs their sound
Little prevails, or rather seems a tune,
Harsh, and of dissonant mood from his complaint,
Unless he feel within
Some source of consolation from above;
665   Secret refreshings, that repair his strength,
And fainting spirits uphold.
      God of our fathers, what is man!
That thou towards him with hand so various,
Or might I say contrarious,

670   Temper'st thy providence through his short course,
Not evenly, as thou rul'st
The angelic orders and inferior creatures mute,
Irrational and brute.
Nor do I name of men the common rout,
675   That wand'ring loose about
Grow up and perish, as the summer fly,
Heads without name no more remembered,
But such as thou hast solemnly elected,
With gifts and graces eminently adorned
680   To some great work, thy glory,
And people's safety, which in part they effect:
Yet toward these thus dignified, thou oft
Amidst their height of noon,
Changest thy countenance, and thy hand with no
     regard
685   Of highest favours past
From thee on them, or them to thee of service.
      Nor only dost degrade them, or remit
To life obscured, which were a fair dismission,
But throw'st them lower than thou didst exalt
     them high,
690   Unseemly falls in human eye,
Too grievous for the trespass or omission,
Oft leav'st them to the hostile sword
Of heathen and profane, their carcases
To dogs and fowls a prey, or else captived:
695   Or to the unjust tribunals, under change of times,
And condemnation of the ingrateful multitude. [2]
If these they scape, perhaps in poverty

---

[1] *patience as the truest fortitude* We may understand from this passage that there is more than one kind of fortitude, patience being the truest; and that the point has been discussed by ancient and modern philosophers. This is in fact the case. From the Stoic philosophers down through the Christian centuries there had been discussion of the role of patience in the ethical and religious life. It had been classified as a kind of fortitude, the other kind being magnanimity. St. Thomas Aquinas, in discussing "fortitude," described magnanimity as a virtue of aggression and patience as a virtue of endurance (*Summa Theologica* Part II, Second Part, questions 123–139). We may say that magnanimity is the kind of fortitude appropriate to the hero of epic, patience the kind appropriate to the Christian saint. There can be little doubt which of the two Milton preferred to celebrate. See *Paradise Lost* 9:27f and 12:569.

---

[2] *their carcases / To dogs and fowls a prey, or else captived: / Or to the unjust tribunals, under change of times, / And condemnation of the ingrateful multitude* These lines express very well the fate of some republicans under the Restoration; see Blair Worden's "Milton, Samson Agonistes, and the Restoration" in *Culture and Society in the Stuart Restoration*, 122f. Worden remarks that the three regicides executed in April 1662 proclaimed that their cause would survive "when the fowls have eaten of our vile bodies."

With sickness and disease thou bow'st them down,
Painful diseases and deformed,
700 In crude old age;
Though not disordinate, yet causeless suffering
The punishment of dissolute days, in fine,
Just or unjust, alike seem miserable,
For oft alike, both come to evil end.
705   So deal not with this once thy glorious champion,
The image of thy strength, and mighty minister.
What do I beg? how hast thou dealt already?
Behold him in this state calamitous, and turn
His labours, for thou canst, to peaceful end.
710   But who is this, what thing of sea or land?
Female of sex it seems,
That so bedecked, ornate, and gay,
Comes this way sailing
Like a stately ship [1]
715 Of Tarsus, bound for th' isles
Of Javan or Gadire
With all her bravery on, and tackle trim,
Sails filled, and streamers waving,
Courted by all the winds that hold them play,
720 An amber scent of odorous perfume
Her harbinger, a damsel train behind;
Some rich Philistian matron she may seem,
And now at nearer view, no other certain
Than Dalila thy wife.

725 *Sam.* My wife, my traitress, let her not come near
      me.

Chor. Yet on she moves, now stands and eyes thee
      fixed,
About t' have spoke, but now, with head declined
Like a fair flower surcharged with dew, she weeps
And words addressed seem into tears dissolved,
730 Wetting the borders of her silken veil:
But now again she makes address to speak.

---

[1] *Like a stately ship* The Israelites were not a sea-going nation, but
some of their enemies were.

Dal. With doubtful feet and wavering resolution
I came, still dreading thy displeasure, Samson,
Which to have merited, without excuse,
735 I cannot but acknowledge; yet if tears
May expiate (though the fact more evil drew
In the perverse event than I foresaw)
My penance hath not slackened, though my pardon
No way assured. But conjugal affection
740 Prevailing over fear, and timorous doubt
Hath led me on desirous to behold
Once more thy face, and know of thy estate.
If aught in my ability may serve
To lighten what thou suffer'st, and appease
745 Thy mind with what amends is in my power,
Though late, yet in some part to recompense
My rash but more unfortunate misdeed.

Sam. Out, out hyena; these are thy wonted arts,
And arts of every woman false like thee,
750 To break all faith, all vows, deceive, betray,
Then as repentant to submit, beseech,
And reconcilement move with feigned remorse,
Confess, and promise wonders in her change,
Not truly penitent, but chief to try
755 Her husband, how far urged his patience bears,
His virtue or weakness which way to assail:
Then with more cautious and instructed skill
Again transgresses, and again submits;
That wisest and best men full oft beguiled
760 With goodness principled not to reject
The penitent, but ever to forgive,
Are drawn to wear out miserable days,
Entangled with a poisonous bosom snake,
If not by quick destruction soon cut off
765 As I by thee, to ages an example.

Dal. Yet hear me Samson; not that I endeavour
To lessen or extenuate my offence,
But that on the other side, if it be weighed
By itself, with aggravations not surcharged,
770 Or else with just allowance counterpoised,

I may, if possible, thy pardon find
The easier towards me, or thy hatred less.
First granting, as I do, it was a weakness
In me, but incident to all our sex,
775 Curiosity, inquisitive, importune
Of secrets, then with like infirmity
To publish them, both common female faults:
Was it not weakness also to make known
For importunity, that is for naught,
780 Wherein consisted all thy strength and safety?
To what I did thou show'dst me first the way.
But I to enemies revealed, and should not.
Nor shouldst thou have trusted that to woman's
        frailty:
Ere I to thee, thou to thyself wast cruel.
785 Let weakness then with weakness come to parle
So near related, or the same of kind,
Thine forgive mine; that men may censure thine
The gentler, if severely thou exact not
More strength from me, than in thyself was found.
790 And what if love, which thou interpret'st hate,
The jealousy of love, powerful of sway
In human hearts, nor less in mine towards thee,
Caused what I did? I saw thee mutable
Of fancy, feared lest one day thou wouldst leave me
795 As her at Timna, sought by all means therefore
How to endear, and hold thee to me firmest:
No better way I saw than by importuning
To learn thy secrets, get into my power
Thy key of strength and safety: thou wilt say,
800 Why then revealed? I was assured by those
Who tempted me, that nothing was designed
Against thee but safe custody, and hold:
That made for me; I knew that liberty
Would draw thee forth to perilous enterprises,
805 While I at home sat full of cares and fears
Wailing thy absence in my widowed bed;
Here I should still enjoy thee day and night
Mine and love's prisoner, not the Philistines',
Whole to myself, unhazarded abroad,
810 Fearless at home of partners in my love.

These reasons in love's law have passed for good,
Though fond and reasonless to some perhaps;
And love hath oft, well meaning, wrought much woe.
Yet always pity or pardon hath obtained.
815 Be not unlike all others, not austere
As thou art strong, inflexible as steel.
If thou in strength all mortals dost exceed,
In uncompassionate anger do not so.

Sam. How cunningly the sorceress displays
820 Her own transgressions, to upbraid me mine!
That malice not repentance brought thee hither,
By this appears: I gave, thou say'st, the example,
I led the way; bitter reproach, but true,
I to myself was false ere thou to me,
825 Such pardon therefore as I give my folly,
Take to thy wicked deed: which when thou seest
Impartial, self-severe, inexorable,
Thou wilt renounce thy seeking, and much rather
Confess it feigned, weakness is thy excuse,
830 And I believe it, weakness to resist
Philistian gold: if weakness may excuse,
What murderer, what traitor, parricide,
Incestuous, sacrilegious, but may plead it?
All wickedness is weakness: that plea therefore
835 With God or man will gain thee no remission.
But love constrained thee; call it furious rage
To satisfy thy lust: love seeks to have love;
My love how couldst thou hope, who took'st the
        way
To raise in me inexpiable hate,
840 Knowing, as needs I must, by thee betrayed?
In vain thou striv'st to cover shame with shame,
Or by evasions thy crime uncover'st more.

Dal. Since thou determin'st weakness for no plea
In man or woman, though to thy own condemning,
845 Hear what assaults I had, what snares besides,
What sieges girt me round, ere I consented;
Which might have awed the best-resolved of men,
The constantest to have yielded without blame.

It was not gold, as to my charge thou lay'st,
850 That wrought with me; thou know'st the magistrates
And princes of my country came in person,
Solicited, commanded, threatened, urged,
Adjured by all the bonds of civil duty
And of religion, pressed how just it was,
855 How honourable, how glorious to entrap
A common enemy, who had destroyed
Such numbers of our nation: and the priest
Was not behind, but ever at my ear,
Preaching how meritorious with the gods
860 It would be to ensnare an irreligious
Dishonourer of Dagon: what had I
To oppose against such powerful arguments?
Only my love of thee held long debate;
And combated in silence all these reasons
865 With hard contest: at length that grounded maxim
So rife and celebrated in the mouths
Of wisest men; that to the public good
Private respects must yield; with grave authority
Took full possession of me and prevailed;
870 Virtue, as I thought, truth, duty so enjoining.

Sam. I thought where all thy circling wiles would end;
In feigned religion, smooth hypocrisy.
But had thy love, still odiously pretended,
Been, as it ought, sincere, it would have taught thee
875 Far other reasonings, brought forth other deeds.
I before all the daughters of my tribe
And of my nation chose thee from among
My enemies, loved thee, as too well thou knew'st,
Too well, unbosomed all my secrets to thee,
880 Not out of levity, but overpowered
By thy request, who could deny thee nothing;
Yet now am judged an enemy. Why then
Didst thou at first receive me for thy husband?
Then, as since then, thy country's foe professed:
885 Being once a wife, for me thou wast to leave

Parents and country; nor was I their subject, [1]
Nor under their protection but my own,
Thou mine, not theirs: if aught against my life
Thy country sought of thee, it sought unjustly,
890 Against the law of nature, law of nations,
No more thy country, but an impious crew
Of men conspiring to uphold their state
By worse than hostile deeds, violating the ends
For which our country is a name so dear;
895 Not therefore to be obeyed. But zeal moved thee;
To please thy gods thou didst it; gods unable
To acquit themselves and prosecute their foes
But by ungodly deeds, the contradiction
Of their own deity, gods cannot be:
900 Less therefore to be pleased, obeyed, or feared,
These false pretexts and varnished colours failing,
Bare in thy guilt how foul must thou appear!

Dal. In argument with men a woman ever
Goes by the worse, whatever be her cause.

905 *Sam.* For want of words no doubt, or lack of breath,
Witness when I was worried with thy peals.

Dal. I was a fool, too rash, and quite mistaken
In what I thought would have succeeded best.
Let me obtain forgiveness of thee, Samson,
910 Afford me place to show what recompense
Towards thee I intend for what I have misdone,
Misguided; only what remains past cure
Bear not too sensibly, nor still insist
To afflict thyself in vain: though sight be lost,
915 Life yet hath many solaces, enjoyed
Where other senses want not their delights

---

[1] *Being once a wife, for me thou wast to leave / Parents and country* Whether in the context of the Hebrew Bible, or of Milton's England, it would have been obvious that in marrying Samson, Dalila renounced her god and society and owed fealty to his society and his God. Modern views and customs are irrelevant to the poem's *meaning*, though not of course to its *significance*. For the distinction between these terms see E.D. Hirsch, *Validity in Interpretation* (New Haven: Yale U P, 1967).

At home in leisure and domestic ease,
Exempt from many a care and chance to which
Eyesight exposes daily men abroad.
920 I to the lords will intercede, not doubting
Their favourable ear, that I may fetch thee
From forth this loathsome prison-house, to abide
With me, where my redoubled love and care
With nursing diligence, to me glad office,
925 May ever tend about thee to old age
With all things grateful cheered, and so supplied,
That what by me thou hast lost thou least shalt
    miss.

Sam. No, no, of my condition take no care;
It fits not; thou and I long since are twain;
930 Nor think me so unwary or accursed
To bring my feet again into the snare
Where once I have been caught; I know thy trains
Though dearly to my cost, thy gins, and toils;
Thy fair enchanted cup, and warbling charms
935 No more on me have power, their force is nulled, [1]
So much of adder's wisdom I have learnt
To fence my ear against thy sorceries. [2]
If in my flower of youth and strength, when all
    men
Loved, honoured, feared me, thou alone could
    hate me
940 Thy husband, slight me, sell me, and forgo me;
How wouldst thou use me now, blind, and thereby
Deceivable, in most things as a child
Helpless, thence easily contemned, and scorned;
And last neglected? How wouldst thou insult
945 When I must live uxorious to thy will
In perfect thraldom, how again betray me,
Bearing my words and doings to the lords
To gloss upon, and censuring, frown or smile?

This jail I count the house of liberty
950 To thine whose doors my feet shall never enter. [3]

Dal. Let me approach at least, and touch thy
    hand.

Sam. Not for thy life, lest fierce remembrance wake
My sudden rage to tear thee joint by joint.
At distance I forgive thee, go with that;
955 Bewail thy falsehood, and the pious works
It hath brought forth to make thee memorable
Among illustrious women, faithful wives:
Cherish thy hastened widowhood with the gold
Of matrimonial treason: so farewell.

960 *Dal.* I see thou art implacable, more deaf
To prayers than winds and seas, yet winds to seas
Are reconciled at length, and sea to shore:
Thy anger, unappeasable, still rages,
Eternal tempest never to be calmed.
965 Why do I humble thus myself, and suing
For peace, reap nothing but repulse and hate?
Bid go with evil omen and the brand
Of infamy upon my name denounced?
To mix with thy concernments I desist
970 Henceforth, nor too much disapprove my own.
Fame if not double-faced is double-mouthed,
And with contrary blast proclaims most deeds,
On both his wings, one black, the other white,
Bears greatest names in his wild airy flight.
975 My name perhaps among the circumcised
In Dan, in Judah, and the bordering tribes,
To all posterity may stand defamed,
With malediction mentioned, and the blot
Of falsehood most unconjugal traduced.
980 But in my country where I most desire,
In Ecron, Gaza, Asdod, and in Gath
I shall be named among the famousest
Of women, sung at solemn festivals,

---

[1] *Thy fair enchanted cup* in allusion to Circe.

[2] *adder's wisdom* deafness; "they are like the deaf adder that stoppeth her ear; Which will not hearken to the voice of charmers, charming never so wisely" (Psalm 58: 4–5).

---

[3] *To thine* compared to thine; a very common idiom in this period.

Living and dead recorded, who to save
985 Her country from a fierce destroyer, chose
Above the faith of wedlock-bands, my tomb
With odours visited and annual flowers.
Not less renowned than in Mount Ephraim,
Jael, who with inhospitable guile
990 Smote Sisera sleeping through the temples nailed. [1]
Nor shall I count it heinous to enjoy
The public marks of honour and reward
Conferred upon me, for the piety
Which to my country I was judged to have shown.
995 At this whoever envies or repines
I leave him to his lot, and like my own.

Chor. She's gone, a manifest serpent by her sting
Discovered in the end, till now concealed.

Sam. So let her go, God sent her to debase me,
1000 And aggravate my folly who committed
To such a viper his most sacred trust
Of secrecy, my safety, and my life.

Chor. Yet beauty, though injurious, hath strange
          power,
After offence returning, to regain
1005 Love once possessed, nor can be easily
Repulsed, without much inward passion felt
And secret sting of amorous remorse.

Sam. Love-quarrels oft in pleasing concord end,
Not wedlock-treachery endangering life.

1010 *Chor.* It is not virtue, wisdom, valour, wit,
Strength, comeliness of shape, or amplest merit
That woman's love can win or long inherit;
But what it is, hard is to say,
Harder to hit
1015 (Which way soever men refer it),
Much like thy riddle, Samson, in one day

Or seven, though one should musing sit; [2]
     If any of these or all, the Timnian bride
Had not so soon preferred
1020 Thy paranymph, worthless to thee compared, [3]
Successor in thy bed,
Nor both so loosely disallied
Their nuptials, nor this last so treacherously
Had shorn the fatal harvest of thy head.
1025 Is it for that such outward ornament
Was lavished on their sex, that inward gifts
Were left for haste unfinished, judgment scant,
Capacity not raised to apprehend
Or value what is best
1030 In choice, but oftest to affect the wrong?
Or was too much of self-love mixed,
Of constancy no root infixed,
That either they love nothing, or not long?
     Whate'er it be, to wisest men and best
1035 Seeming at first all heavenly under virgin veil,
Soft, modest, meek, demure,
Once joined, the contrary she proves, a thorn
Intestine, far within defensive arms
A cleaving mischief, in his way to virtue
1040 Adverse and turbulent, or by her charms
Draws him awry enslaved
With dotage, and his sense depraved
To folly and shameful deeds which ruin ends.
What pilot so expert but needs must wreck
1045 Embarked with such a steers-mate at the helm?
     Favoured of heaven who finds
One virtuous rarely found,
That in domestic good combines:
Happy that house! his way to peace is smooth:
1050 But virtue which breaks through all opposition,

---

[1] *Jael* For the story of Jael and Sisera, see Judges 4.

[2] *Much like thy riddle* See Judges 14.

[3] *paranymph* in Greek antiquity, the "friend of the bridegroom," who accompanied him when he went to fetch home the bride; in modern terms, "best man" at a wedding. The reference is to Judges 14:20. The Septuagint uses a different noun, with the same meaning, at this place. The word comes as a reminder that, though his story is biblical, Milton had Greek drama in mind when writing *Samson*.

And all temptation can remove,
Most shines and most is acceptable above.
　　Therefore God's universal law
Gave to the man despotic power
1055 Over his female in due awe,
Nor from that right to part an hour,
Smile she or lour:
So shall he least confusion draw
On his whole life, not swayed
1060 By female usurpation, nor dismayed. [1]
　　But had we best retire, I see a storm?

Sam. Fair days have oft contracted wind and rain.

Chor. But this another kind of tempest brings.

Sam. Be less abstruse, my riddling days are past.

1065 *Chor.* Look now for no enchanting voice, nor fear
The bait of honeyed words; a rougher tongue
Draws hitherward, I know him by his stride,
The giant Harapha of Gath, his look
Haughty as is his pile high-built and proud.
1070 Comes he in peace? what wind hath blown him
　　hither
I less conjecture than when first I saw
The sumptuous Dalila floating this way:
His habit carries peace, his brow defiance.

Sam. Or peace or not, alike to me he comes.

1075 *Chor.* His fraught we soon shall know, he now
　　arrives.

Har. I come not Samson, to condole thy chance,
As these perhaps, yet wish it had not been,
Though for no friendly intent. I am of Gath,

Men call me Harapha, of stock renowned
1080 As Og or Anak and the Emims old
That Kiriathaim held, thou know'st me now
If thou at all art known. Much I have heard
Of thy prodigious might and feats performed
Incredible to me, in this displeased,
1085 That I was never present on the place
Of those encounters, where we might have tried
Each other's force in camp or listed field: [2]
And now am come to see of whom such noise
Hath walked about, and each limb to survey,
1090 If thy appearance answer loud report.

Sam. The way to know were not to see but taste.

Har. Dost thou already single me? I thought
Gyves and the mill had tamed thee. O that
　　fortune [3]
Had brought me to the field where thou art famed
1095 To have wrought such wonders with an ass's jaw;
I should have forced thee soon wish other arms,
Or left thy carcase where the ass lay thrown:
So had the glory of prowess been recovered
To Palestine, won by a Philistine
1100 From the unforeskinned race, of whom thou bear'st
The highest name for valiant acts, that honour
Certain to have won by mortal duel from thee,
I lose, prevented by thy eyes put out.

Sam. Boast not of what thou wouldst have done,
　　but do
1105 What then thou wouldst, thou seest it in thy
　　hand.

Har. To combat with a blind man I disdain,
And thou hast need much washing to be touched.

---

[1] *not swayed / By female usurpation* "But I suffer not a woman to teach, nor to usurp authority over the man, but to be in silence. For Adam was first formed, then Eve" (I Timothy 2:12–13). JL notes that Milton cites this approvingly in the *Doctrine and Discipline of Divorce*.

[2] *listed field* provided with lists, for tilting.

[3] *Gyves* shackles, fetters.

Sam. Such usage as your honourable lords
Afford me assassinated and betrayed, [1]
1110 Who durst not with their whole united powers
In fight withstand me single and unarmed,
Nor in the house with chamber ambushes
Close-banded durst attack me, no not sleeping,
Till they had hired a woman with their gold
1115 Breaking her marriage faith to circumvent me.
Therefore without feigned shifts let be assigned
Some narrow place enclosed, where sight may give
    thee,
Or rather flight, no great advantage on me;
Then put on all thy gorgeous arms, thy helmet
1120 And brigandine of brass, thy broad habergeon, [2]
Vantbrace and greaves, and gauntlet, add thy spear
A weaver's beam, and seven-times-folded shield, [3]
I only with an oaken staff will meet thee,
And raise such outcries on thy clattered iron,
1125 Which long shall not withhold me from thy head,
That in a little time while breath remains thee,
Thou oft shalt wish thyself at Gath to boast
Again in safety what thou wouldst have done
To Samson, but shalt never see Gath more.

Har. Thou durst not thus disparage glorious arms
1130 Which greatest heroes have in battle worn,
Their ornament and safety, had not spells
And black enchantments, some magician's art
Armed thee or charmed thee strong, which thou
    from heaven
1135 Feign'dst at thy birth was given thee in thy hair,
Where strength can least abide, though all thy hairs
Were bristles ranged like those that ridge the back
Of chafed wild boars or ruffled porcupines.

---

[1] *assassinated* wounded by treachery (*OED* assassinate *v* 3).

[2] *brigandine* chain-mail or plates sewn on canvas or leather; *habergeon* sleeveless coat of mail; *Vantbrace* armour for the forearm (JL); *greaves* armour for the leg below the knee (*OED* greave 2).

[3] *seven-times-folded shield* Compare the seven-fold shield of Turnus in Virgil's *Aeneid* 12:925.

Sam. I know no spells, use no forbidden arts; [4]
1140 My trust is in the living God who gave me
At my nativity this strength, diffused
No less through all my sinews, joints and bones, [5]
Than thine, while I preserved these locks unshorn,
The pledge of my unviolated vow.
1145 For proof hereof, if Dagon be thy god,
Go to his temple, invocate his aid
With solemnest devotion, spread before him
How highly it concerns his glory now
To frustrate and dissolve these magic spells,
1150 Which I to be the power of Israel's God
Avow, and challenge Dagon to the test,
Offering to combat thee his champion bold,
With the utmost of his godhead seconded:
Then thou shalt see, or rather to thy sorrow
1155 Soon feel, whose God is strongest, thine or mine.

Har. Presume not on thy God, whate'er he be,
Thee he regards not, owns not, hath cut off
Quite from his people, and delivered up
Into thy enemies' hand, permitted them
1160 To put out both thine eyes, and fettered send thee
Into the common prison, there to grind
Among the slaves and asses thy comrades,
As good for nothing else, no better service
With those thy boisterous locks, no worthy match
1165 For valour to assail, nor by the sword
Of noble warrior, so to stain his honour,
But by the barber's razor best subdued.

Sam. All these indignities, for such they are
From thine, these evils I deserve and more,
1170 Acknowledge them from God inflicted on me
Justly, yet despair not of his final pardon
Whose ear is ever open; and his eye
Gracious to readmit the suppliant;

---

[4] *I know no spells, use no forbidden arts* an echo of the oath taken by mediaeval knights before a tournament.

[5] *My trust is in the living God* Samson has rediscovered his role as God's champion.

In confidence whereof I once again
1175 Defy thee to the trial of mortal fight,
By combat to decide whose god is God,
Thine or whom I with Israel's sons adore.

Har. Fair honour that thou dost thy God, in
    trusting
He will accept thee to defend his cause,
1180 A murderer, a revolter, and a robber.

Sam. Tongue-doughty giant, how dost thou prove
    me these?

Har. Is not thy nation subject to our lords?
Their magistrates confessed it, when they took
    thee
As a league-breaker and delivered bound
1185 Into our hands: for hadst thou not committed
Notorious murder on those thirty men
At Ascalon, who never did thee harm,
Then like a robber stripp'dst them of their robes?
The Philistines, when thou hadst broke the league,
1190 Went up with armèd powers thee only seeking,
To others did no violence nor spoil.

Sam. Among the daughters of the Philistines
I chose a wife, which argued me no foe;
And in your city held my nuptial feast:
1195 But your ill-meaning politician lords,
Under pretence of bridal friends and guests,
Appointed to await me thirty spies,
Who threatening cruel death constrained the bride
To wring from me and tell to them my secret,
1200 That solved the riddle which I had proposed.
When I perceived all set on enmity,
As on my enemies, wherever chanced,
I used hostility, and took their spoil
To pay my underminers in their coin.
1205 My nation was subjected to your lords.
It was the force of conquest; force with force
Is well ejected when the conquered can.

But I a private person, whom my country
As a league-breaker gave up bound, presumed
1210 Single rebellion and did hostile acts.
I was no private but a person raised
With strength sufficient and command from
    heaven [1]
To free my country; if their servile minds
Me their deliverer sent would not receive,
1215 But to their masters gave me up for nought,
The unworthier they; whence to this day they
    serve.
I was to do my part from heaven assigned,
And had performed it if my known offence
Had not disabled me, not all your force:
1220 These shifts refuted, answer thy appellant
Though by his blindness maimed for high attempts,
Who now defies thee thrice to single fight,
As a petty enterprise of small enforce.

Har. With thee a man condemned, a slave
    enrolled,
1225 Due by the law to capital punishment?
To fight with thee no man of arms will deign.

Sam. Cam'st thou for this, vain boaster, to survey
    me,
To descant on my strength, and give thy verdict?
Come nearer, part not hence so slight informed;
1230 But take good heed my hand survey not thee.

Har. O Baal-zebub! can my ears unused
Hear these dishonours, and not render death?

Sam. No man withholds thee, nothing from thy
    hand
Fear I incurable; bring up thy van,
1235 My heels are fettered, but my fist is free.

---

[1] *I was no private but a person raised* etc.   Samson does not concede
that he is merely a private person; he had been appointed by God.

Har. This insolence other kind of answer fits.

Sam. Go baffled coward, lest I run upon thee,
Though in these chains, bulk without spirit vast,
And with one buffet lay thy structure low,
1240 Or swing thee in the air, then dash thee down
To the hazard of thy brains and shattered sides.

Har. By Astaroth ere long thou shalt lament
These braveries in irons loaden on thee.

Chor. His giantship is gone somewhat crestfall'n,
1245 Stalking with less unconscionable strides,
And lower looks, but in a sultry chafe.

Sam. I dread him not, nor all his giant-brood,
Though fame divulge him father of five sons
All of gigantic size, Goliah chief.

1250 *Chor.* He will directly to the lords, I fear,
And with malicious counsel stir them up
Some way or other yet further to afflict thee.

Sam. He must allege some cause, and offered fight
Will not dare mention, lest a question rise
1255 Whether he durst accept the offer or not,
And that he durst not plain enough appeared.
Much more affliction than already felt
They cannot well impose, nor I sustain;
If they intend advantage of my labours,
1260 The work of many hands, which earns my keeping
With no small profit daily to my owners.
But come what will, my deadliest foe will prove
My speediest friend, by death to rid me hence,
The worst that he can give, to me the best.
1265 Yet so it may fall out, because their end
Is hate, not help to me, it may with mine
Draw their own ruin who attempt the deed.

Chor. O how comely it is and how reviving
To the spirits of just men long oppressed!

1270 When God into the hands of their deliverer
Puts invincible might
To quell the mighty of the earth, the oppressor,
The brute and boisterous force of violent men
Hardy and industrious to support
1275 Tyrannic power, but raging to pursue
The righteous and all such as honour truth;
He all their ammunition
And feats of war defeats
With plain heroic magnitude of mind
1280 And celestial vigour armed,
Their armouries and magazines contemns,
Renders them useless, while
With wingèd expedition
Swift as the lightning glance he executes
1285 His errand on the wicked, who surprised
Lose their defence distracted and amazed.
But patience is more oft the exercise
Of saints, the trial of their fortitude, [1]
Making them each his own deliverer,
1290 And victor over all
That tyranny or fortune can inflict,
Either of these is in thy lot,
Samson, with might endued
Above the sons of men; but sight bereaved
1295 May chance to number thee with those
Whom patience finally must crown.
This idol's day hath been to thee no day of rest,
Labouring thy mind
More than the working day thy hands,
1300 And yet perhaps more trouble is behind.
For I descry this way
Some other tending, in his hand

---

[1] *But patience is more oft the exercise / Of saints* The Chorus's speech deals with the two kinds of fortitude (magnanimity and patience) from lines 1268–96. One may see in the tone of the earlier part a natural elation at the possibility that Samson may yet be capable of heroic action, and in the tone of what follows a sober acceptance of the likelihood that he may have to be content with heroic suffering. There is an irony which will not be apparent to the Danites until after Samson's death: that is, Samson's pulling down of the temple upon himself and the Philistines unites both kinds of fortitude; it is an action which is also a suffering.

A sceptre or quaint staff he bears,
Comes on amain, speed in his look.
1305 By his habit I discern him now
A public officer, and now at hand.
His message will be short and voluble.

Off. Hebrews, the prisoner Samson here I seek.

Chor. His manacles remark him, there he sits.

1310 *Off.* Samson, to thee our lords thus bid me say;
This day to Dagon is a solemn feast,
With sacrifices, triumph, pomp, and games;
Thy strength they know surpassing human rate,
And now some public proof thereof require
1315 To honour this great feast, and great assembly;
Rise therefore with all speed and come along,
Where I will see thee heartened and fresh clad
To appear as fits before the illustrious lords.

Sam. Thou know'st I am an Hebrew, therefore
    tell them,
1320 Our law forbids at their religious rites
My presence; for that cause I cannot come.

Off. This answer, be assured, will not content
    them.

Sam. Have they not sword-players, and every sort
Of gymnic artists, wrestlers, riders, runners,
1325 Jugglers and dancers, antics, mummers, mimics,
But they must pick me out with shackles tired,
And over-laboured at their public mill,
To make them sport with blind activity?
Do they not seek occasion of new quarrels
1330 On my refusal to distress me more,
Or make a game of my calamities?
Return the way thou cam'st, I will not come.

Off. Regard thyself, this will offend them highly.

Sam. Myself? my conscience and internal peace.
1335 Can they think me so broken, so debased
With corporal servitude, that my mind ever
Will condescend to such absurd commands?
Although their drudge, to be their fool or jester,
And in my midst of sorrow and heart-grief
1340 To show them feats, and play before their god,
The worst of all indignities, yet on me
Joined with extreme contempt? I will not come.

Off. My message was imposed on me with speed,
Brooks no delay: is this thy resolution?

1345 *Sam.* So take it with what speed thy message
    needs.

Off. I am sorry what this stoutness will produce.

Sam. Perhaps thou shalt have cause to sorrow
    indeed.

Chor. Consider, Samson; matters now are strained
Up to the height, whether to hold or break;
1350 He's gone, and who knows how he may report
Thy words by adding fuel to the flame?
Expect another message more imperious,
More lordly thundering than thou well wilt bear.

Sam. Shall I abuse this consecrated gift
1355 Of strength, again returning with my hair
After my great transgression, so requite
Favour renewed, and add a greater sin
By prostituting holy things to idols;
A Nazarite in place abominable
1360 Vaunting my strength in honour to their Dagon?
Besides, how vile, contemptible, ridiculous,
What act more execrably unclean, profane?

Chor. Yet with this strength thou serv'st the
    Philistines,
Idolatrous, uncircumcised, unclean.

Sam. Not in their idol-worship, but by labour
Honest and lawful to deserve my food
Of those who have me in their civil power.

Chor. Where the heart joins not, outward acts
    defile not.

Sam. Where outward force constrains, the
    sentence holds
But who constrains me to the temple of Dagon,
Not dragging? the Philistian lords command,
Commands are no constraints. If I obey them,
I do it freely; venturing to displease
God for the fear of man, and man prefer,
Set God behind: which in his jealousy
Shall never, unrepented, find forgiveness.
Yet that he may dispense with me or thee
Present in temples at idolatrous rites
For some important cause, thou need'st not
    doubt.

Chor. How thou wilt here come off surmounts
    my reach.

Sam. Be of good courage, I begin to feel
Some rousing motions in me which dispose
To something extraordinary my thoughts.
I with this messenger will go along,
Nothing to do, be sure, that may dishonour
Our law, or stain my vow of Nazarite.
If there be aught of presage in the mind,
This day will be remarkable in my life
By some great act, or of my days the last.

Chor. In time thou hast resolved, the man returns.

Off. Samson, this second message from our lords
To thee I am bid say. Art thou our slave,
Our captive, at the public mill our drudge,
And dar'st thou at our sending and command
Dispute thy coming? come without delay;

Or we shall find such engines to assail
And hamper thee, as thou shalt come of force,
Though thou wert firmlier fastened than a rock.

Sam. I could be well content to try their art,
Which to no few of them would prove pernicious.
Yet knowing their advantages too many,
Because they shall not trail me through their streets
Like a wild beast, I am content to go.
Masters' commands come with a power resistless
To such as owe them absolute subjection;
And for a life who will not change his purpose?
(So mutable are all the ways of men)
Yet this be sure, in nothing to comply
Scandalous or forbidden in our law.

Off. I praise thy resolution, doff these links:
By this compliance thou wilt win the lords
To favour, and perhaps to set thee free.

Sam. Brethren farewell, your company along
I will not wish, lest it perhaps offend them
To see me girt with friends; and how the sight
Of me as of a common enemy,
So dreaded once, may now exasperate them
I know not. Lords are lordliest in their wine;
And the well-feasted priest then soonest fired
With zeal, if aught religion seem concerned:
No less the people on their holydays
Impetuous, insolent, unquenchable;
Happen what may, of me expect to hear
Nothing dishonourable, impure, unworthy
Our God, our law, my nation, or myself,
The last of me or no I cannot warrant.

Chor. Go, and the holy one
Of Israel be thy guide
To what may serve his glory best, and spread his
    name
Great among the heathen round:
Send thee the angel of thy birth, to stand

Fast by thy side, who from thy father's field
Rode up in flames after his message told
Of thy conception, and be now a shield
1435 Of fire; that spirit that first rushed on thee
In the camp of Dan
Be efficacious in thee now at need.
For never was from heaven imparted
Measure of strength so great to mortal seed,
1440 As in thy wondrous actions hath been seen.
But wherefore comes old Manoa in such haste
With youthful steps? much livelier than erewhile
He seems: supposing here to find his son,
Or of him bringing to us some glad news?

1445 *Man.* Peace with you brethren; my inducement
     hither
Was not at present here to find my son,
By order of the lords new parted hence
To come and play before them at their feast.
I heard all as I came, the city rings
1450 And numbers thither flock, I had no will,
Lest I should see him forced to things unseemly.
But that which moved my coming now, was
     chiefly
To give ye part with me what hope I have
With good success to work his liberty.

1455 *Chor.* That hope would much rejoice us to
     partake
With thee; say reverend sire, we thirst to hear.

Man. I have attempted one by one the lords
Either at home, or through the high street
     passing,
With supplication prone and father's tears
1460 To accept of ransom for my son their prisoner,
Some much averse I found and wondrous harsh,
Contemptuous, proud, set on revenge and spite;
That part most reverenced Dagon and his priests,
Others more moderate seeming, but their aim
1465 Private reward, for which both god and state

They easily would set to sale, a third
More generous far and civil, who confessed
They had enough revenged, having reduced
Their foe to misery beneath their fears,
1470 The rest was magnanimity to remit,
If some convenient ransom were proposed. [1]
What noise or shout was that? it tore the sky.

Chor. Doubtless the people shouting to behold
Their once great dread, captive, and blind before
     them,
1475 Or at some proof of strength before them shown.

Man. His ransom, if my whole inheritance
May compass it, shall willingly be paid
And numbered down: much rather I shall choose
To live the poorest in my tribe, than richest,
1480 And he in that calamitous prison left.
No, I am fixed not to part hence without him.
For his redemption all my patrimony,
If need be, I am ready to forgo
And quit: not wanting him, I shall want nothing.

1485 *Chor.* Fathers are wont to lay up for their sons,
Thou for thy son art bent to lay out all;
Sons wont to nurse their parents in old age,
Thou in old age car'st how to nurse thy son,
Made older than thy age through eyesight lost.

1490 *Man.* It shall be my delight to tend his eyes,
And view him sitting in the house, ennobled
With all those high exploits by him achieved,
And on his shoulders waving down those locks,
That of a nation armed the strength contained:
1495 And I persuade me God had not permitted

---

[1] *Some much averse I found and wondrous harsh* etc. Worden comments that after the Restoration some members of Parliament, "high-flying Anglicans among them, responded to pleas for leniency with bitter vindictiveness, others with personal opportunism, others still with heart-warming magnanimity. The stories told [by Ludlow and Lucy Hutchinson] are strikingly similar to Manoa's" ("Milton, Samson Agonistes, and the Restoration," 120).

His strength again to grown up with his hair
Garrisoned round about him like a camp
Of faithful soldiery, were not his purpose
To use him further yet in some great service,
1500 Not to sit idle with so great a gift
Useless, and thence ridiculous about him.
And since his strength with eyesight was not lost,
God will restore him eyesight to his strength.

Chor. Thy hopes are not ill founded nor seem
      vain
1505 Of his delivery, and thy joy thereon
Conceived, agreeable to a father's love,
In both which we, as next participate. [1]

Man. I know your friendly minds and—O what
      noise!
Mercy of heaven what hideous noise was that!
1510 Horribly loud unlike the former shout.

Chor. Noise call you it or universal groan
As if the whole inhabitation perished,
Blood, death, and deathful deeds are in that noise,
Ruin, destruction at the utmost point.

1515 *Man.* Of ruin indeed methought I heard the
      noise, [2]
O it continues, they have slain my son.

Chor. Thy son is rather slaying them, that outcry
From slaughter of one foe could not ascend.

Man. Some dismal accident it needs must be;
1520 What shall we do, stay here or run and see?

Chor. Best keep together here, lest running thither
We unawares run into danger's mouth.
This evil on the Philistines is fall'n,
From whom could else a general cry be heard?
1525 The sufferers then will scarce molest us here,
From other hands we need not much to fear.
What if his eyesight (for to Israel's God
Nothing is hard) by miracle restored,
He now be dealing dole among his foes,
1530 And over heaps of slaughtered walk his way?

Man. That were a joy presumptuous to be
      thought.

Chor. Yet God hath wrought things as incredible
For his people of old; what hinders now?

Man. He can I know, but doubt to think he will;
1535 Yet hope would fain subscribe, and tempts belief.
A little stay will bring some notice hither.

Chor. Of good or bad so great, of bad the sooner;
For evil news rides post, while good news baits.
And to our wish I see one hither speeding,
1540 An Hebrew, as I guess, and of our tribe.

Messenger. O whither shall I run, or which way fly [3]
The sight of this so horrid spectacle
Which erst my eyes beheld and yet behold;
For dire imagination still pursues me.
1545 But providence or instinct of nature seems,
Or reason though disturbed, and scarce consulted
To have guided me aright, I know not how,
To thee first reverend Manoa, and to these
My countrymen, whom here I knew remaining,
1550 As at some distance from the place of horror,
So in the sad event too much concerned.

---

[1] *as next*   in the sense of "next of kin" (as Danites).

[2] *ruin*   the act of giving way and falling down, on the part of a building (*OED* ruin *v* I 1); for an interesting discussion of this word see Owen Barfield, *Poetic Diction* (London: Faber and Faber, 1952), 113–126.

[3] *O whither shall I run* etc.   In relation to this speech, it is worth recalling what Milton writes in the Argument: "an Hebrew comes in haste confusedly at first; and afterward more distinctly relating the catastrophe."

Man. The accident was loud, and here before thee
With rueful cry, yet what it was we hear not,
No preface needs, thou seest we long to know.

1555 *Mess.* It would burst forth, but I recover breath
And sense distract, to know well what I utter.

Man. Tell us the sum, the circumstance defer.

Mess. Gaza yet stands, but all her sons are fall'n,
All in a moment overwhelmed and fall'n.

1560 *Man.* Sad, but thou know'st to Israelites not saddest
The desolation of a hostile city.

Mess. Feed on that first, there may in grief be
surfeit.

Man. Relate by whom.

Mess.   By Samson.
Man.   That still lessens
The sorrow, and converts it nigh to joy.

1565 *Mess.* Ah Manoa I refrain, too suddenly
To utter what will come at last too soon;
Lest evil tidings with too rude irruption
Hitting thy agèd ear should pierce too deep.

Man. Suspense in news is torture, speak them out.

1570 *Mess.* Then take the worst in brief, Samson is
dead.

Man. The worst indeed, O all my hope's defeated
To free him hence! but death who sets all free
Hath paid his ransom now and full discharge.
What windy joy this day had I conceived
1575 Hopeful of his delivery, which now proves
Abortive as the first-born bloom of spring
Nipped with the lagging rear of winter's frost.

Yet ere I give the reins to grief, say first,
How died he? death to life is crown or shame.
1580 All by him fell thou say'st, by whom fell he,
What glorious hand gave Samson his death's
wound?

Mess. Unwounded of his enemies he fell

Man. Wearied with slaughter then or how?
explain.

Mess. By his own hands.

Man.   Self-violence? what cause
1585 Brought him so soon at variance with himself
Among his foes?

Mess.   Inevitable cause
At once both to destroy and be destroyed;
The edifice where all were met to see him
Upon their heads and on his own he pulled.

1590 *Man.* O lastly over-strong against thyself!
A dreadful way thou took'st to thy revenge.
More than enough we know; but while things yet
Are in confusion, give us if thou canst,
Eye-witness of what first or last was done,
1595 Relation more particular and distinct.

Mess. Occasions drew me early to this city,
And as the gates I entered with sunrise,
The morning trumpets festival proclaimed
Through each high street: little I had dispatched
1600 When all abroad was rumoured that this day
Samson should be brought forth to show the people
Proof of his mighty strength in feats and games;
I sorrowed at his captive state, but minded
Not to be absent at that spectacle.
1605 The building was a spacious theatre,
Half round on two main pillars vaulted high,
With seats where all the lords and each degree

Of sort, might sit in order to behold,
The other side was open, where the throng
1610 On banks and scaffolds under sky might stand;
I among these aloof obscurely stood.
The feast and noon grew high, and sacrifice
Had filled their hearts with mirth, high cheer, and
   wine,
When to their sports they turned. Immediately
1615 Was Samson as a public servant brought,
In their state livery clad; before him pipes
And timbrels, on each side went armèd guards,
Both horse and foot before him and behind
Archers, and slingers, cataphracts and spears. [1]
1620 At sight of him the people with a shout
Rifted the air clamouring their god with praise,
Who had made their dreadful enemy their thrall.
He patient but undaunted where they led him,
Came to the place, and what was set before him
1625 Which without help of eye might be assayed,
To heave, pull, draw, or break, he still performed
All with incredible, stupendious force,
None daring to appear antagonist.
At length for intermission sake they led him
1630 Between the pillars; he his guide requested
(For so from such as nearer stood we heard)
As over-tired to let him lean awhile
With both his arms on those two massy pillars
That to the archèd roof gave main support.
1635 He unsuspicious led him; which when Samson
Felt in his arms, with head a while inclined,
And eyes fast fixed he stood, as one who prayed,
Or some great matter in his mind revolved.
At last with head erect thus cried aloud,
1640 Hitherto, lords, what your commands imposed
I have performed, as reason was, obeying,
Not without wonder or delight beheld.
Now of my own accord such other trial

I mean to show you of my strength, yet greater; [2]
1645 As with amaze shall strike all who behold.
This uttered, straining all his nerves he bowed,
As with the force of winds and waters pent,
When mountains tremble, those two massy pillars
With horrible convulsion to and fro,
1650 He tugged, he shook, till down they came and
   drew
The whole roof after them, with burst of thunder
Upon the heads of all who sat beneath,
Lords, ladies, captains, counsellors, or priests,
Their choice nobility and flower, not only
1655 Of this but each Philistian city round
Met from all parts to solemnize this feast.
Samson with these immixed, inevitably
Pulled down the same destruction on himself;
The vulgar only scaped who stood without. [3]

Chor. O dearly-bought revenge, yet glorious!
1660 Living or dying thou hast fulfilled
The work for which thou wast foretold
To Israel, and now li'st victorious
Among thy slain self-killed
1665 Not willingly, but tangled in the fold,

---

[1] *cataphracts* soldiers in full armour (*OED* cataphract 2); *spears* spearmen.

[2] *of my own accord* The distinction between the inner voice and the promptings of the devices and desires of our own hearts is central to what has been called the crucial question in interpreting *Samson Agonistes*: whether Samson hurled down the pillars because he was divinely propelled or because he was self-motivated. There is more than one level of answer to the view that the words "of my own accord" represent an admission on Samson's part that he does not act by divine commission: (a) the phrase stands not in opposition to divine command but to Philistine command; (b) the phrase occurs in a speech in which Samson addresses the lords of Philistia; it should not therefore be treated as if it were omniscient author commentary. Samson is under no moral obligation of frankness toward his enemies; (c) at a deeper level than the one Samson intends the Philistines to understand, the verb "accord" means to "bring heart to heart" and therefore to reconcile oneself with another; in their hidden meaning the words refer to Samson's own individual empowerment through reconciliation with God. See Rudrum, *Discerning the Spirit*, 253–254.

[3] *The vulgar only scaped who stood without* Note that the common people escape slaughter; those who are killed belong to what historians of the early modern period call "the political nation," that is, those who have the wealth or position to exert political influence.

Of dire necessity, whose law in death conjoined
Thee with thy slaughtered foes in number more
Than all thy life had slain before.

Semichor. While their hearts were jocund and
    sublime,
1670 Drunk with idolatry, drunk with wine,
And fat regorged of bulls and goats,
Chanting their idol, and preferring
Before our living dread who dwells
In Silo his bright sanctuary:
1675 Among them he a spirit of frenzy sent,
Who hurt their minds,
And urged them on with mad desire
To call in haste for their destroyer;
They only set on sport and play
1680 Unweetingly importuned
Their own destruction to come speedy upon
    them.
So fond are mortal men
Fall'n into wrath divine,
As their own ruin on themselves to invite,
1685 Insensate left, or to sense reprobate,
And with blindness internal struck.

Semichor. But he though blind of sight,
Despised and thought extinguished quite,
With inward eyes illuminated
1690 His fiery virtue roused
From under ashes into sudden flame,
And as an evening dragon came, [1]
Assailant on the perchèd roosts,
And nests in order ranged
1695 Of tame villatic fowl; but as an eagle
His cloudless thunder bolted on their heads. [2]
So virtue given for lost,

Depressed, and overthrown, as seemed,
Like that self-begotten bird
1700 In the Arabian woods embossed, [3]
That no second knows nor third,
And lay erewhile a holocaust,
From out her ashy womb now teemed,
Revives, reflourishes, then vigorous most
1705 When most unactive deemed,
And though her body die, her fame survives,
A secular bird ages of lives. [4]

Man. Come, come, no time for lamentation now,
Nor much more cause, Samson hath quit himself
1710 Like Samson, and heroically hath finished
A life heroic, on his enemies
Fully revenged, hath left them years of mourning,
And lamentation to the sons of Caphtor [5]
Through all Philistian bounds. To Israel
1715 Honour hath left, and freedom, let but them
Find courage to lay hold on this occasion,
To himself and father's house eternal fame;
And which is best and happiest yet, all this
With God not parted from him, as was feared,
1720 But favouring and assisting to the end.
Nothing is here for tears, nothing to wail
Or knock the breast, no weakness, no contempt,
Dispraise, or blame, nothing but well and fair,
And what may quiet us in a death so noble.
1725 Let us go find the body where it lies
Soaked in his enemies' blood, and from the
    stream
With lavers pure, and cleansing herbs wash off
The clotted gore. I with what speed the while

---

[1] *an evening dragon*   "not the fire-breathing, flying kind, but a large snake (*OED* 1), such as might enter a barnyard by stealth to prey on domestic *fowl*. Samson entered the temple like a cunning snake, but he struck the Philistines like an *eagle*" (JL).

[2] *villatic fowl*   farmyard fowl.

[3] *that self-begotten bird*   the Phoenix, which is unique (because there is only one living at any time) and an emblem of Christ because of its power of resurrection; the application of this image to Samson supports the arguments of those who see Samson as a "type" of Christ and the poem as a drama of regeneration; *embossed*   imbosked, hidden in a wood (*OED* emboss v^2 1b, this place cited).

[4] *secular*   living for an age or ages (*OED* secular *a* 6).

[5] *the sons of Caphtor*   the Philistines, who had immigrated from Caphtor, thought to be Crete (JL).

(Gaza is not in plight to say us nay)
1730 Will send for all my kindred, all my friends
To fetch him hence and solemnly attend
With silent obsequy and funeral train
Home to his father's house: there will I build him
A monument, and plant it round with shade
1735 Of laurel ever green, and branching palm,
With all his trophies hung, and acts enrolled
In copious legend, or sweet lyric song.
Thither shall all the valiant youth resort,
And from his memory inflame their breasts
1740 To matchless valour, and adventures high:
The virgins also shall on feastful days
Visit his tomb with flowers, only bewailing
His lot unfortunate in nuptial choice,
From whence captivity and loss of eyes.

1745 *Chor.* All is best, though we oft doubt,
What the unsearchable dispose
Of highest wisdom brings about,
And ever best found in the close.
Oft he seems to hide his face,
1750 But unexpectedly returns
And to his faithful champion hath in place
Bore witness gloriously; whence Gaza mourns
And all that band them to resist
His uncontrollable intent,
1755 His servants he with new acquist
Of true experience from this great event
With peace and consolation hath dismissed,
And calm of mind all passion spent.
—1671

Sir John Suckling
1609 – 1641

John Suckling was born at Twickenham in Middlesex (later famously the home of Alexander Pope). His father, Sir John Suckling, was a successful lawyer, who became Secretary of State, a Privy Councillor and a member of Parliament. His mother was Martha Cranfield, sister to Lionel Cranfield, the first Earl of Middlesex. Aubrey reports that Suckling's father was said to be "but a dull fellow," and that "the wit came by the mother." His mother died before Suckling was five years old. Suckling was educated at Trinity College, Cambridge, left without taking a degree, and entered Gray's Inn in 1627. His father's death, shortly afterwards, made Suckling heir to rich estates in three counties; he frequented the court, and became acquainted with such wits as Thomas Carew, Richard Lovelace and William Davenant. Near the end of 1628, Suckling embarked on an extended visit to Europe, visiting Paris first, and then proceeding to Italy. In September 1630 he was back in England and was knighted by Charles I. In July 1631 he joined an expedition which set out from Great Yarmouth to reinforce the army of Gustavus Adolphus. In 1632 he returned to the English court, and threw himself into the pleasures common to rich young men of the time; he was a reckless gambler, and one of the earliest references to Piccadilly is Aubrey's story that his sisters would go there in fear that he would "lose their portions" at its bowling green. He was not without serious interests, however, and knew Lord Falkland, Roger Boyle, Thomas Stanley and other intellectuals of the time. Early in 1637 his "A Sessions of the Poets," in which many of his contemporaries are named, circulated in manuscript. In the same year he went on a jaunt to Bath with Davenant and some others; Aubrey gives an amusing account of this expedition. In 1639 Suckling and his friend Lord Goring undertook to "bring a hundred horse each" for Charles I's Scottish campaign; Suckling is said to have spent twelve thousand pounds, and incurred much ridicule for the expensive and colourful uniforms of his troopers. In 1641 he was suspected of a plot to free Strafford from the Tower, and fled overseas. In Paris he began a love-affair which led to disaster. The lady's previous lover, to gain revenge, accused him of conspiring the death of Philip IV. Suckling was tortured and condemned to the gallows; but he was reprieved because his enemy, in remorse, confessed to his perjury and was himself sentenced to death. Suckling is thought to have committed suicide rather than live in the poverty to which he had become reduced. Little of Suckling's work appeared in his lifetime; a collection was published in 1646 by the leading Royalist publisher, Humphrey Moseley.

❧❧❧

To the Reader [1]

While Suckling's name is in the forehead of this book, these poems can want no preparation: It had been a prejudice to posterity they should have slept longer, and an injury to his own ashes. They that conversed with him alive, and truly (under which notion I comprehend only knowing Gentlemen, his soul being transcendent, and incommunicable to others, but by reflection), will honour these posthume Ideas of their friend: And if any have lived in so much darkness as not to have known so great an ornament of our age, by looking upon these remains with civility and understanding, they may timely yet repent, and be forgiven.

---

[1] from *Fragmenta Aurea* (1646), and written by the publisher, Humphrey Moseley. Moseley also wrote a preface to Suckling's *Last Remains* (1659), which begins: "Among the highest and most refined wits of the Nation, this genteel and princely poet took his generous rise from the Court; where having flourished with splendour and reputation, he lived only long enough to see the sun-set of that Majesty from whose auspicious beams he derived his lustre."

In this age of paper-prostitutions, a man may buy the reputation of some author's into the price of their volume; but know, the name that leadeth into this Elysium is sacred to Art and Honour, and no man that is not excellent in both is qualified a competent judge: For when knowledge is allowed, yet education in the censure of a gentleman requires as many descents as goes to make one; And he that is bold upon his unequal stock to traduce this name, or learning, will deserve to be condemned again into ignorance his original sin, and die in it.

But I keep back the Ingenuous Reader by my unworthy Preface: the gate is open, and thy soul invited to a garden of ravishing variety; admire his wit, that created these for thy delight, while I withdraw into a shade, and contemplate who must follow.

—1646

Song

1

Why so pale and wan fond lover?
    Prithee why so pale?
Will, when looking well can't move her,
    Looking ill prevail?
5   Prithee why so pale?

2

Why so dull and mute young sinner?
    Prithee why so mute?
Will, when speaking well can't win her,
    Saying nothing do't?
10   Prithee why so mute?

3

Quit, quit, for shame, this will not move,
    This cannot take her;
If of her self she will not love,
    Nothing can make her,
15   The Devil take her.
—1638

A Ballad. Upon a Wedding [1]

1

I tell thee Dick, where I have been,
Where I the rarest things have seen,
    O things beyond compare!
Such sights again cannot be found
5 In any part of English ground,
    Be it at wake, or fair.

2

At *Charing-Cross*, hard by the way
Where we (thou know'st) do sell our hay,
    There is a house with stairs;
10 And there did I see coming down
Such folk as are not in our town,
    Forty at least, in pairs.

3

Amongst the rest, one pest'lent fine,
(His beard no bigger though than thine)
15   Walked on before the rest:
Our landlord looks like nothing to him:
The King, (God bless him) 'twould undo him,
    Should he go still so dressed.

4

At Course-a-Park, without all doubt,
20 He should have first been taken out
    By all the maids i'th' town; [2]
Though lusty *Roger* there had been,
Or little *George* upon the green,
    Or *Vincent* of the crown.

---

[1] This poem was probably written for the marriage of John Lord Lovelace. It was first published in *Wits Recreations*.

[2] *Course-a-Park* a country game, in which a girl called out the name of a person of the other sex to chase her (*OED*).

5

25 But wot you what? the youth was going
To make an end of all his wooing; [1]
   The parson for him stayed:
Yet by his leave (for all his haste)
He did not wish so much all past,
30   (Perchance) as did the maid.

6

The maid, (and thereby hangs a tale,
For such a maid no Whitsun-ale
   Could ever yet produce) [2]
No grape that's kindly ripe, could be
35 So round, so plump, so soft as she,
   Nor half so full of juice.

7

Her fingers were so small, the ring
Would not stay on which they did bring,
   It was too wide a peck: [3]
40 And to say truth (for out it must)
It looked like the great collar (just)
   About our young colt's neck.

8

Her feet beneath her petticoat,
Like little mice stole in and out,
45   As if they fear'd the light:
But oh! she dances such a way!
No sun upon an Easter day
   Is half so fine a sight.

9

He would have kissed her once or twice,
50 But she would not, she was so nice,
   She would not do't in sight;
And then she looked as who should say

I will do what I list to day;
   And you shall do't at night.

10

55 Her cheeks so rare a white was on,
No daisy makes comparison,
   (Who sees them is undone)
For streaks of red were mingled there,
Such as are on a Katherine pear,
60   (The side that's next the sun.)

11

Her mouth so small when she doth speak,
Thou'dst swear her teeth her words did break,
   That they might passage get;
But she so handles still the matter,
65 They come as good as ours, or better,
   And are not spoil'd one whit.

12

Her lips were red, and one was thin,
Compar'd to that was next her chin;
   (Some bee had stung it newly.)
70 But (*Dick*) her eyes so guard her face;
I durst no more upon her gaze,
Than on the sun in *July*. [4]

13

If wishing should be any sin,
The parson self had guilty been,
75   (She looked that day so purely;)
And did the youth so oft the feat
At night, as some did in conceit,
   It would have spoil'd him, surely.

14

Passion oh me! how I run on!
80 There's that that would be thought upon,
   (I trow) besides the bride:

---

[1] *wot you what?* Do you know what?

[2] *Whitsun-ale* a parish festival formerly held at Whitsuntide, marked by feasting, sports and merrymaking (*OED* Whitsun).

[3] *too wide a peck* too wide by a good deal (*OED* peck *sb¹* 3).

[4] *July* accented thus as late as Dr. Johnson's time; the modern pronunciation is abnormal and unexplained (*OED*).

The bus'ness of the kitchen great;
For it is fit that men should eat,
    Nor was it there denied.

15

85 Just in the nick the cook knocked thrice,
And all the waiters in a trice
    His summons did obey:
Each serving man with dish in hand,
Marched boldly up, like our train band,
90   Presented, and away.

16

When all the meat was on the table,
What man of knife, or teeth, was able
    To stay to be entreated?
And this the very reason was,
95 Before the parson could say Grace,
    The company was seated.

17

Now hats fly off, and youths carouse;
Healths first go round, and then the house,
    The brides came thick and thick:
100 And when 'twas nam'd another's health,
Perhaps he made it hers by stealth.
    (And who could help it? *Dick*)

18

O'th' sudden up they rise and dance,
Then sit again and sigh, and glance;
105   Then dance again and kiss:
Thus sev'ral ways the time did pass,
Whilst ev'ry woman wished her place,
    And ev'ry man wished his.

19

By this time all were stoln aside
110 To counsel and undress the bride;
    But that he must not know:
But yet 'twas thought he guessed her mind,
And did not mean to stay behind
    Above an hour or so.

20

115 When in he came (*Dick*) there she lay
Like new-faln snow melting away;
    ('Twas time I trow to part)
Kisses were now the only stay;
Which soon she gave, as who should say,
120   Good b'w'y'! with all my heart.

21

But just as Heav'ns would have to cross it,
In came the bridemaids with the posset: [1]
    The bridegroom eat in spite;
For had he left the women to't
125 It would have cost two hours to do't,
    Which were too much that night.

22

At length the candles out, and now
All that they had not done, they do:
    What that is, who can tell?
130 But I believe it was no more
Than thou and I have done before
    With Bridget, and with Nell.
—1640

The Constant Lover

1

Out upon it, I have loved
    Three whole days together;
And am like to love three more,
    If it hold fair weather.

2

5 Time shall moult away his wings
    Ere he shall discover

---

[1] *posset* hot milk curdled with ale, wine or other liquor; often with sugar, spices or other ingredients (*OED* posset *sb*).

In the whole wide world again
    Such a constant lover.

3

But a pox upon't, no praise
10   There is due at all to me:
Love with me had made no stay,
    Had it any been but she.

4

Had it any been but she
    And that very very face,
15 There had been at least ere this
    A dozen dozen in her place.
—1646

A Barley-break [1]

1

Love, Reason, Hate, did once bespeak
    Three mates to play at barley-break;
Love, Folly took; and Reason, Fancy;
And Hate consorts with Pride; so dance they:
5 Love coupled last, and so it fell
That Love and Folly were in hell.

2

They break, and Love would Reason meet,
But Hate was nimbler on her feet;
Fancy looks for Pride, and thither
10 Hies, and they two hug together:

Yet this new coupling still doth tell
That Love and Folly were in hell.

3

The rest do break again, and Pride
Hath now got Reason on her side;
15 Hate and Fancy meet, and stand
Untouched by Love in Folly's hand:
Folly was dull, but Love ran well,
So Love and Folly were in hell.
—1646

Sonnet I

1

Do'st see how unregarded now
    that piece of beauty passes?
There was a time when I did vow
    to that alone;
5   but mark the fate of faces:
That red and white works now no more on me
Than if it could not charm or I not see.

2

And yet the face continues good,
    and I have still desires,
10 Am still the self same flesh and blood,
      as apt to melt
    and suffer from those fires;
Oh! some kind power unriddle where it lies,
Whether my heart be faulty, or her eyes?

3

She every day her Man doth kill,
    and I as often die;
Neither her power then, nor my will
      can question'd be,
    what is the mystery?

---

[1] Barley-break is an old country game. The first word of the title may be a corruption of "parley," "a term used in the games of children, when a truce is demanded"; or it may refer to the fact that the game was played in a field or stack-yard. The game was played by six persons, three of each sex, in couples; one couple were left in the middle (called "hell") and had to catch the others, who were allowed to separate or "break" when hard-pressed, and thus to change partners. If they were caught they had to take their turn in "hell." See *OED* barley *interjec* and barley-break; see also the description in *The Poems of Sir Philip Sidney*, ed. W.A. Ringler (Oxford: Clarendon P, 1962), 495.

20 Sure beauties' empires, like to greater states
Have certain periods set, and hidden fates. [1]
—1646

Sonnet II

1

Of thee (kind boy) I ask no red and white
  to make up my delight,
    no odd becoming graces,
Black eyes, or little know-not-whats, in faces; [2]
5 Make me but mad enough, give me good store
Of Love, for her I court,
        I ask no more,
'Tis love in love that makes the sport.

2

There's no such thing as that we beauty call,
10   it is mere cozenage all; [3]
    for though some long ago
Like't certain colours mingled so and so,
That doth not tie me now from choosing new;
If I a fancy take
15   To black and blue,
That fancy doth it beauty make.

3

'Tis not the meat, but 'tis the appetite
  makes eating a delight,
    and if I like one dish
20 More than another, that a pheasant is;
What in our watches, that in us is found,
So to the height and nick

We up be wound,
No matter by what hand or trick.
—1646

Sonnet III

1

Oh! for some honest lover's ghost,
  Some kind unbodied post
Sent from the shades below.
I strangely long to know
5 Whether the nobler chaplets wear, [4]
Those that their mistress' scorn did bear,
  Or those that were used kindly.

2

For what-so-e'er they tell us here
  To make those sufferings dear,
10   'Twill there I fear be found,
  That to the being crown'd,
T'have lov'd alone will not suffice,
Unless we also have been wise,
  And have our loves enjoy'd.

3

15 What posture can we think him in,
  That here unlov'd again
  Departs, and's thither gone
  Where each sits by his own?
Or how can that *Elysium* be
20 Where I my mistress still must see
  Circled in others' arms?

4

For there the judges all are just,
  And *Sophonisba* must

[1] *Sure beauties' empires.../ Have certain periods set* Compare the proverbial sentence "States have their conversions and periods as well as natural bodies," *The Works of George Herbert*, ed. F.E. Hutchinson (Oxford: Clarendon P, 1941), 361 (no. 1166).

[2] *know-not-whats* an Englishing of the French *je ne sais quoi;* the French phrase occurs in a letter of Suckling's *The Works of Sir John Suckling*, ed. Thomas Clayton, (Oxford: Clarendon P, 1971), 153.

[3] *cozenage* deception (*OED* cozenage b).

[4] *chaplets* wreaths for the head (*OED* chaplet).

Be his whom she held dear; [1]
25 Not his who loved her here:
The sweet *Philoclea* since she died
Lies by her *Pirocles* his side,
Not by *Amphialus*. [2]

5

Some bays (perchance) or myrtle bough
30 For difference crowns the brow
Of those kind souls that were
The noble Martyrs here;
And if that be the only odds,
(As who can tell) ye kinder gods,
35 Give me the Woman here.
—1646

The Wits
(A Sessions of the Poets) [3]

1

A sessions was held the other day,
And *Apollo* himself was at it (they say;)
The laurel that had been so long reserv'd,
Was now to be given to him best deserv'd.
And
5 Therefore the wits of the Town came thither,
'Twas strange to see how they flocked together;
Each strongly confident of his own way,
Thought to carry the laurel away that day.

2

There was *Selden*, and he sat hard by the chair;
10 *Wenman* not far off, which was very fair; [4]
Sands with *Townsend*, for they kept no order;
Digby and *Chillingworth* a little further: [5]
And
There was *Lucan's* translator too, and he
That makes God speak so big in's poetry;
15 *Selwin* and *Waller*, and *Berkeleys* both the brothers;
Jack Vaughan and *Porter*, with divers others. [6]

3

The first that broke silence was good old *Ben*,
Prepared before with Canary wine, [7]
And he told them plainly he desrved the bays,
20 For his were called Works, where others were but
Plays; [8]

---

[1] *Sophonisba* the daughter of Hasdrubal and the wife of Syphax, whom she won over to the Carthaginian cause; when Syphax was overthrown Sophonisba took poison (*OCD*). Suckling refers to her in a letter to his sister, whose husband, apparently not much to be regretted, had committed suicide (*Works*, 149).

[2] *Philoclea...Pirocles...Amphialus* These names occur in Sir Philip Sidney's *Arcadia*.

[3] This poem, written in the summer of 1637, was sung to Charles I during his hunting expedition to the New Forest in late August and early September of that year (*Works*, 266–267). The word "sessions" denotes a trial, whereas "session" denotes only a sitting of a court.

---

[4] *Selden* John Selden (1584–1654), a famous legal scholar, considered to be one of the most learned men of his time; *Wenman* Sir Francis Wenman (fl. 1615–1640), described by Aubrey as an acquaintance of Lord Falkland, whose house at Great Tew, near Oxford, was "like a College, full of learned men."

[5] *Sands* i.e. George Sandys (1578–1644), translator of Ovid's *Metamorphoses* and the first book of the *Aeneid*, and author of a paraphrase of the psalms; *Townsend* i.e. Aurelian Townshend (fl. 1601–1643), author of two masques and a number of poems; *Digby* Sir Kenelm Digby (1603–1665), author of *Observations upon Religio Medici* (1643), and various scientific and philosophical writings; *Chillingworth* William Chillingworth (1602–1644), author of *The Religion of Protestants A Safe Way To Salvation* (1637).

[6] *Lucan's translator* Thomas May (1595–1650). On his importance see David Norbrook, *Writing the English Republic* (Cambridge: Cambridge U P, 1999); *he / That makes God speak so big in's poetry* not identified; Francis Quarles, George Wither, and Phineas Fletcher have been suggested (*Works*, 274); *Selwin* not identified; *Waller* Edmund Waller (1606–1687); *Berkeleys both the brothers* Sir William Berkeley (d. 1677) and John Berkeley, first Baron Berkeley of Stratton (d. 1678); *Jack Vaughan* Sir John Vaughan (1603–1674); *Porter* Endymion Porter (1587–1644).

[7] *good old Ben* Ben Jonson (1572–1637). Ben Jonson died on August 6, 1637, at about the same time as this poem was written. It has been argued that Suckling would not have ridiculed him immediately after his death, but Suckling had long been hostile to Jonson.

[8] *his were called Works, where others were but Plays* The folio *Works of Benjamin Jonson*, 1616, was thought presumptuous, as no other dramatist had published a collection of his plays before this.

And
Bid them remember how he had purg'd the stage
Of errors, that had lasted many an age,
And he hop'd they did think the *Silent Woman*,
The Fox, and the *Alchymist* outdone by no man. [1]

4

25 *Apollo* stopt him there, and bid him not go on,
'Twas merit, he said, and not presumption
Must carry it; at which *Ben* turned about,
And in great choler offered to go out:
But
Those that were there thought it not fit
30 To discontent so ancient a wit;
And therefore *Apollo* call'd him back again,
And made him mine host of his own new Inn. [2]

5

Tom Carew was next, but he had a fault
That would not well stand with a Laureate; [3]
35 His Muse was hard bound, and th'issue of's brain
Was seldom brought forth but with trouble and
pain.
And
All that were present there did agree,
A Laureate's Muse should be easy and free;
Yet sure 'twas not that, but 'twas thought that his
Grace
40 Considered he was well he had a cup-bearer's
place. [4]

6

Will. Davenant asham'd of a foolish mischance
That he had got lately travelling in *France*, [5]
Modestly hoped the handsomness of's Muse
Might any deformity about him excuse. [6]
And
45 Surely the company would have been content,
If they could have found any precedent;
But in all their records either in verse or prose,
There was not one Laureat without a nose.

7

To *Will Berkeley* sure all the wits meant well,
50 But first they would see how his snow would sell: [7]
Will smil'd and swore in their judgements they
went less,
That concluded of merit upon success. [8]
So
Sullenly taking his place again,
He gave way to *Selwin*, that straight stept in;
55 But alas! he had been so lately a wit,
That *Apollo* himself hardly knew him yet.

8

Toby Matthew (pox on 't! how came he there?)
Was busily whispering some-body i'th'ear, [9]
When he had the honour to be nam'd i'the Court:

---

[5] *Will. Davenant* William Davenant (1606–1668); *travelling in France* possibly a euphemism for contracting syphilis, popularly associated (by the English) with France.

[6] *any deformity about him* Aubrey writes of Davenant, "He got a terrible clap of a black handsome wench that lay in Axe-yard, Westminster…which cost him his nose, with which unlucky mischance many wits were too cruelly bold"; *clap* gonorrhea.

[7] *how his snow would sell* It has been conjectured that this is a facetious reference to the frigidity or freedom from sexual impurity of Berkeley's play *The Lost Lady*, which had not yet been performed.

[8] *they… / That concluded of merit upon success* presumably, those who equated popular success with literary merit.

[9] *Toby Matthew* Sir Toby Matthew (1577–1655); *was busily whispering* Anthony à Wood wrote of Matthew that it was his custom always to be whispering in company.

---

[1] *The Silent Woman, The Fox, The Alchemist* all plays by Jonson. *The Fox* is *Volpone*.

[2] *his own new Inn* Jonson's play *The New Inn* failed badly in its first stage production; this was the occasion for his "Ode to Himself."

[3] *Tom Carew* Thomas Carew (1594/5–1640).

[4] *a cup-bearer's place* in allusion to Carew's position as Sewer in Ordinary to Charles I.

60 But Sir, you may thank my Lady *Carlisle* for't; [1]
　　　　　　For
Had not her Character furnished you out
With something of handsome, without all doubt
You and your sorry Lady Muse had been
In the number of those that were not to come in.

9

65 In haste two or three from the Court came in,
And they brought letters (forsooth) from the Queen;
'Twas discreetly done too, for if they had come
Without them, they had scarce been let into the
　　　　room.
　　　　　　This
Made a dispute; for 'twas plain to be seen
70 Each man had a mind to gratify the Queen: [2]
But *Apollo* himself could not think it fit;
There was difference, he said, 'twixt fooling and
　　　　wit.

10

Suckling next was call'd, but did not appear,
And strait one whisperd *Apollo* in's ear,
75 That of all men living he cared not for't,
He loved not the Muses so well as his sport;
　　　　　　And
Prized black eyes, or a lucky hit
At bowls, above all the trophies of wit;
But *Apollo* was angry, and publicly said
80 'Twere fit that a fine were set on his head.

11

Wat Montague now stood forth to his trial,
And did not so much as suspect a denial; [3]
Wise *Apollo* then asked him first of all
If he understood his own pastoral.
　　　　　　For
85 If he could do it, 'twould plainly appear
He understood more than any man there,
And did merit the bays above all the rest,
But the Mounsier was modest, and silence
　　　　confessed.

12

During these troubles, in the crowd was hid
90 One that *Apollo* soon missed, little *Sid*; [4]
And having spied him, call'd him out of the throng,
And advised him in his ear not to write so strong.
　　　　　　Then
Murrey was summon'd, but 'twas urg'd that he
Was chief already of another company. [5]

13

Hales set by himself most gravely did smile [6]
95 To see them about nothing keep such a coil; [7]
Apollo had spied him, but knowing his mind
Past by, and call'd *Falkland* that sat just behind:
　　　　　　But

<hr>

[1] *my Lady Carlisle* Lucy Hay, Countess of Carlisle (1599–1660), was admired by Charles I's courtiers, but not apparently by Suckling. He is uncomplimentary about her in his "Upon my Lady Carlisle's walking in Hampton-Court garden," a poem in dialogue form in which Thomas Carew praises and Suckling dispraises her. Matthew's *Character of the Most Excellent Lady, Lucy Countess of Carlisle*, was circulating in 1636, though not printed until 1660.

[2] *This made a dispute* etc. omitted from the earliest printed copies because of the impropriety of its reference to Henrietta Maria; *gratify* is a double entendre.

[3] *Wat Montague* Walter Montague (?1603–1677). His *The Shepherd's Paradise* was acted by Henrietta Maria and her maids of honour, for the entertainment of Charles I, in January 1633.

[4] *little Sid* Sidney Godolphin (1610–1643), a poet. He was killed in the Civil War. See the chapter "The Death of Sidney Godolphin" in Irene Coltman, *Private Men and Public Causes* (London: Faber and Faber, 1962).

[5] *Murrey* probably William Murray, Gentleman of the Bedchamber and later first Earl of Dysart. In a manuscript of the time he is referred to as "his country's chiefest wit."

[6] *Hales* John Hales (1584–1656).

[7] *keep such a coil* a proverbial phrase, meaning "make such a fuss."

He was of late so gone with Divinity,
100 That he had almost forgot his Poetry, [1]
Though to say the truth (and *Apollo* did know it)
He might have been both his Priest and his Poet.

14

At length who but an Alderman did appear,
At which *Will. Davenant* began to swear;
105 But wiser *Apollo* bid him draw nigher,
And when he was mounted a little higher
He
Openly declared that 'twas the best sign
Of good store of wit to have good store of coin,
And without a syllable more or less said,
110 He put the laurel on the alderman's head.

15

At this all the wits were in such a maze
That for a good while they did nothing but gaze
One upon another, not a man in the place
But had discontent writ in great in his face.
Only
115 The small Poets cleared up again,

Out of hope (as 'twas thought) of borrowing;
But sure they were out, for he forfeits his Crown
When he lends any Poet about the Town.
—1646

A Candle [2]

There is a thing which in the light
Is seldom us'd, but in the night
It serves the maiden female crew,
The ladies, and the good-wives too: [3]
5 They use to take it in their hand,
And then it will uprightly stand;
And to a hole they it apply,
Where by its good will it would die:
It spends, goes out, and still within [4]
10 It leaves its moisture thick and thin.
—1659

---

[1] *Falkland* Lucius Cary, second Viscount Falkland (?1610–1643).
See note on Wenman, above.

---

[2] Facetious poems on the clandestine uses of the candle were common in the period.

[3] *good-wives* mistresses of houses, therefore, married women (*OED* good-wife 1).

[4] *die...spends* Both words were commonly used in the period to refer to orgasm.

Gerrard Winstanley
1609 – ?1676

Born in Lancashire, the son of a mercer (a dealer in fabrics) with puritan sympathies, Winstanley worked in the London cloth trade until his business failed in 1643, when he moved to Cobham in Surrey to earn a living as a farm labourer. Most of the activities and writings (about twenty pamphlets and broadsheets) for which he is known date from the period 1648–1652. Like many other radicals of the revolutionary period, Winstanley disappears from the records after 1660, though he may be the Gerrard Winstanley who died a Quaker and corn chandler in 1676.

Winstanley's early pamphlets participate in the tradition of radical religious mysticism represented by Lawrence Clarkson (in his Seeker and Antinomian phases) and Abiezer Coppe. Like Coppe, Winstanley's search for Scripture's spiritual meaning led to a concern for social justice: Hell, he believed, was a mechanism of control used by clerics and the rich to oppress the poor. But Winstanley is best known for the political revelation that led to the Digger movement, a vision of agrarian communism first proclaimed in *The New Law of Righteousness* (1649) and set out in its most elaborate form in his last publication, *The Law of Freedom in a Platform* (1652). Winstanley argued that men could be free only when private property was abolished, all had access to the land and worked it in common, and no one worked for wages: social and economic inequities, he wrote, were a function of inequities in the distribution of property. While several Digger communes were founded to put these ideas into practice, the most famous was on St. George's Hill, near Winstanley's home in Cobham. Winstanley and others began to till the commons land there in April 1649; alarmed local landowners complained to Thomas Fairfax and the Council of State, who proved not to share their anxieties. But the owners persisted, pursued the Diggers in court, and led a mob to trample their crops. The Diggers resettled nearby, but were finally driven out in 1650. The experiment and the attempts to suppress it were widely reported at the time. The following *Declaration* was the second of two manifestos published to explain the project.

While the Digger movement is best known for Winstanley's political writings, Digger communities around the country produced a variety of texts, including songs written to popularize their cause. In 1650, the Digger community on St. George's Hill published *The Diggers Mirth*, a short pamphlet containing "verses composed and fitted to tunes, for the delight and recreation of all those who Dig, or own that work, in the Commonwealth of England." "The Digger's Song" included here was not among the songs published at the time, but was discovered in the manuscript papers of William Clarke, secretary to Cromwell's Council of War. Like the other Digger songs, its authorship is uncertain, though its similarity to verses scattered in Winstanley's pamphlets has led some to credit him with writing it.

❧❧❧

The Diggers' Song

You noble Diggers all, stand up now, stand up now,
  You noble Diggers all, stand up now,
The waste land to maintain, seeing Cavaliers by name

5 Your digging does disdain, and persons all defame
    Stand up now, stand up now.

Your houses they pull down, stand up now, stand up now,
    Your houses they pull down, stand up now.

Your houses they pull down to fright poor men in
    town,
But the gentry must come down, and the poor
    shall wear the crown.
10   Stand up now, Diggers all.

With spades and hoes and plows, stand up now,
    stand up now,
    With spades and hoes and plows stand up now,
Your freedom to uphold, seeing Cavaliers are bold
To kill you if they could, and rights from you to
    hold.
15   Stand up now, Diggers all.

Their self-will is their law, stand up now, stand
    up now,
    Their self-will is their law, stand up now.
Since tyranny came in they count it now no sin
To make a gaol a gin,[1] to starve poor men therein.
20   Stand up now, stand up now.

The gentry are all round, stand up now, stand up
    now,
    The gentry are all round, stand up now.
The gentry are all round, on each side they are
    found,
Their wisdom's so profound, to cheat us of our
    ground.
25   Stand up now, stand up now.

The lawyers they conjoin, stand up now, stand up
    now,
    The lawyers they conjoin, stand up now,
To arrest you they advise, such fury they devise,
The devil in them lies and hath blinded both their
    eyes.
30   Stand up now, stand up now.

The clergy they come in, stand up now, stand up
    now,
    The clergy they come in, stand up now.
The clergy they come in, and say it is a sin
That we should now begin, our freedom for to win.
35   Stand up now, Diggers all.

The tithe they yet will have, stand up now, stand
    up now,
    The tithes they yet will have, stand up now.
The tithes they yet will have, and lawyers their
    fees crave,
And this they say is brave, to make the poor their
    slave.
40   Stand up now, Diggers all.

'Gainst lawyers and gainst Priests, stand up now,
    stand up now,
    Gainst lawyers and gainst Priests stand up now.
For tyrants they are both even flat against their
    oath,
To grant us they are loath, free meat, and drink,
    and cloth.
45   Stand up now, Diggers all.

The club is all their law, stand up now, stand up
    now,
    The club is all their law, stand up now.
The club is all their law to keep men in awe,
But they no vision saw to maintain such a law.
50   Stand up now, Diggers all.

The Cavaliers are foes, stand up now, stand up
    now,
    The Cavaliers are foes, stand up now;
The Cavaliers are foes, themselves they do disclose
By verses not in prose to please the singing boys
55   Stand up now, Diggers all.

To conquer them by love, come in now, come in
    now,

---

[1] *gin* a snare or trap, or even an engine of torture (*OED* gin *sb*[1] 4, 5).

To conquer them by love, come in now;   60
To conquer them by love, as it does you behove,
For he is King above, no power is like to love.

Glory here Diggers all.

—CA. 1649–50

Anne Bradstreet
ca. 1612 – 1672

Born in 1612, Anne was the second of six children of Thomas and Dorothy Yorke. When she was six years old, her father became page to Lord Compton who was then steward to the fourth Earl of Lincoln, a prominent Puritan. The family moved, as a result, to Sempringham Manor in Lincolnshire, where Anne was educated by tutors and able to access the libraries of both her father and the Earl. She contracted smallpox in 1628, and was married later that year to Simon Bradstreet, son of a non-conformist minister in Lincolnshire, a fortunate union by her own account. In 1630, the Bradstreets and Dudleys set sail for New England, landing at Salem, Massachusetts. They moved immediately to Charlestown, then to Newtown, and finally settled in Ipswich for several years before moving to Andover, where Anne spent the remainder of her life. Thomas Dudley became the governor of Massachusetts colony in 1634, the same year that Anne bore the first of eight children. In 1642, she distributed her first collection of poems in manuscript form. These poems were well received, inspiring the Puritan

divine Cotton Mather to describe her as "a crown to her father." Without her knowledge, Bradstreet's brother-in-law John Woodbridge published her work in England under the title *The Tenth Muse Lately Sprung up in America* (1650). In 1661, Anne had a long and serious illness, but her husband, now secretary of the colony, was required to travel to England on state business. It was during his absence that she wrote her "poetical epistles" to her husband. Her later writing consisted mainly of elegies, occasional meditations and poems of supplication in the face of illness, affliction, and the absence of her family. Bradstreet died of consumption at Andover, September 16, 1672. A second edition of her poems was published posthumously in 1678 (*Several Poems*), but her prose contemplations, meditations and additional poems, preserved by her son Simon (the Andover Manuscript) remained unpublished until 1867. Bradstreet's corpus exhibits a facility in historical, political and religious verse as well as intensity and candour in the expression of personal grief, domestic pleasure and religious faith.

❧❧❧

The Prologue [1]

1

To sing of wars, of captains, and of kings,
  Of cities founded, commonwealths begun,
For my mean pen, are too superior things,
And how they all, or each, their dates have run:
5 Let poets, and historians set these forth,
My obscure verse, shall not so dim their worth.

2

But when my wond'ring eyes, and envious heart,

Great Bartas' sugared lines do but read o'er; [2]
Fool, I do grudge, the Muses did not part
10 'Twixt him and me, that over-fluent store;
A Bartas can do what a Bartas will,
But simple I, according to my skill.

3

From schoolboy's tongue, no rhetoric we expect,
Nor yet a sweet consort, from broken strings,

---

[1] *The Prologue* the Prologue to *The Tenth Muse Lately Sprung up in America* (London, 1650).

[2] *Bartas* Guillaume de Salluste du Bartas, much admired by English Puritans during Bradstreet's youth, was a French soldier and author of *La Sepmaine* (1578) and *La Seconde Sepmaine* (1584), lengthy religious poems noted for encyclopedic presentation of information and Calvinistic didacticism. Joshua Sylvester's translation, *Divine Weeks and Works*, was published in 1621.

15 Nor perfect beauty, where's a main defect,
My foolish, broken, blemished Muse so sings;
And this to mend, alas, no art is able,
'Cause nature made it so irreparable.

4

Nor can I, like that fluent sweet tongued Greek [1]
Who lisped at first, speak afterwards more plain.
20 By art, he gladly found what he did seek,
A full requital of his striving pain:
Art can do much, but this maxim's most sure,
A weak or wounded brain admits no cure.

5

I am obnoxious to each carping tongue,
25 Who says, my hand a needle better fits,
A poet's pen, all scorn, I should thus wrong;
For such despite they cast on female wits:
If what I do prove well, it won't advance,
They'll say it's stol'n, or else, it was by chance.

6

30 But sure the antique Greeks were far more mild,
Else of our sex, why feigned they those nine, [2]
And poesy made, Calliope's own child,
So 'mongst the rest, they placed the arts divine:
But this weak knot they will full soon untie,
35 The Greeks did nought but play the fool and lie.

7

Let Greeks be Greeks, and women what they are,
Men have precedency, and still excel,
It is but vain, unjustly to wage war,
Men can do best, and women know it well;
40 Preeminence in each, and all is yours,
Yet grant some small acknowledgment of ours.

---

[1] *sweet tongued Greek* Demosthenes (384–322 B.C.E.) was considered the greatest of Athenian orators. There is a legend that he overcame a speech defect by declaiming with pebbles in his mouth.

[2] *nine* The Nine Muses are the Greek deities who preside over music, poetry, the arts and sciences. Calliope is Muse of the heroic epic.

8

And oh, ye high flown quills, that soar the skies,
And ever with your prey, still catch your praise,
If e'er you deign these lowly lines, your eyes
45 Give wholesome parsley wreath, I ask no bays:
This mean and unrefined ore of mine, [3]
Will make your glistering gold but more to shine.
—1650

A Dialogue between Old England and New, Concerning their Present Troubles.
Anno 1642

New England.

Alas, dear Mother, fairest queen, and best,
With honor, wealth, and peace, happy and
       blessed;
What ails thee hang thy head, and cross thine arms?
5 And sit i'th dust, to sigh these sad alarms?
What deluge of new woes thus overwhelm
The glories of thy ever famous realm?
What means this wailing tone, this mourning
       guise?
Ah, tell thy daughter, she may sympathize.

10   Old England.

Art ignorant indeed, of these my woes?
Or must my forced tongue these griefs disclose?
And must myself dissect my tattered state,
Which 'mazed Christendom stands wond'ring at?
15 And thou a child, a limb, and dost not feel
My weak'ned fainting body now to reel?
This physic-purging-potion I have taken,
Will bring consumption, or an ague quaking,
Unless some cordial thou fetch from high,
20 Which present help may ease this malady.
If I decease, dost think thou shalt survive?
Or by my wasting state, dost think to thrive?

---

[3] *ore* "stuff" in the 1650 edition.

Then weigh our case, if't be not justly sad,
Let me lament alone, while thou art glad.

25   New England.
And thus, alas, your state you much deplore,
In general terms, but will not say wherefore:
What medicine shall I seek to cure this woe,
If th' wound's so dangerous I may not know?
30 But you perhaps would have me guess it out,
What, hath some Hengist, like that Saxon stout,
By fraud, and force, usurped thy flow'ring
    crown, [1]
And by tempestuous wars thy fields trod down?
Or hath Canutus, that brave valiant Dane, [2]
35 The regal, peaceful scepter from thee ta'en?
Or is't a Norman, whose victorious hand [3]
With English blood bedews thy conquered land?
Or is't intestine wars that thus offend?
Do Maud, and Stephen for the crown contend? [4]

40 Do barons rise, and side against their king? [5]
And call in foreign aid, to help the thing?
Must Edward be deposed, or is't the hour [6]
That second Richard must be clapped i'th'
    Tower? [7]
Or is the fatal jar again begun,
45 That from the red, white pricking roses sprung? [8]
Must Richmond's aid, the nobles now implore, [9]
To come, and break the tushes of the boar?
If none of these, dear mother, what's your woe?
Pray, do not fear Spain's bragging Armado? [10]
50 Doth your ally, fair France, conspire your wrack?
Or, do the Scots play false behind your back?

---

[1] *Hengist* The Anglo-Saxons came to Britain at the invitation of King Vortigern and were granted lands in the eastern part of the island in exchange for military service. When Hengist, the Anglo-Saxon leader, arrived in Kent (449 C.E.), he flooded England with pagan Saxons, eventually deposed Vortigern and succeeded to the kingdom in 455 C.E., reigning until his death in 488 C.E.

[2] *Canutus* Canute (Cnut), King of England, Norway, and Denmark (ca. 995–1035). Battles between the Dane Canute and the Wessex kings resulted in a pact in which Edmund Ironside held Wessex and Canute Mercia. On Edmund's death in 1017, Canute reigned over the realm of England until his death in 1035.

[3] *Norman* Edward the Confessor died in 1066 without an heir. There were two claimants to the throne: the Anglo-Saxon Harold, son of Godwin, and William of Normandy. Harold ruled for forty weeks and a day before William invaded and conquered England.

[4] *Maud, and Stephen* In 1125 Stephen, nephew of Henry I, swore fealty to Henry's daughter Matilda (Maud) as her father's successor. When Stephen proclaimed himself King after Henry's death, he was opposed by Matilda and his reign was troubled by internal wars. Though Matilda imprisoned Stephen for six months in 1141, during which time she reigned as Queen, she left England in 1148, withdrawing her claim to the throne in favour of her son Henry of Anjou. Henry waged war against Stephen until 1153, when Stephen named him as heir.

[5] *Do barons rise…against the king* After the death of his brother Richard I, the Lion-Hearted, John succeeded to England's throne. His tyrannical reign (1199–1216) and aggressive policy against the baronage caused the nobility to unite against him and to compel him to sign the Magna Carta in 1215.

[6] *Edward* Edward II experienced two civil wars during his reign. He defeated Thomas, Earl of Lancaster in 1322, but lost the rebellion led by his queen Isabella and her lover Roger Mortimer. It is believed that he was murdered in 1328.

[7] *second Richard* While still in his minority, Richard II succeeded to the throne after the death of Edward III in 1377. In 1399, when Richard II was in Ireland, Henry of Bolingbroke, son of John of Gaunt, returned from exile and was supported by Parliament in his bid for the throne. Richard II was imprisoned and apparently murdered the following year, making way for the first Lancastrian king, Henry IV.

[8] *red, white pricking roses sprung* The War of the Roses was a series of dynastic wars fought by the rival houses of Lancaster and York for the throne of England. The War began in 1455 with the struggle between Henry IV and Richard Plantagenet, third Duke of York, and ended in 1485 when Henry Tudor defeated Richard III's forces at Bosworth.

[9] *Richmond's aid* Richard III usurped the throne in 1483. Insurrections against him occurred from 1483 onwards until Henry Tudor, Earl of Richmond, arrived with troops and defeated him at Bosworth. Richmond was crowned Henry VII in 1485, the first monarch of the Tudor dynasty.

[10] *Spain's bragging Armado* In 1587, conflicts between England and Spain developed into a war when England offered to support the revolt of the Netherlands against Spanish rule and when the English executed Mary Queen of Scots. Philip II of Spain dispatched an armada in 1588, which was defeated by the forces of Queen Elizabeth I. Despite this defeat, England's war with Spain continued until 1604.

Doth Holland quit you ill, for all your love?
Whence is this storm, from earth, or heaven
    above? [1]
Is't drought, is't famine, or is't pestilence?
55 Dost feel the smart, or fear the consequence?
Your humble child entreats you, show your grief,
Though arms, nor purse she hath, for your relief:
Such is her poverty, yet shall be found
A suppliant for your help, as she is bound.

60   Old England.
I must confess, some of those sores you name,
My beauteous body at this present maim;
But foreign foe, nor feigned friend I fear,
For they have work enough (thou know'st)
    elsewhere;
65 Nor is it Alice's son and Henry's daughter, [2]
Whose proud contention cause this slaughter;
Nor nobles siding, to make John no king
French Lewis unjustly to the crown to bring;
No Edward, Richard to lose rule, and life,
70 Nor no Lancastrians, to renew old strife;
No crook-backed tyrant, now usurps the seat,
Whose tearing tusks did wound, and kill, and
    threat:
No Duke of York nor Earl of March to soil
Their hands in kindred's blood, whom they did
    foil:
75 No need of Tudor, roses to unite,
None knows which is the red, or which the white:
Spain's braving fleet a second time is sunk,
France knows, how of my fury she hath drunk;
By Edward Third, and Henry Fifth of fame,
80 Her lilies in mine arms avouch the same.
My sister Scotland hurts me now no more,
Though she hath been injurious heretofore.

What Holland is, I am in some suspense,
But trust not much unto his excellence;
85 For wants, sure some I feel, but more I fear,
And for the pestilence, who knows how near;
Famine, and plague, two sisters of the sword,
Destruction to a land doth soon afford;
They're for my punishments ordained on high,
90 Unless thy tears prevent it speedily.
But yet, I answer not what you demand,
To show the grievance of my troubled land;
Before I tell the effect, I'll shew the cause,
Which are my sins, the breach of sacred laws;
95 Idolatry, supplanter of a nation,
With foolish superstitious adoration;
And liked, and countenanced by men of might,
The Gospel is trod down, and hath no right;
Church offices are sold, and bought, for gain,
100 That Pope, had hope, to find Rome here again;
For oaths, and blasphemies did ever ear
From Beelzebub himself, such language hear? [3]
What scorning of the saints of the Most High,
What injuries did daily on them lie?
105 What false reports, which nick-names did they take,
Nor for their own, but for their master's sake?
And thou, poor soul, wast jeered among the rest,
Thy flying for the truth I made a jest;
For Sabbath-breaking, and for drunkenness,
110 Did ever land profaneness more express?
From crying bloods, yet cleansed am not I,
Martyrs, and others, dying causelessly:
How many Princely heads on blocks laid down,
For nought, but title to a fading crown?
115 'Mongst all the cruelties which I have done,
Oh, Edward's babes, and Clarence hapless son, [4]

---

[1] *fair France...heaven above?* Bradstreet refers to England's relations with France, Scotland and Holland in general terms in these lines and in ll. 78–84.

[2] ll. 65–84 In these lines Old England recites the account of England's history sketched by New England in ll. 39–52.

---

[3] *Beelzebub* One of the names of Satan; in its Latin and Syriac version it can mean "lord of the flies" (see Matthew 12:24, 27; Mark 3:22, Luke 11:15, 18).

[4] *Edward's babes, and Clarence hapless son* It is believed that Richard III effected the murder of his nephews in order to succeed to the throne.

O Jane, why didst thou die in flow'ring prime, [1]
Because of royal stem, that was thy crime;
For bribery, adultery, for thefts, and lies,
120 Where is the nation, I can't paralyze;
With usury, extortion, and oppression,
These be the Hydras of my stout transgression; [2]
These be the bitter fountains, heads, and roots,
Whence flowed the source, the sprigs, the boughs,
    and fruits;
125 Of more than thou canst hear, or I relate,
That with high hand I still did perpetrate;
For these, were threatened the woeful day,
I mocked the preachers, put it far away;
The sermons yet upon record do stand,
130 That cried, destruction to my wicked land:
These prophets' mouths (alas the while) was
    stopped,
Unworthily, some backs whipped, and ears
    cropped;
Their reverent cheeks, did bear the glorious marks
Of stinking, stigmatizing, Romish clerks;
135 Some lost their livings, some in prison pent,
Some grossly fined, from friends to exile went:
Their silent tongues to heaven did vengeance cry,
Who heard their cause, and wrongs judged
    righteously,
And will repay it sevenfold in my lap,
140 This is forerunner of my after clap,
Nor took I warning by my neighbors' falls,
I saw sad Germany's dismantled walls. [3]

I saw her people famished, nobles slain,
Her fruitful land, a barren heath remain.
145 I saw (unmoved) her armies foiled and fled,
Wives forced, babes tossed, her houses calcined,
I saw strong Rochel yielding to her foe, [4]
Thousands of starved Christians there also.
I saw poor Ireland bleeding out her last, [5]
150 Such cruelty as all reports have past.
My heart obdurate, stood not yet aghast.
Nor sip I of that cup, and just 't may be,
The bottom dregs reserved are for me.

155   New England.
To all you've said, sad mother, I assent
Your fearful sins, great cause there's to lament,
My guilty hands (in part) hold up with you,
A sharer in your punishment's my due,
160 But all you say, amounts to this effect,
Not what you feel, but what you do expect.
Pray in plain terms, what is your present grief,
Then let's join heads, and hands for your relief.

                     Old England.
165 Well, to the matter then, there's grown of late,
'Twixt king and peers a question of state,
Which is the chief, the law, or else the king,
One saith it's he, the other no such thing.
My better part in court of Parliament,
170 To ease my groaning land show their intent,
To crush the proud, and right to each man deal.

---

[1] *O Jane...flow'ring prime* Lady Jane Grey (1538–1554), great-granddaughter of Henry VII, was proclaimed Queen of England July 10, 1553, following the death of Edward VI. She reigned for nine days before Mary Tudor entered London and was proclaimed Queen. Lady Jane was imprisoned and beheaded six months later. Her Protestant piety was memorialized by John Foxe in his *Acts and Monuments* (London, 1563).

[2] *Hydras* Hydra was the fabulous many-headed snake of the marshes of Lerna, whose heads grew again as fast as they were cut off.

[3] *Germany's dismantled walls* During the Thirty Years War (1618–1648), the German Protestant forces in the Palatinate were defeated by the Catholic Princes of Germany and the Hapsburg empire.

[4] *strong Rochel...to her foe* La Rochelle was a Huguenot stronghold during the Wars of Religion (1562–1598). The Huguenots, French Protestant followers of Calvin, however, were ultimately stripped of all political power when La Rochelle fell after a siege of 14 months (1628).

[5] *poor Ireland...out her last* In the winter of 1641, there was a massacre of English Protestants in the Irish rebellion. John Temple's *The Irish Rebellion* (1646) gave a horrific account of the slaughter of English settlers. In Bradstreet's poem *The Four Ages of Man*, Old Age says of the Irish rebellion: "Three hundred thousand slaughtered innocents, / By bloody Popish, hellish miscreants; / Oh may you live, and so you will I trust / To see them swill in blood until they burst" (1678 edition).

To help the Church, and stay the commonweal,
So many obstacles comes in their way,
As puts me to a stand what I should say,
175 Old customs, new prerogatives stood on,
Had they not held law fast, all had been gone,
Which by their prudence stood them in such stead,
They took high Strafford lower by the head, [1]
And to their Laud be't spoke, they held i'th'
    Tower, [2]
180 All England's metropolitan that hour,
This done, an Act they would have passed fain,
No prelate should his bishopric retain; [3]
Here tugged they hard indeed, for all men saw,
This must be done by Gospel, not by law.
185 Next the militia they urged sore,
This was denied, I need not say wherefore.
The King displeased, at York himself absents, [4]
They humbly beg return, show their intents,
The writing, printing, posting to and fro,
190 Shows all was done, I'll therefore let it go.
But now I come to speak of my disaster,
Contention's grown 'twixt subjects and their master:
They worded it so long, they fell to blows,
That thousands lay on heaps, here bleeds my woes.
195 I that no wars, so many years have known,

Am now destroyed, and slaughtered by mine
    own, [5]
But could the field alone this cause decide,
One battle, two or three I might abide,
But these may be beginnings of more woe,
200 Who knows, the worst, the best may overthrow;
Religion, Gospel, here lies at the stake,
Pray now dear child, for sacred Zion's sake,
Oh pity me, in this sad perturbation,
My plundered towns, my houses' devastation,
205 My ravished virgins, and my young men slain,
My wealthy trading fallen, my dearth of grain,
The seed time's come, but ploughman hath no
    hope,
Because he knows not, who shall inn his crop:
The poor they want their pay, their children
    bread,
210 Their woeful mother's tears unpitied.
If any pity in thy heart remain,
Or any childlike love thou dost retain,
For my relief now use thy utmost skill,
And recompense me good, for all my ill.

215   New England
Dear mother cease complaints, and wipe your eyes,
Shake off your dust, cheer up, and now arise,
You are my mother, nurse, I once your flesh,
Your sunken bowels gladly would refresh:
220 Your griefs I pity much, but should do wrong,
To weep for that we both have prayed for long,
To see these latter days of hoped for good,
That Right may have its right, though't be with
    blood;
After dark Popery the day did clear,
225 But now the sun in's brightness shall appear,
Blest be the nobles of thy noble land,
With (ventured lives) for truth's defense that stand,
Blest be thy Commons, who for common good,
And thine infringed laws have boldly stood.

---

[1] *high Strafford* Thomas Wentworth (1593-1641), Earl of Strafford, Lord President of the Council of the North and Lord Deputy of Ireland, was executed for treason on May 12, 1641. Charles I never forgave himself for signing Strafford's death-warrant.

[2] *Laud* an unfriendly pun on the name of William Laud (1573-1645), Archbishop of Canterbury, who was imprisoned in 1641 and executed in 1645 at the age of seventy-three.

[3] *an Act…bishopric retain* The Root and Branch Petition, demanding the abolition of episcopacy, was presented to the House of Commons, December 11, 1640.

[4] *at York himself absents* Charles I left for York in March, 1642, after which Parliament voted to put the kingdom in a state of defence. They soon delivered to Charles I their "Nineteen Propositions" for settlement, which demanded "constitutional liberty." Charles rejected the propositions, claiming that their implementation would cause "a total subversion of the fundamental laws."

[5] *slaughtered by mine own* Here Bradstreet refers to the battles of the first Civil War (1642–1646).

230 Blest be thy counties which do aid thee still
With hearts, and states, to testify their will.
Blest be thy preachers, who do cheer thee on,
O cry, "the sword of God, and Gideon"; [1]
And shall I not on those wish Mero's curse, [2]
235 That help thee not with prayers, arms, and purse,
And for myself, let miseries abound,
If mindless of thy state I e'er be found.
These are the days, the Church's foes to crush,
To root out prelates, head, tail, branch, and rush.
240 Let's bring Baal's vestments out, to make a fire, [3]
Their miters, surplices, and all their tire,
Copes, rochets, crosiers, and such trash, [4]
And let their names consume, but let the flash
Light Christendom, and all the world to see,
245 We hate Rome's whore, with all her trumpery.
Go on brave Essex, show whose son thou art, [5]
Not false to king, nor country in thy heart,
But those that hurt his people and his crown,
By force expel, destroy, and tread them down:
250 Let gaols be filled with th' remnant of that pack,
And sturdy Tyburn loaded till it crack, [6]
And ye brave nobles, chase away all fear,

And to this blessed cause closely adhere
O mother, can you weep, and have such peers.
255 When they are gone, then drown yourself in tears.
If now you weep so much, that then no more,
The briny ocean will o'erflow your shore,
These, these, are they (I trust) with Charles our
King,
Out of all mists, such glorious days will bring,
260 That dazzled eyes beholding much shall wonder
At that thy settled peace, thy wealth and splendor,
Thy Church and weal, established in such
manner,
That all shall joy that thou displayedst thy
banner,
And discipline erected, so I trust,
265 That nursing kings, shall come and lick thy dust:
Then justice shall in all thy courts take place,
Without respect of persons, or of case,
Then bribes shall cease, and suits shall not stick
long,
Patience, and purse of clients for to wrong:
270 Then high commissions shall fall to decay,
And pursuivants and catchpoles want their pay, [7]
So shall thy happy nation ever flourish,
When truth and righteousness they thus shall
nourish.
When thus in peace: thine armies brave send out,
275 To sack proud Rome, and all her vassals rout:
There let thy name, thy fame, thy valor shine,
As did thine ancestors in Palestine,
And let her spoils, full pay, with interest be,
Of what unjustly once she polled from thee,
280 Of all the woes thou canst let her be sped,
Execute to th' full the vengeance threatened.
Bring forth the beast that ruled the world with's
beck, [8]

---

[1] *"the sword of God and Gideon"* "When I blow with a trumpet, I and all that are with me, then blow ye the trumpets also on every side of all the camp, and say, 'The Sword of the Lord, and of Gideon'" (Judges 7:18; see also 7:20).

[2] *Mero's curse* "Curse ye Meroz, said the angel of the Lord, curse ye bitterly the inhabitants thereof; because they came not to the help of the Lord, to the help of the Lord against the mighty" (Judges 5:23). In February, 1642, a fast day was observed in London for the sins of the nation. Steven Marshall preached at Westminster from this very text in Judges; his Meroz sermon was so popular that he was frequently invited to deliver it.

[3] *Baal* the name of a pagan god, most commonly applied to Hadad, the fertility god of Canaan.

[4] *miters...and such trash* the vestments and ritual objects of Laudian Anglicanism.

[5] *brave Essex* Robert Devereux, third Earl of Essex (1591–1646), accepted the command of the main parliamentary army in the first Civil War. He advocated a purely defensive war policy, and suggested reopening peace talks with the King.

[6] *Tyburn* the public gallows in London.

[7] *pursuivants and catchpoles* warrant officers (*OED* pursuivant *sb* 2; catchpole 2).

[8] *Bring forth the beast* The beast described in John's apocalyptic vision of Revelation was frequently associated with Papacy in Puritan rhetoric.

And tear his flesh, and set your feet on's neck,
And make his filthy den so desolate,
285 To th' 'stonishment of all that knew his state,
This done, with brandished swords, to Turkey go,
(For then what is't, but English blades dare do)
And lay her waste, for so's the sacred doom,
And do to Gog, as thou hast done to Rome. [1]
290 Oh Abraham's seed lift up your heads on high.
For sure the day of your redemption's nigh; [2]
The scales shall fall from your long blinded eyes, [3]
And him you shall adore, who now despise,
Then fullness of the nations in shall flow,
295 And Jew and Gentile, to one worship go,
Then follows days of happiness and rest,
Whose lot doth fall to live therein is blest:
No Canaanite shall then be found i'th' land,
And holiness, on horses' bells shall stand, [4]
300 If this make way thereto, then sigh no more,
But if at all, thou didst not see't before.
Farewell dear mother, Parliament, prevail,
And in a while you'll tell another tale.
—1650

---

[1] *Gog* In Ezekiel's vision, Gog of the land of Magog appears as the enemy of Israel against whom God will rain fire and brimstone in the last days (38–39). In Revelation, Satan leads Gog and Magog against the New Jerusalem (20:2). Exegetes have associated Gog with the Anti-Christ. In *Christ Triumphans* John Foxe refers to Gog in his description of Satan's stirring up of the Turks against Palestine and eastern Europe, hence Bradstreet's association of Gog with Turkey.

[2] *Abraham's seed…redemption's nigh* "And if ye be Christ's, then are ye Abraham's seed, and heirs according to the promise" (Galatians 3:29).

[3] *The scales…blinded eyes* "And immediately there fell from his [Saul's] eyes as it had been scales: and he received sight forthwith, and arose, and was baptized" (Acts 9:18).

[4] *holiness on horses' bells* "In that day shall there be upon the bells of the horses, HOLINESS UNTO THE LORD; and the pots in the Lord's house shall be like the bowls before the altar" (Zechariah 14:20).

The Flesh and the Spirit

In secret place where once I stood
Close by the banks of Lacrim flood [5]
I heard two sisters reason on
Things that are past, and things to come;
5 One Flesh was called, who had her eye
On worldly wealth and vanity;
The other Spirit, who did rear
Her thoughts unto a higher sphere:
Sister, quoth Flesh, what liv'st thou on
10 Nothing but meditation?
Doth contemplation feed thee so
Regardlessly to let earth go?
Can speculation satisfy
Notion without reality?
15 Dost dream of things beyond the moon
And dost thou hope to dwell there soon?
Hast treasures there laid up in store
That all in th' world thou count'st but poor?
Art fancy sick, or turned a sot [6]
20 To catch at shadows which are not?
Come, come, I'll show unto thy sense,
Industry hath its recompense.
What canst desire, but thou may'st see
True substance in variety?
25 Dost honor like? Acquire the same,
As some to their immortal fame:
And trophies to thy name erect
Which wearing time shall ne'er deject.
For riches dost thou long full sore?
30 Behold enough of precious store.
Earth hath more silver, pearls and gold,
Than eyes can see, or hands can hold.
Affect's thou pleasure? Take thy fill,
Earth hath enough of what you will.
35 Then let not go, what thou may'st find,
For things unknown, only in mind.

---

[5] *Lacrim* Latin *lacrimae*, "tears."

[6] *sot* fool (*OED* sot *sb*[1] A.1).

Spirit Be still thou unregenerate part,
Disturb no more my settled heart,
For I have vowed (and so will do)
40 Thee as a foe, still to pursue.
And combat with thee will and must,
Until I see thee laid in th' dust.
Sisters we are, yea twins we be,
Yet deadly feud 'twixt thee and me;
45 For from one father are we not,
Thou by old Adam wast begot, [1]
But my arise is from above,
Whence my dear Father I do love.
Thou speak'st me fair, but hat'st me sore,
50 Thy flattering shows I'll trust no more.
How oft thy slave, hast thou me made,
When I believed, what thou hast said,
And never had more cause of woe
Than when I did what thou bad'st do.
55 I'll stop mine ears at these thy charms,
And count them for my deadly harms.
Thy sinful pleasures I do hate,
Thy riches are to me no bait,
Thine honors do, nor will I love;
60 For my ambition lies above.
My greatest honor it shall be
When I am victor over thee,
And triumph shall, with laurel head,
When thou my captive shalt be led,
65 How I do live, thou need'st not scoff,
For I have meat thou know'st not of;
The hidden manna I do eat,
The word of life it is my meat. [2]
My thoughts do yield me more content
70 Than can thy hours in pleasure spent.

Nor are they shadows which I catch,
Nor fancies vain at which I snatch,
But reach at things that are so high,
Beyond thy dull capacity;
75 Eternal substance I do see,
With which enriched I would be:
Mine eye doth pierce the heavens, and see [3]
What is invisible to thee.
My garments are not silk nor gold,
80 Nor such like trash which earth doth hold,
But royal robes I shall have on,
More glorious than the glist'ring sun;
My crown not diamonds, pearls, and gold,
But such as angels' heads enfold.
85 The city where I hope to dwell,
There's none on earth can parallel;
The stately walls both high and strong,
Are made of precious jasper stone;
The gates of pearl, both rich and clear,
90 And angels are for porters there;
The streets thereof transparent gold,
Such as no eye did e'er behold,
A crystal river there doth run,
Which doth proceed from the Lamb's throne:
95 Of life, there are the waters sure,
Which shall remain forever pure,
Nor sun, nor moon, they have no need,
For glory doth from God proceed:
No candle there, nor yet torchlight,
100 For there shall be no darksome night.
From sickness and infirmity,
For evermore they shall be free,
Nor withering age shall e'er come there,
But beauty shall be bright and clear;
105 This city pure is not for thee,
For things unclean there shall not be:
If I of heaven may have my fill,
Take thou the world, and all that will.
—1678

---

[1] *old Adam* "And so it is written, The first man Adam was made a living soul; the last Adam [Christ] was made a quickening spirit" (I Corinthians 15:45).

[2] *The hidden manna...is my meat* "He that has an ear, let him hear what the Spirit saith unto the churches; To him that overcometh will I give to eat of the hidden manna, and will give him a white stone, and in the stone a new name written, which no man knoweth saving he that receiveth it" (Revelation 2:17).

---

[3] ll. 77–106 Bradstreet's description of heaven is based on that found in Revelation 21:10–27 and 22:1–5.

The Author to Her Book

Thou ill-formed offspring of my feeble brain,
 Who after birth did'st by my side remain,
Till snatched from thence by friends, less wise
   than true [1]
Who thee abroad, exposed to public view,
5 Made thee in rags, halting to th' press to trudge,
Where errors were not lessened (all may judge).
At thy return my blushing was not small,
My rambling brat (in print) should mother call,
I cast thee by as one unfit for light,
10 Thy visage was so irksome in my sight;
Yet being mine own, at length affection would
Thy blemishes amend, if so I could: [2]
I washed thy face, but more defects I saw,
And rubbing off a spot, still made a flaw.
15 I stretched thy joints to make thee even feet,
Yet still thou run'st more hobbling than is meet;
In better dress to trim thee was my mind,
But nought save homespun cloth, i' th' house I
   find.
In this array, 'mongst vulgars mayst thou roam,
20 In critics' hands, beware thou dost not come;
And take thy way where yet thou art not known,
If for thy father asked, say, thou hadst none:
And for thy mother, she alas is poor,
Which caused her thus to send thee out of door.
—1678

To My Dear and Loving Husband

If ever two were one, then surely we.
 If ever man were loved by wife, then thee;
If ever wife was happy in a man,
Compare with me ye women if you can.
5 I prize thy love more than whole mines of gold,
Or all the riches that the East doth hold.
My love is such that rivers cannot quench, [3]
Nor ought but love from thee, give recompense.
Thy love is such I can no way repay,
10 The heavens reward thee manifold I pray.
Then while we live, in love let's so persevere,
That when we live no more, we may live ever.
—1678

Another

Phoebus make haste, the day's too long, be
   gone, [4]
The silent night's the fittest time for moan;
But stay this once, unto my suit give ear,
And tell my griefs in either hemisphere:
5 (And if the whirling of thy wheels don't drowned)
The woeful accents of my doleful sound,
If in thy swift career thou canst make stay,
I crave this boon, this errand by the way,
Commend me to the man more loved than life,
10 Show him the sorrows of his widowed wife;
My dumpish thoughts, my groans, my brackish
   tears
My sobs, my longing hopes, my doubting fears,
And if he love, how can he there abide?
My interest's more than all the world beside.
15 He that can tell the stars or ocean sand,

---

[1] *Till snatched…than true* Either Anne's sister Mercy, Mercy's husband Rev. John Woodbridge, or Rev. Nathanial Ward took possession of Bradstreeet's poems and carried them to England, where Bradstreet's brother-in-law John Woodbridge arranged for their publication (*The Tenth Muse*, 1650), despite her claims that she never intended to publish them.

[2] *Would thy blemishes amend* Bradstreet revised and added to her verse after the publication of *The Tenth Muse*. However, she did not live to see the second edition of her work (*Several Poems,* 1678).

[3] *My love is such that rivers cannot quench* "Many waters cannot quench love, neither can the floods drown it: if a man would give all the substance of his house for love, it would be utterly contemned" (Song of Solomon 8:7).

[4] *Phoebus* a name of Apollo, the Sun-god; the sun personified (*OED*).

Or all the grass that in the meads do stand,
The leaves in th' woods, the hail or drops of rain,
Or in a corn-field number every grain,
Or every mote that in the sunshine hops,
20 May count my sighs, and number all my drops:
Tell him, the countless steps that thou dost trace,
That once a day, thy spouse thou mayst embrace;
And when thou canst not treat by loving mouth,
Thy rays afar salute her from the south. [1]
25 But for one month I see no day (poor soul)
Like those far situate under the pole,
Which day by day long wait for thy arise,
O how they joy when thou dost light the skies.
O Phoebus, hadst thou but thus long from thine
30 Restrained the beams of thy beloved shine,
At thy return, if so thou could'st or durst
Behold a chaos blacker than the first.
Tell him here's worse than a confused matter,
His little world's a fathom under water,
35 Nought but the fervor of his ardent beams
Hath power to dry the torrent of these streams.
Tell him I would say more, but cannot well,
Oppressed minds, abruptest tales do tell.
Now post with double speed, mark what I say,
40 By all our loves conjure him not to stay.
—1678

In Memory of my Dear Grandchild
Elizabeth Bradstreet
Who Deceased August, 1665
Being A Year and Half Old

Farewell dear babe, my heart's too much content
Farewell sweet babe, the pleasure of mine eye,
Farewell fair flower that for a space was lent,
Then ta'en away unto eternity.

5 Blest babe why should I once bewail thy fate,
Or sigh thy days so soon were terminate;
Sith thou art settled in an everlasting state.

2

By nature trees do rot when they are grown.
 And plums and apples thoroughly ripe do fall,
10 And corn and grass are in their season mown,
And time brings down what is both strong and tall.
But plants new set to be eradicate,
And buds new blown, to have so short a date,
Is by his hand alone that guides nature and fate.
—1678

Some Verses upon the Burning of Our
House, July 10ᵗʰ, 1666 [2]

In silent night when rest I took
For sorrow near I did not look,
I wakened was with thund'ring noise
And piteous shrieks of dreadful voice.
5 That fearful sound of "fire" and "fire,"
Let no man know is my desire.
I starting up the light did spy,
And to my God my heart did cry
To strengthen me in my distress
10 And not to leave me succourless.
Then coming out beheld a space
The flame consume my dwelling place,
And when I could no longer look
I blest his name that gave and took, [3]
15 That laid my goods now in the dust
Yea so it was, and so 'twas just.
It was his own, it was not mine
Far be it that I should repine,

---

[1] *by loving mouth* presumably "by kissing"; *from the south* i.e. in the winter when, for those of us in the northern hemisphere, the sun moves to the south of the sky.

[2] This poem was included in the Andover Manuscript and remained unpublished until 1867.

[3] *I blest…and took* "Then Job arose…and said, Naked came I out of my mother's womb, and naked shall I return thither: the Lord gave, and the Lord hath taken away; blessed be the name of the Lord" (Job 1:20–21).

He might of all justly bereft,
20 But yet sufficient for us left. [1]
When by the ruins oft I passed
My sorrowing eyes aside did cast
And here and there the places spy
Where oft I sat and long did lie,
25 Here stood that trunk, and there that chest
There lay that store I counted best.
My pleasant things in ashes lie
And them behold no more shall I.
Under the roof no guest shall sit,
30 Nor at thy table eat a bit.
No pleasant tale shall e'er be told
Nor things recounted done of old.
No candle e'er shall shine in thee
Nor bridegroom's voice e'er heard shall be.
35 In silence ever shalt thou lie
Adieu, Adieu, all's vanity.
Then straight I 'gin my heart to chide,
And did thy wealth on earth abide,

Didst fix thy hope on mouldering dust,
40 The arm of flesh didst make thy trust? [2]
Raise up thy thoughts above the sky
That dunghill mists away may fly.
Thou hast a house on high erect,
Framed by that mighty Architect,
45 With glory richly furnished
Stands permanent though this be fled.
It's purchased and paid for too
By him who has enough to do.
A price so vast as is unknown
50 Yet by his gift is made thine own.
There's wealth enough I need no more,
Farewell my pelf, farewell my store. [3]
The world no longer let me love
My hope and treasure lies above.
—(1666)

---

[1] *He might of all justly bereft* an ellipsis for "bereft us."

[2] *arm of flesh* "With him is an arm of flesh; but with us is the Lord our God to help us, and to fight our battles" (II Chronicles 32:8).

[3] *pelf* wealth (*OED* pelf *sb* 3).

Richard Crashaw
1612 – 1649

Richard Crashaw was born in London, the only son of William Crashaw, a notable Puritan preacher and controversialist, a great hater of the Roman communion who in his will declared "Popery" to be "the heap and chaos of all heresies." Perhaps fortunately, William Crashaw did not live to see his son "go over" to Rome. Richard was educated at the Charterhouse, and later entered Pembroke Hall, Cambridge, where he excelled in languages, reading Hebrew, Greek, Latin, Italian and Spanish. Crashaw wrote a number of religious poems during his youth, and in 1634, the year in which he received his B.A., he published his first volume, *Epigrammatum Sacrorum Liber*. This work, published anonymously, contained 185 Latin epigrams. In 1636 Crashaw was admitted to Peterhouse, proceeding to the M.A. degree in 1638. Peterhouse was the centre in Cambridge of Laudian High Anglicanism, and in Crashaw's case the common suspicion that Laudians were on the way to Rome was perhaps justified. Although the precise date of his ordination is unknown, it is known that he was Curate of the church adjoining Peterhouse, Little St. Mary's, in 1639. During the Civil War the chapel at Peterhouse was sacked by Parliamentary forces, and

Crashaw, who supported the Royalist cause, declined to accept the Solemn League and Covenant and was expelled in 1644. In February 1644 Crashaw was in Holland, and then proceeded to France. At a point when the Church of England seemed unlikely to survive, strong inducements were offered to Anglicans in exile to convert to Catholicism. Crashaw was among those who did so, and was relieved from poverty by Queen Henrietta Maria. Several editions of Crashaw's poetry were published in England after his departure. In 1646, a volume of his verse was printed in two parts. The first part was entitled, "Steps to the Temple. Sacred Poems. With other Delights of the Muses" and the second "The Delights of the Muses and other Poems, written on several occasions." Crashaw travelled to Italy in 1648 or 1649 with a letter of recommendation from Queen Henrietta Maria; there he obtained a position under the influential Cardinal Palotta. Letters from various sources suggest that Crashaw's criticism of the Cardinal's retinue resulted in his removal from his post for his own security. In 1649 he was appointed as sub-canon of the Basilica church of Our Lady of Loreto, but died four months later.

❧❧❧

Wishes.
To his (supposed) Mistress

Who ere she be,
  That not impossible she
That shall command my heart and me;

Where ere she lie,
5 Locked up from mortal eye,
In shady leaves of destiny:

Till that ripe birth
Of studied fate stand forth,
And teach her fair steps to our Earth;

10 Till that divine
Idea, take a shrine
Of crystal flesh, through which to shine:

Meet you her my wishes,
Bespeak her to my blisses,
15 And be ye called my absent kisses.

I wish her beauty,
That owes not all his duty
To gaudy tire, or glistering shoo-ty. [1]

Something more than
20 Taffeta or tissue can,
Or rampant feather, or rich fan.

More than the spoil
Of shop, or silkworms' toil
Or a bought blush, or a set smile.

25 A face that's best
By its own beauty dressed,
And can alone commend the rest.

A face made up
Out of no other shop,
30 Than what nature's white hand sets ope. [2]

A cheek where youth,
And blood, with pen of truth
Write, what the reader sweetly ru'th. [3]

A cheek where grows
35 More than a morning rose:
Which to no box his being owes.

Lips, where all day
A lover's kiss may play,
Yet carry nothing thence away.

40 Looks that oppress
Their richest tires but dress
And clothe their simplest nakedness.

Eyes, that displaces
The neighbour diamond, and out faces
45 That sunshine by their own sweet graces.

Tresses, that wear
Jewels, but to declare
How much themselves more precious are.

Whose native ray,
50 Can tame the wanton day
Of gems, that in their bright shades play.

Each ruby there,
Or pearl that dare appear,
Be its own blush, be its own tear.

55 A well tamed heart,
For whose more noble smart,
Love may be long choosing a dart.

Eyes, that bestow
Full quivers on love's bow;
60 Yet pay less arrows than they owe.

Smiles, that can warm
The blood, yet teach a charm,
That chastity shall take no harm.

Blushes, that bin
65 The burnish of no sin,
Nor flames of ought too hot within.

Joys, that confess,
Virtue their mistress,
And have no other head to dress.

70 Fears, fond and flight, [4]
As the coy bride's, when night
First does the longing lover right.

---

[1] *tire* a form of attire, dress, apparel (*OED* attire *sb* 3); also a personal adornment or decoration (*OED* attire *sb* 2); *shoo-ty* ornamental shoe tie.

[2] *ope* form of open (*OED*).

[3] *ru'th* grieves for (*OED* rue *v*[1] 3).

---

[4] *flight* fleeting (*OED* flight *a* 1).

Tears, quickly fled,
And vain, as those are shed
75 For a dying maidenhead.

Days, that need borrow,
No part of their good morrow,
From a fore spent night of sorrow.

Days, that in spite
80 Of darkness, by the light
Of a clear mind are day all night.

Nights, sweet as they,
Made short by lovers' play,
Yet long by th' absence of the day.

85 Life, that dares send
A challenge to his end,
And when it comes say *Welcome Friend.*

Sydnæan showers [1]
Of sweet discourse, whose powers
90 Can crown old Winter's head with flowers,

Soft silken hours,
Open suns; shady bowers,
'Bove all; nothing within that lours. [2]

What ere delight
95 Can make Day's forehead bright;
Or give down to the wings of Night.

In her whole frame,
Have nature all the name,
Art and ornament the shame.

100 Her flattery,
Picture and poesy,
Her counsel her own virtue be.

I wish, her store
Of worth, may leave her poor
105 Of wishes; and I wish—no more.

Now if Time knows
That her whose radiant brows,
Weave them a garland of my vows;

Her whose just bays,
110 My future hopes can raise,
A trophy to her present praise;

Her that dares be,
What these lines wish to see:
I seek no further, it is she.

115 'Tis she, and here
Lo I unclothe and clear,
My wishes' cloudy character.

May she enjoy it,
Whose merit dare apply it,
120 But Modesty dares still deny it.

Such worth as this is,
Shall fix my flying wishes,
And determine them to kisses.

Let her full Glory,
125 My fancies, fly before ye,
Be ye my fictions; but her story.
—1646

---

[1] *Sydnæan showers* in reference to the work of Sir Philip Sidney
(1554–1586).

[2] *lours* looks angry or sullen (*OED* lour *v* 1).

Saint Mary Magdalene
or
The Weeper [1]

L o where a WOUNDED HEART with Bleeding
    EYES conspire.
Is she a FLAMING Fountain, or a Weeping fire! [2]

I

Hail, Sister Springs!
Parents of silver-footed rills!
        Ever bubbling things!
        Thawing crystal! snowy hills,
5 Still spending, never spent! I mean
Thy fair eyes, sweet *Magdalene*!

II

        Heavens thy fair eyes be;
        Heavens of ever-falling stars.
        'Tis seed-time still with thee
        And stars thou sow'st, whose harvest dares
10 Promise the earth to countershine
Whatever makes heaven's forehead fine.

III

        But we are deceived all.
        Stars indeed they are too true;
        For they but seem to fall,
15   As Heaven's other spangles do.

It is not for our earth & us
To shine in things so precious.

IV

        Upwards thou dost weep.
20   Heaven's bosom drinks the gentle stream.
        Where the milky rivers creep,
        Thine floats above; & is the cream.
Waters above th' Heavens, what they be [3]
We are taught best by thy *Tears* & thee.

V

25   Every morn from hence
        A brisk Cherub something sips
        Whose sacred influence
        Adds sweetness to his sweetest lips.
Then to his music. And his song
30 Tastes of this breakfast all day long.

VI

        Not in the Evening's eyes
        When they red with weeping are
        For the Sun that dies,
        Sits Sorrow with a face so fair,
35 No where but here did ever meet
Sweetness so sad, sadness so sweet.

VII

        When Sorrow would be seen
        In her brightest majesty
        (For she is a Queen)
40   Then is she dressed by none but thee.
Then, & only then, she wears
Her proudest pearls; I mean, thy *Tears*.

VIII

        The Dew no more will weep
        The Primrose's pale cheek to deck,
45   The Dew no more will sleep
        Nuzzled in the Lily's neck;

[1] Mary Magdalene, a follower of Christ who attended his crucifixion (John 19:25), was the first person he appeared to after the resurrection (John 20:1–18). An extensive legend grew around her, connecting her (often without evidence) with other stories in the New Testament. She was identified with Mary the sister of Martha (Luke 10:38–42, John 11:1–47) and the sinful woman who anointed the feet of Jesus with perfume and dried them with her hair (Luke 7:36–50). Her association with the latter figure resulted in numerous depictions of her weeping for her sins. She became known as The Weeper.

[2] This couplet, placed here in the 1648 edition, precedes the poem on a separate page in 1652. The present text is based upon the editions of 1648 and 1652.

[3] *Waters above th' Heavens*   The reference is to Genesis 1:7.

Much rather would it be thy *Tear,*
And leave them both to tremble here.

IX

There's no need at all
50   That the balsam-sweating bough [1]
So coyly should let fall
His med'cinable tears; for now
Nature hath learn't to extract a dew
More sovereign & sweet from you.

X

55   Yet let the poor drops weep
(Weeping is the ease of woe)
Softly let them creep,
Sad that they are vanquish't so.
They, though to others no relief,
60   Balsam may be, for their own grief.

XI

Such the maiden gem
By the purpling vine put on,
Peeps from her parent stem
And blushes at the bridegroom sun.
65   This watery blossom of thy eyn, [2]
Ripe, will make the richer wine.

XII

When some new bright guest
Takes up among the stars a room,
And Heaven will make a feast,
70   Angels with crystal vials come
And draw from these full eyes of thine
Their master's water: their own wine.

XIII

Golden though he be,
Golden Tagus murmurs tho; [3]
75   Were his way by thee,
Content & quiet he would go.
So much more rich would he esteem
Thy silver, than his golden stream.

XIV

Well does the May that lies
80   Smiling in thy cheeks, confess
The April in thine eyes.
Mutual sweetness they express.
No April ere lent kinder showers,
Nor May returned more faithful flowers.

XV

85   O cheeks! Beds of chaste loves
By your own showers seasonably dash't
Eyes! nests of milky doves
In your own wells decently washt,
O wit of love! that thus could place
90   Fountain & Garden in one face.

XVI

O sweet contest; of woes
With loves, of tears with smiles disputing!
O fair, & Friendly Foes,
Each other kissing & confuting!
95   While rain & sunshine, cheeks & eyes
Close in kind contrarieties.

XVII

But can these fair Floods be
Friends with the bosom fires that fill thee
Can so great flames agree
100   Eternal tears should thus distil thee!
O floods, o fires! o suns o showers!
Mixed & made friends by Love's sweet powers.

---

[1] *balsam* an aromatic oily or resinous medicinal preparation for healing wounds or soothing pain (*OED* balsam *sb* 2).

[2] *eyn* form of the word eyes (*OED* eye *sb*).

---

[3] *Tagus* The river Tagus flows from eastern Spain, across Spain and Portugal, reaching the Atlantic Ocean at Lisbon.

XVIII

'Twas his well-pointed dart
That digg'd these wells, & dressed this Vine;
105 And taught the wounded *Heart*
The way into these weeping Eyn.
Vain loves avant! bold hands forbear! [1]
The Lamb hath dipp't his white foot here.

XIX

And now where're he strays,
110 Among the Galilean mountains, [2]
Or more unwelcome ways,
He's followed by two faithful fountains;
Two walking baths; two weeping motions;
Portable, & compendious oceans.

XX

O thou, thy lord's fair store!
115 In thy so rich & rare expenses,
Even when he show'd most poor,
He might provoke the wealth of princes.
What prince's wanton'st pride e're could
120 Wash with silver, wipe with gold.

XXI

Who is that King, but he
Who calls't his Crown to be called thine,
That thus can boast to be
Waited on by a wandering mine,
125 A voluntary mint, that strows [3]
Warm silver showers where 're he goes!

XXII

O precious Prodigal! [4]
Fair spend-thrift of thy self! thy measure

XXIII

(Merciless love!) is all.
130 Even to the last Pearl in thy treasure.
All places, times, & objects be
Thy tear's sweet opportunity.

Does the day-star rise?
Still thy stars do fall & fall
135 Does Day close his eyes?
Still the *Fountain* weeps for all.
Let night or day do what they will,
Thou hast thy task; thou weepest still.

XXIV

Does thy song lull the air?
140 Thy falling tears keep faith full time.
Does thy sweet-breath'd prayer
Up in clouds of incense climb?
Still at each sigh, that is, each stop,
A bead, that is, *A Tear,* does drop.

XXV

145 At these thy weeping gates,
(Watching their wat'ry motion)
Each winged moment waits,
Takes his *Tear,* & gets him gone.
By thine Eye's tinct ennobled thus [5]
150 Time lays him up; he's precious.

XXVI

Not, so long she lived,
Shall thy tomb report of thee;
But, so long she grieved,
Thus must we date thy memory.
155 Others by moments, months, & years
Measure their ages; thou, by *Tears.*

XXVII

So do perfumes expire.
So sigh tormented sweets, oppressed

---

[1] *avant* form of avaunt; be gone! Be off! Away! (*OED* avaunt 1).

[2] *Galilean* Jesus was raised in Nazareth, a town in Galilee (Luke 2:39, 40), where he also began his ministry (Luke 4:14–30).

[3] *strows* form of *strews*: scatters, spreads loosely (*OED* strew *v* 1).

[4] *Prodigal* one who spends money extravagantly (*OED* prodigal *sb* 1).

---

[5] *tinct* a transmuting elixir (*OED* tinct *sb* 3).

With proud unpitying fire.
160   Such Tears the suffering Rose that's vexed
With ungentle flames does shed,
Sweating in a too warm bed.

XXVIII

     Say, ye bright brothers,
     The fugitive sons of those fair Eyes
165   Your fruitful mothers!
     What make you here? what hopes can tice [1]
You to be born? what cause can borrow
You from those nests of noble sorrow?

XXIX

     Whither away so fast?
170   For sure the sordid earth
     Your sweetness cannot taste
     Nor does the dust deserve your birth.
Sweet, whither haste you then? o say
Why you trip so fast away?

XXX

175   We go not to seek,
     The darlings of Aurora's bed, [2]
     The rose's modest cheek
     Nor the violet's humble head.
Though the Field's eyes too *Weepers* be
180   Because they want such *Tears* as we.

XXXI

     Much less mean we to trace
     The fortune of inferior gems,
     Preferred to some proud face
     Or perched upon fear'd diadems.
185   Crowned heads are toys. We go to meet
A worthy object, our lord's *Feet.*
—1652

---

[1]   *tice*   a form of entice (*OED* tice).

[2]   *Aurora*   the Roman goddess of the dawn and hence the rising light
of the morning (*OED* Aurora 1,2).

A Hymn to the Name and Honour
of the Admirable Saint Teresa [3]

Love, thou art absolute sole lord
  Of *Life* and *Death.* To prove the word,
We'll now appeal to none of all
Those thy old soldiers, great and tall,
5   Ripe men of martyrdom, that could reach down
With strong arms, their triumphant crown;
Such as could with lusty breath
Speak loud into the face of death
Their great *Lord's* glorious name, to none
10   Of those whose spacious bosoms spread a throne
For *Love* at large to fill: spare blood and sweat;
And see him take a private seat,
Making his mansion in the mild
And milky soul of a soft child.
15   Scarce has she learn't to lisp the name
Of Martyr; yet she thinks it shame
Life should so long play with that breath
Which spent can buy so brave a death. [4]
She never undertook to know
20   What death with love should have to do;
Nor has she e're yet understood
Why to show love, she should shed blood
Yet though she cannot tell you why,
She can *love,* & she can *die.*
25   Scarce has she blood enough to make
A guilty sword blush for her sake;
Yet has she a *heart* dares hope to prove

---

[3]   Saint Teresa of Avila (1515–1582) was one of the most celebrated
mystics and women of the Roman Catholic Church. She instigated the
Carmelite Reform, returning the Carmelite Order to its original
austerity and enclosure, with contemplation as the primary focus of the
nuns. Despite substantial opposition from both civic and religious
sources, Teresa established sixteen convents in Spain. Her writings
include a spiritual autobiography and several mystical works. Gian
Lorenzo Bernini (1598–1680) sculpted an image of her in a moment
of mystical insight, being pierced by the arrow of divine light, in his
white marble masterpiece "The Ecstasy of Saint Teresa."

[4]   *so brave a death*   Teresa writes in her autobiography of her desire as
a child to become a martyr.

How much less strong is *death* than *love*.
   Be love but there; let poor six years
30 Be posed with the maturest fears [1]
Man trembles at, you straight shall find
Love knows no nonage, nor the *mind*. [2]
'Tis *love,* not *years* or *limbs* that can
Make the Martyr, or the man.
35   *Love* touched her *heart,* & lo it beats
High, & burns with such brave heats;
Such thirsts to die, as dares drink up,
A thousand cold deaths in one cup.
Good reason. For she breathes all fire.
40 Her weak breast heaves with strong desire
Of what she may with fruitless wishes
Seek for amongst her *mother's* kisses.
   Since 'tis not to be had at home
She'll travel to a Martyrdom.
45 No home for hers confesses she
But where she may a Martyr be.
   She'll to the Moors; & trade with them,
For this unvalued diadem. [3]
She'll offer them her dearest breath,
50 With *Christ's* Name in't, in change for death.
She'll bargain with them; & will give
Them *God;* teach them how to live
In him: or, if they this deny,
For him she'll teach them how to *die.*
55 So shall she leave amongst them sown
Her *Lord's* blood; or at least her own.
   Farewell then, all the world! Adieu.
Teresa is no more for you.
Farewell, all pleasures, sports, & joys,
60 (Never till now esteemed toys)
Farewell what ever dear may be,

Mother's arms or *father's* knee
Farewell house, & farewell home!
She's for the Moors, & *Martyrdom.*
65   *Sweet,* not so fast! lo thy fair Spouse
Whom thou seekst with so swift vows,
Calls thee back, & bids thee come
T'embrace a milder *Martyrdom.*
   Blest powers forbid, Thy tender life
70 Should bleed upon a barbarous knife;
Or some base hand have power to race [4]
Thy breast's chaste cabinet, & uncase
A soul kept there so sweet, o no;
Wise Heaven will never have it so.
75 *Thou* art Love's victim; & must die
A death more mystical & high.
Into Love's arms thou shalt let fall
A still-surviving funeral.
His is the *dart* must make the *death*
80 Whose stroke shall taste thy hallowed breath;
A dart thrice dipped in that rich flame
Which writes thy spouse's radiant Name [5]
Upon the roof of Heav'n; where ay
It shines, & with a sovereign ray
85 Beats bright upon the burning faces
Of souls which in that name's sweet graces
Find everlasting smiles. So rare,
So spiritual, pure, & fair
Must be th'immortal instrument
90 Upon whose choice point shall be sent
A life so loved; & that there be
Fit executioners for thee,
The fair'st & first-born sons of fire
Blest *Seraphim,* shall leave their quire [6]
95 And turn Love's soldiers, upon *thee*
To exercise their archery.
   O how oft shalt thou complain
Of a sweet & subtle *pain.*

---

[1] *posed with* placed against (*OED* pose *v*[1] 4a).

[2] *nonage* the condition of being underage; the period of legal infancy; minority (*OED* nonage *sb* [1]1).

[3] *She'll to the Moors...unvalued diadem* Living in an age in which martyrdoms were rare, Teresa and her brother believed that in order to become martyrs they would have to travel to a place where Christianity was unpopular (*Life*, Chapter 1).

---

[4] *race* to cut or slash (*OED* race *v*[3] 1).

[5] *thy spouse's radiant Name* Jesus Christ.

[6] *quire* A form of the word "choir" (*OED* choir).

Of intolerable *joys;*
100 Of a *death,* in which who dies
Loves his death, & dies again.
And would for ever so be slain.
And lives, & dies; & knows not why
To live, but that he thus may never leave to *die.*
105   How kindly will thy gentle *heart*
Kiss the sweetly-killing *dart!*
And close in his embraces keep
Those delicious Wounds, that weep
Balsam to heal themselves with. Thus
110 When these thy *deaths,* so numerous,
Shall all at last die into one,
And melt thy Soul's sweet mansion;
Like a soft lump of incense, hasted
By too hot a fire, & wasted
115 Into perfuming clouds, so fast
Shalt thou exhale to Heaven at last
In a resolving *sigh,* & then
O what? Ask not the tongues of men.
Angels cannot tell, suffice,
120 Thy self shall feel thine own full joys
And hold them fast for ever. There
So soon as thou shalt first appear,
The *moon* of maiden stars, thy white
Mistress, attended by such bright [1]
125 Souls as thy shining self, shall come
And in her first ranks make thee room;
Where 'mongst her snowy family
Immortal welcomes wait for thee.
    O what delight, when revealed *Life* shall stand [2]
130 And teach thy lips heav'n with his hand;
On which thou now may'st to thy wishes
Heap up thy consecrated kisses.
What joys shall seize thy soul, when she
Bending her blessed eyes on thee
135 (Those second smiles of Heav'n) shall dart

Her mild rays through thy melting heart!
    Angels, thy old friends, there shall greet thee
Glad at their own home now to meet thee.
    All thy good *Works* which went before
140 And waited for thee, at the door,
Shall own thee there; & all in one
Weave a constellation
Of *crowns,* with which the *King* thy spouse
Shall build up thy triumphant brows.
145   All thy old woes shall now smile on thee
And thy pains sit bright upon thee
All thy sorrows here shall shine,
All thy *suff'rings* be divine.
Tears shall take comfort, & turn gems
150 And *wrongs* repent to *diadems.*
Ev'n thy *deaths* shall live; & new
Dress the soul that erst they slew.
Thy wounds shall blush to such bright scars
As keep account of the *Lamb's* wars.
155   Those rare *Works* where thou shalt leave writ,
Love's noble history, with wit
Taught thee by none but him, while here
They feed our souls, shall clothe *thine* there.
Each heavenly word by whose hid flame
160 Our hard hearts shall strike fire, the same
Shall flourish on thy brows, & be
Both fire to us & flame to thee;
Whose light shall live bright in thy *face*
By glory, in our hearts by grace.
165   Thou shalt look round about, & see
Thousands of crowned Souls throng to be
Themselves thy crown. Sons of thy vows
The virgin-births with which thy sovereign spouse
Made fruitful thy fair soul, go now
170 And with them all about thee bow
To Him, put on (he'll say) put on
(My rosy love) that thy rich zone [3]
Sparkling with the sacred flames
Of thousand souls, whose happy names

---

[1] *The moon of maiden stars, thy white / Mistress*   the Virgin Mary.

[2] *revealed Life*   Jesus Christ ("I am the way, and the truth, and the life"— John 14:6).

---

[3] *zone*   a girdle or belt (*OED* zone *sb* 3).

175 Heav'n keeps upon thy score. (Thy bright
Life brought them first to kiss the light
That kindled them to stars.) And so
Thou with the *Lamb,* thy lord, shalt go;
And whereso'ere he sets his white

180 Steps, walk with *Him* those ways of light
Which who in death would live to see,
Must learn in life to die like thee.
—1648, 1652

John Cleveland
1613 – 1658

John Cleveland was the son of an impoverished charity school usher, who was in 1621 given a clerical living, from which, because he was a Royalist, he was ejected by the Parliament of 1644–1645. Like other poets of the time, Cleveland seems to have owed much to the instruction in Greek and Latin of his school teacher, Richard Vynes. Cleveland was an undergraduate at Christ's College, Cambridge, and then moved on to St. John's College, of which he became a Fellow in 1634. As he did not take holy orders, he was compelled by the statutes of his college to choose to become a lawyer or a physician; in fact he seems to have studied both law and medicine, and was generally regarded as an ornament of the college. When Cromwell was a candidate for Cambridge in the Long Parliament, Cleveland opposed him, and when Cromwell won the election by one vote, declared that "that single vote hath ruined the whole kingdom." As a Royalist, Cleveland was in 1645 ejected from his fellowship, and went to the Royalist army at Oxford, where he won a reputation for his personality and his verse. He was at Newark when the Royalist garrison there surrendered, and was thought notable enough by the King's enemies to be singled out in their propaganda sheet, the "Kingdom's Weekly Intelligencer," in which his employment was described as being "to gather all college rents within the power of the king's forces in those parts, which he distributes to such as are turned out of their fellowships at Cambridge for their malignancy." "The King's Disguise" and "The Rebel Scot" express powerfully Cleveland's sense of betrayal and disgust at the course of events; he is said to have predicted immediately that the Scots would betray Charles.

After the fall of Newark, Cleveland, unemployed and impoverished, was supported by fellow Royalists. According to Aubrey, he became great friends with Samuel Butler, the author of the immensely popular *Hudibras,* published after the Restoration. In 1655 Cleveland was arrested in Norwich on charges which included consorting with known Royalists and Papists, and imprisoned in Great Yarmouth for three months, after which he was released after writing a letter to Cromwell. Thereafter he depended for a living mainly on teaching, so that neither his legal nor his medical training contributed to his support. He died before the Restoration.

Cleveland took certain aspects of "metaphysical" style to extremes, and some anthologists have understandably represented him by his more accessible pieces. This is, however, a disservice to serious readers. The tortuous wit of his more important work is the play of a fundamentally serious mind contemplating momentous events, and as such is worth our attention.

❧

The King's Disguise [1]

And why so coffin'd in this vile disguise,
Which who but sees blasphemes thee with his eyes?

5 My twins of light within their pent-house shrink,
And hold it their allegiance to wink. [2]
Oh for a state-distinction to arraign

---

[1] The occasion of this bitter poem was Charles I's leaving Oxford, disguised as a gentleman's servant, on April 27, 1646 and surrendering himself to the Scots on May 5. The earliest extant manuscript version dates from January 1647. Henry Vaughan's "The King Disguised, written about the same time that Mr. John Cleveland wrote his," should also be consulted. The notes which follow are much indebted, in spite of occasional disagreement, to Brian Morris and Eleanor Withington, eds., *The Poems of John Cleveland* (Oxford: Clarendon P, 1967).

[2] *to wink* to close. *OED* wink *v* 1 1 and 5 are relevant.

Charles of high treason 'gainst my Sovereign.
What an usurper to his Prince is wont,
Cloister and shave him, he himself hath don't.
His muffled fabric speaks him a recluse,
10 His ruins prove it a religious house. [1]
The Sun hath mew'd his beams from off his lamp,
And Majesty defac'd the Royal stamp. [2]
Is't not enough thy Dignity's in thrall,
But thou'lt transcribe it in thy shape and all?
15 As if thy Blacks were of too faint a die,
Without the tincture of Tautology.
Flay an Egyptian for his Cassock skin
Spun of his Country's darkness, line't within
With Presbyterian budge, that drowsy trance,
20 The Synod's sable, foggy ignorance:
Nor bodily nor ghostly Negro could
Rough-cast thy figure in a sadder mould. [3]
This Privy-chamber of thy shape would be
But the Close mourner to thy Royalty. [4]
25 Then break the circle of thy Tailor's spell,
A Pearl within a rugged Oyster's shell. [5]

Heaven, which the Minster of thy Person owns, [6]
Will fine thee for Dilapidations.
Like to a martyr'd Abbey's coarser doom,
30 Devoutly alter'd to a Pigeon room:
Or like the College by the changeling rabble,
Manchester's Elves, transform'd into a Stable. [7]
Or if there be a profanation higher,
Such is the Sacrilege of thine Attire. [8]
35 By which th'art half depos'd, thou look'st like one
Whose looks are under Sequestration. [9]
Whose Renegado form, at the first glance,
Shews like the self-denying Ordinance. [10]
Angel of light, and darkness too, I doubt,
40 Inspir'd within, and yet posses'd without.
Majestic twilight in the state of grace,
Yet with an excommunicated face.
Charles and his Mask are of a different mint,
A Psalm of mercy in a miscreant print.
45 The Sun wears Midnight, Day is beetle-brow'd,
And Lightning is in Kelder of a cloud. [11]
Oh the accurst Stenography of fate! [12]
The Princely Eagle shrunk into a Bat.
What charm, what magic vapour can it be

[1] *His muffled fabric…house*   OED fabric *sb* I 1 and 3b make it clear that the word could apply both to a building and to the human body; both meanings are relevant here; *ruins* reminds us that the dissolution of the monasteries during Henry VIII's reformation was much in mind to Cleveland's contemporaries, because the Roundheads defaced what they regarded as idolatrous ornamentation in churches.

[2] *The Sun…Royal stamp*   These lines rely on the analogy (in the "Elizabethan world picture") between the Sun in the heavens and the King on earth; *mew'd* shed (*OED* mew *v* [1] c).

[3] *Flay…mould*   i.e. if you were to flay; *darkness* one of the plagues of Egypt: Exodus 10:21–23; *Presbyterian budge* Presbyterians were anathema to Royalists of Cleveland's stamp; *budge* to be understood by reference to its meaning as noun and adjective (OED budge *sb* [1] a kind of fur and budge *a* 1 pompous, stiff, formal); *that drowsy…ignorance* in apposition to *budge* and so explaining more precisely what Cleveland means us to understand by that word; *Synod* a Presbyterian assembly (*OED* synod 1 b).

[4] *Close mourner*   deep mourners (*OED* close *a* 11b).

[5] *rugged*   "The Rugged-Oyster…is of a dull ash colour" (*OED* rugged *a* [1] 2).

[6] *Minster*   monastery, monastery church, temple; see the various senses in *OED*. King Charles is especially consecrated by God, and being disguised is like a holy building in need of repair.

[7] *Manchester's elves*   a reference to the Puritan take-over of the Universities; the Earl of Manchester was ordered in 1644 to "purify" Cambridge; the "elves" are his troops, a "changeling rabble" because they had turned away from their allegiance to the King.

[8] *Sacrilege…Attire*   The subject-matter and tone of this poem indicates the importance attached to the visual symbols of monarchy.

[9] *Sequestration*   an emotive word in the language of the time. Many of the Anglican clergy were deprived of their livings. See *OED* sequestration 4. Under "sequestrator" *OED* quotes Cleveland: "He is the State's Cormorant."

[10] *self-denying Ordinance*   an Act passed in 1645 preventing anybody from simultaneously holding a command in the Army and a seat in either House of Parliament.

[11] *Kelder*   womb, from the Dutch word for a cellar. Vaughan and Brome followed Cleveland in using the word.

[12] *Stenography*   shorthand. *OED* quotes this line as the first figurative use of the word.

That checks his rays to this Apostasy? [1]
It is no subtle film of tiffany air,
No Cob-web vizard, such as Ladies wear,
When they are veiled on purpose to be seen,
Doubling their lustre by their vanquished Screen: [2]
No, the false scabbard of a prince is tough
And three-piled darkness, like the smokey slough
Of an imprisoned flame, 'tis *Faux* in grain,
Dark lantern to our bright meridian. [3]
Hell belched the damp, the Warwick-Castle-vote
Rang *Britain's* curfew, so our light went out. [4]
The black offender, should he wear his sin
For penance, could not have a darker skin.
Thy visage is not legible, the letters,
Like a Lord's name, writ in fantastic fetters:
Clothes where a Switzer might be buried quick,
As overgrown as the Body Politic. [5]
False beard enough, to fit a stage's plot,
For that's the ambush of their wit, God wot.
Nay all his properties so strange appear, [6]
Y' are not i' th' presence, though the King be
    there.

A Libel is his dress, a garb uncouth,
Such as the *Hue* and *Cry* once purged at mouth. [7]
Scribbling Assasinate, thy lines attest
An ear-mark due; Cub of the Blatant Beast, [8]
Whose breath before 'tis syllabled for worse,
Is blasphemy unfledg'd, a callow curse.
The Laplanders when they would sell a wind
Wafting to hell, bag up thy phrase, and bind
It to the Barque, which at the voyage end
Shifts Poop, and breeds the colic in the fiend. [9]
But I'le not dub thee with a glorious scar,
Nor sink thy Sculler with a Man of War. [10]
The black-mouth'd *Si quis* and this slandering suit,
Both do alike in picture execute. [11]
But since w' are all called Papists, why not date
Devotion to the rags thus consecrate. [12]
As Temples use to have their Porches wrought

---

[1] *Apostasy* abandonment of religious faith or moral allegiance (*OED* apostasy 1, with other senses relevant); *rays* Cleveland is returning to the Sun-King parallel; there is too an Eagle-King parallel, the Eagle being "the king of birds."

[2] *It is no subtle film…Screen* Cleveland seems to be playing here on the etymological relation between *tiffany* (muslin, cobweb lawn) and *theophany*, since manifestations of God always conceal as well as reveal. See *OED* tiffany 1 and 2.

[3] *Faux* Guy Fawkes, the first person discovered in the Gunpowder Plot (1605), was represented in prints as entering the House of Parliament bearing a dark lantern.

[4] *the Warwick-Castle-vote* In 1646 Parliament commanded that the King should be sent to Warwick Castle. The Scots did not comply; but Cleveland is seeing the vote as extinguishing the power of the monarchy.

[5] *Clothes…Body Politic* Members of the Swiss Guard (employed then by various European monarchs and to this day in the Vatican) were notoriously large; Charles I was a small man. Events have shown that the Body Politic has grown too large in relation to its Head, the King.

[6] *properties* in the double sense of "stage properties" and "attributes of the King."

---

[7] *Hue and Cry Mercurius Britanicus* issued a Hue and Cry after the King in its issue of July 28 – August 4, 1645; one editor was imprisoned and the other forced to apologize. *OED* hue and cry: outcry calling for the pursuit of a felon.

[8] *An ear-mark due* Cropping of the ears, in part or in whole, was a punishment meted out under Charles I to those deemed to have published seditious libel. Three authors of anti-episcopal pamphlets, Burton, Bastwicke and Prynne, were so punished in 1637; *Blatant Beast* a symbol of calumny, which appears in several books of Spenser's *The Faerie Queene*.

[9] Compare Vaughan's reference to Lapland witches in "Upon A Cloak," line 90. Among other activities, they sold winds to sailors. The Hue and Cry of *Britanicus* would sicken the devil himself.

[10] The sense is roughly "You are too insignificant to be honoured with my attention"; *dub* is to invest [somebody] with a new dignity or title (*OED* dub *v* [1] 2).

[11] *black-mouth'd* slanderous, calumnious (*OED*); *Si quis* "If anyone"; the beginning of notices on the doors of churches asking if anyone knew good reason why a person should not be admitted to Holy Orders; the point is that such notices invite slander. The couplet is not entirely clear; *in picture* may suggest execution at one remove, as a picture is an imitation rather than a real person; *this slandering suit* perhaps referring to Charles's disguise.

[12] *w' are all called Papists* a common Puritan charge against those Anglicans who accepted Archbishop Laud's views on ceremonies.

With Sphinxes, creatures of an antick draught, [1]
And puzzling Portraitures, to shew that there
90 Riddles inhabited, the like is here.

But pardon Sir, since I presume to be
Clark of this Closet to Your Majesty; [2]
Me thinks in this your dark mysterious dress
I see the Gospel couched in Parables.
95 The second view my purblind fancy wipes,
And shews Religion in its dusky types.
Such a Text Royal, so obscure a shade
Was *Solomon* in Proverbs all arrayed. [3]

Now all ye brats of this expounding age,
100 To whom the spirit is in pupillage;
You that damn more then ever *Sampson* slew,
And with his engine, the same jaw-bone too: [4]
How is't *Charles* 'scapes your Inquisition free,
Since bound up in the Bible's Livery?
105 Hence cabinet-intruders, pick-locks hence, [5]
You that dim jewels with your Bristol-sense: [6]
And Characters, like Witches, so torment,
Till they confess a guilt, though innocent.
Keys for this Cypher you can never get,
110 None but *S. Peter's* ope's this Cabinet. [7]
This Cabinet, whose aspect would benight

Critic spectators with redundant light.
A Prince most seen, is least: What Scriptures call
The Revelation, is most mystical.
115 Mount then thou shadow royal, and with haste
Advance thy morning star, *Charles's* overcast.
May thy strange journey contradictions twist,
And force fair weather from a Scottish mist.
Heaven's Confessors are pos'd, those star-ey'd Sages,
120 To interpret an Eclipse thus riding stages. [8]
Thus *Israel*-like he travels with a cloud,
Both as a conduct to him, and a shroud.
But oh! he goes to *Gibeon,* and renews
A league with mouldy bread, and clouted shoes. [9]
—1647

The Rebel Scot [10]

How? Providence? and yet a Scottish crew? [11]
Then Madam Nature wears black patches
too: [12]
What? shall our Nation be in bondage thus
Unto a Land that truckles under us?
5 Ring the bells backward; I am all on fire,

---

[1] *Sphinxes* emblematic of the inscrutable. For sculpted sphinxes, see *OED* sphinx 2; *antick* antique; *draught* here, "representation in sculpture"; this place is cited under *OED* draught *sb* X 27b.

[2] *Clark etc.* A Clerk of the Closet was an ecclesiastic in private attendance upon a monarch, a royal confessor (*OED* clerk *sb* 6c).

[3] *Me thinks...arrayed* The suggestion is that the disguise points to a mystery, as do "types" in religion; but the word *arrayed* points beyond "*Solomon* in Proverbs" to Matthew 6:29 and Solomon arrayed in all his glory, in contrast to the humble disguise of the King.

[4] *with...the same jaw-bone too* with the jaw-bone of an ass. See Judges 15:15.

[5] *cabinet-intruders* in reference to the publication of letters written by Charles, said to have been taken from a cabinet captured at the Battle of Naseby.

[6] *Bristol-sense* in reference to the "Bristol diamond" (*OED* Bristol 3). To have *Bristol-sense* is to suspect that all jewels are false; in this case the jewel is Charles.

[7] Only St. Peter will be able to interpret the character of the King.

---

[8] *pos'd* puzzled; *Eclipse* another reference to the Sun-King parallel; Charles is eclipsed by his disguise; *stages* divisions of a journey (*OED* stage *sb* IV).

[9] See Joshua 9:3–15, especially verse 5; *clouted* patched. The point of the last line is that the Scots were no more to be trusted than the inhabitants of Gibeon who deceived Joshua.

[10] The Scottish army entered England on January 19, 1644. Morris and Withington consider that the poem may have been written before the event, in view of the fact that Pym, mentioned in l. 10, died on December 8, 1643. Their view is that "the tone of the passage suggests that Pym is still alive." I fail to see that it does.

[11] *Providence* the cry of the New Model Army.

[12] *patches* small pieces of silk or court-plaster, worn on the face to conceal blemishes or to show off the complexion (*OED* patch *sb* [1] 2). That is, it is unnatural for the Scots to rise up against the King. The next two lines express an English view of the inferiority of the Scots.

Not all the buckets in a Country Choir [1]
Shall quench my rage. A Poet should be fear'd
When angry, like a Comet's flaming beard. [2]
And where's the Stoic can his wrath appease
10 To see his Country sick of *Pym's* disease; [3]
By Scotch Invasion to be made a prey
To such Pig-wiggin *Myrmidons* as they? [4]
But that there's charm in verse, I would not quote
The name of *Scot*, without an antidote;
15 Unless my head were red, that I might brew [5]
Invention there that might be poison too.
Were I a drowsy Judge, whose dismal Note
Disgorgeth halters, as a Juggler's throat
Doth ribands: could I (in Sir Emp'rick's tone) [6]
20 Speak Pills in phrase, and quack destruction:
Or roar like *Marshall*, that *Geneva*-Bull, [7]
Hell and damnation a pulpit full:
Yet to express a *Scot*, to play that prize, [8]

Not all those mouth-Granadoes can suffice. [9]
25 Before a *Scot* can properly be cursed,
I must (like *Hocus*) swallow daggers first. [10]
  Come keen *Iambicks*, with your Badger's feet, [11]
And Badger-like, bite till your teeth do meet.
Help ye tart Satirists, to imp my rage,
30 With all the Scorpions that should whip this age. [12]
Scots are like witches; do but whet your pen,
Scratch till the blood come; they'll not hurt you
    then. [13]
Now as the Martyrs were enforc'd to take
The shapes of beasts, like hypocrites, at stake,
35 I'le bait my *Scot* so; yet not cheat your eyes,
A *Scot* within a beast is no disguise. [14]
  No more let *Ireland* brag, her harmless nation
Fosters no Venom, since the Scots' Plantation: [15]
Nor can ours feign'd Antiquity maintain;

---

[1] *Ring the bells backward* that is, beginning with the bass bell, as was done to warn of fire; *Choir* fire-buckets were kept in the choirs of churches.

[2] *a Comet's flaming beard* Comets were thought to presage disasters.

[3] *Pym* John Pym was a great Parliamentary leader. He was said at the time to have died of a disease induced by lice; Cleveland's point is that England is being overrun by the Scots as Pym was by lice.

[4] *Pig-wiggin Myrmidons* Myrmidons were originally a race of war-like men of ancient Thessaly; the word had come to mean "hired ruffians" by Cleveland's time; *Pig-wiggin* variously spelled and obscure in origin, but obviously a term of contempt; see *OED* pigwidgin. *OED* records no sense very satisfactory for this context; Dr. Johnson came close when he called it "a kind of cant word for anything petty or small"; I have no doubt that the exact sense Cleveland had in mind is conveyed in Edwin Brough's letter to *The Times* of June 7, 1923 when he listed it as one of the names given to the runt of a litter of pigs or dogs.

[5] *Unless my head were red* By tradition Judas had red hair, and so it was taken as signifying evil qualities.

[6] *Sir Emp'rick* a quack doctor.

[7] *Marshall* Stephen Marshall was a famous Puritan preacher, who became chief chaplain to the New Model Army.

[8] *play that prize* act that part (*OED* prize *sb*[2] b).

[9] *mouth-Granadoes* explosive speeches (by analogy with hand-grenade).

[10] *Hocus* a conjuror or juggler; the word is an abbreviation of *Hocus-pocus*, the origin of which is uncertain.

[11] *Iambicks, with your Badger's feet* Sir Thomas Browne discusses the opinion that the "Badger hath the legs of one side shorter than of the other" in *Pseudodoxia Epidemica* Book 3, Chapter 5.

[12] *imp* to improve the capacities of, as the flight of a falcon was improved by feathers engrafted in the wing. For *scorpions*, see I Kings 12:11.

[13] *Scratch till the blood come* Witches were thought to be unable to harm anybody who had drawn their blood; see *I Henry VI*, I.v.6: "Blood will I draw on thee, thou art a witch."

[14] *the Martyrs* Christians were blamed by Nero for a great fire in Rome in 64 C.E., and many were put to death, some by being clothed in animal skins and "thrown to the lions": *like hypocrites* but not really so, because they were forced to assume a false appearance; *Scot within a beast* a reference to the custom of painting the body with shapes of beasts, no disguise because they are truly beastly. Cleveland is seeing himself as an English dog baiting the Scottish bear.

[15] *Ireland…no Venom* a reference to the tradition that St. Patrick cleared all Ireland of snakes; *the Scots' Plantation* Ireland was colonized under both Elizabeth and James; it is estimated that 40,000 Scots settled in Ulster between 1610 and 1640, beginning the Presbyterian domination of that province and leading to the religio-political difficulties of our own time.

40 Since they came in, *England* hath wolves again. [1]
The Scot that kept the Tower, might have shown
(Within the grate of his own breast alone)
The Leopard and the Panther; and engrossed [2]
What all those wild Collegiates had cost
45 The honest High-shoes, in their Termly Fees, [3]
First to the savage Lawyer, next to these.
Nature her self doth Scotch-men beasts confess,
Making their Country such a wilderness:
A Land that brings in question and suspense
50 God's omnipresence, but that CHARLES came
            thence:
But that *Montrose* and *Crawford's* loyal band [4]
Aton'd their sins, and christ'ned half the Land.
Nor is it all the Nation hath these spots;
There is a Church, as well as *Kirk* of Scots:
55 As in a picture, where the squinting paint
Shews Fiend on this side, and on that side Saint. [5]
He that saw Hell in's melancholy dream,
And in the twilight of his Fancy's theme,
Scar'd from his sins, repented in a fright,
60 Had he view'd Scotland, had turn'd Proselyte.[6]

A land where one may pray with cursed intent,
O may they never suffer banishment!
Had *Cain* been *Scot*, God would have chang'd his
            doom,
Not forc'd him wander, but confin'd him home. [7]
65 Like Jews they spread, and as infection fly,
As if the Devil had Ubiquity.
Hence 'tis, they live at Rovers; and defy [8]
This or that Place, Rags of Geography.
They're citizens o'th world; they're all in all,
70 Scotland's a Nation Epidemical.
And yet they ramble not to learn the Mode
How to be dressed, or how to lisp abroad,
To return knowing in the Spanish shrug, [9]
Or which of the Dutch States a double Jug
75 Resembles most, in Belly, or in Beard: [10]
(The Card by which the Mariners are steer'd.) [11]
No; the *Scots-Errant* fight, and fight to eat;
Their Estrich-stomachs make their swords their
            meat: [12]
Nature with Scots as tooth-drawers hath dealt,
80 Who use to hang their teeth upon their belt. [13]
Yet wonder not at this their happy choice;
The serpent's fatal still to *Paradise*.

---

[1] *England hath wolves*   There were no wolves in Cleveland's England, but their extirpation was more recent than was thought. Dryden, in *The Hind and the Panther*, also identified Presbyterians with wolves.

[2] *The Scot that kept the Tower*   Sir William Balfour, dismissed in 1641 from his post as Lieutenant of the Tower, became a commander on the Parliamentary side; *The Leopard and the Panther*   associated with lust and treachery; in Cleveland's time the Tower was a menagerie as well as a prison.

[3] *honest High-shoes*   country people, who wore high shoes against mud; Cleveland means that when they come to London to consult their lawyers and see the animals in their Tower, Balfour could exhibit himself and take their money.

[4] *Montrose* and *Crawford*   Scottish noblemen who fought for the King.

[5] *the squinting paint…Saint*   referring to satirical pictures, common in the Reformation.

[6] *He that saw Hell*   The specific reference is unclear; it would be all too easy, and probably inaccurate, to suggest Dante; *had turn'd Proselyte*   the suggestion is that Scotland is worse than Hell, since to change from one religion to another is a stronger course of action than merely to repent.

[7] *Had Cain been Scot* etc.   Morris and Withington say that these are the most famous lines in Cleveland. For Cain, see Genesis 4:1–15.

[8] *at Rovers*   at random (the term is originally from archery, where it had a rather different meaning).

[9] *the Spanish shrug*   Writers of the time were uninhibited in references to the habits of other nations; the body-language of inhabitants of the Mediterranean countries was a frequent subject of remark.

[10] *the Dutch States*   leaders of the United Netherlands; *a double Jug* etc.   the point is, to know which of the leaders looks like a two-pint jug (or the reference may be to a toby-jug, shaped like a human figure).

[11] *The Card* etc.   in reference to the preceding five lines; these social observations form the chart (card) by which travellers find their way around the world.

[12] *Estrich-stomachs*   There are many references in the period to the indiscriminate appetite of the ostrich.

[13] *to hang their teeth upon their belt*   as tooth-drawers were depicted at the time.

Sure *England* hath the Hemerods, and these [1]
On the North Postern of the patient seize,
85 Like Leeches: thus they physically thirst [2]
After our blood, but in the cure shall burst.
Let them not think to make us run o'th' score,
To purchase Villeinage, as once before,
When an Act past, to stroke them on the head,
90 Call them good subjects, buy them ginger-
       bread. [3]
Nor gold, nor Acts of Grace; 'tis steel must tame
The stubborn *Scot*: A Prince that would reclaim
Rebels by yielding, doth like him (or worse)
Who saddled his own back to shame his horse.
95   Was it for this you left your leaner soil,
Thus to lard Israel with Egypt's spoil? [4]
They are the Gospel's Life-guard; but for them,
The garrison of new Jerusalem,
What would the brethren do? the Cause! the Cause!
100 Sack-possets, and the Fundamental Laws! [5]
Lord! what a goodly thing is want of shirts!
How a Scotch-stomach, and no meat, converts!
They wanted food and raiment; so they took
Religion for their Seamstress and their Cook.
105 Unmask them well; their honours and estate,
As well as conscience, are sophisticate. [6]
Shrive but their Titles, and their money poise,
A Laird and twenty pence pronounc'd with noise,
When construed, but for a plain yeoman go,

110 And a good sober two-pence; and well so. [7]
Hence then you proud Impostors, get you gone,
You Picts in Gentry and Devotion: [8]
You scandal to the stock of Verse! a race
Able to bring the Gibbet in disgrace.
115 *Hyperbolus* by suffering did traduce
The Ostracism, and sham'd it out of use. [9]
The Indian that heaven did forswear,
Because he heard the Spaniards were there,
Had he but known what Scots in hell had been,
120 He would *Erasmus*-like have hung between. [10]
My Muse hath done. A Voider for the nonce! [11]
I wrong the Devil, should I pick the bones.
That dish is his: for when the Scots decease,
Hell like their Nation feeds on Barnacles.
125   A Scot, when from the Gallow-Tree got loose,
       Drops into *Styx*, and turns a Soland-Goose. [12]
—1647

---

[1] *Hemerods* A haemorrhoid (variously spelled) could refer to both an affliction of the anus and to a serpent whose bite caused unstoppable bleeding.

[2] *physically thirst* that is, as if the thirst were the result of a medical ailment.

[3] *run o'th' score* get into debt; *as once before* etc. a reference to an Act of February 1641, by which the Scots were voted a gratuity of £300,000.

[4] *Egypt's spoil?* Exodus 12:36.

[5] *the Cause* and *the Fundamental Laws* Puritan slogans, mocked after the Restoration in works such as *Hudibras*.

[6] *sophisticate* not genuine, dishonest (OED sophisticate *ppl a* 1 and 3).

[7] *Shrive* question, examine (*OED* shrive 7); *two-pence* the English penny was worth about ten Scotch pence.

[8] *Picts* Compare the reference in Marvell's *Horatian Ode*.

[9] *Ostracism* a method of temporary banishment practised in ancient Greece (*OED*). *Hyperbolus* was a demagogue who tried to banish others; instead he suffered banishment himself.

[10] *Erasmus-like* Aubrey wrote that "They were wont to say that Erasmus was Interdependent between Heaven and Hell, till, about the year 1655, the Conclave at Rome dammed him for a Heretique, after he had been dead 120 years" (*Aubrey's Brief Lives*, ed. Oliver Lawson Dick, London: Secker and Warburg, 1960, 103).

[11] *Voider* a utensil in which dirty dishes and scraps of food are placed when clearing the table after a meal (*OED* voider 3); *for the nonce* for the occasion.

[12] *Barnacles…Soland-Goose* It was still widely believed at the time that trees in the Orkney Islands bore barnacles that dropped into the water and turned into Soland geese. For other references see *OED* Solan 2.

Epitaph on the Earl of Strafford [1]

Here lies Wise and Valiant Dust,
  Huddled up 'twixt Fit and Just:
Strafford, who was hurried hence
'Twixt Treason and Convenience.
He spent his Time here in a Mist;
A *Papist*, yet a *Calvinist*. [2]
His Prince's nearest Joy, and Grief.
He had, yet wanted all Relief. [3]
The Prop and Ruin of the State;
The People's violent Love, and Hate:
One in extremes lov'd and abhor'd.
Riddles lie here; or in a word, [4]

Here lies Blood; and let it lie
Speechless still, and never cry. [5]
—1647

The General Eclipse [6]

Ladies that guild the glittering Noon
  And by Reflection mend his Ray,
Whose Beauty makes the sprightly Sun
To dance, as upon Easter-day;
    What are you now the Queen's away?

Courageous Eagles, who have whet
Your eyes upon Majestic Light,
And thence deriv'd such Martial heat,
That still your Looks maintain the Fight;
    What are you since the King's Goodnight? [7]

Cavalier-buds, whom Nature teems,
As a Reserve for *England's* Throne,
Spirits whose double edge redeems
The last Age, and adorns your own;
    What are you now the Prince is gone? [8]

---

[1] The Earl of Strafford was executed on May 12, 1641. This poem has been regarded as probably by Cleveland. For discussion see Morris and Withington, xxxiii. There it is said to be unlike any of Cleveland's genuine poems, "but considering the extreme tact enjoined by the event upon a Fellow of St. John's not yet irretrievably committed to the King's cause, it is what one might expect: a trail of consciously clever antitheses, half shielding and sophisticating the pathos of bloody 'riddles.' That Cleveland felt the full shock of the trial is evident from other allusions to Strafford scattered throughout his works." For the attribution to Clemen Paman (1612–1664), see Peter Davidson, *Poetry and Revolution* (Oxford: Clarendon P, 1998), 363, 547.

[2] *A Papist, yet a Calvinist* Cleveland, as a Fellow of St. John's College, Cambridge, which was also Strafford's college, may have heard that Strafford, thought of by the people as a "Papist," was in fact a Calvinist.

[3] *wanted* lacked; *Relief* punning on various senses of the word. Strafford was a wealthy landowner, so *OED* relief [2] 1 ("payment…made to the overlord") would apply; as someone who was tried and executed, and whose King signed his death-warrant, he might be said to lack "assistance in time of danger" (*OED* relief [2] 4). G.M. Trevelyan described the trial, attainder and execution of Strafford as a "high tragedy, unsurpassed for historical and human interest in the political annals of any time or land," and "the bitterest humiliation of Charles's life" (*A Shortened History of England*, Harmondsworth: Penguin Books, 1976 reprint, 298).

[4] *Riddles lie here* Compare "The King's Disguise," l. 90.

[5] The last couplet represents a prayer that the blood of Strafford will not result in a blood-bath for the nation. Compare *Macbeth* III.iv: "It will have blood; they say, blood will have blood"; for the notion that guiltily shed blood cries out see Genesis 4:8-11 and Luke 11:49-51.

[6] This poem, not certainly by Cleveland, is described by Morris and Withington as "one of the many variations" on Wotton's famous lyric, "You meaner beauties of the Night."

[7] The imagery of this stanza may be understood by reference to the "eagle" imagery in "The King's Disguise." There has been disagreement as to whether *the King's Goodnight* refers to Charles I's surrender to the Scots in May 1646 or to his execution in January 1649. Morris and Withington favour the former, and argue that a date of May-June 1646 would not be contradicted by any other reference in the poem. I disagree, for reasons given below.

[8] *the Prince* In the light of the thought-pattern of this and the following stanza, which has to do with succession, this seems more likely to refer to the King's eldest son than to any other possible candidate.

As an obstructed Fountain's head
Cuts the Entail off from the Streams,
And Brooks are disinherited;
Honour and Beauty are mere Dreams,
20   Since *Charles* and *Mary* lost their Beams. [1]

Criminal Valors! who commit
Your Gallantry, whose *Pæan* brings [2]
A Psalm of Mercy after it;
In this sad Solstice of the King's, [3]
25   Your Victory hath mew'd her wings. [4]

See how your Soldier wears his Cage
Of Iron, like the Captive Turk, [5]
And as the Guerdon of his Rage!
See how your glimmering Peers do lurk,
30   Or at the best work journey-work!

Thus 'tis a General Eclipse,
And the whole world is all a-mort; [6]
Only the House of Commons trips
The Stage in a Triumphant sort, [7]
35   Now e'n *John Lilburn* take 'em for't. [8]
—1677

[1] *Mary*   Charles I's Queen, Henrietta Maria.

[2] *who commit / Your Gallantry*   The stanza refers to the Roundheads; this probably means that they send their gallantry to prison (where it will not trouble them by being operative in the world) and/or that they refer it to a Committee to avoid personal responsibility (*OED* commit *v* 2,3,4).

[3] *whose Pæan...after it*   The Roundheads were known for an addiction to the Psalms. *A Psalm of Mercy*   sung on the scaffold. The Roundheads could swing from psalms of praise to psalms of mercy without changing their tune. In this context (of scaffold reference) *this sad Solstice of the King's* seems more likely to refer to his death than to his giving himself up to the Scots.

[4] *mew'd*   shed; presumably the sense is that the Roundheads' victory is hollow.

[5] The allusion is to Bajazeth in Marlowe's *Tamburlaine* Part I, IV. ii.

[6] *all a-mort*   sick to death.

[7] *sort*   manner (*OED* sort *sb* [2] III 21). *Only the House of Commons* suggests the exclusion of both the monarchy and the Lords, indicating a date after the votes of February 1649 abolishing the monarchy and the House of Lords. In the previous stanza *glimmering* indicates a faint, that is fading, light; *journey-work*   work done for wages, with connotations of servility and inferiority (*OED* journey-work).

[8] *Lilburn*   John Lilburne, a political agitator and influential pamphleteer, fought for Parliament from 1642 to 1645, but became disillusioned, as Barry Coward writes, with "the failure of the Long Parliament and the Westminster Assembly to bring about a 'godly reformation'." In 1645 he left the Army and expressed his disillusion in November 1646 with the pamphlet *London's Liberty in Chains*. It is not easy to say with any certainty what this line means. The *e'n* (even) reflects the fact that Lilburne had been a supporter of Parliament, but as it stands the line has two problems: (a) the grammatical mood of "take" appears to be optative, but that yields a problematic sense and (b) the meaning of "take" in either case (is it an ellipsis for "take to task"?). I suspect a misprint; if we emend to "takes" that yields a clear indicative sense, and the suggested ellipsis makes sense in relation to events of the first half of 1649. Although Lilburne was in the Tower in May 1649, the Commons took it for granted that the "disorders and mutinies" of that month were "occasioned by his means," and sent 400 men of two regiments known to be hostile to him to guard the Tower. Lilburne and his friends were segregated from other prisoners and "deprived of pen, ink and paper" (Pauline Gregg, *Free-born John*, London, 1961, 280).

Samuel Butler
1613 – 1680

Little is known of Samuel Butler's life. The son of a Worcestershire farmer and clerk, he was educated at King's School, Worcester, and according to one source proceeded to Cambridge, although no records of his matriculation have been found. Butler worked as a clerk in various households including that of one of Cromwell's generals, Sir Samuel Luke, on whom the figure of Hudibras may be based. His first publication, when he was forty-seven, was an anonymous tract supporting the Stuart cause. In 1661 Butler held a stewardship to Richard Vaughan, Earl of Carbery, at Ludlow Castle, but he held this position only briefly. In December 1661 the first part of *Hudibras* was published and Butler achieved instant fame. The poem delighted the court, but apparently little was done to help Butler financially. The second part of *Hudibras* was printed a year later, and the third section was introduced at the end of 1677. Butler's financial position appears to have deteriorated after he resigned his post at Ludlow, and Charles did little to alleviate his situation until 1677 when Butler was finally awarded a pension, three years before he died of consumption.

୧୬୬

Hudibras
(Excerpts)

THE FIRST PART
CANTO I

THE ARGUMENT

Sir Hudibras *his passing worth,*
The manner how he sallied forth:
His arms and equipage are shown;
His horse's virtues, and his own.
Th' adventure of the Bear and Fiddle
Is sung, but breaks off in the middle.

When *civil* Fury first grew high,
    And men fell out they knew not why;
When hard words, *Jealousies* and *Fears,*
Set folks together by the ears,
5 And made them fight, like mad or drunk,
For Dame *Religion* as for punk, [1]
Whose honesty they all durst swear for,

Though not a man of them knew wherefore:
When *Gospel-trumpeter,* surrounded
10 With long-eared rout, to battle sounded,
And pulpit, drum ecclesiastic,
Was beat with fist, instead of a stick:
Then did Sir *Knight* abandon dwelling,
And out he rode a Colonelling.

15 A wight he was, whose very sight would [2]
Entitle him *Mirror of Knighthood;* [3]
That never bent his stubborn knee
To any thing but Chivalry,
Nor put up blow, but that which laid
20 Right worshipful on shoulder-blade:
Chief of domestic knights and errant,
Either for chartel or for warrant: [4]
Great on the bench, great in the saddle,
That could as well bind o're, as swaddle:
25 Mighty he was at both of these,

---

[1] *punk* a prostitute, strumpet, harlot (*OED* punk *sb*[1]).

[2] *wight* a human being, man or woman, person (*OED* wight *sb* 2).

[3] *Mirror of Knighthood* a Spanish romance translated into English in the late sixteenth century.

[4] *chartel* a written challenge, a letter of defiance (*OED* cartel *sb* 1).

And styled of war as well as peace.
(So some rats of amphibious nature,
Are either for the Land or Water.)
But here our Authors make a doubt,
30 Whether he were more wise, or stout.
Some hold the one, and some the other:
But howso'er they make a pother,
The difference was so small, his Brain
Outweighed his Rage but half a grain:
35 Which made some take him for a tool
That Knaves do work with, call'd a Fool.
And offer to lay wagers, that
As *Montaigne,* playing with his Cat, [1]
Complains she thought him but an Ass,
40 Much more she would Sir *Hudibras.*
(For that's the name our valiant knight
To all his challenges did write.)
But they're mistaken very much,
'Tis plain enough he was no such.
45 We grant, although he had much wit,
H' was very shy of using it,
As being loath to wear it out,
And therefore bore it not about,
Unless on Holy-days, or so,
50 As men their best apparel do.
Beside 'tis known he could speak *Greek,*
As naturally as pigs squeak:
That *Latin* was no more difficile,
Than to a blackbird 'tis to whistle.
55 Being rich in both he never scanted
His bounty unto such as wanted;
But much of either would afford
To many that had not one word.
For *Hebrew* roots, although th' are found
60 To flourish most in barren ground,
He had such plenty, as sufficed
To make some think him circumcised:

And truly so perhaps, he was
'Tis many a pious Christian's case.
65 He was in *Logic* a great critic
Profoundly skill'd in Analytic.
He could distinguish, and divide
A hair 'twixt South and South-west side:
On either which he would dispute,
70 Confute, change hands, and still confute.
He'd undertake to prove by force
Of argument, a man's no horse.
He'd prove a buzzard is no fowl,
And that a *Lord* may be an owl;
75 A calf an *Alderman,* a Goose a *Justice,*
And rooks *Committee-men* and *Trustees.* [2]
He'd run in debt by disputation,
And pay with ratiocination.
All this by syllogism, true [3]
80 In mood and figure, he would do.

For *Rhetoric,* he could not ope
His mouth, but out there flew a trope:
And when he happened to break off
I'th' middle of his speech, or cough,
85 H' had hard words ready, to shew why,
And tell what rules he did it by.
Else when with greatest art he spoke,
You'd think he talked like other folk.
For all a rhetorician's rules
90 Teach nothing but to name his tools.
His ordinary rate of speech
In loftiness of sound was rich,
A *Babylonish* dialect,
Which learned pedants much affect.
95 It was a particoloured dress

---

[1] *Montaigne, playing with his cat* In his essay *An Apology for Raymond Sebonde,* Montaigne writes, "when I play with my cat, who knows if I am not a pastime to her more than she is to me" (Donald Frame, *The Complete Essays of Montaigne*: Stanford, 1958, p.331).

[2] *rooks* cheats, swindlers (*OED* rook *sb*[1] 2b) To rook is to clean of money by fraud, extortion, or other means (*OED* rook *v*[1]1); *Committee men* men who facilitated the appropriation and sale of lands owned by Royalists or the Church on behalf of Parliament.

[3] *syllogism* specious reasoning, used in humorous allusion to its sense in logic (*OED* syllogism 1b).

Of patched and piebald languages
'Twas *English* cut on *Greek* and *Latin,*
Like Fustian heretofore on Satin. [1]
It had an odd promiscuous tone,
100 As if h' had talked three parts in one.
Which made some think, when he did gabble,
Th' had heard three labourers of *Babel;* [2]
Or *Cerberus* himself pronounce [3]
A leash of languages at once.
105 This he as volubly would vent,
As if his stock would ne're be spent.
And truly to support that charge
He had supplies as vast and large.
For he could coin or counterfeit
110 New words, with little or no wit:
Words so debased and hard, no stone
Was hard enough to touch them on.
And when with hasty noise he spoke 'em,
The ignorant for current took 'em.
115 That had the Orator who once,
Did fill his mouth with pebble stones [4]
When he harangued; but known his phrase
He would have used no other ways.

In *Mathematics* he was greater
120 Than *Tycho Brahe* or *Erra Pater:* [5]
For he by geometric scale
Could take the size of *pots* of *ale;*

Resolve by sines and tangents straight, [6]
If bread or butter wanted weight;
125 And wisely tell what hour o'th' day
The clock does strike, by *Algebra.*

Besides he was a shrewd *Philosopher,*
And had read every text and gloss over:
What e're the crabbed'st author hath
130 He understood b'implicit Faith,
What ever *Sceptic* could inquire for;
For every why he had a wherefore:
Knew more than forty of them do,
As far as words and terms could go.
135 All which he understood by rote,
And as occasion served, would quote;
No matter whether right or wrong:
They might be either said or sung.
His notions fitted things so well,
140 That which was which he could not tell:
But oftentimes mistook the one
For th'other, as Great Clerks have done.
He could reduce all things to acts
And knew their natures by abstracts,
145 Where entity and quiddity, [7]
The ghosts of defunct bodies, fly;
Where truth in person does appear,
Like words congealed in Northern Air.

He knew *what's what,* and that's as high
150 As *Metaphysic wit can fly.*
In *School-Divinity* as able
As he that hight *Irrefragable;* [8]
Profound in all the nominal
And real ways beyond them all,

[1] *Fustian* coarse cloth made of cotton and flax; also, inflated, turgid or inappropriately lofty language (*OED* fustian *sb* 1 and 2).

[2] *Babel* Genesis 11:1-9. The attempt to build a tower that would reach heaven was punished by God through a fragmentation of one universal language into many languages.

[3] *Cerberus* the many-headed dog that guards the underworld in Greek mythology.

[4] *the Orator who once...pebble stones* Plutarch writes in his *Lives* that the great orator Demosthenes overcame speech defects by speaking with pebbles in his mouth.

[5] *Tycho Brahe or Erra Pater* Tycho Brache, a Danish astronomer of the sixteenth century, designed the "Tychonic" system of the universe. Erra Pater was the alleged author of a sixteenth-century almanac which contained medical advice and weather predictions based on astrology.

[6] *Resolve by sines and tangents* The sine, the tangent and the secant are the three fundamental trigonometrical functions. See *OED* sine 2.

[7] *quiddity* the real nature or essence of a thing; that which makes a thing what it is (*OED* quiddity *sb*[1]1).

[8] *As he that hight Irrefragable* Alexander of Hales, a Franciscan theologian of the twelfth and thirteenth centuries, was known as the *Doctor Irrefragabilis.*

155 And with as delicate a hand
Could twist as tough a Rope of Sand.
And weave fine cobwebs, fit for skull
That's empty when the Moon is full;
Such as take lodgings in a Head
160 That's to be let unfurnished.
He could raise scruples dark and nice,
And after solve 'em in a trice:
As if Divinity had catched
The itch, of purpose to be scratched;
165 Or, like a Mountebank, did wound
And stab her self with doubts profound,
Only to shew with how small pain
The sores of faith are cured again;
Although by woeful proof we find,
170 They always leave a scar behind.
He knew the seat of Paradise,
Could tell in what degree it lies:
And, as he was disposed, could prove it,
Below the moon, or else above it:
175 What *Adam* dreamt of when his bride
Came from her closet in his side: [1]
Whether the Devil tempted her
By a *high Dutch* interpreter:
If either of them had a navel;
180 Who first made music malleable:
Whether the Serpent at the Fall
Had cloven feet, or none at all.
All this, without a gloss or comment,
He would unriddle in a moment
185 In proper terms, such as men smatter
When they throw out and miss the matter.

.   .   .   .

A *Squire* he had whose name was *Ralph*,
That in th' adventure went his half.
(Though writers, for more stately tone,
455 Do call him *Ralpho;* 'tis all one:
And when we can with metre safe,
We'll call him so, if not plain *Raph*.

_____
1 *What Adam dreamt of…closet in his side*   Genesis 3:7–4:24.

For rhyme the rudder is of verses,
With which like ships they steer their courses.)
460 An equal stock of wit and valor
He had laid in, by birth a tailor.
The mighty *Tyrian* Queen that gained [2]
With subtle shreds a tract of land,
Did leave it with a castle fair
465 To his great ancestor, her heir:
From him descended cross-legged knights,
Famed for their faith and warlike fights
Against the bloody cannibal,
Whom they destroyed both great and small.
470 This sturdy Squire had as well
As the bold *Trojan* knight, seen hell, [3]
Not with a counterfeited pass
Of Golden Bough, but true gold-lace.
His *knowledge* was not far behind
475 The knight's, but of another kind,
And he another way came by it:
Some call it *Gifts,* and some *New light;* [4]
A Liberal Art, that costs no pains
Of study, industry, or brains.
480 His wits were sent him for a token,
But in the carriage cracked and broken.
Like commendation nine-pence, crooked
With to and from my love, it looked.
He ne're considered it, as loath
485 To look a gift-horse in the mouth;
And very wisely would lay forth
No more upon it than 'twas worth.
But as he got it freely, so
He spent it frank and freely too.
490 For saints themselves will sometimes be
Of gifts that cost them nothing, free.
By means of this, with *hem* and *cough,*
Prolongers to enlightened Snuff,

_____
2 *The mighty Tyrian Queen*   Dido (Virgil, *Aeneid,* i. 367–8).

3 *the bold Trojan knight*   Aeneas (Virgil, *Aeneid,* vi. 187ff). Aeneas used a magical golden bough to access the underworld.

4 *Some call it Gifts, and some New light*   The sectarians used both the terms "gifts" and "new light" to refer to divine inspiration.

He could deep Mysteries unriddle,
495 As easily as thread a needle;
For as of vagabonds we say,
That they are ne're beside their way:
Whate're men speak by this *new Light,*
Still they are sure to be i'th' right.
500 'Tis a *dark-lantern* of the spirit,
Which none see by but those that bear it:
A Light that falls down from on high,
For spiritual trades to cozen by: [1]
An *Ignis Fatuus,* that bewitches, [2]
505 And leads men into pools and ditches,
To make them dip themselves, and sound
For Christendom in dirty pond; [3]
To dive like wild fowl for Salvation,
And fish to catch Regeneration. [4]
510 This Light inspires, and plays upon
The nose of Saint, like bagpipe-drone,
And speaks through hollow empty soul;
As through a trunk, or whisp'ring hole,
Such language as no mortal ear
515 But spiritual eaves-droppers can hear.
So Phœbus or some friendly Muse [5]
Into small poet's song infuse;
Which they at second-hand rehearse
Through reed or bagpipe, verse for verse.

520 Thus *Ralph* became infallible,
As three or four-legg'd oracle,
The ancient cup, or modern chair;

Spoke truth point-blank, though unaware:
For mystic learning, wondrous able
525 In Magic, *Talisman,* and *Cabal,* [6]
Whose primitive tradition reaches
As far as *Adam's* first green breeches:
Deep-sighted in Intelligences,
Ideas, Atoms, Influences;
530 And much of *Terra Incognita,* [7]
Th'intelligible world could say:
A deep occult philosopher,
As learn'd as the wild Irish are,
Or Sir Agrippa, for profound [8]
535 And solid lying much renown'd:
He *Anthroposophus,* and *Floud,* [9]
And *Jacob Behmen* understood; [10]
Knew many an amulet and charm,
That would do neither good nor harm:
540 In *Rosicrucian* lore as learned, [11]

---

[1] *cozen* to cheat, defraud by deceit (*OED* cozen *v* 1).

[2] *Ignis Fatuus* a thing that deludes or misleads by means of fugitive appearances (*OED* will o' the wisp *fig.* 1); also marsh fire, marsh light (*OED* marsh 4). Referred to under several names in early modern literature, reflecting the hazards of cross-country travel in those days.

[3] *To make them dip...in dirty pond* refers to baptism by immersion as opposed to the sprinkling of water used to baptize by the established Protestant church.

[4] *Regeneration* in religious use: the process or fact of being born again in a spiritual sense, the state resulting from this (*OED* regeneration 2).

[5] *Phœbus* one of the names for Apollo, a Greek god associated with music among other things.

[6] *Cabal* the name given in post-biblical Hebrew to the oral tradition handed down from Moses to the Rabbis of the Mishnah and the Talmud (*OED* cabbala 1).

[7] *Terra Incognita* unknown land (commonly used in early cartography).

[8] *Sir Agrippa* Heinrich Cornelius Agrippa von Nettesheim (1486–1535), philosopher and cabalist who published a work celebrating hermetic beliefs and later renounced his former faith in magic.

[9] *Anthroposophus* Thomas Vaughan (1621–1666), brother to Henry Vaughan the poet, wrote a number of hermetic texts; *Floud* Robert Fludd (1574–1637), hermetic philosopher. These four writers represented mystical nonsense to those of a more rationalist bent, like Butler and, after him, Jonathan Swift. Of one of Vaughan's works, Swift wrote that it was "a piece of the most unintelligable Fustian, that, perhaps, was ever published in any Language."

[10] *Jacob Behmen* Jacob Boehme (1575–1624), a Silesian mystic, many of whose works were translated into English in the 1640s and 1650s. The unintelligibility of his style makes him fair game for Butler's satire, but there are also passages of penetrating spiritual insight which won the admiration of William Law in the eighteenth century and S.T. Coleridge in the nineteenth.

[11] *Rosicrucian* The Rosicrucians were reputedly the members of a society or order founded in the late fifteenth century by one Christian Rosencreuz. They were said to claim various forms of secret and magic knowledge, such as the transmutation of metals, the prolongation of life, and power over the elements. See *OED* rosicrucian *sb* 1.

As he that *Verè adeptus* earned. [1]
He understood the speech of birds [2]
As well as they themselves do words:
Could tell what subtlest *Parrots* mean,
545 That speak and think contrary clean;
What *Member* 'tis of whom they talk
When they cry *Rope*, and *Walk, Knave, walk.*
He'd extract numbers out of matter,
And keep them in a glass, like water,
550 Of sov'reign pow'r to make men wise;
For dropped in blurred, thick-sighted eyes,
They'd make them see in darkest night,
Like owls, though purblind in the light.
By help of these (as he professed)
555 He had *First Matter* seen undressed:
He took her naked all alone,
Before one rag of *Form* was on.
The chaos too he had descry'd,
And seen quite through, or else he ly'd:
560 Not that of paste-board which men shew
For groats at *Fair* of *Bartholmew;* [3]
But its great grandsire, first o'th' name,
Whence that and Reformation came:
Both Cousin-germans, and right able
565 T'inveigle and draw in the rabble. [4]
But *Reformation* was, some say,
O'th' younger house to *Puppet-play.*
He could foretell whats'ever was

By consequence to come to pass.
570 As death of great men, alterations,
Diseases, battles, inundations.
All this without th'eclipse of Sun,
Or dreadful Comet, he hath done,
By inward light, a way as good,
575 And easy to be understood.
But with more lucky hit than those
That use to make the Stars depose,
Like Knights o'th' Post, and falsely charge [5]
Upon themselves what others forge:
580 As if they were consenting to
All mischief in the world men do:
Or like the Dev'l, did tempt and sway 'em
To rogueries, and then betray 'em.
They'll search a Planet's house, to know
585 Who broke and robbed a house below:
Examine *Venus,* and the *Moon,*
Who stole a thimble or a spoon:
And though they nothing will confess,
Yet by their very looks can guess,
590 And tell what guilty aspect bodes,
Who stole, and who received the goods.
They'll question *Mars,* and by his look
Detect who 'twas that nimm'd a cloak: [6]
Make *Mercury* confess and peach
595 Those thieves which he himself did teach.
They'll find i'th' Physiognomies
O'th' Planets all men's destinies:
Like him that took the doctor's bill,
And swallowed it instead o'th' pill.
600 Cast the Nativity o'th' question, [7]
And from positions to be guessed on,
As sure as if they knew the moment
Of native's birth, tell what will come on't.
They'll feel the pulses of the Stars,

---

[1] *Verè adeptus*   adept in truth. The word *adept* was used and assumed by alchemists who professed to have attained the great secret (*OED* adept *sb* b).

[2] One of the alleged magical powers of the Rosicrucians was the ability to understand the speech of animals and birds.

[3] *Fair of Bartholmew*   Bartholomew's fair, founded in the twelfth century by the prior of St. Bartholomew, was held at the end of August. By the seventeenth century the fair had become a spectacle of noisy entertainment, trade and celebration. The playwright Ben Jonson wrote a drama, *Bartholomew Fair*, about the corruption and chicanery of the event.

[4] *Cousin-germans*   persons or things closely related or allied to another; near relatives (*OED* cousin-german *fig* 2).

---

[5] *Knights o' th'Post*   notorious perjurers; those who get their living by giving false evidence (*OED* knight of the Post).

[6] *nimm'd a cloak*   stole a cloak; *nim* to steal (*OED* nim *v* 3).

[7] *Nativity*   birth considered astrologically; a horoscope (*OED* nativity 4). *Native* is the subject of the horoscope (*OED* native *sb* 2).

605　To find out agues, coughs, catarrhs;
　　And tell what crisis does divine
　　The rot in sheep, or mange in swine:
　　In men what gives or cures the itch,
　　What makes them cuckolds, poor or rich:
610　What gains or loses, hangs or saves;
　　What makes men great, what fools or knaves;
　　But not what wise, for only of those

　　The Stars (they say) cannot dispose,
　　No more then can the Astrologians.
615　There they say right, and like true *Trojans*.
　　This Ralpho knew, and therefore took
　　The other Course, of which we spoke.
　　—1662

Rowland Watkyns
ca. 1614 – 1664

Rowland Watkyns was a native of Herefordshire. His parentage has not been established with absolute certainty. However, a pedigree from the Heraldic Visitation of Hereford, 1634, refers to a Rowland Watkins who was the third son of Samuell Watkins and Sibell Parry (both spellings of the surname occurring in the pedigree). The "most dear and pious Uncle, Mr. James Parry, Parson of Tedstone," to whom Watkyns dedicated a poem, was probably Sibell's brother. The Rowland of this pedigree had three brothers and four sisters; the eldest son, James, is described as having been aged 26 in 1634. Rowland's place in the family cannot be determined exactly, though the format of the pedigree suggests that at least one sister as well as two brothers were born before him. His wife's name is not known. He wrote "an epitaph" upon "his beloved daughter, Susanna," who was born in 1655 and died in 1658. A son matriculated at Jesus College, Oxford. His name, Samuel, that of Rowland's father in the pedigree cited above, strengthens the case that the pedigree refers to the poet. There is no record that Watkyns graduated from either university, but he is likely to have been an undergraduate at Jesus College, Oxford, which had a strong Welsh connection.[1]

Watkyns became the vicar of Llanfrynach, four miles south-east of Brecon, in 1635. He was dispossessed of his living, probably in 1648, one of several clergy so treated by the Brecon Sequestration Committee before the Act for the Propagation of the Gospel in Wales came into effect in 1650. He was restored to his living at the Restoration, and held it until his death. Watkyns's *Flamma Sine Fumo* (1662) is divided into three sections: a collection of verse mostly on religious and ethical themes; seventy-three *Proverbial Sentences* in couplets; and *A Looking-Glasse for the Sicke, or signs of several Diseases, With their Cures and Remedies*. The poems reveal a Laudian Anglican contemptuous of "the New Illiterate lay-Teachers." Like his neighbour, the better-known poet Henry Vaughan, Watkyns wrote on Christ's Nativity, the feast disliked by so many Puritans, and on the Virgin Mary.

There is no known record of political activism, beyond poems apparently addressed in manuscript to Royalist acquaintances. Whereas Vaughan kept up a constant stream of publication from 1646 to 1655, Watkyns did not publish his poems until 1662, when it had become not merely safe but possibly advantageous to do so.

A Looking-Glasse for the Sicke suggests that Watkyns may have practised as a physician while he was deprived of his living, and so have been in competition with Vaughan. In relation to contemporary medical controversy, they took opposing positions. Watkyns advocated herbal and questioned "mineral" cures; the Vaughan brothers practised Paracelsian or "chymical" medicine. Such differences may underlie an apparent antipathy between the two men, indicated by the fact that no reference to Watkyns appears in Vaughan's work, while a poem prefaced to *Flamma Sine Fumo* contains rather transparently veiled, and certainly hostile, references to Vaughan.

Watkyns's work has no great aesthetic appeal, but is interesting in relation to contemporary doctrinal and social conflicts, and enhances our knowledge of Royalist society in Breconshire during the interregnum.

---

[1] The pedigree is reprinted in Paul C. Davies's edition of *Flamma Sine Fumo* (Cardiff: U of Wales P, 1968), p. xii. However, Davies considered the identification with the Rowland of that pedigree to be "hazardous." For the reasons here given, I consider it virtually certain that the identification is correct.

෨෧෨

To the Reader

I am not eagle ey'd to face the Sun,
My mind is low, and so my verse doth run.
I do not write of stars to make men wonder.
Or plancts how remote they move asunder.
5 My shallow river thou may'st ford with ease,
Ways, which are fair, and plain can ne'er
    displease. [1]
—1662

The Anabaptist

Ostende Anabaptistam, & ego ostendam monstrum. [2]

What wouldst thou have? a King, a Lord, a
    Knight,
A Bishop, Priest are monsters in thy sight;
No Church, nor Altar, and no Law must be
To dictate but thy conscience unto thee.
5 If thou art displeas'd with Laws Divine, and Civil,
I know not what will fit thee, but the Devil.
—1662

Upon the mournful death of our late Soveraign Lord Charles the first, King of England, &c.

I read of a Confessor, and a King,
A King, and Martyr is a stranger thing.
Our *Charles* was both: A King both just, and wise,
A holy Martyr, and sweet sacrifice:
5 Thieves did consent to kill the just; but why?
When that the Wolf is Judge, the Lamb must die?
He went to *Canaan* for three Kingdoms' good,
Through the red-sea of his own sacred blood: [3]
Thus *John* the Baptist died, that holy one,
10 Whilst *Herod* did usurp King *David's* throne. [4]
By his beheading it may well be said,
Three kingdoms by injustice lost their head; [5]
If e'er I shall the aid of saints implore,
Thy shrine alone (good *Charles*) I will adore;
15 Lord, let my soul unto thy Kingdom come,
To see King *Charles* crown'd for his Martyrdom.
—1662

---

[1] In this prefatory poem, Watkyns seems to have had Henry Vaughan in mind. Consider the first line, in relation to Vaughan's statement in "The Star" that "eagles eye not stars"; the third, in relation to the fact that the words "star" and "stars" occur forty-six times in *Silex Scintillans*; and the last, in relation to the fact that Vaughan, in the title of *Olor Iscanus* ("The Swan of Usk"), laid claim to be the poet of a river. For more on the relationship of Vaughan and Watkyns, see Alan Rudrum, "Resistance, Collaboration and Silence: Henry Vaughan and Breconshire Royalism" in *The English Civil Wars in the Literary Imagination*, ed. Claude J. Summers and Ted-Larry Pebworth (Columbia: U of Missouri P, 1999), pp. 102–118.

[2] *Ostende Anabaptistam, & ego ostendam monstrum* "Show me an Anabaptist, and I will show you a monster." The word Anabaptist was properly used to designate religious groups who refused to allow their children to be baptized and instituted adult baptism. See the article "Anabaptists" in *ODCC*. The word was used rather loosely as a term of abuse in this period, to refer to various groups of radical sectaries; the content of the poem suggests that Watkyns may have had the Quakers in mind.

[3] *He went to Canaan* etc. The Exodus (the escape of the Israelites from captivity in Egypt) was read by Christians as a type of the escape of the Christian soul from the snares of the devil, with Joshua prefiguring Jesus. Watkyns is writing within a Royalist tradition which saw Charles I not merely as a martyr but as a Christ-like figure.

[4] *Thus John the Baptist died* etc. As was common at the time, Watkyns is interpreting the events of his own time in the light of biblical history.

[5] *Three kingdoms* England, Scotland and Ireland.

The Common People [1]

Neutrum modò, mas modo vulgus. [2]

The many-headed *Hydra*, or the people,
   Now build the church, then pull down bells
      and steeple:
Today for learned bishops, and a king,
They shout with one consent: tomorrow sing
5 A different note: One while the people cry
To Christ *Hosanna*; then him crucify:
And thus the wavering multitude will be
Constant in nothing but inconstancy:
When these together swarm, the kingdom fears;
10 They are as fierce as tigers, rude as bears.
   —1662

The holy Sepulchre

Christ is our Rock, who in a rock is lain,
   The lesser rock the greater doth contain:
Out of a rock they newly hewed his grave,
The new man Christ thus a new tomb must
      have:[3]
5 No creature might repose or lay his head,
Without presumption, in the Creator's bed:
The lily of the valley, *Sharon's* rose, [4]
His fragrant grave in a sweet garden chose.
This rock did shelter Christ two days; but he
10 An everlasting refuge is to me:
He is the Rock, that doth our souls relieve

With water, which doth life eternal give. [5]
—1662

The new illiterate Lay-Teachers [6]

Εχας, ἔχας ἔϛε βέβηλοι [7]

Why trouble you religion's sacred stream,
   And tear Christ's coat, which had no rent,
      or seam?
And you do patch it too with ragged clouts
Of false opinions, and fantastic doubts.
5 The skillful husbandman must till, and sow,
That ground's ill dressed, where blind men hold
      the plough.
Now in the Temple every saucy Jack
Opens his shop, and shows his pedlar's pack.
Instead of candles we enjoy the snuff,
10 For precious balm we have but kitchen-stuff.
The ruder sort are by these teachers led,
Who acorns eat, and might have better bread;
If this a propagation shall be found,
These build the house, which pull it to the
      ground; [8]

---

[1] Expressions of contempt for the common people were not peculiar to Royalists; they are to be found on both sides of the political conflict.

[2] "The common people, now masculine, now neither the one thing nor the other."

[3] *The new man* in reference to Christ as "the second Adam."

[4] *the lily of the valley, Sharon's rose* "I am the rose of Sharon, and the lily of the valleys" (Song of Solomon 2:1). Christians interpreted the Song as an allegory of Christ's love for his Bride, the Church; and the understanding was that Christ was the lily and the rose. More recently, these words are understood to have been spoken by the bride; see the New English Bible.

[5] *He is the Rock* etc. "they drank of that spiritual Rock that followed them, and that Rock was Christ" (I Corinthians 10:4).

[6] *The new illiterate Lay-Teachers* Members of radical religious groups, believing in the doctrine of the "inner light," and that preaching was "a gift of the Spirit," held that a university education was not necessary for a preacher. Several of the Anglican clergy in Watkyns' vicinity were dispossessed of their livings, as he was; but in many cases they were not replaced. This poem suggests that nevertheless radical sectarian preachers, perhaps itinerants, did hold forth from their pulpits.

[7] Εχας, ἔχας ἔϛε βέβηλοι "Far off, far off, o profane ones." Paul C. Davies notes that this was a formula recited at the beginning of the Mysteries to warn off the uninitiated (*Flamma Sine Fumo* p. 158).

[8] *propagation* The reference is to "An Act for the Better Propagation and Preaching of the Gospel in Wales," ordered by Parliament in February, 1649. Henry Vaughan, in his *Life of Paulinus*, wrote that Paulinus "preferred the indignation and hatred of the multitude to their love, he would not buy their friendship with the loss of Heaven, nor call those Saints and propagators, who were Devils and destroyers" (quoted from F.E. Hutchinson, *Henry Vaughan: A Life and Interpretation*, Oxford: Clarendon P, 1947, p. 115).

15   This is mere hocus-pocus; a strange slight,
    By putting candles out, to gain more light. [1]
    Mad men by virtue of this propagation,
    Have Bedlam left, and preach'd for Reformation.
    And they might well turn preachers, for we had
20   Many that were more foolish, and more mad.
    The tinker being one of excellent mettle,
    Begins to sound his doctrine with his kettle.
    And the laborious ploughman I bewail,
    Who now doth thresh the pulpit with his flail.
25   The lousy tailor with his holy thimble
    Doth patch a sermon up most quick and nimble.
    He doth his skill, and wisdom much express,
    When with his goose he doth the Scripture press. [2]
    The chandler now a man of light we find,
30   His candle leaves a stinking snuff behind.
    The apothecary, who can give a glister

    Unto a holy brother or a sister;
    Hath one dram of the spirit, and can pray,
    Or preach, and make no scruple of his way.
35   Thus false coin doth for current money pass.
    And precious stones are valued less than glass.
    Not disputation, but a rigid law
    Must keep these frantic sectarists in awe. [3]
    The itch of disputation will break out
40   Into a scab of error; which without
    Some speedy help will soon infect and run
    Through all the flock, where it hath once begun.
    I will take heed in these bad times, and care
    To shut my shop, but keep my constant ware.
45   Lord let thy tender vine no longer bleed,
    Call home thy shepherds which thy lambs may
      feed.
    —1662

---

[1] *mere hocus-pocus* the deceptive patter of a conjuror (*OED* Hocus-Pocus).

[2] *his goose* the tailor's smoothing iron (*OED* goose *sb* 5).

---

[3] *Not disputation*, etc. This couplet foreshadows the harsh penal laws against Non-conformists passed after the Restoration.

For none commends his judgement, that doth
    choose
That which a blind man only could refuse;
75 Such are the Towers which th'hoary Temples
    grace [1]
Of Cibele, when all her heavenly race [2]
Do homage to her, yet she cannot boast
Amongst that numerous, and celestial host,
More heroes than can Windsor, nor doth Fame's
80 Immortal book record more noble names.
Not to look back so far, to whom this Isle
Must owe the glory of so brave a pile;
Whether to Caesar, Albanact, or Brute,
The British Arthur, or the Danish Knute, [3]
85 (Though this of old no less contest did move,
Then when for *Homer*'s birth seven cities strove) [4]
(Like him in birth, thou shouldst be like in Fame,
As thine his fate, if mine had been his Flame.)
But whoso'ere it was, nature design'd
90 First a brave place, and then as brave a mind;
Nor to recount those several Kings, to whom
It gave a Cradle, or to whom a Tomb;
But thee (great *Edward*) and thy greater son, [5]
He that the lilies wore, and he that won, [6]
95 And thy *Bellona,* who deserves her share [7]

In all thy glories; of that royal pair [8]
Which waited on thy triumph, she brought one,
Thy son the other brought, and she that son;
Nor of less hopes could her great offspring prove,
100 A Royal Eagle cannot breed a Dove.
Then didst thou found that Order: whether love [9]
Or victory thy Royal thoughts did move,
Each was a noble cause, nor was it less
I'th institution, than the great success,
105 Whilst every part conspires to give it grace,
The King, the Cause, the Patron, and the place, [10]
Which foreign Kings, and Emperors esteem
The second honour to their Diademe.
Had thy great destiny but given thee skill,
110 To know as well, as power to act her will,
That from those Kings, who then thy captives were,
In after-times should spring a Royal pair, [11]
Who should possess all that thy mighty power,
Or thy desires more mighty did devour;
115 To whom their better fate reserves what ere
The Victor hopes for, or the vanquished fear;
That blood, which thou and thy great grandsire
    shed,
And all that since these sister nations bled,
Had been unspilt, had happy Edward known
120 That all the blood he spilt, had been his own;
Thou hadst extended through the conquer'd East,
Thine and the Christian name, and made them blest
To serve thee, while that loss this gain would bring,
Christ for their God, and *Edward* for their King;
125 When thou that Saint thy Patron didst design,
In whom the Martyr, and the Soldier join;

---

[1] *hoary* ancient; venerable from age, time-honoured (*OED* hoary *a* 1c).

[2] *Cibele* often referred to as mother of the gods (*OCD*).

[3] *Albanact...Brute...Knute* According to legend, Brute (or Brutus), the great grandson of the Trojan Aeneus, was one of the founding fathers of Britain, settling in England in the twelfth century B.C.E. Knute (or Canute) was a king of Denmark in the eleventh century who led a number of Viking raids into England.

[4] *Homer* The birthplace of the Greek author Homer was frequently disputed (*OCD*).

[5] *great Edward* Edward III of England.

[6] *He that the lilies wore* Edward claimed the French throne, and the French lily, through his mother, Isabella of France; *he that won* Edward's son, the Black Prince.

[7] *Bellona* Queen Philippa, wife of Edward III.

---

[8] *that royal pair* David II of Scotland was captured while Philippa was overseeing England in the absence of her son and husband. John II of France was captured by the Black Prince at the battle of Poitiers.

[9] *didst thou found that Order* Edward III created the Order of the Garter in 1348.

[10] *the patron* St. George is the patron saint of England.

[11] *a Royal pair* Charles I, of the Scottish royal house of Stuart; Henrietta Maria, daughter of Henri IV of France.

And when thou didst within the Azure round, [1]
(Who evil thinks may evil him confound) [2]
The English armies encircle, thou didst seem
130 But to foretell, and prophesy of him, [3]
Who has within that Azure round confin'd
These Realms, which Nature for their bound
    design'd.
That bound which to the world's extremest ends,
Endless herself, her liquid arms extends;
135 In whose heroic face I see the Saint
Better expressed, than in the liveliest paint;
That fortitude which made him famous here,
That heavenly piety, which Saints him there,
Who when this Order he forsakes, may he
140 Companion of that sacred Order be.
Here could I fix my wonder, but our eyes,
Nice as our tastes, affect varieties;
And though one please him most, the hungry guest
Tastes every dish, and runs through all the feast;
145 So having tasted *Windsor,* casting round
My wandring eye, an emulous Hill doth bound [4]
My more contracted sight, whose top of late
A chapel crown'd, till in the common fate [5]
The neighbouring Abbey fell, (may no such storm
150 Fall on our times, where ruin must reform.)
Tell me (my Muse) what monstrous dire offence,
What crime could any Christian King incense [6]
To such a rage? was't Luxury, or Lust?
Was he so temperate, so chaste, so just?
155 Were these their crimes? they were his own, much
    more.

But they (alas) were rich, and he was poor;
And having spent the treasures of his Crown,
Condemns their Luxury, to feed his own;
And yet this act, to varnish o're the shame
160 Of sacrilege, must bear devotion's name;
And he might think it just, the cause, and time
Considered well; for none commits a crime,
Appearing such, but as 'tis understood,
A real, or at least a seeming good.
165 While for the Church his learned pen disputes, [7]
His much more learned sword his pen confutes;
Thus to the Ages past he makes amends,
Their charity destroys, their faith defends. [8]
Then did Religion in a lazy Cell,
170 In empty, airy contemplations dwell;
And like the block unmoved lay, but ours
As much too active like the stork devours.
Is there no temperate Region can be known,
Betwixt their frigid, and our Torrid Zone?
175 Could we not wake from that lethargic dream,
But to be restless in a worse extreme?
And for that lethargy was there no cure,
But to be cast into a calenture? [9]
Can knowledge have no bound, but must advance
180 So far, to make us wish for ignorance?
And rather in the dark to grope our way,
Than led by a false guide to err by day?
Parting from thence 'twixt anger, shame, and fear
Those for what's past, and this for what's too near:
185 My eye descending from the Hill surveys
Where Thames amongst the wanton valleys
    strays; [10]
Thames the most lov'd of all the Ocean's sons,
By his old sire to his embraces runs,

---

[1] *Azure round*   the badge of the Garter. Azure is the blue colour in coats of arms (*OED* azure *a* 3).

[2] the motto of the Order of the Garter: *Honi soit quy mal y pense.*

[3] *But to foretell, and prophesy of him*   Charles I.

[4] *emulous Hill*   St. Anne's Hill, a smaller hill near to Cooper's Hill.

[5] *A chapel crown'd*   Chertsey Abbey, a Benedictine monastery. After the English Reformation, Henry VIII suppressed and ransacked the monasteries.

[6] *Christian King*   Henry VIII.

---

[7] *his learned pen disputes*   a reference to the religious writings of Henry VIII.

[8] an allusion to Henry's title *Fidei Defensor,* still borne by British monarchs.

[9] *calenture*   fever (*OED* calenture 2).

[10] *Thames*   The Thames runs 210 miles from the Cotswolds through London to the North Sea.

190 Hasting to pay his tribute to the Sea,
Like mortal life to meet Eternity:
And though his clearer sand no golden veins,
Like *Tagus* and *Pactolus* streams contains, [1]
His genuine, and less guilty wealth t'explore,
Search not his bottom, but behold his shore;
195 O're which he kindly spreads his spacious wing,
And hatches plenty for th'ensuing Spring,
Nor with a furious, and unruly wave,
Like profuse Kings, resumes the wealth he gave:
No unexpected inundations spoil
200 The mower's hopes, nor mock the plowman's toil:
Then like a lover he forsakes his shores,
Whose stay with jealous eyes his spouse implores,
Till with a parting kiss he saves her tears,
And promising return, secures her fears;
205 As a wise King first settles fruitful peace
In his own Realms, and with their rich increase
Seeks war abroad, and then in triumph brings
The spoils of Kingdoms, and the Crowns of Kings:
So Thames to *London* doth at first present
210 Those tributes, which the neighbouring countries
    sent;
But at his second visit from the East,
Spices he brings, and treasures from the West;
Finds wealth where 'tis, and gives it where it wants,
Cities in deserts, woods in cities plants,
215 Rounds the whole Globe, and with his flying towers
Brings home to us, and makes both Indies ours:
So that to us no thing, no place is strange
Whilst thy fair bosom is the world's Exchange:
O could my verse freely and smoothly flow,
220 As thy pure flood, heav'n should no longer know
Her old *Eridanus,* thy purer stream [2]
Should bathe the gods, and be the poets' theme.
Here Nature, whether more intent to please

Us or herself with strange varieties,
225 (For things of wonder give no less delight
To the wise maker's, than beholder's sight.
Though these delights from several causes move,
For so our children, thus our friends we love.)
Wisely she knew the harmony of things,
230 As well as that of sounds, from discords springs;
Such was the discord, which did first disperse
Form, order, beauty through the universe;
While dryness moisture, coldness heat resists,
All that we have, and that we are subsists:
235 While the steep horrid roughness of the wood
Strives with the gentle calmness of the flood.
Such huge extremes when Nature doth unite,
Wonder from thence results, from thence delight;
The stream is so transparent, pure, and clear,
240 That had the self-enamour'd youth gaz'd here, [3]
So fatally deceiv'd he had not been,
While he the bottom, not his face had seen.
And such the roughness of the Hill, on which
Diane her toils, and *Mars* his tents might pitch. [4]
245 And as our surly supercilious lords,
Big in their frowns, and haughty in their words,
Look down on those, whose humble fruitful pain
Their proud, and barren greatness must sustain:
So looks the Hill upon the stream, between
250 There lies a spacious, and a fertile Green;
Where from the woods, the Dryades oft meet [5]
The Nayades, and with their nimble feet [6]
Soft dances lead, although their airy shape
All but a quick Poetic sight escape;
255 There Faunus and Sylvanus keep their Courts, [7]

---

[3] *the self-enamour'd youth* Narcissus, a beautiful youth who loved no one until he saw his own reflection in water and fell in love with that; finally he pined away and died (*OCD*).

[4] *Diane* a Roman goddess associated with the hunt.

[5] *Dryades* nymphs supposed to inhabit trees (*OED* dryad 1).

[6] *Nayades* river nymphs (*OED* naiades).

[7] *Faunus* god of the herdsmen, often identified with Inuus, fertilizer of cattle, and with Pan. He was primarily of the forests (*OCD*); *Sylvanus* Roman god of uncultivated land (*OCD*).

---

[1] *Tagus and Pactolus* rivers famous in antiquity for their golden sands.

[2] *Eridanus* mythical river often associated with the Po (*OCD*); also used in astronomy as a name for a large constellation of stars in the Southern Hemisphere.

And thither all the horrid host resorts,
(When like the elixir, with his evening beams, [1]
The Sun has turn'd to gold the silver streams)
To graze the ranker mead, that noble herd, [2]
260 On whose sublime, and shady fronts is rear'd
Nature's great masterpiece, to shew how soon
Great things are made, but sooner much undone.
Here have I seen our *Charles*, when great affairs [3]
Give leave to slacken, and unbend his cares,
265 Chasing the royal Stag; the gallant beast,
Rous'd with the noise, 'twixt hope and fear
 distressed,
Resolves 'tis better to avoid, than meet
His danger, trusting to his winged feet:
But when he sees the dogs, now by the view
270 Now by the scent his speed with speed pursue,
He tries his friends, among the lesser herd,
Where he but lately was obey'd, and feared,
Safety he seeks; the herd unkindly wise,
Or chases him from thence, or from him flies;
275 Like a declining Statesman, left forlorn
To his friends' pity, and pursuers' scorn;
Wearied, forsaken, and pursued, at last
All safety in despair of safety plac't;
Courage he thence assumes, resolv'd to bear
280 All their assaults, since 'tis in vain to fear;
But when he sees the eager chase renew'd,
Himself by dogs, the dogs by men pursu'd;
When neither speed, nor art, nor friends, nor force
Could help him, towards the stream he bends his
 course;
285 Hoping those lesser beasts would not assay [4]
An Element more merciless then they:
But fearless they pursue, nor can the flood

Quench their dire thirst, (alas) they thirst for blood.
As some brave *Hero,* whom his baser foes
290 In troops surround, now these assail, now those,
Though prodigal of life, disdains to die [5]
By vulgar hands, but if he can descry
Some nobler foe's approach, to him he calls
And begs his fate, and then contented falls:
295 So the tall stag, amids the lesser hounds
Repels their force, and wounds returns for wounds,
Till *Charles* from his unerring hand lets fly
A mortal shaft, then glad and proud to die
By such a wound, he falls, the crystal flood
300 Dying he dyes, and purples with his blood:
This a more innocent, and happy chase
Than when of old, but in the self-same place,
Fair Liberty pursued, and meant a prey
To tyranny, here turn'd, and stood at bay.
305 When in that remedy all hope was plac't,
Which was, or should have been at least, the last.
For armed subjects can have no pretence
Against their Princes, but their just defence;
And whether then, or no, I leave to them
310 To justify, who else themselves condemn.
Yet might the face be just, if we may guess
The justness of an action from success,
Here was that Charter seal'd, wherein the Crown [6]
All marks of arbitrary power lays down:
315 Tyrant and Slave, those names of hate and fear,
The happier style of King and Subject bear:
Happy, when both to the same center move;
When Kings give liberty, and Subjects love.
Therefore not long in force this Charter stood
320 Wanting that seal, it must be seal'd in blood.
The Subjects arm'd, the more their Princes gave,
But this advantage took, the more to crave:
Till Kings by giving, give themselves away,
And even that power, that should deny, betray.
325 "Who gives constrain'd, but his own fear reviles,

---

[1] *elixir* by which metals were thought to change into gold (*OED* elixir *sb* 1).

[2] *ranker mead* a more luxurious meadow (*OED* rank *a* A III 10), (*OED* mead[2] a).

[3] *Charles* Charles I.

[4] *assay* attack, assault, assail (*OED* assay *v* 14).

---

[5] *prodigal* lavish in the disposal of things (*OED a* prodigal A 3).

[6] *Charter* the Magna Carta, signed in 1215 by King John, limited the power of the monarchy.

Not thank'd, but scorn'd; nor are they gifts, but
    spoils,"
And they, whom no denial can withstand,
Seem but to ask, while they indeed command.
Thus all to limit Royalty conspire,
330 While each forgets to limit his desire.
Till kings like old *Antaeus* by their fall, [1]
Being forc't, their courage from despair recall,
When a calm river rais'd with sudden rains,
Or snows dissolv'd o'reflows th'adjoining plains,
335 The husbandmen with high rais'd banks secure [2]
Their greedy hopes, and this he can endure.
But if with bays, and dams they strive to force,
His channel to a new, or narrow course,
No longer then within his banks he dwells,
340 First to a torrent, then a deluge swells;

Stronger, and fiercer by restraint, he roars,
And knows no bound, but makes his powers his
    shores:
Thus Kings by grasping more than they can hold,
First made their Subjects by oppressions bold,
345 And popular sway by forcing Kings to give
More, than was fit for Subjects to receive,
Ran to the same extreme; and one excess
Made both, by stirring to be greater, less;
Nor any way, but seeking to have more,
350 Makes either lose, what each possessed before.
Therefore their boundless power let Princes draw
Within the channel, and the shores of Law,
And may that Law, which teaches Kings to sway
Their Sceptres, teach their Subjects to obey.
—1642

---

[1] *Antaeus* a mythical king of Libya, and son of the Earth, who compelled all strangers to wrestle with him. If they managed to throw him to the ground, he would gain strength from his mother, the Earth. He was finally killed by Hercules who lifted him from the ground before crushing him to death (*OCD*).

[2] *husbandmen* men who till or cultivate the soil; farmers (*OED* husbandman 1a).

Richard Lovelace
1618 –1656/7

Richard Lovelace came of an old Kentish family. His father, Sir William, who had been knighted by James I, was killed in battle in Holland, leaving a widow and a large family, the eldest child being the future Cavalier poet. Lovelace was educated at Oxford, and in his account of notable Oxford graduates Anthony à Wood described him as "being then accounted the most amiable and beautiful person that ever eye beheld," and also of "innate modesty, virtue and courtly deportment which made him… much admired by the female sex." He was created Master of Arts prematurely, "at the request of a great lady belonging to the queen," universities then being every bit as responsive to external pressures as they are now. During his residence at Oxford Lovelace wrote a play, *The Scholar, a Comedy,* and also began his career as a writer of lyric. Lovelace became active in the Royalist interest before the outbreak of civil war, taking part in the Scottish expedition of 1639. In 1642 he undertook to deliver to Parliament the famous Kentish petition on the King's behalf, though he knew of its similarity to a previous petition which Parliament had ordered to be burnt by the common hangman. As a result he was committed to the Gatehouse at Westminster, where he wrote "To Althea, from Prison," regarded by contemporaries as a masterpiece and frequently reprinted. There are good reasons to believe that "To Lucasta. From Prison," once thought to have been written during his second period of imprisonment, was also written at this time. He was released after about seven weeks, and, though constrained himself by the conditions of his release, provided money to his brothers for the King's cause.

Between 1642 and 1646 he spent a considerable time in the Low Countries, returning at least twice to England. His interest in painting (he was admitted to the Freedom of the Painters Company in 1647) was no doubt strengthened during that time. After his release he lived for a time in London, on good terms with many "wits" of the time, but was later with the King in Oxford. He left England after the fall of that city in 1646, and fought for the French against Spain. He was back in England by 1648, and was soon imprisoned again, probably because of fears aroused by the uprising in Kent at Christmas 1647, provoked by the county committee's attempt to prohibit celebration of that feast. His book of verse, *Lucasta,* was licensed in February 1648 but publication was not allowed until May 1649. Andrew Marvell, in one of the dedicatory poems prefaced to the volume, considers why it should have been subject to such censorship. Lovelace seems to have spent his fortune in personal extravagance and in serving the King, and may have died in poverty in Gunpowder Alley in London, a known resort of "indigent refugees, lurking papists and delinquents." He died sometime between the summer of 1656 and the autumn of 1657. A second volume, *Lucasta. Posthume Poems,* dated 1659 but actually published in 1660, was seen through the press by his brother Dudley, along with *Elegies Sacred to the Memory of the Author: By several of his Friends.* The second *Lucasta* is generally thought to have nothing equal to the best poems in the 1649 volume; however, there are some interesting poems in which such creatures as an ant, a snail, a falcon, and a fly are discussed as emblems of the human political world.

❧❧❧

To Lucasta, Going to the Wars

I

Tell me not (sweet) I am unkind,
  That from the nunnery
Of thy chaste breast, and quiet mind,
  To war and arms I fly. [1]

II

5 True; a new mistress now I chase,
  The first foe in the field;
And with a stronger faith embrace
  A sword, a horse, a shield. [2]

III

Yet this inconstancy is such,
10 As you too shall adore;
I could not love thee (dear) so much,
  Lov'd I not honour more.
—1649

The Grasshopper

To my Noble Friend, Mr. Charles Cotton [3]

ODE
I

Oh thou that swing'st upon the waving hair
  Of some well-filled oaten beard,
Drunk ev'ry night with a delicious tear

Dropt thee from Heav'n, where now th' art
  reared.

II

5 The joys of earth and air are thine entire,
  That with thy feet and wings dost hop and fly;
And when thy poppy works thou dost retire
  To thy carved acron-bed to lie. [4]

III

Up with the day, the sun thou welcomst then,
10 Sportst in the gilt-plats of his beams,
And all these merry days mak'st merry men,
  Thy self, and melancholy streams.

IV

But ah the sickle! Golden ears are cropped;
  Ceres and *Bacchus* bid good night;
15 Sharp frosty fingers all your flowers have topped,
  And what scythes spared, winds shave off
    quite.

V

Poor verdant fool! And now green ice! thy joys
  Large and as lasting, as thy perch of grass,
Bid us lay in 'gainst winter, rain, and poise
20 Their floods, with an o'erflowing glass.

VI

Thou best of *men* and *friends*! we will create
  A genuine summer in each other's breast;
And spite of this cold time and frozen fate
  Thaw us a warm seat to our rest.

VII

25 Our sacred hearths shall burn eternally
  As vestal flames, the North-wind, he
Shall strike his frost-stretched wings, dissolve and fly
  This *Ætna* in epitome.

---

[1] *the nunnery* etc. This is a good example of Royalist coat-trailing, like similar apparently approving references to Roman Catholicism in Herrick and Vaughan.

[2] The poem evokes an earlier, "heroic" age, removed from the actualities of contemporary combat (the English cavalry did not carry shields, for example); this historical inaccuracy is suggestive of chivalrous attachment to the Royalist cause.

[3] Charles Cotton was a poet. In this poem, a translation of a Greek lyric attributed in the period to Anacreon, Lovelace expresses a common theme of the defeated Royalist, the retreat into private life, personal friendship, and the cup that cheers. The grasshopper is an extended metaphor of the impermanence of prosperity.

[4] *when thy poppy works* when you become sleepy, as if under the influence of opium; *acron* obsolete form of acorn (*OED*).

VIII

Dropping *December* shall come weeping in,
　　Bewail th' usurping of his reign;
30 But when in showers of old Greek we begin,
　　Shall cry, he hath his crown again!

IX

Night as clear *Hesper* shall our tapers whip
　　From the light casements where we play,
35 And the dark hag from her black mantle strip,
　　And stick there everlasting day.

X

Thus richer than untempted kings are we,
　　That asking nothing, nothing need:
Though Lord of all what seas embrace; yet he
40 　　That wants himself, is poor indeed.
—1649

To Lucasta. From Prison [1]
An Epode

I

Long in thy shackles, liberty,
　I ask not from these walls, but thee;
Left for a while another's bride
　　To fancy all the world beside.

II

5 Yet ere I do begin to love,
　　See! How I all my objects prove;
Then my free soul to that confine,
　　'Twere possible I might call mine.

III

First I would be in love with *Peace*,
10 　　And her rich swelling breasts increase;

But how alas! how may that be,
　　Despising Earth, will she love me?

IV

Faine would I be in love with *War*,
　　As my dear just avenging star;
15 But War is loved so ev'ry where,
　　Ev'n he disdains a lodging here.

V

Thee and thy wounds I would bemoan
　　Fair thorough-shot *Religion*;
But he lives only that kills thee,
20 　　And who so binds thy hands, is free.

VI

I would love a *Parliament*
　　As a main prop from Heaven sent;
But ah! Who's he that would be wedded
　　To the fairest body that's beheaded? [2]

VII

25 Next would I court my *Liberty,*
　　And then my birth-right, *Property;*
But can that be, when it is known
　　There's nothing you can call your own?

VIII

A *Reformation* I would have,
30 　　As for our griefs a *sovereign* salve;
That is, a cleansing of each wheel
　　Of state, that yet some rust doth feel:

IX

But not a Reformation so,
　　As to reform were to o'erthrow;
35 Like watches by unskilful men
　　Disjointed, and set ill again.

---

[1] This poem was almost certainly composed during Lovelace's first imprisonment, in 1642. The poem asks for liberty from Lucasta in order to find other objects of love.

[2] *the fairest body that's beheaded* presumably in reference to Parliament's repudiation of the authority of the King.

X

The *Public Faith* I would adore,
But she is bankrupt of her store; [1]
Nor how to trust her can I see,
For she that cozens all, must me.

40

XI

Since then none of these can be
Fit objects for my Love and me;
What then remains, but th' only spring
Of all our loves and joys? The KING.

XII

He who being the whole Ball
Of Day on Earth, lends it to all; [2]
When seeking to eclipse his right,
Blinded, we stand in our own light.

45

XIII

And now an universal mist
Of error is spread o'er each breast,
With such a fury edged, as is
Not found in th' inwards of th' abyss.

50

XIV

Oh from thy glorious starry wain
Dispense on me one sacred beam
To light me where I soon may see
How to serve you, and you trust me. [3]
—1649

55

To my Worthy Friend Mr. Peter Lilly;
on that excellent Picture of his Majesty, and the
Duke of York, drawn by him at Hampton-Court [4]

I

See! what a *clouded Majesty!* and eyes
Whose glory through their mist doth brighter
   rise!
See! what an humble bravery doth shine,
And grief triumphant breaking through each
   line;
How it commands the face! so sweet a scorn
Never did *happy misery* adorn!
So sacred a contempt! that others show
To this, (oth' height of all the wheel) below;
That mightiest monarchs by this shaded book
May copy out their proudest, richest look.

5

10

Whilst the true *Eaglet* this quick lustre spies,
And by his *Sun's* enlightens his own eyes; [5]
He cares his cares, his burthen feels, then straight
Joys that so lightly he can bear such weight;
Whilst either either's passion doth borrow,
And both do grieve the same victorious sorrow.

15

These my best *Lilly* with so bold a spirit
And soft a grace, as if thou didst inherit
For that time all their greatness, and didst draw
With those brave eyes your *Royal Sitters* saw.

20

Not as of old, when a rough hand did speak
A strong aspect, and a fair face, a weak;

---

[1] *Public Faith* "In order to finance the militia Parliament published 'proposals for the bringing in of money, or plate, to maintain horse, horsemen and arms.' 'And they further declared that whosoever brought in money or plate...should be repaid their money with interest of 8 per cent, for which they did engage the public faith'" (Clarendon, quoted by John Wilders, *Samuel Butler: Hudibras*, Oxford: Clarendon P, 1967, p. 352).

[2] *He who...Of Day on Earth* Lovelace is thinking in terms of the analogy between the sun in the heavens and the king on earth.

[3] It is possible that when he wrote this poem, Lovelace was already contemplating making his submission to Parliament with a view to obtaining his release from prison. The question of whether the King could thereafter trust him might well have been on his mind.

[4] The picture praised in this poem recorded one of the occasions when Charles, imprisoned at Hampton Court, was allowed to see his children. It is an interesting painting, regarded by art historians as marking a landmark in Lely's career. For an excellent, and complicating, discussion of both the painting and this poem, see Lois Potter, *Secret Rites and Secret Writing: Royalist Literature 1641–1660* (Cambridge: Cambridge U P, 1989), 65–71.

[5] *the true Eaglet* Again Lovelace is playing on the Sun-King parallel, and on the perception that eagles could gaze directly at the sun. In this case the "eaglet" is the future James II.

When only a black beard cried Villain, and
By *Hieroglyphicks* we could understand;
25 When crystal typified in a white spot,
And the bright ruby was but one red blot;
Thou dost the things *orientally* the same,
Not only paintst its colour, but its *flame*:
Thou sorrow canst design without a tear, [1]
30 And with the Man his very *Hope* or *Fear*;
So that th' amazed world shall henceforth find
None but my *Lilly* ever drew a *Mind*.
—1649

To Althea, From Prison [2]

SONG

I

When Love with unconfined wings
   Hovers within my gates;
And my divine *Althea* brings
   To whisper at the grates:
5 When I lie tangled in her hair,
   And fettered to her eye;
The *Gods* that wanton in the air,
   Know no such liberty. [3]

II

When flowing cups run swiftly round
10   With no allaying *Thames*,
Our careless heads with roses bound,
   Our hearts with loyal flames;
When thirsty grief in wine we steep,
   When healths and draughts go free,
15 Fishes that tipple in the deep,
   Know no such liberty.

III

When (like committed linnets) I
   With shriller throat shall sing
The sweetness, mercy, majesty,
20   And glories of my King;
When I shall voice aloud, how good
   He is, how great should be;
Enlarged winds that curl the flood,
   Know no such liberty.

IV

25 Stone walls do not a prison make,
   Nor iron bars a cage;
Minds innocent and quiet take
   That for an hermitage;
If I have freedom in my love,
30   And in my soul am free;
Angels alone that soar above,
   Enjoy such liberty.
—1649

The Ant [4]

1

Forbear thou great good husband, little Ant;
   A little respite from thy flood of sweat;
Thou, thine own horse and cart, under this plant
   Thy spacious tent, fan thy prodigious heat;
5 Down with thy double load of that one grain;
It is a granary for all thy train.

2

Cease large example of wise thrift a while,
   (For thy example is become our law) [5]
And teach thy frowns a seasonable smile:

---

[1] *Thou sorrow canst design without a tear*   Lovelace is here suggesting Lely's independence of crudely emblematic pointers, that is, his skill in psychological portraiture.

[2] This poem circulated in manuscript for seven years before it was published; at least six manuscripts survive.

[3] *Gods*   "birds" in some manuscripts.

---

[4] This poem does not merely flaunt Royalist liberality and love of pleasure, but suggests that Lovelace has given real thought to the opposition between two value systems.

[5] *For thy example is become our law*   This line points to the ant's meaning as an emblem of Puritanism.

10 So *Cato* sometimes the nak'd Florals saw. [1]
And thou almighty foe, lay by thy sting,
Whilst thy unpaid musicians, crickets, sing.

3

Lucasta, She that holy makes the day,
   And 'stils new life in fields of fueillemort: [2]
15 Hath back restor'd their verdure with one ray,
   And with her eye bid all to play and sport.
Ant to work still; Age will thee truant call;
And to save now, th' art worse than prodigal.

4

Austere and *Cynic!* not one hour t'allow,
20   To lose with pleasure what thou gotst with
      pain:
But drive on sacred festivals, thy plow;
   Tearing high-ways with thy o'er charged wain.
Not all thy life time one poor minute live,
And thy o'er laboured bulk with mirth relieve?

5

25 Look up then miserable ant, and spy
   Thy fatal foes, for breaking of her law,
Hov'ring above thee, Madam, *Margaret Pie*,
   And her fierce Servant, Meagre, Sir *John Daw:*
Thy self and storehouse now they do store up,
30 And thy whole harvest too within their crop.

6

Thus we unthrifty thrive within Earth's tomb,
   For some more rav'nous and ambitious jaw:

The *grain* in th' *ants*, the *ants* in the *pie's* womb,
   The *pie* in th' *hawk's*, the *hawks* ith' *eagle's*
      maw:
35 So scattering to hoard 'gainst a long day,
Thinking to save all, we cast all away.
—1660

To a Lady with child
that asked an Old Shirt

And why an honoured ragged shirt, that shows,
   Like tattered ensigns, all its body's blows?
Should it be swathed in a vest so dire,
It were enough to set the child on fire;
5 Dishevelled queens should strip them of their
      hair,
And in it mantle the new rising heir:
Nor do I know ought worth to wrap it in,
Except my parchment upper-coat of skin:
And then expect no end of its chaste tears,
10 That first was rolled in down, now furs of
      bears.
   But since to Ladies 't hath a custom been
Linen to send, that travail and lie in;
To the nine Sempstresses, my former friends, [3]
I sued, but they had nought but shreds and ends.
15 At last, the jolli'st of the three times three,
Rent th' apron from her smock, and gave it me,
'Twas soft and gentle, subtly spun no doubt;
Pardon my boldness, Madam; *Here's the clout.*
—1660

---

[1] *Cato sometimes the nak'd Florals saw* Lovelace understands Puritan objection to festivals as based upon their connection to pagan customs; this line is historically inaccurate but reflects the fact that "rather than prevent a popular custom, [Cato] left the theatre" (*Poems of Richard Lovelace*, ed. C.H. Wilkinson, Oxford: Clarendon P, 1930, p. 300).

[2] *fueillemort* of a faded colour (*Poems*, p. 300).

---

[3] *the nine Sempstresses, my former friends* that is, the nine Muses. He has no shirt to give her, so he offers her this poem.

Abraham Cowley
1618 – 1667

Abraham Cowley was the seventh child of Thomas Cowley, a London stationer. He was born after his father's death, and probably named after his godfather. When he was about ten he opened Spenser's *Faerie Queene* by chance, was "infinitely delighted" and resolved to be a poet himself. One of the most precocious of English poets, he was fifteen when *Poetical Blossoms* was published in 1633, but much of it may have been ready for the press two years earlier. Rumour of its impending publication may have been the occasion of the sonnet "How soon hath Time," by Milton, who was ten years older. 1633 was also notable as the year when the poems of John Donne and George Herbert first achieved print publication. Cowley has been thought of as the last of "the school of Donne." Cowley was educated at Westminster School and in 1636 went up to Trinity College, Cambridge, where he became a close friend of Richard Crashaw and of William Hervey, the first cousin of Henry Jermyn, who was to become Henrietta Maria's secretary and eventually Earl of St. Albans. This connection was later to become important to Cowley. As a young man, Cowley was ambitious for fame as a poet, imagining himself crossing the Alps of success as "the Muse's Hannibal." This ambition may explain his unwise attempt to write a religious epic, the *Davideis*, which was never completed. In 1642 he wrote a comedy, *The Guardian*, for a visit to Cambridge of the Prince of Wales; any hopes of becoming a professional dramatist were dashed by Parliament's banning of all stage performances shortly afterwards. In 1644 he was deprived of his position at Cambridge by the Earl of Manchester's commission, which required subscription to the Solemn League and Covenant. By then Cowley had already departed for Oxford, at that point in the hands of the Royalists; he became a member of the Great Tew circle which congregated around Lord Falkland, and was regarded as a leading Royalist poet. In the early summer of 1643 he began work on a long poem, *The Civil War*, which he abandoned after the first battle of Newbury (September 20, 1643) when it became apparent that history was providing the wrong plot.

Henrietta Maria left England in April 1644, never to see Charles I again. Some time before June 1646 Cowley was in Paris, in Jermyn's household. For several years he managed Henrietta Maria's correspondence (in cipher) with Charles, and, after Charles's death, with the Duke of York. Cowley may have been responsible for drawing Crashaw to the attention of Henrietta Maria. In Paris he is likely to have met Thomas Hobbes, whose philosophy, it has been argued, was important for the development of Cowley's poetic; he also met the diarist John Evelyn, who was to become a great friend, and Edmund Waller, his chief rival as a love poet. Having earlier declared his ambition to be "the Muse's Hannibal," he now decided that he would be "Love's Columbus." His poems in *The Mistress* (1647) provoked Dr. Johnson to say that they "might have been written for penance by a hermit, or for hire by a philosophical rhymer who had only heard of another sex."

In 1651 Cowley went to Scotland with letters for Charles II, and then to Jersey, still a Royalist stronghold, with a mission to sell Crown lands there to raise funds for the royal exiles. Hyde, later to be Lord Chancellor and the most powerful subject in the first years of the Restoration, suspected that Cowley had skimmed off a disproportionate commission. By the summer of 1654 he was back in England, with Cromwell's permission, studying medicine, perhaps as a cover, and now suspected by both sides. In April 1655 he was seized on suspicion of a plot against Cromwell, and only released when his friend, the doctor Charles Scarborough, put up a thousand pounds as warranty for his good behaviour. Like Lovelace, Cowley seems to have been profoundly affected by imprisonment, and the publication he prepared while incarcerated was to ensure that his years of work as a Royalist agent were not rewarded as he had hoped after the Restoration. The *Poems* of 1656, with its famous preface and the often enigmatic Pindaric Odes, have received a good deal of critical attention, in the hope that they might yield a sense of what Cowley's true political opinions were, and whether they were revealed or masked in the preface. His biographer, Bishop Sprat, wrote that he believed "that it would be a meritorious service to the King if any man who was known to have followed his interest could insinuate into the usurpers' minds that men of his principles were now willing to be quiet, and could persuade the poor oppressed Royalists to conceal their affections for better occasions." Unfortunately for Cowley, neither Hyde nor Charles saw it that way, Hyde being angered at the apparent desertion of the Royalist cause expressed in the preface and Charles perhaps concerned by the apparent endorsement of the assassination of a ruler in the "Brutus" ode. It is worth noting, though, that the *Poems* of 1656, like *The Mistress* of 1647, were published by Humphrey Moseley, the leading Royalist publisher of the period.

After his release from prison, Cowley lived in London under surveillance from both sides. He was admitted to the degree of "doctor of physick" at Oxford in December 1657, but there is no evidence that he ever practised. A more notable defector from the Royalist cause at that time was the Duke of Buckingham, who was an admirer of Cowley's work and became a consistent supporter. Another important friend made at this time was Thomas Sprat, still an undergraduate at Wadham College, Oxford, as was the future Earl of Rochester. When it finally became clear that Charles II would be restored to the throne, Cowley tried to rid himself of the suspicion caused by the *Poems* of 1656, writing a long letter to Ormonde at the royal headquarters in Brussels on December 26, 1659. He received no direct help from Charles, but the King did order Trinity College to reinstate him in his fellowship and Cowley was allowed to resume his service to Jermyn. His suit for the mastership of the Savoy, a lucrative sinecure which had been promised him by Charles I, was unsuccessful; his poem in response to this disappointment, "The Complaint," cannot be regarded as a model of stoic fortitude. However, Cowley was far from impoverished during the seven years that remained to him after the Restoration. He had the income from his Cambridge fellowship, a profitable association with Davenant in the newly revived London theatre, with two of his own plays quite popular, and, from 1662, a substantial grant of lands from Henrietta Maria. Moreover, he continued to lead an active intellectual life, with friends among those who founded the Royal Society. He was among those who floated a plan to regularize the English language, and he turned his retirement from affairs of state to good account by becoming a keen amateur gardener, with the help of his friend John Evelyn. His essays, among the most attractive of his writings, are the product of these retired years. He was regarded, by the time of his death, as the greatest poet of his age, and according to Evelyn "near one hundred coaches of noblemen and persons of quality" attended his funeral. He was buried in Westminster Abbey next to Chaucer and Spenser.

☙☙☙

The Wish

1

Well then; I now do plainly see,
   This busy world and I shall ne'r agree;
The very *honey* of all earthly joy
  Does of all meats the soonest *cloy*,
5   And they (methinks) deserve my pity,

Who for it can endure the stings,
  The *crowd*, and *buzz*, and *murmurings*
   Of this great *hive*, the City.

2

  Ah, yet ere I descend to th' grave
10 May I a *small house*, and *large garden* have!
And a *few friends*, and *many books*, both true,
  Both wise, and both delightful too!

And since *Love* ne'r will from me flee,
A *mistress* moderately fair,
15 And good as *guardian-angels* are,
Only belov'd, and loving me!

3

Oh, *fountains*, when in you shall I
My self, eased of unpeaceful thoughts, espy?
Oh *fields!* Oh *woods!* when, when shall I be made
20 The happy *tenant* of your shade?
Here's the spring-head of *pleasure's* flood;
Here's wealthy *Nature's Treasury*,
Where all the *riches* lie, that she
Has coined and stamped for good.

4

25 *Pride* and *Ambition* here,
Only in *far fetched metaphors* appear;
Here nought but *winds* can hurtful *murmurs*
scatter,
And nought but *Echo flatter.*
The *gods*, when they descended, hither
30 From heaven did always choose their way;
And therefore we may boldly say,
That 'tis the *way* too *thither.*

5

How happy here should I,
And one dear *She*, live, and embracing die?
35 *She* who is all the world, and can exclude
In *deserts solitude.*
I should have then this only fear,
Lest men, when they my pleasures see,
Should hither throng to live like me,
40 And so make a *city* here.
—1647

The Grasshopper [1]

Happy *insect*, what can be
In happiness compared to thee?
Fed with nourishment divine,
The dewy *morning's* gentle *wine!*
5 *Nature* waits upon thee still,
And thy verdant cup does fill,
'Tis filled where ever thou dost tread,
Nature self's thy Ganymede. [2]
Thou dost drink, and dance, and sing;
10 Happier than the happiest *King!*
All the *fields* which thou dost see,
All the *plants* belong to *thee*,
All that *summer hours* produce,
Fertile made with early juice.
15 Man for thee does sow and plow;
Farmer he, and *landlord thou!*
Thou dost innocently joy;
Nor does thy *luxury* destroy;
The *shepherd* gladly heareth thee,
20 More harmonious than he.
Thee country hinds with gladness hear,
Prophet of the ripened year!
Thee *Phoebus* loves, and does inspire;
Phoebus in himself thy *sire.*
25 To thee of all things upon earth,
Life is no longer than thy *mirth.*
Happy *insect*, happy thou,
Dost neither *age*, nor *winter* know.
But when thou'st drunk, and danced, and sung,
30 Thy fill, the flowry leaves among
(*Voluptuous*, and *wise* with all,
Epicurean animal!)
Sated with thy *summer feast*,
Thou retir'st to endless *rest.*
—1656

---

[1] Compare Lovelace's poem of the same title.

[2] *Ganymede*   a Trojan youth, whom Zeus made his cupbearer.

The Innocent Ill

1

Though all thy gestures and discourses be
    Coined and stamped by *Modesty*,
    Though from thy *tongue* ne'er slipped away
One word which *nuns* at th' *altar* might not say,
5   Yet such a sweetness, such a grace
      In all thy *speech* appear,
     That what to th' *eye* a beauteous face,
      That thy *tongue* is to th' *ear*.
    So cunningly it wounds the heart,
10   It strikes such heat through ev'ry part,
That thou a *tempter* worse then *Satan* art.

2

Though in thy thoughts scarce any tracks have been
    So much as of *Original* Sin,
15   Such charms thy *beauty* wears as might
Desires in dying confessed *Saints* excite.
     Thou with strange *adultery*
      Dost in each breast a *brothel keep*;
     Awake all men do *lust* for thee,
20   And some *enjoy* thee when they *sleep*.
    Ne'er before did *woman* live,
    Who to such *multitudes* did give
The *root* and cause of *sin*, but only *Eve*.

3

Though in thy breast so quick a *pity* be,
25   That a *fly's death's* a *wound* to thee.
     Though savage, and rock-hearted those
Appear, that weep not even *romances'* woes.
     Yet ne'er before was tyrant known,
      Whose rage was of so large extent,
30   The ills thou dost are *whole* thine own,
Thou'rt *principal* and *instrument*;
    In all the deaths that come from you,
    You do the *treble office* do
Of *judge*, of *torturer*, and of *weapon* too.

4

35 Thou *lovely instrument* of *angry Fate*,
     Which *God* did for our faults create!
     Thou *pleasant, universal ill*,
Which *sweet* as *health*, yet like a *plague* dost kill!
     Thou kind, well-natured *tyranny!*
40 Thou *chaste* committer of a *rape!*
     Thou *voluntary destiny*,
      Which no man *can*, or *would* escape!
    So gentle, and so glad to spare,
    So wondrous good, and wondrous fair,
45 (We know) even the *destroying angels* are.
—1656

On the Death of Mr. Crashaw

Poet and *Saint*! to thee alone are given
  The two most sacred *names* of *Earth* and
    Heaven.
The hard and rarest *union* which can be
Next that of *Godhead* with *Humanity*. [1]
5 Long did the *Muses* banished *slaves* abide,
And built vain *Pyramids* to mortal pride;
Like *Moses* thou (though spells and charms
    withstand)
Hast brought them nobly home back to their *Holy*
    Land.
    Ah wretched *we*, poets of *Earth!* but *thou*
10 Wert *living* the same *poet* which thou'rt *now*.
Whilst *angels* sing to thee their airs divine,
And joy in an applause so great as *thine*.
Equal society with them to hold,
Thou need'st not make *new songs*, but say the *old*.
15 And they (kind spirits!) shall all rejoice to see
How little less then *they*, *exalted man* may be.
Still the old *heathen gods* in *numbers* dwell,
The *heavenliest* thing on *Earth* still keeps up *Hell*.
Nor have we yet quite purged the *Christian land*;

---

[1] *[the union] of Godhead with Humanity* as in the traditional Christian understanding of Jesus.

20 Still *idols* here, like *calves* at *Bethel* stand.
And though *Pan's death* long since all *oracles*
    broke, [1]
Yet still in rhyme the *fiend Apollo* spoke:
Nay with the worst of heathen dotage we
(Vain men!) the *monster woman deify*;
25 Find *stars*, and tie our *fates* there in a *face*,
And *Paradise* in them by whom we *lost* it, place.
What different faults corrupt our *Muses* thus?
Wanton as girls, as *old wives, fabulous!*
     Thy spotless *Muse*, like *Mary*, did contain
30 The boundless *Godhead*; she did well disdain
That her *eternal verse* employed should be
On a less subject than *eternity*;
And for a sacred *mistress* scorned to take,
But her whom *God* himself scorned not his *spouse*
    to make.
35 It (in a kind) *her miracle* did do;
A fruitful *mother* was, and *virgin* too.
     How well (blest Swan) did fate contrive thy
        death;
And made thee render up thy tuneful breath
In thy great *mistress'* arms? thou most divine
40 And richest *offering* of *Loretto's shrine!*
Where like some holy *sacrifice* t'expire,
A *fever* burns thee, and *love* lights the *fire*.
Angels (they say) brought the famed *chapel* there,
And bore the sacred load in triumph through the
    air.
45 'Tis surer much they brought thee there, and *they*,
And *thou*, their charge, went *singing* all the way.
     Pardon, my *Mother Church*, if I consent
That *angels* led him when from *thee* he went,
For even in *error* sure no *danger* is
50 When joined with so much *piety* as *his*.
Ah, mighty *God*, with shame I speak't, and grief,
Ah that our greatest *faults* were in *belief!*
And our weak *reason* were even weaker yet,

---

[1] *Pan's death...all oracles broke* in reference to the tradition that
idolatrous gods and oracles were destroyed by Christ; see Milton, *On
the Morning of Christ's Nativity.*

Rather than thus our *wills* too strong for it.
55 His *faith* perhaps in some nice tenents might
Be wrong; his *life*, I'm sure, was *in the right*. [2]
And I myself a *Catholic* will be,
So far at least, great *Saint*, to *pray* to thee. [3]
     Hail, *bard triumphant!* and some care bestow
60 On *us*, the *poets militant* below! [4]
Opposed by our old encmy, adverse *Chance*,
Attacked by *envy*, and by *ignorance*,
Enchained by *beauty*, tortured by *desires*,
Exposed by *tyrant-love* to savage *beasts* and *fires*.
65 Thou from low earth in nobler *flames* didst rise,
And like *Elijah*, mount *alive* the skies. [5]
Elisha-like (but with a wish much less, [6]
More fit thy *greatness*, and my *littleness*)
Lo here I beg (I whom thou once didst prove
70 So humble to *esteem*, so good to *love*)
Not that thy *spirit* might on me *doubled* be,
I ask but *half* thy mighty *spirit* for me.
And when my *Muse* soars with so strong a wing,
'Twill learn of things *divine*, and first of *thee* to
    sing.
—1656

---

[2] *nice tenents* fine points of theology. Cowley has to deal with the
fact that Crashaw had converted to Roman Catholicism.

[3] *to pray to thee* Roman Catholics addressed intercessory prayers to
the saints; the Reformed religions considered this an idolatrous
practice.

[4] *bard triumphant...poets militant* in allusion to the Church
Triumphant (the host of Christians who died in the faith and are
considered to be in Heaven) and the Church Militant (the Church
here on earth, still battling against evil).

[5] *like Elijah, mount alive the skies* "there appeared a chariot of fire,
and horses of fire...And Elijah went up by a whirlwind into heaven"
(II Kings 2:11).

[6] *Elisha-like* Elisha asked for a "double portion" of Elijah's spirit (II
Kings 2:9).

To Mr. Hobbes

1

Vast *bodies* of *philosophy*
   I oft have seen, and read,
     But all are *bodies dead*,
   Or *bodies* by *art fashioned*;
5 I never yet the *living soul* could see,
     But in thy *books* and *thee*.
       'Tis only *God* can know
   Whether the fair *Idea* thou dost show
   Agree entirely with his *own* or no.
10   This I dare boldly tell,
   'Tis so *like Truth*, 'twill serve our turn as well.
Just, as in *Nature*, their *proportions* be,
   As full of *concord* their *variety*,
   As *firm* the parts upon their *center* rest,
15 And all so *solid* are, that they at least
   As much as *Nature*, *emptiness* detest.

2

Long did the mighty *Stagirite* retain
   The *universal intellectual reign*; [1]
   Saw his own country's short-lived *leopard* slain;
20 The stronger *Roman-eagle* did outfly,
   Oftner *renewed* his *age*, and saw that *die*.
Mecca itself, in spite of *Mahumet*, possessed,
   And chased by a wild *deluge* from the east,
   His *monarchy* new-planted in the *west*.
25 But as in time each great imperial race
   Degenerates, and gives some new one place:
     So did this noble *Empire* waste,
     Sunk by degrees from glories past,
   And in the *school-men's* hands it perished quite at
     last. [2]
30   Then nought but words it grew,

And those all barb'rous too, [3]
   It perished, and it vanished there,
The *life* and *soul* breathed out became but empty
   air.

3

The *fields* which answered well the *ancients' plow*,
35 Spent and out-worn return no *harvest* now,
   In barren *age* wild and unglorious lie,
     And boast of *past fertility*,
   The *poor relief* of *present poverty*.
     Food and *fruit* we must now want:
40   Unless new *lands* we *plant*.
We break up *tombs* with *sacrilegious hands*,
     Old *rubbish* we remove;
To walk in *ruins*, like vain *ghosts*, we love,
     And with fond *divining wands*,
45   We search among the *dead*
     For treasures *buried*;
   Whilst still the *liberal Earth* does hold
So many *virgin mines* of *undiscovered gold*.

4

The *Baltic*, *Euxin*, and the *Caspian*,
50 And slender-limbed *Mediterranean*,
   Seem narrow *creeks* to *thee*, and only fit.
For the poor wretched *fisher-boats* of *Wit*.
Thy nobler *vessel* the vast *ocean* tries,
     And nothing sees but *seas* and *skies*,
55   'Till unknown *regions* it descries,
Thou great *Columbus* of the *golden lands* of *new*
   philosophies.
     Thy task was harder much than his,
     For thy learned *America* is
   Not only found out first by thee,
60 And rudely left to *future Industry*,
     But thy *eloquence* and thy *wit*
Has *planted*, *peopled*, *built*, and *civilized* it.

---

[1] *the mighty Stagirite* Aristotle, who was born at Stageira. He was a vastly influential philosopher for centuries, and an important aspect of early modern intellectual life was the attempt to dethrone his philosophy.

[2] *the school-men* the scholastic philosophers of the Middle Ages.

---

[3] *barb'rous* like the speech of barbarians. See the interesting entry under barbarous *a* (*OED*).

5

I little thought before,
(Nor, being my *own self* so *poor*,
65   Could comprehend so vast a *store*)
That all the *wardrobe* of rich *eloquence*
Could have afforded half enough,
Of *bright*, of *new*, and *lasting* stuff,
To clothe the mighty *limbs* of thy *gigantic sense*.
70 Thy solid *reason* like the *shield* from heaven
To the *Trojan Hero* given, [1]
Too strong to take a mark from any mortal dart,
Yet shines with *gold* and *gems* in every part,
And *wonders* on it graved by the learn'd hand of
Art;
75   A *shield* that gives delight
Even to the *enemies'* sight,
Then, when they're sure to lose the *combat* by't.

6

Nor can the *snow* which now cold *Age* does shed
Upon thy reverend head,
80 Quench or allay the noble *fires* within,
But all which thou hast *been*,
And all that *youth* can *be*, thou'rt yet,
So fully still dost thou
Enjoy the *manhood*, and the *bloom* of *wit*,
85 And all the *natural heat*, but not the *fever* too.
So *contraries* on *Ætna's* top conspire,
Here hoary *frosts*, and by them breaks out *fire*;
A secure *peace* the *faithful neighbours* keep,
Th' embolden'd *snow* next to the *flames* does
sleep.
90   And if we weigh, like *thee*,
Nature, and *causes*, we shall see
That thus it *needs must be*.
To things *immortal Time* can do no wrong,

And that which never is *to die*, for ever must be
young.
—1656

Brutus

1

Excellent *Brutus*, of all human race
The best, 'till *Nature* was improved by *Grace*, [2]
'Till men above *themselves faith* raised more
Than *reason* above *beasts* before.
5 Virtue was thy *life's center*, and from thence
Did *silently* and *constantly* dispense
The gentle vigorous *influence*
To all the wide and fair *circumference*:
And all the *parts* upon it leaned so easily,
10 Obeyed the mighty *force* so *willingly*,
That none could discord or disorder see
In all their *contrariety*.
Each had his motion natural and free,
And the *whole* no more *moved* than the *whole*
world could be.

2

15 From thy strict Rule some think that thou didst
swerve
(*Mistaken honest men*) in *Cæsar's* blood; [3]
What *mercy* could the *tyrant's life* deserve,
From him who killed *himself* rather than serve? [4]
Th' *heroic exaltations* of *good*
20   Are so far from *understood*,
We count them *vice*: Alas our *sight's* so ill,
That things which swiftest *move* seem to stand *still*.
We look not upon *Virtue* in her height,
On her supreme *idea*, brave and bright,

---

[1] *the shield from heaven / To the Trojan Hero given* In Virgil's *Aeneid*, Book 8.615 ff., there is an elaborate description of the shield Vulcan makes for Aeneas, with its depiction of Roman history culminating in the Battle of Actium.

[2] *'till Nature was improved by Grace* until the Christian dispensation. See the ending of the poem.

[3] *Cæsar's blood* For a vivid portrayal of the role of Brutus in the assassination, see Shakespeare's *Julius Caesar*.

[4] *him who killed himself* Brutus killed himself after being defeated by Octavian and Antony.

25   In the *original light*:
      But as her *beams* reflected pass
Through our own *nature* or ill *custom's glass*.
      And 'tis no wonder so,
      If with dejected eye
30   In standing *pools* we seek the *sky*,
That *stars* so high *above* should seem to us *below*.

3

      Can we stand by and see
Our *mother* robbed, and bound, and ravished be,
      Yet not to her assistance stir,
35 Pleas'd with the *strength* and *beauty* of the
      ravisher?
Or shall we fear to kill him, if before
      The *cancelled name* of *friend* he bore?
      Ingrateful Brutus do they call?
Ingrateful Cæsar who could *Rome* enthral!
40 An act more barbarous and unnatural
(In th' exact balance of true *virtue* tried)
Than his *successor Nero's parricide*! [1]
      There's none but *Brutus* could deserve
      That all men else should *wish* to *serve*,
45 And *Cæsar's* usurped place to him should proffer;
None can deserve 't but he who would *refuse* the
      offer.

4

Ill Fate assumed a *body* thee t' affright,
And wrapt itself i' th' terrors of the *night*;
I'll meet thee at Philippi, said the *spright*:
50   *I'll meet thee there*, saidst *thou*,
      With such a *voice*, and such a *brow*,
As put the trembling *ghost* to sudden flight;
      It vanished as a *taper's* light
      Goes out when *spirits* appear in sight.

55 One would have thought t' had heard the
      morning crow,
      Or seen her well-appointed *star*
Come marching up the *eastern hill* afar.
Nor durst it in *Philippi's* field appear,
      But *unseen* attacked thee there.
60 Had it presum'd in any shape thee to oppose,
Thou wouldst have forced it back upon thy foes:
      Or slain't like *Cæsar*, though it be
A *Conqu'ror* and a *Monarch* mightier far than
      he.

5

What joy can *human things* to us afford,
65 When we see perish thus by odd events,
      Ill men, and wretched *accidents*,
The best *cause* and best *man* that ever drew a
      sword?
          When we see
The false *Octavius*, and wild *Antony*,
      God-like *Brutus*, conquer *thee*?
70 What can we say but thine own *tragic word*,
That *Virtue*, which had worshipped been by thee
As the most solid *good*, and greatest *deity*,
      By this fatal proof became
      An idol only, and a *name*.
75   Hold noble *Brutus*, and restrain
The bold voice of thy generous *disdain*:
      These mighty *gulfs* are yet
Too deep for all thy *judgment* and thy *wit*.
80 The *time's* set forth already which shall quell
Stiff *Reason*, when it offers to *rebel*;
      Which these great *secrets* shall unseal,
      And new *philosophies* reveal.
A few years more, so soon hadst thou not died,
85 Would have confounded *human virtue's* pride,
      And show'd thee a *God crucified*.
—1656

---

[1] *Nero's parricide!* Agrippina, the wife of the Emperor Claudius, persuaded him to adopt her son Nero; four years later Claudius died; it was generally believed that Agrippina handed him a dish of poisonous mushrooms (see *OCD* articles on Nero and Claudius).

To the Royal Society

1

Philosophy the great and only heir
Of all that human knowledge which has been
Unforfeited by man's rebellious sin,
    Though full of years he do appear,
5 (Philosophy, I say, and call it, he,
For whatsoe'er the painter's fancy be,
    It a male-virtue seems to me)
Has still been kept in nonage till of late,
Nor managed or enjoyed his vast estate:
10 Three or four thousand years one would have
        thought,
To ripeness and perfection might have brought
    A science so well bred and nursed,
And of such hopeful parts too at the first.
But, oh, the guardians and the tutors then,
15 (Some negligent, and some ambitious men)
Would ne'er consent to set him free,
Or his own natural powers to let him see,
Lest that should put an end to their authority.

2

That his own business he might quite forget,
20 They amused him with the sports of wanton wit,
With the desserts of poetry they fed him,
Instead of solid meats t' increase his force;
Instead of vigorous exercise they led him
Into the pleasant labyrinths of ever-fresh discourse:
25   Instead of carrying him to see
The riches which do hoarded for him lie
    In Nature's endless treasury,
    They chose his eye to entertain
    (His curious but not covetous eye)
30 With painted scenes, and pageants of the brain.
Some few exalted spirits this latter age has shown,
That laboured to assert the liberty
(From guardians, who were now usurpers grown)
Of this old *minor* still, captived philosophy;
35   But 'twas rebellion called to fight

For such a long-oppressed right.
Bacon at last, a mighty man, arose
    Whom a wise King and Nature chose
    Lord Chancellor of both their laws, [1]
40 And boldly undertook the injured pupil's cause.

3

Authority, which did a body boast,
Though 'twas but air condensed, and stalked about,
Like some old giant's more gigantic ghost,
    To terrify the learned rout
45 With the plain magic of true Reason's light,
    He chased out of our sight,
Nor suffered living men to be misled
    By the vain shadows of the dead:
To graves, from whence it rose, the conquered
        phantom fled;
50   He broke that monstrous god which stood
In midst of th' orchard, and the whole did claim,
    Which with a useless scythe of wood, [2]
    And something else not worth a name,
    (Both vast for show, yet neither fit
55   Or to defend, or to beget;
    Ridiculous and senseless terrors!) made
Children and superstitious men afraid.
    The orchard's open now, and free;
Bacon has broke that scarecrow deity;
60   Come, enter, all that will,
Behold the ripened fruit, come gather now your fill.
    Yet still, methinks, we fain would be
    Catching at the forbidden tree,
    We would be like the deity,
65 When truth and falsehood, good and evil, we
Without the senses' aid within ourselves would see;

---

[1] *Bacon* Francis Bacon's philosophy was influential upon the group which founded the Royal Society, and for that reason he has been regarded as the father of English experimental science.

[2] *scythe* The form "sith" in early editions is closer to the etymologically correct "sithe." The scythe was an attribute of Time and of Death (*OED* scythe *sb*).

For 'tis God only who can find
All Nature in his mind.

4

From words, which are but pictures of the thought,
70 (Though we our thoughts from them perversely
        drew)
To things, the mind's right object, he it brought,
Like foolish birds to painted grapes we flew;
He sought and gathered for our use the true;
And when on heaps the chosen bunches lay,
75 He pressed them wisely the mechanic way,
Till all their juice did in one vessel join,
Ferment into a nourishment divine,
        The thirsty soul's refreshing wine.
Who to the life an exact piece would make,
80 Must not from other's work a copy take;
        No, not from Rubens or van Dyke; [1]
Much less content himself to make it like
Th' ideas and the images which lie
In his own fancy, or his memory.
85   No, he before his sight must place
        The natural and living face;
        The real object must command
Each judgment of his eye, and motion of his
        hand.

5

From these and all long errors of the way,
90 In which our wandring predecessors went,
And like th' old Hebrews many years did stray
        In deserts but of small extent,
Bacon, like Moses, led us forth at last,
        The barren wilderness he past,
95   Did on the very border stand
        Of the blessed promised land,
And from the mountain's top of his exalted wit,

Saw it himself, and showed us it.
But life did never to one man allow
100 Time to discover worlds, and conquer too;
Nor can so short a line sufficient be
To fathom the vast depths of Nature's sea:
        The work he did we ought t' admire,
        And were unjust if we should more require
105 From his few years, divided 'twixt th' excess
Of low affliction, and high happiness.
For who on things remote can fix his sight,
That's always in a triumph, or a fight?

6

From you, great champions, we expect to get
110 These spacious countries but discovered yet;
Countries where yet instead of Nature, we
Her images and idols worshipped see:
These large and wealthy regions to subdue,
Though Learning has whole armies at command,
115   Quartered about in every land,
A better troop she ne'er together drew.
        Methinks, like Gideon's little band,
        God with design has picked out you,
To do these noble wonders by a few: [2]
120 When the whole host he saw, they are (said he)
        Too many to o'ercome for me;
        And now he chooses out his men,
        Much in the way that he did then:
        Not those many whom he found
125   Idly extended on the ground,
        To drink with their dejected head
The stream just so as by their mouths it fled:
        No, but those few who took the waters up,
And made of their laborious hands the cup.

7

130 Thus you prepared; and in the glorious fight
        Their wondrous pattern too you take:
Their old and empty pitchers first they brake,
And with their hands then lifted up the light.

---

[1] *Rubens or van Dyke* Sir Peter Paul Rubens (1588–1640) and Sir
Anthony van Dyck (1599–1641), both very important in the history
of English painting. See Margaret Whinney and Oliver Millar, *English
Art 1625–1714* (Oxford: Clarendon P, 1957).

---

[2] *Gideon's little band* See Judges 7.

Io! Sound too the trumpets here!
135 Already your victorious lights appear;
New scenes of Heaven already we espy,
And crowds of golden worlds on high;
Which from the spacious plains of earth and sea
    Could never yet discovered be
140 By sailor's or Chaldean's watchful eye. [1]
Nature's great works no distance can obscure,
No smallness her near objects can secure
    Y' have taught the curious sight to press
    Into the privatest recess
145 Of her imperceptible littleness.
    Y' have learn'd to read her smallest hand,
And well begun her deepest sense to understand.

8

Mischief and true dishonour fall on those
Who would to laughter or to scorn expose
150 So virtuous and so noble a design, [2]
So human for its use, for knowledge so divine.
The things which these proud men despise, and
        call
    Impertinent, and vain, and small,
Those smallest things of Nature let me know,
155 Rather than all their greatest actions do.
Whoever would deposed truth advance
    Into the throne usurped from it,
Must feel at first the blows of ignorance,
    And the sharp points of envious wit.
160 So when by various turns of the celestial dance,
    In many thousand years
    A star, so long unknown, appears,
Though Heaven itself more beauteous by it grow,
It troubles and alarms the world below,
165 Does to the wise a star, to fools a meteor show.

9

With courage and success you the bold work begin;
    Your cradle has not idle been:
None e'er but *Hercules* and you could be
At five years age worthy a history. [3]
170   And ne'er did fortune better yet
    Th' historian to the story fit:
    As you from all old errors free
And purge the body of philosophy;
    So from all modern follies he
175 Has vindicated eloquence and wit.
His candid style like a clean stream does slide,
    And his bright fancy all the way
    Does like the sunshine in it play;
It does like Thames, the best of rivers, glide,
180 Where the god does not rudely overturn,
    But gently pour the crystal urn,
And with judicious hand does the whole current
    guide.
T' has all the beauties Nature can impart,
And all the comely dress without the paint of art.
—1667

Sors Virgiliana

Aeneid Book 4, verse 615

By a bold people's stubborn arms oppressed,
Forced to forsake the land which he possessed,
Torn from his dearest son, let him in vain
Beg help, and see his friends unjustly slain:
5 Let him to bold unequal terms submit,
In hopes to save his Crown; but lose both it
And life at once: untimely let him die
And on an open stage unburied lie.
—1692

---

[1] *Chaldean* one skilled in occult learning; an astrologer (*OED* Chaldean B *sb*).

[2] *to laughter or to scorn* The experiments conducted by members of the Royal Society were satirized from its earliest days and well into the eighteenth century.

---

[3] *a history* Thomas Sprat's *History of the Royal Society* was published in 1667.

Of Solitude

1

Hail, old patrician trees, so great and good!
    Hail ye plebeian under wood!
      Where the poetic birds rejoice,
And for their quiet nests and plenteous food,
5   Pay with their grateful voice.

2

Hail, the poor Muses' richest manor seat!
    Ye country houses and retreat,
      Which all the happy gods so love,
That for you oft they quit their bright and great
10   Metropolis above.

3

Here Nature does a house for me erect,
    Nature the wisest architect,
      Who those fond artists does despise
That can the fair and living trees neglect;
15   Yet the dead timber prize.

4

Here let me careless and unthoughtful lying,
    Hear the soft winds above me flying,
      With all their wanton boughs dispute,
And the more tuneful birds to both replying,
20   Nor be myself too mute.

5

A silver stream shall rule his waters near,
    Gilt with the sun-beams here and there
      On whose enamelled bank I'll walk,
And see how prettily they smile, and hear
25   How prettily they talk.

6

Ah wretched, and too solitary he
    Who loves not his own company!
      He'll feel the weight of't many a day
Unless he call in sin or vanity
30   To help to bear't away.

7

Oh Solitude, first state of human-kind!
    Which blest remained till man did find
      Even his own helper's company.
As soon as two (alas!) together joined,
35   The serpent made up three.

8

Though God himself, through countless ages thee
    His sole companion chose to be,
      Thee, sacred Solitude alone,
Before the branchy head of number's tree
40   Sprang from the trunk of one. [1]

9

Thou (though men think thine an unactive part)
    Dost break and tame th'unruly heart,
      Which else would know no settled pace,
Making it move, well managed by thy art,
45   With swiftness and with grace.

10

Thou the faint beams of reason's scattered light,
    Dost like a burning-glass unite,
      Dost multiply the feeble heat,
And fortify the strength, till thou dost bright
50   And noble fires beget.

11

Whilst this hard truth I teach, methinks, I see
    The monster London laugh at me,
      I should at thee too, foolish city,
If it were fit to laugh at misery,
55   But thy estate I pity.

---

[1] *Before the branchy head of number's tree / Sprang from the trunk of one*
before the unity of God brought forth the multiplicity of the phenomenal world.

12

Let but thy wicked men from out thee go,
　And all the fools that crowd the so,
　Even thou who dost thy millions boast,

60　A village less then Islington wilt grow,
　　A solitude almost.
　—1668

Alexander Brome
1620 — 1666

Brome was an attorney by profession, but during the civil wars became notable for his polemical pieces, written from an ardently Royalist perspective, against the Rump Parliament. To compare his work, with its Cavalier addiction to drinking songs, with that of Henry Vaughan, is to realize that Royalists came in more than one shape. During the Interregnum Brome edited the work of the dramatist Richard Brome, to whom he was not related, and wrote a play of his own, *The Cunning Lovers*. He also contributed commendatory poems to one of the major Royalist publishing events of the period, the 1647 edition of Beaumont and Fletcher's works. However, his *Songs and Poems* were not collected until after the Restoration, in 1661.

❧❧❧

The Levellers rant [1]

1

To the *Hall,* to the *hall,*
  For justice we call,
On the King and his pow'rful adherents and
    friends,
Who still have endeavoured, but we work their
    ends.
5 'Tis we will pull down what e're is above us,
And make them to fear us, that never did love us,
  We'll level the proud and make every degree.
  To our Royalty bow the knee,
    'Tis no less then treason,
10   'Gainst freedom and reason
  For our brethren to be higher then we.

2

  First the thing, call'd a King,
  To judgement we bring,
And the spawn of the court, that were prouder
    than he,
15 And next the two Houses united shall be, [2]
It does to the Romish religion enveigle, [3]

For the state to be two-headed like the spread-
    eagle. [4]
  We'll purge the superfluous members away,
  They are too many Kings to sway,
20   And as we all teach,
    'Tis our Liberties' breach,
  For the Freeborn Saints to obey.

3

  Not a Claw, in the Law,
  Shall keep us in awe;
25 We'll have no cushion-cuffers to tell us of hell, [5]
For we are all gifted to do it as well, [6]
'Tis freedom that we do hold forth to the Nation
To enjoy our fellow-creatures as at the creation;
  The carnal men's wives are for men of the spirit,
30   Their wealth is our own by merit,
    For we that have right,
    By the Law called Might,
  Are the Saints that must judge and inherit.
—1661

---

[1] *The Levellers* The Levellers sought reforms which reflected their belief in the equality of all men.

[2] *the two Houses* the House of Lords and the House of Commons.

[3] *enveigle* i.e. inveigle, to entice, allure, seduce (*OED* inveigle *v*2).

---

[4] *two-headed like the spread-eagle* The double-headed eagle was the traditional emblem of Imperial power; the speaker wants to reduce government to one "head," the Commons.

[5] *cushion-cuffer* a preacher who indulges in violent actions (*OED* cushion 11).

[6] The Levellers believed that all men should have the right to preach.

The New-Courtier

1

Since it must be so,
  Then so let it go,
Let the giddy-brain'd times turn round,
Since we have no King, let the goblet be crown'd,
5   Our Monarchy thus we'll recover;
      While the pottles are weeping, [1]
        We'll drench our sad souls
        In big-bellied bowls,
      Our sorrows in sack shall lie steeping,
10 And we'll drink till our eyes do run over.
        And prove it by reason
        That it can be no Treason
        To drink and to sing
A mournival of healths to our new-crown'd King. [2]

2

15   Let us all stand bare,
        In the presence we are,
Let our noses like bonfires shine,
Instead of the conduits, let the pottles run wine,
      To perfect this new Coronation,
20   And we that are loyal,
        In drink, shall be peers.
        While that face, that wears
      Pure Claret, looks like the blood-royal
And out-stares the Bores of the Nation.
25   In sign of obedience,
        Our oaths of allegiance
        Beer-glasses shall be,
And he that tipples ten 's of the Nobility.

3

      But if in this reign,
30   The halberted train [3]
Or the Constable should rebel,
And should make their twibill'd militia to swell, [4]
      And against the King's party raise arms,
        Then the Drawers like Yeomen
35   Of the Guard, with quart-pots,
          Shall fuddle the sots,
        While we make 'um both cuckolds and
          freemen,
      And on their wives beat up alarums. [5]
        Thus as each health passes,
40   We'll triple the glasses,
          And hold it no sin,
To be loyal and drink in defence of our King.
—1661

The Saints' Encouragement [6]

1

Fight on brave soldiers for the cause,
    Fear not the Cavaliers;
Their threatnings are as senseless, as
    Our jealousies and fears.
5 'Tis you must perfect this great work,
    And all Malignants slay, [7]
You must bring back the King again
    The clean contrary way.

---

[1] *pottles* measures of capacity for liquids, equal to two quarts or half a gallon (*OED* pottle 1 b).

[2] *mournival* a set of four (*OED* mournival 2).

[3] *halberted train* a train of soldiers armed with halberts, weapons which were a combination of a spear and a battle-ax (*OED* halbert *sb* 1).

[4] *twibill'd militia* a militia armed with double-edged battle-axes (*OED* twibil 3).

[5] *alarums* a variant spelling of alarms (*OED*).

[6] It was part of the Puritans' rhetoric to style themselves "saints"; Royalists like Vaughan expressed indignation, those like Brome amusement.

[7] *Malignants* applied between 1641 and 1660 by the supporters of the Parliament and the Commonwealth to the supporters of Charles I (*OED* malignant *sb* 1b).

2

'Tis for Religion that you fight,
10   And for the Kingdom's good,
By robbing Churches, plundering men,
    And shedding guiltless blood. [1]
Down with the Orthodoxal train, [2]
    All Loyal Subjects slay;
15 When these are gone we shall be blessed
    The clean contrary way.

3

When *Charles* we've bankrupt made like us,
    Of Crown and power bereft him;
And all his loyal subjects slain,
20   And none but Rebels left him.
When we've beggar'd all the Land,
    And sent our trunks away,
We'll make him then a glorious Prince,
    The clean contrary way.

4

25 'Tis to preserve his Majesty,
    That we against him fight,
Nor are we ever beaten back,
    Because our cause is right,
If any make a scruple on't,
30   Our Declarations say
Who fight for us, fight for the King,
    The clean contrary way.

5

At *Keynton, Branford, Plymouth, York*, [3]
    And diverse places more;
35 What victories we Saints obtained,
    The like ne're seen before.
How often we Prince *Rupert* killed, [4]
    And bravely won the day,
The wicked Cavaliers did run
40   The clean contrary way.

6

The true Religion we maintain,
    The Kingdom's peace, and plenty;
The privilege of Parliament
    Not known to one of twenty:
45 The ancient Fundamental Laws; [5]
    And teach men to obey
Their lawful sovereign, and all these,
    The clean contrary way.

7

We subjects' Liberties preserve,
50   By prisonment and plunder,
And do enrich our selves and state
    By keeping the wicked under.
We must preserve Mechanics now [6]

---

[1] *And for the Kingdom's good…shedding guiltless blood* The visible symbols of ritual worship, seen as popish by those who rejected Laudian Anglicanism, were removed from churches, sometimes violently, during the turbulence before the Civil War and during the interregnum.

[2] *Orthodoxal train* the church hierarchy. Some sectarians supported the concept of equality within the church.

[3] *At Keynton, Branford, Plymouth, York* Keynton is a reference to the battle of Edgehill, which was fought in October 1642. Brentford [Branford] was occupied by the King in November 1642. At the beginning of 1643 York was held by the Royalists and Plymouth was held by Parliament.

[4] *How often we Prince Rupert killed* Charles I's nephew, Prince Rupert, successfully led the King's cavalry in a series of battles until his defeat in July 1644 at Marston Moor. In November 1644 Rupert was appointed Commander-in-Chief of the King's armies, but was dismissed after he surrendered Bristol to the Parliamentarians in the following September. He was sent into exile after the Parliamentary victory.

[5] *The ancient Fundamental Laws* Brome is alluding to Parliament's frequent references to the monarchy's transgression of a "fundamental law" which was never specifically explained.

[6] *Mechanics* those involved in manual labour or skill (*OED* mechanic *sb* 1). Radical sectaries allowed uneducated laymen to preach to their congregations.

To lecturize and pray;
55 By them the Gospel is advanced,
The clean contrary way.

8

And though the King be much misled
By that malignant crew; [1]
He'll find us honest, and at last,
60 Give all of us our due.
For we do wisely plot, and plot
Rebellion to destroy,
He sees we stand for peace and truth,
The clean contrary way.

9

65 The public faith shall save our souls,
And good out-works together, [2]
And ships shall save our lives that stay,
Only for wind and weather.
But when our faith and works fall down,
70 And all our hopes decay,
Our Acts will bear us up to heaven,
The clean contrary way.
—1661

A Satire on the Rebellion

Urge me no more to sing. I am not able
To raise a note, songs are abominable.
Yea *David's* psalms do now begin to be
Turn'd out of Church, by hymns *extempore*. [3]
5 No accents are so pleasant now as those
That are caesura'd through the pastor's nose. [4]

I'll only weep our misery and ruth,
I am no Poet, for I speak the truth.
Behold a self against it self doth fight,
10 And the left hand prevails above the right.
The grumbling guts, i'th' belly of the State,
Unthankful for the wholesome food they ate,
Belch at their head, and do begin to slight
The Cates, to which they had an appetite. [5]
15 They long for kickshaws, and new fangled dishes, [6]
Not which all love, but which each fancy wishes.
Behold a glorious *Phoebus* tumbling down, [7]
While the rebellious bears usurp the Crown.
Behold a team of *Phaetons* aspire [8]
20 To guide the Sun, and set the World on fire.
All goes to wrack, and it must needs be so,
When those would run, that know not how to go.
Behold a lawful Sovereign to whose mind
Dishonesty's a stranger, now confined
25 To the anarchic pow'r of those whose reason
Is flat rebellion, and their truth is Treason.
Behold the loyal Subjects pill'd and poll'd, [9]
And from *Algere* to *Tunis* bought and sold.
Their goods sequestred by a legal stealth,
30 The private robb'd t'uphold the Commonwealth, [10]
And those the only plunderers are grown
Of others' states, that had none of their own. [11]

---

[1] *malignant crew* that is the King's advisors, often considered responsible for his actions.

[2] *out-works* outer defences or outposts (*OED* outwork *sb* 1).

[3] *Turn'd out of Church, by hymns extempore* The psalms were part of the Anglican liturgy of the Book of Common Prayer. In 1644 the use of the liturgy was discontinued in the two Houses in favor of extempore prayer.

[4] *caesura'd* nonce-word, from the noun (*OED* caesura *v* 3).

[5] *Cates* bought provisions or victuals, usually more delicate or dainty than those of home production (*OED* cate *sb*[1] 1).

[6] *kickshaws* a fancy dish in cookery (*OED* kickshaw 1).

[7] *Phoebus* a name of Apollo as the Sun god; the sun personified.

[8] *Phaetons* The son of Helios the Sun god, Phaeton persuaded his father to let him guide the solar chariot for one day. Phaeton was too weak to control the horses that pulled the chariot, and in order to minimize damage to the world, Zeus killed him with a thunderbolt.

[9] *pill'd and poll'd* pillaged and robbed (*OED* pill *v*[1] III. 9).

[10] *The private robb'd t'uphold the Commonwealth* The Sequestration Ordinance of March, 1643, enabled Parliament to seize the estates of the King's supporters. The profits were forwarded to the treasury at Guildhall. It was widely suspected that some members of the Commons used this opportunity to increase their personal wealth.

[11] *states* property, possessions; one's private means; linked to estate (*OED* state *sb* 36).

Robbers no more by night in secret go,
They have a License now for what they do.
35   If any to the rulers do complain,
They know no other godliness but gain.
Nor give us any plaster for the sore
Of paying much, but only paying more.
What ere we do or speak, how ere we live,
40   All is acquitted if we will but give;
They sit in bulwarks, and do make the laws
But fair pretences to a fouler cause,
And horse-leech-like cry give, what ere they say, [1]

Or sing, the burden of their song is Pay.
45   How wretched is that State! how full of woe,
When those that should preserve, do overthrow!
When they rule us, and ore them money reigns,
Who still cry Give, and always gape for gains!
But on those Judges lies a heavy curse,
50   That measure crimes by the delinquent's purse.
     The time will come when they do cease to live,
     Some will cry Take, as fast as they cri'd Give.
—1661

---

[1] *horse-leech* a rapacious, insatiable person (*OED* horse-leech *sb* 3).

Lucy Hutchinson
1620 – ca. 1675

Lucy Apsley Hutchinson was born in the Tower of London, the daughter of Lucy St. John and Sir Allen Apsley, Lieutenant of the Tower. While pregnant with Lucy, her mother dreamt of a star settling in her hand as she walked in the garden. Lucy's father interpreted this to mean that she would bear "a daughter of some extraordinary eminency." In an autobiographical fragment, Lucy paints herself as a particularly bright child, eagerly reading and listening to sermons by the age of four. At seven, she was instructed by eight tutors in language, music, dancing, writing and needlework, yet was continually drawn into the world of texts, eventually displaying competence in French, Latin, Greek and Hebrew. It was her pleasure in writing "witty songs and amorous sonnets" that drew the attentions of her future husband, John Hutchinson, who was compelled to make her acquaintance after detecting a "rationality in the sonnet, beyond the customary reach of a she-wit." Though struck down with smallpox in 1638, later that year she wed Hutchinson, by whom she had eight children. In 1640, Lucy moved to Owthorpe, the Hutchinson family home, where she soon turned her attention to the translation of the six books of Lucretius. Although this translation, written in the schoolroom of her children, was not published, it enjoyed circulation amongst friends. Such tranquillity was soon interrupted by the turbulence of the civil wars. Hutchinson, a Parliamentarian, was governor of the castle in Nottingham, and in 1646 assumed a seat in the Long Parliament. Appointed one of the judges at the trial of the King, he was to sign Charles I's death sentence, an act which led to his imprisonment in the Tower after the Restoration. When he was removed to Sandown Castle in Kent in 1663, the unhealthy conditions weakened his health and, despite Lucy's daily visits and medical efforts, he died the following year. To console herself, Lucy became her husband's biographer. In the *Memoirs of Colonel Hutchinson*, Hutchinson emerges as virtuous and valorous, suffering saint and noble warrior. The *Memoirs* do not, however, merely eulogize but offer a compelling and detailed, if partisan, account of the Civil War. Prefaced to the *Memoirs* is a fragment of "The Life of Mrs. Hutchinson," strangely more forthcoming on the history of Britain than it is on the childhood of Lucy or the workings of her mind. In later life, Lucy Hutchinson wrote two religious treatises, *On the Principles of Christian Religion* and *On Theology*, for the benefit of her children, yet never ventured to publish any of her work. She had once declared that silence was the most becoming virtue in women, which may well explain her distaste for publication. The date of Lucy Hutchinson's death is unknown.

⁊⁊⁊

"All Sorts of Men" [1]

All sorts of men through various labours press
To the same end, contented quietness;

Great princes vex their labouring thoughts to be
Possessed of an unbounded sovereignty;
5 The hardy soldier doth all toils sustain
That he may conquer first, and after reign;
Th'industrious merchant ploughs the angry seas
That he may bring home wealth, and live at ease.

---

[1] Hutchinson's editor, the Reverend Julius Hutchinson, writes that this poem was found: "in the small book containing her own life, and most probably composed by her during her husband's retirement from public business to his seat at Owthorpe." The classical source for the genre of the retirement poem is Horace's Epode II, *Beatus ille* ("The Happy Man"), a lyric which contrasts the peace and contentment of country living with the vexations of urban life. Ben Jonson's translation of this epode, "The Praises of a Country Life," and Katherine Philips's "A Country Life" are among the many early modern versions of the Horatian retirement poem.

These none of them attain; for sweet repose
10   But seldom to the splendid palace goes;
A troop of restless passions wander there,
And only private lives are free from care.
Sleep to the cottage bringeth happy nights,
But to the court hung round with flaring lights,
15   Which th' office of the vanished day supply,
His image only comes to close the eye,
But gives the troubled mind no ease of care,
While country slumbers undisturbed are;
Where, if the active fancy dreams present,
20   They bring no horrors to the innocent.
Ambition doth incessantly aspire,
And each advance leads on to new desire;
Nor yet can riches av'rice satisfy,
For want and wealth together multiply:
25   Nor can voluptuous men more fulness find,
For enjoyed pleasures leave their stings behind.
He's only rich who knows no want; he reigns
Whose will no severe tyranny constrains;
And he alone possesseth true delight
30   Whose spotless soul no guilty fears affright.
This freedom in the country life is found,
Where innocence and safe delights abound.
Here man's a prince; his subjects ne'er repine
When on his back their wealthy fleeces shine:
35   If for his appetite the fattest die,
Those who survive will raise no mutiny:
His table is with home-got dainties crowned,
With friends, not flatterers, encompassed round;

No spies nor traitors on his trencher wait,[1]
40   Nor is his mirth confined to rules of state;
An armed guard he neither hath nor needs,
Nor fears a poisoned morsel when he feeds;
Bright constellations hang above his head,
Beneath his feet are flow'ry carpets spread;
45   The merry birds delight him with their songs,
And healthful air his happy life prolongs;
At harvest merrily his flocks he shears,
And in cold weather their warm fleeces wears;
Unto his ease he fashions all his clothes;
50   His cup with uninfected liquor flows:
The vulgar breath doth not his thoughts elate,
Nor can he be o'erwhelmed by their hate.
Yet, if ambitiously he seeks for fame,
One village feast shall gain a greater name
55   Than his who wears the imperial diadem,
Whom the rude multitude do still condemn.
Sweet peace and joy his blest companions are;
Fear, sorrow, envy, lust, revenge, and care,
And all that troop which breeds the world's offence.
60   With pomp and majesty, are banished thence.
What court then can such liberty afford?
Or where is man so uncontrolled a lord?
—1806

---

[1] *trencher* a serving plate and that food which it bears (*OED* trencher[1] II.2,4).

Andrew Marvell
1621 – 1678

Marvell was the son of a Yorkshire clergyman, who was appointed Lecturer in Holy Trinity Church, Hull, in 1624. He was educated at Hull Grammar School and in 1633 went up to Trinity College, Cambridge. His first published verse was in a congratulatory volume of poems in Latin and Greek on the birth of a child to Charles I and Henrietta Maria. In 1639 he became B.A. and converted briefly to Catholicism. His father, finding him in London, sent him back to Cambridge, which he left in 1641, the year of his father's death. Between 1642 and 1647 he travelled in Holland, France, Italy, and Spain. During part of the period 1650–1652 he was tutor to Lord Fairfax's daughter Mary; in 1653 he was recommended by Milton for the post of Assistant Latin Secretary to the Council of State, but was not appointed. In 1653 he became tutor to William Dutton, who was later a ward of Cromwell's; in 1656 he was in France with Dutton, and was there described as "a notable English Italo-Macchiavellian." In 1657 he was appointed Latin Secretary to the Council of State, where he received the same stipend as Milton. In 1659 he was elected Member of Parliament for Hull, a position he held for almost twenty years. In 1662–63 he was in Holland for eleven months; in July 1663 he went as secretary to the Earl of Carlisle on an embassy to Russia, Sweden, and Denmark, returning in January of 1665. Much of Marvell's writing was published anonymously or pseudonymously; a reward was offered for information as to the author or printer of his *An Account of the Growth of Popery and Arbitrary Government*, 1677. Marvell died suddenly in 1678. Aubrey wrote, "Some suspected that he was poisoned by the Jesuits, but I cannot be positive." In 1681 *Miscellaneous Poems* "By Andrew Marvell Esq; Late Member of the Honourable House of Commons" was published.[1]

For Marvell see also Aubrey, *Brief Lives*.

⁊⁊

Flecknoe, an English Priest at Rome [2]

Obliged by frequent visits of this man,
  Whom as priest, poet, and musician,
I for some branch of *Melchizédek* took [3]
(Though he derives himself from *my Lord*
    Brooke); [4]
5 I sought his lodging, which is at the sign

Of *The Sad Pelican;* subject divine
For poetry.[5] There, three staircases high,
Which signifies his triple property,
I found at last a chamber, as 'twas said,
10 But seemed a coffin set on the stairs' head
Not higher than seven, nor larger than three feet;
Only there was nor ceiling, nor a sheet, [6]
Save that the ingenious door did, as you come,
Turn in, and show to wainscot half the room.
15 Yet of his state no man could have complained,
There being no bed where he entertained:
And though within one cell so narrow pent,

---

[1] In preparing this selection, the following printed editions were consulted: *The Poems of Andrew Marvell*, ed. H.M. Margoliouth, second edition (Oxford: Clarendon P, 1952), and *Andrew Marvell: The Complete Poems*, ed. Elizabeth Story Donno (Harmondsworth: Penguin Classics, 1985).

[2] Richard Flecknoe (d. 1678?) was in Rome during Lent of 1645 and 1646. He was a priest, and his notoriety as a bad poet explains the title of John Dryden's *Mac Flecknoe*.

[3] *Melchizédek* as a type of one who holds multiple offices; he was both king and priest (Genesis 14:18).

---

[4] *Lord Brooke* Fulke Greville, first Lord Brooke (d. 1628), about whose work Flecknoe wrote commendary verses.

[5] *Pelican* thought to feed its young with its own flesh and blood, and hence an emblem of Christ.

[6] *ceiling* wainscoting.

He'd *stanzas* for a whole *apartément.* [1]
    Straight without further information,
20 In hideous verse, he, in a dismal tone,
Begins to exorcise, as if I were
Possessed; and sure the *Devil* brought me there.
But I, who now imagined myself brought
To my last trial, in a serious thought
25 Calmed the disorders of my youthful breast,
And to my martyrdom preparèd rest.
Only this frail ambition did remain,
The last distemper of the sober brain,
That there had been some present to assure
30 The future ages how I did endure:
And how I, silent, turned my burning ear
Towards the verse; and when that could not hear,
Held him the other; and unchangèd yet,
Asked still for more, and prayed him to repeat:
35 Till the tyrant, weary to persecute,
Left off, and tried t'allure me with his lute.
    Now as two instruments, to the same key
Being tuned by art, if the one touchèd be
The other opposite as soon replies,
40 Moved by the air and hidden sympathies;
So while he with his gouty fingers crawls
Over the lute, his murm'ring belly calls,
Whose hungry guts to the same straitness twined
In echo to the trembling strings repined.
45   I, that perceived now what his music meant,
Asked civilly if he had eat this Lent.
He answered yes, with such and such an one.
For he has this of generous, that alone
He never feeds, save only when he tries
50 With gristly tongue to dart the passing flies.
I asked if he eat flesh. And he, that was
So hungry that, though ready to say *Mass,*
Would break his fast before, said he was sick,
And the *ordinance* was only politic.
55 Nor was I longer to invite him scant,
Happy at once to make him Protestant,

And silent. Nothing now our dinner stayed
But till he had himself a body made—
I mean till he were dressed; for else so thin
60 He stands, as if he only fed had been
With consecrated wafers: and the *Host*
Hath sure more flesh and blood than he can boast.
This *basso relievo* of a man, [2]
Who as a camel tall, yet easily can
65 The needle's eye thread without any stitch,
(His only impossible is to be rich),
Lest his too subtle body, growing rare,
Should leave his soul to wander in the air,
He therefore circumscribes himself in rimes;
70 And swaddled in's own papers seven times,
Wears a close jacket of poetic buff,
With which he doth his third dimension stuff.
Thus armèd underneath, he over all
Does make a primitive *sottana* fall; [3]
75 And above that yet casts an antique cloak,
Worn at the first Council of *Antioch,* [4]
Which by the *Jews* long hid, and disesteemed,
He heard of by tradition, and redeemed.
But were he not in this black habit decked,
80 This half-transparent man would soon reflect
Each colour that he passed by, and be seen,
As the *chameleon,* yellow, blue, or green.
    He dressed, and ready to disfurnish now
His chamber, whose compactness did allow
85 No empty place for complimenting doubt,
But who came last is forced first to go out;
I meet one on the stairs who made me stand,
Stopping the passage, and did him demand.
I answered, "He is here, *Sir;* but you see
90 You cannot pass to him but thorough me."
He thought himself affronted, and replied,
"I whom the palace never has denied

---

[1] *stanzas* In Italian, "stanza" means both poetic stanza and room.

[2] *basso relievo* bas or low relief sculpture, in which the forms have shape but little depth.

[3] *sottana* cassock (Italian).

[4] *Council of Antioch* held in the year 321.

Will make the way here;" I said, "*Sir*, you'll do
Me a great favour, for I seek to go."
95 He gathering fury still made sign to draw;
But himself there closed in a scabbard saw
As narrow as his sword's; and I, that was
Delightful, said, "There can no body pass
Except by penetration hither, where
100 Two make a crowd; nor can three persons here
Consist but in one substance." Then, to fit
Our peace, the priest said I too had some wit.
To prov't, I said, "The place doth us invite
By its own narrowness, Sir, to unite."
105 He asked me pardon; and to make me way
Went down, as I him followed to obey.
But the propitiatory priest had straight
Obliged us, when below, to celebrate
Together our atonement: so increased
110 Betwixt us two the dinner to a feast.

    Let it suffice that we could eat in peace;
And that both poems did and quarrels cease
During the table; though my new-made friend
Did, as he threatened, ere 'twere long intend
115 To be both witty and valiant: I, loath,
Said 'twas too late, he was already both.

    But now, alas, my first tormentor came,
Who satisfied with eating, but not tame,
Turns to recite; though judges most severe
120 After the assize's dinner mild appear,
And on full stomach do condemn but few,
Yet he more strict my sentence doth renew,
And draws out of the black box of his breast
Ten quire of paper in which he was dressed.
125 Yet that which was a greater cruelty
Than *Nero's* poem, he calls charity: [1]
And so the *pelican* at his door hung

Picks out the tender bosom to its young.
    Of all his poems there he stands ungirt
130 Save only two foul copies for his shirt: [2]
Yet these he promises as soon as clean.
But how I loathed to see my neighbour glean
Those papers which he peelèd from within
Like white flakes rising from a leper's skin!
135 More odious than those rags which the French
    youth
At ordinaries after dinner show'th
When they compare their *chancres* and *poulains*. [3]
Yet he first kissed them, and after takes pains
To read; and then, because he understood
140 Not one word, thought and swore that they were
    good.
But all his praises could not now appease
The provoked author, whom it did displease
To hear his verses, by so just a curse,
That were ill made, condemned to be read, worse:
145 And how (impossible) he made yet more
Absurdities in them than were before.
For he his untuned voice did fall or raise
As a deaf man upon a viol plays,
Making the half points and the periods run
150 Confuseder than the atoms in the sun.
Thereat the poet swelled, with anger full,
And roared out, like *Perillus* in's own *bull*: [4]
"*Sir*, you read false." "That, any one but you,
Should know the contrary." Whereat, I, now
155 Made mediator, in my room, said, "Why,
To say that you read false, *Sir*, is no lie."
Thereat the waxen youth relented straight;
But saw with sad despair that 'twas too late.
For the disdainful poet was retired
160 Home, his most furious satire to have fired
Against the rebel, who, at this struck dead,

---

[1] *a greater cruelty / Than Nero's poem* "While [Nero] was singing no one was allowed to leave the theatre even for the most urgent reasons. And so it is said that some women gave birth to children there, while many who were worn out with listening and applauding, secretly leaped from the wall, since the gates at the entrance were closed, or feigned death and were carried out as for burial" (Suetonius, *Lives of the Caesars*, 6.23.2).

[2] *foul copies* the contemporary term for an author's manuscript drafts, but here with an implication of more literal foulness.

[3] *poulains* sores, from venereal disease.

[4] *Perillus* the inventor, and first victim, of a brazen bull in which the tyrant Phalaris (ruled Sicily ca. 570–564 B.C.E.) roasted his victims.

Wept bitterly as disinherited.
Who should commend his mistress now? Or who
Praise him? Both difficult indeed to do
165 With truth. I counselled him to go in time,
Ere the fierce poet's anger turned to rime.
    He hasted; and I, finding myself free,
As one 'scaped strangely from captivity,
Have made the chance be painted; and go now
170 To hang it in *Saint Peter's* for a vow.
    —1681 (MID-1640s?)

The Coronet

When for the thorns with which I long, too
    long,
With many a piercing wound,
    My Saviour's head have crowned,
I seek with garlands to redress that wrong:
5   Through every garden, every mead,
I gather flowers (my fruits are only flowers),
    Dismantling all the fragrant towers
That once adorned my shepherdess's head.
And now when I have summed up all my store,
10   Thinking (so I myself deceive)
    So rich a chaplet thence to weave
As never yet the King of Glory wore:
    Alas, I find the serpent old
    That, twining in his speckled breast,
15   About the flowers disguised does fold,
    With wreaths of fame and interest.
Ah, foolish man, that wouldst debase with them,
And mortal glory, Heaven's diadem!
But Thou who only couldst the serpent tame,
20 Either his slippery knots at once untie,
And disentangle all his winding snare;
Or shatter too with him my curious frame, [1]

And let these wither, so that he may die,
Though set with skill and chosen out with care:
25 That they, while Thou on both their spoils dost
    tread,
May crown thy feet, that could not crown thy head.
    —1681

The Gallery

1

Clora, come view my soul, and tell
Whether I have contrived it well.
Now all its several lodgings lie
Composed into one Gallery;
5 And the great *arras*-hangings, made
Of various faces, by are laid; [2]
That, for all furniture, you'll find
Only your picture in my mind.

2

Here thou are painted in the dress
10 Of an inhuman murderess;
Examining upon our hearts
Thy fertile shop of cruel arts: [3]
Engines more keen than ever yet
Adorned a tyrant's cabinet;
15 Of which the most tormenting are
Black eyes, red lips, and curlèd hair.

3

But, on the other side, th'art drawn
Like to *Aurora* in the dawn;
When in the East she slumbering lies,
20 And stretches out her milky thighs;
While all the morning choir does sing,
And *manna* falls, and roses spring;

[1] *my curious frame* the "coronet" that is the poem itself, a devotional garland formed of flowers (poetic tropes) rescued from his secular love poetry (the "fragrant towers" of line 7), but which, like the secular verse, is wound up with the snake of self-interest and desire for fame; *curious* clever, skillful, ingenious (*OED* curious *a* 4).

[2] *arras* a rich tapestry fabric, in which figures and scenes are woven in colours (*OED* arras 1).

[3] *Examining* testing.

And, at thy feet, the wooing doves
Sit pérfecting their harmless loves.

4

25 Like an enchantress here thou show'st,
Vexing thy restless lover's ghost;
And, by a light obscure, dost rave
Over his entrails, in the cave;
Divining thence, with horrid care,
30 How long thou shalt continue fair;
And (when informed) them throw'st away,
To be the greedy vulture's prey.

5

But, against that, thou sit'st afloat
Like *Venus* in her pearly boat.
35 The *halcyons*, calming all that's nigh,
Betwixt the air and water fly; [1]
Or, if some rolling wave appears,
A mass of ambergris it bears.
Nor blows more wind than what may well
40 Convoy the perfume to the smell. [2]

6

These pictures and a thousand more
Of thee my gallery do store
In all the forms thou canst invent
Either to please me, or torment:
45 For thou alone to people me,
Art grown a numerous colony;
And a collection choicer far
Than or *Whitehall's* or *Mantua's* were. [3]

7

But, of these pictures and the rest,
50 That at the entrance likes me best:
Where the same posture, and the look
Remains, with which I first was took:
A tender shepherdess, whose hair
Hangs loosely playing in the air,
55 Transplanting flowers from the green hill,
To crown her head, and bosom fill.
—1681

The Definition of Love

1

My love is of a birth as rare
As 'tis for object strange and high:
It was begotten by Despair
Upon Impossibility.

2

5 Magnanimous Despair alone
Could show me so divine a thing,
Where feeble Hope could ne'er have flown
But vainly flapped its tinsel wing.

3

And yet I quickly might arrive
10 Where my extended soul is fixed, [4]
But Fate does iron wedges drive,
And always crowds itself betwixt.

4

For Fate with jealous eye does see
Two perfect loves, nor lets them close: [5]
15 Their union would her ruin be,
And her tyrannic power depose.

---

[1] *halcyons* birds which were fabled to charm the wind and waves so that the sea was specially calm during the time of the winter solstice (*OED* halcyon *sb* A).

[2] *Convoy* convey (*OED* convoy *v. trans.* II 5).

[3] *Whitehall's or Mantua's* Charles I had bought the paintings of Vincenzo Gonzaga, Duke of Mantua, adding them to his own fine art collection at Whitehall.

---

[4] *extended soul* an oxymoron, since extension is a quality of matter. Donne employed a similar conceit in "A Valediction, forbidding mourning," lines 21–24.

[5] *close* conjoin; unite (*OED* close *v* III 10 *trans.*).

5

And therefore her decrees of steel
Us as the distant Poles have placed,
(Though Love's whole world on us doth wheel)
20   Not by themselves to be embraced,

6

Unless the giddy heaven fall,
And earth some new convulsion tear;
And, us to join, the world should all
Be cramped into a *planisphere*. [1]

7

25   As lines (so loves) *oblique* may well
Themselves in every angle greet:
But ours so truly *parallel*,
Though infinite, can never meet.

8

Therefore the love which us doth bind,
30   But Fate so enviously debars,
Is the conjunction of the mind,
And opposition of the stars. [2]
—1681

To His Coy Mistress

Had we but world enough, and time,
This coyness Lady were no crime.
We would sit down, and think which way
To walk, and pass our long love's day.
5   Thou by the *Indian Ganges'* side
Shouldst *rubies* find: I by the tide

Of *Humber* would complain. I would [3]
Love you ten years before the Flood:
And you should, if you please, refuse
10   Till the conversion of the *Jews*. [4]
My vegetable love should grow
Vaster than empires, and more slow. [5]
An hundred years should go to praise
Thine eyes, and on thy forehead gaze.
15   Two hundred to adore each breast:
But thirty thousand to the rest.
An age at least to every part,
And the last age should show your heart:
For, Lady, you deserve this state;
20   Nor would I love at lower rate.
      But at my back I always hear
Time's wingèd chariot hurrying near:
And yonder all before us lie
Deserts of vast Eternity.
25   Thy beauty shall no more be found;
Nor, in thy marble vault, shall sound
My echoing song: then worms shall try
That long-preserved virginity:
And your quaint honour turn to dust;
30   And into ashes all my lust. [6]
The grave's a fine and private place,
But none, I think, do there embrace.

---

[1] *planisphere* a chart formed by the projection of a sphere onto a plane (*OED* planisphere).

[2] *conjunction* union, connection; in astrology and astronomy, an apparent proximity of two planets or other heavenly bodies (*OED* conjunction 1,3); *opposition* in astrology and astronomy, the relative position of two heavenly bodies when exactly opposite to each other as seen from the earth's surface (*OED* opposition 1,3).

[3] *Humber* in allusion to Marvell's residence in Hull; see any map of England.

[4] *conversion of the Jews* which was expected to take place shortly before the Day of Judgement.

[5] *vegetable love* The soul was thought to have three parts: the vegetative, the animal or sensitive, and the rational. The vegetative soul controlled growth. In this conceit, the poet's love would not be capable of physical sensation.

[6] *quaint* *OED* remarks that in many examples from this period the exact meaning is difficult to determine. It might suggest "unusual," "old-fashioned," or "affected." See the various adjectival senses. It is also possible that Marvell had in mind the medieval sense, referring to the vagina, used by Chaucer in *The Miller's Tale*; *honour* chastity (*OED* honour *sb* 3).

Now, therefore, while the youthful hue [1]
Sits on thy skin like morning dew,
35 And while thy willing soul transpires
At every pore with instant fires,
Now let us sport us while we may;
And now, like amorous birds of prey,
Rather at once our time devour,
40 Than languish in his slow-chapped power. [2]
Let us roll all our strength, and all
Our sweetness, up into one ball:
And tear our pleasures with rough strife,
Thorough the iron gates of life. [3]
45 Thus, though we cannot make our sun
Stand still, yet we will make him run. [4]
—1681

An Horatian Ode Upon Cromwell's Return From Ireland [5]

The forward youth that would appear [6]
Must now forsake his *Muses* dear,
Nor in the shadows sing

His numbers languishing. [7]
5 'Tis time to leave the books in dust,
And oil th' unusèd armour's rust:
Removing from the wall
The corslet of the hall.
So restless Cromwell could not cease [8]
10 In the inglorious arts of peace,
But through adventrous war
Urgèd his active star.
And, like the three-forked lightning, first
Breaking the clouds where it was nursed,
15 Did thorough his own side [9]
His fiery way divide.
(For 'tis all one to courage high
The emulous or enemy:
And with such to inclose
20 Is more than to oppose.)
Then burning through the air he went,
And palaces and temples rent:
And Caesar's head at last
Did through his laurels blast. [10]
25 'Tis madness to resist or blame
The force of angry heaven's flame:
And, if we would speak true,
Much to the man is due,
Who, from his private gardens, where
30 He lived reservèd and austere,
As if his highest plot
To plant the bergamot, [11]
Could by industrious valour climb

---

[1] *hue* Some editors prefer "glue" here; Margoliouth argues that the word already had its modern meaning and would be inadmissible in this context (*The Poems and Letters of Andrew Marvell.* 2 vols., Oxford: Clarendon P, 1927, 3rd edn. 1971).

[2] *slow-chapped* slowly devouring (*OED* chapped *ppl.a* [2]).

[3] *gates* the traditional reading. Elizabeth Donno considers that "grates" is correct (*Andrew Marvell. The Complete Poems*, ed. Elizabeth Story Donno, Harmondsworth: Penguin Books, 1972 [1987 reprint], p. 235).

[4] *we cannot make our sun / Stand still* The *source* of this may be Joshua 10:12, but the *context* is in Ovid, *Amores* I:13 and in poems closer to Marvell's time, such as Donne's *The Sun Rising*. The point is that lovers want time to pass slowly.

[5] Cromwell returned from Ireland in May 1650, and entered Scotland on July 22. The fact that lines 105–108 look forward to an invasion of Scotland suggests that the poem was composed in June and/or July of that year. It was cancelled from most copies of the 1681 Folio, presumably because of its political stance.

[6] *forward* prompt, eager, ardent (*OED* forward *a* 6,6c,7); *appear* emerge into public life (*OED* appear *v* 1,5).

---

[7] *numbers* metrical periods or feet; hence, lines, verses (*OED* numbers sb. IV 18); *languishing* suggestive of love poetry.

[8] *cease* remain at rest (*OED* cease *v* I,2).

[9] *thorough his own side* referring to the fact that Cromwell succeeded against rival Parliamentary leaders.

[10] *Caesar's head at last / Did through his laurels blast* Every Caesar was entitled to wear a laurel wreath. Traditionally, lightning did not strike laurel; but Cromwell (represented here as a natural force, like lightning) has struck down Charles I.

[11] *bergamot* an especially fine kind of pear, known as "prince's pear" (*OED* bergamot).

To ruin the great work of time,
35   And cast the kingdoms old
         Into another mould.
Though Justice against Fate complain,
And plead the ancient Rights in vain:
         But those do hold or break
40   As men are strong or weak.
Nature, that hateth emptiness,
Allows of penetration less: [1]
         And therefore must make room
         Where greater spirits come,
45 What field of all the Civil Wars,
Where his were not the deepest scars? [2]
         And *Hampton* shows what part
         He had of wiser art,
Where, twining subtle fears with hope,
50   He wove a net of such a scope,
         That *Charles* himself might chase
         To *Carisbrooke's* narrow case: [3]
That thence the Royal Actor born
The *Tragic Scaffold* might adorn:
55   While round the armèd bands
         Did clap their bloody hands.
He nothing common did or mean
Upon that memorable scene: [4]
         But with his keener eye

60   The axe's edge did try: [5]
Nor called the *gods* with vulgar spite
To vindicate his helpless right,
         But bowed his comely head,
         Down, as upon a bed.
65 This was that memorable hour
Which first assured the forcèd power. [6]
         So when they did design
         The Capitol's first line,
A bleeding head where they begun,
70   Did fright the architects to run;
         And yet in that the State
         Foresaw its happy fate. [7]
And now the Irish are ashamed
To see themselves in one year tamed: [8]
75   So much one man can do,
         That does both act and know.
They can affirm his praises best,
And have, though overcome, confessed
         How good he is, how just,
80   And fit for highest trust: [9]
Nor yet grown stiffer with command,
But still in the Republic's hand:
         How fit he is to sway
         That can so well obey.
85 He to the Commons' feet presents
A kingdom, for his first year's rents:
         And, what he may, forbears
         His fame, to make it theirs:
And has his sword and spoils ungirt,
90   To lay them at the public's skirt.

---

[1] *Nature…of penetration less*   "Nature abhors a vacuum"; and is even more hostile to two bodies occupying the same space at the same time.

[2] *the deepest scars*   Cromwell received no serious injury on the battlefield; presumably the reference is to the scars he inflicted. There is classical precedent for this idiom.

[3] *Hampton…Carisbrooke's narrow case*   Charles fled from his confinement at Hampton Court to Carisbrooke Castle on the Isle of Wight. The Governor was afraid to give him sanctuary, and so he fell once more into the hands of his enemies. At the time people thought that Cromwell had plotted Charles's flight and recapture, but there is no evidence that he did.

[4] The words "scaffold" and "scene" were both used to denote a stage; Marvell's description has been understood both as a description of a stage tragedy enacted in "real life" and as an allusion to the popularity of acting at Charles's court, which was strongly criticized by some Puritans.

[5] *try*   test (*OED* try *v* 7).

[6] *assured*   secured (*OED* assured *ppl. a.* A1).

[7] *So when…happy Fate*   Livy and other classical authors tell that when the foundations of the temple of Jupiter Capitolium were being dug, an undecayed man's head was found, which was taken as an omen of the success of Rome; "bleeding" and "fright" are Marvell's additions, relating to his contemporary situation.

[8] *one year*   Cromwell landed in Dublin on August 15, 1649.

[9] *How good he is, how just*   It seems unlikely that the Irish would have lavished any such praise upon Cromwell.

So when the falcon high
Falls heavy from the sky,
She, having killed, no more does search
But on the next green bough to perch,
95   Where, when he first does lure,
    The falc'ner has her sure.
What may not then our isle presume
While Victory his crest does plume?
    What may not others fear
100   If thus he crowns each year?
A Caesar, he, ere long to Gaul,
To Italy an Hannibal, [1]
    And to all states not free
    Shall *climactéric* be. [2]
105 The *Pict* no shelter now shall find
Within his parti-coloured mind, [3]
    But from this valour sad [4]
    Shrink underneath the plaid:
Happy, if in the tufted brake
110 The English hunter him mistake, [5]
    Nor lay his hounds in near
    The Caledonian deer.
But thou, the Wars' and Fortune's son,
March indefatigably on,
115   And for the last effect
    Still keep thy sword erect:
Besides the force it has to fright
The spirits of the shady night, [6]

120 The same arts that did *gain*
A *power*, must it *maintain*. [7]
—1681

The Picture of Little T.C. in a Prospect of Flowers

1

See with what simplicity
This nymph begins her golden days!
In the green grass she loves to lie,
And there with her fair aspect tames
5 The wilder flowers, and gives them names:
But only with the roses plays;
    And them does tell
What colour best becomes them, and what smell.

2

Who can foretell for what high cause
10 This Darling of the Gods was born!
Yet this is she whose chaster laws
The wanton Love shall one day fear,
And, under her command severe,
See his bow broke and ensigns torn.
15   Happy, who can
Appease this virtuous enemy of man!

3

O, then let me in time compound, [8]
And parley with those conquering eyes;
Ere they have tried their force to wound,
20 Ere, with their glancing wheels, they drive
In triumph over hearts that strive,
And them that yield but more despise.

---

[1] *Caesar, Hannibal* invaders of Gaul and Italy. The reference is probably to an expectation that Cromwell would take action against Roman Catholic powers in Europe.

[2] *climacteric* marking an epoch (*OED* climacteric A 1b, this place cited).

[3] *The Pict...parti-coloured mind* Referring to the Scots as Picts, Marvell is punning (in "parti-coloured" and "plaid") on the supposed derivation of Pict from the Latin *pingere,* to represent, paint or embroider.

[4] *sad* steadfast; valiant (*OED* sad *a* 2,3).

[5] *mistake* because of the plaid, thought of as camouflage.

[6] *to fright / The spirits of the shady night* The cross-hilt of the sword was thought to ward off evil spirits.

---

[7] The ending of the poem, with its reminder that Cromwell came to power by unconstitutional means, may be seen as realistic or pessimistic about England's future..

[8] *compound* come to terms with, but also with a political resonance in the period: Royalists compounded by paying a fine to avoid confiscation of their estates.

Let me be laid,
Where I may see thy glories from some shade.

4

25 Meantime, whilst every verdant thing
Itself does at thy beauty charm,
Reform the errors of the spring;
Make that the tulips may have share
Of sweetness, seeing they are fair;
30 And roses of their thorns disarm:
        But most procure
That violets may a longer age endure.

5

But, O young beauty of the woods,
Whom Nature courts with fruits and flowers,
35 Gather the flowers, but spare the buds;
Lest *Flora* angry at thy crime, [1]
To kill her infants in their prime,
Do quickly make th'example yours;
        And, ere we see,
40 Nip in the blossom all our hopes and thee.
      —1681 (WRITTEN EARLY 1650S?)

The Nymph Complaining
for the Death of Her Fawn

The wanton troopers riding by [2]
Have shot my fawn, and it will die.
Ungentle men! They cannot thrive
To kill thee. Thou ne'er didst alive
5 Them any harm: alas, nor could
Thy death yet do them any good.
I'm sure I never wished them ill;
Nor do I for all this; nor will:
But if my simple prayers may yet
10 Prevail with heaven to forget

Thy murder, I will join my tears
Rather than fail. But, O my fears!
It cannot die so. Heaven's King
Keeps register of every thing:
15 And nothing may we use in vain.
E'en beasts must be with justice slain,
Else men are made their *deodands*. [3]
Though they should wash their guilty hands
In this warm life-blood, which doth part
20 From thine, and wound me to the heart,
Yet could they not be clean: their stain
Is dyed in such a purple grain,
There is not such another in
The world, to offer for their sin.
25   Unconstant *Sylvio*, when yet
I had not found him counterfeit,
One morning (I remember well),
Tied in this silver chain and bell
Gave it to me: nay, and I know
30 What he said then; I'm sure I do.
Said he, "Look how your huntsman here
Hath taught a fawn to hunt his *dear*."
But *Sylvio* soon had me beguiled.
This waxèd tame, while he grew wild,
35 And quite regardless of my smart,
Left me his fawn, but took his heart.
     Thenceforth I set myself to play
My solitary time away
With this: and very well content,
40 Could so mine idle life have spent.
For it was full of sport; and light
Of foot, and heart; and did invite
Me to its game; it seemed to bless
Itself in me. How could I less
45 Than love it? O I cannot be
Unkind, t'a beast that loveth me.
     Had it lived long, I do not know
Whether it too might have done so

---

[1] *Flora* Roman goddess of flowers.

[2] *troopers* first used of soldiers in the Scottish army that invaded England in 1640 (*OED* trooper).

[3] *deodands* literally, things given to God; in English law, personal possessions forfeited in expiation because they caused a person's death (*OED* deodand).

As *Sylvio* did: his gifts might be
50 Perhaps as false or more than he.
But I am sure, for ought that I
Could in so short a time espy,
Thy love was far more better than
The love of false and cruel men.
55   With sweetest milk, and sugar, first
I it at mine own fingers nursed.
And as it grew, so every day
It waxed more white and sweet than they.
It had so sweet a breath! And oft
60 I blushed to see its foot more soft,
And white (shall I say than my hand?)
Nay, any lady's of the land.
    It is a wondrous thing, how fleet
'Twas on those little silver feet.
65 With what a pretty skipping grace,
It oft would challenge me the race:
And when 't had left me far away,
'Twould stay, and run again, and stay.
For it was nimbler much than hinds;
70 And trod, as on the foúr winds. [1]
    I have a garden of my own
But so with roses overgrown,
And lilies, that you would it guess
To be a little wilderness.
75 And all the springtime of the year
It only lovèd to be there.
Among the beds of lilies, I
Have sought it oft, where it should lie;
Yet could not, till itself would rise,
80 Find it, although before mine eyes.
For, in the flaxen lilies' shade,
It like a bank of lilies laid.
Upon the roses it would feed,
Until its lips e'en seemed to bleed:
85 And then to me 'twould boldly trip,
And print those roses on my lip.
But all its chief delight was still

On roses thus itself to fill:
And its pure virgin limbs to fold
90 In whitest sheets of lilies cold.
Had it lived long, it would have been
Lilies without, roses within.
    O help! O help! I see it faint:
And die as calmly as a saint.
95 See how it weeps. The tears do come
Sad, slowly dropping like a gum.
So weeps the wounded balsam: so
The holy frankincense doth flow.
The brotherless *Heliades* [2]
100 Melt in such amber tears as these.
    I in a golden *vial* will
Keep these two crystal tears; and fill
It till it do o'erflow with mine;
Then place it in *Diana's* shrine. [3]
105   Now my sweet fawn is vanished to
Whither the swans and turtles go:
In fair *Elysium* to endure,
With milk-white lambs, and ermines pure.
O do not run too fast: for I
110 Will but bespeak thy grave, and die.
    First my unhappy statue shall
Be cut in marble; and withal,
Let it be weeping too: but there
Th'engraver sure his art may spare,
115 For I so truly thee bemoan,
That I shall weep though I be stone: [4]
Until my tears, still dropping, wear
My breast, themselves engraving there.
There at my feet shalt thou be laid,
120 Of purest alabaster made:

---

[2] *Heliades*   the daughters of Helios (the sun); their grief over the death of their brother Phaethon led to their transformation into poplar trees and their tears into amber.

[3] *Diana's shrine*   Diana was the Roman goddess of chastity and hunting.

[4] *though I be stone*   like Niobe, whose pride in the number of her children caused their deaths; her grief led Zeus to transform Niobe into a weeping stone.

---

[1] *four*   disyllabic, as elsewhere in Marvell, and as in the north of England to this day.

For I would have thine image be
    White as I can, though not as thee.
—1681 (WRITTEN EARLY 1650s?)

Upon the Hill and Grove at Bilbrough

To the Lord Fairfax

1

See how the archèd earth does here
Rise in a perfect hemisphere!
The stiffest compass could not strike
A line more circular and like;
5 Nor softest pencil draw a brow
So equal as this hill does bow.
It seems as for a model laid,
And that the world by it was made.

2

Here learn, ye mountains more unjust,
10 Which to abrupter greatness thrust, [1]
That do with your hook-shouldered height
The earth deform and heaven fright,
For whose excrescence, ill-designed,
Nature must a new centre find, [2]
15 Learn here those humble steps to tread,
Which to securer glory lead.

3

See what a soft access and wide
Lies open to its grassy side;
Nor with the rugged path deters
20 The feet of breathless travellers.
See then how courteous it ascends,
And all the way it rises bends;
Nor for itself the height does gain,
But only strives to raise the plain.

4

25 Yet thus it all the field commands,
And in unenvied greatness stands,
Discerning further than the cliff
Of heaven-daring *Tenerife*. [3]
How glad the weary seamen haste
30 When they salute it from the mast! [4]
By night the Northern Star their way
Directs, and this no less by day.

5

Upon its crest this mountain grave
A plump of agèd trees does wave. [5]
35 No hostile hand durst ere invade
With impious steel the sacred shade.
For something always did appear
Of the *great Master's* terror there: [6]
And men could hear his armour still
40 Rattling through all the grove and hill.

6

Fear of the *Master*, and respect
Of the great *Nymph*, did it protect,
Vera the *Nymph* that him inspired, [7]
To whom he often here retired,
45 And on these oaks engraved her name;
Such wounds alone these woods became:
But ere he well the barks could part
'Twas writ already in their heart.

7

For they ('tis credible) have sense
50 As we, of love and reverence,

---

[1] *unjust* irregular (*OED* unjust *a* 4 *Obs.*). The ethical sense is also intended.

[2] *excrescence* abnormal, morbid or disfiguring outgrowth (*OED* excrescence 3).

[3] *Tenerife* a mountain peak in the Canaries, over 12,000 feet.

[4] *How glad…mast!* Grosart cites Markham's *Life of the Great Lord Fairfax*: "On Bilbrough hill, 145 feet above the sea, there was then a great clump of trees, which was a landmark for ships going up the Humber…".

[5] *plump* clump or bunch (*OED* plump *sb*[1] c).

[6] in allusion to Fairfax's military prowess.

[7] *Vera the Nymph that him inspired* Fairfax's wife was the daughter of Sir Horace Vere.

And underneath the coarser rind
The *genius* of the house do bind. [1]
Hence they successes seem to know,
And in their *Lord's* advancement grow;
55 But in no memory were seen,
As under this, so straight and green;

8

Yet now no further strive to shoot,
Contented if they fix their root.
Nor to the wind's uncertain gust,
60 Their prudent heads too far intrust.
Only sometimes a fluttering breeze
Discourses with the breathing trees,
Which in their modest whispers name
Those acts that swelled the cheek of fame.

9

65 "Much other groves," say they, "than these
And other hills him once did please.
Through groves of pikes he thundered then,
And mountains raised of dying men.
For all the *civic garlands* due
70 To him, our branches are but few.
Nor are our trunks enow to bear
The *trophies* of one fertile year."

10

'Tis true, ye trees, nor ever spoke
More certain *oracles* in oak. [2]
75 But peace, (if you his favour prize):
That courage its own praises flies.
Therefore to your obscurer seats
From his own brightness he retreats:
Nor he the hills without the groves,
80 Nor height, but with retirement, loves.
—1681

---

[1] *genius of the house*   its controlling spirit (*OED* genius 1).

[2] *oracles in oak*   in allusion to the grove of oaks at Dodona.

Upon Appleton House

To my Lord Fairfax

1

Within this sober frame expect
Work of no foreign architect,
That unto caves the quarries drew,
And forests did to pastures hew,
5 Who of his great design in pain
Did for a model vault his brain,
Whose columns should so high be raised
To arch the brows that on them gazed.

2

Why should of all things Man unruled
10 Such unproportioned dwellings build?
The Beasts are by their Dens expressed:
And Birds contrive an equal Nest;
The low-roofed tortoises do dwell
In cases fit of tortoise shell:
15 No creature loves an empty space;
Their bodies measure out their place.

3

But He, superfluously spread,
Demands more room alive than dead;
And in his hollow palace goes
20 Where winds (as he) themselves may lose;
What need of all this marble crust
T'impark the wanton mote of dust,
That thinks by breadth the world t'unite
Though the first builders failed in height? [3]

4

25 But all things are composèd here
Like Nature, orderly and near:
In which we the dimensions find
Of that more sober age and mind,
When larger-sizèd men did stoop

---

[3] Genesis 11:1–9 (the Tower of Babel).

30 To enter at a narrow loop;
As practising, in doors so strait
To strain themselves through Heaven's Gate. [1]

5

And surely when the after age
Shall hither come in pilgrimage,
35 These sacred places to adore,
By Vere and Fairfax trod before, [2]
Men will dispute how their extent
Within such dwarfish confines went:
And some will smile at this, as well
40 As Romulus his bee-like cell. [3]

6

Humility alone designs
Those short but admirable lines,
By which, ungirt and unconstrained,
Things greater are in less contained.
45 Let others vainly strive t'immure
The circle in the quadrature! [4]
These *holy Mathematics* can
In every figure equal man.

7

Yet thus the laden house does sweat,
50 And scarce endures the *Master* great:
But where he comes the swelling hall
Stirs, and the square grows spherical,
More by his *Magnitude* distressed,
Then he is by its straitness pressed:
55 And too officiously it slights
That in itself which him delights.

8

So Honour better Lowness bears,
Than that unwonted greatness wears:
Height with a certain grace does bend,
60 But low things clownishly ascend.
And yet what needs there here excuse,
Where everything does answer use?
Where neatness nothing can condemn,
Nor Pride invent what to contemn?

9

65 A stately *Frontispiece of Poor* [5]
Adorns without the open door:
Nor less the rooms within commends
Daily new *furniture of friends*.
The house was built upon the place
70 Only as for a mark of grace;
And for an *Inn* to entertain
Its Lord a while, but not remain.

10

Him Bishop's Hill or Denton may, [6]
Or Bilbrough, better hold than they:
75 But Nature here hath been so free
As if she said, "Leave this to me."
Art would more neatly have defaced
What she had laid so sweetly waste,
In fragrant gardens, shady woods,
80 Deep meadows, and transparent floods.

11

While with slow eyes we these survey,
And on each pleasant footstep stay,
We opportunely may relate
The progress of this house's fate.

---

[1] *As practising…Heaven's Gate* Matthew 7:13–14.

[2] *Vere and Fairfax* Lord Fairfax and his wife Anne, daughter of Sir Horace Vere.

[3] *his bee-like cell* an ellipsis for beehive-like. A thatched hut, the traditional dwelling of Romulus, was preserved on the Palatine Hill at Rome.

[4] *Let others…quadrature!* "Squaring the circle" was a proverbially difficult problem in mathematics.

[5] *Frontispiece* literally, the facade of a building; more usually applied to the decorated entrance (*OED* frontispiece *sb* 1). As in "To Penshurst," the charity of the house's owner is stressed.

[6] *Bishop's Hill or Denton* other houses belonging to the family.

85 A *Nunnery* first gave it birth [1]
    (For *Virgin Buildings* oft brought forth); [2]
    And all that neighbour-ruin shows
    The quarries whence this dwelling rose.

12

    Near to this gloomy cloister's gates
90 There dwelt the blooming virgin *Thwaites*,
    Fair beyond measure, and an heir
    Which might deformity make fair.
    And oft she spent the summer suns
    Discoursing with the subtle nuns.
95 Whence in these words one to her weaved, [3]
    (As 'twere by chance) thoughts long conceived.

13

    "Within this holy leisure we
    Live innocently, as you see.
    These walls restrain the world without,
100 But hedge our liberty about.
    These bars inclose that wider den
    Of those wild Creatures callèd Men.
    The cloister outward shuts its gates,
    And, from us, locks on them the grates.

14

105 "Here we, in shining armour white,
    Like *Virgin Amazons* do fight.
    And our chaste *Lamps* we hourly trim,
    Lest the great *Bridegroom* find them dim. [4]
    Our *orient* breaths perfumèd are
110 With incense of incessant prayer.

    And holy-water of our tears
    Most strangely our complexion clears.

15

    "Not tears of grief; but such as those
    With which calm pleasure overflows;
115 Or pity, when we look on you
    That live without this happy Vow.
    How should we grieve that must be seen
    Each one a *Spouse*, and each a *Queen*, [5]
    And can in *Heaven* hence behold
120 Our brighter robes and crowns of gold?

16

    "When we have prayèd all our beads, [6]
    Someone the holy *Legend* reads; [7]
    While all the rest with needles paint
    The face and graces of the *Saint*.
125 But what the linen can't receive
    They in their lives do interweave.
    This work the saints best represents;
    That serves for altar's ornaments.

17

    "But much it to our work would add
130 If here your hand, your Face we had:
    By it we would *Our Lady* touch;
    Yet thus She you resembles much.
    Some of your features, as we sewed,
    Through every *Shrine* should be bestowed.
135 And in one beauty we would take
    Enough a thousand *Saints* to make.

18

    "And (for I dare not quench the fire
    That me does for your good inspire)
    'Twere sacrilege a man t'admit

---

[1] *A nunnery...birth* The house came into the Fairfax family at the dissolution of the monasteries in 1542.

[2] *Virgin Buildings oft brought forth* Commissions enquiring into the state of religious houses before the Dissolution of the Monasteries naturally found that vows of chastity had not always been kept.

[3] *subtle, weaved* a good example of Marvell's verbal wit. The word "subtle" derives from the Latin for "finely woven" (*OED* subtle *a* 1).

[4] *Bridegroom* Matthew 25:1–13.

[5] *Each one a spouse* Nuns are regarded as being married to Christ.

[6] *prayèd all our beads* recited the Rosary in its entirety.

[7] *legend* the life of a saint, as in Donne's "The Canonization." It was customary for a nun or monk to read aloud at meal-times or while others were occupied in the kind of work described here.

140 To holy things, for heaven fit.
I see the *Angels* in a Crown
On you the lilies showering down: [1]
And around about you glory breaks,
That something more than human speaks.

19

145 "All beauty, when at such a height,
Is so already consecrate.
Fairfax I know; and long ere this
Have marked the youth, and what he is.
But can he such a *Rival* seem
150 For whom you Heav'n should disesteem?
Ah, no! and 'twould more honour prove
He your *Devoto* were, than love. [2]

20

"Here live belovèd, and obeyed:
Each one your Sister, each your Maid.
155 And, if our rule seem strictly penned,
The Rule itself to you shall bend.
Our *Abbess* too, now far in age,
Doth your succession near presage.
How soft the yoke on us would lie,
160 Might such fair hands as yours it tie!

21

"Your voice, the sweetest of the choir,
Shall draw *Heav'n* nearer, raise us higher.
And your example, if our Head,
Will soon us to perfection lead.
165 Those virtues to us all so dear,
Will straight grow sanctity when here:
And that, once sprung, increase so fast
Till miracles it work at last.

22

"Nor is our *Order* yet so nice, [3]
170 Delight to banish as a vice.
Here pleasure piety doth meet;
One pérfecting the other sweet.
So through the mortal fruit we boil
The sugar's uncorrupting oil: [4]
175 And that which perished while we pull,
Is thus preservèd clear and full

23

"For such indeed are all our arts,
Still handling Nature's finest parts.
Flowers dress the altars; for the clothes,
180 The sea-born amber we compose;
Balms for the grieved we draw; and pastes
We mold, as baits for curious tastes. [5]
What need is here of Man? unless
These as sweet sins we should confess.

24

185 "Each Night among us to your side
Appoint a fresh and Virgin Bride;
Whom if *our Lord* at midnight find,
Yet neither should be left behind.
Where you may lie as chaste in bed,
190 As pearls together billeted,
All night embracing arm in arm
Like crystal pure with cotton warm.

25

"But what is this to all the store
Of joys you see, and may make more!
195 Try but a while, if you be wise:
The trial neither costs, nor ties."
Now, *Fairfax*, seek her promised faith:
Religion that dispensèd hath,

---

[1] *lilies* emblematic of chastity.

[2] *Devoto* devotee, in a religious sense; see *OED* devoto *sb* A.

[3] *nice* "strict…in conduct" (*OED* nice *a* 7d).

[4] *uncorrupting* preserving.

[5] *curious* "difficult to satisfy…fastidious" (*OED* curious *a* 2).

Which she henceforward does begin; [1]
200 The nun's smooth tongue has sucked her in.

26

Oft, though he knew it was in vain,
Yet would he valiantly complain.
"Is this that *Sanctity* so great,
An *Art* by which you finelier cheat?
205 Hypocrite witches, hence avaunt,
Who though in prison yet enchant!
Death only can such thieves make fast,
As rob though in the dungeon cast.

27

"Were there but, when this House was made,
210 One stone that a just hand had laid,
It must have fall'n upon her head
Who first thee from thy faith misled.
And yet, how well soever meant,
With them 'twould soon grow fraudulent:
215 For like themselves they alter all,
And vice infects the very wall.

28

"But sure those buildings last not long,
Founded by folly, kept by wrong.
I know what fruit their gardens yield,
220 When they it think by night concealed.
Fly from their vices. 'Tis thy state, [2]
Not thee, that they would consecrate.
Fly from their ruin. How I fear,
Though guiltless, lest thou perish there."

29

225 What should he do? He would respect
Religion, but not Right neglect:

For first Religion taught him right,
And dazzled not but cleared his sight.
Sometimes resolved, his Sword he draws,
230 But reverenceth then the Laws:
For justice still that courage led;
First from a Judge, then Soldier bred.

30

Small honour would be in the storm.
The court him grants the lawful form;
235 Which licensed either peace or force,
To hinder the unjust divorce.
Yet still the *Nuns* his right debarred,
Standing upon their holy guard.
Ill-counselled women, do you know
240 Whom you resist, or what you do?

31

Is not this he whose offspring fierce
Shall fight through all the universe;
And with successive valour try
France, Poland, either Germany;
245 Till one, as long since prophesied,
His horse through conquered Britain ride?
Yet, against Fate, his Spouse they kept,
And the great race would intercept. [3]

32

Some to the breach against their foes
250 Their *Wooden Saints* in vain oppose.
Another bolder stands at push
With their old *Holy-Water Brush*.
While the disjointed *Abbess* threads
The jingling chain-shot of her *Beads*.
255 But their loud'st cannon were their lungs;
And sharpest weapons were their tongues. [4]

---

[1] *Now, Fairfax, seek…does begin* seek her promised word, from which religion, which she now begins, has dispensed her. (This does not mean that she has been converted to Christianity, but that she has begun the life of a "religious.")

[2] *state* estate.

---

[3] *the great race would intercept* They would prevent William Fairfax and Isabel Thwaites from founding a family.

[4] Marvell, firmly Protestant and anti-Catholic, clearly enjoyed writing this section on the house's history.

33

But, waving these aside like flies,
Young *Fairfax* through the wall does rise.
Then th' unfrequented vault appeared,
260 And superstitions vainly feared.
The *Relics* false were set to view;
Only the Jewels there were true—
But truly bright and holy *Thwaites*
That weeping at the *Altar* waits.

34

265 But the glad youth away her bears,
And to the *Nuns* bequeaths her tears:
Who guiltily their Prize bemoan,
Like gypsies that a child had stolen.
Thenceforth (as when the Enchantment ends,
270 The Castle vanishes or rends)
The wasting Cloister with the rest
Was in one instant dispossessed.

35

At the demolishing, this seat
To *Fairfax* fell as by escheat. [1]
275 And what both *Nuns* and *Founders* willed
'Tis likely better thus fulfilled.
For if the *Virgin* proved not theirs,
The *Cloister* yet remainèd hers.
Though many a *Nun* there made her vow,
280 'Twas no *Religious House* till now.

36

From that blest bed the *Hero* came,
Whom *France* and *Poland* yet does fame: [2]
Who, when retirèd here to peace,
His warlike Studies could not cease;
285 But laid these gardens out in sport

In the just figure of a fort;
And with five bastions it did fence,
As aiming one for every sense.

37

When in the *East* the morning ray
290 Hangs out the Colours of the Day,
The Bee through these known Allies hums, [3]
Beating the *Dian* with its *drums*. [4]
Then flowers their drowsy eyelids raise,
Their silken ensigns each displays,
295 And dries its pan yet dank with dew,
And fills its flask with odours new. [5]

38

These, as their *Governor* goes by,
In fragrant volleys they let fly;
And to salute their *Governess*
300 Again as great a charge they press:
None for the *Virgin Nymph*; for she [6]
Seems with the flowers a flower to be.
And think so still! though not compare [7]
With breath so sweet, or cheek so fair.

39

305 Well shot, ye firemen! Oh how sweet,
And round your equal fires do meet,
Whose shrill report no ear can tell,
But echoes to the eye and smell.
See how the flowers, as at *Parade*,

---

[1] *as by escheat* This legal term is a polite way of saying that the land was given to Fairfax at the Dissolution.

[2] *the Hero* The reference seems naturally to apply to the son of William and Isabella, Sir Thomas Fairfax; arguments have been made for it referring to his son or to his grandson, who was Marvell's patron.

---

[3] *Allies* The primary meaning is probably "alleys," but the old spelling allows for an appropriate military pun.

[4] *Dian* "a trumpet-call or drum-roll in the early morning" (*OED*).

[5] *pan* the part of the musket-lock which contains the priming; *flask* powder-flask.

[6] *Governor* Lord Fairfax; *Governess* Lady Fairfax; *Virgin Nymph* their daughter Mary, between twelve and fourteen when Marvell was employed as her tutor.

[7] *not compare* Elizabeth Donno reads this as an imperative, telling the flowers not to vie with Mary; alternatively, it may be read as an elliptical indicative (they do not compare with her, for she is superior).

310 Under their *Colours* stand displayed:
Each *Regiment* in order grows,
That of the tulip, pink, and rose.

40

But when the vigilant *Patrol*
Of stars walks round about the *Pole*,
315 Their leaves, that to the stalks are curled,
Seem to their staves the *ensigns* furled.
Then in some flower's belovèd hut
Each bee as sentinel is shut,
And sleeps so too: but, if once stirred,
320 She runs you through, nor asks *the Word*. [1]

41

Oh thou, that dear and happy isle
The garden of the world ere while,
Thou *Paradise* of foúr seas,
Which *Heaven* planted us to please,
325 But, to exclude the world, did guard
With watery if not flaming sword;
What luckless Apple did we taste,
To make us mortal, and thee waste?

42

Unhappy! shall we never more
330 That sweet *Militía* restore,
When gardens only had their towers,
And all the garrisons were flowers,
When roses only arms might bear,
And men did rosy garlands wear?
335 Tulips, in several colours barred,
Were then the *Switzers* of our *Guard*. [2]

43

The *Gardener* had the *Soldier's* place,
And his more gentle Forts did trace.

The nursery of all things green
340 Was then the only *Magazine*.
The *winter quarters* were the stoves,
Where he the tender plants removes.
But war all this doth overgrow;
We ordnance plant and powder sow.

44

345 And yet there walks one on the sod
Who, had it pleasèd him and *God*,
Might once have made our gardens spring
Fresh as his own and flourishing.
But he preferred to the *Cinque Ports*
350 These five imaginary forts,
And, in those half-dry trenches, spanned
Power which the ocean might command. [3]

45

For he did, with his utmost skill,
Ambition weed, but *Conscience* till—
355 *Conscience*, that heaven-nursèd plant,
Which most our earthly gardens want.
A prickling leaf it bears, and such
As that which shrinks at every touch; [4]
But flowers eternal, and divine,
360 That in the Crowns of Saints do shine.

46

The sight does from these *Bastions* ply,
Th' invisible *Artillery*;
And at proud *Cawood Castle* seems [5]
To point the *battery* of its beams.
365 As if it quarrelled in the seat

---

[1] *nor* an alternative reading, giving an opposite sense, is *or; the Word* the password.

[2] *Switzers of our Guard* in reference to the black, yellow and red stripes of the uniform of the Swiss guards at the Vatican.

[3] In this section Marvell is reflecting on the part played by Fairfax in the Civil War and its aftermath. Fairfax, who had been Commander-in-Chief of the Parliamentary forces, resigned and retired to his estates in Yorkshire in June 1650.

[4] *shrinks at every touch* in reference to the so-called "sensitive plant."

[5] *Cawood Castle* seat of the Archbishop of York, two miles from Nun Appleton.

Th' ambition of its *Prelate* great. [1]
But o'er the meads below it plays,
Or innocently seems to graze.

47

And now to the *Abyss* I pass
370 Of that unfathomable Grass,
Where Men like Grasshoppers appear,
But Grasshoppers are Giants there:
They, in their squeaking laugh, contemn
Us as we walk more low than them:
375 And, from the precipices tall
Of the green spires, to us do call.

48

To see men through this meadow dive,
We wonder how they rise alive,
As, under water, none does know
380 Whether he fall through it or go.
But, as the mariners that sound,
And show upon their lead the ground,
They bring up flow'rs so to be seen,
And prove they've at the bottom been.

49

385 No Scene that turns with Engines strange
Does oftener than these meadows change. [2]
For when the sun the grass hath vexed,
The tawny mowers enter next;
Who seem like *Israelites* to be,
390 Walking on foot through a green sea.
To them the grassy deeps divide,
And crowd a lane to either side. [3]

50

With whistling scythe, and elbow strong,
These massacre the grass along:

395 While one, unknowing, carves the *rail*, [4]
Whose yet unfeathered quills her fail.
The edge all bloody from its breast
He draws, and does his stroke detest,
Fearing the flesh untimely mowed
400 To him a fate as black forebode.

51

But bloody *Thestylis*, that waits
To bring the mowing camp their cates, [5]
Greedy as kites has trussed it up, [6]
And forthwith means on it to sup:
405 When on another quick she lights,
And cries, "He called us *Israelites*;
But now, to make his saying true,
Rails rain for quails, for manna, dew." [7]

52

Unhappy birds! what does it boot
410 To build below the grass's root;
When lowness is unsafe as height,
And chance o'ertakes what 'scapeth spite?
And now your orphan parents' call
Sounds your untimely Funeral.
415 Death-trumpets creak in such a note,
And 'tis the *Sourdine* in their throat. [8]

53

Or sooner hatch or higher build:
The Mower now commands the Field,
In whose new traverse seemeth wrought
420 A camp of battle newly fought:
Where, as the meads with hay, the plain
Lies quilted o'er with bodies slain:

---

[1] *quarrelled* found fault with (transitive).

[2] *Scene…Engines strange* in reference to the elaborate stage effects of Court masques.

[3] *Israelites…sea* Exodus 14. Some Parliamentarians saw the victory over Charles I in terms of the Israelites' escape from Pharaoh.

[4] *rail* land-rail or corncrake (*OED* rail *sb* [3]).

[5] *cates* provisions. Compare "caterer."

[6] *kites* The kite is a bird of prey; the word was used figuratively of rapacious persons.

[7] *for* instead of; *manna* Exodus 16:10–15.

[8] *Sourdine* a muted trumpet (*OED*).

The women that with forks it fling,
Do represent the pillaging.

54

425 And now the careless victors play,
Dancing the triumphs of the hay; [1]
Where every mower's wholesome heat
Smells like an *Alexander's sweat*.
Their females fragrant as the mead
430 Which they in *Fairy Circles* tread:
When at their dance's end they kiss,
Their new-made hay not sweeter is.

55

When after this 'tis piled in cocks,
Like a calm sea it shows the rocks,
435 We wondering in the river near
How boats among them safely steer.
Or, like the *desert Memphis sand*,
Short *Pyramids* of hay do stand.
And such the *Roman Camps* do rise
440 In hills for soldiers' obsequies. [2]

56

This *Scene* again withdrawing brings
A new and empty face of things,
A levelled space, as smooth and plain
As cloths for *Lilly* stretched to stain. [3]
445 The world when first created sure
Was such a table rase and pure. [4]
Or rather such is the *Toril*
Ere the bulls enter at Madril. [5]

57

450 For to this naked equal flat,
Which *Levellers* take pattern at,
The villagers in common chase
Their cattle, which it closer rase;
And what below the scythe increased
Is pinched yet nearer by the beast.
455 Such, in the painted world, appeared
Davenant with th' universal herd. [6]

58

They seem within the polished grass
A landskip drawn in looking-glass,
And shrunk in the huge pasture show
460 As spots, so shaped, on faces do—
Such fleas, ere they approach the eye,
In multiplying glasses lie. [7]
They feed so wide, so slowly move,
As *Constellations* do above.

59

465 Then, to conclude these pleasant acts,
Denton sets ope its *cataracts*, [8]
And makes the Meadow truly be
(What it but seemed before) a Sea.
For, jealous of its Lord's long stay,
470 It tries t'invite him thus away.
The river in itself is drowned,
And isles the astonished cattle round.

60

Let others tell the *Paradox*,
How eels now bellow in the ox;
475 How horses at their tails do kick,

---

[1] *hay* a pun, since the hay is also a country dance.

[2] *Roman Camps…obsequies* These burial mounds are actually British in origin.

[3] *Lilly* the famous painter Sir Peter Lely. Pepys spells his name in the same way.

[4] *rase* blank tablet (*tabula rasa*).

[5] *Toril* bull-ring; *Madril* Madrid.

[6] *Davenant…herd* in reference to *Gondibert* 2:6; Davenant describes a painting of the Six Days of Creation in which a "universal herd" appears on the Sixth Day.

[7] *Such fleas…lie* Fleas on the glass look like mere dots until they are viewed through the microscope.

[8] *Denton* an estate on the River Wharfe thirty miles from Nun Appleton. Margoliouth remarks that the meadows are still liable to flood.

Turned as they hang to leeches quick;
How boats can over bridges sail;
And fishes do the stables scale.
How *salmons* trespassing are found;
480 And pikes are taken in the pound. [1]

61

But I, retiring from the flood,
Take sanctuary in the wood,
And, while it lasts, myself embark
In this yet green, yet growing ark,
485 Where the first carpenter might best
Fit timber for his keel have pressed. [2]
And where all creatures might have shares,
Although in armies, not in pairs.

62

The double wood of ancient stocks,
490 Linked in so thick, an union locks,
It like two pedigrees appears,
On th' one hand Fairfax, th' other Vere's: [3]
Of whom though many fell in war,
Yet more to heaven shooting are:
495 And, as they Nature's cradle decked,
Will in green age her hearse expect.

63

When first the eye this forest sees
It seems indeed as *Wood* not *Trees*:
As if their neighbourhood so old
500 To one great trunk them all did mould.
There the huge bulk takes place, as meant
To thrust up a *fifth element*,
And stretches still so closely wedged
As if the night within were hedged.

64

505 Dark all without it knits; within
It opens passable and thin;
And in as loose an order grows,
As the *Corinthean Porticoes*.
The arching boughs unite between
510 The columns of the temple green;
And underneath the wingèd choirs
Echo about their tunèd fires.

65

The *Nightingale* does here make choice
To sing the trials of her voice.
515 Low shrubs she sits in, and adorns
With music high the squatted thorns.
But highest oaks stoop down to hear,
And listening elders prick the ear.
The thorn, lest it should hurt her, draws
520 Within the skin its shrunken claws.

66

But I have for my music found
A sadder, yet more pleasing sound:
The *stock-doves*, whose fair necks are graced
With nuptial rings, their ensigns chaste;
525 Yet always, for some cause unknown,
Sad pair unto the elms they moan.
O why should such a couple mourn,
That in so equal flames do burn!

67

Then as I careless on the bed
530 Of gelid *strawberries* do tread,
And through the hazels thick espy
The hatching *throstle's* shining eye,
The *heron* from the ash's top,
The eldest of its young lets drop,
535 As if it stork-like did pretend
That *Tribute* to *its Lord* to send.

---

[1] *pound*   an enclosure for stray cattle (*OED*).

[2] *the first carpenter*   See the story of Noah's Ark in Genesis 6–7.

[3] *like two pedigrees*   The two woods are joined, like the Fairfax and Vere families.

68

But most the *Hewel's* wonders are,
Who here has the *Holtfelster's* care. [1]
He walks still upright from the root,
540 Measuring the timber with his foot,
And all the way, to keep it clean,
Doth from the bark the woodmoths glean.
He, with his beak, examines well
Which fit to stand and which to fell.

69

545 The good he numbers up, and hacks,
As if he marked them with the axe.
But where he, tinkling with his beak,
Does find the hollow oak to speak,
That for his building he designs,
550 And through the tainted side he mines.
Who could have thought the *tallest Oak*
Should fall by such a *feeble stroke*! [2]

70

Nor would it, had the Tree not fed
A *Traitor-worm*, within it bred,
555 (As first our *Flesh* corrupt within
Tempts impotent and bashful *Sin*).
And yet that *Worm* triumphs not long,
But serves to feed the *hewel's* young,
While the oak seems to fall content,
560 Viewing the treason's punishment.

71

Thus I, *easy Philosopher*,
Among the Birds and *Trees* confer.
And little now to make me wants
Or of the fowls, or of the plants:
565 Give me but wings as they, and I
Straight floating on the air shall fly:

[1] *Hewel* the green woodpecker; *Holtfelster* i.e. holt-feller, wood-cutter. This is the only use of the word recorded in *OED*.

[2] *tallest Oak...feeble stroke!* This, in combination with the following stanza, has been seen as a reflection on the fate of Charles I.

Or turn me but, and you shall see
I was but an inverted tree.

72

Already I begin to call
570 In their most learn'd original:
And where I language want, my signs
The bird upon the bough divines;
And more attentive there doth sit
Than if she were with lime-twigs knit.
575 No leaf does tremble in the wind
Which I, returning, cannot find.

73

Out of these scattered *Sibyl's* leaves
Strange *Prophecies* my fancy weaves: [3]
And in one history consumes,
580 Like *Mexique paintings*, all the *Plumes*. [4]
What *Rome, Greece, Palestine,* ere said
I in this light *Mosaic* read. [5]
Thrice happy he who, not mistook,
Hath read in *Nature's mystic book*. [6]

74

585 And see how chance's better wit
Could with a mask my studies hit! [7]
The oak leaves me embroider all,
Between which caterpillars crawl:
And Ivy, with familiar trails,

[3] *Sibyl* "one or other of certain women of antiquity...reputed to possess powers of prophecy" (*OED*).

[4] *Mexique paintings* pictures made with feathers, described in Thomas Powell's *Humane Industry* (1661).

[5] *Mosaic* that is, in this mosaic formed by the light shining through the leaves, with a pun: the first five books of the Bible were attributed to Moses.

[6] *Nature's mystic book* Nature was regarded as "God's second book"; *Thrice happy he* perhaps in compliment to Fairfax, who was interested in the hermetic books. Attributed to "Hermes the thrice-great," they had much to say about *Nature's mystic book*.

[7] *with a mask my studies hit!* fit me up with a disguise or clothing suitable to my studies.

590 Me licks, and clasps, and curls, and hales.
Under this *antic Cope* I move
Like some great *Prelate of the Grove*. [1]

75

Then, languishing with ease, I toss
On pallets swoll'n of velvet moss,
595 While the wind, cooling through the boughs,
Flatters with air my panting brows.
Thanks for my rest, ye *Mossy Banks*;
And unto you *cool Zephyrs* thanks,
Who, as my hair, my thoughts too shed,
600 And winnow from the chaff my head.

76

How safe, methinks, and strong, behind
These trees have I encamped my mind:
Where Beauty, aiming at the Heart,
Bends in some tree its useless dart;
605 And where the World no certain shot
Can make, or me it toucheth not.
But I on it securely play,
And gall its horsemen all the day.

77

Bind me, ye *woodbines*, in your twines,
610 Curl me about, ye gadding *vines*, [2]
And, oh, so close your circles lace,
That I may never leave this place:
But lest your fetters prove too weak,
Ere I your silken bondage break,
615 Do you, O *brambles*, chain me too,
And, courteous *briars*, nail me through.

78

Here in the morning tie my chain,
Where the two woods have made a lane,
While, like a *guard* on either side,
620 The trees before their *Lord* divide;
This, like a long and equal thread,
Betwixt two *labyrinths* does lead.
But where the floods did lately drown,
There at the evening stake me down.

79

625 For now the waves are fall'n and dried,
And now the meadows fresher dyed,
Whose grass, with moister colour dashed,
Seems as green silks but newly washed.
No serpent new nor crocodile
630 Remains behind our little Nile,
Unless itself you will mistake,
Among these meads the only snake. [3]

80

See in what wanton harmless folds
It everywhere the meadow holds;
635 And its yet muddy back doth lick,
Till as a *crystal mirror* slick,
Where all things gaze themselves, and doubt
If they be in it or without.
And for his shade which therein shines,
640 *Narcissus*-like, the *Sun* too pines.

81

Oh what a pleasure 'tis to hedge
My temples here with heavy sedge,
Abandoning my lazy side,
Stretched as a bank unto the tide,
645 Or to suspend my sliding foot
On th' osier's underminèd root,
And in its branches tough to hang,
While at my lines the fishes twang!

---

[1] *antic Cope* "antic" and "antique" were interchangeable spellings; the former could mean "grotesque"; "cope" could refer to a variety of church-men's garments; Marvell would have known that Milton had used the same phrase in *Apology for Smectymnuus*, 1642.

[2] *gadding vines* Milton's phrase in "Lycidas," published in 1637 at Cambridge, when Marvell was there.

---

[3] *itself* "our little Nile." The river's course is "serpentine."

82

But now away my hooks, my quills,
650 And angles—idle utensíls. [1]
The young Maria walks tonight:
Hide, trifling youth, thy pleasures slight.
'Twere shame that such judicious eyes
Should with such toys a man surprise;
655 *She,* that already is the law
Of all her sex, her age's awe.

83

See how loose Nature, in respect
To her, itself doth recollect;
And everything so whisht and fine,
660 Starts forthwith to its *bonne mine.* [2]
The *Sun* himself, of *Her* aware,
Seems to descend with greater care;
And lest she see him go to bed,
In blushing clouds conceals his head.

84

665 So when the shadows laid asleep
From underneath these banks do creep,
And on the river as it flows
With *eben shuts* begin to close;
The modest *halcyon* comes in sight, [3]
670 Flying betwixt the day and night;
And such an horror calm and dumb,
Admiring Nature does benumb.

85

The viscous air, wheres'e'er She fly,
Follows and sucks her azure dye;
675 The jellying stream compacts below,
If it might fix her shadow so;
The stupid fishes hang, as plain [4]

As *flies in crystal* overta'en;
And men the silent *Scene* assist, [5]
680 Charmed with the *Sapphire-wingèd Mist.*

86

Maria such, and so doth hush
The *world,* and through the ev'ning rush.
No new-born *Comet* such a train
Draws through the sky, nor star new-slain.
685 For straight those giddy rockets fail,
Which from the putrid earth exhale,
But by her *flames,* in *Heaven* tried,
Nature is *wholly vitrified.* [6]

87

'Tis *She* that to these gardens gave
690 That wondrous beauty which they have;
She straightness on the woods bestows;
To *Her* the Meadow sweetness owes;
Nothing could make the river be
So crystal pure but only *She*;
695 *She* yet more pure, sweet, straight, and fair,
Than gardens, woods, meads, rivers are.

88

Therefore what first *She* on them spent,
They gratefully again present:
The meadow carpets where to tread;
700 The garden flow'rs to crown *Her* head;
And for a glass the limpid brook,
Where *She* may all her beauties look;
But, since *She* would not have them seen,
The wood about *her* draws a screen.

---

[1] *quills* floats; *angles* fishing tackle.

[2] *bonne mine* good appearance; *bonne* is disyllabic.

[3] *eben shuts* black shutters; *halcyon* kingfisher.

[4] *stupid* stupified.

---

[5] *assist* stand by (*OED* assist *v* I).

[6] *vitrified* perfected by being turned into glass; a "sea of glass" occurs several times in Revelation (e.g. 4:6); see also Henry Vaughan ("L'Envoy," line 12), for the image of all Nature being vitrified. As Elizabeth Donno points out, a lady's power over a landscape was a standard *topos.*

89

705 For *She*, to higher beauties raised,
Disdains to be for lesser praised.
She counts her beauty to converse
In all the languages as *hers*; [1]
Nor yet in those *herself* employs
710 But for that *wisdom*, not the *noise*;
Nor yet that *wisdom* would affect,
But as 'tis *Heaven's dialect*.

90

Blest Nymph! that couldst so soon prevent
Those *Trains* by Youth against thee meant:
715 Tears (wat'ry shot that pierce the mind);
And *sighs* (Love's cannon charged with wind);
True Praise (that breaks through all defence);
And *feigned complying Innocence*;
But knowing where this *Ambush* lay,
720 She 'scaped the safe, but roughest way.

91

This 'tis to have been from the first
In a *Domestic Heaven* nursed,
Under the *Discipline* severe
Of *Fairfax*, and the starry *Vere*;
725 Where not one object can come nigh
But pure, and spotless as the eye;
And *Goodness* doth itself entail
On *Females*, if there want a *Male*.

92

Go now, fond Sex, that on your Face
730 Do all your useless Study place,
Nor once at Vice your Brows dare knit
Lest the smooth Forehead wrinkled sit:
Yet your own Face shall at you grin,
Thorough the black-bag of your skin, [2]

735 When *knowledge* only could have filled
And *Virtue* all those *furrows tilled*.

93

Hence *She* with graces more divine
Supplies beyond her *sex* the *line*;
And like a *sprig of mistletoe*
740 On the *Fairfacian Oak* does grow;
Whence, for some universal good,
The *Priest* shall cut the sacred bud,
While her *glad Parents* most rejoice,
And make their *Destiny* their *Choice*. [3]

94

745 Meantime, ye fields, springs, bushes, flowers,
Where yet She leads her studious hours,
(Till Fate her worthily translates,
And find a *Fairfax* for our *Thwaites*),
Employ the means you have by Her,
750 And in your kind yourselves prefer;
That, as all *Virgins* she precedes,
So you all *woods, streams, gardens, meads*.

95

For you, *Thessalian Tempe's Seat*
Shall now be scorned as obsolete;
755 *Aranjuez*, as less, disdained; [4]
The *Bel-Retiro* as constrained; [4]
But name not the *Idalian Grove*—
For 'twas the seat of wanton love— [5]
Much less the Dead's *Elysian Fields*,
760 Yet nor to them your Beauty yields.

---

[1] *all the languages* In a 1651 poem to his friend Robert Witty, Marvell writes that "Celia whose English doth more richly flow / Than *Tagus* …Now learns the tongues of *France* and *Italy*." "Celia" seems likely to refer to Mary Fairfax.

[2] *black-bag* mask. The meaning is that knowledge and virtue make a woman more attractive than do cosmetics.

---

[3] *glad Parents…Destiny their Choice* In 1657 Mary married the second Duke of Buckingham, son of the disastrous favourite of James I and Charles I, and himself described by David Ogg as setting "a standard of ducal independence and vagary never since approached." He was the Zimri of Dryden's *Absalom and Achitophel*.

[4] *Thessalian Tempe's Seat* celebrated as a *locus amoenus* (delightful place) by classical poets; *Aranjuez* and *Bel-Retiro* both royal residences in Spain.

[5] *Idalian Grove* in Cyprus, haunt of Venus.

96

'Tis not, what once it was, *the World*,
But a rude heap together hurled,
All negligently overthrown,
Gulfs, deserts, precipices, stone. [1]
765 Your lesser *World* contains the same,
But in more decent order tame;
You Heaven's Centre, Nature's lap,
And Paradise's only Map. [2]

97

But now the *Salmon-Fishers* moist
770 Their *leathern boats* begin to hoist,
And, like *Antipodes* in shoes,
Have shod their *heads* in their *canoes*. [3]
How *Tortoise-like*, but not so slow,
These rational *Amphibii* go! [4]
775 Let's in: for the dark *Hemisphere*
Does now like one of them appear.
—1681

The Garden

1

How vainly men themselves amaze
To win the palm, the oak, or bays, [5]
And their uncessant labours see
Crowned from some single herb or tree,
5 Whose short and narrow vergèd shade
Does prudently their toils upbraid,
While all flow'rs and all trees do close
To weave the garlands of repose.

2

Fair Quiet, have I found thee here,
10 And Innocence, thy sister dear!
Mistaken long, I sought you then
In busy companies of men.
Your sacred plants, if here below,
Only among the plants will grow.
15 Society is all but rude,
To this delicious solitude.

3

No white nor red was ever seen [6]
So am'rous as this lovely green.
Fond lovers, cruel as their flame,
20 Cut in these trees their mistress' name.
Little, alas, they know, or heed,
How far these beauties hers exceed!
Fair trees! wheres'e'er your barks I wound,
No name shall but your own be found.

4

25 When we have run our passion's heat,
Love hither makes his best retreat.
The *gods*, that mortal beauty chase,
Still in a tree did end their race.
Apollo hunted *Daphne* so,
30 Only that she might laurel grow.
And *Pan* did after *Syrinx* speed,
Not as a nymph, but for a reed. [7]

---

[1] Margoliouth considered that this means that since Nun Appleton set a new standard, the world had become by comparison a rude heap; perhaps, but an allusion to "the world turned upside down" by civil strife is also likely.

[2] *lesser World* the "microcosm" of Nun Appleton.

[3] *Antipodes in shoes* "The Antipodes wear their shoes on their heads" (Cleveland, *Square Cap*, line 19). *Antipodes*: literally, "having the feet opposite" (*OED*).

[4] *rational Amphibii* The salmon-fishers are creatures of both land and water. Sir Thomas Browne had described man as "that great and true amphibium."

[5] *the palm, the oak, or bays* wreaths; the traditional awards for military, political, or poetic achievement; the "bays" are laurel bays.

---

[6] *white nor red* emblematic of female beauty.

[7] two myths about the pursuit of fame and the metamorphosis of desire into art. Chased by Apollo, god of poetry, Daphne turned into the laurel tree that became his sacred emblem. Chased by Pan, the god of flocks and shepherds, Syrinx turned into a reed, the basis of the pan-pipe, emblem of pastoral poetry.

5

What wondrous life is this I lead!
Ripe apples drop about my head;
35 The luscious clusters of the vine
Upon my mouth do crush their wine;
The nectarine, and curious peach,
Into my hands themselves do reach;
Stumbling on melons, as I pass,
40 Ensnared with flowers, I fall on grass.

6

Meanwhile the mind, from pleasures less,
Withdraws into its happiness:
The mind, that ocean where each kind
Does straight its own resemblance find, [1]
45 Yet it creates, transcending these,
Far other worlds, and other seas,
Annihilating all that's made
To a green thought in a green shade.

7

Here at the fountain's sliding foot,
50 Or at some fruit-tree's mossy root,
Casting the body's vest aside,
My soul into the boughs does glide:
There like a bird it sits, and sings,
Then whets, and combs its silver wings; [2]
55 And, till prepared for longer flight,
Waves in its plumes the various light.

8

Such was that happy garden-state,
While man there walked without a mate:
After a place so pure, and sweet,
60 What other help could yet be meet!
But 'twas beyond a mortal's share
To wander solitary there:

Two paradises 'twere in one
To live in paradise alone.

9

65 How well the skilful gardener drew
Of flowers and herbs this dial new, [3]
Where from above the milder sun
Does through a fragrant zodiac run;
And, as it works, the industrious bee
70 Computes its time as well as we.
How could such sweet and wholesome hours
Be reckoned but with herbs and flowers!
—1681 (EARLY 1650s?)

On a Drop of Dew

See how the orient dew,
Shed from the bosom of the morn
Into the blowing roses,
Yet careless of its mansion new,
5 For the clear region where 'twas born
Round in itself incloses:
And in its little globe's extent,
Frames as it can its native element.
How it the purple flow'r does slight,
10 Scarce touching where it lies,
But gazing back upon the skies,
Shines with a mournful light,
Like its own tear,
Because so long divided from the sphere.
15 Restless it rolls and unsecure,
Trembling lest it grow impure,
Till the warm sun pity its pain,
And to the skies exhale it back again.
So the soul, that drop, that ray
20 Of the clear fountain of eternal day,
Could it within the human flow'r be seen,
Remembering still its former height,
Shuns the sweet leaves and blossoms green,

---

[1] alluding to the belief that the sea contained a counterpart for every plant and animal on land.

[2] *whets* preens.

[3] *dial* sundial; the garden itself is an hourly and seasonal clock.

And recollecting its own light,
25 Does, in its pure and circling thoughts, express
The greater heaven in an heaven less.
In how coy a figure wound,
Every way it turns away:
So the world excluding round,
30 Yet receiving in the day,
Dark beneath, but bright above,
Here disdaining, there is love.
How loose and easy hence to go,
How girt and ready to ascend,
35 Moving but on a point below,
It all about does upwards bend.
Such did the manna's sacred dew distill,
White and entire, though congealed and chill,
Congealed on earth: but does, dissolving, run,
40 Into the glories of th'almighty sun.
—1681

A Dialogue between the Soul and Body

Soul

O, who shall from this dungeon raise
A soul, enslaved so many ways?
With bolts of bones, that fettered stands
In feet, and manacled in hands.
5 Here blinded with an eye; and there
Deaf with the drumming of an ear.
A soul hung up, as 'twere, in chains
Of nerves, and arteries, and veins,
Tortured, besides each other part,
10 In a vain head, and double heart.

Body

O, who shall me deliver whole,
From bonds of this tyrannic soul?
Which, stretched upright, impales me so,
That mine own precipice I go; [1]

15 And warms and moves this needless frame [2]
(A fever could but do the same),
And, wanting where its spite to try,
Has made me live to let me die,
A body that could never rest,
20 Since this ill spirit it possessed.

Soul

What magic could me thus confine
Within another's grief to pine?
Where, whatsoever it complain,
I feel, that cannot feel, the pain,
25 And all my care itself employs,
That to preserve, which me destroys:
Constrained not only to endure
Diseases, but, what's worse, the cure:
And ready oft the port to gain,
30 Am shipwrecked into health again.

Body

But physic yet could never teach
The maladies thou me dost reach:
Whom first the cramp of hope does tear,
And then the palsy shakes of fear;
35 The pestilence of love does heat,
Or hatred's hidden ulcer eat;
Joy's cheerful madness does perplex,
Or sorrow's other madness vex;
Which knowledge forces me to know,
40 And memory will not forgo.
What but a soul could have the wit
To build me up for sin so fit?
So architects do square and hew,
Green trees that in the forest grew.
—1681 (WRITTEN LATE 1640S-EARLY 1650S?)

---

[1] *mine own precipice I go* explained by Marvell's use of the same image in his *Rehearsal Transpros'd*: "After he was stretch'd to such an height in his own fancy, that he could not look down from top to toe but his Eyes dazzled at the precipice of his stature" (1,64).

[2] *needless* having no need.

The Mower against Gardens

Luxurious man, to bring his vice in use,
　　Did after him the world seduce,
And from the fields the flowers and plants allure,
　　Where nature was most plain and pure.
5　He first enclosed within the gardens square
　　A dead and standing pool of air,
And a more luscious earth for them did knead,
　　Which stupified them while it fed.
The pink grew then as double as his mind;
10　　The nutriment did change the kind.
With strange perfumes he did the roses taint,
　　And flowers themselves were taught to paint.
The tulip, white, did for complexion seek,
　　And learned to interline its cheek:
15　Its onion root they then so high did hold,
　　That one was for a meadow sold. [1]
Another world was searched, through oceans new,
　　To find the *Marvel of Peru*. [2]
And yet these rarities might be allowed
20　　To man, that sovereign thing and proud,
Had he not dealt between the bark and tree, [3]
　　Forbidden mixtures there to see.
No plant now knew the stock from which it came;
　　He grafts upon the wild the tame:
That th' uncertain and adulterate fruit
25　　Might put the palate in dispute.
His green *seraglio* has its eunuchs too,
　　Lest any tyrant him outdo.
And in the cherry he does nature vex,
　　To procreate without a sex.
30　'Tis all enforced, the fountain and the grot,
　　While the sweet fields do lie forgot:
Where willing Nature does to all dispense

A wild and fragrant innocence:
And *fauns* and *fairies* do the meadows till,
35　　More by their presence than their skill.
Their statues, polished by some ancient hand,
　　May to adorn the gardens stand:
But howsoe'er the figures do excel,
　　The *gods* themselves with us do dwell.
—1681

Damon the Mower

1

Hark how the Mower *Damon* sung,
　　With love of *Juliana* stung!
While everything did seem to paint
The scene more fit for his complaint.
5　Like her fair eyes the day was fair,
But scorching like his am'rous care.
Sharp like his scythe his sorrow was,
And withered like his hopes the grass.

2

"Oh what unusual heats are here,
10　Which thus our sunburned meadows sear!
The grasshopper its pipe gives o'er;
And hamstringed frogs can dance no more.
But in the brook the green frog wades;
And grasshoppers seek out the shades.
15　Only the snake, that kept within,
Now glitters in its second skin.

3

"This heat the sun could never raise,
Nor Dog Star so inflame the days.
It from an higher beauty grow'th,
20　Which burns the fields and mower both:
Which mads the dog, and makes the sun
Hotter than his own *Phaëton*. [4]

----

[1] *For a meadow sold*　referring to the "tulip mania" in Holland in the 1630s, during which spectacular prices were paid for some bulbs.

[2] *Marvel of Peru*　a multi-coloured tropical flower.

[3] *between the bark and tree*　proverbial expression for interfering activity, here made literal through the reference to grafting.

----

[4] *Phaëton*　He set the world on fire when driving the chariot of his father, the sun god.

Not *July* causeth these extremes,
But *Juliana's* scorching beams. [1]

4

25 "Tell me where I may pass the fires
Of the hot day, or hot desires.
To what cool cave shall I descend,
Or to what gelid fountain bend?
Alas! I look for ease in vain,
30 When remedies themselves complain.
No moisture but my tears do rest,
Nor cold but in her icy breast.

5

"How long wilt thou, fair shepherdess,
Esteem me, and my presents less?
35 To thee the harmless snake I bring,
Disarmèd of its teeth and sting;
To thee *chameleons*, changing hue,
And oak leaves tipped with honey dew.
Yet thou, ungrateful, hast not sought
40 Nor what they are, nor who them brought.

6

"I am the Mower *Damon*, known
Through all the meadows I have mown.
On me the morn her dew distills
Before her darling daffodils.
45 And, if at noon my toil me heat,
The sun himself licks off my sweat.
While, going home, the evening sweet
In cowslip-water bathes my feet.

7

"What, though the piping shepherd stock
50 The plains with an unnumbered flock,
This scythe of mine discovers wide
More ground than all his sheep do hide.
With this the golden fleece I shear

Of all these closes every year.
55 And though in wool more poor than they,
Yet am I richer far in hay.

8

"Nor am I so deformed to sight,
If in my scythe I lookèd right;
In which I see my picture done,
60 As in a crescent moon the sun.
The deathless fairies takes me oft
To lead them in their dances soft:
And, when I tune myself to sing,
About me they contract their ring.

9

65 "How happy might I still have mowed,
Had not Love here his thistles sowed!
But now I all the day complain,
Joining my labour to my pain;
And with my scythe cut down the grass,
70 Yet still my grief is where it was:
But, when the iron blunter grows,
Sighing, I whet my scythe and woes."

10

While thus he threw his elbow round,
Depopulating all the ground,
75 And, with his whistling scythe, does cut
Each stroke between the earth and root,
The edgèd steel by careless chance
Did into his own ankle glance;
And there among the grass fell down,
80 By his own scythe, the Mower mown.

11

"Alas!" said he, "these hurts are slight
To those that die by love's despite.
With shepherd's-purse, and clown's-all-heal, [2]
The blood I staunch, and wound I seal.
85 Only for him no cure is found,

---

[1] *July* accented on the first syllable; the modern English pronunciation is abnormal and unexplained (*OED*).

[2] *shepherd's-purse, and clown's-all-heal* herbs traditionally used to stanch bleeding and to heal wounds.

Whom *Juliana's* eyes do wound.
'Tis death alone that this must do:
For Death thou art a Mower too."
—1681

The Mower to the Glow-worms

1

Ye living lamps, by whose dear light
The nightingale does sit so late,
And studying all the summer night,
Her matchless songs does meditate;

2

5   Ye country comets, that portend
No war, nor prince's funeral,
Shining unto no higher end
Than to presage the grass's fall;

3

Ye glow-worms, whose officious flame
10 To wandering mowers shows the way,
That in the night have lost their aim,
And after foolish fires do stray; [1]

4

Your courteous lights in vain you waste,
Since *Juliana* here is come,
15 For she my mind hath so displaced
That I shall never find my home.
—1681

The Mower's Song

1

My mind was once the true survey
Of all these meadows fresh and gay,
And in the greenness of the grass
Did see its hopes as in a glass;

---

[1] *foolish fires* a literal translation of *ignes fatui* (will-o'-the-wisps), but also, figuratively, the fires of passion.

5   When *Juliana* came, and she
What I do to the grass, does to my thoughts and me.

2

But these, while I with sorrow pine,
Grew more luxuriant still and fine,
That not one blade of grass you spied,
10 But had a flower on either side;
When *Juliana* came, and she
What I do to the grass, does to my thoughts and me.

3

Unthankful meadows, could you so
A fellowship so true forgo,
15 And in your gaudy May-games meet,
While I lay trodden under feet?
When *Juliana* came, and she
What I do to the grass, does to my thoughts and me.

4

But what you in compassion ought,
20 Shall now by my revenge be wrought:
And flow'rs, and grass, and I and all,
Will in one common ruin fall.
For *Juliana* comes, and she
What I do to the grass, does to my thoughts and me.

5

And thus, ye meadows, which have been
Companions of my thoughts more green,
Shall now the heraldry become
With which I will adorn my tomb;
For *Juliana* comes, and she
30 What I do to the grass, does to my thoughts and me.
—1681

The Character of Holland

*H*olland, that scarce deserves the name of *land*,
As but the off-scouring of the *British sand*;
And so much earth as was contributed

By *English pilots* when they heaved the lead;
5   Or what by th' ocean's slow alluvion fell [1]
Of shipwrecked cockle and the mussel shell;
This indigested vomit of the sea
Fell to the *Dutch* by just propriety. [2]
   Glad then, as miners that have found the ore,
10   That with mad labour fished the *land* to *shore*,
And dived as desperately for each piece
Of earth, as if't had been of *ambergris*,
Collecting anxiously small loads of clay,
Less than what building swallows bear away,
15   Or than those pills which sordid beetles roll,
Transfusing into them their dunghill soul.
   How did they rivet, with gigantic piles,
Thorough the centre their new-catchèd miles,
And to the stake a struggling country bound,
20   Where barking waves still bait the forcèd ground,
Building their *wat'ry Babel* far more high
To reach the sea, than those to scale the *sky*.
   Yet still his claim the injured ocean laid,
And oft at leap-frog o'er their steeples played:
25   As if on purpose it on land had come
To show them what's their *Mare Liberum*. [3]
A daily deluge over them does boil;
The earth and water play at *level-coil*; [4]
The fish oftimes the burger dispossessed,
30   And sat not as a meat but as a guest.
And oft the *tritons* and the *sea nymphs* saw
Whole shoals of *Dutch* served up by *cabillau*; [5]
Or as they over the new level ranged
For pickled *herring*, pickled *Heeren* changed.
35   Nature, it seemed, ashamed of her mistake,

Would throw their land away at *duck* and *drake*. [6]
   Therefore *necessity*, that first made *kings*,
Something like *government* among them brings.
For as with *pygmies*, who best kills the *crane*,
40   Among the *hungry*, he that treasures *grain*,
Among the *blind*, the one-eyed *blinkard* reigns,
So rules among the *drownèd*, he that *drains*.
Not who first sees the *rising sun* commands,
But who could first discern the *rising land*s.
45   Who best could know to pump an earth so leak
Him they their *Lord* and *country's Father* speak.
To make a *bank* was a great *plot of state*;
Invent a *shovel*, and be *magistrate*.
Hence some small *dyke-grave* unperceived invades [7]
50   The *power*, and grows, as 'twere, a *King of Spades*.
But for less envy some *joint states* endures,
Who look like a *Commission of the Sewers*.
For these *Half-anders*, half wet, and half dry,
Nor bear *strict service*, nor *pure liberty*. [8]
55   'Tis probable *Religion* after this
Came next in order, which they could not miss.
How could the *Dutch* but be converted, when
Th'*Apostles* were so many fishermen?
Besides, the waters of themselves did rise,
60   And, as their land, so them did re-baptize,
Though *herring* for their *god* few voices missed,
And *Poor-John* to have been th' *Evangelist*. [9]
Faith, that could never twins conceive before,
Never so fertile, spawned upon this shore,
65   More pregnant than their *Marg'ret*, that laid down
For *Hans-in-Kelder* of a whole *Hans-town*. [10]
   Sure when *Religion* did itself embark,
And from the *East* would *Westward* steer its ark,

---

[1] *alluvion* alluvium; the gradual build-up of land deposited as sediment (*OED* alluvion 1, 3–5).

[2] *just propriety* appropriately (because of their drinking habits).

[3] *Mare Liberum* the freedom of the seas; the title of a book (1609) by the Dutch jurist Hugo Grotius.

[4] *level-coil* a game in which "each player is in turn driven from his seat and supplanted by another" (*OED* level-coil).

[5] *cabillau* codfish (French).

[6] *duck and drake* a game of skipping stones; figuratively, to squander (*OED* duck and drake 1–2).

[7] *dyke-grave* Dutch official responsible for inspecting the dykes.

[8] *Half-anders* as opposed to Holl (whole)-anders.

[9] *Poor-John* dried salt fish (*OED* Poor John 1).

[10] A Dutch woman reputedly gave birth to 365 children at one time; *Hans-in-kelder* "Hans-in-the-cellar," an unborn child (Dutch).

It struck, and splitting on this unknown ground,
70 Each one thence pillaged the first piece he found:
Hence *Amsterdam*, *Turk-Christian-Pagan-Jew*,
Staple of sects and mint of schism grew,
That *bank of conscience*, where not one so strange
Opinion but finds credit, and exchange.
75 In vain for *Catholics* ourselves we bear;
The *Universal Church* is only there. [1]

Nor can civility there want for *tillage*,
Where wisely for their *court* they chose a *village*. [2]
How fit a title clothes their *governors*,
80 Themselves the *Hogs*, as all their subjects *Bores*! [3]

Let it suffice to give their country fame
That it had one *Civilis* called by name,
Some fifteen hundred and more years ago; [4]
But surely never any that *was* so.

85 See but their *mermaids* with their *tails of fish*,
Reeking at *church* over the *chafing-dish*: [5]
A vestal turf enshrined in earthen ware
Fumes through the loopholes of a wooden square.
Each to the *temple* with these *altars* tend
90 (But still does place it at her *western end*),
While the fat steam of *female sacrifice*
Fills the *priest's nostrils* and puts out his *eyes*.

Or what a spectacle the *skipper gross*,
A *water-Hercules butter-coloss*,
95 *Tunned* up with all their several *towns of Beer*, [6]
When staggering upon some land, *snick* and
    sneer,
They try, like statuaries, if they can

Cut out each other's *Athos* to a man: [7]
And carve in their large bodies, where they please,
100 The arms of the *United Provinces*.

But when such amity at home is showed,
What then are their confederacies abroad?
Let this one court'sy witness all the rest:
When their whole navy they together pressed—
105 Not Christian captives to redeem from bands,
Or intercept the Western golden sands—
No, but all ancient rights and leagues must vail, [8]
Rather than to the *English* strike their sail;
To whom their weather-beaten *province* owes
110 Itself—when as some greater vessel tows
A cockboat tossed with the same wind and fate—
We buoyed so often up their *sinking state*.

Was this *Jus Belli & Pacis*? Could this be [9]
Cause why their *burgomaster of the sea* [10]
115 Rammed with gun powder, flaming with brand
    wine,
Should raging hold his linstock to the mine,
While, with feigned *treaties*, they invade by stealth
Our sore new circumcisèd *Commonwealth*?
Yet of his vain attempt no more he sees
120 Than of *case-butter* shot and *bullet-cheese*.
And the torn navy staggered with him home, [11]
While the sea laughed itself into a foam.
'Tis true since that (as fortune kindly sports),
A wholesome danger drove us to our ports, [12]
125 While half their banished keels the tempest tossed,

---

[1] *Catholics…Universal Church*   The English church, which retained bishops, and hence the "apostolic succession," regarded itself as Catholic. Dutch cities offered a rare degree of religious toleration, hence their popularity as refuges for religious exiles.

[2] *a village*   The Hague.

[3] *Hogs…Bores*   punning on "hoog" (high), part of the title used by the ruling Dutch States-General, and Boers.

[4] *Civilis*   Gaius Julius Civilis, a noble Batavian who led a revolt against the Romans in 69–70 C.E.

[5] *chafing-dish*   referring to the small stoves used in Dutch churches.

[6] *Beer*   punning on the common Dutch town prefix "Bier."

[7] *cut each other's Athos*   An ancient sculptor proposed to carve Mount Athos into the shape of Alexander; Dutch skippers, by implication, were large as well as belligerent.

[8] *vail*   salute or show respect to by lowering the flag (*OED* vail v² I).

[9] *Jus Belli & Pacis*   the law of war and peace, the title of another work (1625) by Hugo Grotius.

[10] *their burgomaster of the sea*   the Dutch Admiral Martin Harpertzoon Van Tromp (1597–1653).

[11] *staggered with him home*   in an engagement with the English in May 1652, the Dutch lost two ships.

[12] In November 1652, the Dutch inflicted severe damage on the English fleet; Marvell puts the loss in the best possible light.

Half, bound at home in prison to the frost:
That ours meantime at leisure might careen,
In a calm winter, under skies serene,
As the obsequious air and waters rest,
130 Till the dear *halcyon* hatch out all its nest.
The *Commonwealth* doth by its losses grow;
And, like its own seas, only ebbs to flow.
Besides, that very agitation laves,
And purges out the corruptible waves.
135　　And now again our armèd *Bucentore* [1]
Doth yearly their *sea nuptials* restore.
And now their *hydra* of *seven provinces*
Is strangled by our *infant Hercules*. [2]
Their tortoise wants its vainly stretchèd neck;
140 Their navy all our conquest or our wreck;
Or, what is left, their *Carthage* overcome
Would render fain unto our better *Rome*,
Unless our *Senate*, lest their youth disuse
The war, (but who would?) peace, if begged, refuse.
145　　For now of nothing may our *state* despair,
Darling of heaven, and of men the care;
Provided that they be what they have been,
Watchful abroad, and honest still within.
For while our *Neptune* doth a *trident* shake,
150 Steeled with those piercing heads—*Deane,*
　　Monck, and Blake— [3]
And while *Jove* governs in the highest sphere,
Vainly in *Hell* let *Pluto* domineer.
—1665 AND 1672 (LINES 1-100), 1681 (1653)

---

[1] *Bucentore* the ceremonial galley used to celebrate the annual marriage of Venice to the sea.

[2] *infant Hercules* "infant" because the Commonwealth was but "new circumcised" (l. 118); killing the multi-headed hydra was Hercules' second labour.

[3] The three British Generals-at-Sea, Richard Deane (1610–1653), Robert Blake (1599–1657), and George Monck (1608–1670).

Bermudas

Where the remote *Bermudas* ride
In th' Ocean's bosom unespied
From a small boat, that rowed along,
The listening Winds received this song.
5　　"What should we do but sing his praise
That led us through the watery maze,
Unto an isle so long unknown, [4]
And yet far kinder than our own?
Where he the huge sea-monsters wracks,
10 That lift the deep upon their backs,
He lands us on a grassy stage,
Safe from the storms, and prelate's rage.
He gave us this eternal spring,
Which here enamels everything,
15 And sends the fowl to us in care,
On daily visits through the air.
He hangs in shades the orange bright,
Like golden lamps in a green night,
And does in the pom'granates close
20 Jewels more rich than Ormus shows. [5]
He makes the figs our mouths to meet,
And throws the melons at our feet,
But apples plants of such a price, [6]
No tree could ever bear them twice.
25 With cedars, chosen by his hand,
From Lebanon, he stores the land,
And makes the hollow seas, that roar,
Proclaim the ambergris on shore. [7]
He cast (of which we rather boast)
30 The gospel's pearl upon our coast, [8]

---

[4] *an isle...unknown* The group of islands in the North Atlantic was discovered by Juan Bermudez in 1515.

[5] *Ormus* Compare Milton's "the wealth of Ormus and of Ind" (*PL* 2.2). Ormus, in the Persian Gulf, was famous as a jewel market.

[6] *apples* pineapples.

[7] *Proclaim* make known (*OED* proclaim *v.* 4 *fig.*); *ambergris* a wax-like substance found floating in tropical seas, used in perfumery (*OED* ambergris).

[8] *The gospel's pearl* See Matthew 13:45–46.

And in these rocks for us did frame
A temple, where to sound his name.
Oh let our voice his praise exalt,
Till it arrive at heaven's vault:
35 Which thence (perhaps) rebounding, may
Echo beyond the Mexique Bay."
    Thus sung they, in the English boat,
An holy and a cheerful note,
And all the way, to guide their chime,
40 With falling oars they kept the time. [1]
—1681

The First Anniversary of the Government under His Highness the Lord Protector [2]

Like the vain curlings of the wat'ry maze,
  Which in smooth streams a sinking weight
    does raise,
So Man, declining always, disappears
In the weak circles of increasing years;
5 And his short tumults of themselves compose,
While flowing Time above his head does close.
    Cromwell alone with greater vigour runs,
(Sun-like) the stages of succeeding suns:
And still the day which he doth next restore,
10 Is the just wonder of the day before.
Cromwell alone doth with new lustre spring,
And shines the jewel of the yearly ring.
    'Tis he the force of scattered Time contracts,
And in one year the work of ages acts:
15 While heavy monarchs make a wide return,
Longer, and more malignant than Saturn: [3]

And though they all Platonic years should reign, [4]
In the same posture would be found again.
Their earthy projects under ground they lay,
20 More slow and brittle than the China clay: [5]
Well may they strive to leave them to their son,
For one thing never was by one king done.
Yet some more active for a frontier town,
Taken by proxy, beg a false renown;
25 Another triumphs at the public cost,
And will have won, if he no more have lost;
They fight by others, but in person wrong,
And only are against their subjects strong;
Their other wars seem but a feigned contést,
30 This common enemy is still oppressed;
If conquerors, on them they turn their might;
If conquered, on them they wreak their spite:
They neither build the Temple in their days,
Nor matter for succeeding founders raise; [6]
35 Nor sacred prophecies consult within,
Much less themself to pérfect them begin;
No other care they bear of things above,
But with astrologers divine of Jove
To know how long their planet yet reprieves
40 From the deservèd fate their guilty lives:
Thus (image-like) an useless time they tell,
And with vain sceptre, strike the hourly bell,
Nor more contribute to the state of things,
Than wooden heads unto the viol's strings.
45   While indefatigable Cromwell hies,
And cuts his way still nearer to the skies,
Learning a music in the region clear,
To tune this lower to that higher sphere.

---

[1] In the last two lines Marvell wittily reverses the usual relationship between sailors' shanties and their work. Here the work is subsidiary to the song of praise.

[2] Oliver Cromwell accepted the Instrument of Government, the constitution that made him Lord Protector, in December 1653.

[3] *Saturn* the planet with the longest orbit known at the time; traditionally considered astrologically unfavourable.

[4] *Platonic years* the period that would end when all heavenly bodies returned to their original positions, calculated between 26,000 and 36,000 years.

[5] *China clay* porcelain, the preparation of which was thought to involve burying the clay for an extended period.

[6] Contrasting modern monarchs with David and Solomon (I Chronicles 28–29).

So when *Amphion* did the lute command, [1]
50 Which the god gave him, with his gentle hand,
The rougher stones, unto his measures hewed,
Danced up in order from the quarries rude;
This took a lower, that an higher place,
As he the treble altered, or the bass:
55 No note he struck, but a new stone was laid,
And the great work ascended while he played.

　　The listening structures he with wonder eyed,
And still new stops to various time applied:
Now through the strings a martial rage he throws,
60 And joining straight the Theban tower arose;
Then as he strokes them with a touch more sweet,
The flocking marbles in a palace meet;
But, for he most the graver notes did try,
Therefore the temples reared their columns high:
65 Thus, ere he ceased, his sacred lute creates
Th' harmonious city of the seven gates.

　　Such was that wondrous order and consent,
When *Cromwell* tuned the ruling Instrument, [2]
While tedious statesmen many years did hack,
70 Framing a liberty that still went back,
Whose num'rous gorge could swallow in an hour
That island, which the sea cannot devour:
Then our *Amphion* issues out and sings,
And once he struck, and twice, the powerful
　　strings.
75 　　The Commonwealth then first together came,
And each one entered in the willing frame;
All other matter yields, and may be ruled;
But who the minds of stubborn men can build?
No quarry bears a stone so hardly wrought,
80 Nor with such labour from its centre brought;
None to be sunk in the foundation bends,
Each in the house the highest place contends,
And each the hand that lays him will direct,

And some fall back upon the architect;
85 Yet all composed by his attractive song,
Into the animated city throng.
　　The Commonwealth does through their
　　　centres all
Draw the circumf'rence of the public wall;
The crossest spirits here do take their part,
90 Fast'ning the contignation which they thwart; [3]
And they, whose nature leads them to divide,
Uphold, this one, and that the other side;
But the most equal still sustain the height,
And they as pillars keep the work upright,
95 While the resistance of opposèd minds,
The fabric (as with arches) stronger binds,
Which on the basis of a senate free,
Knit by the roof's protecting weight, agree.
　　When for his foot he thus a place had found,
100 He hurls e'er since the world about him round, [4]
And in his several aspects, like a star,
Here shines in peace, and thither shoots in war,
While by his beams observing princes steer,
And wisely court the influence they fear.
105 O would they rather by his pattern won
Kiss the approaching, not yet angry Son; [5]
And in their numbered footsteps humbly tread
The path where holy oracles do lead;
How might they under such a captain raise
110 The great designs kept for the latter days!
But mad with reason (so miscalled) of state
They know them not, and what they know not,
　　hate.
Hence still they sing hosanna to the whore,
And her, whom they should massacre, adore:

---

[1] *Amphion*　In classical myth, Amphion built a wall around Thebes by playing his lyre (given him by the god Hermes) with such skill that the stones moved of their own accord.

[2] *Instrument*　with a pun on the Instrument of Government, the constitution that established Cromwell as Lord Protector.

[3] *contignation*　frame (*OED* contignation 2). This passage plays on architectural metaphors to suggest that the presence of opposing interests within a country paradoxically provides strength when the government is framed as a commonwealth.

[4] *his foot*　The Greek mathematician Archimedes reportedly claimed that, given a place to stand and a lever long enough, he could move the world.

[5] See Psalm 2:10–12.

115 But Indians, whom they should convert, subdue;
Nor teach, but traffic with, or burn the Jew. [1]
  Unhappy princes, ignorantly bred,
By malice some, by error more misled,
If gracious heaven to my life give length,
120 Leisure to time, and to my weakness strength,
Then shall I once with graver accents shake
Your regal sloth, and your long slumbers wake:
Like the shrill huntsman that prevents the east,
Winding his horn to kings that chase the beast.
125   Till then my muse shall hollo far behind
Angelic *Cromwell* who outwings the wind,
And in dark nights, and in cold days alone
Pursues the monster thorough every throne: [2]
Which shrinking to her *Roman* den impure,
130 Gnashes her gory teeth; nor there secure.
  Hence oft I think if in some happy hour
High grace should meet in one with highest
    power,
And then a seasonable people still
Should bend to his, as he to heaven's will,
135 What we might hope, what wonderful effect
From such a wished conjuncture might reflect.
Sure, the mysterious work, where none withstand,
Would forthwith finish under such a hand:
Foreshortened time its useless course would stay,
140 And soon precipitate the latest day.
But a thick cloud about that morning lies,
And intercepts the beams of mortal eyes,
That 'tis the most which we determine can,
If these the times, then this must be the man.
145 And well he therefore does, and well has guessed,
Who in his age has always forward pressed;
And knowing not where heaven's choice may
    light,

Girds yet his sword, and ready stands to fight;
But men, alas, as if they nothing cared,
150 Look on, all unconcerned, or unprepared;
And stars still fall, and still the dragon's tail
Swinges the volumes of its horrid flail.
For the great justice that did first suspend
The world by sin, does by the same extend.
155 Hence that blest day still counterpoisèd wastes,
The ill delaying what th'elected hastes;
Hence landing nature to new seas is tossed,
And good designs still with their authors lost.
  And thou, great *Cromwell*, for whose happy
    birth
160 A mould was chosen out of better earth;
Whose saint-like mother we did lately see
Live out an age, long as a pedigree; [3]
That she might seem (could we the Fall dispute),
T'have smelled the blossom, and not eat the fruit;
165 Though none does of more lasting parents grow,
Yet never any did them honour so,
Though thou thine heart from evil still unstained,
And always hast thy tongue from fraud refrained;
Thou, who so oft through storms of thundering
    lead
170 Hast born securely thine undaunted head,
Thy breast through poniarding conspiracies,
Drawn from the sheath of lying prophecies;
Thee proof beyond all other force or skill,
Our sins endanger, and shall one day kill.
175   How near they failed, and in thy sudden fall
At once assayed to overturn us all. [4]
Our brutish fury struggling to be free,
Hurried thy horses while they hurried thee,
When thou hadst almost quit thy mortal cares,
180 And soiled in dust thy crown of silver hairs.
  Let this one sorrow interweave among

---

[1] The conversion of the Jews was thought to be a necessary prelude to the arrival of Judgement Day; with this in mind, Cromwell in 1655 formally readmitted Jews into England, from which they had been banned since 1290.

[2] *monster* the Whore of Babylon (Revelation 17:5), identified by Protestant commentators with the Roman Catholic church.

[3] Cromwell's mother Elizabeth died in November 1654, at the age of ninety-four.

[4] *thy sudden fall* In September 1654, Cromwell survived a potentially fatal accident when he overturned while driving a coach with six horses in Hyde Park.

The other glories of our yearly song.
Like skilful looms, which through the costly
    thread
Of purling ore, a shining wave do shed:
185 So shall the tears we on past grief employ,
Still as they trickle, glitter in our joy.
So with more modesty we may be true,
And speak, as of the dead, the praises due:
While impious men deceived with pleasure short,
190 On their own hopes shall find the fall retort.
    But the poor beasts, wanting their noble
        guide,
(What could they more?) shrunk guiltily aside.
First wingèd Fear transports them far away,
And leaden Sorrow then their flight did stay.
195 See how they each his towering crest abate,
And the green grass, and their known mangers
    hate,
Nor through wide nostrils snuff the wanton air,
Nor their round hoofs, or curlèd manes compare;
With wand'ring eyes, and restless ears they stood,
200 And with shrill neighings asked him of the wood.
    Thou, *Cromwell*, falling, not a stupid tree,
Or rock so savage, but it mourned for thee:
And all about was heard a panic groan,
As if that Nature's self were overthrown.
205 It seemed the earth did from the centre tear;
It seemed the sun was fall'n out of the sphere:
Justice obstructed lay, and reason fooled;
Courage disheartened, and religion cooled.
A dismal silence through the palace went,
210 And then loud shrieks the vaulted marbles rent,
Such as the dying chorus sings by turns,
And to deaf seas, and ruthless tempests mourns,
When now they sink, and now the plundering
    streams
Break up each deck, and rip the oaken seams.
215   But thee triumphant hence the fiery car,
And fiery steeds had borne out of the war,
From the low world, and thankless men above,
Unto the kingdom blest of peace and love:

We only mourned ourselves, in thine ascent,
220 Whom thou hadst left beneath with mantle rent.
    For all delight of life thou then didst lose,
When to command, thou didst thyself depose;
Resigning up thy privacy so dear,
To turn the headstrong people's charioteer;
225 For to be *Cromwell* was a greater thing,
Than ought below, or yet above a king:
Therefore thou rather didst thyself depress,
Yielding to rule, because it made thee less.
    For, neither didst thou from the first apply
230 Thy sober spirit unto things too high,
But in thine own fields exercised'st long,
An healthful mind within a body strong;
Till at the seventh time thou in the skies,
As a small cloud, like a man's hand, didst rise; [1]
235 Then did thick mists and winds the air deform,
And down at last thou poured'st the fertile storm,
Which to the thirsty land did plenty bring,
But, though forewarned, o'ertook and wet the
    King.
    What since he did, an higher force him pushed
240 Still from behind, and yet before him rushed,
Though undiscerned among the tumult blind,
Who think those high decrees by man designed.
'Twas Heaven would not that his power should
    cease,
But walk still middle betwixt war and peace:
245 Choosing each stone, and poising every weight,
Trying the measures of the breadth and height;
Here pulling down, and there erecting new,
Founding a firm state by proportions true.
    When *Gideon* so did from the war retreat, [2]
250 Yet by the conquest of two kings grown great,
He on the peace extends a warlike power,
And *Isr'el* silent saw him raze the tower;
And how he *Succoth's* Elders durst suppress,

---

[1] *the seventh time…didst rise* recalling Elijah, who obtained rain for a drought-stricken Israel (I Kings 18:44).

[2] *Gideon* see Judges 8:9.

With thorns and briars of the wilderness.
255 No king might ever such a force have done;
Yet would not he be Lord, nor yet his son.
    Thou with the same strength, and an heart as
        plain,
Didst (like thine olive) still refuse to reign, [1]
Though why should others all thy labour spoil,
260 And brambles be anointed with thine oil,
Whose climbing flame, without a timely stop,
Had quickly levelled every cedar's top?
Therefore first growing to thyself a law,
Th' ambitious shrubs thou in just time didst awe.
265   So have I seen at sea, when whirling winds,
Hurry the bark, but more the seamen's minds,
Who with mistaken course salute the sand,
And threatening rocks misapprehend for land,
While baleful *Tritons* to the shipwreck guide,
270 And corposants along the tackling slide, [2]
The passengers all wearied out before,
Giddy, and wishing for the fatal shore,
Some lusty mate, who with more careful eye
Counted the hours, and every star did spy,
275 The helm does from the artless steersman strain,
And doubles back unto the safer main.
What though a while they grumble discontent,
Saving himself, he does their loss prevent.
    'Tis not a freedom, that where all command;
280 Nor tyranny, where one does them withstand:
But who of both the bounders knows to lay
Him as their father must the state obey.
    Thou, and thine house (like Noah's eight) did
        rest, [3]
Left by the wars' flood on the mountains' crest:
285 And the large vale lay subject to thy will,
Which thou but as an husbandman wouldst till:

And only didst for others plant the vine
Of liberty, not drunken with its wine.
    That sober liberty which men may have,
290 That they enjoy, but more they vainly crave:
And such as to their parents' tents do press,
May show their own, not see his nakedness.
    Yet such a *Chammish* issue still does rage, [4]
The shame and plague both of the land and age,
295 Who watched thy halting, and thy fall deride,
Rejoicing when thy foot had slipped aside,
That their new king might the fifth sceptre shake, [5]
And make the world, by his example, quake: [6]
Whose frantic army should they want for men
300 Might muster heresies, so one were ten.
What thy misfortune, they the spirit call,
And their religion only is to fall.
Oh *Mahomet*! now couldst thou rise again,
Thy falling-sickness should have made thee reign, [7]
305 While *Feake* and *Simpson* would in many a tome,
Have writ the comments of thy sacred foam:
For soon thou mightst have passed among their
    rant [8]
Were't but for thine unmovèd tulipant; [9]
As thou must needs have owned them of thy band
310 For prophecies fit to be Alcoraned.

---

[1] *like thine olive* referring to the parable in Judges 9:7–15, in which the olive, like *Oliver* Cromwell, refused the offer of kingship.

[2] *corposants* St. Elmo's fire.

[3] *Noah's eight* Cromwell's family, like Noah's (with his wife, three sons and their wives), consisted at the time of eight people (his wife, two sons, and four daughters).

[4] *Chammish* like Ham, Noah's second son, who was cursed for uncovering his father's nakedness (Genesis 9:20–25); his "issue" are the various radical groups conflated together in the lines following (Fifth Monarchists, Quakers, and Ranters) who show their "father" Cromwell similar disrespect.

[5] *fifth sceptre* referring to the Fifth Monarchy men, a radical religious sect who opposed Cromwell after the establishment of the Protectorate; Christopher Feake and John Simpson (see l. 305) were Fifth Monarchists imprisoned in 1654 for sedition.

[6] *quake* probably a glancing reference to the Quakers, founded by George Fox in the late 1640s.

[7] *falling sickness* epilepsy.

[8] *rant* probably a reference to the Ranters, a loosely (if at all) organized group of radical religious writers much demonized in the early 1650s for their antinomianism. For more information, see the selections from Abiezer Coppe and Lawrence Clarkson.

[9] *tulipant* turban.

Accursèd locusts, whom your king does spit
Out of the centre of th' unbottomed pit;
Wand'rers, adult'rers, liars, *Munster's* rest, [1]
Sorcerers, atheists, Jesuits possessed;
315 You who the scriptures and the laws deface
With the same liberty as points and lace; [2]
Oh race most hypocritically strict!
Bent to reduce us to the ancient Pict;
Well may you act the *Adam* and the *Eve*; [3]
320 Ay, and the serpent too that did deceive.

But the great captain, now the danger's o'er,
Makes you for his sake tremble one fit more;
And, to your spite, returning yet alive
Does with himself all that is good revive.

325 So when first man did through the morning
        new
See the bright sun his shining race pursue,
All day he followed with unwearied sight,
Pleased with that other world of moving light;
But thought him when he missed his setting
        beams,
330 Sunk in the hills, or plunged below the streams.
While dismal blacks hung round the universe,
And stars (like tapers) burned upon his hearse:
And owls and ravens with their screeching noise
Did make the fun'rals sadder by their joys.
335 His weeping eyes the doleful vigils keep,
Not knowing yet the night was made for sleep:
Still to the west, where he him lost, he turned,
And with such accents as despairing mourned:
"Why did mine eyes once see so bright a ray;
340 Or why day last no longer than a day?"
When straight the sun behind him he descried,
Smiling serenely from the further side.

So while our star that gives us light and heat,

345 Seemed now a long and gloomy night to threat,
Up from the other world his flame he darts,
And princes (shining through their windows)
        starts,
Who their suspected counsellors refuse,
And credulous ambassadors accuse.
"Is this", saith one, "the nation that we read
350 Spent with both wars, under a captain dead, [4]
Yet rig a navy while we dress us late,
And ere we dine, raze and rebuild their state?
What oaken forests, and what golden mines!
What mints of men, what union of designs!
355 (Unless their ships, do, as their fowl proceed
Of shedding leaves, that with their ocean breed). [5]
Theirs are not ships, but rather arks of war
And beakèd promontories sailed from far;
Of floating islands a new hatchèd nest;
360 A fleet of worlds, of other worlds in quest;
An hideous shoal of wood-leviathans,
Armed with three tier of brazen hurricanes,
That through the centre shoot their thundering
        side
And sink the earth that does at anchor ride.
365 What refuge to escape them can be found,
Whose wat'ry leaguers all the world surround? [6]
Needs must we all their tributaries be,
Whose navies hold the sluices of the sea.
The ocean is the fountain of command,
370 But that once took, we captives are on land.
And those that have the waters for their share,
Can quickly leave us neither earth nor air.
Yet if through these our fears could find a pass,
Through double oak, and lined with treble brass,
375 That one man still, although but named, alarms
More than all men, all navies, and all arms.

---

[1] *Munster's rest*   the remainders or dregs of Munster, the German city taken over in the 1530s by a group of Anabaptists whose beliefs (including common ownership of property and polygamy) made them a byword for socially dangerous religious fanaticism.

[2] *points and lace*   for fastening hose.

[3] *act the Adam and the Eve*   by going naked.

---

[4] *both wars*   the British civil wars and the first Anglo-Dutch War of 1652–54.

[5] *as their fowl proceed / Of shedding leaves*   referring to the belief that Solan geese (gannets) were generated from certain kinds of leaves (in other versions, from barnacles) that fell in the water.

[6] *watery leaguers*   sea-based beseigers.

Him, in the day, him, in late night I dread,
And still his sword seems hanging o'er my head.
The nation had been ours, but his one soul
380 Moves the great bulk, and animates the whole.
He secrecy with number hath enchased,
Courage with age, maturity with haste:
The valiant's terror, riddle of the wise,
And still his falchion all our knots unties.
385 Where did he learn those arts that cost us dear?
Where below earth, or where above the sphere?
He seems a king by long succession born,
And yet the same to be a king does scorn.
Abroad a king he seems, and something more,
390 At home a subject on the equal floor.
O could I once him with our title see,
So should I hope that he might die as we.
But let them write his praise that love him best,
It grieves me sore to have thus much confessed."
395   Pardon, great Prince, if thus their fear or spite
More than our love and duty do thee right.
I yield, nor further will the prize contend,
So that we both alike may miss our end:
While thou thy venerable head dost raise
400 As far above their malice as my praise,
And as the *Angel* of our commonweal,
Troubling the waters, yearly mak'st them heal.
—1655

On Mr. Milton's "Paradise Lost" [1]

When I beheld the poet blind, yet bold,
    In slender book his vast design unfold,
Messiah crowned, *God's* reconciled decree,
Rebelling *Angels*, the Forbidden Tree,
5 Heaven, Hell, Earth, Chaos, all; the argument
Held me a while, misdoubting his intent
That he would ruin (for I saw him strong)
The sacred truths to fable and old song,

(So *Sampson* groped the temple's posts in spite)
10 The world o'erwhelming to revenge his sight.
    Yet as I read, soon growing less severe,
I liked his project, the success did fear;
Through that wide field how he his way should
    find
O'er which lame faith leads understanding blind;
15 Lest he perplexed the things he would explain,
And what was easy he should render vain.
    Or if a work so infinite he spanned,
Jealous I was that some less skilful hand
(Such as disquiet always what is well,
20 And by ill imitating would excel)
Might hence presume the whole Creation's day
To change in scenes, and show it in a play. [2]
    Pardon me, *mighty poet*, nor despise
My causeless, yet not impious, surmise.
25 But I am now convinced that none will dare
Within thy labours to pretend a share.
Thou hast not missed one thought that could be
    fit,
And all that was improper dost omit:
So that no room is here for writers left,
30 But to detect their ignorance or theft.
That majesty which through thy work doth reign
Draws the devout, deterring the profane.
And things divine thou treatst of in such state
As them preserves, and thee, inviolate.
35 At once delight and horror on us seize,
Thou sing'st with so much gravity and ease;
And above human flight dost soar aloft,
With plume so strong, so equal, and so soft.
The *bird* named from that *paradise* you sing
40 So never flags, but always keeps on wing. [3]

---

[1] This poem was published in the second edition of *Paradise Lost* (1674).

[2] *less skilful hand...show it in a play* alluding to John Dryden, who published his heroic drama *The State of Innocence* in 1677, but had it licensed for publication in 1674. According to John Aubrey, when Dryden asked Milton for permission to put his epic into rhyme, Milton gave him leave "to tag" his verses (see ll. 49–50).

[3] The bird of paradise was popularly believed to be always in flight.

Where couldst thou words of such a compass
    find?
Whence furnish such a vast expanse of mind?
Just Heaven thee, like *Tiresias*, to requite,
Rewards with *prophecy* thy loss of sight. [1]
45   Well mightst thou scorn thy readers to allure
With tinkling rhyme, of thine own sense secure;
While the *Town-Bayes* writes all the while and
    spells, [2]
And like a pack-horse tires without his bells.
Their fancies like our bushy points appear,

50 The poets tag them; we for fashion wear. [3]
I too transported by the *mode* offend,
And while I meant to *praise* thee, must *commend.* [4]
Thy verse created like thy theme sublime,
In number, weight, and measure, needs not
    rhyme.
—1674

[1] *Tiresias* a legendary Theban prophet to whom Milton compares himself in *Paradise Lost* 3.33–34.

[2] *Town-Bayes* John Dryden.

[3] "Points" were the ribbons or cords that held up hose; "tags" were the bands of metal, often decorative (hence "bushy points") used to keep them from unraveling. Like tagged points, rhymes were fashionable, decorative, and came in pairs.

[4] That is, the exigencies of rhyme ("the mode") compel the use of one word rather than another.

Henry Vaughan
1621 — 1695

Henry Vaughan was the elder of two twins. His twin brother Thomas was to become the most notable "hermetic" author in England after Robert Fludd, and intellectually the two brothers had much in common. Though the family was well connected, their father was a younger son, and they were not wealthy, and became less so, in all likelihood, as a result of their intransigent Royalism during the Civil War. Henry and Thomas were educated by a clergyman, Matthew Herbert, a few miles from the family home, and then went to Oxford, though certain evidence of Vaughan's residence there is lacking. It has generally been assumed that the twins went to Oxford at the same time, but there is some reason to

believe that Henry may have gone up a little later than his younger brother. Like many elder sons, Henry did not take a degree, but proceeded to London to study at the Inns of Court. The outbreak of the Civil War caused him to return to his native Wales, where he spent most of the rest of his life, making his living as a physician. His work reflects deep religious feeling and a strong engagement on the side of the Royalism and Anglicanism which were defeated in the Civil War. He was a bookish man who also took a strong and informed interest in natural history; one occupation of his later years was writing the common English names of plants in the margins of a book on herbal medicine.

ᴄᴚᴇᴚ

(From *Poems with the Tenth Satire
of Juvenal Englished*)
extract from [1]

A Rhapsody

Should we go now a wandering, we should
    meet
With catchpoles, whores, & carts in every
    street: [2]
Now when each narrow lane, each nook & cave, [3]
Sign-posts, & shop-doors, pimp for every knave, [4]
5 When riotous sinful plush, and tell-tale spurs [5]
Walk Fleet street, & the Strand, when the soft stirs
Of bawdy, ruffled silks, turn night to day;
And the loud whip, and coach scolds all the way;
When lust of all sorts, and each itchy blood
10 From the Tower-wharf to Cymbeline, and Lud, [6]
Hunts for a mate, and the tired footman reels
'Twixt chair-men, torches, & the hackney wheels.
—1646

---

[1] Space forbids printing the whole poem; the extract given is a good example of a manner which Vaughan virtually abandoned in his major work, *Silex Scintillans*.

[2] *catchpoles* officers who arrested for debt; bum-bailiffs. *OED* notes that it has been a word of contempt since at least the sixteenth century.

[3] *nook* "an out-of-the-way corner in or among buildings" (*OED* nook *sb* 3b); *cave* probably used in the Latin sense of a hollow place, a den.

---

[4] *Sign-posts…pimp for every knave* The narrow lanes, shop doors and so on act as pimps on behalf of knaves, i.e. they are conducive to vice and bring profit to those who live by knavery.

[5] *tell-tale* because the spurs clank.

[6] *From the Tower-wharf to Cymbeline, and Lud* from east to west of the City of London. Statues of the "early kings" were placed on Ludgate in 1260, and renewed in 1586 when Ludgate was rebuilt.

(From *Olor Iscanus*)

Upon a Cloak Lent Him
by Mr. J. Ridsley [1]

Here, take again thy *sack-cloth*! and thank
    heaven [2]
Thy courtship hath not killed me; is't not even [3]
Whether we die by piecemeal, or at once
Since both but ruin, why then for the nonce [4]
5 Didst husband my afflictions, and cast o'er
Me this forced *hurdle* to inflame the score? [5]
Had I near *London* in this *rug* been seen
Without doubt I had executed been
For some bold *Irish* spy, and cross a sledge [6]
10 Had lain messed up for their *four gates* and *bridge*. [7]
When first I bore it, my oppressed feet
Would needs persuade me, 'twas some *leaden*
    sheet; [8]
Such deep impressions, and such dangerous holes
Were made, that I began to doubt my soles,
15 And every step (so near necessity)
Devoutly wished some honest cobbler by,
Besides it was so short, the *Jewish* rag

Seemed circumcised, but had a *Gentile* shag. [9]
Hadst thou been with me on that day, when we
20 Left craggy *Beeston*, and the fatal *Dee*, [10]
When beaten with fresh storms, and late mishap
It shared the office of a *cloak*, and *cap*,
To see how 'bout my clouded head it stood
Like a thick *turband*, or some lawyer's *hood*,
25 While the stiff, hollow pleats on every side
Like *conduit-pipes* rained from the *bearded hide*,
I know thou wouldst in spite of that day's fate
Let loose thy mirth at my new shape and state,
And with a shallow smile or two profess
30 Some *Sarazin* had lost the *clouted dress*. [11]
Didst ever see the *good wife* (as they say)
March in her short cloak on the *Christening* day,
With what soft motions she salutes the Church,
And leaves the bedrid mother in the lurch;
35 Just so jogged I, while my dull horse did trudge
Like a circuit-beast plagued with a gouty judge. [12]
    But this was civil. I have since known more
And worser pranks: one night (as heretofore
Th' hast known) for want of change (a thing
    which I
40 And *Bias* used before me) I did lie [13]
Pure *Adamite*, and simply for that end
Resolved, and made this for my bosom-*friend*.
O that thou hadst been there next morn, that I

---

[1] This poem indicates a sociability and sense of humour in Vaughan that is downplayed in *Silex Scintillans*. Ridsley has not been identified.

[2] *sack-cloth* the garb of Christian penitents, therefore a gibe at the discomfort of the cloak.

[3] *courtship* courtesy (*OED* courtship 1b).

[4] *both* that is, dying by piecemeal, or at once.

[5] *forced hurdle* sardonically: "a hurdle forced into service as a cloak."

[6] *Irish* because rugs were made in Ireland; *cross a sledge* across a sledge; see *OED* sledge *sb* [2] 2b: "formerly used for conveying condemned persons to execution."

[7] *messed up* chopped up (*OED* mess *v* 1); *their four gates and bridge* Parts of the dismembered bodies of executed criminals were often exhibited over the city gates and on London Bridge as a deterrent to law-breaking.

[8] *leaden sheet* in reference to the weight of the cloak; *sheet* carries on the connotations of *sack-cloth* in l. 1, since a sheet was also a penitential garment.

[9] *but…a Gentile shag* It was not short in respect of its nap; see *OED* shag *sb* [1] 1c.

[10] *craggy Beeston, and the fatal Dee* Beeston Castle surrendered to the Parliamentarians in November 1645; after they had surrendered, the Royalists were allowed to march out across the River Dee to Denbigh.

[11] *Sarazin* Muslim; *clouted* patched.

[12] *circuit-beast* the horse ridden by the judge as he travelled his circuit.

[13] *a thing…Bias…before me* The reference is to Adamite (naked) and to the saying attributed to Bias of Priene. When Priene was besieged, and everyone gathered together his possessions for flight, Bias made no such preparations, and when asked why, said, "I carry all my possessions with me."

Might teach thee new *Micro-cosmo-graphy*! [1]
45 Thou wouldst have ta'en me, as I naked stood,
For one of the *seven pillars* before the flood, [2]
Such *characters* and *hieroglyphics* were
In one night worn, that thou mightst justly swear
I'd slept in *cere-cloth,* or at *Bedlam* where [3]
50 The mad men lodge in straw, I'll not forbear
To tell thee all, his wild *impress* and *tricks* [4]
Like *Speed's* old *Britons* made me look, or *Picts*; [5]
His villainous, biting, *wire-embraces*
Had sealed in me more strange forms and faces [6]
55 Than *children* see in dreams, or thou hast read
In *arras, puppet-plays,* and *ginger-bread,* [7]
With *angled schemes,* and *crosses* that bred fear [8]
Of being handled by some *conjurer,*
And nearer thou wouldst think (such *strokes* were
      drawn)
60 I'd been some rough statue of *Fetter-lane,* [9]
Nay, I believe, had I that instant been

By *surgeons* or *apothecaries* seen,
They had condemned my razed skin to be
Some walking *Herbal,* or *Anatomy.* [10]
65 But (thanks to the day!) 'tis off. I'd now advise
Thee friends to put this piece to merchandize;
The *pedlars* of our age have business yet,
And gladly would against the *Fair-day* fit
Themselves with such a *roof,* that can secure
70 Their *wares* from *dogs* and *cats* rained in shower,
It shall perform; or if this will not do
'Twill take the *ale-wives* sure; 'twill make them
      two [11]
Fine rooms of *one,* and spread upon a stick
Is a partition without lime or brick.
75 *Horned* obstinacy! how my heart doth fret [12]
To think what *mouths* and *elbows* it would set
In a wet day! have you for two pence e'er [13]
Seen King *Harry's* Chapel at *Westminster,*
Where in their dusty gowns of *brass* and *stone*
80 The judges lie, and marked you how each one [14]
In sturdy marble-plets about the knee [15]
Bears up to show his legs and symmetry?
Just so would this; that I think't weaved upon
Some stiffnecked *Brownist's* exercising loom. [16]

---

[1] *Micro-cosmo-graphy* the description of the microcosm or man (*OED*). The coarseness of the cloak marked his body with as many lines as there are on a map of the macrocosm or "greater world."

[2] *one of the seven pillars before the flood* This appears to be an echo of Proverbs 9:1; but "before the flood" suggests rather the *two* inscribed pillars supposed to have survived the flood; see Josephus, *Jewish Antiquities* I.ii. 3.

[3] *cere-cloth* cloth impregnated with wax or a glutinous substance, used both in surgery and as a winding-sheet for corpses; *Bedlam* the hospital of St. Mary of Bethlehem in London, used as a mental asylum.

[4] *his* its; also in l. 53. *his* as a neuter possessive was in use throughout the century.

[5] *Speed's old Britons...or Picts* In his *History of Great Britain* (1611), Speed mentions elaborate tattooing as characteristic of the ancient Britons and the Picts.

[6] *sealed* impressed.

[7] *arras* tapestry; *ginger-bread* often made in fantastic shapes and elaborately decorated.

[8] *angled schemes, and crosses* astronomical or magical diagrams used by "conjurors" or magicians.

[9] *rough statue of Fetter-lane* Edward Marshall, a stone-cutter, lived in Fetter Lane. His roughed-out statues may have been a feature of the street.

[10] *Herbal, or Anatomy* Books on botany and anatomy were often elaborately illustrated.

[11] *take* captivate (*OED* take *v* 10).

[12] *Horned obstinacy* probably exclaiming on the stiffness of the cloak, inflexible as horn.

[13] *how my heart...wet day* Probably Vaughan is thinking of the cloak as stiff enough to be used in setting broken bones and pretending to want it for that purpose on a wet day, when roads would be dangerously slippery.

[14] *each one* each gown.

[15] *plets* pleats. Modernization would probably distort Vaughan's pronunciation. See *OED* plait, pleat and plet.

[16] *Some stiffnecked Brownist's exercising loom* The Brownists were a Puritan sect, followers of Robert Browne. Weavers tended towards Puritanism; *stiffnecked* obstinate; as a Laudian Anglican Vaughan would have been unsympathetic to Puritans; *exercising* in ironic reference to the sense "preaching, or prophesying" (*OED* exercise *v* 10c).

85 O that thou hadst it when this juggling fate
    Of soldiery first seized me! at what rate
    Would I have bought it then, what was there but
    I would have given for the *compendious hut*?
    I do not doubt but (if the weight could please,)
90 'Twould guard me better than a *Lapland-lease*, [1]
    Or a *German* shirt with enchanted lint
    Stuffed through, and the devil's *beard* and *face*
            weaved in't. [2]
        But I have done. And think not, friend, that I
    This freedom took to jeer thy courtesy,
95 I thank thee for't, and I believe my muse
    So known to thee, thou'lt not suspect abuse;
    She did this, 'cause (perhaps) thy *love* paid thus
    Might with my *thanks* out-live thy *cloak*, and *us*.
    —1651

From *Silex Scintillans* (1650)

Regeneration

I

A ward, and still in bonds, one day [3]
            I stole abroad,
    It was high-spring, and all the way
        Primrosed, and hung with shade; [4]
5   Yet, was it frost within,
            And surly winds

---

[1] *Lapland-lease* Compare Habington's "Your Lordship then shall walk as safe, as if a Lapland witch…preserved you shot-free" (quoted *OED* Lapland); *lease* is probably a synecdoche for "woven garment." See *OED* lease *sb* [4] 2: "the crossing of the warp-threads in a loom."

[2] *Or a German shirt…weaved in't* Reginald Scot gives the method of making "a waistcoat of proof" in *Discovery of Witchcraft*, 1584, p. 231. Vaughan's *devil's beard* and *face* draws upon that description.

[3] *A ward, and still in bonds* The literal meaning is that the protagonist is not of legal age, and is bound to follow the commands of his guardian. In the metaphorical meaning, the guardian may be God, and the bondage may be to sin.

[4] *Primrosed* Compare *Hamlet* I.iii.50 ("primrose path of dalliance") and *Macbeth* II.iii.21 ("primrose way to the everlasting bonfire").

Blasted my infant buds, and sin
        Like clouds eclipsed my mind.

2

    Stormed thus, I straight perceived my spring
10   Mere stage, and show,
    My walk a monstrous, mountained thing
        Rough-cast with rocks, and snow;
            And as a pilgrim's eye
            Far from relief,
15 Measures the melancholy sky
        Then drops, and rains for grief,

3

    So sighed I upwards still; at last
            'Twixt steps, and falls
    I reached the pinnacle, where placed
20   I found a pair of scales,
        I took them up and laid
            In the one late pains,
    The other smoke, and pleasures weighed
        But proved the heavier grains; [5]

4

25 With that, some cried, *Away;* straight I
            Obeyed, and led
    Full east, a fair, fresh field could spy [6]
        Come called it, *Jacob's bed*; [7]
            A Virgin-soil, which no
30   Rude feet ere trod,
    Where (since he stepped there,) only go
        Prophets, and friends of God. [8]

---

[5] This stanza may be regarded as the literary rendering of an emblem, probably a variation on Francis Quarles, *Emblems* (1639), Book I, Emblem iv, in which the pleasures and honours of the world are balanced against a bubble, and found to be "altogether lighter than vanity."

[6] *Full east* towards the place of rebirth. Vaughan draws upon the "Easter" connotations of "east" in half a dozen other poems.

[7] *Jacob's bed* Genesis 28:10-22.

[8] *Prophets, and friends of God* Wisdom of Solomon 7:27.

5

Here, I reposed; but scarce well set,
    A grove descried
35 Of stately height, whose branches met
    And mixed on every side;
    I entered, and once in
      (Amazed to see't,)
Found all was changed, and a new spring
40   Did all my senses greet;

6

The unthrift Sun shot vital gold [1]
    A thousand pieces,
And heaven its azure did unfold
    Chequered with snowy fleeces,
45   The air was all in spice [2]
    And every bush
A garland wore; thus fed my eyes
    But all the ear lay hush.

7

Only a little fountain lent
50   Some use for ears,
And on the dumb shades language spent
    The music of her tears;
    I drew her near, and found
    The cistern full
55 Of divers stones, some bright, and round
    Others ill-shaped, and dull. [3]

8

The first (pray mark,) as quick as light
    Danced through the flood,

But, the last more heavy than the night
60   Nailed to the centre stood;
    I wondered much, but tired
    At last with thought,
My restless eye that still desired
    As strange an object brought;

9

65 It was a bank of flowers, where I descried
    (Though 'twas mid-day,)
Some fast asleep, others broad-eyed
    And taking in the ray, [4]
    Here musing long, I heard
70   A rushing wind
Which still increased, but whence it stirred
    No where I could not find; [5]

10

I turned me round, and to each shade
    Dispatched an eye,
75 To see, if any leaf had made
    Least motion, or reply,
    But while I listening sought
    My mind to ease
By knowing, where 'twas, or where not,
80   It whispered; *Where I please.*

Lord, then said I, *On me one breath,
And let me die before my death!*

Song of Solomon 4:16
*Arise O north, and come thou south-wind, and blow
upon my garden, that the spices thereof may flow out.*
—1650

---

[1] *vital gold* The discovery of gold occurs in other early modern conversion narratives, for example those by Jacob Boehme and Vaughan's brother Thomas, who in *Lumen de Lumine* writes of "certain pieces of gold, which she had left behind her."

[2] *all in spice* Song of Solomon 4:16, a passage Vaughan recalls many times.

[3] *stones* emblematic of souls. The bright and round ones (roundness connoting perfection) are those which have "danced" in the cleansing baptismal waters; the others are nailed to the centre of the earth, where Hell was traditionally thought to be.

---

[4] *the ray* God, and Christ, were traditionally symbolized by the Sun.

[5] *rushing wind* See Acts 2:1-2 and John 3:8. It seems likely that Vaughan intended "Nor where" in accordance with John 3:8 to which the passage obviously refers.

The Retreat [1]

Happy those early days! when I
Shined in my Angel-infancy.
Before I understood this place
Appointed for my second race, [2]
Or taught my soul to fancy aught
But a white, celestial thought,
When yet I had not walked above
A mile, or two, from my first love, [3]
And looking back (at that short space,)
Could see a glimpse of his bright face;
When on some *gilded cloud,* or *flower*
My gazing soul would dwell an hour,
And in those weaker glories spy
Some shadows of eternity;
Before I taught my tongue to wound
My conscience with a sinful sound,
Or had the black art to dispense
A several sin to every sense,
But felt through all this fleshly dress
Bright *shoots* of everlastingness. [4]
    O how I long to travel back
And tread again that ancient track!
That I might once more reach that plain,
Where first I left my glorious train,
From whence the enlightened spirit sees
That shady city of palm trees; [5]

But (ah!) my soul with too much stay
Is drunk, and staggers in the way.
Some men a forward motion love,
But I by backward steps would move,
And when this dust falls to the urn
In that state I came return.
—1650

"Joy of my life! while left me here" [6]
¶ [7]

1

Joy of my life! while left me here,
        And still my love!
How in thy absence thou dost steer
        Me from above!
        A life well led
        This truth commends,
        With quick, or dead
        It never ends.

2

Stars are of mighty use: the night
        Is dark, and long;
The road foul, and where one goes right,
        Six may go wrong.
        One twinkling ray
        Shot o'er some cloud,
        May clear much way
        And guide a crowd.

3

God's saints are shining lights: who stays
        Here long must pass

---

[1] The theme of the innocence of childhood had religio-political implications at the time, since it was opposed to Calvinist doctrine. See also Vaughan's poem "Child-hood," and Traherne.

[2] *my second race* In his *Mount of Olives* Vaughan wrote of comparing "my appointed time here with the portion preceding it, and the eternity to follow." The "pre-existence" of the soul, clearly implied in this poem, was another disputed doctrine.

[3] *my first love* See Revelation 2:4. Vaughan echoes this passage in several poems, referring sometimes to Christ, sometimes to the Holy Spirit.

[4] *shoots of everlastingness* The phrase, brilliantly transformed, is borrowed from Owen Felltham, *Resolves* (1634).

[5] *That I might…palm trees* Deuteronomy 34:1–4.

---

[6] This poem seems likely to refer to Vaughan's younger brother William, who died in 1648. The date of Vaughan's first wife's death is unknown, but she was probably alive when the 1650 *Silex Scintillans* was published.

[7] Poems of mourning in *Silex Scintillans* are headed with a pilcrow, or paragraph mark. Vaughan may have used this printer's device, common in Bibles of the period, to suggest that these poems had a special significance for him.

O'er dark hills, swift streams, and steep ways
20   As smooth as glass;
        But these all night
        Like candles, shed
        Their beams, and light
        Us into bed.

                        4
25 They are (indeed,) our pillar-fires [1]
        Seen as we go,
    They are that City's shining spires [2]
        We travel to;
        A swordlike gleam
30   Kept man for sin
        First *out*; this beam [3]
        Will guide him *in*.

—1650

The Morning-Watch [4]

O joys! Infinite sweetness! with what flowers, [5]
    And shoots of glory, my soul breaks, and
        buds!
            All the long hours
            Of night, and rest
5   Through the still shrouds
            Of sleep, and clouds,

This dew fell on my breast; [6]
        O how it *bloods*,
    And *spirits* all my earth! hark! In what rings,
10 And *hymning circulations* the quick world [7]
            Awakes, and sings;
            The rising winds,
            And falling springs,
            Birds, beasts, all things
15   Adore him in their kinds. [8]
            Thus all is hurled [9]
    In sacred *hymns*, and *order*, the great *chime* [10]
    And *symphony* of nature. Prayer is [11]
            The world in tune,
20   A spirit-voice,
            And vocal joys
            Whose *echo* is heaven's bliss. [12]
            O let me climb [13]
    When I lie down! The pious soul by night
25 Is like a clouded star, whose beams though said
            To shed their light
            Under some cloud
            Yet are above,
            And shine, and move
30   Beyond that misty shroud.

---

[1] *pillar-fires* Exodus 13:21.

[2] *that City's shining spires* See the description of the heavenly Jerusalem in Revelation 21.

[3] *A swordlike...First out* Genesis 3:24.

[4] For the title see Exodus 14:24. A marginal note in AV (1649) explains "about the last three hours of the night." This would be from 3:00 hrs to 6:00 hrs; *watch* also had the sense of a religious observance (*OED* watch *sb* 2). Given the theme of the harmony of creation, the fact that the poem falls into nine sections (regarding each set of long and each set of short lines as a section) seems significant; there were nine orders of angels and nine planetary spheres.

[5] *O joys! Infinite sweetness!* Herbert's "The Holy Scriptures I" begins "O book! infinite sweetness!" Vaughan may be implying that the Book of Nature, like the Scriptures, contains divine lessons.

[6] *This dew fell on my breast* In *The Mount of Olives* Vaughan writes "sanctify...my heart with the dew of thy divine Spirit."

[7] *the quick world* In *Anthroposophia Theomagica* Thomas Vaughan writes that "the world, which is God's building, is full of spirit, quick, and living."

[8] *in their kinds* according to their natures. His view that the "creatures" praise God on their own account sets Vaughan apart from Herbert.

[9] *hurled* Given the notion that the order of the world is exhibited in circular motion, this is probably to be understood as "whirled." For the association between the two words, see *OED* "whirl" and "hurl."

[10] *chime* "a system of which all the parts are in harmony" (*OED* chime *sb* [1] 7 *fig*).

[11] *symphony* in the Latin sense, derived from the Greek, of concord, harmony.

[12] *Whose echo is heaven's bliss* Heaven's bliss is the answer to prayer.

[13] *O let me climb* that is, pray; compare "Isaac's Marriage" 44–45.

So in my bed
That curtained grave, though sleep, like ashes, hide
My lamp, and life, both shall in thee abide.
—1650

"And do they so?"

Romans 8:19
Etenim res creatae exerto capite observantes
expectant revelationem Filiorum Dei [1]

1

And do they so? have they a sense
    Of ought but influence? [2]
Can they their heads lift, and expect,
    And groan too? why the elect [3]
5 Can do no more: my volumes said
    They were all dull, and dead,
They judged them senseless, and their state
    Wholly inanimate. [4]
    Go, go; seal up thy looks,
10   And burn thy books.

2

I would I were a stone, or tree,
    Or flower by pedigree,
Or some poor high-way herb, or spring
    To flow, or bird to sing!
15 Then should I (tied to one sure state,)
    All day expect my date; [5]

But I am sadly loose, and stray
    A giddy blast each way;
    O let me not thus range!
20   Thou canst not change.

3

Sometimes I sit with thee, and tarry
    An hour, or so, then vary.
Thy other creatures in this scene
    Thee only aim, and mean;
25 Some rise to seek thee, and with heads
    Erect peep from their beds;
Others, whose birth is in the tomb,
    And cannot quit the womb,
    Sigh there, and groan for thee,
30   Their liberty.

4

O let not me do less! shall they
    Watch, while I sleep, or play?
Shall I thy mercies still abuse
    With fancies, friends, or news?
35 O brook it not! thy blood is mine,
    And my soul should be thine
O brook it not! why wilt thou stop
    After whole showers one drop?
    Sure, thou wilt joy to see
40   Thy sheep with thee.
—1650

"I walked the other day"
¶

1

I walked the other day (to spend my hour) [6]
    Into a field
Where I sometimes had seen the soil to yield
    A gallant flower, [7]

---

[1] "For the creatures, watching with lifted head, wait for the revelation of the sons of God." The Latin of the epigraph is from Beza's translation of Romans; Vaughan probably chose the translation of an important Calvinist in a sardonic spirit, as the poem is opposed to Calvinist views on the "creatures" as expressed in a number of English biblical commentaries.

[2] *influence* that is, of the stars upon earthly things.

[3] *elect* In the Calvinist world-view, people were either "elect" or "reprobate," destined by God to heaven or to hell from the beginning of time.

[4] *inanimate* See n. 7 to "The Morning Watch."

[5] *my date* the day of my death.

[6] *my hour* probably, regular hour of meditation.

[7] *A gallant flower* Compare George Herbert, "Peace," 13–15.

5　But winter now had ruffled all the bower
　　　　And curious store
　　I knew there heretofore.

2

　　Yet I whose search loved not to peep and peer
　　　　I'the face of things [1]
10　Thought with my self, there might be other springs
　　　　Besides this here
　　Which, like cold friends, sees us but once a year,
　　　　And so the flower
　　Might have some other bower.

3

15　Then taking up what I could nearest spy
　　　　I digged about
　　That place where I had seen him to grow out,
　　　　And by and by
　　I saw the warm recluse alone to lie
20　　　Where fresh and green
　　He lived of us unseen.

4

　　Many a question intricate and rare
　　　　Did I there strow,
　　But all I could extort was, that he now
25　　　Did there repair
　　Such losses as befell him in this air
　　　　And would ere long
　　Come forth most fair and young.

5

　　This passed, I threw the clothes quite o'er his
　　　head, [2]
30　　　And stung with fear
　　Of my own frailty dropped down many a tear
　　　　Upon his bed,

Then sighing whispered, *Happy are the dead!* [3]
　　　　What peace doth now
35　　*Rock him asleep below!*

6

　　And yet, how few believe such doctrine springs
　　　　From a poor root
　　Which all the winter sleeps here under foot
　　　　And hath no wings
40　To raise it to the truth and light of things,
　　　　But is still trod
　　By every wandering clod.

7

　　O thou! whose spirit did at first inflame
　　　　And warm the dead,
45　And by a sacred incubation fed
　　　　With life this frame
　　Which once had neither being, form, nor name,
　　　　Grant I may so
　　Thy steps track here below, [4]

8

50　That in these masques and shadows I may see [5]
　　　　Thy sacred way,
　　And by those hid ascents climb to that day
　　　　Which breaks from thee
　　Who art in all things, though invisibly;
55　　　Show me thy peace,
　　Thy mercy, love, and ease,

9

　　And from this care, where dreams and sorrows reign
　　　　Lead me above
　　Where light, joy, leisure, and true comforts move

---

[1] *whose search…face of things* who preferred not to be superficial.

[2] *I threw…o'er his head* that is, replaced the soil over the plant.

---

[3] *Happy are the dead!* "Blessed are the dead which die in the Lord" (Revelation 14:13).

[4] *Thy steps track here below* that is, in observation of and meditation upon the creatures.

[5] *masques and shadows* perhaps a significant pun, involving the notion of mask: concealment and masque: stage representation. The idea is that the natural world both conceals and reveals God, who is, to quote another poem of Vaughan's, "in all things, though invisibly."

60   Without all pain,
There, hid in thee, show me his life again
          At whose dumb urn
        Thus all the year I mourn.
—1650

From *Silex Scintillans* (1655)

"They are all gone into the world of light!"

¶

They are all gone into the world of light!
    And I alone sit ling'ring here;
Their very memory is fair and bright,
    And my sad thoughts doth clear.

5 It glows and glitters in my cloudy breast
    Like stars upon some gloomy grove,
Or those faint beams in which this hill is dressed,
    After the sun's remove.

10 I see them walking in an air of glory,
    Whose light doth trample on my days:
My days, which are at best but dull and hoary,
    Mere glimmering and decays.

O holy hope! and high humility,
15   High as the Heavens above!
These are your walks, and you have showed them
    me
        To kindle my cold love,

Dear, beauteous death! the jewel of the just,
    Shining nowhere, but in the dark;
20 What mysteries do lie beyond thy dust;
    Could man outlook that mark!

He that hath found some fledged bird's nest, may
    know
    At first sight, if the bird be flown;

But what fair well, or grove he sings in now,
25   That is to him unknown. [1]

And yet, as Angels in some brighter dreams
    Call to the soul, when man doth sleep: [2]
So some strange thoughts transcend our wonted
    themes,
        And into glory peep.

30 If a star were confined into a tomb [3]
    Her captive flames must needs burn there;
But when the hand that locked her up, gives room,
    She'll shine through all the sphere.

O Father of eternal life, and all
35   Created glories under thee!
Resume thy spirit from this world of thrall
    Into true liberty.

Either disperse these mists, which blot and fill
    My perspective (still) as they pass, [4]
40 Or else remove me hence unto that hill,
    Where I shall need no glass. [5]
—1655

---

[1] *He that hath found...to him unknown* The bird is a common symbol for the soul; *fair well, or grove* The well and the grove are two of Vaughan's favourite details from Old Testament landscape.

[2] *And yet, as Angels...when man doth sleep* Sir Thomas Browne wrote, "That there should be divine dreams seems unreasonably doubted by Aristotle" (*Works,* ed. Keynes, vol III, p. 230).

[3] *tomb* The tomb was one of Vaughan's metaphors for the body.

[4] *perspective* telescope.

[5] *glass* that is, of the telescope; see also "For now we see through a glass, darkly; but then face to face" (I Corinthians 13:12).

Cock-Crowing

Father of lights! what sunny seed, [1]
What glance of day hast thou confined
Into this bird? To all the breed
This busy ray thou hast assigned;
5   Their magnetism works all night, [2]
     And dreams of Paradise and light.

Their eyes watch for the morning hue,
Their little grain expelling night [3]
So shines and sings, as if it knew
10 The path unto the house of light.
     It seems their candle, howe'r done,
     Was tinned and lighted at the sun. [4]

If such a tincture, such a touch,
So firm a longing can impower
15 Shall thy own image think it much
To watch for thy appearing hour?
     If a mere blast so fill the sail, [5]
     Shall not the breath of God prevail? [6]

O thou immortal light and heat!
20 Whose hand so shines through all this frame,
That by the beauty of the seat,

We plainly see, who made the same. [7]
     Seeing thy seed abides in me,
     Dwell thou in it, and I in thee.

25 To sleep without thee, is to die;
Yea, 'tis a death partakes of hell:
For where thou dost not close the eye
It never opens, I can tell.
     In such a dark, Egyptian border, [8]
30   The shades of death dwell and disorder.

If joys, and hopes, and earnest throes,
And hearts, whose pulse beats still for light
Are given to birds; who, but thee, knows
A love-sick soul's exalted flight?
35   Can souls be tracked by any eye
     But his, who gave them wings to fly?

Only this veil which thou hast broke, [9]
And must be broken yet in me,
This veil, I say, is all the cloak
40 And cloud which shadows thee from me.
     This veil thy full-eyed love denies,
     And only gleams and fractions spies. [10]

O take it off! make no delay,
But brush me with thy light, that I
45 May shine unto a perfect day,
And warm me at thy glorious Eye!

---

[1] *Father of lights* "Every good gift…cometh down from the Father of lights" (James 1:17); *sunny seed* "For [the Soul] is guided by…a seed or glance of light, descending from the first Father of lights" (Thomas Vaughan, *Anima Magica Abscondita*). Cornelius Agrippa had asserted the "solary" nature of the cock in *Three Books of Occult Philosophy* I:23.

[2] *magnetism* the faculty implanted by God in the bird which makes light attractive to it. The word was "used of other attractive forces formerly confused with magnetism" (*OED*).

[3] *expelling night* In hermetic thought "influence" was two-directional, between microcosm and macrocosm.

[4] *tinned* kindled. Thomas Vaughan refers to "the secret candle of God, which he hath tinned in the elements" (*Lumen de Lumine*).

[5] *a mere blast* a mere puff of wind. See *OED* blast *sb* 2.

[6] *the breath of God* Genesis 2:7.

[7] *Whose hand so shines…who made the same* Romans 1:20: "For the invisible things [of God] are…understood by the things that are made."

[8] *Egyptian border* Exodus 10:21.

[9] *veil* Various biblical passages are relevant: II Corinthians 3:13–16; I Corinthians 11:24; Hebrews 10:20.

[10] *This veil…only gleams and fractions spies* "This veil denies God's full-eyed love, and only spies it in gleams and fractions." Compare I Corinthians 13:9–10.

O take it off! or till it flee,
Though with no lily, stay with me! [1]

—1655

The Knot [2]

Bright Queen of Heaven! God's Virgin Spouse
　　The glad world's blessed maid!
Whose beauty tied life to thy house,
　　And brought us saving aid.

5　Thou art the true loves-knot; by thee
　　God is made our ally, [3]
And man's inferior essence he
　　With his did dignify.

For coalescent by that band
10　　We are his body grown, [4]
Nourished with favours from his hand
　　Whom for our head we own.

And such a knot, what arm dares loose,
　　What life, what death can sever?
15　Which us in him, and him in us
　　United keeps for ever. [5]

—1655

---

[1] *Though with no lily, stay with me!* See Song of Solomon 2:16. "In this Song, Solomon…describeth the perfect love of Jesus Christ…and the faithful soul, for his church" (headnote in a Bible of 1649).

[2] The Virgin Mary is addressed as the knot of peace in one mediaeval hymn, and as the knot of love in another.

[3] *ally* combining two senses, "associated by treaty" and "kinsman" (*OED* ally *sb* 5). In view of the title it is relevant that the word is derived from Latin *ad* to and *ligare* to bind, fasten; and that "united" (l. 16) and "untied" are anagrams.

[4] *coalescent…his body grown* Christians regard the Church as the Body of Christ. See I Corinthians 10:17.

[5] Romans 8:35–39 is the background of this stanza, and reminds us of the political context of Vaughan's verse.

The Night

John 3:2

Through that pure *Virgin-shrine*, [6]
　That sacred veil drawn o'er thy glorious
　　　noon [7]
That men might look and live as glow-worms shine,
　　And face the moon:
5　　Wise *Nicodemus* saw such light
　　As made him know his God by night.

Most blest believer he!
Who in that land of darkness and blind eyes
Thy long expected healing wings could see, [8]
10　　When thou didst rise,
　　And what can never more be done,
　　Did at mid-night speak with the Sun!

O who will tell me, where
He found thee at that dead and silent hour!
15　What hallowed solitary ground did bear
　　So rare a flower, [9]
　　Within whose sacred leaves did lie
　　The fullness of the Deity.

No mercy-seat of gold,
20　No dead and dusty *Cherub*, nor carved stone,
But his own living works did my Lord hold
　　And lodge alone;

---

[6] *Virgin-shrine* This phrase refers both to the night sky and to Christ's earthly body. The night sky contains the moon, Diana; the application of the phrase to Christ in his earthly existence is more complex.

[7] *That sacred veil* See Hebrews 10:20 ("the veil, that is to say, his flesh"); *thy glorious noon* Implicit in the phrase is the traditional image of Christ as the Sun of Righteousness.

[8] *healing wings* See Malachi 4:2.

[9] *So rare a flower* In the imagery of the poem the stress is upon Christ's indwelling in natural phenomena, rather than upon a particular historical and personal manifestation.

Where *trees* and *herbs* did watch and peep [1]
And wonder, while the *Jews* did sleep.

25   Dear night! This world's defeat;
The stop to busy fools; care's check and curb;
The day of Spirits; my soul's calm retreat [2]
      Which none disturb!
Christ's progress, and his prayer time; [3]
30   The hours to which high Heaven doth chime.

God's silent, searching flight:
When my Lord's head is filled with dew, and all [4]
His locks are wet with the clear drops of night;
      His still, soft call;
35   His knocking time; the soul's dumb watch,
When Spirits their fair kindred catch.

Were all my loud, evil days
Calm and unhaunted as is thy dark Tent,
Whose peace but by some *Angel's* wing or voice
40   Is seldom rent;
Then I in Heaven all the long year
Would keep, and never wander here.

But living where the sun
Doth all things wake, and where all mix and tire
45 Themselves and others, I consent and run
      To every mire,
And by this world's ill-guiding light,
Err more than I can do by night.

There is in God (some say)
50 A deep, but dazzling darkness; as men here [5]
Say it is late and dusky, because they
      See not all clear;
O for that night! where I in him
Might live invisible and dim.
  —1655

The Book [6]

Eternal God! maker of all
That have lived here, since the man's fall;
The Rock of ages! in whose shade
They live unseen, when here they fade.

5 Thou knew'st this *paper*, when it was
Mere *seed*, and after that but *grass*; [7]
Before 'twas *dressed* or *spun*, and when
Made *linen*, who did *wear* it then:
What were their lives, their thoughts & deeds
10 Whether good *corn*, or fruitless *weeds*.

Thou knew'st this *tree*, when a green *shade*
Covered it, since a *cover* made, [8]
And where it flourished, grew and spread,
15 As if it never should be dead.

Thou knew'st this harmless *beast*, when he
Did live and feed by thy decree
On each green thing; then slept (well fed)
Clothed with this *skin*, which now lies spread
20 A *covering* o'er this aged book,

[1] *trees and herbs did watch and peep* Compare "And do they so?" in which Vaughan attributes a conscious spiritual expectation to the non-human creation.

[2] *The day of Spirits* Into one of his translations Vaughan interpolates "Paracelsus writes,…that the night is the working time of Spirits" (see L.C. Martin, ed., *Works*, Oxford, 1957, 305 and note).

[3] *Christ's…prayer time* Vaughan refers to Mark 1:35.

[4] *filled with dew* Song of Solomon 5:2.

[5] *A deep, but dazzling darkness* Behind these lines lie such passages as I John 4:2 as elaborated by Dionysius the Areopagite.

[6] To see the world of Nature *as* a book was a commonplace; Vaughan's originality is to see it *in* a book.

[7] *paper…grass* Paper was made from linen, which was made from flax (Vaughan uses the word "grass" in its general sense, which was common enough).

[8] *tree…a cover made* The cover of the book was made of thin boards, covered with leather.

Which makes me wisely weep and look
On my own dust; mere dust it is,
But not so dry and clean as this.
Thou knew'st and saw'st them all and though
25 Now scattered thus, dost know them so.

O knowing, glorious spirit! when
Thou shalt restore trees, beasts and men,
When thou shalt make all new again,
Destroying only death and pain, [1]
30 Give him amongst thy works a place,
Who in them loved and sought thy face!
—1655

From *Thalia Rediviva* (1678)

To His Books

B right books! the *perspectives t*o our weak
sights: [2]
The clear *projections* of discerning lights.
Burning and shining *thoughts*; man's posthume
day: [3]
The *track* of fled souls, and their *Milky-Way.*
5 The dead *alive* and *busy*, the still *voice*

Of enlarged spirits, kind heaven's white *decoys*. [4]
Who lives with you, lives like those knowing
flowers,
Which in commerce with *light*, spend all their
hours:
Which shut to *clouds*, and *shadows* nicely shun;
10 But with glad haste unveil to *kiss* the sun. [5]
Beneath you all is dark and a dead night;
Which whoso lives in, wants both health and
sight.
By sucking you, the wise (like *bees*) do grow
15 Healing and rich, though this they do most slow:
Because most choicely, for as great a store
Have we of *books*, as bees of *herbs*, or more.
And the great task to *try*, then know the good:
To discern *weeds*, and judge of wholesome *food*,
20 Is a rare, scant performance; for *man* dies
Oft ere 'tis done, while the *bee* feeds and flies.
But you were all choice *flowers*, all set and dressed
By old, sage *florists*, who well knew the best.
And I amidst you all am turned a *weed!*
25 Not wanting knowledge, but for want of heed.
Then thank thy self *wild fool*, that wouldst not be
Content to know—what was too much for thee!
—1678

---

[1] *O knowing…death and pain* The belief, expressed here, in the restitution of all things at the last day was a popular element in Renaissance hermeticism. It was regarded as false and heretical by many in Vaughan's England, especially so by neo-Calvinist commentators on Romans 8:19–22. See relevant passages in Thomas Edwards, *Gangraena.*

[2] *perspectives* magnifying glasses.

[3] *man's posthume day* the idea being that authors live on in their books.

---

[4] *Bright books…white decoys* This device of piling up comparisons is a feature of Welsh poetry, known as *dyfalu.* Compare Herbert, "Prayer" (I).

[5] *those knowing flowers…kiss the sun* flowers such as the daisy and the marigold.

Margaret Cavendish, Duchess of Newcastle
1623 – 1673

Margaret Cavendish was born in Colchester, Essex, the youngest of eight children of Sir Thomas Lucas, a wealthy landowner, and Elizabeth Leighton. In "A True Relation of my Birth, Breeding, and Life" Margaret recalls that she was raised by her mother after her father's death in accordance with "her birth and the nature of her sex" *(Nature's Pictures*, 1656). Her education, however, was limited to the traditional "feminine arts," a condition which Cavendish laments throughout her writings. When Queen Henrietta Maria appeared in Oxford in 1643, Margaret had a "great desire to be one of her maids of honour," and having obtained permission from her mother, she travelled to Oxford to become her attendant. Soon after her departure, Margaret's mother and brothers were sequestered from their estate and plundered of their goods. Elizabeth Lucas, however, managed to maintain Margaret in good condition to avoid her shameful exit from court. When the court went into exile in France (1644), Margaret met the exiled widower William Cavendish, Marquis (later Duke) of Newcastle, thirty years her senior (a selection from his writing is included in this anthology). Despite the difference in age, William successfully wooed Margaret, drawn, as she claims, to her "bashful fears which many condemned," for he would "choose such a wife as he might bring to his own humours; and not such a one as was wedded to self-conceit, or one that had been tempered to the humours of another." They were married in Paris in 1645. From Paris, they travelled to Rotterdam where they resided for six months until settling in Antwerp, where they remained until the Restoration. There were no children of the marriage.

In 1651, Margaret returned to England in an attempt to save William's estates. However, her application for funds from the sequestration committee was unsuccessful, and but for the assistance of Charles Cavendish, William's brother, they would have had little means of support. The same year, Margaret returned to Antwerp where she lived lavishly on credit. She published her first book of poetry, *Poems and Fancies*, in 1653. She followed this publication with collections of philosophical epistles and treatises, and short prose fictional works before returning to England in 1660. After her return, Margaret spent much of her time at the Newcastle estate writing closet drama, social and philosophical essays, poetry, prose fiction, and her husband's biography.

Viewed as an eccentric because of her unusual dress, her novel scientific notions, and her desire to write for publication, Margaret was criticized by many of her contemporaries including Samuel Pepys and Dorothy Osborne. However, her work was celebrated in some quarters. She was praised by such contemporary female authors as Katherine Philips and Bathsua Makin. Margaret's strengths as a writer lie in her refusal to operate within social and literary convention. She self-consciously engaged in generic innovation, adopted positions in the "masculine" discourses of natural philosophy and history, and challenged the philosophical conceptions of Descartes, Hobbes, More, and Van Helmont. Cavendish was a member of the political rearguard and the philosophical vanguard, and her writing exhibits a struggle between conservative and radical impulses, most notably in her treatment of women and of the non-human world. Margaret Cavendish died in London and was buried in Westminster Abbey.

⬥⬥⬥

The Poetress's Hasty Resolution

Reading my verses, I liked them so well,
Self-love did make my judgement to rebel:
Thinking them so good, I thought more to write;
Considering not how others would them like.
5 I writ so fast, I thought, if I lived long,
A pyramid of fame to build thereon.
Reason observing which way I was bent,
Did stay my hand, and asked me what I meant;
Will you, said she, thus waste your time in vain;
10 On that which in the world small praise shall gain?
For shame leave off, said she, the printer spare,
He'll lose by your ill poetry, I fear;
Besides the world hath already such a weight
Of useless books, as it is over fraught.
15 Then pity take, do the world a good turn,
And all you write cast in the fire, and burn.
Angry I was, and Reason struck away,
When I did hear, what she to me did say.
Then all in haste I to the press it sent,
20 Fearing Persuasion might my book prevent:
But now 'tis done, with grief repent do I,
Hang down my head with shame, blush sigh, and
    cry.
Take pity, and my drooping spirits raise,
Wipe off my tears with handkerchiefs of praise.
—1653

A Discourse of Beasts

Who knows, but beasts, as they do lie,
In meadows low, or else on mountains high,
But that they do contemplate on the sun,
And how his daily, yearly circles run.
5 Whether the sun about the earth doth rove,
Or else the earth upon its own poles move.
And in the night, when twinkling stars we see,
Like man, imagines them all suns to be.
And may like man, stars, planets number well,
10 And could they speak, they might their motions tell.

And how the planets in each orb do move:
'Gainst their astrology no man can prove.
For they may know the stars and their aspects,
What influence they cast, and their effects.
—1653

The Hunting of the Hare [1]

Betwixt two ridges of plowed-land, lay Wat,
Pressing his body close to earth lay squat.
His nose upon his two forefeet close lies,
Glaring obliquely with his great grey eyes.
5 His head he always sets against the wind;
If turn his tail his hairs blow up behind:
Which he too cold will grow, but he is wise,
And keeps his coat still down, so warm he lies.
Thus resting all the day, till sun doth set,
10 Then riseth up, his relief for to get.
Walking about until the sun doth rise,
Then back returns, down in his form he lies. [2]
At last, poor Wat was found, as he there lay,
By huntsmen, with their dogs which came that way.
15 Seeing, gets up, and fast begins to run,
Hoping some ways the cruel dogs to shun.
But they by nature have so quick a scent,
That by their nose they trace what way he went.
And with their deep, wide mouths set forth a cry,
20 Which answered was by echoes in the sky.
Then Wat was struck with terror, and with fear,
Thinks every shadow still the dogs they were.
And running out some distance from the noise,
To hide himself, his thoughts he new employs. [3]
25 Under a clod of earth in sandpit wide,
Poor Wat sat close, hoping himself to hide.

---

[1] This poem is one of the most remarkable expressions of empathy for the non-human to be found in the period.

[2] *form* the nest or lair in which a hare crouches (*OED* form *sb* II.21a).

[3] This couplet was changed in the 1668 edition to: "And running out some distance from their cry,/ To hide himself, his thoughts he did employ."

There long he had not sat, but straight his ears
The winding horns, and crying dogs he hears:[1]
Starting with fear, up leaps, then doth he run,
30 And with such speed, the ground scarce treads upon.
Into a great thick wood he straight way gets,
Where underneath a broken bough he sits.
At every leaf that with the wind did shake,
Did bring such terror, made his heart to ache.
35 That place he left, to champian plains he went, [2]
Winding about, for to deceive their scent.
And while they snuffling were, to find his track,
Poor Wat, being weary, his swift pace did slack.
On his two hinder legs for ease did sit,
40 His forefeet rubbed his face from dust, and sweat.
Licking his feet, he wiped his ears so clean,
That none could tell that Wat had hunted been.
But casting round about his fair great eyes,
The hounds in full career he near him spies:
45 To Wat it was so terrible a sight,
Fear gave him wings, and made his body light.
Though weary was before, by running long,
Yet now his breath he never felt more strong.
Like those that dying are, think health returns,
50 When 'tis but a faint blast, which life out burns.
For spirits seek to guard the heart about,
Striving with death, but death doth quench them
    out.
Thus they so fast came on, with such loud cries,
That he no hopes hath left, nor help espies.
55 With that the winds did pity poor Wat's case,
And with their breath the scent blew from the place.
Then every nose is busily employed,
And every nostril is set open, wide:
And every head doth seek a several way,
60 To find what grass, or track, the scent on lay.
Thus quick industry, that is not slack,
Is like to witchery, brings lost things back.

For though the wind had tied the scent up close,
A busy dog thrust in his snuffling nose:
65 And drew it out, with it did foremost run,
Then horns blew loud, for th' rest to follow on.
The great slow hounds, their throats did set a base,
The fleet swift hounds, as tenors next in place;
The little beagles they a treble sing,
70 And through the air their voice a round did ring!
Which made a consort, as they ran along;[3]
If they but words could speak, might sing a song,
The horns kept time, the hunters shout for joy,
And valiant seem, poor Wat for to destroy:
75 Spurring their horses to a full career,
Swim rivers deep, leap ditches without fear;
Endanger life, and limbs, so fast will ride,
Only to see how patiently Wat died.
For why, the dogs so near his heels did get,
80 That they their sharp teeth in his breech did set.
Then tumbling down, did fall with weeping eyes,
Gives up his ghost, and thus poor Wat he dies.
Men whooping loud, such acclamations make,
As if the devil they did prisoner take.
85 When they do but a shiftless creature kill;
To hunt, there needs no valiant soldier's skill.
But man doth think that exercise, and toil,
To keep their health, is best, which makes most spoil.
Thinking that food, and nourishment so good,
90 And appetite, that feeds on flesh and blood.
When they do lions, wolves, bears, tigers see,
To kill poor sheep, straight say, they cruel be.
But for themselves all creatures think too few,
For luxury, wish God would make them new.
95 As if that God made creatures for man's meat,
To give them life, and sense, for man to eat;
Or else for sport, or recreation's sake,
Destroy those lives that God saw good to make:
Making their stomachs, graves, which full they fill
100 With murdered bodies, that in sport they kill.

---

[1] *winding* blowing (*OED* wind *sb*[1] II.12a).

[2] *champian plains* plains unbroken by hills or wood; an expanse of level open country; possibly a field of battle as the chief scene of military operations (*OED* champian *a* A.1,5a).

[3] *consort* a harmonious combination of voices and instruments (*OED* consort *sb*[2] II.3b).

Yet man doth think himself so gentle, mild,
When he of creatures is most cruel wild.
And is so proud, thinks only he shall live,
That God a god-like nature did him give.
105 And that all creatures for his sake alone,
Was made for him, to tyrannize upon.
—1653

The Pastime of the Queen of the Fairies, when she comes upon earth out of the center

This lovely sweet, and beauteous Fairy Queen,
Begins to rise, when vesper's star is seen.[1]
For she is kin unto the god of night,
So to Diana, and the stars so bright.[2]
5 And so to all the rest in some degrees,
Yet not so near relation as to these.
As for Apollo, she disclaims him quite,[3]
And swears she ne'er will come within his light.
For they fell out about some foolish toy,
10 Where ever since in him she takes no joy.
She saith, he always doth more harm than good,
If that his malice were true understood.
For he brings dearths by parching up the ground,
And sucks up waters, that none can be found.
15 He makes poor man in fev'rish plagues to lie,
His arrows hot, both man and beast do die.
So that to him she never will come near,
But hates to see, when that his beams appear.
This makes the cock her notice give, they say,
20 That when he rises, she may go her way.
And makes the owl her favourite to be,
Because Apollo's face she hates to see.

Owls sleep all day, yet hollow in the night,[4]
Make acclamations that they're out of sight.
25 So doth the glowworm all day hide her head,
But lights her taper-tail, when he's a bed,
To wait upon the fairest Fairy Queen,
Whilst she is sporting on the meady green.
Her pastime only is when she's on earth,
30 To pinch the sluts, which make Hobgoblin mirth:[5]
Or changes children while the nurses sleep,
Making the father rich, whose child they keep.
This hobgoblin is the Queen of Fairies' fool,
35 Turning himself to horse, cow, tree, or stool;
Or anything to cross by harmless play,
As leading travellers out of their way,
Or kick down pails of milk, cause cheese not turn,
Or hinder butter's coming in the churn:
40 Which makes the farmer's wife to scold, and fret,
That she the cheese, and butter cannot get.
Then holds he up the hens' rumps, as they say,
Because their eggs too soon they should not lay.
The good wife sad, squats down upon a chair,
45 Not at all thinking it was Hob the fair:
Where frowning sits; then Hob gives her the slip,
And down she falls, whereby she hurts her hip.
And many pranks, which Hob plays on our stage,
With his companion Tom Thumb, the Queen's page;
50 Who doth like piece of fat in pudding lie,
50 There almost chokes the eater, going awry.
And when he's down, the guts, their wind blows out,
Putting the standers by into a rout.
Thus shames the eater with a foul disgrace,
That never after dare he show his face.
55 Besides, in many places puts himself,

---

1 *vesper's star*   the evening star (*OED* vesper I.1).

2 *Diana*   the moon goddess, patroness of virginity and of hunting.

3 *Apollo*   the sun-god of the Greeks and Romans; the patron of music and poetry.

4 *hollow*   halloo; that is, cry out loud (*OED* halloo *v* 1a).

5 *Hobgoblin*   a mischievous tricksy imp or sprite, potentially a terrifying apparition (*OED* hobgoblin *sb* 1).

As bags, budgets, being a little elf,[1]
To make his bearers start away with fear,
To think that anything alive is there.
In this, the Queen of Fairies takes delight,
60 In summer's even, and in winter's night;
And when that she is weary of these plays,
She takes her coach, and goeth on her ways;
Unto her paradise, the center deep,
Which is the storehouse rich of nature sweet.
—1653

Her Descending Down

The stately palace in which the Queen dwells,
Whose fabric is built of hodmandod shells,[2]
The hangings thereof a rainbow that's thin,
Which seems wondrous fine, if one enter in;
5 The chambers are made of amber that's clear,
Which gives a sweet smell, if fire be near:
Her bed a cherry-stone, carved throughout,
And with butterfly's wing hung about:
Her sheets are made of a dove's eyes skin,
10 Her pillow a violet bud laid therein:
The large doors are cut of transparent glass,
Where the Queen may be seen, as she doth pass.
The doors are locked fast with silver pins,
The Queen's asleep, and now our day begins.
15 Her time in pleasure passes thus away,
And shall do so, until the world's last day.
—1653

"I Language want"

I language want, to dress my fancies in,
The hair's uncurled, the garments loose, and thin;
Had they but silver lace to make them gay,
Would be more courted than in poor array.
5 Or had they art, might make a better show;
But they are plain, yet cleanly do they go.
The world in bravery doth take delight,
And glittering shows do more attract the sight;
And everyone doth honour a rich hood,
10 As if the outside made the inside good.
And every one doth bow, and give the place,
Not for the man's sake, but the silver lace.
Let me entreat in my poor book's behalf,
That all may not adore the golden calf.
15 Consider pray, gold hath no life therein,
And life in nature is the richest thing.
So fancy is the soul in poetry,
And if not good, a poem ill must be.
Be just, let fancy have the upper place,
20 And then my verses may perchance find grace.
If flattering language all the passions rule,
Then sense, I fear, will be a mere dull fool.
—1653

---

[1] *budgets* pouches, bags, wallets, usually of leather (*OED* budget *sb* 1a).

[2] *hodmandod shells* shells of snails (*OED* hodmandod *a* 1).

John Dryden
1631 – 1700

John Dryden was born in Northamptonshire of a Puritan family. He was a King's Scholar at Westminster School from 1644–1650 and then went up to Trinity College, Cambridge. Thomas Hill, a Presbyterian graduate of Emmanuel College, Cambridge (notable for its Puritan tendencies) was the preacher at the local church during Dryden's boyhood, became a regular preacher at Westminster Abbey while Dryden was at the school, and became Master of Trinity College while Dryden was an undergraduate there. Dryden's "lifelong distrust of the clergy" has been ascribed to his long acquaintance with this earnest and long-winded preacher, and his views on church and state to the influence of Richard Busby, who was Headmaster of Westminster from 1638 until 1695. The fact that Busby, a Royalist and Laudian Anglican, was allowed to keep his place after the Royalist defeat, might be taken as evidence of his relative unimportance; in fact as Headmaster of the most important school in England, he was a prominent figure. Dryden's earliest publication, "Upon the death of the Lord Hastings," is an extravagantly baroque poem, demonstrating Dryden's acquaintance with the aesthetic of Charles I's court. However, families like Dryden's benefited from the so-called "retreat from revolution" which followed the execution of Charles I, that is from the defence of private property and the opposition to the extension of democracy. When Cromwell became Lord Protector in 1653, Dryden's kinsman Sir Gilbert Pickering was appointed to the Council of State and Dryden seems to have been given government employment, though just what he did remains obscure. He walked in Cromwell's funeral procession with Milton and Marvell. The "Heroic Stanzas" consecrated to the memory of Cromwell (1659) suggest that Dryden no more foresaw the return of monarchy than did most of his contemporaries. When the Restoration did occur, however, he foresaw, and positioned himself to take advantage of the fact, that it was likely to bring about increased patronage for the arts, and that stage plays would become popular. He became the leading dramatist and political satirist of the Restoration period, but recognized Milton's pre-eminence in classical epic. His non-dramatic verse takes the public sphere for its themes, and two important poems, *Religio Laici* and *The Hind and the Panther*, set forth his position as an Anglican and as a convert to Roman Catholicism. His religious views are consonant with a lifelong dislike of the kind of religious dissent which "turned the world upside down" during his boyhood. As a Roman Catholic, Dryden lost his position at the "Glorious Revolution" in 1688, and from then on made his living by translations of the great classical poets, so heralding the transition from reliance on patronage to reliance on income derived from the sale of his books.

❧❧❧

Annus Mirabilis [1]

The Year of Wonders 1666

DUKE OF ALBEMARLE'S BATTLE, FIRST DAY [2]

Our fleet divides, and straight the Dutch appear,
In number and a famed commander bold:
215 The narrow seas can scarce their navy bear,
Or crowded vessels can their soldiers hold.

---

[1] *Annus Mirabilis* 1666 had been expected to be in some way extraordinary, because 666 is the number of the beast (Revelation 13:18). The Dutch War and the Fire of London were seen as fulfilments of prophecy. The poem represents Dryden's attempt at a "modern epic," that is one without myth and legend. Charles II was so gratified by *Annus Mirabilis* that he made Dryden Poet Laureate.

[2] This extract represents stanzas 54–71 (lines 213–284).

The duke, less numerous, but in courage more,
On wings of all the winds to combat flies;
His murdering guns a loud defiance roar
220 And bloody crosses on his flag-staffs rise.

Both furl their sails and strip them for the fight;
Their folded sheets dismiss the useless air;
Th' *Elean* plains could boast no nobler sight,
When struggling champions did their bodies
    bare. [1]

225 Borne each by other in a distant line,
The sea-built forts in dreadful order move:
So vast the noise, as if not fleets did join,
But lands unfixed and floating nations strove.

Now passed, on either side they nimbly tack;
230 Both strive to intercept and guide the wind:
And in its eye more closely they come back
To finish all the deaths they left behind.

On high-raised decks the haughty *Belgians* ride,
Beneath whose shade our humble frigates go;
235 Such port the *elephant* bears, and so defied
By the *rhinoceros*, her unequal foe.

And as the build, so different is the fight;
Their mounting shot is on our sails designed:
Deep in their hulls our deadly bullets light
240 And through the yielding planks a passage find.

Our dreaded admiral from far they threat
Whose battered rigging their whole war receives.
All bare, like some old oak which tempests beat,
He stands, and sees below his scattered leaves.

245 Heroes of old when wounded shelter sought;
But he, who meets all danger with disdain,

E'en in their face his ship to anchor brought
And steeple-high stood propped upon the main.

At this excess of courage, all amazed,
250 The foremost of his foes a while withdraw.
With such respect in entered *Rome* they gazed
Who on high chairs the godlike fathers saw.

And now, as where *Patroclus'* body lay,
Here *Trojan* chiefs advanced, and there the *Greek*,
255 Ours o'er the duke their pious wings display,
And theirs the noblest spoils of *Britain* seek.

Meantime, his busy mariners he hastes
His shattered sails with rigging to restore;
And willing pines ascend his broken masts,
260 Whose lofty heads rise higher than before.

Straight to the *Dutch* he turns his dreadful prow
More fierce the important quarrel to decide:
Like swans, in long array his vessels show,
Whose crests, advancing, do the waves divide.

265 They charge, recharge, and all along the sea
They drive, and squander the huge *Belgian* fleet.
Berkeley alone, not making equal way,
Did a like fate with lost *Creusa* meet. [2]

The night comes on, we eager to pursue
270 The combat still, and they ashamed to leave:
Till the last streaks of dying day withdrew,
And doubtful moonlight did our rage deceive.

In the *English* fleet each ship resounds with joy
And loud applause of their great leader's fame:
275 In fiery dreams the *Dutch* they still destroy,
And, slumbering, smile at the imagined flame.

---

[1] *Th' Elean plains*   scene of the ancient Olympic games.

[2] *not making equal way*   Some copies read "who nearest danger lay."

Not so the *Holland* fleet, who, tired and done,
Stretched on their decks like weary oxen lie:
Faint sweats all down their mighty members run,
280 (Vast bulks, which little souls but ill supply.)

In dreams they fearful precipices tread,
Or, shipwrecked, labour to some distant shore,
Or in dark churches walk among the dead:
They wake with horror, and dare sleep no more.

DIGRESSION CONCERNING SHIPPING AND NAVIGATION [1]

By viewing nature, nature's handmaid, art,
Makes mighty things from small beginnings
 grow:
Thus fishes first to shipping did impart
620 Their tail the rudder, and their head the prow.

Some log, perhaps, upon the waters swam,
A useless drift, which, rudely cut within,
And hollowed, first a floating trough became,
And cross some rivulet *passage* did begin.

625 In shipping such as this the *Irish kern*,
And untaught *Indian*, on the stream did glide:
Ere sharp-keeled boats to stem the flood did learn,
Or fin-like oars did spread from either side.

Add but a sail, and *Saturn* so appeared, [2]
630 When from lost empire he to exile went,
And with the golden age to *Tiber* steered,
Where coin and first commerce he did invent.

Rude as their ships was navigation then,
No useful compass or meridian known:
635 Coasting, they kept the land within their ken,
And knew no north but when the pole-star shone.

Of all who since have used the open sea,
Than the bold *English* none more fame have won:
Beyond the year, and out of heaven's highway,
640 They make discoveries where they see no sun.

But what so long in vain, and yet unknown,
By poor mankind's benighted wit is sought,
Shall in this age to *Britain* first be shown,
And hence be to admiring nations taught.

645 The ebbs of tides and their mysterious flow
We as art's elements shall understand,
And as by line upon the ocean go,
Whose paths shall be familiar as the land,

Instructed ships shall sail to quick commerce, [3]
650 By which remotest regions are allied;
Which makes one city of the universe,
Where some may gain and all may be supplied.

Then, we upon our globe's last verge shall go
And view the ocean leaning on the sky
655 From thence our rolling neighbours we shall
 know
And on the lunar world securely pry.
—1667

Absalom and Achitophel

si propius stes
te capiet magis.
[if you stand nearer it will attract you more]

TO THE READER

It is not my intention to make an apology for my poem: some will think it needs no excuse, and others will receive none. The design, I am sure, is honest; but he who draws his pen for one party must expect to make enemies of the other. For wit

---

[1] This extract represents stanza 155–164 (lines 617–656).

[2] *Saturn* brought arts and laws to Italy (*Aeneid* 8.3319ff).

[3] *Instructed* By a more exact measure of Longitude (Dryden's note).

and fool are consequents of Whig and Tory; and every man is a knave or an ass to the contrary side. There's a treasury of merits in the fanatic church, as well as in the Papist; and a pennyworth to be had of saintship, honesty, and poetry, for the lewd, the factious, and the blockheads; but the longest chapter in Deuteronomy has not curses enough for an anti Bromingham.' My comfort is, their manifest prejudice to my cause will render their judgment of less authority against me. Yet if a poem have a genius, it will force its own reception in the world; for there's a sweetness in good verse, which tickles even while it hurts, and no man can be heartily angry with him who pleases him against his will. The commendation of adversaries is the greatest triumph of a writer, because it never comes unless extorted. But I can be satisfied on more easy terms: if I happen to please the more moderate sort, I shall be sure of an honest party, and, in all probability, of the best judges; for the least concerned are commonly the least corrupt. And I confess, I have laid in for those by rebating the satire (where justice would allow it) from carrying too sharp an edge. They who can criticise so weakly as to imagine I have done my worst, may be convinced, at their own cost, that I can write severely with more ease than I can gently. I have but laughed at some men's follies, when I could have declaimed against their vices; and other men's virtues I have commended as freely as I have taxed their crimes. And now, if you are a malicious reader, I expect you should return upon me that I affect to be thought more impartial than I am. But if men are not to be judged by their pro fessions, God forgive you commonwealth's-men for professing so plausibly for the government. You cannot be so unconscionable as to charge me for not subscribing of my name; for that would reflect too grossly upon your own party, who never dare, though they have the advantage of a jury to secure them. If you like not my poem, the fault may, possibly, be in my writing (though it is hard for an author to judge against himself); but, more probably, it is in your morals, which cannot bear the truth of it. The violent, on both sides, will condemn the character of Absalom, as either too favourably or too hardly drawn. But they are not the violent whom I desire to please. The fault on the right hand is to extenuate, palliate, and indulge, and, to confess freely, I have endeavoured to commit it. Besides the respect which I owe his birth, I have a greater for his heroic virtues, and David himself could not be more tender of the young man's life than I would be of his reputation. But since the most excellent natures are always the most easy, and, as being such, are the soonest perverted by ill counsels, especially when baited with fame and glory; it is no more a wonder that he withstood not the temptations of Achitophel, than it was for Adam not to have resisted the two devils, the serpent and the woman. The conclusion of the story I purposely forbore to prosecute, because I could not obtain from myself to show Absalom unfortunate. The frame of it was cut out but for a picture to the waist, and if the draft be so far true, it is as much as I designed.

Were I the inventor, who am only the historian, I should certainly conclude the piece with the reconcilement of Absalom to David. And who knows but this may come to pass? Things were not brought to an extremity where I left the story; there seems yet to be room left for a composure; hereafter there may only be for pity. I have not so much as an uncharitable wish against Achitophel, but am content to be accused of a good-natured error, and to hope with Origen, that the Devil himself may at last be saved. For which reason, in this poem, he is neither brought to set his house in order, nor to dispose of his person afterwards as he in wisdom shall think fit. God is infinitely merciful; and his vicegerent is only not so, because he is not infinite. The true end of satire is the amendment of vices by correction. And he who writes honestly is no more an enemy to the offender, than the physician to the patient, when he prescribes harsh remedies to an inveterate disease; for those are only in order to prevent the surgeon's work of an *ense rescindendum*, which I wish not to my very enemies. To conclude all: if the body politic have any analogy to the natural, in my weak judgment, an act of oblivion were as necessary in a hot, distempered state, as anopiate would be in a raging fever.

ABSALOM AND ACHITOPHEL [1]

In pious times, ere priest-craft did begin, [2]
Before polygamy was made a sin;
When man on many multiplied his kind,
Ere one to one was cursedly confined:
5　When Nature prompted, and no law denied
Promiscuous use of concubine and bride;
Then Israel's monarch after Heaven's own heart,
His vigorous warmth did variously impart
To wives and slaves: and, wide as his command,
10　Scattered his Maker's image through the land.
Michal, of royal blood, the crown did wear,
A soil ungrateful to the tiller's care: [3]
Not so the rest; for several mothers bore
To godlike David, several sons before.
15　But since like slaves his bed they did ascend,
No true succession could their seed attend.
Of all this numerous progeny was none
So beautiful, so brave as Absolom:

Whether, inspired by some diviner lust,
20　His father got him with a greater gust; [4]
Or that his conscious destiny made way,
By manly beauty, to imperial sway.
Early in foreign fields he won renown,
With kings and states allied to Israel's crown:
25　In peace the thoughts of war he could remove,
And seemed as he were only born for love.
Whate'er he did was done with so much ease,
In him alone 'twas natural to please.
His motions all accompanied with grace;
30　And paradise was opened in his face.
With secret joy, indulgent David viewed
His youthful image in his son renewed:
To all his wishes nothing he denied,
And made the charming Annabel his bride. [5]
35　What faults he had (for who from faults is free?)
His father could not, or he would not see.
Some warm excesses which the law forbore,
Were construed youth that purged by boiling o'er:
And Amnon's murder, by a specious name,
40　Was called a just revenge for injured fame. [6]
Thus praised and loved the noble youth remained,
While David, undisturbed, in Sion reigned. [7]
But life can never be sincerely blest:
Heaven punishes the bad, and proves the best. [8]
45　The Jews, a headstrong, moody, murmuring race,
As ever tried th' extent and stretch of grace;
God's pampered people whom, debauched with
　　ease,
No king could govern, nor no God could please; [9]

---

[1] Dryden uses the biblical story of the rebellion of Absalom against his father, David (II Samuel 13–18), to allegorize the threat of the Duke of Monmouth, an illegitimate son of Charles II, against the King. James Duke of York, Charles's brother and heir, was Catholic. The political and religious strife occasioned by the Popish plot (1678) initiated by Titus Oates created a tumultuous atmosphere, which the Earl of Shaftesbury took as opportunity to have Monmouth crowned King. Charles managed the situation by dissolving Parliament.

[2] *priest-craft* the exercise of priestly responsibilities; the arts used by worldly & ambitious priests.

[3] Daughter of Saul and one of David's wives. She was childless, as was Catherine of Braganza, Charles II's Queen. See II Samuel 6:12–23.

---

[4] *gust* relish (*OED* gust *sb* [2] 4).

[5] *Annabel* Anne, Countess of Buccleuch (1651–1732).

[6] Amnon, Absalom's half-brother, raped Tamar, Absalom's sister, and was murdered as a result (II Samuel 13:28–29). There is presumably a reference to an act of violence with which Monmouth was associated, but nothing is certainly known.

[7] *Sion* that is, Jerusalem; here, London.

[8] *proves* tries, tests.

[9] *debauched* seduced from allegiance (*OED* debauch *v* 1); corrupted (*OED* debauch *v* 2).

(Gods they had tried of every shape and size
50 That God-smiths could produce, or priests
        devise:)
    These Adam-wits, too fortunately free,
    Began to dream they wanted liberty; [1]
    And when no rule, no precedent was found
    Of men, by laws less circumscribed and bound,
55 They led their wild desires to woods and caves,
    And thought that all but savages were slaves.
    They who when Saul was dead, without a blow,
    Made foolish Ishbosheth the crown forgo; [2]
    Who banished David did from Hebron bring,
60 And with a general shout proclaimed him King: [3]
    Those very Jews, who, at their very best,
    Their humour more than loyalty expressed,
    Now, wondered why so long they had obeyed
    An idol monarch which their hands had made:
65 Thought they might ruin him they could create;
    Or melt him to that golden calf, a state. [4]
    But these were random bolts: no formed design,
    Nor interest made the factious crowd to join:
    The sober part of Israel, free from stain,
70 Well knew the value of a peaceful reign,
    And, looking backward with a wise affright,
    Saw seams of wounds, dishonest to the sight;
    In contemplation of whose ugly scars,
    They cursed the memory of civil wars.
75 The moderate sort of men, thus qualified,
    Inclined the balance to the better side:
    And David's mildness managed it so well,
    The bad found no occasion to rebel.
    But when to sin our biased nature leans,

80 The careful devil is still at hand with means;
    And providently pimps for ill desires.
    The Good Old Cause revived, a plot requires: [5]
    Plots, true or false, are necessary things,
    To raise up Commonwealths, and ruin kings.
85   Th' inhabitants of old Jerusalem
    Were Jebusites: the town so called from them; [6]
    And their's the native right—
    But when the chosen people grew more strong, [7]
    The rightful cause at length became the wrong:
90 And every loss the men of Jebus bore,
    They still were thought God's enemies the more.
    Thus worn and weakened, well or ill content,
    Submit they must to David's government:
    Impoverished and deprived of all command,
95 Their taxes doubled as they lost their land,
    And, what was harder yet to flesh and blood,
    Their gods disgraced, and burnt like common
        wood.
    This set the heathen priesthood in a flame;
    For priests of all religions are the same:
100 Of whatsoe'er descent their godhead be,
    Stock, stone, or other homely pedigree, [8]
    In his defence his servants are as bold
    As if he had been born of beaten gold.
    The Jewish Rabbins, though their enemies,
105 In this conclude them honest men and wise:
    For 'twas their duty, all the learned think,
    T'espouse his cause by whom they eat and drink.
    From hence began that Plot, the nation's curse,
    Bad in itself, but represented worse; [9]
110 Raised in extremes, and in extremes decried;
    With oaths affirmed, with dying vows denied.

---

[1] *Adam-wits* The name Adam was used figuratively of the unregenerate condition or character (*OED*). Dryden is recalling the story of Adam and Eve and the forbidden fruit (Genesis 2–3).

[2] *Saul* Cromwell; *Ishbosheth* Richard Cromwell.

[3] *proclaimed him King* Charles was restored to the throne in 1660.

[4] *that golden calf, a state* in reference to the golden calf worshipped by the Jews while Moses was on Mt. Sinai (Exodus 32). The language of idolatry was used both by Royalists, as here, and by their opponents. Republicans regarded the restored monarchy as an idol.

---

[5] *The Good Old Cause* that is, the cause of the Commonwealth.

[6] Jebus was the original name of Jerusalem. Here, "Jebusites" refer to Roman Catholics.

[7] *the chosen people* in the biblical source, the Jews; here, the Protestants.

[8] *Stock* wood (*OED* stock 1b).

[9] *that Plot* the Popish plot.

Not weighed or winnowed by the multitude; [1]
But swallowed in the mass, unchewed and crude. [2]
Some truth there was, but dashed and brewed
   with lies;
115 To please the fools, and puzzle all the wise.
Succeeding times did equal folly call,
Believing nothing, or believing all.
Th' Egyptian rites the Jebusites embraced;
Where gods were recommended by their taste. [3]
120 Such savoury deities must needs be good,
As served at once for worship and for food.
By force they could not introduce these gods;
For ten to one in former days was odds.
So fraud was used, (the sacrificer's trade):
125 Fools are more hard to conquer than persuade.
Their busy teachers mingled with the Jews,
And raked for converts, even the court and
   stews: [4]
Which Hebrew priests the more unkindly took,
Because the fleece accompanies the flock. [5]
130 Some thought they God's anointed meant to slay
By guns, invented since full many a day:
Our author swears it not; but who can know
How far the Devil and Jebusites may go?
This Plot, which failed for want of common
   sense,
135 Had yet a deep and dangerous consequence:
For, as when raging fevers boil the blood,
The standing lake soon floats into a flood;
And every hostile humour, which before
Slept quiet in its channels, bubbles o'er:
140 So, several factions from this first ferment,
Work up to foam, and threat the government.

Some by their friends, more by themselves
   thought wise,
Opposed the power to which they could not rise.
Some had in courts been great, and thrown from
   thence,
145 Like fiends were hardened in impenitence.
Some, by their monarch's fatal mercy, grown,
From pardoned rebels kinsmen to the throne;
Were raised in power and public office high:
Strong bands, if bands ungrateful men could tie.
150   Of these the false Achitophel was first:
A name to all succeeding ages cursed. [6]
For close designs, and crooked counsels fit; [7]
Sagacious, bold, and turbulent of wit;
Restless, unfixed in principles and place;
155 In power unpleased, impatient of disgrace:
A fiery soul, which working out its way,
Fretted the pygmy body to decay,
And o'er informed the tenement of clay. [8]
A daring pilot in extremity;
160 Pleased with the danger, when the waves went
   high
He sought the storms; but for a calm unfit,
Would steer too nigh the sands, to boast his wit.
Great wits are sure to madness near allied,
And thin partitions do their bounds divide;
165 Else, why should he, with wealth and honour blest,
Refuse his age the needful hours of rest?
Punish a body which he could not please;
Bankrupt of life, yet prodigal of ease?
And all to leave what with his toil he won,
170 To that unfeathered, two legged thing, a son:
Got, while his soul did huddled notions try; [9]
And born a shapeless lump, like anarchy.

---

[1] *winnowed* cleared of worthless elements (*OED* winnow *v* 1b).

[2] *crude* uncooked; undigested (*OED* crude *a* 2, 3).

[3] *Th' Egyptian rites...recommended by their taste* The reference is to Catholicism, and the consumption of bread and wine in the Mass.

[4] *stews* brothels.

[5] *the fleece* a common metaphor in the period for financial compensation, especially in the form of commissions, bribes, and tithes.

[6] *Achitophel* the Earl of Shaftesbury, who agitated to have Monmouth crowned king.

[7] *close designs* concealed, secret designs (*OED* close *a* 4a).

[8] *o'er informed* over-animated (*OED* inform *v* 3a).

[9] *huddled* confused, crowded together without order (*OED* huddled *ppl.a*).

In friendship false, implacable in hate:
Resolved to ruin or to rule the state.
175 To compass this the triple bond he broke; [1]
The pillars of the public safety shook:
And fitted Israel for a foreign yoke.
Then seized with fear, yet still affecting fame, [2]
Usurped a patriot's all-atoning name.
180 So easy still it proves in factious times,
With public zeal to cancel private crimes:
How safe is treason, and how sacred ill,
Where none can sin against the people's will:
Where crowds can wink, and no offence be known,
185 Since in another's guilt they find their own.
Yet fame deserved no enemy can grudge;
The statesman we abhor, but praise the judge.
In Israel's courts ne'er sat an Abbethdin [3]
With more discerning eyes, or hands more clean:
190 Unbribed, unsought, the wretched to redress;
Swift of dispatch, and easy of access.
Oh, had he been content to serve the Crown,
With virtues only proper to the gown;
Or, had the rankness of the soil been freed
195 From cockle, that oppressed the noble seed: [4]
David for him his tuneful harp had strung,
And Heaven had wanted one immortal song.
But wild Ambition loves to slide, not stand;
And Fortune's ice prefers to Virtue's land:
200 Achitophel, grown weary to possess
A lawful Fame, and lazy Happiness;
Disdained the golden fruit to gather free,

And lent the crowd his arm to shake the tree. [5]
Now, manifest of crimes contrived long since,
205 He stood at bold defiance with his Prince: [6]
Held up the buckler of the people's cause, [7]
Against the Crown; and skulked behind the
    laws.
The wished occasion of the Plot he takes,
Some circumstances finds, but more he makes.
210 By buzzing emissaries fills the ears
Of listening crowds with jealousies and fears
Of arbitrary counsels brought to light,
And proves the King himself a Jebusite:
Weak arguments! which yet he knew full well,
215 Were strong with people easy to rebel.
For, governed by the moon, the giddy Jews
Tread the same track when she the prime renews: [8]
And once in twenty years, their scribes record,
By natural instinct they change their Lord.
220 Achitophel still wants a chief, and none
Was found so fit as warlike Absalom: [9]
Not, that he wished his greatness to create,
(For politicians neither love nor hate:)
But, for he knew his title not allowed,
225 Would keep him still depending on the crowd:
That kingly power, thus ebbing out, might be
Drawn to the dregs of a democracy.
Him he attempts with studied arts to please,
And sheds his venom, in such words as these:
230   Auspicious Prince! at whose nativity
Some royal planet ruled the southern sky;

---

[1] *the triple bond* an alliance of England, Sweden, and Holland against France (formed in 1668).

[2] *affecting* aspiring toward (*OED* affect *v* 1).

[3] *Abbethdin* senior judge in the Jewish civil court (Shaftesbury was Lord Chancellor).

[4] *rankness* abundance (*OED* rank *a* 2) or overabundance (*OED* rank *a* 6a). The word is chosen carefully; several senses apply; *cockle* in reference to plants that grow in cornfields, varying according to location (*OED* cockle *sb*[1] 1); there is an implied reference to the Parable of the Sower.

[5] *the golden fruit* recalling Eden's forbidden fruit and the golden apples of the Hesperides.

[6] *manifest* clearly guilty of (*OED* manifest *a* 2).

[7] *buckler* originally a small round shield used defensively (*OED* buckler *sb* 1); often associated with the champion in a confrontation (*OED* buckler *sb* 5).

[8] *prime* lunar cycle of nineteen years (*OED* prime *sb*[1] 4b).

[9] *wants* lacks, is in need of.

Thy longing country's darling and desire;
Their cloudy pillar and their guardian fire: [1]
Their second Moses, whose extended wand
235 Divides the seas, and shows the promised land:
Whose dawning day in every distant age
Has exercised the sacred prophet's rage:
The people's prayer, the glad diviner's theme,
The young men's vision, and the old men's dream!
240 Thee, Saviour, thee, the nation's vows confess;
And, never satisfied with seeing, bless:
Swift, unbespoken pomps, thy steps proclaim,
And stammering babes are taught to lisp thy
      name. [2]
How long wilt thou the general joy detain;
245 Starve, and defraud the people of thy reign?
Content ingloriously to pass thy days
Like one of Virtue's fools that feeds on praise,
Till thy fresh glories, which now shine so bright,
Grow stale and tarnish with our daily sight.
250 Believe me, royal youth, thy fruit must be
Or gathered ripe, or rot upon the tree.
Heaven has to all allotted, soon or late,
Some lucky revolution of their fate,
Whose motions, if we watch and guide with skill,
255 (For human good depends on human will),
Our fortune rolls, as from a smooth descent,
And from the first impression takes the bent:
But if unseized, she glides away like wind;
And leaves repenting Folly far behind.
260 Now, now she meets you, with a glorious prize,
And spreads her locks before her as she flies.
Had thus old David, from whose loins you spring,
Not dared, when Fortune called him, to be King,
At Gath an exile he might still remain, [3]

265 And Heaven's anointing oil had been in vain. [4]
Let his successful youth your hopes engage,
But shun th' example of declining age:
Behold him setting in his western skies,
The shadows lengthning as the vapours rise.
270 He is not now, as when on Jordan's sand
The joyful people thronged to see him land,
Cov'ring the beach, and blackning all the strand: [5]
But, like the Prince of Angels, from his height
Comes tumbling downward with diminished light;
275 Betrayed by one poor plot to public scorn,
(Our only blessing since his cursed return);
Those heaps of people which one sheaf did bind,
Blown off and scattered by a puff of wind.
What strength can he to your designs oppose,
280 Naked of friends, and round beset with foes?
If Pharaoh's doubtful succour he should use,
A foreign aid would more incense the Jews: [6]
Proud Egypt would dissembled friendship bring;
Foment the war, but not support the King:
285 Nor would the royal party e'er unite
With Pharaoh's arms, t'assist the Jebusite;
Or if they should, their interest soon would break,
And with such odious aid make David weak.
All sorts of men by my successful arts,
290 Abhorring kings, estrange their altered hearts
From David's rule: and 'tis the general cry,
'Religion, commonwealth, and liberty.'
If you, as champion of the public good,
Add to their arms a chief of royal blood,
295 What may not Israel hope, and what applause
Might such a general gain by such a cause?
Not barren Praise alone, that gaudy flower,
Fair only to the sight, but solid power;
And nobler is a limited command,
300 Giv'n by the love of all your native land,

[1] *Their cloudy pillar and their guardian fire* During the Exodus, the Israelites were led by a cloud by day, and by a pillar of fire by night.

[2] *unbespoken* spontaneous; a pomp is a triumphal or ceremonial procession (*OED* pomp *sb 2*).

[3] *At Gath an exile he might still remain* David took refuge from Saul in Gath (I Samuel 27: 1–7); the latter part of Charles II's exile was spent in Brussels.

[4] *Heaven's anointing oil* See I Samuel 6: 1–13: God rejects Saul and commands Samuel to anoint David.

[5] *on Jordan's sand* recollecting the scene when Charles landed at Dover upon his restoration.

[6] *Pharaoh's doubtful succour* the dubious aid of Louis XIV of France.

Than a successive title, long, and dark,
Drawn from the mouldy rolls of Noah's Ark."
 What cannot praise effect in mighty minds,
When flattery soothes, and when ambition blinds!
305 Desire of power, on earth a vicious weed,
Yet, sprung from high, is of celestial seed:
In God 'tis glory: and when men aspire,
'Tis but a spark too much of heavenly fire.
Th' ambitious youth, too covetous of fame,
310 Too full of angel's metal in his frame; [1]
Unwarily was led from virtue's ways;
Made drunk with honour, and debauched with
  praise. [2]
Half loath, and half consenting to the ill,
(For loyal blood within him struggled still)
315 He thus replied—"And what pretence have I
To take up arms for public liberty?
My father governs with unquestioned right;
The faith's defender, and mankind's delight:
Good, gracious, just, observant of the laws;
320 And Heaven by wonders has espoused his cause.
Whom has he wronged in all his peaceful reign?
Who sues for justice to his throne in vain?
What millions has he pardoned of his foes,
Whom just revenge did to his wrath expose?
325 Mild, easy, humble, studious of our good;
Inclined to mercy, and averse from blood.
If mildness ill with stubborn Israel suit,
His crime is God's beloved attribute.
What could he gain, his people to betray,
330 Or change his right for arbitrary sway?
Let haughty Pharaoh curse with such a reign,
His fruitful Nile, and yoke a servile train.
If David's rule Jerusalem displease,

The Dog-star heats their brains to this disease. [3]
335 Why then should I, encouraging the bad,
Turn rebel and run popularly mad? [4]
Were he a tyrant who, by lawless might,
Oppressed the Jews, and raised the Jebusite,
Well might I mourn; but Nature's holy bands
340 Would curb my spirits, and restrain my hands:
The people might assert their liberty;
But what was right in them, were crime in me.
His favour leaves me nothing to require;
Prevents my wishes, and outruns desire. [5]
345 What more can I expect while David lives,
All but his kingly diadem he gives;
And that":—But there he paused; then sighing,
  said—
"Is justly destined for a worthier head.
For when my father from his toils shall rest,
350 And late augment the number of the blest,
His lawful issue shall the throne ascend,
Or the collateral line where that shall end. [6]
His brother, though oppressed with vulgar spite,
Yet dauntless, and secure of native right,
355 Of every royal virtue stands possessed;
Still dear to all the bravest and the best.
His courage foes, his friends his truth proclaim;
His loyalty the king, the world his fame.
His mercy e'en th' offending crowd will find,
360 For sure he comes of a forgiving kind.
Why should I then repine at Heaven's decree;
Which gives me no pretence to royalty?
Yet O that Fate, propitiously inclined,

---

[3] *The Dog-star heats their brains* The re-appearance of Sirius in late summer was associated in ancient times with fever and madness. Compare the beginning of Pope's *Epistle to Dr. Arbuthnot.*

[4] *run popularly mad* run into the madness of pandering to the majority.

[5] *Prevents* anticipates, goes before. Compare the Collect for Easter Sunday in the Book of Common Prayer, with its reference to God's special grace preventing us and putting into our minds good desires.

[6] *the collateral line* descended from the same stock, but in a different line (*OED* collateral *a* 4).

---

[1] *angel's metal* the "stuff" of which man—or angel—is made (*OED* metal *sb* 1f). The apparent compliment is double-edged; the angel Satan's pride and ambition led him to rebel against God.

[2] *debauched* See the note to line 47.

Had raised my birth, or had debased my mind;
365 To my large soul not all her treasure lent,
And then betrayed it to a mean descent.
I find, I find my mounting spirits bold,
And David's part disdains my mother's mould. [1]
Why am I scanted by a niggard birth? [2]
370 My soul disclaims the kindred of her earth:
And made for empire, whispers me within;
'Desire of greatness is a godlike sin.' "
    Him staggering so when Hell's dire agent found,
While fainting Virtue scarce maintained her
    ground, [3]
375 He pours fresh forces in, and thus replies:
    "Th' eternal God, supremely good and wise,
Imparts not these prodigious gifts in vain:
What wonders are reserved to bless your reign?
Against your will your arguments have shown,
380 Such virtue's only given to guide a throne.
Not that your father's mildness I contemn;
But manly force becomes the diadem.
'Tis true, he grants the people all they crave;
And more perhaps than subjects ought to have:
385 For lavish grants suppose a monarch tame,
And more his goodness than his wit proclaim.
But when should people strive their bonds to
    break,
If not when kings are negligent or weak?
Let him give on till he can give no more,
390 The thrifty Sanhedrin shall keep him poor: [4]

And every shekel which he can receive,
Shall cost a limb of his prerogative. [5]
To ply him with new plots, shall be my care,
Or plunge him deep in some expensive war;
395 Which when his treasure can no more supply,
He must, with the remains of kingship, buy.
His faithful friends, our jealousies and fears [6]
Call Jebusites; and Pharaoh's pensioners:
Whom when our fury from his aid has torn,
400 He shall be naked left to public scorn.
The next successor, whom I fear and hate,
My arts have made obnoxious to the state;
Turned all his virtues to his overthrow,
And gained our elders to pronounce a foe. [7]
405 His right, for sums of necessary gold,
Shall first be pawned, and afterwards be sold:
Till time shall ever-wanting David draw,
To pass your doubtful title into law:
If not, the people have a right supreme
410 To make their kings; for kings are made for them.
All empire is no more than power in trust,
Which when resumed, can be no longer just.
Succession, for the general good designed,
In its own wrong a nation cannot bind:
415 If altering that, the people can relieve,
Better one suffer, than a nation grieve.
The Jews well know their power: ere Saul they
    chose,
God was their King, and God they durst depose.
Urge now your piety, your filial name,
420 A father's right, and fear of future fame,
The public good, that universal call,
To which e'en Heav'n submitted, answers all.
Nor let his love enchant your generous mind;

[1] *David's part disdains my mother's mould* That is, his royal inheritance predominates over his mother's humble birth.

[2] *scanted* diminished (*OED* scanted *ppl.a*); *niggard* miserly. Monmouth felt himself to be short-changed by the fact that his mother was a commoner, and his father's mistress, not his queen. He would have done well to count his blessings, as his fate was to be executed for rebelling against James II.

[3] *Him staggering so when Hell's dire agent found* The Miltonic inversion signals the fact that this is in parts a "heroic" satire, dealing with momentous events; *staggering* beginning to doubt or waver (*OED* stagger *v* 2).

[4] *Sanhedrin* Jerusalem's most authoritative judicial council, which here stands for Parliament.

[5] *his prerogative* the Royal prerogative, that is the Crown's special privileges (*OED* prerogative *sb* 1a). It is thematic to Stuart history that successive Parliaments used their power of controlling the King's money-supply in order to check the powers of the crown.

[6] *jealousies and fears* Dryden, writing in the Stuart interest, here recalls a phrase common in pre-Restoration Parliamentary pamphlets.

[7] prevailed upon, or caused, elders to pronounce him an enemy.

Not one, but all mankind's epitome.
Stiff in opinions, always in the wrong;
Was everything by starts, and nothing long:
But, in the course of one revolving moon,
550 Was chemist, fiddler, statesman, and buffoon:
Then all for women, painting, rhyming, drinking;
Besides ten thousand freaks that died in thinking. [1]
Blest madman, who could every hour employ,
With something new to wish, or to enjoy!
555 Railing and praising were his usual themes;
And both (to show his judgment) in extremes:
So over-violent, or over-civil,
That every man, with him, was god or devil.
In squandering wealth was his peculiar art:
560 Nothing went unrewarded, but desert.
Beggared by fools, whom still he found too late:
He had his jest, and they had his estate. [2]
He laughed himself from court, then sought relief
By forming parties, but could ne'er be chief:
565 For, spite of him, the weight of business fell
On Absalom and wise Achitophel:
Thus, wicked but in will, of means bereft,
He left not faction, but of that was left.
      Titles and names 'twere tedious to rehearse
570 Of lords, below the dignity of verse.
Wits, warriors, commonwealth's-men, were the
      best:
Kind husbands and mere nobles all the rest.
And therefore, in the name of dullness, be
The well-hung Balaam and cold Caleb free.
575 And canting Nadab let oblivion damn, [3]

Who made new porridge for the Paschal Lamb. [4]
Let friendship's holy band some names assure:
Some their own worth, and some let scorn secure.
Nor shall the rascal rabble here have place,
580 Whom kings no titles gave, and God no grace:
Not bull-faced Jonas, who could statutes draw
To mean rebellion, and make treason law. [5]
But he, though bad, is followed by a worse,
The wretch who Heaven's anointed dared to
      curse.
585 Shimei, whose youth did early promise bring
Of zeal to God and hatred to his King; [6]
Did wisely from expensive sins refrain,
And never broke the Sabbath, but for gain:
Nor ever was he known an oath to vent,
590 Or curse unless against the government.
Thus, heaping wealth, by the most ready way
Among the Jews, which was to cheat and pray;
The city, to reward his pious hate
Against his master, chose him magistrate:
595 His hand a vare of justice did uphold; [7]
His neck was loaded with a chain of gold.
During his office, treason was no crime;
The sons of Belial had a glorious time: [8]

---

[1] *freaks* whims.

[2] *still* always

[3] For Balaam, see Numbers 22–24; for Caleb, see Numbers 13–14; for Nadab, see Leviticus 10:1–2. Balaam is possibly Theophilus Hastings, Earl of Huntingdon; Caleb is Arthur Capel, Earl of Essex; Nadab is William, Lord Howard of Esrick (*canting Nadab* because he was formerly a preacher).

---

[4] *Who made new porridge for the Paschal Lamb* who did away with the Book of Common Prayer; *porridge* (a hotchpotch) was a contemptuous term used by opponents of the Book of Common Prayer; *the Paschal Lamb* is Jesus whose sacrifice on the cross is commemorated in the Holy Communion.

[5] *Jonas* Sir William Jones, largely responsible for both the Exclusion Bill (against James's succession) and the prosecutor of those accused in the Popish plot.

[6] *Shimei* See II Samuel 16:5–13, a lively episode in which Shimei curses and stones David while he flees from the rebellious Absalom; here Slingsby Bethel, responsible for Shaftesbury's avoiding charges of treason.

[7] *vare* a rod, staff or wand, carried as a symbol of authority (*OED* vare sb 2).

[8] *sons of Belial* a biblical phrase referring to reprobate, dissolute or uncouth persons. See Deuteronomy 13:13, Judges 19:22, I Samuel 2:12.

For Shimei, though not prodigal of pelf, [1]
600 Yet loved his wicked neighbour as himself:
When two or three were gathered to declaim
Against the monarch of Jerusalem,
Shimei was always in the midst of them.
And if they cursed the King when he was by,
605 Would rather curse than break good company.
If any durst his factious friends accuse,
He packed a jury of dissenting Jews,
Whose fellow-feeling, in the godly cause,
Would free the suffering saint from human laws.
610 For laws are only made to punish those,
Who serve the King, and to protect his foes.
If any leisure time he had from power,
(Because 'tis sin to misemploy an hour),
His business was, by writing, to persuade
615 That kings were useless, and a clog to trade:
And, that his noble style he might refine,
No Rechabite more shunned the fumes of wine. [2]
Chaste were his cellars, and his shrieval board
The grossness of a city feast abhorred: [3]
620 His cooks, with long disuse, their trade forgot;
Cool was his kitchen, though his brains were hot.
Such frugal virtue malice may accuse,
But sure 'twas necessary to the Jews:
For towns once burnt, such magistrates require
625 As dare not tempt God's providence by fire.
With spiritual food he fed his servants well,
But free from flesh, that made the Jews rebel:
And Moses' laws he held in more account,
For forty days of fasting in the Mount. [4]
630   To speak the rest, who better are forgot,
Would tire a well breathed witness of the plot:

Yet, Corah, thou shalt from oblivion pass; [5]
Erect thy self, thou monumental brass:
High as the serpent of thy metal made, [6]
635 While nations stand secure beneath thy shade.
What though his birth were base, yet comets rise
From earthy vapours ere they shine in skies.
Prodigious actions may as well be done
By weaver's issue as by prince's son.
640 This arch-attestor for the public good,
By that one deed ennobles all his blood.
Who ever asked the witnesses' high race,
Whose oath with martyrdom did Stephen grace? [7]
Ours was a Levite, and as times went then,
645 His tribe were God Almighty's gentlemen.
Sunk were his eyes, his voice was harsh and loud,
Sure signs he neither choleric was, nor proud: [8]
His long chin proved his wit; his saintlike grace
A church vermilion, and a Moses' face; [9]
650 His memory, miraculously great,
Could plots exceeding man's belief, repeat;
Which, therefore cannot be accounted lies,
For human wit could never such devise.
Some future truths are mingled in his book;
655 But where the witness failed, the Prophet spoke:
Some things like visionary flights appear;
The Spirit caught him up, the Lord knows where:
And gave him his rabbinical degree

---

[1] *pelf* money, wealth, riches, filthy lucre (*OED* pelf *sb* 3).

[2] *No Rechabite more shunned the fumes of wine* Rachab's descendants refused to drink wine (Jeremiah 35).

[3] *shrieval* belonging to a sheriff.

[4] *the Mount* Mount Sinai, where Moses received God's commandments during a forty day fast (Exodus 34:28).

[5] *Corah* After challenging Moses and Aaron, he was swallowed up by the earth (Numbers 16); here, Titus Oates, the manufacturer of the Popish Plot.

[6] *the serpent of thy metal made* Israelites complaining against God and bitten by serpents as punishment were saved when Moses erected a brass serpent for them to look upon (Numbers 21:4–9); *thy metal* because Oates was a brazen liar.

[7] *Stephen* "a man full of faith and of the Holy Ghost" was martyred as a result of false witnesses (Acts 6–7).

[8] *choleric* ill-tempered (*OED* choleric *a* 3).

[9] *a Moses' face* After receiving the commandments, Moses' face shone (Exodus 34:29–30).

Unknown to foreign university. [1]
660 His judgment yet his memory did excel;
Which pieced his wondrous evidence so well,
And suited to the temper of the times;
Then groaning under Jebusitic crimes.
Let Israel's foes suspect his heavenly call,
665 And rashly judge his writ apocryphal; [2]
Our laws for such affronts have forfeits made:
He takes his life, who takes away his trade.
Were I myself in witness Corah's place,
The wretch who did me such a dire disgrace,
670 Should whet my memory, though once forgot,
To make him an appendix of my plot.
His zeal to Heaven made him his Prince despise,
And load his person with indignities:
But zeal peculiar privilege affords;
675 Indulging latitude to deeds and words;
And Corah might for Agag's murder call,
In terms as coarse as Samuel used to Saul. [3]
What others in his evidence did join,
(The best that could be had for love or coin),
680 In Corah's own predicament will fall:
For witness is a common name to all.
 Surrounded thus with friends of every sort,
Deluded Absalom forsakes the court:
Impatient of high hopes, urged with renown,
685 And fired with near possession of a crown:
Th' admiring crowd are dazzled with surprise,
And on his goodly person feed their eyes:
His joy concealed, he sets himself to show;
On each side bowing popularly low:
690 His looks, his gestures, and his words he frames,
And with familiar ease repeats their names.
Thus formed by nature, furnished out with arts,

He glides unfelt into their secret hearts:
Then with a kind compassionating look,
695 And sighs, bespeaking pity ere he spoke,
Few words he said; but easy those and fit:
More slow than Hybla drops, and far more
 sweet. [4]
 "I mourn, my countrymen, your lost estate;
Though far unable to prevent your fate:
700 Behold a banished man, for your dear cause
Exposed a prey to arbitrary laws!
Yet O! that I alone could be undone,
Cut off from empire, and no more a son!
Now all your liberties a spoil are made;
705 Egypt and Tyrus intercept your trade,
And Jebusites your sacred rites invade. [5]
My father, whom with reverence yet I name,
Charmed into ease, is careless of his fame:
And, bribed with petty sums of foreign gold,
710 Is grown in Bathsheba's embraces old: [6]
Exalts his enemies, his friends destroys:
And all his power against himself employs.
He gives, and let him give, my right away:
But why should he his own and yours betray?
715 He, only he, can make the nation bleed,
And he alone from my revenge is freed.
Take then my tears" (with that he wiped his eyes)
"'Tis all the aid my present power supplies:
No court informer can these arms accuse,
720 These arms may sons against their father's use,
And, tis my wish, the next successor's reign
May make no other Israelite complain."
 Youth, beauty, graceful action, seldom fail:
But common interest always will prevail:
725 And pity never ceases to be shown
To him who makes the people's wrongs his own.
The crowd, (that still believe their kings oppress)

---

[1] *his rabbinical degree* Titus Oates pretended to have academic qualifications which he did not possess, thus anticipating a form of deception popular in the twentieth century.

[2] *apocryphal* literally, excluded from the sacred writings; therefore, not certainly to be trusted.

[3] *And Corah might...as Samuel used to Saul* After Saul had shown him mercy, Samuel hewed Agag to pieces. See I Samuel 15.

---

[4] *Hybla* a Sicilian honey celebrated for its sweetness.

[5] *Egypt and Tyrus* France and Holland.

[6] For David's adultery with Bathsheba, see II Samuel 11. The reference here is to the Duchess of Portsmouth, one of Charles's mistresses.

With lifted hands their young Messiah bless:
Who now begins his progress to ordain
730 With chariots, horsemen, and a numerous train:
From east to west his glories he displays,
And, like the sun, the promised land surveys.[1]
Fame runs before him as the morning star;
And shouts of joy salute him from afar:
735 Each house receives him as a guardian god;
And consecrates the place of his abode:
But hospitable treats did most commend
Wise Issachar, his wealthy western friend. [2]
This moving court, that caught the people's eyes,
740 And seemed but pomp, did other ends disguise:
Achitophel had formed it, with intent
To sound the depths, and fathom, where it went,
The people's hearts; distinguish friends from foes;
And try their strength, before they came to blows:
745 Yet all was coloured with a smooth pretence
Of specious love, and duty to their Prince.
Religion, and redress of grievances,
Two names that always cheat and always please,
Are often urged; and good King David's life
750 Endangered by a brother and a wife. [3]
Thus in a pageant show a plot is made;
And peace itself is war in masquerade.
Oh foolish Israel! never warned by ill,
Still the same bait, and circumvented still!
755 Did ever men forsake their present ease,
In midst of health imagine a disease;
Take pains contingent mischiefs to foresee,
Make heirs for monarchs, and for God decree?
What shall we think! Can people give away
760 Both for themselves and sons, their native sway?
Then they are left defenceless, to the sword

Of each unbounded, arbitrary lord:
And laws are vain, by which we right enjoy,
If kings unquestioned can those laws destroy.
765 Yet, if the crowd be judge of fit and just,
And kings are only officers in trust,
Then this resuming cov'nant was declared
When kings were made, or is for ever barred:
If those who gave the scepter, could not tie
770 By their own deed their own posterity,
How then could Adam bind his future race?
How could his forfeit on mankind take place?
Or how could heavenly justice damn us all,
Who ne'er consented to our father's fall?
775 Then kings are slaves to those whom they
command,
And tenants to their people's pleasure stand.
Add, that the power for property allowed,
Is mischievously seated in the crowd:
For who can be secure of private right,
780 If sovereign sway may be dissolved by might?
Nor is the people's judgment always true:
The most may err as grossly as the few.
And faultless kings run down, by common cry,
For vice, oppression, and for tyranny.
785 What standard is there in a fickle rout,
Which, flowing to the mark, runs faster out?
Nor only crowds, but Sanhedrins may be
Infected with this public lunacy: [4]
And share the madness of rebellious times,
790 To murder monarchs for imagined crimes. [5]
If they may give and take whene'er they please,
Not kings alone, (the Godhead's images),
But government itself at length must fall
To Nature's state; where all have right to all.
795 Yet, grant our lords the people kings can make,
What prudent men a settled throne would shake?
For whatsoe'er their sufferings were before,
That change they covet makes them suffer more.

---

[1] *From east to west his glories he displays* Monmouth journeyed through England in 1680, hoping to attract popular support.

[2] *Issachar* Jacob's son. See Genesis 49:14–15. Here, the wealthy Thomas Thynne of Longleat, who entertained Monmouth on his progress.

[3] *Endangered by a brother and a wife* Oates accused both Charles's Queen and his brother James of conspiring to kill him.

---

[4] *Sanhedrins* See line 390 and note.

[5] *To murder monarchs for imagined crimes* Charles I was executed in 1649.

All other errors but disturb a state;
800 But innovation is the blow of Fate.
If ancient fabrics nod, and threat to fall,
To patch the flaws, and buttress up the wall, [1]
Thus far 'tis duty; but here fix the mark: [2]
For all beyond it is to touch our ark.
805 To change foundations, cast the frame anew,
Is work for rebels, who base ends pursue:
At once divine and human laws control;
And mend the parts by ruin of the whole.
The tampering world is subject to this curse,
810 To physic their disease into a worse. [3]
    Now what relief can righteous David bring?
How fatal 'tis to be too good a king!
Friends he has few, so high the madness grows,
Who dare be such, must be the people's foes:
815 Yet some there were, e'en in the worst of days;
Some let me name, and naming is to praise.
    In this short file Barzillai first appears; [4]
Barzillai, crowned with honour and with years:
Long since, the rising rebels he withstood
820 In region's waste, beyond the Jordan's flood:
Unfortunately brave to buoy the state;
But sinking underneath his master's fate:
In exile with his godlike prince he mourned;
For him he suffered, and with him returned.
825 The court he practised, not the courtier's art:
Large was his wealth, but larger was his heart:
Which well the noblest objects knew to choose,
The fighting warrior, and recording Muse.
His bed could once a fruitful issue boast:
830 Now more than half a father's name is lost.
His eldest hope, with every grace adorned,

By me (so Heaven will have it) always mourned,
And always honoured, snatched in manhood's
    prime
By unequal fates, and Providence's crime: [5]
835 Yet not before the goal of honour won,
All parts fulfilled of subject and of son;
Swift was the race, but short the time to run.
O narrow circle, but of power divine,
Scanted in space, but perfect in thy line!
840 By sea, by land, thy matchless worth was known;
Arms thy delight, and war was all thy own:
Thy force, infused, the fainting Tyrians propped: [6]
And haughty Pharaoh found his fortune stopped. [7]
O ancient honour! O unconquered hand,
845 Whom foes unpunished never could withstand!
But Israel was unworthy of thy name:
Short is the date of all immoderate fame.
It looks as Heaven our ruin had designed,
And durst not trust thy fortune and thy mind.
850 Now, free from Earth, thy disencumbered soul
Mounts up, and leaves behind the clouds and
    starry pole:
From thence thy kindred legions mayst thou
    bring
To aid the guardian angel of thy King.
Here stop my Muse, here cease thy painful flight;
855 No pinions can pursue immortal height: [8]
Tell good Barzillai thou canst sing no more,
And tell thy soul she should have fled before;
Or fled she with his life, and left this verse
To hang on her departed patron's hearse?
860 Now take thy steepy flight from Heaven, and see [9]
If thou canst find on earth another he;
Another he would be too hard to find,
See then whom thou canst see not far behind.

---

[1] *nod*   sway (*OED* nod *v* 3).

[2] *mark*   boundary (*OED* mark *sb* 1).

[3] *To physic their disease into a worse*   Dryden was intelligent enough to observe that in his time, as occasionally in our own, medical treatment was more dangerous than the disease treated.

[4] *Barzillai*   loyal to David during Absalom's rebellion (II Samuel 17:27–9; 19:31–9). Here, James Butler, Duke of Ormond (1610–1688), a model of loyalty to the crown.

---

[5] *unequal*   unjust.

[6] *Tyrians*   here, the Dutch.

[7] *haughty Pharaoh*   Louis XIV of France.

[8] *pinions*   wings.

[9] *steepy*   precipitous.

Zadok the priest, whom, shunning power and
    place,
865 His lowly mind advanced to David's grace: [1]
With him the Sagan of Jerusalem, [2]
Of hospitable soul and noble stem;
Him of the western dome, whose weighty sense
Flows in fit words and heavenly eloquence. [3]
870 The prophets' sons by such example led,
To learning and to loyalty were bred: [4]
For colleges on bounteous kings depend,
And never rebel was to arts a friend.
To these succeed the pillars of the laws,
875 Who best could plead and best can judge a cause.
Next them a train of loyal peers ascend:
Sharp judging Adriel the Muses' friend,
Himself a Muse—In Sanhedrin's debate
True to his Prince; but not a slave of state [5]
880 Whom David's love with honours did adorn,
That from his disobedient son were torn.
Jotham of piercing wit and pregnant thought, [6]
Endued by nature, and by learning taught [7]
To move assemblies, who but only tried
885 The worse awhile, then chose the better side;

Nor chose alone, but turned the balance too;
So much the weight of one brave man can do.
Hushai, the friend of David in distress, In public
storms of manly steadfastness; [8]
890 By foreign treaties he informed his youth;
And joined experience to his native truth.
His frugal care supplied the wanting throne,
Frugal for that, but bounteous of his own:
'Tis easy conduct when exchequers flow,
895 But hard the task to manage well the low:
For sovereign power is too depressed or high,
When kings are forced to sell, or crowds to buy.
Indulge one labour more my weary Muse,
For Amiel, who can Amiel's praise refuse? [9]
900 Of ancient race by birth, but nobler yet
In his own worth, and without title great:
The Sanhedrin long time as chief he ruled,
Their reason guided and their passion cooled;
So dext'rous was he in the crown's defence,
905 So formed to speak a loyal nation's sense,
That as their band was Israel's tribes in small,
So fit was he to represent them all.
Now rasher charioteers the seat ascend,
Whose loose careers his steady skill commend:
910 They like th' unequal ruler of the day, [10]
Misguide the seasons and mistake the way; [11]
While he withdrawn at their mad labour smiles,

---

[1] *Zadok the priest* Zadok and the Levites followed David out of the city when he was threatened by Absalom, but David commanded that they remain. The reference is to William Sancroft (1617–1693), Dean of St. Paul's and afterwards Archbishop of Canterbury.

[2] *the Sagan of Jerusalem* The Sagan, deputy to the Jewish high priest, was the second highest temple functionary. The reference is to Henry Compton (1632–1713). Bishop of London from 1675, he supervised the Protestant education of James's children and opposed the Exclusion Bill.

[3] *Him of the western dome* John Dolben (1625–1686), Dean of Westminster from 1662.

[4] *The prophets' sons* the boys of Westminster School, probably the most influential school in seventeenth-century England, where Dryden, like Cowley, had been a King's Scholar.

[5] *Adriel* See I Samuel 18,19. The reference is to John Sheffield, Earl of Mulgrave (1648–1721), Dryden's patron.

[6] *Jotham* Jotham denounced Abimelech, the would-be usurper. The reference is to George Savile (1633–1695), trusted associate of Charles II.

[7] *Endued* endowed (*OED* endow *v* 7).

---

[8] *Hushai, the friend of David in distress* Hushai collaborated with David against Absalom during David's exile by staying in Jerusalem to spy on and mislead Absalom (II Samuel 15:32–7, 16:16–19, 17:5–16). The reference is to Lawrence Hyde (1642–1711), who opposed the exclusion of James from succession and, as one of Charles II's treasury commissioners, assisted Dryden financially.

[9] *Amiel* Amiel brought David supplies during his exile (II Samuel 17: 27–9). As Speaker in the House of Commons (1673–1678) Edward Seymour (1633–1708) strove to further the cause of the court; he opposed Exclusion.

[10] *unequal* not equal or capable of rule; inadequate (*OED* unequal 2b).

[11] *th' unequal ruler of the day* an allusion to Phaethon, son of Helios or Apollo. Phaethon asked to convey the Sun across the sky, but he could not control the immortal horses and threatened to set the world ablaze until Zeus killed him with a thunderbolt.

10 To settle the succession of the state:
And, pondering which of all his sons was fit
To reign, and wage immortal war with wit;
Cried, "'Tis resolved; for Nature pleads that he
Should only rule, who most resembles me:
15 Shadwell alone my perfect image bears,
Mature in dullness from his tender years.
Shadwell alone, of all my sons, is he
Who stands confirmed in full stupidity.
The rest to some faint meaning make pretence,
20 But Shadwell never deviates into sense.
Some beams of wit on other souls may fall,
Strike through and make a lucid interval;
But Shadwell's genuine night admits no ray,
His rising fogs prevail upon the day:
25 Besides, his goodly fabric fills the eye, [1]
And seems designed for thoughtless majesty:
Thoughtless as monarch oaks, that shade the plain,
And, spread in solemn state, supinely reign. [2]
Heywood and Shirley were but types of thee,
30 Thou last great prophet of tautology: [3]
Even I, a dunce of more renown than they,
Was sent before but to prepare thy way:
And, coarsely clad in Norwich drugget, came
To teach the nations in thy greater name. [4]
35 My warbling lute, the lute I whilom strung [5]
When to King John of Portugal I sung, [6]
Was but the prelude to that glorious day,
When thou on silver Thames did'st cut thy way,
With well-timed oars before the royal barge,

40 Swelled with the pride of thy celestial charge;
And big with hymn, commander of an host,
The like was ne'er in Epsom blankets tost. [7]
Methinks I see the new Arion sail, [8]
The lute still trembling underneath thy nail.
45 At thy well-sharpened thumb from shore to shore
The treble squeaks for fear, the basses roar:
Echoes from Pissing-Ally, "Shadwell" call, [9]
And "Shadwell" they resound from Ashton Hall. [10]
About thy boat the little fishes throng,
50 As at the morning toast, that floats along.
Sometimes as prince of thy harmonious band
Thou wield'st thy papers in thy threshing hand.
St. Andre's feet ne'er kept more equal time, [11]
Not ev'n the feet of thy own *Psyche*'s rhyme:
55 Though they in number as in sense excel;
So just, so like tautology they fell,
That, pale with envy, Singleton forswore
The lute and sword, which he in triumph bore, [12]
And vowed he ne'er would act Villerius more. [13]
60 Here stopped the good old sire, and wept for joy
In silent raptures of the hopeful boy.
All arguments, but most his plays, persuade,
That for anointed dullness he was made.

---

[1] *goodly fabric* large bulk; see *OED* fabric *sb* 3b.

[2] *supinely* indolently (*OED* supinely *adv* 2).

[3] *Heywood and Shirley were but types of thee* Thomas Heywood (?1570–1641) and James Shirley (1596–1666) were dramatists; a type is "a thing which prefigures, anticipates, or symbolizes another imperfectly" (*OED* type *sb* 1 1b).

[4] *Norwich drugget* Drugget is coarse woolen cloth (*OED* drugget *sb* 1a); Shadwell was a Norfolk man.

[5] *whilom* once (OED *adv* 2).

[6] *King John of Portugal* who, according to Flecknoe, had been his patron.

[7] *Epsom blankets* In Shadwell's *Virtuoso*, Sir Samuel Hearty, who believed himself to be a wit, was tossed in a blanket; there is also a reference to an affray in Epsom of June 1676, when several men, among them Rochester and Etherege, tossed in a blanket fiddlers who had refused to play for them.

[8] According to Greek mythology, Arion was a celebrated musician who, returning from a profitable visit to Italy and Sicily, was thrown overboard by sailors, and was rescued by dolphins (*OCD*).

[9] *Pissing-Ally* near the Strand.

[10] *Ashton Hall* possibly a reference to the house of Edmund Ashton, one of Shadwell's friends.

[11] *St. Andre* choreographer of Shadwell's opera, *Psyche*.

[12] *Singleton* a musician at the Royal Theatre.

[13] *Villerius* character in William Davenant's opera *Siege of Rhodes* (1656).

Close to the walls which fair Augusta bind, [1]
65 (The fair Augusta much to fears inclined)
An ancient fabric, raisd t'inform the sight,
There stood of yore, and Barbican it hight: [2]
A watchtower once; but now, so fate ordains,
Of all the pile an empty name remains.
70 From its old ruins brothel-houses rise,
Scenes of lewd loves, and of polluted joys,
Where their vast courts the mother-strumpets keep,
And, undisturbed by watch, in silence sleep.
Near these a nursery erects its head,
75 Where queens are formed, and future heroes bred;
Where unfledged actors learn to laugh and cry,
Where infant punks their tender voices try, [3]
And little Maximins the gods defy. [4]
Great Fletcher never treads in buskins here,
80 Nor greater Johnson dares in socks appear. [5]
But gentle Simkin just reception finds
Amidst this monument of vanished minds: [6]
Pure clenches, the suburban Muse affords, [7]
And Panton waging harmless war with words.
85 Here Flecknoe, as a place to Fame well known,
Ambitiously designed his Shadwell's throne.
For ancient Decker prophesied long since, [8]
That in this pile should reign a mighty prince,
Born for a scourge of wit, and flail of sense:
90 To whom true dullness should some *Psyches* owe,

But worlds of *Misers* from his pen should flow;
Humorists and *Hypocrites* it should produce, [9]
Whole Raymond families, and tribes of Bruce. [10]
    Now Empress Fame had published the renown
95 Of Shadwell's coronation through the town.
Rous'd by report of Fame, the nations meet,
From near Bun-Hill, and distant Watling-street. [11]
No Persian carpets spread th' imperial way,
But scattered limbs of mangled poets lay:
100 From dusty shops neglected authors come,
Martyrs of pies, and relics of the bum. [12]
Much Heywood, Shirley, Ogilby there lay, [13]
But loads of Shadwell almost choked the way.
Bilked stationers for yeomen stood prepared,
105 And Herringman was captain of the guard. [14]
The hoary prince in majesty appeared,
High on a throne of his own labours reared.
At his right hand our young Ascanius sat [15]
Rome's other hope, and pillar of the state.
110 His brows thick fogs, instead of glories, grace,
And lambent dullness played around his face. [16]
As Hannibal did to the altars come,
Sworn by his sire a mortal foe to Rome; [17]
So Shadwell swore, nor should his vow be vain,
115 That he till death true dullness would maintain;

---

[1] *Augusta* "the old name of London" (Dryden's note to *Annus Mirabilis*, line 1177).

[2] *Barbican it hight* It was called the Barbican; a fortification in the wall of London.

[3] *punks* prostitutes (*OED* punk *sb* 1).

[4] *little Maximins* Maximin was the raging atheist emperor in Dryden's *Tyrannic Love* (1670).

[5] *Great Fletcher…greater Jonson* John Fletcher (1579–1625) and Ben Jonson (1572–1637); *buskins…socks* Buskins were the high boots worn by tragic actors; socks were the low shoes or slippers of Athenian comedy.

[6] *Simkin* simpleton, a common name for a character in a farce.

[7] *clenches* word-plays (*OED* clench *sb* II 4).

[8] *Decker* a London dramatist (1572–1632).

[9] *Misers, Humorists,* and *Hypocrites* the titles of early plays by Shadwell.

[10] *Raymond families, and tribes of Bruce* Raymond and Bruce were characters in Shadwell's works.

[11] *Bun-Hill…Watling-street* Bunhill was in the City; Watling Street was a Roman road, a section of which ran through London.

[12] *Martyrs of pies, and relics of the bum* Unsold printed sheets were used to line pie-plates or as toilet paper.

[13] John Ogilby (1600–1676) translated Homer and Virgil.

[14] *Bilked stationers* publishers who lost money by their authors; Henry Herringman published both Shadwell and Dryden.

[15] *Ascanius* the son of Aeneas, he typified the ideal Roman youth (*OCD*).

[16] *lambent* playing lightly over the surface (*OED* lambent *a* 1b).

[17] *Hannibal* the Carthaginian general, whose father made him swear never to be a friend to Rome (*OCD*).

And in his father's right, and realm's defence,
Ne'er to have peace with wit, nor truce with sense.
The King himself the sacred unction made, [1]
As King by office, and as priest by trade:
120 In his sinister hand, instead of ball, [2]
He placed a mighty mug of potent ale;
Love's Kingdom to his right he did convey,
At once his sceptre and his rule of sway; [3]
Whose righteous lore the prince had practised
    young,
125 And from whose loins recorded Psyche sprung.
His temples, last, with poppies were o'erspread, [4]
That nodding seemed to consecrate his head:
Just at that point of time, if Fame not lie,
On his left hand twelve reverend owls did fly.
130 So Romulus, 'tis sung, by Tiber's brook,
Presage of sway from twice six vultures took. [5]
Th' admiring throng loud acclamations make,
And omens of his future empire take.
The sire then shook the honours of his head,
135 And from his brows damps of oblivion shed [6]
Full on the filial dullness: long he stood,
Repelling from his breast the raging God;
At length burst out in this prophetic mood:
    "Heavens bless my son, from Ireland let him
    reign
140 To far Barbados on the western main;
Of his dominion may no end be known,
And greater than his father's be his throne.
Beyond Loves Kingdom let him stretch his pen;
He paused, and all the people cried "Amen."

145 Then thus, continued he, "My son, advance
Still in new impudence, new ignorance.
Success let others teach, learn thou from me
Pangs without birth, and fruitless industry.
Let Virtuosos in five years be writ;
150 Yet not one thought accuse thy toil of wit.
Let gentle George in triumph tread the stage, [7]
Make Dorimant betray, and Loveit rage; [8]
Let Cully, Cockwood, Fopling, charm the pit,
And in their folly show the writer's wit. [9]
155 Yet still thy fools shall stand in thy defence,
And justify their author's want of sense.
Let 'em be all by thy own model made
Of dullness, and desire no foreign aid:
That they to future ages may be known,
160 Not copies drawn, but issue of thy own.
Nay let thy men of wit too be the same,
All full of thee, and differing but in name;
But let no alien Sedley interpose
To lard with wit thy hungry Epsom prose. [10]
165 And when false flowers of rhetoric thou would'st
    cull,
Trust Nature, do not labour to be dull;
But write thy best, and top; and, in each line,
Sir Formal's oratory will be thine. [11]
Sir Formal, though unsought, attends thy quill,
170 And does thy northern dedications fill. [12]
Nor let false friends seduce thy mind to fame,
By arrogating Jonson's hostile name.
Let father Flecknoe fire thy mind with praise,
And Uncle Ogilby thy envy raise.

---

[1] *the sacred unction*   the sacramental oil used in coronation ceremonies.

[2] *In his sinister hand, instead of ball*   in his left hand, instead of the ball which symbolized the world in the coronation ceremony.

[3] *Love's Kingdom*   one of Flecknoe's plays (1664).

[4] *poppies*   instead of laurels, soporifics; an allusion to the fact that Shadwell took opium.

[5] *twice six vultures*   Plutarch relates that Romulus was allowed to choose the site of Rome because he saw twelve vultures to Remus's six.

[6] *honours*   adornments (*OED* honour *sb* 6b).

[7] *gentle George*   Sir George Etherege (1636–1692), dramatist.

[8] *Dorimant...Loveit*   characters in Etherege's well-known play *The Man of Mode* (1676).

[9] *Cully, Cockwood, Fopling*   other characters from Etherege's comedies.

[10] Sir Charles Sedley (1638–1701) wrote a prologue to Shadwell's *Epsom Wells* and was said to have assisted in its composition.

[11] *Sir Formal*   Sir Formal Trifle, a character in Shadwell's *Virtuoso*.

[12] *northern dedications*   Shadwell dedicated several works to the Duke and Duchess of Newcastle.

175 Thou art my blood, where Jonson has no part;
    What share have we in nature, or in art?
    Where did his wit on learning fix a brand,
    And rail at arts he did not understand?
    Where made he love in Prince Nicander's vein, [1]
180 Or swept the dust in *Psyche*'s humble strain?
    Where sold he bargains, 'whip-stitch', 'kiss my arse',
    Promised a play and dwindled to a farce?
    When did his muse from Fletcher scenes purloin,
    As thou whole Eth'rege dost transfuse to thine?
185 But so transfused as oil on water's flow,
    His always float above, thine sinks below.
    This is thy province, this thy wondrous way,
    New humours to invent for each new play:
    This is that boasted bias of thy mind,
190 By which one way, to dullness, 'tis inclined.
    Which makes thy writings lean on one side still,
    And ,in all changes, that way bends thy will.
    Nor let thy mountain belly make pretence
    Of likeness; thine's a tympany of sense. [2]
195 A tun of man in thy large bulk is writ, [3]
    But sure thou'rt but a kilderkin of wit. [4]
    Like mine, thy gentle numbers feebly creep,
    Thy tragic Muse gives smiles, thy comic sleep.
    With whate'er gall thou sett'st thy self to write,
200 Thy inoffensive satires never bite.
    In thy felonious heart, though venom lies,
    It does but touch thy Irish pen, and dies.
    Thy genius calls thee not to purchase fame

    In keen iambics, but mild anagram: [5]
205 Leave writing plays, and choose for thy command
    Some peaceful province in acrostic land. [6]
    There thou mayest wings display and altars raise, [7]
    And torture one poor word ten thousand ways.
    Or if thou would'st thy different talents suit,
210 Set thy own songs, and sing them to thy lute."
    He said, but his last words were scarcely heard,
    For Bruce and Longvil had a Trap prepared,
    And down they sent the yet declaiming bard. [8]
    Sinking he left his drugget robe behind,
215 Borne upwards by a subterranean wind.
    The mantle fell to the young prophet's part, [9]
    With double portion of his father's art.
    —1682

---

[1] *Prince Nicander's vein*   Nicander is a character in *Psyche*.

[2] *tympany*   a swelling often figured as a disease; bombast (*OED* tympany 2).

[3] *tun*   large cask for liquids (*OED* tun *sb* 1).

[4] *kilderkin*   a cask for liquids, fish etc.; half a barrrel (*OED* kilderkin 1).

---

[5] *keen iambics*   biting satiric verse (*OED* iambic B *sb*); compare Cleveland, "The Rebel Scot," lines 27–28: "Come keen *Iambicks,* with your Badger's feet, / And Badger-like, bite till your teeth do meet."

[6] *Some peaceful province in acrostic land*   An acrostic is a poem whose initial letters spell out a word.

[7] *wings display and altars raise*   Dryden is thinking of Herbert's "Easter Wings" and "The Altar."

[8] *Bruce and Longvil*   In *The Virtuoso*, Clarinda and Miranda lower Sir Formal through a trapdoor while he speaks. Bruce and Longvil are audience to the trick.

[9] While Elijah, carried in a chariot of fire upon a whirlwind, was borne to heaven, his mantle descended upon his successor, Elisha (II Kings 2: 9–14).

Religio Laici
or A Layman's Faith [1]

Ornari res ipsa negat; contenta doceri [2]

THE PREFACE

A poem with so bold a title, and a name prefixed, from which the handling of so serious a subject would not be expected, may reasonably oblige the author, to say somewhat in defence both of himself, and of his undertaking. In the first place, if it be objected to me that being a layman, I ought not to have concerned myself with speculations, which belong to the profession of divinity; I could answer, that perhaps, laymen, with equal advantages of parts and knowledge, are not the most incompetent judges of sacred things; but in the due sense of my own weakness and want of learning, I plead not this: I pretend not to make my self a judge of faith, in others, but only to make a confession of my own; I lay no unhallowed hand upon the ark;[3] but wait on it, with the reverence that becomes me at a distance: In the next place I will ingenuously confess, that the helps I have used in this small treatise, were many of them taken from the works of our own reverend divines of the Church of England; so that the weapons with which I combat irreligion, are already consecrated; though I suppose they may be taken down as lawfully as the sword of Goliah was by David,[4] when they are to be employed for the common cause, against the enemies of piety. I intend not by this to entitle them to any of my errors;[5] which, yet, I hope are only those of charity to mankind; and such as my own charity has caused me to commit, that of others may more easily excuse. Being naturally inclined to scepticism in philosophy, I have no reason to impose my opinions, in a subject which is above it: But whatever they are, I submit them with all reverence to my Mother Church, accounting them no further mine, than as they are authorized, or at least, uncondemned by her. And, indeed, to secure my self on this side, I have used the necessary precaution, of showing this paper before it was published to a judicious and learned friend, a man indefatigably zealous in the service of the Church and State: and whose writings, have highly deserved of both. He was pleased to approve the body of the discourse, and I hope he is more my friend, than to do it out of complaisance:[6] 'Tis true he had too good a taste to like it all; and amongst some other faults recommended to my second view, what I have written, perhaps too boldly on St. Athanasius:[7] which he advised me wholly to omit. I am sensible enough that I had done more prudently to have followed his opinion:[8] But then I could not have satisfied myself, that I had done honestly not to have written what was my own. It has always been my thought, that heathens, who never did, nor without miracle could hear of the name of Christ were yet in a possibility of salvation. Neither will it enter easily into my belief, that before the coming of our Saviour, the

---

[1] This poem was occasioned by a translated work of biblical criticism, Father Richard Simon's *Critical History of the Old Testament*. Simon's discussion of the problems of the biblical text, with its many manuscript variants, concludes that they justify Catholicism's interpreting the bible in the light of its own traditions. Dryden saw that discussion of textual problems could lead to denial of the supernatural authority of scripture, and in the poem presents himself as an Anglican whose faith is biblically based. In the poem Dryden attacks Deism, Catholic authoritarianism, and the Dissenters. There is some irony here, because Dryden ended his days as a Roman Catholic.

[2] "My subject is content to be taught; and scorns adornment" (Manilius, *Astronomica* 3.39).

[3] See I Chronicles 13:9–10, where Uzza touches the ark and is killed as a result.

[4] After David has killed Goliath, he receives Goliath's sword from Abimelech (I Samuel 21:8–9).

[5] *to entitle them* impute to them (*OED* 5c).

[6] *complaisance* courtesy.

[7] *Athanasius* See note, p. 995.

[8] *sensible* aware, cognizant (*OED* 11a).

whole world, excepting only the Jewish nation, should lie under the inevitable necessity of everlasting punishment, for want of that revelation, which was confined to so small a spot of ground as that of Palestine. Among the sons of Noah we read of one only who was accursed; and if a blessing in the ripeness of time was reserved for Japhet, (of whose progeny we are,) it seems unaccountable to me, why so many generations of the same offspring, as preceded our saviour in the flesh, should be all involved in one common condemnation, and yet that their posterity should be entitled to the hopes of salvation: As if a bill of exclusion[1] had passed only on the fathers, which debarred not the sons from their succession. Or that so many ages had been delivered over to Hell, and so many reserved for Heaven, and that the Devil had the first choice, and God the next. Truly I am apt to think, that the revealed religion which was taught by Noah to all his sons, might continue for some ages in the whole posterity. That afterwards it was included wholly in the family of Sem is manifest: but when the progenies of Cham and Japhet swarmed into colonies, and those colonies were subdivided into many others; in process of time their descendants lost by little and little the primitive and purer rites of divine worship, retaining only the notion of one deity; to which succeeding generations added others: (for men took their degrees in those ages from conquerors to Gods.) Revelation being thus eclipsed to almost all Mankind, the light of Nature as the next in dignity was substituted; and that is it which St. Paul concludes to be the rule of the heathens; and by which they are hereafter to be judged. If my supposition be true, then the consequence which I have assumed in my poem may be also true; namely, that deism, or the principles of natural worship,[2] are only the faint remnants or dying flames of revealed religion in the posterity of Noah: And that our modern philosophers, nay and some of our philosophising divines have too much exalted the faculties of our souls, when they have maintained that by their force, Mankind has been able to find out that there is one supreme agent or intellectual being which we call God:[3] that praise and prayer are his due worship; and the rest of those deducements, which I am confident are the remote effects of revelation, and unattainable by our discourse,[4] I mean as simply considered, and without the benefit of divine illumination. So that we have not lifted up ourselves to God, by the weak pinions of our Reason, but he has been plead to descend to us; and what Socrates said of him, what Plato writ, and the rest of the heathen philosophers of several nations, is all no more than the twilight of revelation, after the sun of it was set in the race of Noah. That there is something above us, some principle of motion, our reason can apprehend, though it cannot discover what it is, by its own virtue. And indeed 'tis very improbable, that we, who by the strength of our faculties cannot enter into the knowledge of any being, not so much as of our own, should be able to find out by them, that Supreme Nature, which we cannot otherwise define, than by saying it is infinite; as if infinite were definable, or infinity a subject for our narrow understanding. They who would prove religion by Reason, do but weaken the cause which they endeavour to support: 'tis to take away the pillars from our faith, and to prop it only with a twig: 'tis to design a tower like that of Babel,[5] which if it were

---

[1] an attempt (1680–81) to keep James from becoming King.

[2] Deists contend that a supreme being set the world in motion and that our rationality is sufficient to discover this and bring us to worship Him. They reject a more 'conventional' Christian stress on supernatural revelation.

[3] *intellectual being* apprehended only through our intellect (OED 2).

[4] *discourse* reasoning; rationality (OED 2).

[5] See Genesis 2.

possible (as it is not) to reach Heaven, would come to nothing by the confusion of the workmen. For every man is building a several way;[1] impotently conceited of his own model, and his own materials: Reason is always striving, and always at a loss, and of necessity it must so come to pass, while 'tis exercised about that which is not its proper object. Let us be content at last, to know God, by his own methods; at least so much of him, as he is pleased to reveal to us, in the sacred Scriptures; to apprehend them to be the word of God, is all our reason has to do; for all beyond it is the work of faith, which is the seal of Heaven impressed upon our human understanding.

And now for what concerns the Holy Bishop Athanasius,[2] the preface of whose creed seems inconsistent with my opinion; which is, that heathens may possibly be saved; in the first place I desire it may be considered that it is the preface only, not the creed itself, which, (till I am better informed) is of too hard a digestion for my charity. 'Tis not that I am ignorant how many several texts of Scripture seemingly support that cause; but neither am I ignorant how all those texts may receive a kinder, and more mollified interpretation. Every man who is read in church history, knows that belief was drawn up after a long contestation with Arius,[3] concerning the divinity of our blessed Saviour, and his being one substance with the Father; and that thus compiled, it was sent abroad among the Christian churches, as a kind of test, which whosoever took, was looked on as an orthodox believer. 'Tis manifest from hence, that the heathen part of the empire was not concerned in it: for its business was not to distinguish betwixt pagans and Christians, but betwixt heretics and true believers. This, well considered, takes off the heavy weight of censure, which I would willingly avoid from so venerable a man; for if this proportion, whosoever will be saved, be restrained only, to those to whom it was intended, and for whom it was composed, I mean the Christians; then the anathema,[4] reaches not the heathens, who had never heard of Christ, and were nothing interested in that dispute. After all, I am far from blaming even that prefatory addition to the creed, and as far from cavilling at the continuation of it in the liturgy of the Church; where on the days appointed, 'tis publicly read:[5] for I suppose there is the same reason for it now, in opposition to the Socinians,[6] as there was then against the Arians; the one being a heresy, which seems to have been refined out of the other; and with how much more plausibility of reason it combats our religion, with so much more caution to be avoided: and therefore the prudence of our Church is to be commended which has interposed her authority for the recommendation of this creed. Yet to such as are grounded in the true belief, those explanatory creeds, the Nicene[7] and this of Athanasius might perhaps be spared: for what is supernatural, will always be a mystery in spite of exposition: and for my own part the plain Apostle's Creed, is most suitable to my weak understanding; as the simplest diet is the most easy of digestion.

I have dwelt longer on this subject than I intended; and longer than, perhaps, I ought; for having laid down, as my foundation, that the

---

[1] *several* separate, distinct.

[2] Bishop of Alexandria, St. Athanasius (296–373) opposed the Arian heresy (below). Before he begins his written argument, Athanasius asserts that all those who do not hold the Catholic faith are automatically condemned to oblivion.

[3] An Alexandrian presbyter, Arius (256–336) opposed the idea that Christ was divine (consubstantial with God), as well as the doctrine of the Trinity (the idea that father, son, and the Holy Spirit together constitute one God).

[4] *anathema* God's curse, whereby a person is consigned to Satan.

[5] The *Book of Common Prayer* assigns certain days when the Athanasian creed should be used instead of the Apostle's Creed.

[6] *Socinians* Renaissance sect which accepted Arian claims.

[7] statement of Christian belief conceived at the first Council of Nicea, to combat the Arian heresy.

scripture is a rule; that in all things needful to salvation, it is clear, sufficient, and ordained by God Almighty for that purpose, I have left myself no right to interpret obscure places, such as concern the possibility of eternal happiness to heathens: because whatsoever is obscure is concluded not necessary to be known.

But, by asserting the scripture to be the canon of our faith, I have unavoidably created to myself two sorts of enemies: The Papists indeed, more directly, because they have kept the scripture from us, what they could; and have reserved to themselves a right of interpreting what they have delivered under the pretence of infallibility: and the fanatics more collaterally, because they have assumed what amounts to an infallibility in the private spirit: and have detorted those texts of scripture, which are not necessary to salvation, to the damnable uses of sedition, disturbance and destruction of the civil government. To begin with the Papists, and to speak freely, I think them the less dangerous (at least in appearance) to our present state; for not only the penal laws are in force against them, and their number is contemptible; but also their peerage and commons are excluded from parliaments, and consequently those laws in no probability of being repealed. A general and uninterrupted plot of their clergy, ever since the Reformation, I suppose all protestants believe. For 'tis not reasonable to think but that so many of their orders, as were ousted from their fat possessions, would endeavour a reentrance against those whom they account heretics. As for the late design, Mr. Coleman's letters, for ought I know are the best evidence; and what they discover, without wire-drawing their sense, or malicious glosses, all men of reason conclude credible.[1] If there be any thing more than this required of me, I must believe it as well as I am able, in spite of the witnesses, and out of a decent

conformity to the votes of parliament: For I suppose the fanatics will not allow the private spirit in this case: Here the infallibility is at least in one part of the government; and our understandings as well as our wills are represented. But to return to the Roman Catholics, how can we be secure from the practice of Jesuited Papists in that religion? For not two or three of that Order, as some of them would impose upon us, but almost the whole body of them are of opinion, that their infallible master has a right over kings, not only in spirituals but temporals. Not to name Mariana, Bellarmine, Emanuel Sa, Molina, Santarel, Simancha, and at the least twenty others of foreign countries; we can produce of our own nation, Campian, and Doleman or Parsons, besides many are named whom I have not read, who all of them attest this doctrine, that the Pope can depose and give away the right of any sovereign prince, *si vel paulum deflexerit*, if he shall never so little warp: but if he once comes to be excommunicated, then the bond of obedience is taken off from subjects; and they may and ought to drive him like another Nebuchadnezzar, *ex hominum Christianorum Dominatu*, from exercising dominion over Christians: and to this they are bound by virtue of divine precept, and by all the ties of conscience under no less penalty than damnation. If they answer me (as a learned priest has lately written,) that this doctrine of the Jesuits is not *de fide* [an article of faith], and that consequently they are not obliged by it, they must pardon me, if I think they have nothing to the purpose; for 'tis a Maxim in their church, where points of faith are not decided, and that doctors are of contrary opinions, they may follow which part they please; but more safely the most received and most authorized. And their champion Bellarmine has told the world, in his apology, that the King of England is a vassal to the Pope, *ratione directi Dominii*, and that he holds in

---

[1] Edward Coleman, executed in 1678 for conspiring to re-establish Catholicism in England.

villeinage of his Roman landlord.[1] Which is no new claim put in for England. Our chronicles are his authentic witnesses, that King John was deposed by the same plea, and Philip Augustus admitted tenant. And which makes the more for Bellarmine, the French king was again ejected when our King submitted to the church, and the crown received under the sordid condition of a vassalage.

'Tis not sufficient for the more moderate and well-meaning Papists, (of which I doubt not there are many) to produce the evidences of their loyalty to the late King, and to declare their innocency in this plot; I will grant their behaviour in the first, to have been as loyal and as brave as they desire; and will be willing to hold them excused as to the second, (I mean when it comes to my turn, and after my betters; for 'tis a madness to be sober alone, while the nation continues drunk:) but that saying of their father Cres:[2] is still running in my head, that they may be dispensed with in their obedience to an heretic prince, while the necessity of the times shall oblige them to it: (for that [as another of them tells us,] is only the effect of Christian prudence) but when once they shall get power to shake him off, an heretic is no lawful king, and consequently to rise against him is no rebellion. I should be glad therefore, that they would follow the advice which was charitably given them by a reverend prelate of our church; namely, that they would join in a public act of disowning and detesting those Jesuitick principles; and subscribe to all doctrines which deny the Pope's authority of deposing kings, and releasing subjects from their oath of allegiance: to which I should think they might easily be induced, if it be true that this present Pope has condemned the doctrine of king-killing (a thesis of the Jesuits) amongst others *ex Cathedra* (as they call it) or in open consistory.

Leaving them, therefore, in so fair a way (if they please themselves) of satisfying all reasonable men, of their sincerity and good meaning to the government, I shall make bold to consider that other extreme of our religion, I mean the fanatics, or schismatics, of the English church. Since the Bible has been translated into our tongue, they have used it so, as if their business was not to be saved but to be damned by its contents. If we consider only them, better had it been for the English nation, that it had still remained in the original Greek and Hebrew, or at least in the honest Latin of St. Jerome, than that several texts in it, should have been prevaricated to the destruction of that government, which put it into so ungrateful hands.

How many heresies the first translation of Tyndal produced in few years,[3] let my Lord Herbert's history of Henry the Eighth inform you; insomuch that for the gross errors in it, and the great mischiefs it occasioned, a sentence passed on the first edition of the Bible, too shameful almost to be repeated. After the short reign of Edward the Sixth (who had continued to carry on the Reformation, on other principles than it was begun) every one knows that not only the chief promoters of that work, but many others, whose consciences would not dispense with popery, were forced, for fear of persecution, to change climates: from whence returning at the beginning of Queen Elizabeth's reign, many of them who had been in France, and at Geneva, brought back the rigid opinions and imperious discipline of Calvin, to graft upon our Reformation. Which, though they cunningly concealed at first (as well knowing how nauseously that drug would go down in a lawful monarchy, which was prescribed for a rebellious commonwealth), yet they always kept it in reserve; and were never wanting to themselves either in court or parliament, when either they had any prospect of a

---

[1] *villeinage* tenure in service to a feudal lord.

[2] *Cres* Hugh Cressy, English chaplain to Queen Catherine.

[3] *Tyndal* William Tyndale (?1490–1536); his translation provided the basis for most of the Authorized version.

numerous party of fanatic members in the one, or the encouragement of any favourite in the other, whose covetousness was gaping at the patrimony of the church. They who will consult the works of our venerable Hooker,[1] or the account of his life, or more particularly the letter written to him on this subject, by George Cranmer, may see by what gradations they proceeded; from the dislike of cap and surplice, the very next step was admonitions to the parliament against the whole government ecclesiastical: then came out volumes in English and Latin in defence of their tenets: and immediately, practices were set on foot to erect their discipline without authority. Those not succeeding, satire and railing was the next: And Martin Mar-Prelate (the Marvel of those times) was the first Presbyterian scribbler, who sanctified libels and scurrility to the use of the good old cause.[2] Which was done (says my author) upon this account; that (their serious treatises having been fully answered and refuted) they might compass by railing what they had lost by reasoning; and when their cause was sunk in court and parliament, they might at least hedge in a stake amongst the rabble: for to their ignorance all things are wit which are abusive; but if church and state were made the theme, then the doctoral degree of wit was to be taken at Billingsgate: even the most saintlike of the party, though they durst not excuse this contempt and vilifying of the government, yet were pleased, and grinned at it with a pious smile; and called it a judgment of God against the hierarchy. Thus sectaries, we may see, were born with teeth, foul-mouthed and scurrilous from their infancy: and if spiritual pride, venom, violence, contempt of superiors and slander had been the marks of orthodox belief; the Presbytery and the rest of our schismatics, which are their spawn, were always the most visible church in the Christian world.

'Tis true, the government was too strong at that time for a rebellion; but to show what proficiency they had made in Calvin's school, even then their mouths watered at it: for two of their gifted brotherhood (Hacket and Coppinger) as the story tells us, got up into a pease-cart, and harangued the people, to dispose them to an insurrection, and to establish their discipline by force:[3] so that however it comes about, that now they celebrate Queen Elizabeth's birth-night, as that of their saint and patroness; yet then they were for doing the work of the Lord by arms against her; and in all probability, they wanted but a fanatic Lord Mayor and two sheriffs of their party to have compassed it.

Our venerable Hooker, after many admonitions which he had given them, toward the end of his preface, breaks out into this prophetic speech. "There is in every one of these considerations most just cause to fear, lest our hastiness to embrace a thing of so perilous consequence (meaning the 'Presbyterian discipline') should cause posterity to feel those evils, which as yet are more easy for us to prevent, than they would be for them to remedy."

How fatally this Cassandra has foretold we know too well by sad experience: the seeds were sown in the time of Queen Elizabeth, the bloody harvest ripened in the reign of King Charles the Martyr: and because all the sheaves could not be carried off without shedding some of the loose grains, another crop is too like to follow; nay I fear 'tis unavoidable if the conventiclers be permitted still to scatter.

A man may be suffered to quote an adversary to our religion, when he speaks truth: and 'tis the observation of Meimbourg in his *History of Calvinism,* that where-ever that discipline was planted and embraced, rebellion, civil war and misery attended

---

[1] *Hooker* Richard Hooker (?1554–1600); his *Of the Laws of Ecclesiastical Polity* was the standard defence of the Church of England.

[2] *Martin Mar-Prelate* the pseudonymous author of a series of surreptitiously printed anti-episcopal tracts (1588–89); Dryden links their use of satire to the polemical work of Andrew Marvell.

[3] *Hacket and Coppinger* a self-proclaimed Messiah and his disciple; William Hacket was executed in 1591, Edmund Coppinger died in prison in 1592.

it. And how indeed should it happen otherwise? Reformation of church and state has always been the ground of our divisions in England. While we were Papists, our Holy Father rid us, by pretending authority out of the scriptures to depose princes, when we shook off his authority, the sectaries furnished themselves with the same weapons, and out of the same magazine, the Bible. So that the scriptures, which are in themselves the greatest security of governors, as commanding express obedience to them, are now turned to their destruction; and never since the Reformation has there wanted a text of their interpreting to authorize a rebel. And 'tis to be noted by the way, that the doctrines of king-killing and deposing, which have been taken up only by the worst party of the Papists, the most frontless flatterers of the Pope's authority, have been espoused, defended and are still maintained by the whole body of nonconformists and republicans. 'Tis but dubbing themselves the People of God, which 'tis the interest of their preachers to tell them they are, and their own interest to believe; and after that, they cannot dip into the Bible, but one text or another will turn up for their purpose: If they are under persecution (as they call it,) then that is a mark of their election; if they flourish, then God works miracles for their deliverance, and the saints are to possess the earth.

They may think themselves to be too roughly handled in this paper; but I who know best how far I could have gone on this subject, must be bold to tell them they are spared: though at the same time I am not ignorant that they interpret the mildness of a writer to them, as they do the mercy of the government; in the one they think it fear, and conclude it weakness in the other. The best way for them to confute me, is, as I before advised the Papists, to disclaim their principles, and renounce their practices. We shall all be glad to think them true Englishmen when they obey the King, and true Protestants when they conform to the church discipline.

It remains that I acquaint the reader, that the verses were written for an ingenious young gentleman my friend; upon his translation of *The Critical History of the Old Testament*, composed by the learned Father Simon: the verses therefore are addressed to the translator of that work, and the style of them is, what it ought to be, epistolary.[1]

If any one be so lamentable a critic as to require the smoothness, the numbers and the turn of heroic poetry in this poem; I must tell him, that if he has not read Horace, I have studied him, and hope the style of his epistles is not ill imitated here. The expressions of a poem, designed purely for instruction, ought to be plain and natural, and yet majestic: for here the poet is presumed to be a kind of law-giver, and those three qualities which I have named are proper to the legislative style. The florid, elevated and figurative way is for the passions; for love and hatred, fear and anger, are begotten in the soul by showing their objects out of their true proportion; either greater than the life, or less; but instruction is to be given by showing them what they naturally are. A man is to be cheated into passion, but to be reasoned into truth.

Religio Laici
(excerpts)

Dim, as the borrow'd beams of moon and stars
To lonely, weary, wandering travellers,
Is Reason to the soul: and as on high,
Those rolling fires discover but the sky
Not light us here; so Reason's glimmering ray
Was lent, not to assure our doubtful way,
But guide us upward to a better day.
And as those nightly tapers disappear
When day's bright Lord ascends our hemisphere;
So pale grows Reason at religion's sight;
So dies, and so dissolves in supernatural light.

1 *my friend* Henry Dickinson.

Some few, whose lamp shone brighter, have been
   led
From cause to cause, to Nature's secret head;
And found that one first principle must be:
15 But what, or who, that UNIVERSAL HE;
Whether some soul encompassing this ball
Unmade, unmod'd; yet making, moving all;
Or various atoms interfering dance
Leapt into form, (the noble work of chance;)
20 Or this great all was from eternity;
Not ev'n the stagirite himself could see;
And Epicurus guess'd as well as he:
As blindly grop'd they for a future state;
As rashly judg'd of providence and fate:
25 But least of all could their endeavours find
What most concern'd the good of humane kind: [1]
For happiness was never to be found;
But vanish'd from 'em, like enchanted ground.
One thought content the good to be enjoy'd:
30 This, every little accident destroy'd:
The wiser madmen did for virtue toil:
A thorny, or at best a barren soil:
In pleasure some their glutton souls would steep;
But found their line too short, the well too deep;
35 And leaky vessels which no bliss cou'd keep.
Thus, anxious thoughts in endless circles roll,
Without a centre where to fix the soul:
In this wild maze their vain endeavours end.
How can the less the greater comprehend?
40 Or finite reason reach infinity?
For what cou'd fathom GOD were more than he.
   The Deist thinks he stands for firmer ground;
Cries ευρεκα: the might secret's found:
God is that spring of good; supreme, and best;
45 We, made to serve, and in that service blest;
If so, some rules of worship must be given,
Distributed alike to all by Heaven:
Else God were partial, and to some deny'd
The means his justice shou'd for all provide.

50 This general worship is to PRAISE, and PRAY:
One part to borrow blessings, one to pay:
And when frail Nature slides into offence,
The sacrifice for crimes is penitence.
Yet, since th' effects of providence, we find
55 Are variously dispens'd to humane kind;
That vice triumphs, and virtue suffers here,
(A brand that sovereign justice cannot bear;)
Our reason prompts us to a future state:
The last appeal from fortune, and from fate:
60 Where God's all-righteous ways will be declar'd;
The bad meet punishment, the good, reward.
   Thus Man by his own strength to Heaven
      wou'd soar: [2]
And wou'd not be oblig'd to God for more.
Vain, wretched creature, how art thou misled
65 To think thy wit these God-like notions bred!
These truths are not the product of thy mind,
But dropped from Heaven, and of a nobler kind.
Reveal'd religion first inform'd thy sight,
And Reason saw not, till faith sprung the light.
70 Hence all thy natural worship takes the source:
'Tis revelation what thou thinkst discourse.
Else, how com'st thou to see these truths so clear,
Which so obscure to heathens did appear?
Not Plato these, nor Aristotle found:
75 Nor he whose wisdom oracles renown'd. [3]
Hast thou a wit so deep, or so sublime,
Or canst thou lower dive, or higher climb?
Canst thou, by reason, more of God-head know
Than Plutarch, Seneca, or Cicero?
80 Those giant wits, in happier ages born,
(When arms, and arts did Greece and Rome adorn)
Knew no such system: no such piles cou'd raise
Of natural worship, built on pray'r and praise,
To one sole GOD.
85 Nor did remorse, to expiate sin, prescribe:
But slew their fellow creatures for a bribe:

---

[1] "Opinions of the several sects of philosophers concerning the *summum bonum*" (Dryden's marginal note).

[2] "Of revealed religion" (Dryden's marginal note).

[3] "Socrates" (Dryden's marginal note).

To the Memory of Mr. Oldham [1]

Farewell, too little and too lately known,
Whom I began to think and call my own;
For sure our souls were near allied; and thine
Cast in the same poetic mould with mine.
5 One common note on either lyre did strike,
And knaves and fools we both abhorred alike:
To the same goal did both our studies drive,
The last set out the soonest did arrive. [2]
Thus *Nisus* fell upon the slippery place,
10 While his young friend perform'd and won the
       race. [3]
O early ripe! to thy abundant store
What could advancing age have added more?
It might (what Nature never gives the young)
Have taught the numbers of thy native tongue. [4]
15 But satire needs not those, and wit will shine
Through the harsh cadence of a rugged line.
A noble error, and but seldom made,
When poets are by too much force betrayed.
Thy generous fruits, though gathered ere thy prime
20 Still shewed a quickness; and maturing time
But mellows what we write to the dull sweets of
       Rime.
Once more, hail and farewell; farewell thou young,
But ah too short, *Marcellus* of our tongue; [5]
Thy brows with ivy, and with laurels bound;

25 But fate and gloomy night encompass thee
       around.
—1684

Juvenal's Sixth Satire
(excerpts)

THE EMPRESS MESSALINA

This was a private crime; but you shall hear
What fruits the sacred brows of monarchs
       bear:
The good old sluggard but began to snore,
When, from his side, up rose the imperial whore; [6]
165 She, who preferred the pleasures of the night
To *pomps*, that are but impotent delight,
Strode from the palace, with an eager pace,
To cope with a more masculine embrace.
Muffled she marched, like *Juno* in a cloud,
170 Of all her train but one poor wench allowed;
One whom in secret service she could trust,
The rival and companion of her lust.
To the known brothel-house she takes her way,
And for a nasty room gives double pay;
175 That room in which the rankest harlot lay.
Prepared for fight, *expectingly* she lies,
With heaving breasts, and with desiring eyes.
The fair unbroken belly lay displayed
Where once the brave *Britannicus* was laid.
180 Bare was her bosom, bare the field of lust,
Eager to swallow every sturdy thrust.
Still as one drops, another takes his place,
And baffled, still succeeds to like disgrace.
At length, when friendly darkness is expired,
185 And every strumpet from her cell retired,
She lags behind and lingering at the gate,
With a *repining* sigh submits to fate;
All filth without, and all afire within,
Tired with the toil, *unsated* with the sin.

---

[1] John Oldham the satirist, who was about thirty when he died.

[2] *The last set out the soonest did arrive* probably a studied ambiguity: Oldham was born later than Dryden, but died earlier; but the primary meaning is that Oldham achieved poetic excellence at an earlier stage in his life than Dryden did in his.

[3] *Nisus* etc. See Virgil, *Aeneid* 5.295ff. "Euryalus famed for beauty and flower of youth, Nisus for tender love of the boy." In a race, Nisus was leading but slipped; in rising, "not forgetful" of his friend, he tripped the person behind him, thus allowing Euryalus to win "by grace of his friend."

[4] *the numbers of thy native tongue* more harmonious English versification.

[5] *Marcellus* son of Octavia, sister of Augustus; see Virgil, *Aeneid*, 860ff.

---

[6] *good old sluggard* Claudius. Juvenal "tells the famous story of Messalina, wife to Claudius" (Dryden's note)

190 Old Caesar's bed the modest matron seeks,
  The steam of lamps still hanging on her checks
In ropy smut; thus foul, and thus *bedight*,
She brings him back the product of the night.

THE LEARNED WIFE

575   But of all plagues, the greatest is untold;
The *book-learned* wife, in Greek and Latin bold;
The critic-dame, who at her table sits,
Homer and Virgil quotes, and weighs their wits,
And pities Dido's agonising fits.
580 She has so far the ascendant of the board,
The prating pedant puts not in one word;
The man of law is nonplussed in his suit,
Nay, every other female tongue is mute.
Hammers and beating anvils you would swear,
585 And Vulcan, with his whole militia, there.
Tabors and trumpets, cease; for she alone
Is able to redeem the labouring moon.
E'en wit's a burden, when it talks too long;
But she, who has no continence of tongue,
590 Should walk in breeches, and should wear a
    beard,
And mix among the philosophic herd.
O what a midnight curse has he, whose side
Is pestered with a mood and figure bride!
Let mine, ye Gods! (if such must be my fate,)
595 No logic learn, nor history translate,
But rather be a quiet, humble fool;
I hate a wife to whom I go to school,
Who climbs the grammar-tree, distinctly knows
Where noun, and verb, and participle grows;
600 Corrects her country-neighbour; and, abed,
For breaking Priscian's breaks her husband's head.

THE GAUDY GOSSIP

  The gaudy gossip, when she's set agog,
In jewels dressed, and at each ear a bob,
Goes flaunting out, and in her trim of pride,
605 Thinks all she says or does is justified.

When poor, she's scarce a tolerable evil;
But rich, and fine, a wife's a very devil.
  She duly, once a month, renews her face;
Meantime it lies in daub and hid in grease.
610 Those are the husband's nights; she craves her
    due,
He takes fat kisses, and is stuck in glue.
But to the loved adulterer when she steers,
Fresh from the bath, in brightness she appears:
For him the rich Arabia sweats her gum,
615 And precious oils from distant Indies come,
How haggardly soe'er she looks at home.
The eclipse then vanishes, and all her face
Is opened, and restored to every grace;
The crust removed, her cheeks as smooth as silk
620 Are polished with a wash of asses' milk;
And should she to the furthest north be sent,
A train of these attend her banishment.
But hadst thou seen her plastered up before,
'Twas so unlike a face, it seemed a sore.
625   'Tis worth our while, to know what all the day
They do, and how they pass their time away;
For, if o'ernight the husband has been slack,
Or counterfeited sleep, and turned his back,
Next day, be sure, the servants go to wrack.
630 The chambermaid and dresser are called whores,
The page is stripped, and beaten out of doors;
The whole house suffers for the master's crime,
And he himself is warned to wake another time.
  She hires tormentors by the year; she treats
635 Her visitors, and talks, but still she beats.
Beats while she paints her face, surveys her gown,
Casts up the day's account, and still beats on:
Tired out, at length, with an outrageous tone,
She bids them in the devil's name be gone.
640 Compared with such a proud, insulting dame,
Sicilian tyrants may renounce their name.
For if she hastes abroad to take the air,
Or goes to Isis' church, (the bawdy house of
    prayer)
She hurries all her handmaids to the task;

645 Her head, alone, will twenty dressers ask.
Psecas, the chief, with breast and shoulders bare,
Trembling, considers every sacred hair;
If any straggler from his rank be found,
A pinch must for the mortal sin compound.
650 Psecas is not in fault; but in the glass,
The dame's offended at her own ill face.
That maid is banished; and another girl
More dexterous manages the comb and curl.
The rest are summoned on a point so nice,
655 And first the grave old woman gives advice;
The next is called, and so the turn goes round,
As each for age, or wisdom, is renowned:
Such counsel, such deliberate care they take,
As if her life and honour lay at stake:
660 With curls on curls, they build her head before,
And mount it with a formidable tower.
A giantess she seems; but look behind,
And then she dwindles to the pigmy kind.
Duck-legged, short-waisted, such a dwarf she is,
665 That she must rise on tiptoes for a kiss.
Meanwhile her husband's whole estate is spent;
He may go bare, while she receives his rent.
She minds him not; she lives not as a wife,
But like a bawling neighbour, full of strife:
670 Near him in this alone, that she extends
Her hate to all his servants and his friends.
—1693

Juvenal's Tenth Satire
(excerpts)

SEJANUS

In his own age, Democritus could find
Sufficient cause to laugh at humankind:
75 Learn from so great a wit; a land of bogs
With ditches fenced, a heaven fat with fogs,
May form a spirit fit to sway the state,
And make the neighbouring monarchs fear their
fate.

He laughs at all the vulgar cares and fears;
80 At their vain triumphs, and their vainer tears:
An equal temper in his mind he found,
When fortune flattered him and when she
frowned.
'Tis plain from hence that what our vows request
Are hurtful things, or useless at the best.
85 Some ask for envied power; which public hate
Pursues, and hurries headlong to their fate:
Down go the titles; and the statue crowned,
Is by base hands in the next river drowned.
The guiltless horses, and the chariot wheel,
90 The same effects of vulgar fury feel:
The smith prepares his hammer for the stroke,
While the lunged bellows hissing fire provoke.
Sejanus, almost first of Roman names,
The great Sejanus crackles in the flames:
95 Formed in the forge, the pliant brass is laid
On anvils; and of head and limbs are made,
Pans, cans, and piss-pots, a whole kitchen trade.
Adorn your doors with laurels; and a bull,
Milk white, and large, lead to the Capitol;
100 Sejanus with a rope is dragged along,
The sport and laughter of the giddy throng;
"Good lord!" they cry, "what Ethiop lips he has;
How foul a snout, and what a hanging face!"
By heaven, I never could endure his sight!
105 But say, how came his monstrous crimes to light?
What is the charge, and who the evidence,
(The saviour of the nation and the prince?)
Nothing of this; but our old Caesar sent
A noisy letter to his parliament.
110 'Nay, sirs, if Caesar writ, I ask no more;
He's guilty, and the question's out of door.
How goes the mob? (for that's a mighty thing,)
When the king's trump, the mob are for the king;
They follow fortune, and the common cry
115 Is still against the rogue condemned to die
But the same very mob, that rascal crowd,
Had cried "Sejanus," with a shout as loud,
Had his designs (by fortune's favour blest)

Succeeded, and the prince's age oppressed.
120 But long, long since, the times have changed their
        face,
The people grown degenerate and base;
Not suffered now the freedom of their choice
To make their magistrates, and sell their voice.
Our wise forefathers, great by sea and land,
125 Had once the power and absolute command;
All offices of trust themselves disposed;
Raised whom they pleased, and whom they
        pleased deposed:
But we who give our native rights away
And our enslaved posterity betray
130 Are now reduced to beg an alms, and go
On holidays to see a puppet-show.
"There was a damned design," cries one, "no
        doubt,
For warrants are already issued out:
I met Brutidius in a mortal fright,
135 He's dipped for certain, and plays least in sight;
I fear the rage of our offended prince,
Who thinks the senate slack in his defence.
Come, let us haste, our loyal zeal to show,
And spurn the wretched corpse of Caesar's foe:
140 But let our slaves be present there; lest they
Accuse their masters, and for gain betray.
Such were the whispers of those jealous times,
About Sejanus' punishment and crimes.
Now tell me truly, wouldst thou change thy fate,
145 To be, like him, first minister of state?
To have thy levees crowded with resort,
Of a depending, gaping, servile court;
Dispose all honours of the sword and gown,
Grace with a nod, and ruin with a frown;
150 To hold thy prince in pupilage, and sway
That monarch, whom the mastered world obey?
While he, intent on secret lusts alone,
Lives to himself, abandoning the throne;
Cooped in a narrow isle, observing dreams
155 With flattering wizards, and erecting schemes!
I well believe thou wouldst be great as he,

For every man's a fool to that degree:
All wish the dire prerogative to kill;
E'en they would have the power, who want the
        will:
160 But wouldst thou have thy wishes understood,
To take the bad together with the good?
Wouldst thou not rather choose a small renown,
To be the mayor of some poor paltry town;
Bigly to look, and barbarously to speak;
165 To pound false weights, and scanty measures
        break?
Then, grant we that Sejanus went astray
In every wish, and knew not how to pray;
For he who grasped the world's exhausted store
Yet never had enough, but wished for more,
170 Raised a top-heavy tower, of monstrous height,
Which, mouldering, crushed him underneath the
        weight.
—1693

The Secular Masque [1]

Enter Janus.

JANUS
*C*hronos, *Chronos*, mend thy pace,
    An hundred times the rolling sun
Around the radiant belt has run
In his revolving race.
5 Behold, behold, the goal in sight,
Spread thy fans, and wing thy flight.

Enter Chronos, *with a scythe in his hand, and a
great globe on his back, which he sets down at his
entrance.*

---

[1] The title refers to the turn of the century (see *OED a* secular III 5).
Dryden wrote a prologue, epilogue and this "masque" as additions to
"an old play of Fletcher's, called the Pilgrim" (from a letter of
Dryden's, April 11, 1700). There is a story that Dryden died on the
third night of performance, which would date the first night as April
29, 1700 (Kinsley, *Poems*, p. 2082).

CHRONOS

Weary, weary of my weight,
Let me, let me drop my freight,
    And leave the world behind.
I could not bear
Another year
The load of human-Kind.

Enter Momus *Laughing.*

MOMUS

Ha! ha! ha! Ha! ha! ha! well hast thou done,
    To lay down thy pack,
    And lighten thy back,
The world was a Fool, e'er since it begun,

And since neither Janus, nor Chronos, nor I,
    Can hinder the crimes,
    Or mend the bad times,
'Tis better to laugh than to cry.

Chorus of all three *'Tis better to laugh than to cry.*

JANUS

Since Momus comes to laugh below,
    Old Time begin the show,
That he may see, in every scene,
What changes in this age have been,

CHRONOS

Then goddess of the silver bow begin.

Horns, or Hunting-Music within.
Enter Diana.

DIANA

With horns and with hounds I waken the day,
And hie to my woodland walks away;
I tuck up my robe, and am buskined soon,
And tie to my forehead a waxing moon.

I course the fleet stag, unkennel the fox,
And chase the wild goats o'er summits of
    rocks,
With shouting and hooting we pierce through
    the sky;
And Echo turns hunter, and doubles the cry.

CHORUS OF ALL

35 With shouting and hooting, we pierce through
    the sky,
And Echo turns hunter, and doubles the cry.

JANUS

Then our age was in its prime,

CHRONOS

Free from rage.

DIANA

—And free from crime.

MOMUS

A very merry, dancing, drinking,
Laughing, quaffing, and unthinking time.

CHORUS OF ALL

Then our age was in its prime,
Free from rage, and free from crime,
A very merry, dancing, drinking,
45 *Laughing, quaffing, and unthinking time.*

Dance of Diana's Attendants.
Enter Mars.

MARS

Inspire the vocal brass, inspire;
The world is past its infant age:
    Arms and Honour,
    Arms and Honour,
    Set the martial mind on fire,
    And kindle manly rage.

40

50

Mars has looked the sky to red;
And Peace, the lazy good, is fled.
Plenty, Peace, and Pleasure fly;
55   The Sprightly Green
In *Woodland*-walks, no more is seen;
The sprightly green, has drunk the Tyrian dye.

CHORUS OF ALL
Plenty, Peace, &c.

MARS
Sound the trumpet, beat the drum,
60   Through all the world around;
Sound a reveille, sound, sound,
The warrior god is come.

CHORUS OF ALL
Sound the Trumpet, &c.

MOMUS
Thy sword within the scabbard keep,
65   And let mankind agree;
Better the world were fast asleep,
      Than kept awake by thee.
The fools are only thinner,
      With all our cost and care;
70   But neither side a winner,
      For things are as they were.

CHORUS OF ALL
The Fools are only, &c.

Enter Venus.

VENUS
Calms appear, when storms are past;
      Love will have his hour at last:
75   Nature is my kindly care;
Mars destroys, and I repair;
Take me, take me, while you may,
Venus comes not ev'ry day.

CHORUS OF ALL
Take her, take her, &c.

CHRONOS
80   The world was then so light,
I scarcely felt the Weight;
Joy rul'd the day, and love the night.
But since the queen of pleasure left the ground,
    I faint, I lag
And feebly drag
85   The pond'rous Orb around.

MOMUS
      All, all, of a piece throughout;
Pointing
to Diana   Thy chase had a beast in view;
to Mars   Thy wars brought nothing about;
to Venus   Thy lovers were all untrue.

JANUS
90   'Tis well an old Age is out

CHRONOS
And time to begin a new.

CHORUS OF ALL
All, all, of apiece throughout
Thy chase had a beast in view
Thy wars brought nothing about
95 *Thy lovers were all untrue.*
'Tis well an old Age is out,
And time to begin a new.

Dance of Huntsmen, Nymphs, Warriors and
Lovers.
—1700

Katherine Philips
1632 – 1664

Katherine Philips's parents were John Fowler, a prosperous London merchant, and Katherine Oxenbridge. According to John Aubrey, "she had read the Bible through before she was full four years old" and "could have brought away a sermon in her memory." At eight years of age, she was sent to a fashionable boarding school in Hackney, where she was instructed by the famous Presbyterian schoolmistress, Mrs. Salmon. Though raised in a Puritan family, she made friendships during her schooldays that drew her into the literary milieu of the London Cavaliers. When in 1646 her widowed mother married Sir Richard Philips of Picton Castle in Pembrokeshire, the family moved to Wales. Two years later, Katherine married Colonel James Philips, a kinsman of Sir Richard's and a prominent Parliamentarian in west Wales. He was thirty-eight years her senior. The couple settled at Cardigan Priory, where she bore a son (1655), who died in infancy, and a daughter (1656).

Early in her marriage, Philips formed a "Society of Friendship" whose members, despite her husband's political affiliations, were Royalists. Those adopted into the Society received pseudonyms, Katherine's being "Orinda." When her husband was appointed as a Commissioner under the Act for the Propagation of the Gospel in Wales, she continued to participate in Cavalier literary circles. In 1662, Philips visited Dublin where she was befriended by Roger Boyle, Earl of Orrery, who urged her to translate Corneille's *La Mort de Pompée*. Philips's *Pompey*, first performed on February 10, 1663 in Dublin, was critically acclaimed. When an unauthorized edition of her poems was published in 1664, she denied responsibility for the volume, and the printer quickly withdrew it from sale. The same year, Philips traveled to London where she contracted smallpox and died, leaving unfinished a translation of Corneille's *Horace*.

In 1667, her poems and translations were published posthumously by her friend Sir Charles Cotterel ("Poliarchus"), Master of Ceremonies at the Court of Charles II. In 1705, Cotterel published his correspondence with Philips under the title *Letters from Orinda to Poliarchus*. The literary reputation of Philips, the "Matchless Orinda," flourished after her death. She became a symbol of female literary achievement, figuring in the poetry and prose of her contemporaries as the model of female authorship.

❧❧❧

Upon the Double Murder of K. Charles I in Answer to a Libelous Copy of Rimes by Vavasour Powell [1]

I think not on the state, nor am concerned
Which way soever the great helm is turned:
But as that son whose father's danger nigh

5   Did force his native dumbness, and untie
The fettered organs; so this is a cause
That will excuse the breach of nature's laws.
Silence were now a sin, nay passion now
Wise men themselves for merit would allow.
What noble eye could see (and careless pass)
10   The dying lion kicked by every ass? [2]
Has Charles so *broke God's laws*, he must not have
A quiet crown, nor yet a quiet grave?
Tombs have been sanctuaries; thieves lie there

[1] Powell, a Fifth Monarchist, held the post of Approver of Ministers under the Propagation Act. Philips's biographer notes that while he was staying at Cardigan Priory in the early 1650s, Powell wrote an anti-monarchical poem about the dead King (Patrick Thomas, *Katherine Philips ['Orinda']*. Cardiff: U of Wales P, 1988, 23).

[2] *dying lion* The Scottish lion was the dominant image on the Stuart coat of arms; hence, the Stuart monarch was often figured as a lion.

Secure from all their penalty and fear.
15 Great Charles his double misery was this,
Unfaithful friends, ignoble enemies.
Had any heathen been this prince's foe,
He would have wept to see him injured so.
His title was his crime, they'd reason good
20 To quarrel at the right they had withstood.
He broke God's laws, and therefore he must die;
And what shall then become of thee and I?
Slander must follow treason; but yet stay,
Take not our reason with our king away.
25 Though you have seized upon all our defence,
Yet do not sequester our common sense. [1]
Christ will be King, but I ne'er understood
His subjects built his kingdom up with blood,
Except their own; or that he would dispense
30 With his commands, though for his own defence.
Oh! to what height of horror are they come
Who dare pull down a crown, tear up a tomb?
—1667

On the Numerous Access of the English to wait upon the King in Flanders [2]

Hasten, great prince, unto thy British Isles,
Or all thy subjects will become exiles.
To thee they flock, thy presence is their home,
As Pompey's camp, where'er it moved, was Rome. [3]
5 They that asserted thy just cause go hence
To testify their joy and reverence;
And those that did not, now, by wonder taught,
Go to confess and expiate their fault. [4]

So that if thou dost stay, thy gasping land
10 Itself will empty on the Belgic sand: [5]
Where the affrighted Dutchman does profess
He thinks it an invasion, not address.
As we unmonarched were for want of thee,
So till thou come we shall unpeopled be.
15 None but the close fanatic will remain, [6]
Who by our loyalty his ends will gain:
And he th'exhausted land will quickly find
As desolate a place as he designed.
For England (though grown old with woes) will see
20 Her long denied and sovereign remedy.
So when old Jacob could but credit give
That his prodigious Joseph still did live,
(Joseph that was preserved to restore
Their lives that would have taken his before)
25 *It is enough,* (said he) *to Egypt I*
Will go, and see him once before I die. [7]
—1667

On the 3 of September, 1651 [8]

As when the glorious magazine of light
Approaches to his canopy of night, [9]
He with new splendour clothes his dying rays,
And double brightness to his beams conveys;
5 And (as to brave and check his ending fate)
Puts on his highest looks in's lowest state, [10]
Dressed in such terror as to make us all

---

[1] *sequester* confiscate, take forcible possession of (*OED* sequester *v* 2).

[2] *King* Charles II. En route to England, Charles left Brussels for Holland on March 30, 1660.

[3] *As Pompey's camp...was Rome* Roman general and consul Gnaeus Pompeius (106–48 B.C.E.) ruled officially in Spain and unofficially in Gaul, Africa, the East and parts of Italy until his murder in Egypt.

[4] *expiate* extinguish the guilt of (*OED* expiate *v* 3).

[5] *Belgic* of or pertaining to the Netherlands (*OED* belgic *a* Ab).

[6] *close* secret (*OED* close A.4a).

[7] *So when old...I die* Jacob's favorite son Joseph was sold into slavery by his jealous brothers who told their father he had been killed. Joseph rose to prominence in Egypt and saved his family from famine. When Jacob was told Joseph lived, he said, "It is enough; Joseph my son is yet alive: I will go and see him before I die" (Genesis 45:28).

[8] Charles II was defeated at the battle of Worcester on September 3rd.

[9] *magazine* repository (*OED* magazine *sb* 1a).

[10] *brave and check* defy and arrest.

Be anti-Persians, and adore his fall; [1]
Then quits the world depriving it of day,
10 While every herb and plant does droop away:
So when our gasping English royalty
Perceived her period was now drawing nigh,
She summons her whole strength to give one
    blow,
To raise herself, or pull down others too.
15 Big with revenge and hope she now spake more
Of terror than in many months before;
And musters her attendants, or to save
Her from, or else attend her to, the grave: [2]
Yet but enjoyed the miserable fate
20 Of setting majesty, to die in state.
Unhappy kings, who cannot keep a throne,
Nor be so fortunate to fall alone!
Their weight sinks others: Pompey could not fly,
But half the world must bear him company;
25 And captived Sampson could not life conclude,
Unless attended with a multitude. [3]
Who'd trust to greatness now, whose food is air,
Whose ruin sudden, and whose end despair?
Who would presume upon his glorious birth,
30 Or quarrel for a spacious share of earth,
That sees such diadems become so cheap,
And heroes tumble in a common heap?
Oh give me virtue then, which sums up all,
And firmly stands when crowns and scepters fall.
—1667

Friendship's Mystery, To My Dearest Lucasia [4]

1

Come, my Lucasia, since we see
  That miracles men's faith do move, [5]
By wonder and by prodigy
    To the dull angry world let's prove
5   There's a religion in our love.

2

For though we were designed t'agree,
    That fate no liberty destroys,
But our election is as free
    As angels, who with greedy choice
10   Are yet determined to their joys.[6]

3

Our hearts are doubled by the loss,
    Here mixture is addition grown;
We both diffuse, and both engross: [7]
    And we whose minds are so much one,
15   Never, yet ever are alone.

4

We court our own captivity
    Than thrones more great and innocent:
'Twere banishment to be set free,
    Since we wear fetters whose intent
20   Not bondage is, but ornament.

---

[1] *anti-Persians* in reference to the Indo-Iranian cult of Mithras, understood as a sun-god.

[2] *or...or* either...or.

[3] *And captived....a multitude* Blinded and imprisoned after his defeat at the hands of the Philistine agent Delilah, Samson pulled down the pillars which held up the house filled with Philistines, killing his enemies and himself (Judges 16).

---

[4] *Friendship's Mystery* friendship as a religious rite or a sacrament (*OED* mystery [1] 3).

[5] *Lucasia* the name assigned to Anne Owen on her formal acceptance into the "Society of Friendship" December 29, 1651.

[6] *For though we...their joys* Though the speaker and Lucasia are designed by nature to be of one mind (*OED* agree *v* IV.9), as the angels are determined to worship God, yet their ability to choose (*OED* election 2a) is not lessened thereby, for they elect the fate for which they are predestined.

[7] *diffuse* extend, spread out (*OED* diffuse *v.* 3); *engross* collect together, condense (*OED* engross *v* II.4a,III.8).

5

Divided joys are tedious found,
    And griefs united easier grow:
We are ourselves but by rebound,
    And all our titles shuffled so,
25   Both princes, and both subjects too.

6

Our hearts are mutual victims laid,
    While they (such power in friendship lies)
Are altars, priests, and off'rings made:
    And each heart which thus kindly dies, [1]
30   Grows deathless by the sacrifice.
—1667

A Retired Friendship, To Ardelia [2]

1

Come, my Ardelia, to this bower,
    Where kindly mingling souls awhile
Let's innocently spend an hour,
    And at all serious follies smile.

2

5   Here is no quarreling for crowns,
        Nor fear of changes in our fate;
No trembling at the great one's frowns,
        Nor any slavery of state.

3

Here's no disguise nor treachery,
10   Nor any deep concealed design;
From blood and plots this place is free,
        And calm as are those looks of thine.

4

Here let us sit and bless our stars,
    Who did such happy quiet give,

15   As that removed from noise of wars
        In one another's hearts we live.

5

Why should we entertain a fear
    Love cares not how the world is turned:
If crowds of dangers should appear,
20   Yet friendship can be unconcerned.

6

We wear about us such a charm,
    No horror can be our offence;
For mischief's self can do no harm
    To friendship or to innocence.

7

25   Let's mark how soon Apollo's beams
        Command the flocks to quit their meat, [3]
And not entreat the neighbouring streams
        To quench their thirst, but cool their heat.

8

In such a scorching age as this
30   Who would not ever seek a shade,
Deserve their happiness to miss,
    As having their own peace betrayed.

9

But we (of one another's mind
    Assured) the boisterous world disdain;
35   With quiet souls and unconfined
        Enjoy what princes wish in vain.
—1667

Wiston Vault

And why this vault and tomb? Alike we must
    Put off distinction, and put on our dust.
Nor can the stateliest fabric help to save
From the corruptions of a common grave;

---

[1] *kindly*   readily or congenially (*OED* kindly *adv.* I.1c).

[2] *Ardelia*   Ardelia's identity is not known.

[3] *Apollo's beams*   sunbeams; Apollo is the god of the sun.

5 Nor for the resurrection more prepare
Than if the dust were scattered into air.
What then? Th' ambition's just, say some, that we
May thus perpetuate our memory.
Ah false vain task of art! Ah poor weak man!
10 Whose monument does more than's merit can: [1]
Who by his friends' best care and love's abused,
And in his very epitaph accused:
For did they not suspect his name would fall,
There would not need an epitaph at all.
15 But after death too I would be alive,
And shall, if my Lucasia do, survive.
I quit these pomps of death, and am content,
Having her heart to be my monument:
Thou ne'er stone to me, 'twill stone for me prove,
20 By the peculiar miracles of love.
There I'll inscription have which no tomb gives,
Not, *Here Orinda lies*, but, *Here she lives*.
—1667

To My Excellent Lucasia,
On Our Friendship

I did not live until this time
Crowned my felicity,
When I could say without a crime,
I am not thine, but thee. [2]

5 This carcass breathed, and walked, and slept,
So that the world believed
There was a soul the motions kept; [3]
But they were all deceived.

For as a watch by art is wound
10 To motion, such was mine:

But never had Orinda found
A soul till she found thine; [4]

Which now inspires, cures and supplies, [5]
And guides my darkened breast:
15 For thou art all that I can prize,
My joy, my life, my rest.

No bridegroom's nor crown-conqueror's mirth
To mine compared can be:
They have but pieces of this earth,
20 I've all the world in thee.

Then let our flames still light and shine,
And no false fear control,
As innocent as our design,
Immortal as our soul.
—1667

A Country Life [6]

How sacred and how innocent
A country-life appears,
How free from tumult, discontent,
From flattery or fears!
5 This was the first and happiest life,
When man enjoyed himself;
Till pride exchanged peace for strife,
And happiness for pelf. [7]
'Twas here the poets were inspired,
10 Here taught the multitude;

---

[1] *than's* than his.

[2] *I did not live…but thee* Until this time when my happiness was perfected, I could not truly say "I am not yours, but you."

[3] *carcass* the body as a lifeless shell from which the soul has fled (*OED* carcass *sb* 4).

[4] *Orinda* the pseudonym of Katherine Philips.

[5] *inspires* breathes life into (*OED* inspire *v* I.2b).

[6] *A Country Life* The classical source for the retirement poem is Horace's Epode II, *Beatus ille* ("The Happy Man"), a lyric which contrasts the peace and contentment of country living with the vexations of urban life. Compare Ben Jonson's translation of this Epode, "The Praises of a Country Life" and Lucy Hutchinson's "All Sorts of Men."

[7] *pelf* wealth (*OED* pelf *sb* 3).

The brave they here with honour fired, [1]
    And civilized the rude.
That golden age did entertain
    No passion but of love;
15 The thoughts of ruling and of gain
    Did ne'er their fancies move.
None then did envy neighbour's wealth,
    Nor plot to wrong his bed:
Happy in friendship and in health,
20   On roots, not beasts, they fed.
They knew no law nor physic then,
    Nature was all their wit.
And if there yet remain to men
    Content, sure this is it.
25 What blessings doth this world afford
    To tempt or bribe desire?
Her courtship is all fire and sword,
    Who would not then retire?
Then welcome dearest solitude,
30   My great felicity;
Though some are pleased to call thee rude,
    Thou art not so, but we.
Them that do covet only rest,
    A cottage will suffice:
35 It is not brave to be possessed
    Of earth, but to despise. [2]
Opinion is the rate of things,
    From hence our peace doth flow;
I have a better fate than kings,
40   Because I think it so.
When all the stormy world doth roar
    How unconcerned am I?
I cannot fear to tumble lower
    Who never could be high.
45 Secure in these unenvied walls
    I think not on the state,
And pity no man's case that falls
    From his ambition's height.

Silence and innocence are safe;
50   A heart that's nobly true
At all these little arts can laugh [3]
    That do the world subdue.
While others revel it in State,
    Here I'll contented sit,
55 And think I have as good a fate
    As wealth and pomp admit.
Let some in courtship take delight,
    And to th'Exchange resort; [4]
Then revel out a winter's night,
60   Not making love, but sport.
These never know a noble flame,
    'Tis lust, scorn, or design:
While vanity plays all their game,
    Let peace and honour mine.
65 When the inviting spring appears,
    To Hyde Park let them go, [5]
And hasting thence be full of fears
    To lose Spring-Garden show. [6]
Let others (nobler) seek to gain
70   In knowledge happy fate,
And others busy them in vain
    To study ways of State.
But I, resolved from within,
    Confirmed from without,
75 In privacy intend to spin
    My future minutes out.
And from this hermitage of mine

---

[1] *fired* inspired with passion (*OED* fire *v*[1] 3a).

[2] *brave* worthy (*OED* brave *a* A.3a).

---

[3] *arts* stratagems (*OED* art *sb* III.14).

[4] *Exchange* The New Exchange, a bazaar on the south side of the Strand, was a popular market best known for its haberdashery and millinery shops.

[5] *Hyde Park* People "toured" Hyde Park in hopes of catching a glimpse of prominent members of the court.

[6] *Spring-Garden* The Spring Garden was then a part of St. James's Park. In her *Memoirs*, Lady Anne Halkett writes that in her youth (before 1644) she did "walk in the Spring Garden sometimes (before it grew something scandalous by the abuse of some)" (Oxford, 1979, p.11).

I banish all wild toys, [1]
And nothing that is not divine
80   Shall dare to tempt my joys.
There are below but two things good,
        Friendship and honesty,
And only those of all I would
        Ask for felicity.
85 In this retired and humble seat
        Free from both war and strife,
I am not forced to make retreat
        But choose to spend my life.
—1667

Orinda to Lucasia parting
October 1661 at London

Adieu dear object of my love's excess,
        And with thee all my hopes of happiness,
With the same fervent and unchangèd heart
Which did its whole self once to thee impart,
5   (And which though fortune has so sorely bruised,
Would suffer more, to be from this excused)
I to resign thy dear converse submit,
Since I can neither keep, nor merit it.
Thou hast too long to me confinèd been,
10 Who ruin am without, passion within.
My mind is sunk below thy tenderness,
And my condition does deserve it less;
I'm so entangled and so lost a thing
By all the shocks my daily sorrow bring,
15 That would'st thou for thy old Orinda call
Thou hardly could'st unravel her at all.
And should I thy clear fortunes interline
With the incessant miseries of mine?
No, no, I never loved at such a rate
20 To tie thee to the rigours of my fate,
As from my obligations thou art free,
Sure thou shalt be so from my injury,
Though every other worthiness I miss,

Yet I'll at least be generous in this.
25 I'd rather perish without sigh or groan,
Than thou should'st be condemned to give me one;
Nay in my soul I rather could allow
Friendship should be a sufferer, than thou;
Go then, since my sad heart has set thee free,
30 Let all the loads and chains remain on me.
Though I be left the prey of sea and wind,
Thou being happy wilt in that be kind;
Nor shall I my undoing much deplore,
Since thou art safe, whom I must value more.
35 Oh! mayst thou ever be so, and as free
From all ills else, as from my company,
And may the torments thou hast had from it
Be all that heaven will to thy life permit.
And that they may thy virtue service do,
40 Mayst thou be able to forgive them too:
But though I must this sharp submission learn,
I cannot yet unwish thy dear concern.
Not one new comfort I expect to see,
I quit my joy, hope, life, and all but thee;
45 Nor seek I thence ought that may discompose
That mind where so serene a goodness grows.
I ask no inconvenient kindness now,
To move thy passion, or to cloud thy brow;
And thou wilt satisfy my boldest plea
50 By some few soft remembrances of me,
Which may present thee with this candid thought,
I meant not all the troubles that I brought.
Own not what passion rules, and fate does crush,
But wish thou couldst have done 't without a blush,
55 And that I had been, ere it was too late,
Either more worthy, or more fortunate.
Ah who can love the thing they cannot prize?
But thou mayst pity though thou dost despise.
Yet I should think that pity bought too dear,
60 If it should cost those precious eyes a tear.
        Oh may no minute's trouble thee possess,
But to endear the next hour's happiness;
And mayst thou when thou art from me removed,
Be better pleased, but never worse beloved:

---

[1] *toys* amusements (*OED* toy *sb* I.2).

65 Oh pardon me for pouring out my woes
In rhyme now, that I dare not do 't in prose.
For I must love whatever is called dear,
And thy assistance all that loss to bear,
And have more cause than ere I had before,
70 To fear that I shall never see thee more.
—1667

Orinda Upon Little Hector Philips [1]

1

Twice forty months of wedlock I did stay, [2]
Then had my vows crowned with a lovely
boy,
And yet in forty days he dropped away, [3]
O swift vicissitude of human joy.

2

5 I did but see him and he disappeared,
I did but pluck the rosebud and it fell,
A sorrow unforeseen and scarcely feared,
For ill can mortals their afflictions spell. [4]

3

And now (sweet babe) what can my trembling
heart
10 Suggest to right my doleful fate or thee,
Tears are my muse and sorrow all my art,
So piercing groans must be thy elegy.

4

Thus whilst no eye is witness of my moan,
I grieve thy loss (Ah boy too dear to live)
15 And let the unconcerned world alone,
Who neither will, nor can refreshment give.

---

1 *Hector Philips* Hector Philips was born on April 23, 1655 and died
May 2, 1655.

2 *Twice forty months in wedlock* Philips was married in August, 1648;
stay wait (*OED* stay v^1 I.9).

3 *in forty days* within forty days.

4 *spell* discover (*OED* spell v^2 I.2a).

5

An off'ring too for thy sad tomb I have,
Too just a tribute to thy early hearse,
Receive these gasping numbers to thy grave, [5]
20 The last of thy unhappy mother's verse. [6]
—1667

Orinda to Lucasia

Observe the weary birds ere night be done,
How they would fain call up the tardy sun,
With feathers hung with dew,
And trembling voices too.
5 They court their glorious planet to appear,
That they may find recruits of spirits there.
The drooping flowers hang their heads,
And languish down into their beds: [7]
While brooks more bold and fierce than they,
10 Wanting those beams, from whence
All things must drink influence,
Openly murmur and demand the day. [8]

2

Thou my Lucasia art far more to me,
Than he to all the underworld can be; [9]
From thee I've heat and light,
Thy absence makes my night.
But ah! my friend, it now grows very long,
The sadness weighty, and the darkness strong:
My tears (its dew) dwell on my cheeks,
20 And still my heart thy dawning seeks,
And to thee mournfully it cries,

---

5 *numbers* metrical periods or feet; hence, lines, verses (*OED* number
sb IV 18b).

6 *The last...mother's verse* Philips in fact continued to write verse
until her death.

7 *recruits of spirits* a fresh supply of the vital or animating principle
(*OED* recruit *sb* I.3c; spirit *sb* I.1).

8 *influence* the ethereal fluid which streams from the stars to act
upon all things sublunary (*OED* influence *sb* 2a).

9 *he* the sun.

That if too long I wait,
    Ev'n thou mayst come too late,
And not restore my life, but close my eyes.
—1667

A Married State [1]

A married state affords but little ease:
    The best of husbands are so hard to please.
This in wives' careful faces you may spell, [2]
Though they dissemble their misfortunes well.
5   A virgin state is crowned with much content,
It's always happy as it's innocent.

No blustering husbands to create your fears,
No pangs of childbirth to extort your tears,
No children's cries for to offend your ears,
10 Few worldly crosses to distract your prayers.
Thus are you freed from all the cares that do
Attend on matrimony and a husband too.
Therefore, madam, be advised by me:
Turn, turn apostate to love's levity. [3]
15 Suppress wild nature if she dare rebel,
There's no such thing as leading apes in hell. [4]
—(WRITTEN BEFORE 1648)

---

[1] Not included in any early-modern printed edition of Philips's works, this poem is one of two handwritten on a single sheet (Orielton MSS Box 24, National Library of Wales). It was written before 1648. Compare Jane Barker's "A Virgin Life."

[2] *spell* decipher (*OED* spell v^2 2b).

[3] *apostate* one who forsakes her moral allegiance (*OED* apostate *sb* A1).

[4] *leading apes in hell* the fancied consequence of dying an old maid.

Philo-Philippa
fl. 1663

Katherine Philips's *Pompey*, an English translation of Corneille's *La Mort de Pompée*, was first performed at the Theatre Royal, Smock Alley, Dublin, on February 10, 1663. The play was well received. In a letter to Sir Charles Cotterell ("Poliarchus"), Philips describes the response: "I have had many letters and copies of verses sent me, some from acquaintance[s], and some from strangers, to compliment me upon *Pompey*, which, were I capable of vanity, would even surfeit me with it; for they are so full of flattery, that I have not the confidence to send

them to you. One of them, who pretends to be a woman, writes very well, but I cannot imagine who the author is, nor by any inquiry I can make, have hitherto been able to discover" (April 8, 1663). The poem written by this unknown Irish woman, to whom Cotterell assigned the name "Philo-Philippa," was included among the commendatory poems which prefaced the 1667 edition of Philips's *Poems*. "To the Excellent Orinda" explicitly challenges the dominant conceptions of gender and authorship in seventeenth-century England.

※※※

To the Excellent Orinda

Let the male poets their male Phoebus
   choose, [1]
Thee I invoke, Orinda, for my Muse;
He could but force a branch, Daphne her tree
Most freely offers to her sex and thee,
5 And says to verse, so unconstrained as yours,
Her laurel freely comes, your fame secures:
And men no longer shall with ravished bays
Crown their forced poems by as forced a praise. [2]
   Thou glory of our sex, envy of men,
10 Who are both pleased and vexed with thy bright
    pen:
Its lustre doth entice their eyes to gaze,
But men's sore eyes cannot endure its rays;
It dazzles and surprises so with light,
To find a noon where they expected night:

15 A woman translate *Pompey*! which the famed
Corneille with such art and labour framed! [3]
To whose close version the wits club their sense,
And a new lay poetic SMEC springs thence! [4]
Yes, that bold work a woman dares translate,
20 Not to provoke, nor yet to fear men's hate.
Nature doth find that she hath erred too long,
And now resolves to recompense that wrong:
Phoebus to Cynthia must his beams resign,
The rule of day and wit's now feminine. [5]
25   That sex, which heretofore was not allowed
To understand more than a beast, or crowd;
Of which problems were made, whether or no

---

[1] *Phoebus* Apollo, the sun god, and patron of music and poetry.

[2] *He could ...a praise* Sworn to virginity, Daphne was transformed into a laurel tree to escape the sexual advances of Apollo, who created a crown from one of the tree's branches. Thereafter, the laurel crown was bestowed on those distinguished for excellence in poetry.

---

[3] *Pompey* Corneille's *La Mort de Pompée* (Paris, 1644).

[4] *To whose..their sense* In 1663, Sir William Davenant produced an English translation of Corneille's *Pompée* collaboratively written by the "Wits" Edmund Waller, Sidney Godolphin, Charles Sackville, Sir Charles Sedley and Sir Edward Filmer; *club* combine (*OED* club *v* 6); *SMEC* In 1641, Stephen Marshal, Edmund Calamy, Thomas Young, Matthew Newcomen and William Spurstow co-authored an anti-episcopal pamphlet and published it under their initials: "Smectymnuus."

[5] *Cynthia* the goddess of the moon.

Women had souls; but to be damned, if so; [1]
Whose highest contemplation could not pass,
30   In men's esteem, no higher than the glass;
And all the painful labours of their brain,
Was only how to dress and entertain:
Or, if they ventured to speak sense, the wise
Made that, and speaking ox, like prodigies. [2]
35   From these thy more than masculine pen hath
         reared
Our sex; first to be praised, next to be feared.
And by the same pen forced, men now confess,
To keep their greatness, was to make us less.
    Men know of how refined and rich a mould
40   Our sex is framed, what sun is in our gold: [3]
They know in lead no diamonds are set,
And jewels only fill the cabinet. [4]
Our spirits purer far than theirs, they see; [5]
By which even men from men distinguished be:
45   By which the soul is judged, and does appear
Fit or unfit for action, as they are.
    When in an organ various sounds do stroke,
Or grate the ear, as birds sing, or toads croak;
The breath, that voices every pipe, 's the same,
50   But the bad metal doth the sound defame.
So, if our souls by sweeter organs speak,
And theirs with harsh false notes the air do break;
The soul's the same, alike in both doth dwell,

'Tis from her instruments that we excel. [6]
55   Ask me not then, why jealous men debar
Our sex from books in peace, from arms in war;
It is because our parts will soon demand
Tribunals for our persons, and command. [7]
    Shall it be our reproach, that we are weak,
60   And cannot fight, nor as the school-men speak?
Even men themselves are neither strong nor wise,
If limbs and parts they do not exercise.
    Trained up to arms, we Amazons have been,
And Spartan virgins strong as Spartan men:
65   Breed women but as men, and they are these;
Whilst Sybarit men are women by their ease. [8]
Why should not brave Semiramis break a lance,
And why should not soft Ninias curl and dance? [9]
Ovid in vain bodies with change did vex,
70   Changing her form of life, Iphis changed sex, [10]
Nature to females freely doth impart
That, which the males usurp, a stout, bold heart.
Thus hunters female beasts fear to assail;
And female hawks more metalled than the male: [11]
75   Men ought not then courage and wit engross,

---

[1] *That sex…damned, if so* Compare Elizabeth Johnson's criticism of those who render women "mere slaves, perfect Turkish wives, without properties, or sense or souls" ("Preface" *Poems…Written by Philomela*, 1696).

[2] *like prodigies* similar prodigies, that is, things out of the ordinary course of nature (*OED* prodigy 2).

[3] *what sun…our gold* The ancients believed that threads of gold were woven into the earth by the sun.

[4] *cabinet* a case for the safe custody of jewels; *fig.* the body (*OED* cabinet *sb* I.5,1b).

[5] *spirits* the vital principle (or breath of life) which gives life to the physical organism (*OED* spirit *sb.* I.1); Philo-Philippa relies on St. Paul's division of persons into body, soul and spirit (I Thessalonians 5:23). Compare Speght's "Both man and woman of three parts consist, / Which Paul doth body, soul and spirit call" ("A Dream" ll.127–128).

[6] *So if our souls…we excel* Philo-Philippa echoes Cornelius Agrippa's belief that while "there is no preeminence of nobility (between man and woman, by the essence of the soul) of one above the other," "as for the exercise and operation of the soul, the illustrious sex of women, infinitely almost excels the rough and unpolished generation of men" (*Of the nobility and preeminence of the female sex* [1532], translated by Edward Fleetwood in 1652 and entitled *The Glory of Women*).

[7] *parts* abilities (*OED* part *sb* II.12).

[8] *Sybarit* inhabitants of Sybaris whose epicureanism was proverbial.

[9] *Semiramis* in Greek legend, the daughter of the Syrian goddess Derceto. After the death of her second husband, Ninus, king of Assyria, she ruled Assyria and was renowned in war; *Ninias* the son of Ninus and Semiramis. He is described by Bradstreet as "A Prince wedded to ease and to delight" ("The Four Monarchies" I.149–182).

[10] *Iphis* In Ovid's *Metamorphoses* (Book IX), the impoverished Ligdus tells his pregnant wife Telethusa that if she bears a daughter, the child must die. When she bears a daughter, she disguises the child as a boy and names "him" Iphis. When Ligdus arranges Iphis's marriage, Telethusa prays to Isis for assistance and Iphis is transformed into a young man.

[11] *metalled* spirited (*OED* mettle *sb* 2).

Whilst the fox lives, the lion, or the horse. [1]
Much less ought men both to themselves confine,
Whilst women, such as you, Orinda, shine.
      That noble friendship brought thee to our coast,
80 We thank Lucasia, and thy courage boast. [2]
Death in each wave could not Orinda fright,
Fearless she acts that friendship she did write:
Which manly virtue to their sex confined,
Thou rescuest to confirm our softer mind;
85 For there's required (to do that virtue right)
Courage, as much in friendship as in fight.
The dangers we despise, doth this truth prove,
Though boldly we not fight, we boldly love.
      Engage us unto books, Sappho comes forth,
90 Though not of Hesiod's age, of Hesiod's worth. [3]
If souls no sexes have, as 'tis confessed,
'Tis not the he or she makes poems best:
Nor can men call these verses feminine,
Be the sense vigorous and masculine.
95 'Tis true, Apollo sits as judge of wit,
But the nine female learned troop are it: [4]
Those laws, for which Numa did wise appear,
Wiser Ægeria whispered in his ear. [5]
The Gracchi's mother taught them eloquence; [6]

100 From her breasts courage flowed, from her brain
      sense;
And the grave beards, who heard her speak in
      Rome,
Blushed not to be instructed, but o'ercome.
Your speech, as hers, commands respect from all,
Your very looks, as hers, rhetorical:
105 Something of grandeur in your verse men see,
That they rise up to it as majesty.
The wise and noble Orrery's regard,
Was much observed, when he your poem heard: [7]
All said, a fitter match was never seen,
110 Had Pompey's widow been Arsamne's queen. [8]
      Pompey, who greater than himself's become,
Now in your poem, than before in Rome;
And much more lasting in the poet's pen,
Great princes live, than the proud towers of men.
115 He thanks false Egypt for its treachery,
Since that his ruin is so sung by thee; [9]
And so again would perish, if withal,
Orinda would but celebrate his fall.
Thus pleasingly the bee delights to die,
120 Foreseeing, he in amber tomb shall lie.
If that all Egypt, for to purge its crime,
Were built into one pyramid o'er him,
Pompey would lie less stately in that hearse,
Than he doth now, Orinda, in thy verse:
125 This makes Cornelia for her Pompey vow,
Her hand shall plant his laurel on thy brow:
So equal in their merits were both found,
That the same wreath poets and princes crowned:

---

[1] *engross*   attribute exclusively to themselves (*OED* engross *v* II.4c).

[2] *Lucasia*   Anne Lewis Owen of Pembrokeshire. When in 1662 Anne married her second husband, Colonel Marcus Trevor, Philips accompanied them to their new home in Ireland.

[3] *Sappho*   the Greek poet of Lesbos (b. 612 B.C.E.) whose work was collected into nine books; *Hesiod*   the ancient Greek poet (fl. 700 B.C.E.), often coupled or contrasted with Homer as the other chief representative of early epic.

[4] *nine female learned troop*   the nine Muses, the Greek deities who preside over music, poetry, the arts and sciences.

[5] *Those laws...in his ear*   Numa, according to legend king of Rome after Romulus. Later Romans attrributed many of their religious institutions to him. Legends recount that he received counsel from the nymph Ægeria.

[6] *Gracchi's mother*   Cornelia (second century B.C.E.), the daughter of P. Scipio Africanus and the mother of the social reformers Tiberius and Gaius Gracchus. She was considered the model Roman matron, and her epistles, admired by Cicero, were accounted models of style.

---

[7] *Orrery's regard*   While in Ireland, Philips met Roger Boyle, Earl of Orrery (1621–1679) and Lord Lieutenant of Ireland. One of the pioneers of heroic drama, he encouraged Philips to translate Corneille's *Pompée*.

[8] *Pompey's widow*   Cornelia (fl. 48 B.C.E.), the daughter of Metellus Scipio, is praised in Plutarch's *Lives*: "She was well versed in literature, in playing the lyre, and in geometry, and had been accustomed to listen to philosophical discourses with profit." *Arsamne* unidentified.

[9] *false Egypt...treachery*   After he was defeated by Caesar at Pharsalus, Pompey (106–48 B.C.E.) fled the field of battle, was joined by his wife Cornelia, and sailed to Egypt. He was stabbed to death as he landed.

And what on that great captain's brow was dead,
130 She joys to see re-flourished on thy head.
    In the French rock Cornelia first did shine,
But shined not like herself till she was thine:
Poems, like gems, translated from the place
Where they first grew, receive another grace.
135 Dressed by thy hand, and polished by thy pen,
She glitters now a star, but jewel then:
No flaw remains, no cloud, all now is light
Transparent as the day, bright parts more bright.
Corneille, now made English, so doth thrive,
140 As trees transplanted do much lustier live. [1]
Thus ore digged forth, and by such hands as thine
Refined and stamped, is richer than the mine.
Liquors from vessel into vessel poured,
Must lose some spirits, which are scarce restored: [2]
145 But the French wines, in their own vessel rare,
Poured into ours, by thy hand, spirits are;
So high in taste, and so delicious,
Before his own Corneille thine would choose.
He finds himself enlightened here, where shade
150 Of dark expression his own words had made:
There what he would have said, he sees so writ,
As generously, to just decorum fit.
When in more words than his you please to flow,
Like a spread flood, enriching all below,
155 To the advantage of his well meant sense,
He gains by you another excellence.
To render word for word, at the old rate,
Is only but to construe, not translate:
In your own fancy free, to his sense true,
160 We read Corneille, and Orinda too:
And yet ye both are so the very same,
As when two tapers joined make one bright flame.
And sure the copier's honour is not small,

When artists doubt which is original.
165   But if your fettered Muse thus praised be,
What great things do you write when it is free?
When it is free to choose both sense and words,
Or any subject the vast world affords?
A gliding sea of crystal doth best show
170 How smooth, clear, full, and rich your verse doth
    flow:
Your words are chosen, culled, not by chance writ, [3]
To make the sense, as anagrams do hit.
Your rich becoming words on the sense wait,
As Maids of Honour on a Queen of State.
175 'Tis not white satin makes a verse more white,
Or soft; iron is both, write you on it.
Your poems come forth cast, no file you need,
At one brave heat both shaped and polished.
    But why all these encomiums of you, [4]
180 Who either doubts, or will not take as due?
Renown how little you regard, or need,
Who like the bee, on your own sweets doth feed?
    There are, who like weak fowl with shouts fall
    down,
Dozed with an army's acclamation: [5]
185 Not able to endure applause, they fall,
Giddy with praise, their praise's funeral.
But you, Orinda, are so unconcerned,
As if when you, another we commend.
Thus, as the sun, you in your course shine on,
190 Unmoved with all our admiration:
    Flying above the praise you shun, we see
    Wit is still higher by humility.
—1667

---

[1] *lustier* in the sense of having greater vigour and fertility (*OED* lust *sb* 6).

[2] *spirits* extracts, essences (*OED* spirit *sb* v.22).

[3] *culled* selected (*OED* cull *v*[1] 1).

[4] *encomiums* formal or high-flown expressions of praise (*OED* encomium).

[5] *dozed with* stupefied by (*OED* dozed *ppl.a*).

Thomas Traherne
1637 – 1674

Little is known about Traherne's life. He was the son of a Herefordshire shoemaker, of a Welsh family. He would have been five when the Civil War broke out, and Hereford was in the thick of the conflict, changing hands three times. It is possible that both of Traherne's parents died when he was young; nothing is heard of them, and Traherne and his brother Philip seem to have been adopted by an innkeeper, Philip Traherne senior. Traherne graduated from Brasenose College, one of the more Puritan of the Oxford colleges, in 1656, and was appointed rector of Credenhill near Hereford in 1657. He was ordained as an Anglican priest at the Restoration in 1660, and is known to have been a member of a religious circle centred upon a devout woman, Susanna Hopton. He kept in contact with Oxford, and his work *Roman Forgeries*, published in 1673, may represent work towards a Bachelor of Divinity degree. He became B.D. in 1669. While he retained his rectorship at Credenhill until his death, in 1669 he moved to London, as private chaplain to Sir Orlando Bridgeman, Lord Keeper of the Privy Seal. He was buried at Teddington in Middlesex.

The works by which Traherne is now best known, his poems and *Centuries of Meditation*, were not published in his lifetime. The manuscripts were found on two bookstalls, in different streets, in 1897, by a scholar who recognized that they were the work of the same writer. Many of the poems exist in two versions, one "improved" by Traherne's brother Philip. At first they were thought to be by Vaughan, because of some thematic similarities; but in fact Vaughan and Traherne are stylistically far apart, and Vaughan is by far the better poet, which is not to say that Traherne's work is without interest. The prose work, *Centuries of Meditation*, is generally considered to be superior to the verse.

There has been a good deal of excitement among scholars and devotees of Traherne in recent years, because manuscripts keep on turning up. In 1967, for example, his *Commentaries of Heaven* were discovered on a burning trash-heap by a man searching for car parts. He emigrated to Canada, and fifteen years after the discovery the manuscript was identified as Traherne's. Another manuscript of devotional prose was discovered in the late 1990s.

☙☙☙

Wonder

I

How like an Angel came I down!
    How bright are all things here!
When first among his Works I did appear
    O how their GLORY me did crown?
5 The World resembled his *Eternity*,
    In which my soul did walk;
And ev'ry thing that I did see,
    Did with me talk.

2

  The skies in their magnificence,
10   The lively, lovely air;
Oh how divine, how soft, how sweet, how fair!
    The stars did entertain my sense,
And all the Works of GOD so bright and pure,
    So rich and great did seem,
15   As if they ever must endure,
    In my esteem.[1]

---

[1] *In my esteem* in my valuation of them, that is, that they were "divine" (lines 11 and 24).

3

A native health and innocence
    Within my bones did grow,[1]
And while my GOD did all his glories show,
20   I felt a vigour in my sense
That was all SPIRIT. I within did flow
    With seas of life, like wine;
I nothing in the World did know,
    But 'twas divine.

4

25   Harsh ragged objects were concealed,
        Oppressions tears and cries,
Sins, griefs, complaints, dissensions, weeping
        eyes,
    Were hid: and only things revealed,
Which heav'nly spirits, and the Angels prize,
30   The state of innocence
And bliss, not trades and poverties,
        Did fell my sense.

5

The streets were paved with golden stones,
    The boys and girls were mine,
35 Oh how did all their lovely faces shine!
    The sons of men were Holy Ones.
Joy, Beauty, Welfare did appear to me,
        And ev'ry thing which here I found,
While like an Angel I did see,
40   Adorned the ground.

6

Rich diamond and pearl and gold
    In ev'ry place was seen;
Rare splendors, yellow, blue, red, white and
        green,
    Mine eyes did ev'rywhere behold,

45 Great wonders clothed with glory did appear,
    Amazement was my bliss.
That and my wealth was ev'rywhere:
    No joy to this! [2]

7

Cursed and devised proprieties,[3]
50   With Envy, Avarice
And Fraud, those fiends that spoil even Paradise,[4]
    Fled from the splendor of mine eyes.
And so did hedges, ditches, limits, bounds,
    I dreamed not ought of those,
55   But wandered over all men's grounds,
        And found repose.

8

Proprieties themselves were mine,
    And hedges ornaments;
Walls, boxes, coffers, and their rich contents
60   Did not divide my joys, but shine.
Clothes, ribbons, jewels, laces, I esteemed
    My joys by others worn;
For me they all to wear them seemed
    When I was born.[5]

—1903

---

[1] *A native health and innocence*   in opposition to the Calvinist notion of "original sin," which might be summed up by Psalm 51:5, "Behold, I was shapen in wickedness: and in sin hath my mother conceived me." The theme of the innocence of childhood is one of those common to Vaughan and Traherne.

[2] *to this*   compared to this; a very common idiom of the period.

[3] *proprieties*   properties, here and in line 57. In stanzas seven and eight Traherne is making the point that the child does not understand the commercial notion of "ownership," but enjoys everything just as if it were his own. A twentieth-century author has written that a painting is "really" owned, not by the wealthy person who has been able to buy it, but by those best able to appreciate it.

[4] *Envy, Avarice / And Fraud, those fiends that spoil even Paradise* Compare the representation of Satan and the rebel angels in *Paradise Lost*. Fraud involves misrepresentation, and Satan and his followers are frequently represented as liars, for example in Revelation 12:9, "Satan, which deceiveth the whole world," and *Paradise Lost* 1:367 ("falsities and lies") and 5:243 ("deceit and lies").

[5] *For me*   for my sake.

Innocence

1

But that which most I wonder at, which most
I did esteem my bliss, which most I boast,
And ever shall enjoy, is that within
    I felt no stain, nor spot of sin.

5   No darkness then did overshade,
    But all within was pure and bright,
    No guilt did crush, nor fear invade
    But all my soul was full of light.

    A joyful sense and purity
10   Is all I can remember.
    The very night to me was bright,
    'Twas summer in December.

2

A serious meditation did employ
My soul within, which taken up with joy
15 Did seem no outward thing to note, but fly
    All objects that do feed the eye.

    While it those very objects did
    Admire, and prize, and praise, and love,
    Which in their glory most are hid,
20   Which presence only doth remove.

    Their constant daily presence I
        Rejoicing at, did see;
    And that which takes them from the eye
    Of others, offered them to me.

3

25 No inward inclination did I feel
    To avarice or pride: my soul did kneel
    In admiration all the day. No lust, nor strife,
        Polluted then my infant life.

30 No fraud nor anger in me moved
    No malice jealousy or spite;
    All that I saw I truly loved.
    Contentment only and delight

    Were in my soul. O Heav'n! what bliss
        Did I enjoy and feel!
35 What powerful delight did this
    Inspire! for this I daily kneel.

4

Whether it be that Nature is so pure,
And Custom only vicious; or that sure
God did by miracle the guilt remove,
40   And make my soul to feel his love,

    So early: Or that 'twas one day,
    Where in this happiness I found;
    Whose strength and brightness so do ray,
    That still it seemeth to surround.

45 What ere it is, it is a light
        So endless unto me
    That I a world of true delight
    Did then and to this day do see.

5

The prospect was the gate of Heav'n, that day
50 The ancient light of Eden did convey
Into my soul: I was an Adam there,
    A little Adam in a sphere

    Of joys! O there my ravished sense
    Was entertained in Paradise,
55 And had a sight of Innocence.
    All was beyond all bound and price.

    An antepast of Heaven sure![1]
        I on the earth did reign.

---

[1] *An antepast*   a foretaste.

Within, without me, all was pure,
60   I must become a child again.[1]
—1903

The Preparative [2]

1

My body being dead, my limbs unknown;[3]
   Before I skilled to prize
      Those living stars mine eyes,[4]
Before my tongue or cheeks were to me shown,
5   Before I knew my hands were mine,
Or that my sinews did my members join,
      When neither nostril, foot, nor ear,
As yet was seen, or felt, or did appear;
      I was within
10   A house I knew not, newly clothed with skin.

2

Then was my soul my only all to me,
      A living endless eye,
      Far wider than the sky
Whose power, whose act, whose essence was to see.
15   I was an inward *sphere of light*,
Or an interminable orb of *sight*,

An endless and a living day,
A vital Sun that round about did *ray*
      All life and sense,
20   A naked simple pure *Intelligence*.

3

I then no thirst nor hunger did conceive,
      No dull necessity,
      No want was known to me;
Without disturbance then I did receive
25   The fair *ideas* of all things,[5]
And had the honey even without the stings,
      A meditating inward eye
Gazing at quiet did within me lie,
      And ev'ry thing
30   Delighted me that was their heav'nly king.[6]

4

For *sight* inherits beauty, *hearing* sounds,
      The *nostril* sweet perfumes,
      All *tastes* have hidden rooms
Within the *tongue*; and *feeling feeling* wounds
35   With pleasure and delight; but I
Forgot the rest, and was all sight, or eye.
      Unbodied and devoid of care,
Just as in Heav'n the holy Angels are,
      For simple sense
40   Is Lord of all created excellence.

---

[1] *I must become a child again*   Compare Matthew 18:3, "Except ye be converted, and become as little children, ye shall not enter into the kingdom of heaven." See also John 3:1–8.

[2]   The original title of this poem was "The Vision," which was then erased in favour of the present title. There is a subsequent poem called "The Vision," and it has been suggested that Traherne might have intended the two to be a "double poem." The word "preparative" occurs in the first line of "The Vision," and the two poems are linked thematically, dealing with sight as the sense through which we receive divine intimations. Retirement (line 69 of this poem) or "flight" (the first line of "The Vision") are the preparatives for the proper religious understanding of what the eye perceives. Implicit in all this is the concept of the natural or "phenomenal" world as "God's second book."

[3] *dead*   lacking sensation. Traherne is writing, accurately or not, about the earliest state of infancy.

[4] *Before I skilled to prize*   before I understood how to value (*OED* skill *v*[1] 4).

[5] *ideas*   in the Platonic sense, the "idea" being the eternally existing pattern or archetype of any class of things, of which the individual things in that class are imperfect copies, and from which they derive their existence (*OED* idea *sb* 1). Traherne means that he was able to apprehend perfection. Traherne, like many English intellectuals of the time, was much taken with Platonic and neo-Platonic conceptions.

[6] *And ev'ry thing / Delighted me that was their heav'nly king*   This conception of the individual as godlike seems to have been too strong for Traherne's brother Philip; he altered these lines to "And all things fair / Delighted me that was to be their heir." The next stanza might be taken as Traherne's justification of the statement embodied in these lines.

5

Being thus prepared for all felicity,
    Not prepossessed with dross,
    Nor stiffly glued to gross
And dull materials that might ruin me,
45   Not fettered by an iron fate
With vain affections in my earthy state
    To anything that might seduce
My sense, or misemploy it from its use
        I was as free
50 As if there were nor sin, nor misery

6

Pure empty powers that did nothing loath,
    Did like the fairest glass,
    Or spotless polished brass,
Themselves soon in their object's image clothe.
55   Divine impressions when they came,
Did quickly enter and my soul inflame.
    'Tis not the object, but the light
That maketh Heaven; 'tis a purer sight.
        Felicity
60 Appears to none but them that purely see.[1]

7

A disentangled and a naked sense
    A mind that unpossessed,
    A disengaged breast,
An empty and a quick intelligence
65   Acquainted with the Golden Mean,
An even spirit pure and serene,
    Is that where Beauty, Excellence,
And Pleasure keep their Court of Residence.
        My Soul retire,
70 Get free, and so thou shalt even all admire.
    —1903

---

[1] *Felicity / Appears to none but them that purely see*   Compare Jacob Boehme, "the right man regenerate and renewed in Christ is…in the Paradise of God" (Epistle 25:14). Many of Boehme's works were translated into English in the seventeenth century and had considerable influence. Compare also Blake, "If the doors of perception were cleansed, every thing would appear as it is: infinite" (*The Marriage of Heaven and Hell*, Plate 14).

The Instruction

Spew out thy filth, thy flesh abjure,
  Let not contingents thee defile;
For transients only are impure,
    And empty things thy soul beguile.

5 Unfelt, unseen let those things be,
    Which to thy spirits were unknown,
When to thy blessed infancy
    The World, thy Self, thy God, was shown.

All that is great and stable stood
10   Within thy harmless view at first;
All that in visibles is good,
    Or pure, or fair, or unaccursed.

Whatever else thou now dost see
    In custom, action, or desire,
15 Is but a part of misery
    Wherein all men at once conspire.
    —1903

The Demonstration

1

The highest things are easiest to be shown,
  And only capable of being *known*.[2]
    A mist involves the eye,
    While in the middle it doth lie;
    And till the ends of things are seen,
5 The way's uncertain that doth stand between.
    As in the air we see the clouds
    Like winding sheets, or shrouds;

---

[2] *The highest things are…/ only capable of being known*   That is, only the highest things are capable of being known. This is a Platonic concept; the "ideas" (see note to previous poem) are accessible to our intellects, but their copies in the phenomenal world are not. Plato's argument was that only the ideas are unchanging; of their embodiments in the phenomenal world we can only have opinion, not knowledge, because we cannot have knowledge of that which is constantly changing.

Which though they nearer are obscure
10 The Sun, which higher far, is far more pure.

2

Its very brightness makes it near the eye,
Though many thousand leagues beyond the sky.
　　Its beams by violence
　　Invade, and ravish distant sense.
15　　Only extremes and heights are known; [1]
No certainty, where no perfection 's shown.
　　Extremities of blessedness
　　　Compel us to confess
　　A GOD indeed, whose excellence,
20 In all his Works, must needs succeed all sense.

3

And for this cause incredibles alone
May be by demonstration to us shown.
　　　Those things that are most bright
　　　Sun-like appear in their own light.
25　　And nothing 's truly seen that 's mean:
Be it a sand, an acorn, or a bean,
　　　It must be clothed with endless glory,
　　　　Before its perfect story
　　　(Be the spirit ne'er so clear)
30 Can in its Causes and its Ends appear.

4

What can be more incredible then this,
Where may we find a more profound abyss?
　　　What heav'nly height can be
　　　Transcendent to this summity!
35　　What more desirable object can
Be offered to the soul of hungering man!
　　　His gifts as they to us come down
　　　　Are infinite, and crown
　　　The soul with strange fruitions; yet
40 Returning from us they more value get. [2]

5

And what than this can be more plain and clear
What truth then this more evident appear!
　　　The GODHEAD cannot prize
　　　The Sun at all, nor yet the skies,
45　　Or air, or earth, or trees, or seas,
Or stars, unless the soul of man they please.
　　　He neither sees with human eyes
　　　　Nor needs himself seas skies
　　　Or Earth, or anything: He draws
50 No breath, nor eats or drinks by Nature's laws.

6

The joy and pleasure which his soul doth take
In all his Works, is for his creatures' sake.
　　　So great a certainty
　　　We in this holy doctrine see
55　　That there could be no worth at all
In anything material great or small
　　　Were not some creature more alive,
　　　　When it might worth derive,
　　　GOD is the spring whence things came forth
60 Souls are the fountains of their real worth.

7

The joy and pleasure which his soul doth take
In all his Works is for his creatures' sake
　　　Yet doth he take delight
　　　That's altogether infinite
65　　In them even as they from him come
For such his love and goodness is, the sum
　　　Of all his happiness doth seem,
　　　　At least in his esteem,
　　　In that delight and joy to lie
70 Which is his blessed creatures' melody.

---

[1] *No certainty, where no perfection 's known*　See the previous note.

[2] *unless the soul of man they please*　This idea, that God cannot take pleasure in his Creation unless it pleases human beings, might have been adopted, or adapted, from Boehme. In his philosophy the seventh or final form of Nature is called "figure." In this state Nature has evolved properly, the creatures stand marked with the signature of God, as being to his honour and glory; and mankind's ability to apprehend the creatures as they are marked with God's signature marks the achievement of highest consciousness, regarded as one of the ends of the creative process. Traherne's thinking on this matter is nicely encapsulated in lines 59–60.

8

In them he sees, and feels, and smells, and lives,
In them affected is to whom he gives:
    In then ten thousand ways,
    He all his works again enjoys,
75   All things from Him to Him proceed
By them; are his in them: as if indeed
    His Godhead did itself exceed.
    To them He all conveys;
    Nay even Himself: He is the End
80 To whom in them Himself, and all things tend.
    —1903

The Anticipation [1]

I

My contemplation dazzles in the End
  Of all I comprehend,[2]
    And soars above all heights,
Diving into the depths of all delights.
5   Can He become the End,
    To whom all creatures tend?
Who is the Father of all infinites!
Then may He benefit receive from things,
And be *not Parent only* of all springs.

2

10 The End doth want the means, and is the cause,
    Whose sake, by Nature's laws,

Is that for which they are.[3]
Such sands, such dangerous rocks we must beware
    From all eternity
15   A perfect deity
Most great and blessed he doth still appear.
His Essence Perfect was in all its Features
He ever Blessed in his Joys and Creatures.

3

From everlasting he these joys did need,
20   And all these joys proceed
    From Him eternally.
From everlasting his felicity
    Complete and perfect was:
    Whose bosom is the glass,
25 Wherein we all things everlasting see.
His Name is NOW, his Nature is forever.
None can his creatures from their Maker Sever.

4

The End in him from everlasting is
    The Fountain of all bliss.
30   From everlasting it
Efficient was, and influence did emit,[4]
    That caused all. Before
    The world, we do adore
This glorious End. Because all benefit
35 From it proceeds. Both are the very same.
The End and Fountain differ but in name.

5

That so the End should be the very Spring,
    Of ev'ry glorious thing;
    And that which seemeth last,

---

[1] This poem represents a more philosophical exposition of ideas announced in "The Demonstration." It stands here as a rare representative, in this anthology, of a class of poems quite common in the seventeenth century, that is the attempt to express or explore explicitly philosophical ideas. Henry More, for example, wrote what might be described as a Spenserian epic of philosophical ideas. By contrast, "ideas" in Donne are usually there by way of illustration of arguments about sex or religion, rather than for their own sake. The title of the poem probably refers to its chief idea, that the First Cause is also (and therefore "anticipates") the Final Cause.

[2] *the End* that is, the "final cause." Traherne's vision is teleological, in the sense that everything is seen as having a divinely implanted purpose, toward which it is pressing.

[3] *doth want* lacks; *Whose sake…/ Is that for which they are* that is, things exist for the sake of their end, or final cause. The rest of the stanza appears to be rejecting the idea, in that particular form. The burden of the poem is that God is both the beginning and the end of all creatures.

[4] *From everlasting it / Efficient was* That is, the final cause and the efficient cause are identical; this is clearly stated in line 36: "The End and Fountain differ but in name."

40 The Fountain and the Cause; attained so fast,
   That it was first; and moved
   The efficient, who so loved
All worlds and made them for the sake of this
It shows the End complete before, and is
45 A perfect token of his perfect bliss.

6

The End complete, the means must needs be so.
   By which we plainly know,
   From all Eternity,
The means whereby God is, must perfect be.
50   God is himself the means,
   Whereby he doth exist:
And as the Sun by shining 's clothed with beams,
So from himself to all his glory streams,
Who is a Sun, yet what himself doth list.[1]

7

55 His endless wants and his enjoyments be
   From all eternity;
   Immutable in him:
They are his joys before the Cherubim.[2]
   His wants appreciate all, [3]
60   And being infinite,
Permit no being to be mean or small
That he enjoys, or is before his sight.
His satisfactions do his wants delight.

8

Wants are the Fountains of Felicity;
65   No joy could ever be
   Were there no want. No bliss

No sweetness perfect were it not for this.
   Want is the greatest pleasure
   Because it makes all treasure.
70 O what a wonderful profound abyss
Is God! In whom eternal wants and treasures
Are more delightful 'cause they both are pleasures.

9

He infinitely wanteth all his joys;
   (No want the soul o'er cloys.)
75   And all those wanted pleasures
He infinitely hath. What endless measures,
   What heights and depths may we
   In his felicity
Conceive! Whose very wants are endless pleasures,
80 His life in wants and joys is infinite.
And both are felt as his supreme delight.

10

He 's not like us; possession doth not cloy,
   Nor sense of want destroy.
   Both always are together:
85 No force can either from the other sever.
   Yet there 's a space between
   That 's endless. Both are seen
Distinctly still, and both are seen for ever.
As soon as e'er he wanteth all his bliss,
90 His bliss, though everlasting, in him is.

11

His essence is all act: he did, that he
   All act might always be.
   His Nature burns like fire;
His goodness infinitely doth desire,
95   To be by all possessed;
   His love makes others blest.
It is the glory of his high estate,
And that which I forever more admire,
He is an act that doth communicate.

---

[1] *Who is a Sun, yet what himself doth list*   That is, God is the Sun, and whatever else he chooses to be. See *OED* list *v*[1] and compare John 3:8, "The wind bloweth where it listeth."

[2] *his joys before the Cherubim*   God's joys as shown to the cherubim. The cherubim were the second order of angels according to the pseudo-Dionysius; they excelled especially in knowledge, as here, the knowledge of the joys of God. See *OED* cherub.

[3] *appreciate all*   are the cause of value in all things.

12

100 From all to all eternity he is
    That act: an act of bliss:
    Wherein all bliss to all,
That will receive the same, or on him call,
    Is freely given: from whence
105   'Tis easy even to sense,
To apprehend that all receivers are
In him, all gifts, all joys, all eyes, even all
At once, that ever will, or shall appear.

13

He is the means of them, they not of him.
110   The Holy Cherubim
    Souls, Angels from him came
Who is a glorious bright and living flame,
    That on all things doth shine,
    And makes their face devine.

115 And Holy, Holy, Holy, is his Name.
    He is the means both of himself and all,
Whom we the Fountain, Means and End do call.

14

In whom as in the Fountain all things are,
    In whom all things appear
120   As in the Means, and End
From whom they all proceed, to whom they tend.
    By whom they are made ours
    Whose souls are spacious bowers
Of all like his. Who ought to have a sense
125 Of all our wants, of all his excellence,
That while we all, we him might comprehend.
—1903

Charles Sackville, Earl of Dorset
1638 – 1706

A favourite of Charles II, Sackville was noted primarily for the life of dissipation he lived with Sir Charles Sedley and the other rakes of the Restoration court. He withdrew from the court during the reign of James II, but became politically active once more after the Revolution, supporting William and acting as regent several times during the King's absences. He was a friend and patron to poets, and his own poems, published with Sedley's in 1701, were praised by Dryden and Matthew Prior; Dryden also dedicated several poems to him. "My Opinion" reflects the power struggle in the early 1680s between the King's brother, the Catholic James, Duke of York (later James II), and the King's illegitimate eldest son (by his Welsh mistress Lucy Walter), James, Duke of Monmouth. In 1685, Monmouth landed at Lyme Regis with about 150 men, declared his uncle James II a usurper, and claimed the throne for himself; his troops were eventually slaughtered by the Royal army and he was executed on Tower Hill.

ഌ

My Opinion

1

After thinking this fortnight of Whig and of
   Tory,
This to me is the long and the short of the story:
They are all fools or knaves, and they keep up this
   pother
On both sides, designing to cheat one another.

2

5 Poor Rowley (whose maxims of state are a riddle)
Has plac'd himself much like the pin in the
   middle; [1]
Let which corner soever be tumbl'd down first,
'Tis ten thousand to one but he comes by the
   worst.

3

'Twixt brother and bastard (those Dukes of
10   renown) [2]
He'll make a wise shift to get rid of his crown;

Had he half common sense (were it ne'er so uncivil)
He'd have had 'em long since tipp'd down to the
   Devil. [3]

4

The first is a Prince well-fashion'd, well-featur'd,
No bigot to speak of, not false, nor ill-natur'd;
15 The other for government can't be unfit,
He's so little a fop, and so plaguy a wit. [4]

5

Had I this soft son, and this dangerous brother,
I'd hang up the one, then I'd piss upon t'other;
20 I'd make this the long and the short of the story:
The fools might be Whigs, none but knaves should
   be Tories.
—(ca. 1681)

---

[1] *Rowley* Charles II; Rowley was the name of a famously prolific stallion of the period.

[2] the Duke of York (later James II) and James Scott, Duke of Monmouth, Charles II's illegitimate son.

---

[3] *tipp'd* a term from the game of skittles (ninepins), a form of bowling; used when one pin knocks down another by falling or rolling against it, as distinguished from being knocked down directly by the ball. The image completes the metaphor introduced in the second stanza of the King as the pin between the two rivals.

[4] The entire stanza is ironic: the Prince (Duke of York) was unattractive and a notorious bigot; Monmouth was considered a dullard.

Sir Charles Sedley
?1639 – 1701

Sir Charles Sedley was the youngest and posthumous son of the Baronet of Southfleet in Kent. His two elder brothers died childless, and Charles inherited the title and estates of his father. He entered Wadham College, Oxford in 1655–56, but did not take a degree. In 1657 Sedley married Catherine Savage, daughter of Earl Rivers. Their daughter, Catherine, was later to become the favourite mistress of Charles II's brother, James. Sedley became a member of Parliament after the Restoration. A number of scandals were associated with him, generally related to his drinking habits. His literary reputation did not suffer, however, and his work was praised by Charles II, Rochester, Buckingham, Dryden and others. Sedley's literary work was highly varied, consisting of essays, speeches, translations, poetry, and tragic and comedic drama. Sedley narrowly escaped death in 1680 when his skull was fractured by the collapsing roof of the tennis-court in the Haymarket. After Charles II died in 1685, Sedley rarely appeared in London. A number of his plays were published in his lifetime, one of his parliamentary speeches appeared in a broadside, and a few of his short works appeared in miscellanies. After his death numerous editions of Sedley's collected works were published. Indeed there were six versions published in the eighteenth century alone.

જઠજ

Young Coridon and Phillis

Young Coridon and Phillis
   Sat in a Lovely Grove;
Contriving Crowns of Lilies,
   Repeating Tales of Love:
5 And something else, but what I dare not name.

But as they were a Playing,
   She ogled so the Swain;[1]
It sav'd her plainly saying
   Let's kiss to ease our Pain:
10 And something else, but what I dare not name.

A thousand times he kiss'd her,
   Laying her on the Green;
But as he farther press'd her,
   Her pretty Leg was seen:
15 And something else, but what I dare not name.

So many Beauties removing,
   His Ardour still increas'd;
And greater Joys pursuing,
   He wander'd o'er her Breast:
20 And something else, but what I dare not name.

A last Effort she trying,
   His passion to withstand;
Cry'd, but it was faintly crying,
   Pray take away your Hand:
25 And something else, but what I dare not name.

Young Coridon grown bolder,
   The Minute would improve;
This is the time he told her,
   To shew you how I love;
30 And something else, but what I dare not name.

The Nymph seem'd almost dying,
   Dissolv'd in amorous heat;
She kiss'd and told him sighing,

---

[1] *Swain* a man, a youth; a boy (*OED* swain).

My Dear your Love is great:
35 And something else, but what I dare not name.

But Phillis did recover
    Much sooner than the Swain;
She blushing ask'd her Lover,
    Shall we not kiss again:
40 And something else, but what I dare not name.

Thus Love his Revels keeping,
    'Til Nature at a stand;
From talk they fell to Sleeping,
    Holding each others Hand;
45 And something else, but what I dare not name.
    —1694

Aphra Behn
1640 – 1689

Little is certainly known about the early life of Aphra Behn. There are several biographical accounts, which present conflicting versions of her lineage, birthplace and youth. Within a decade of her death were published: *An Account of the Life of the Incomparable Mrs. Behn* (1696), *Memoirs of the Life of Mrs. Behn* (1696) and *The History of the Life and Memoirs of Mrs. Behn* (1698). These and other early references have led biographers to conclude that Aphra Behn was born in Harbledon near Canterbury on July 10, 1640, daughter to Bartholomew Johnson and Elizabeth Denham. It is believed that she spent several years in her early twenties (ca. 1663–64) in Surinam, where she met William Scot. Some time in 1664, she was married to a Mr. Behn, possibly a city merchant of Dutch extraction, who died of the plague in 1665. In August, 1666, during the Dutch war, she was dispatched as an official government spy to Antwerp, with a mission to persuade William Scot to act as a double agent. She returned to England in 1667 heavily in debt, and was briefly imprisoned in London. Despite repeated petitions, she received no compensation for her services, and undertook to live by the pen, writing at least eighteen plays. While her theatrical career dominated the first decade of her professional writing, Behn also produced translations from Latin and French, and wrote popular verse and prose fiction. As a writer of drama, novels, epistles, and poetry, she explored a variety of highly charged subjects not common in Restoration literature: female sexuality, lust, seduction, incest, rape. The themes upon which she wrote drew criticism from churchmen. Bishop Burnet wrote to Anne Wharton: "she is so abominably vile a woman, and rallies not only all Religion but all Virtue in so odious and obscene a manner, that I am heartily sorry that she has writ any thing in your commendation." Perhaps because of the subversive nature of her drama and prose fiction, Behn's role as Tory apologist most evident in her occasional verse has received less critical attention. Aphra Behn died in London and was buried in Westminster Abbey. Of her life and burial, Virginia Woolf was to write: "All women together ought to let flowers fall upon the tomb of Aphra Behn which is, most scandalously but rather appropriately, in Westminster Abbey, for it was she who earned them the right to speak their minds."

❦❧❦

Song
"I Led my Silvia to a Grove"

I led my Silvia to a grove,
Where all the boughs did shade us
The sun itself, though it had strove
It could not have betrayed us.
5 The place secured from human eyes
No other fear allows,
But when the winds do gently rise;
And kiss the yielding boughs.

Down there we sat upon the moss,
10 And did begin to play,
A thousand wanton tricks to pass,
The heat of all the day.
A many kisses I did give,
And she returned the same,
15 Which made her willing to receive;
That which I dare not name.

My greedy eyes no aids required,
To tell their amorous tale,
On her that was already fired:
20 'Twas easy to prevail.

I did but kiss and clasp her round,
Whilst they my thoughts expressed, [1]
And laid her gently on the ground:
Oh! who can guess the rest.
—1672

The Golden Age.
A Paraphrase on a Translation
out of French [2]

I

Blest age! when ev'ry purling stream
Ran undisturbed and clear, [3]
When no scorned shepherds on your banks were
    seen,
Tortured by love, by jealousy, or fear;
When an eternal spring dressed ev'ry bough,
And blossoms fell, by new ones dispossessed;
These their kind shade affording all below,
And those a bed where all below might rest.
The groves appeared all dressed with wreaths of
    flowers,
And from their leaves dropped aromatic showers,
Whose fragrant heads in mystic twines above,
Exchanged their sweets, and mixed with thousand
      kisses,
   As if the willing branches strove
   To beautify and shade the grove
   Where the young wanton gods of love
Offer their noblest sacrifice of blisses.

II

Calm was the air, no winds blew fierce and loud,
The sky was dark'ned with no sullen cloud;
But all the heav'ns laughed with continued light,
And scattered round their rays serenely bright.
   No other murmurs filled the ear
   But what the streams and rivers purled,
When silver waves o'er shining pebbles curled;
   Or when young Zephyrs fanned the gentle
     breeze, [4]
   Gath'ring fresh sweets from balmy flow'rs
     and trees,
Then bore 'em on their wings to perfume all the
    air:
   While to their soft and tender play,
   The gray-plumed natives of the shades
 Unwearied sing till love invades,
Then bill, then sing again, while love and music
   makes the day. [5]

III

   The stubborn plough had then,
   Made no rude rapes upon the virgin earth;
Who yielded of her own account her plenteous
    birth;
   Without the aids of men;
   As if within her teeming womb,
   All nature, and all sexes lay,
   Whence new creations every day
   Into the happy world did come:
   The roses filled with morning dew;
    Bent down their loaded heads,
   T'adorn the careless shepherds' grassy beds
While still young opening buds each moment grew
And as those withered, dressed his shaded couch
    anew;
   Beneath whose boughs the snakes securely dwelt,
   Not doing harm, nor harm from others felt;
   With whom the nymphs did innocently play,

---

[1] *Whilst* original "whose they my"; 1673, 1684 "Whilst those his";
1707 "And thus his."

[2] an expanded adaptation of the opening chorus from *Aminta* (1573),
a pastoral play by Torquato Tasso (1544–1595). The French version
of the play from which Behn worked is not yet known.

[3] *purling* rippling; murmuring (*OED* purling *ppl.a*).

[4] *Zephyrs* soft, gentle winds (*OED* zephyr 2).

[5] *gray-plumed natives* turtle-doves; *bill* stroke bill with bill; caress
(*OED* bill *v²* 2,3).

No spiteful venom in the wantons lay; [1]
But to the touch were soft, and to the sight were
  gay.

IV

50 Then no rough sound of war's alarms,
  Had taught the world the needless use of arms:
    Monarchs were uncreated then,
    Those arbitrary rulers over men;
    Kings that made laws, first broke 'em, and the
      gods
  By teaching us religion first, first set the world at
    odds:

55 Till then ambition was not known,
    That poison to content, bane to repose;
    Each swain was lord o'er his own will alone,
    His innocence religion was, and laws.
    Nor needed any troublesome defence
60 Against his neighbours' insolence.
    Flocks, herds, and every necessary good
    Which bounteous nature had designed for food,
    Whose kind increase o'er-spread the meads and
      plains,
  Was then a common sacrifice to all th'agreeing
    swains. [2]

V

65 Right and property were words since made,
    When power taught mankind to invade:
    When pride and avarice became a trade;
    Carried on by discord, noise and wars,
    For which they bartered wounds and scars;
70 And to enhance the merchandise, miscalled it,
      Fame,
    And rapes, invasions, tyrannies,
    Was gaining of a glorious name:
    Styling their savage slaughters, victories;

Honour, the error and the cheat
75 Of the ill-natured busy great,
    Nonsense, invented by the proud,
    Fond idol of the slavish crowd,
    Thou wert not known in those blest days
  Thy poison was not mixed with our unbounded
    joys;
80 Then it was glory to pursue delight,
    And that was lawful all, the pleasure did invite,
    Then 'twas the amorous world enjoyed its reign;
    And tyrant Honour strove t' usurp in vain.

VI

The flow'ry meads the rivers and the groves,
85 Were filled with little gay-winged loves: [3]
    That ever smiled and danced and played,
    And now the woods, and now the streams invade,
    And where they came all things were gay and glad:
    When in the myrtle groves the lovers sat
90 Oppressed with a too fervent heat;
    A thousand Cupids fanned their wings aloft,
  And through the boughs the yielded air would
    waft: [4]
    Whose parting leaves discovered all below,
95 And every god his own soft power admired,
    And smiled and fanned, and sometimes bent his
      bow;
    Where e'er he saw a shepherd uninspired.
    The nymphs were free, no nice, no coy disdain,
    Denied their joys, or gave the lover pain; [5]
    The yielding maid but kind resistance makes;
100 Trembling and blushing are not marks of shame,
      But the effect of kindling flame:
    Which from the sighing burning swain she takes,
    While she with tears all soft, and downcast eyes,
  Permits the charming conqueror to win the
    prize.

---

[1] *wantons* playful people (*OED* wanton *sb* B.2a).

[2] *swains* shepherds; also, country gallants (*OED* swain *sb* 4,5).

---

[3] *gay-winged lovers* Cupids.

[4] *waft* blow softly (*OED* waft *v*[1] 6c).

[5] *nice* affectedly modest (*OED* nice 5a).

VII

105 The lovers thus, thus uncontrolled did meet,
    Thus all their joys and vows of love repeat:
        Joys which were everlasting, ever new
        And every vow inviolably true;
    Not kept in fear of gods, no fond religious cause,
110   Nor in obedience to the duller laws.
        Those fopperies of the gown were then not
          known,
        Those vain, those politic curbs to keep man in; [1]
    Who by a fond mistake created that a sin;
    Which freeborn we, by right of nature claim our
        own? [2]
115   Who but the learned and dull moral fool
    Could gravely have foreseen, man ought to live by
        rule?

VIII

    Oh cursed Honour! thou who first didst damn,
        A woman to the sin of shame; [3]
        Honour! that rob'st us of our gust,
120   Honour! that hind'red mankind first,
    At love's eternal spring to squench his amorous
        thirst. [4]
        Honour! who first taught lovely eyes the art,
        To wound, and not to cure the heart:
    With love to invite, but to forbid with awe,
125   And to themselves prescribe a cruel law;
        To veil 'em from the lookers on,
        When they are sure the slave's undone,
    And all the charmingst part of beauty hid;
    Soft looks, consenting wishes, all denied.
130   It gathers up the flowing hair,

    That loosely plaid with wanton air. [5]
    The envious net, and stinted order hold,
    The lovely curls of jet and shining gold,
    No more neglected on the shoulders hurled: [6]
135 Now dressed to tempt, not gratify the world,
    Thou miser Honour hord'st the sacred store,
    And starv'st thy self to keep thy votaries poor. [7]

IX

    Honour! that put'st our words that should be free
        Into a set formality.
140 Thou base debaucher of the generous heart,
    That teachest all our looks and actions art;
        What love designed a sacred gift,
        What nature made to be possessed,
        Mistaken Honour, made a theft,
145   For glorious love should be confessed:
    For when confined, all the poor lover gains,
    Is broken sighs, pale looks, complaints, and pains.
    Thou foe to pleasure, nature's worst disease,
        Thou tyrant over mighty kings,
150 What mak'st thou here in shepherds' cottages;
    Why troublest thou, the quiet shades and springs?
        Be gone, and make thy famed resort
          To princes' palaces;
    Go deal and chaffer in the trading court,
155 That busy market for phantastic things; [8]
    Be gone and interrupt the short retreat,
        Of the illustrious and the great;
        Go break the politician's sleep,
        Disturb the gay ambitious fool,
160   That longs for scepters, crowns, and rule,
    Which not his title, nor his wit can keep;
    But let the humble honest swain go on,

---

[1] *fopperies of the gown* absurdities of the law (*OED* foppery 1b); *politic curbs* political restraints (*OED* curb *sb* I.2; politic A.2b).

[2] *fond* foolishly credulous (*OED* fond *a* 2).

[3] *Honour* reputation; here the meaning is closest to reputation for chastity (*OED* honour *sb* 1c, 3a).

[4] *gust* relish (*OED* gust *sb*² 4); *to squench* to satisfy; but also to extinguish (*OED* squench *v* 3,1).

[5] *plaid* played (*OED* plaid); possibly a pun on "plait," a braided tress of hair (*OED* plait *sb* 2a).

[6] *stinted* appointed (*OED* stinted *ppl.a* 1).

[7] *votaries* devout worshippers (*OED* votary I.2).

[8] *chaffer* buy or sell (*OED* chaffer *v* 1a); *phantastic* fanciful or illusory (*OED* fantastic *a* A.1,.2; phantasm *sb* I.1b,II.4b).

In the blest paths of the first rate of man; [1]
   That nearest were to gods allied,
165 And formed for love alone, disdained all other
   pride.

          x

Be gone! and let the Golden Age again,
    Assume its glorious reign;
   Let the young wishing maid confess,
   What all your arts would keep concealed:
170   The mystery will be revealed,
And she in vain denies, whilst we can guess,
She only shows the jilt to teach man how,
To turn the false artillery on the cunning foe. [2]
   Thou empty vision hence, be gone,
175   And let the peaceful swain love on;
The swift paced hours of life soon steal away:
   Stint not ye gods his short lived joy.
The spring decays, but when the winter's gone,
   The trees and flowers anew come on. [3]
180 The sun may set, but when the night is fled,
   And gloomy darkness does retire,
   He rises from his wat'ry bed:
All glorious, gay, all dressed in amorous fire.
   But Sylvia when your beauties fade,
185 When the fresh roses on your cheeks shall die,
   Like flowers that wither in the shade,
Eternally they will forgotten lie,
And no kind spring their sweetness will supply.
When snow shall on those lovely tresses lie
190 And your fair eyes no more shall give us pain,
   But shoot their pointless darts in vain.
What will your duller honour signify?
Go boast it then! and see what numerous store
Of lovers, will your ruined shrine adore.
195   Then let us Sylvia yet be wise,

---

[1] *first rate*   original state.

[2] *shows the jilt*   to play the role of the cheat or harlot (*OED* jilt *v* 1; jilt *sb* 1).

[3] *come*   emended from "comes."

And the gay hasty minutes prize:
The sun and spring receive but our short light,
Once set, a sleep brings an eternal night.
—1684

Song
"Love Armed" [4]

Love in fantastic triumph sat,
  Whilst bleeding hearts around him flowed,
For whom fresh pains he did create,
And strange tyrannic power he showed;
5 From thy bright eyes he took his fire,
Which round about, in sport he hurled;
But 'twas from mine, he took desire,
Enough to undo the amorous world.

From me he took his sighs and tears,
10 From thee his pride and cruelty;
From me his languishments and fears,
And every killing dart from thee;
Thus thou and I, the god have armed,
And set him up a deity;
15 But my poor heart alone is harmed,
Whilst thine the victor is, and free.
—1684

On a Juniper Tree, Cut Down
to Make Busks [5]

Whilst happy I triumphant stood,
  The pride and glory of the wood;

---

[4] first performed in 1677 as the opening song in Act I of *Abdelazer; or, the Moor's Revenge*.

[5] *On a Juniper Tree...Busks* A busk was a strip of wood or other rigid material passed down the front of a corset to stiffen and support it. Formerly and still applied to the whole corset (*OED* busk *sb* [1]). The juniper tree is a hardy spreading low tree, having awl-shaped prickly leaves and bluish-black berries, with a pungent taste, yielding a volatile oil used in medicine. The seeds and wood of the juniper were formerly burnt as purifiers of the air, and the coal of juniper wood was fabled to have a wonderful power of remaining glowing (*OED* juniper 1a).

My aromatic boughs and fruit,
Did with all other trees dispute.
5 Had right by nature to excel,
In pleasing both the taste and smell:
But to the touch I must confess,
Bore an ungrateful sullenness.
My wealth, like bashful virgins, I
10 Yielded with some reluctancy;
For which my value should be more,
Not giving easily my store.
My verdant branches all the year
Did an eternal beauty wear;
15 Did ever young and gay appear.
Nor needed any tribute pay,
For bounties from the god of day:
Nor do I hold supremacy,
(In all the wood) o'er every tree.
20 But even those too of my own race,
That grow not in this happy place.
But that in which I glory most,
And do myself with reason boast,
Beneath my shade the other day,
25 Young Philocles and Cloris lay,
Upon my root she leaned her head,
And where I grew, he made their bed:
Whilst I the canopy more largely spread.
Their trembling limbs did gently press,
30 The kind supporting yielding grass:
Ne'er half so blest as now, to bear
A swain so young, a nymph so fair:
My grateful shade I kindly lent,
And every aiding bough I bent
35 So low, as sometimes had the bliss
To rob the shepherd of a kiss,
Whilst he in pleasures far above
The sense of that degree of love:
Permitted every stealth I made,
40 Unjealous of his rival shade.
I saw 'em kindle to desire,
Whilst with soft sighs they blew the fire:
Saw the approaches of their joy,

He growing more fierce, and she less coy,
45 Saw how they mingled melting rays,
Exchanging love a thousand ways.
Kind was the force on every side,
Her new desire she could not hide:
Nor would the shepherd be denied.
50 Impatient he waits no consent
But what she gave by languishment,
The blessed minute he pursued;
Whilst love, her fear, and shame subdued; [1]
And now transported in his arms,
55 Yields to the conqueror all her charms,
His panting breast, to hers now joined,
They feast on raptures unconfined;
Vast and luxuriant, such as prove
The immortality of love.
60 For who but a divinity,
Could mingle souls to that degree;
And melt 'em into ecstasy.
Now like the Phoenix, both expire, [2]
While from the ashes of their fire,
65 Sprung up a new, and soft desire.
Like charmers, thrice they did invoke,
The god, and thrice new vigour took.
Nor had thy mystery ended there,
But Cloris reassumed her fear,
70 And chid the swain, for having pressed,
What she alas would not resist:
Whilst he in whom love's sacred flame,
Before and after was the same,
Fondly implored she would forget
75 A fault, which he would yet repeat.
From active joys with shame they haste,
To a reflection on the past; [3]
A thousand times my covert bless,

---

[1] *Whilst...subdued* 1680; 1684 omits this line.

[2] *Phoenix* a mythical bird, fabled to be the only one of its kind, that lives five or six hundred years in the Arabian desert, after which it burns itself on a funeral pyre, only to emerge from its ashes to live through another cycle of years.

[3] *shame* 1680; "some" in the 1684 edition.

That did secure their happiness:
80 Their gratitude to every tree
They pay, but most to happy me;
The shepherdess my bark caressed,
Whilst he my root, love's pillow, kissed;
And did with sighs, their fate deplore,
85 Since I must shelter them no more;
And if before my joys were such,
In having heard, and seen too much,
My grief must be as great and high,
When all abandoned I shall be,
90 Doomed to a silent destiny.
No more the charming strife to hear,
The shepherd's vows, the virgin's fear:
No more a joyful looker on,
Whilst love's soft battle's lost and won.
95   With grief I bowed my murmuring head,
And all my crystal dew I shed.
Which did in Cloris pity move,
(Cloris whose soul is made of love;)
She cut me down, and did translate,
100 My being to a happier state.
No martyr for religion died
With half that unconsidering pride;
My top was on that altar laid,
Where love his softest offerings paid:
105 And was as fragrant incense burned,
My body into busks was turned:
Where I still guard the sacred store,
And of love's temple keep the door.
—1684

The Disappointment [1]

I

One day the amorous Lysander,
  By an impatient passion swayed,

---

[1] This poem is loosely based on the first part of de Cantenac's poem "Sur une Impuissance" (*Recueil de diverses poesies choisies*, Amsterdam, 1661), which was translated into English and included in *Wit and Drollery. Jovial Poems* (1682) as "The Lost Opportunity Recovered."

Surprised fair Cloris, that loved maid,
Who could defend herself no longer.
5 All things did with his love conspire;
That gilded planet of the day,
In his gay chariot drawn by fire,
Was now descending to the sea,
And left no light to guide the world,
10 But what from Cloris' brighter eyes was hurled.

II

In a lone thicket made for love,
Silent as yielding maid's consent,
She with a charming languishment,
Permits his force, yet gently strove;
15 Her hands his bosom softly meet,
But not to put him back designed,
Rather to draw 'em on inclined:
Whilst he lay trembling at her feet,
Resistance 'tis in vain to show;
20 She wants the power to say—*Ah! What d' ye do?*

III

Her bright eyes sweet, and yet severe,
Where love and shame confus'dly strive,
Fresh vigor to Lysander give;
And breathing faintly in his ear,
25 She cried—*Cease, cease—your vain desire,*
Or I'll call out—What would you do?
My dearer honour even to you
I cannot, must not give—retire,
Or take this life, whose chiefest part
30 *I gave you with the conquest of my heart.*

IV

But he as much unused to fear,
As he was capable of love,
The blessed minutes to improve,
Kisses her mouth, her neck, her hair;
35 Each touch her new desire alarms,
His burning trembling hand he pressed
Upon her swelling snowy breast,

While she lay panting in his arms.
All her unguarded beauties lie
40 The spoils and trophies of the enemy.

V

And now without respect or fear,
He seeks the object of his vows,
(His love no modesty allows)
By swift degrees advancing—where
45 His daring hand that altar seized,
Where gods of love do sacrifice.
That awful throne, that paradise
Where rage is calmed, and anger pleased,
That fountain where delight still flows,
50 And gives the universal world repose.

VI

Her balmy lips encount'ring his,
Their bodies, as their souls, are joined;
Where both in transports unconfined
Extend themselves upon the moss.
55 Cloris half dead and breathless lay;
Her soft eyes cast a humid light,
Such as divides the day and night;
Or falling stars, whose fires decay:
And now no signs of life she shows,
60 But what in short-breathed sighs returns and goes.

VII

He saw how at her length she lay,
He saw her rising bosom bare;
Her loose thin robes, through which appear
A shape designed for love and play;
65 Abandoned by her pride and shame,
She does her softest joys dispense,
Off'ring her virgin-innocence
A victim to love's sacred flame;
While the o'er-ravished shepherd lies
70 Unable to perform the sacrifice.

VIII

Ready to taste a thousand joys,
The too transported hapless swain
Found the vast pleasure turned to pain;
Pleasure which too much love destroys:
75 The willing garments by he laid,
And heaven all opened to his view,
Mad to possess, himself he threw
On the defenceless lovely maid.
But Oh what envying god conspires
80 To snatch his power, yet leave him the desire!

IX

Nature's support, (without whose aid
She can no human being give)
Itself now wants the art to live;
Faintness its slack'ned nerves invade:
85 In vain th' enraged youth essayed
To call its fleeting vigor back,
No motion 'twill from motion take;
Excess of love his love betrayed:
In vain he toils, in vain commands;
90 The insensible fell weeping in his hand.

X

In this so amorous cruel strife,
Where love and fate were too severe,
The poor Lysander in despair
Renounced his reason with his life:
95 Now all the brisk and active fire
That should the nobler part inflame,
Served to increase his rage and shame,
And left no spark for new desire:
Not all her naked charms could move
100 Or calm that rage that had debauched his love.

XI

Cloris returning from the trance
Which love and soft desire had bred,

Her timorous hand she gently laid
(Or guided by design or chance)
105 Upon that fabulous Priapas, [1]
That potent God, as poets feign;
But never did young shepherdess,
Gath'ring of fern upon the plain,
More nimbly draw her fingers back,
110 Finding beneath the verdant leaves a snake:

XII

Then Cloris her fair hand withdrew,
Finding that god of her desires
Disarmed of all his awful fires,
And cold as flow'rs bathed in the morning-dew.
115 Who can the nymph's confusion guess?
The blood forsook the hinder place,
And strewed with blushes all her face,
Which both disdain and shame expressed:
And from Lysander's arms she fled,
120 Leaving him fainting on the gloomy bed.

XIII

Like lightning through the grove she hies,
Or Daphne from the Delphic god, [2]
No print upon the grassy road
She leaves, t' instruct pursuing eyes.
125 The wind that wantoned in her hair,
And with her ruffled garments played,
Discovered in the flying maid
All that the gods e'er made, if fair.
So Venus, when her love was slain, [3]
130 With fear and haste flew o'er the fatal plain.

XIV

The nymph's resentments none but I
Can well imagine or condole:
But none can guess Lysander's soul,
But those who swayed his destiny.
135 His silent griefs swell up to storms,
And not one god his fury spares;
He cursed his birth, his fate, his stars;
But more the shepherdess's charms,
Whose soft bewitching influence
140 Had damned him to the hell of impotence.
—1684

On the Death of the late Earl of Rochester [4]

Mourn, mourn, ye Muses, all your loss deplore, [5]
The young, the noble Strephon is no more.
Yes, yes, he fled quick as departing light,
And ne'er shall rise from death's eternal night,
5 So rich a prize the Stygian gods ne'er bore, [6]
Such wit, such beauty, never graced their shore.
He was but lent this duller world t'improve
In all the charms of poetry, and love;
Both were his gift, which freely he bestowed,
10 And like a god, dealt to the wond'ring crowd.
Scorning the little vanity of fame,
'Spite of himself attained a glorious name.
But oh! in vain was all his peevish pride,
The sun as soon might his vast lustre hide,
15 As piercing, pointed, and more lasting bright,
As suffering no vicissitudes of night.
    Mourn, mourn, ye Muses, all your loss deplore,
        The young, the noble Strephon is no more.

---

[1] *Priapus* the Greek and Roman god of procreation; hence also of gardens and vineyards; also a representation of the male generative organ—a phallus (*OED* priapus 1,3a).

[2] *Daphne from the Delphic god* Daphne, fleeing the sexual advances of Apollo, was turned into a laurel tree in response to her prayer for assistance.

[3] *Venus, when her love was slain* Adonis was slain by a boar while hunting.

[4] *Earl of Rochester* John Wilmot, Earl of Rochester (1647–1680); see the headnote to his work.

[5] *Muses* The nine Muses are the Greek deities who preside over various fields of creative activity.

[6] *Stygian gods* gods of the underworld (the river Styx was one of the rivers of the underworld).

Now uninspired upon your banks we lie,
20 Unless when we would mourn his elegy;
His name's a genius that would wit dispense,
And give the theme a soul, the words a sense.
But all fine thought that ravished when it spoke,
With the soft youth eternal leave has took;
25 Uncommon wit that did the soul o'ercome,
Is buried all in Strephon's worshipped tomb;
Satire has lost its art, its sting is gone,
The fop and cully now may be undone; [1]
That dear instructing rage is now allayed,
30 And no sharp pen dares tell 'em how they've strayed;
Bold as a god was every lash he took,
But kind and gentle the chastising stroke.
    Mourn, mourn, ye youths, whom fortune has
        betrayed,
        The last reproacher of your vice is dead.

35 Mourn, all ye beauties, put your cyprus on, [2]
The truest swain that e'er adored you's gone;
Think how he loved, and writ, and sighed, and
    spoke,
Recall his mien, his fashion, and his look. [3]
By what dear arts the soul he did surprise,
40 Soft as his voice, and charming as his eyes.
Bring garlands all of never-dying flowers,
Bedewed with everlasting falling showers;
Fix your fair eyes upon your victimed slave,
Sent gay and young to his untimely grave.
45 See where the noble swain extended lies,
Too sad a triumph of your victories;
Adorned with all the graces heaven e'er lent,
All that was great, soft, lovely, excellent

You've laid into his early monument.
50   Mourn, mourn, ye beauties, your sad loss
            deplore,
        The young, the charming Strephon is no
            more.

Mourn, all ye little gods of love, whose darts
Have lost their wonted power of piercing hearts;
Lay by the gilded quiver and the bow,
55 The useless toys can do no mischief now,
Those eyes that all your arrows points inspired,
Those lights that gave ye fire are now retired,
Cold as his tomb, pale as your mother's doves; [4]
Bewail him then oh all ye little loves,
60 For you the humblest votary have lost [5]
That ever your divinities could boast;
Upon your hands your weeping heads decline,
And let your wings encompass round his shrine;
In stead of flowers your broken arrows strow,
65 And at his feet lay the neglected bow.
    Mourn, all ye little gods, your loss deplore
        The soft, the charming Strephon is no
            more.

Large was his fame, but short his glorious race,
70 Like young Lucretius and died apace. [6]
So early roses fade, so over all
They cast their fragrant scents, then softly fall,
While all the scattered perfumed leaves declare,
How lovely 'twas when whole, how sweet, how fair.
75 Had he been to the Roman empire known,

---

[1] *fop* a conceited person, a pretender to wit, wisdom or accomplishments (*OED* fop *sb* 2); *cully* a simpleton (*OED* cully *sb slang* or *colloq.* 1).

[2] *cyprus* a light, transparent material (originally transported from or through Cyprus) resembling cobweb lawn or crape much used for habiliments of mourning (*OED* cypress³ *Obs.* 1c).

[3] *mien* the air, bearing, carriage or manner of a person, as expressive of character or mood (*OED* mien *sb*¹ a).

---

[4] *mother's doves* The chariot of Venus is traditionally represented as drawn by doves.

[5] *votary* a devoted admirer (*OED* votary *sb* II.5).

[6] *Lucretius* poet and philosopher (ca. 94–55 B.C.E.). In *De Rerum Natura* Lucretius expounded Epicureanism to counter fears about the intervention of gods in this life and the punishment of the soul in the next. St. Jerome alleged that Lucretius was poisoned by a love-philtre, wrote the poem during lucid intervals, and eventually committed suicide. Thomas Creech, a close friend of Aphra Behn to whom she dedicated two poems, produced the first English translation of all six books of *De Rerum Natura* in 1682.

When great Augustus filled the peaceful throne; [1]
Had he the noble wond'rous poet seen,
And known his genius, and surveyed his mien,
(When wits, and heroes graced divine abodes,)
80 He had increased the number of their gods;
The royal judge had temples reared to's name,
And made him as immortal as his fame;
In love and verse his Ovid he 'ad outdone, [2]
And all his laurels, and his Julia won. [3]
85   Mourn, mourn, unhappy world, his loss deplore,
        The great, the charming Strephon is no
                more.
—1685

A Pindaric on the Death of our Late Sovereign: With an Ancient Prophecy on His Present Majesty [4]

I

Sad was the morn', the sadder week began,
    And heavily the god of day came on:
From ominous dreams my wondering soul
        looked out,
And saw a dire confusion round about.
5   My bed like some sad monument appeared,

Round which the mournful statues wring their
        hands and weep;
Distracted objects all! with mighty grief, prepared
    To rouse me from my painful sleep.
    Not the sad bards that wailed Jerusalem's woes,
10 (With wild neglect throughout the peopled street,
With a prophetic rage affrighting all they meet) [5]
Had mightier pangs of sorrow, mightier throes;
Ah! wretch, undone they cry! awake forlorn,
The king! the king is dead! rise! rise and mourn.

II

15   Again I bid 'em tell their sorrow's theme,
        Again they cry, *The king! the king is dead!*
Extended, cold and pale, upon the royal bed;
    Again I heard, and yet I thought it dream.
        Impossible! (I raving cry)
20   That such a monarch! such a god should die!
    And no dire warning to the world be given:
No hurricanes on earth! no blazing fires in heaven!
    The sun and tide their constant courses keep:
    That cheers the world with its life-giving reign,
25 This hastes with equal motion to the deep;
And in its usual turns revives the banks again,
        And in its soft and easy way,
    Brings up no storms or monsters from the sea,
No showers of blood, no temple's vale is rent,
30 But all is calm, and all is innocent.
    When nature in convulsions should be hurled,
    And fate should shake the fabric of the world;
Impossible! Impossible I cry!
*So great a king! so much a god! so silently should
    die!* [6]

[1] *Augustus* C. Octavius (63 B.C.E.–14 C.E.), ruler of Rome and the Roman Empire for over forty years. Virgil, Horace and Ovid were amongst the poets of his reign.

[2] *Ovid* Publius Ovidius Naso, poet (43 B.C.E.–17 C.E.), was best known in the Restoration for his love poems (*Amores*) and his poems on seduction and intrigue (*Ars Amatoria*), although references to his epic poem *Metamorphoses* were many. The leading poet in Rome by 8 C.E., he was suddenly banished by Augustus for some indiscretion, the specific nature of which is not known.

[3] *Julia* Julia (39 B.C.E.–14 C.E.), the only daughter of Augustus and Scribonia, was exiled by her father for committing adultery during her third marriage to Tiberius. Macrobius gives an account of her gentle disposition, learning and wit. It was commonly believed that Julia was the model for Corinna, to whom Ovid addressed love poems.

[4] Charles II died February 6, 1685. Despite various attempts by the Whigs to enact the Exclusion Bill (to prevent his brother James's succession), James II succeeded him.

[5] *Not the sad bards…all they meet* Behn refers to the Old Testament prophets who were called to "proclaim the word" of the Lord. Such proclamations were conventionally oracles of divine destruction and punishment, but a promise of salvation typically followed judgment.

[6] *Impossible! (I raving cry)…silently should die* (ll. 19–34) It was generally believed that the death of a monarch would be marked by some sign in the natural world (e.g. eclipse, comet), just as Christ's death was marked by an earthquake and the tearing of the veil in the temple (Matthew 27:50–51).

III

35 True I divined! when lo a voice arrived,
Welcome as that which did the crowd surprise,
When the dead Lazarus from the tomb revived,
And saw a pitying god attend his rise! [1]
Our Sovereign lives! it cried! rise and adore!
40 *Our Sovereign lives! Heaven adds one wonder more,*
To the miraculous history of his num'rous store:
Sudden as thought, or winged light'ning flies,
This chased the gloomy terrors from our eyes,
And all from sorrows, fall to sacrifice.
45 Whole hecatombs of vows the altars crown, [2]
To clear our sins that brought this vengeance down;
So the Great Saviour of the world did fall,
A bleeding victim to atone for all!
Nor were the blest apostles more revived,
50 When in the resurrection they beheld
Their faith established, and their Lord survived,
And all the holy prophecies fulfilled.
Their mighty love, by mighty joy they showed!
And if from feebler faith before,
55 They did the deity, and man adore:
What must they pay, when He confirmed the God?
Who having finished all His wonders here,
And full instructions given,
To make his bright divinity more clear;
60 Transfigured all to glory, mounts to heaven!

IV

So fell our earthly god! so loved, so mourned,

So like a god again returned. [3]
For of his message, yet a part was unperformed,
But oh! our prayers and vows were made too late,
65 The sacred dictates were already past;
And open laid the mighty book of fate,
Where the great MONARCH read his life's short date;
And for eternity prepared in haste.
He saw in th' everlasting chains
70 Of long past time and numerous things,
The fates, vicissitudes, and pains,
Of mighty monarchies, and mighty kings;
And blest his stars that in an age so vain,
Where zealous mischiefs, frauds, rebellions, reign:
75 Like Moses, he had led the murm'ring crowd,
Beneath the peaceful rule of his almighty wand;
Pulled down the golden calf to which they bowed,
And left 'em safe, entering the promised land;
And to good JOSHUA, now resigns his sway,
80 JOSHUA, by heaven and nature pointed out to lead the way. [4]

V

Full of wisdom and the power of God,
The royal PROPHET now before him stood:

---

[3] *So like...again returned* After his stroke of February 2, 1685, Charles II appeared to have a temporary remission of his illness and hopes of his recovery were made public.

[4] *Like Moses...lead the way* (ll. 75–80) Behn figures Charles II and James, Duke of York, as antitypes of Moses and Joshua respectively. Moses rescued the Israelites from captivity in Egypt and led them through the wilderness for forty years despite their murmuring. When Moses climbed Mount Sinai to receive the Ten Commandments, the Israelites fell into idolatry, worshiping a golden calf. Angered, Moses smashed the tablets of the Law, and was prevented from entering the Promised Land of Canaan as a result (Exodus 2–32). Behn omits the sin and punishment of Moses in her allusion. After advising Moses on the laws of inheritance (Numbers 27:11), God instructed him to lay hands on Joshua as a sign that he was his heir apparent (Numbers 27:18–23). Joshua was also called directly by God to lead the Israelites into the Promised Land (Joshua 1:1–2).

---

[1] *When the dead Lazarus...attend his rise* John 11:1–44.

[2] *hecatombs* a sacrifice of many victims; a great number of persons, animals or things, presented as an offering, or devoted to destruction; loosely, a large number or quantity (*OED* hecatomb *sb* 2).

On whom his hands the dying MONARCH laid,
And wept with tender joy, and blest and said:
85 *To thee, kind aid in all my fates and powers,*
Dear partner of my sad and softest hours,
Thy parting king and brother recommends
His frighted nations, and his mourning friends,
Take to thy pious care, my faithful flock.
90   *And though the shelt'ring cedar fade,*
Regard said he, *regard my tender stock:*
        The noble stems may shoot and grow
        To grace the spacious plains, and bow
Their spreading branches round thee a defensive
      shade.
95 The royal SUCCESSOR to all he hears
With sighs assented, and confirming tears.
Much more he spoke! much more he had
      expressed,
But that the charming accents of his tongue
Flew upwards, to compose a heav'nly song,
100 And left his speaking eyes to bless and tell the rest,
His eyes so much adored! whose less'ning light
Like setting suns that hasten on the night;
(Lending their glories to another sphere)
        Those sacred lights are fading here,
105 Whilst every beam above informs a star,

VI

      Which shall a nobler business know,
And influence his best loved friends below.
But oh!
No human thought can paint the grief and
      love,
110 With which the parting heroes strove.
Sad was the scene, soft looks the voice supplies,
Anguish their hearts, and languishment their
      eyes;
Not god-like Jonathan with greater pain,
Sighed his last farewell to the royal swain; [1]

115 While awful silence filled the gloomy place,
And death and midnight hung on every face.
And now the fatal hour came on,
And all the blessed powers above,
In haste to make him ALL their own,
120 Around the royal bed in shining order move.
Once more he longs to see the breaking day,
The last his mortal eyes shall e'er behold,
      And oft he asked if no kind ray,
            Its near approach foretold.
125   And when he found 'twas dawning in,
(With the cold tide of death that flowed all o'er)
Draw, draw, said he, *this cloud that hangs between,*
      And let me take my last adieu;
      Oh let me take my last—last view,
130 *For I shall never, never see it more.*
And now—
Officious angels catch his dying sighs,
And bear 'em up in triumph to the skies,
Each forms a soul! of the divinest dress!
135 For new-born kings and heroes to possess.
The last, that from the sacred fabric flew,
Made CHARLES a god! and JAMES a monarch too.
—1685

To the fair Clarinda, who made Love to me, imagined more than Woman

Fair lovely maid, or if that title be
      Too weak, too feminine for nobler thee,
Permit a name that more approaches truth:
And let me call thee, lovely charming youth.
5 This last will justify my soft complaint,
While that may serve to lessen my constraint;
And without blushes I the youth pursue,
When so much beauteous woman is in view,
Against thy charms we struggle but in vain
10 With thy deluding form thou giv'st us pain,
While the bright nymph betrays us to the swain.

---

[1] *God-like Jonathan…royal swain* Jonathan, the eldest son of King
Saul, made a covenant of friendship with David, who was to be the
next Israelite king (I Samuel 18), and risked his own life to defend

David against the anger of his father (I Samuel 20).

In pity to our sex sure thou wert sent,
That we might love, and yet be innocent:
For sure no crime with thee we can commit;
15 Or if we should—thy form excuses it.
For who, that gathers fairest flowers believes
A snake lies hid beneath the fragrant leaves.

    Thou beauteous wonder of a different kind,
Soft Cloris with the dear Alexis joined;

20 When e'er the manly part of thee, would plead
Thou tempts us with the image of the maid,
While we the noblest passions do extend
The love to Hermes, Aphrodite the friend. [1]
—1688

---

[1] *Hermes, Aphrodite* Hermaphroditus, a bisexual divinity, was the offspring of Hermes (messenger of the gods) and Aphrodite (goddess of love, beauty and fertility).

John Wilmot, Earl of Rochester
1647 – 1680

Though born into the nobility, Rochester inherited little, but he could call upon the goodwill of Charles II, at first because his father had helped the King after the Royalist defeat at the battle of Worcester, and later because the King found him amusing. At Wadham College, Oxford, he began to demonstrate poetic ability, and contributed to a university collection on the restoration of Charles II, and to another on the death of Princess Mary of Orange (1661). On leaving Oxford he went on an extended journey through France and Italy with a tutor, returning in 1664. In 1665 he volunteered for service on the *Royal Katherine,* and took part in an attack on Dutch ships in the Danish harbour of Bergen. On more than one occasion he exhibited bravery under fire.

The court of Charles II was not distinguished for adherence to puritan morality, and Rochester soon became known for drunkenness and sexual profligacy. Towards the end of his life, when ill health occasioned by his excesses brought him to a more thoughtful frame of mind, he declared that at one period he had been constantly drunk for five years together. Nevertheless, he retained his considerable poetic ability. Rochester's verse is textually complex: while he did publish a few poems in his lifetime, his work circulated primarily in manuscript and was shaped by the fluidity of manuscript transmission. A professionally produced scribal anthology was the source behind the printed editions that appeared shortly after his death. Though much of his verse might be thought offensive, to suppress it is to suppress a source of insight into an aspect of Charles II's court which occasioned racy contemporary memoirs and has inspired historical novelists and popularizing historians ever since. In his own time, it was not only the "official" puritans who disapproved of the licentiousness of the court of Charles II; it caused distress to a good many Royalists, even those like Pepys whose own lives were not beyond reproach. During his final illness, Rochester sent for Gilbert Burnet to come and hear his confession. Burnet's *Some Passages on the Life and Death of John, Earl of Rochester* (1680) has been popular reading for students of the period ever since.

☙❧☙

Song [1]

Quoth the Duchess of Cleveland to counselor Knight, [2]
"I'd fain have a prick, knew I how to come by 't.

I desire you'll be secret and give your advice:
Though cunt be not coy, reputation is nice."

5 "To some cellar in Sodom Your Grace must retire [3]
Where porters with black-pots sit round a coal-fire;
There open your case, and Your Grace cannot fail
Of a dozen of pricks for a dozen of ale."

"Is 't so?" quoth the Duchess. "Aye, by God!" quoth the whore.
10 "Then give me the key that unlocks the back door,

---

[1] The dates given for this and the following poems are those of the earliest printed texts. For more complete information see David M. Vieth, ed., *Complete Poems* (New Haven: Yale U P, 1968), 171–220; Peter Beal, *Index of English Literary Manuscripts* vol. 2, pt. 2 (London: Mansell, 1993), 225–87; and the textual apparatus in Harold Love, ed., *Works* (Oxford: Oxford U P, 1998).

[2] *Duchess of Cleveland* Barbara Palmer, formerly Countess of Castlemaine. One of the most important mistresses of Charles II in the decade after the Restoration, she had several other lovers; *Knight* Mary Knight, singer and minor mistress of Charles II.

[3] *Sodom* in reference to a disreputable district of London.

For I'd rather be fucked by porters and car-men [1]
Than thus be abused by Churchill and Jermyn." [2]
—1680

Upon His Leaving His Mistress

'Tis not that I am weary grown
   Of being yours, and yours alone;
But with what face can I incline
To damn you to be only mine?
5   You, whom some kinder power did fashion,
      By merit and by inclination,
      The joy at least of one whole nation.

Let meaner spirits of your sex
With humbler aims their thoughts perplex,
10 And boast if by their arts they can
Contrive to make *one* happy man;
      Whilst, moved by an impartial sense,
      Favors like nature you dispense
      With universal influence.

15 See, the kind seed-receiving earth
To every grain affords a birth.
On her no showers unwelcome fall
Her willing womb retains 'em all.
      And shall my Celia be confined?
20   No! Live up to thy mighty mind,
      And be the mistress of mankind.
—1680

A Satire Against Reason and Mankind

Were I (who to my cost already am
   One of those strange, prodigious
         creatures, man)

---

[1] *car-men* drivers of horse-drawn carts.

[2] *Churchill and Jermyn* John Churchill, who later became the Duke of Marlborough; Henry Jermyn, Master of the Horse to the Duke of York. On July 30, 1667, Pepys goes into some detail on the King quarrelling with her on Jermyn's account.

A spirit free to choose, for my own share,
What case of flesh and blood I pleased to wear,
5 I'd be a dog, a monkey, or a bear,
Or anything but that vain animal
Who is so proud of being rational.
      The senses are too gross, and he'll contrive
A sixth, to contradict the other five,
10 And before certain instinct, will prefer
Reason, which fifty times for one does err;
Reason, an *ignis fatuus* in the mind, [3]
Which, leaving light of nature, sense, behind,
Pathless and dangerous wandering ways it takes
15 Through error's fenny bogs and thorny brakes;
Whilst the misguided follower climbs with pain
Mountains of whimseys, heaped in his own brain;
Stumbling from thought to thought, falls
         headlong down
Into doubt's boundless sea, where, like to drown,
20 Books bear him up awhile, and make him try
To swim with bladders of philosophy;
In hopes still to o'ertake th' escaping light,
The vapor dances in his dazzling sight
Till, spent, it leaves him to eternal night.
25 Then old age and experience, hand in hand,
Lead him to death, and make him understand,
After a search so painful and so long,
That all his life he has been in the wrong.
Huddled in dirt the reasoning engine lies,
30 Who was so proud, so witty, and so wise.
      Pride drew him in, as cheats their bubbles catch,
And made him venture to be made a wretch.
His wisdom did his happiness destroy,
Aiming to know that world he should enjoy.
35 And wit was his vain, frivolous pretense
Of pleasing others at his own expense,
For wits are treated just like common whores:
First they're enjoyed, and then kicked out of doors.
The pleasure past, a threatening doubt remains
40 That frights th' enjoyer with succeeding pains.

---

[3] *ignis fatuus* a thing that misleads by means of fugitive appearances (*OED* will o' the wisp *fig* 1).

Women and men of wit are dangerous tools,
And ever fatal to admiring fools:
Pleasure allures, and when the fops escape,
'Tis not that they're belov'd, but fortunate,
45 And therefore what they fear at heart, they hate.
     But now, methinks, some formal band and
        beard [1]
Takes me to task. Come on, sir; I'm prepared.
    "Then, by your favor, anything that's writ
Against this gibing, jingling knack called wit
50 Likes me abundantly; but you take care
Upon this point, not to be too severe.
Perhaps my muse were fitter for this part,
For I profess I can be very smart
On wit, which I abhor with all my heart.
55 I long to lash it in some sharp essay,
But your grand indiscretion bids me stay
And turns my tide of ink another way.
    "What rage ferments in your degenerate mind
To make you rail at reason and mankind?
60 Blest, glorious man! to whom alone kind heaven
An everlasting soul has freely given,
Whom his great Maker took such care to make
That from himself he did the image take
And this fair frame in shining reason dressed
65 To dignify his nature above beast;
Reason, by whose aspiring influence
We take a flight beyond material sense,
Dive into mysteries, then soaring pierce
The flaming limits of the universe,
70 Search heaven and hell, find out what's acted there,
And give the world true grounds of hope and fear."
    Hold, mighty man, I cry, all this we know
From the pathetic pen of Ingelo,
From Patrick's *Pilgrim*, Sibbes' soliloquies, [2]

75 And 'tis this very reason I despise:
This supernatural gift, that makes a mite
Think he's the image of the infinite,
Comparing his short life, void of all rest,
To the eternal and the ever blest;
80 This busy, puzzling stirrer-up of doubt
That frames deep mysteries, then finds 'em out,
Filling with frantic crowds of thinking fools
Those reverend bedlams, colleges and schools;
Borne on whose wings, each heavy sot can pierce
85 The limits of the boundless universe;
So charming ointments make an old witch fly
And bear a crippled carcass through the sky.
'Tis this exalted power, whose business lies
In nonsense and impossibilities,
90 This made a whimsical philosopher
Before the spacious world, his tub prefer, [3]
And we have modern cloistered coxcombs who
Retire to think, 'cause they have nought to do.
    But thoughts are given for action's government;
95 Where action ceases, thought's impertinent.
Our sphere of action is life's happiness,
And he who thinks beyond, thinks like an ass.
Thus, whilst against false reasoning I inveigh,
I own right reason, which I would obey:
100 That reason which distinguishes by sense
And gives us rules of good and ill from thence,
That bounds desires with a reforming will
To keep 'em more in vigor, not to kill.
Your reason hinders, mine helps to enjoy,
105 Renewing appetites yours would destroy.
My reason is my friend, yours is a cheat;
Hunger calls out, my reason bids me eat;
Perversely, yours your appetite does mock:
This asks for food, that answers, "What's o'clock?"
110 This plain distinction, sir, your doubt secures:
'Tis not true reason I despise, but yours.
    Thus I think reason righted, but for man,
I'll ne'er recant; defend him if you can.

---

[1] *some formal band and beard* some pedantic scholar or clergyman.

[2] *From the pathetic pen...Sibbes' soliloquies* Nathaniel Ingelo (ca. 1621–1683), author of sermons, poetry and a religious romance; Simon Patrick (1626–1707), author of *The Parable of the Pilgrim*; Richard Sibbes (1577–1635), Puritan divine who published sermons and verse.

[3] *a whimsical philosopher* Diogenes the Cynic.

For all his pride and his philosophy,
115 'Tis evident beasts are, in their degree,
As wise at least, and better far than he.
Those creatures are the wisest who attain,
By surest means, the ends at which they aim.
If therefore Jowler finds and kills his hares
120 Better than Meres supplies committee chairs, [1]
Though one's a statesman, th' other but a hound,
Jowler, in justice, would be wiser found.
     You see how far man's wisdom here extends;
Look next if human nature makes amends:
125 Whose principles most generous are, and just,
And to whose morals you would sooner trust.
Be judge yourself, I'll bring it to the test:
Which is the basest creature, man or beast?
Birds feed on birds, beasts on each other prey,
130 But savage man alone does man betray.
Pressed by necessity, they kill for food;
Man undoes man to do himself no good.
With teeth and claws by nature armed, they hunt
Nature's allowance, to supply their want.
135 But man, with smiles, embraces, friendship, praise,
Inhumanly his fellow's life betrays;
With voluntary pains works his distress,
Not through necessity, but wantonness.
     For hunger or for love they fight and tear,
140 Whilst wretched man is still in arms for fear.
For fear he arms, and is of arms afraid,
By fear to fear successively betrayed;
Base fear, the source whence his best passions came:
His boasted honor, and his dear-bought fame;
145 That lust of power, to which he's such a slave,
And for the which alone he dares be brave;
To which his various projects are designed;
Which makes him generous, affable, and kind;
For which he takes such pains to be thought wise,
150 And screws his actions in a forced disguise,
Leading a tedious life in misery
Under laborious, mean hypocrisy.

---
[1] *Meres*   Sir Thomas Meres (1635–1715) was often Chairman when
the House of Commons sat as a committee of the whole.

Look to the bottom of his vast design,
Wherein man's wisdom, power, and glory join:
155 The good he acts, the ill he does endure,
'Tis all from fear, to make himself secure.
Merely for safety, after fame we thirst,
For all men would be cowards if they durst.
     And honesty's against all common sense:
160 Men must be knaves, 'tis in their own defence.
Mankind's dishonest; if you think it fair
Amongst known cheats to play upon the square,
You'll be undone.
Nor can weak truth your reputation save:
165 The knaves will all agree to call you knave.
Wronged shall he live, insulted o'er, oppressed,
Who dares be less a villain than the rest.
     Thus, sir, you see what human nature craves:
Most men are cowards, all men should be knaves.
170 The difference lies, as far as I can see,
Not in the thing itself, but the degree,
And all the subject matter of debate
Is only: Who's a knave of the first rate?

     All this with indignation have I hurled
175 At the pretending part of the proud world,
Who, swollen with selfish vanity, devise
False freedoms, holy cheats, and formal lies
Over their fellow slaves to tyrannize.
     But if in Court so just a man there be
180 (In Court a just man, yet unknown to me)
Who does his needful flattery direct,
Not to oppress and ruin, but protect
(Since flattery, which way soever laid,
Is still a tax on that unhappy trade);
185 If so upright a statesman you can find,
Whose passions bend to his unbiased mind,
Who does his arts and policies apply
To raise his country, not his family,
Nor, whilst his pride owned avarice withstands,
190 Receives close bribes through friends' corrupted
          hands—
     Is there a churchman who on God relies;

Whose life, his faith and doctrine justifies?
Not one blown up with vain prelatic pride, [1]
Who, for reproof of sins, does man deride;
195 Whose envious heart makes preaching a pretense,
With his obstreperous, saucy eloquence,
To chide at kings, and rail at men of sense;
None of that sensual tribe whose talents lie
In avarice, pride, sloth, and gluttony;
200 Who hunt good livings, but abhor good lives;
Whose lust exalted to that height arrives
They act adultery with their own wives,
And ere a score of years completed be,
Can from the lofty pulpit proudly see
205 Half a large parish their own progeny;
Nor doting bishop who would be adored
For domineering at the council board,
A greater fop in business at fourscore,
Fonder of serious toys, affected more,
210 Than the gay, glittering fool at twenty proves
With all his noise, his tawdry clothes, and loves;
    But a meek, humble man of honest sense,
Who, preaching peace, does practice continence;
Whose pious life's a proof he does believe
215 Mysterious truths, which no man can conceive.
If upon earth there dwell such God-like men,
I'll here recant my paradox to them,
Adore those shrines of virtue, homage pay,
And, with the rabble world, their laws obey.
220   If such there be, yet grant me this at least:
Man differs more from man, than man from beast.
—1679 (ll. 1–173), 1680

The Disabled Debauchee [2]

As some brave admiral, in former war
Deprived of force, but pressed with courage still,

Two rival fleets appearing from afar,
    Crawl to the top of an adjacent hill;

5 From whence, with thoughts full of concern, he views
    The wise and daring conduct of the fight,
Whilst each bold action to his mind renews
    His present glory and his past delight;

From his fierce eyes flashes of fire he throws,
10   As from black clouds when lightning breaks away;
Transported, thinks himself amidst the foes,
    And absent, yet enjoys the bloody day;

So, when my days of impotence approach,
    And I'm by pox and wine's unlucky chance
15 Forced from the pleasing billows of debauch
    On the dull shore of lazy temperance,

My pains at least some respite shall afford
    While I behold the battles you maintain
When fleets of glasses sail about the board,
20   From whose broadsides volleys of wit shall rain.

Nor let the sight of honorable scars,
    Which my too forward valor did procure,
Frighten new-listed soldiers from the wars:
    Past joys have more than paid what I endure.

25 Should any youth (worth being drunk) prove nice,
    And from his fair inviter meanly shrink,
'Twill please the ghost of my departed vice
    If, at my counsel, he repent and drink.

Or should some cold-complexioned sot forbid,
30   With his dull morals, our bold night-alarms,
I'll fire his blood by telling what I did
    When I was strong and able to bear arms.

I'll tell of whores attacked, their lords at home;
    Bawds' quarters beaten up, and fortress won;

---

[1] *prelatic* A prelate is a high-ranking church dignitary.

[2] The verse-form of this poem is that of the heroic stanza, that is, an iambic pentameter quatrain, rhyming abab. Here used satirically, it was commonly used in the period for serious works.

35 Windows demolished, watches overcome;
    And handsome ills by my contrivance done.

Nor shall our love-fits, Chloris, be forgot,
    When each the well-looked linkboy strove
        t' enjoy, [1]
And the best kiss was the deciding lot
40   Whether the boy fucked you, or I the boy.

With tales like these I will such thoughts inspire
    As to important mischief shall incline:
I'll make him long some ancient church to fire,
    And fear no lewdness he's called to by wine.

45 Thus, statesmanlike, I'll saucily impose,
    And safe from action, valiantly advise;
Sheltered in impotence, urge you to blows,
    And being good for nothing else, be wise.
—1680

Song

By all love's soft, yet mighty powers,
    It is a thing unfit
That men should fuck in time of flowers, [2]
    Or when the smock's beshit.

5 Fair nasty nymph, be clean and kind,
    And all my joys restore
By using paper still behind
    And sponges for before.

My spotless flames can ne'er decay
10   If after every close,
My smoking prick escape the fray
    Without a bloody nose.

If thou wouldst have me true, be wise
    And take to cleanly sinning;

15 None but fresh lovers' pricks can rise
    At Phyllis in foul linen.
—1680

The Imperfect Enjoyment [3]

Naked she lay, clasped in my longing arms,
I filled with love, and she all over charms;
Both equally inspired with eager fire,
Melting through kindness, flaming in desire.
5 With arms, legs, lips close clinging to embrace,
She clips me to her breast, and sucks me to her
    face.
Her nimble tongue, Love's lesser lightning, played
Within my mouth, and to my thoughts conveyed
Swift orders that I should prepare to throw
10 The all-dissolving thunderbolt below.
My fluttering soul, sprung with the pointed kiss,
Hangs hovering o'er her balmy brinks of bliss.
But whilst her busy hand would guide that part
Which should convey my soul up to her heart,
15 In liquid raptures I dissolve all o'er,
Melt into sperm, and spend at every pore.
A touch from any part of her had done 't:
Her hand, her foot, her very look's a cunt.
    Smiling, she chides in a kind murmuring
        noise,
20 And from her body wipes the clammy joys,
When, with a thousand kisses wandering o'er
My panting bosom, "Is there then no more?"
She cries. "All this to love and rapture's due;
Must we not pay a debt to pleasure too?"
25   But I, the most forlorn, lost man alive,
To show my wished obedience vainly strive:
I sigh, alas! and kiss, but cannot swive.
Eager desires confound my first intent,
Succeeding shame does more success prevent,

---

[1] *linkboy* a boy employed to carry a link (a torch made of tow and pitch) to light passengers along the street (*OED* link-boy *sb* 3).

[2] *flowers* the menstrual discharge (*OED* flower *sb* 2b).

---

[3] Rochester's contribution to a group of contemporary poems treating sexual disappointment, all loosely inspired by Ovid, *Amores*, III.vii; see Aphra Behn's "The Disappointment."

30 And rage at last confirms me impotent.
Ev'n her fair hand, which might bid heat return
To frozen age, and make cold hermits burn,
Applied to my dead cinder, warms no more
Than fire to ashes could past flames restore.
35 Trembling, confused, despairing, limber, dry,
A wishing, weak, unmoving lump I lie.
This dart of love, whose piercing point, oft tried,
With virgin blood ten thousand maids have dyed;
Which nature still directed with such art
40 That it through every cunt reached every heart—
Stiffly resolved, 'twould carelessly invade
Woman or man,[1] nor ought its fury stayed:
Where'er it pierced, a cunt it found or made—
Now languid lies in this unhappy hour,
45 Shrunk up and sapless like a withered flower.

    Thou treacherous, base deserter of my flame,
False to my passion, fatal to my fame,
Through what mistaken magic dost thou prove
So true to lewdness, so untrue to love?
50 What oyster-cinder-beggar-common whore
Didst thou e'er fail in all thy life before?
When vice, disease, and scandal lead the way,
With what officious haste dost thou obey!
Like a rude, roaring hector in the streets
55 Who scuffles, cuffs, and justles all he meets,
But if his King or country claim his aid,
The rakehell villain shrinks and hides his head;
Ev'n so thy brutal valor is displayed,
Breaks every stew,[2] does each small whore invade,
60 But when great Love the onset does command,
Base recreant to thy price, thou dar'st not stand.
Worst part of me, and henceforth hated most,
Through all the town a common fucking post,
On whom each whore relieves her tingling cunt
65 As hogs on gates do rub themselves and grunt,
Mayst thou to ravenous chancres be a prey,
Or in consuming weepings waste away;

---

[1] *or man* Some manuscripts read "Woman, nor man" (the heterosexual reading); another, less textually reliable group offers "or boy."

[2] *stew* (more often stews) brothel.

May strangury and stone thy days attend;[3]
May'st thou ne'er piss, who didst refuse to spend
70 When all my joys did on false thee depend.
    And may ten thousand abler pricks agree
    To do the wronged Corinna right for thee.[4]
—1680

A Ramble in St. James's Park [5]

Much wine had passed, with grave discourse
Of who fucks who, and who does worse[6]
(Such as you usually do hear
From those that diet at the Bear),[7]
5 When I, who still take care to see
Drunkenness relieved by lechery,
Went out into St. James's Park
To cool my head and fire my heart.
But though St. James has th' honor on 't,
10 'Tis consecrate to prick and cunt.
There, by a most incestuous birth,
Strange woods spring from the teeming earth;
For they relate how heretofore,
When ancient Pict began to whore,
15 Deluded of his assignation
(Jilting, it seems, was then in fashion),
Poor pensive lover, in this place
Would frig upon his mother's face;
Whence rows of mandrakes tall did rise
20 Whose lewd tops fucked the very skies.[8]
Each imitative branch does twine

---

[3] *strangury and stone* diseases of the urinary tract.

[4] *Corinna* Ovid's principal mistress in *Amores*.

[5] *Ramble* defined by Samuel Johnson as "to rove loosely in lust"; the "ramble poem" was a popular satirical sub-genre in the period.

[6] For a contemporary poem that takes this kind of "grave discourse" for its subject, see "Court Satire."

[7] *the Bear* a tavern.

[8] *ancient Pict...very skies* This passage parodies Edmund Waller's "On the Park at St. James's" (1660), which celebrated the planting of new trees in the park by Charles II.

In some loved fold of Aretine, [1]
And nightly now beneath their shade
Are buggeries, rapes, and incests made.
25 Unto this all-sin-sheltering grove
Whores of the bulk and the alcove, [2]
Great ladies, chambermaids, and drudges,
The ragpicker, and heiress trudges.
Car-men, divines, great lords, and tailors,
30 Prentices, poets, pimps, and jailers,
Footmen, fine fops do here arrive,
And here promiscuously they swive.
    Along these hallowed walks it was
That I beheld Corinna pass.
35 Whoever had been by to see
The proud disdain she cast on me
Through charming eyes, he would have swore
She dropped from heaven that very hour,
Forsaking the divine abode
40 In scorn of some despairing god.
But mark what creatures women are:
How infinitely vile, when fair!
    Three knights o' th' elbow and the slur [3]
With wriggling tails made up to her.
45   The first was of your Whitehall blades,
Near kin t' th' Mother of the Maids; [4]
Graced by whose favor he was able
To bring a friend t' th' Waiters' table, [5]

Where he had heard Sir Edward Sutton
50 Say how the King loved Banstead mutton; [6]
Since when he'd ne'er be brought to eat
By 's good will any other meat.
In this, as well as all the rest,
He ventures to do like the best,
55 But wanting common sense, th' ingredient
In choosing well not least expedient,
Converts abortive imitation
To universal affectation.
Thus he not only eats and talks
60 But feels and smells, sits down and walks,
Nay looks, and lives, and loves by rote,
In an old tawdry birthday coat.
    The second was a Gray's Inn wit, [7]
A great inhabiter of the pit, [8]
65 Where critic-like he sits and squints,
Steals pocket handkerchiefs, and hints,
From 's neighbor, and the comedy,
To court, and pay, his landlady.
    The third, a lady's eldest son
70 Within few years of twenty-one,
Who hopes from his propitious fate,
Against he comes to his estate,
By these two worthies to be made
A most accomplished tearing blade.
75   One, in a strain 'twixt tune and nonsense,
Cries, "Madam, I have loved you long since.
Permit me your fair hand to kiss";
When at her mouth her cunt cries, "Yes!"
In short, without much more ado,
80 Joyful and pleased, away she flew,
And with these three confounded asses
From park to hackney coach she passes.

---

[1] *Aretine* referring to the illustrations of sexual postures that accompanied sixteenth-century editions of sonnets by Pietro Aretino.

[2] *bulk...alcove* referring to women of the lowest and highest social standings: bulks were stalls that projected out from shop fronts (*OED* bulk sb²); the alcove was the part of a room of state in which the monarch's bed was placed.

[3] *knights o' th' elbow and the slur* gamblers; to slur was to throw dice so that they did not roll (hence, to cheat at dice).

[4] *The first* Rochester sketches the character of a would-be courtier. Whitehall Palace was the home of the Restoration court, to which this young man has gained entrance by being related to the governess of the Queen's maids of honour.

[5] *Waiters' table* not the table for those who served food (a position of some honour), but for those who more generally "waited" on the King.

---

[6] *Sutton...mutton* Sir Edward Sutton was a Gentleman of the Privy Chamber. Since "mutton" was slang for prostitute, our young man may have misunderstood Sutton's reference to the King's fondness for mutton from Banstead Downs, Surrey.

[7] *Gray's Inn* one of the Inns of Court, London's centre for legal education and an important site of literary production.

[8] *great inhabiter of the pit* a frequent theatre-goer.

So a proud bitch does lead about
Of humble curs the amorous rout,
85 Who most obsequiously do hunt
The savory scent of salt-swoln cunt.
Some power more patient now relate
The sense of this surprising fate.
Gods! that a thing admired by me
90 Should fall to so much infamy.
Had she picked out, to rub her arse on,
Some stiff-pricked clown or well-hung parson,
Each job of whose spermatic sluice
Had filled her cunt with wholesome juice,
95 I the proceeding should have praised
In hope sh' had quenched a fire I raised.
Such natural freedoms are but just:
There's something generous in mere lust.
But to turn damned abandoned jade
100 When neither head nor tail persuade;
To be a whore in understanding,
A passive pot for fools to spend in!
The devil played booty, sure, with thee
To bring a blot on infamy.
105   But why am I, of all mankind,
To so severe a fate designed?
Ungrateful! Why this treachery
To humble, fond, believing me,
Who gave you privilege above
110 The nice allowances of love?
Did ever I refuse to bear
The meanest part your lust could spare?
When your lewd cunt came spewing home
Drenched with the seed of half the town,
115 My dram of sperm was supped up after
For the digestive surfeit water. [1]
Full gorgèd at another time
With a vast meal of nasty slime
Which your devouring cunt had drawn
120 From porters' backs and footmen's brawn,
I was content to serve you up

My ballock-full for your grace cup, [2]
Nor ever thought it an abuse
While you had pleasure for excuse—
125 You that could make my heart away
For noise and color, and betray
The secrets of my tender hours
To such knight-errant paramours,
When, leaning on your faithless breast,
130 Wrapped in security and rest,
Soft kindness all my powers did move,
And reason lay dissolved in love!
        May stinking vapors choke your womb
Such as the men you dote upon!
135 May your depravèd appetite,
That could in whiffling fools delight,
Beget such frenzies in your mind
You may go mad for the north wind,
And fixing all your hopes upon 't
140 To have him bluster in your cunt,
Turn up your longing arse t' th' air
And perish in a wild despair!
But cowards shall forget to rant,
Schoolboys to frig, old whores to paint;
145 The Jesuits' fraternity
Shall leave the use of buggery;
Crab-louse, inspired with grace divine,
From earthly cod to heaven shall climb;
Physicians shall believe in Jesus,
150 And disobedience cease to please us,
Ere I desist with all my power
To plague this woman and undo her.
But my revenge will best be timed
When she is married that is limed. [3]
155 In that most lamentable state
I'll make her feel my scorn and hate:
Pelt her with scandals, truth or lies,
And her poor cur with jealousies,

---

[1] *surfeit water* a remedy for overdrinking or overeating.

[2] *grace cup* a final drink, consumed after grace has been said to end the meal.

[3] *limed* technical term for the impregnation, or coupling, of a bitch (*OED* lime *v* [3]).

160 Till I have torn him from her breech,
While she whines like a dog-drawn bitch;
Loathed and despised, kicked out o' th' Town
Into some dirty hole alone,
To chew the cud of misery
And know she owes it all to me.
165   And may no woman better thrive
        That dares profane the cunt I swive!
—1680

A Song of a Young Lady to her Ancient Lover

Ancient person, for whom I
    All the flattering youth defy,
Long be it ere thou grow old,
Aching, shaking, crazy, cold;
5   But still continue as thou art,
        Ancient person of my heart.

On thy withered lips and dry,
Which like barren furrows lie,
Brooding kisses I will pour
10   Shall thy youthful heat restore
(Such kind showers in autumn fall,
And a second spring recall);
        Nor from thee will ever part,
        Ancient person of my heart.

15   Thy nobler part, which but to name
In our sex would be counted shame,
By age's frozen grasp possessed,
From his ice shall be released,
And soothed by my reviving hand,
20   In former warmth and vigor stand.
All a lover's wish can reach
For thy joy my love shall teach,
And for thy pleasure shall improve
All that art can add to love.

25   Yet still I love thee without art,
Ancient person of my heart.
—1691

Signior Dildo [1]

You ladies all of merry England
    Who have been to kiss the Duchess's hand,
Pray, did you lately observe in the show
A noble Italian called Signior Dildo?

5   This signior was one of Her Highness's train,
And helped to conduct her over the main;
But now she cries out, "To the Duke I will go!
I have no more need for Signior Dildo."

At the Sign of the Cross in St. James's Street, [2]
10   When next you go thither to make yourselves sweet
By buying of powder, gloves, essence, or so,
You may chance t' get a sight of Signior Dildo.

You'll take him at first for no person of note
Because he appears in a plain leather coat,
15   But when you his virtuous abilities know,
You'll fall down and worship Signior Dildo.

My Lady Southesk, heavens prosper her for 't! [3]
First clothed him in satin, then brought him to
    Court;
But his head in the circle he scarcely durst show,
20   So modest a youth was Signior Dildo.

---

[1] This poem was occasioned by the marriage of James, Duke of York, to Mary of Modena. After a proxy wedding in Italy, the Duchess was met by the Duke at Dover on November 21, 1673, and the marriage ceremony was repeated.

[2] *St. James's Street* a fashionable street close by St. James's Palace, the Duke's residence.

[3] *Lady Southesk* Ann Hamilton, wife of the Earl of Southesk, was rumored to be one of the mistresses of the Duke of York.

The good Lady Suffolk, thinking no harm,
Had got this poor stranger hid under her arm.
Lady Betty by chance came the secret to know, [1]
And from her own mother stole Signior Dildo.

25 The Countess of Falmouth, of whom people tell,
Her footmen wear shirts of a guinea an ell, [2]
Might save the expense if she did but know
How lusty a swinger is Signior Dildo.

By the help of this gallant the Countess of Ralph [3]
30 Against the fierce Harrys preserved herself safe.
She stifled him almost beneath her pillow,
So closely sh' embraced Signior Dildo.

Our dainty fine duchesses have got a trick
To dote on a fool for the sake of his prick:
35 The fops were undone, did Their Graces but know
The discretion and vigor of Signior Dildo.

That pattern of virtue, Her Grace of Cleveland,
Has swallowed more pricks than the ocean has sand;
But by rubbing and scrubbing so large it does grow,
40 It is fit for just nothing but Signior Dildo.

The Duchess of Modena, though she looks high [4]
With such a gallant is contented to lie,
And for fear the English her secrets should know,
For a Gentleman Usher took Signior Dildo.

45 The countess o' th' Cockpit (Who knows not her
     name? [5]
She's famous in story for a killing dame),
When all her old lovers forsake her, I trow
She'll then be contented with Signior Dildo.

Red Howard, red Sheldon, and Temple so tall [6]
50 Complain of his absence so long from Whitehall;
Signior Bernard has promised a journey to go [7]
And bring back his countryman Signior Dildo.

Doll Howard no longer with 's Highness must
     range, [8]
And therefore is proffered this civil exchange:
55 Her teeth being rotten, she smells best below,
And needs must be fitted for Signior Dildo.

St. Albans, with wrinkles and smiles in his face, [9]
Whose kindness to strangers becomes his high place,
In his coach and six horses is gone to Borgo [10]
60 To take the fresh air with Signior Dildo.

Were this signior but known to the citizen fops,
He'd keep their fine wives from the foremen of
     shops;
But the rascals deserve their horns should still grow
For burning the Pope and his nephew Dildo.

---

[1] *Lady Suffolk* wife of the Earl of Suffolk; *Lady Betty* Elizabeth Howard, the daughter of Lady Barbara Suffolk.

[2] *The Countess of Falmouth* Mary Bagot, widow of the Earl of Falmouth; *an ell* the English ell was forty-five inches (*OED* ell 1).

[3] *Countess of Ralph* Elizabeth, wife of Ralph Montagu, who later became Earl and Duke of Montagu. Rhyming "Ralph" with "safe" is an English upper class pronunciation.

[4] *Duchess of Modena* Laura d'Este, Regent of Modena and mother of Mary of Modena, the new wife of James, Duke of York.

[5] *The countess o' th' Cockpit* The reference is uncertain. Some speculate that she was Anna Maria, widow of Francis Talbot, Earl of Shrewsbury, others that she was Nell Gwyn.

[6] *Red Howard, red Sheldon, and Temple so tall* Anne Howard, Frances Sheldon and Phillipa Temple, Maids of Honor to the Queen.

[7] *Signior Bernard* possibly Don Bernardo de Salinas, a Spanish diplomat.

[8] *Doll Howard* Dorothy Howard, sister to Anne Howard and Maid of Honor to the Queen.

[9] *St. Albans* Henry Jermyn, Earl of St. Albans. See the notes to the preceding poem.

[10] *Borgo* an Italian town close to Modena.

65   Tom Killigrew's wife, north Holland's fine
       flower, [1]
At the sight of this signior did fart and belch sour,
And her Dutch breeding farther to show,
Says, "Welcome to England, Mynheer Van
     Dildo!"

He civilly came to the Cockpit one night,
70   And proffered his service to fair Madam Knight. [2]
Quoth she, "I intrigue with Captain Cazzo; [3]
Your nose in mine arse, good Signior Dildo!"

This signior is sound, safe, ready, and dumb
As ever was candle, carrot, or thumb;
75   Then away with these nasty devices, and show
How you rate the just merits of Signior Dildo.

Count Cazzo, who carries his nose very high,
In passion he swore his rival should die;
Then shut up himself to let the world know
80   Flesh and blood could not bear it from Signior
     Dildo.

A rabble of pricks who were welcome before,
Now finding the Porter denied 'em the door,

Maliciously waited his coming below
And inhumanly fell on Signior Dildo.

85   Nigh wearied out, the poor stranger did fly,
And along the Pall Mall they followed full cry;
The women, concerned, from every window
Cried, "Oh! for heavens' sake, save Signior
     Dildo!"

The good Lady Sandys burst into a laughter [4]
90   To see how the ballocks came wobbling after,
And had not their weight retarded the foe,
Indeed 't had gone hard with Signior Dildo.
—1703

Impromptu on Charles II

God bless our good and gracious King,
  Whose promise none relies on;
Who never said a foolish thing,
    Nor ever did a wise one.
—1707

---

[1] *Tom Killigrew's wife* Charlotte, wife of Tom Killigrew the playwright, was First Lady of the Queen's Privy Chamber.

[2] *Madam Knight* Mary Knight; singer and mistress of Charles II.

[3] *Cazzo* colloquial Italian for "penis."

[4] *Lady Sandys* Lady Lucy Sandys was an acquaintance of Nell Gwyn and frequently at Court.

Elinor James

pub. 1675 – 1715

The polemical pamphleteer Elinor James was the working partner of her husband Thomas James, a successful London printer. Described by her contemporary John Dunton as a "she-state-politician," James wrote and self-published over twenty-three polemical broadsheets and pamphlets dedicated, for the most part, to the defence of the Anglican Church and conservative politics. Her staunch support of James II and her resistance to the settlement of the Glorious Revolution resulted in a conviction for "dispersing scandalous and reflective papers"; as a result, she was briefly committed to Newgate in December, 1689. While James's publications frequently offer religious and political advice to monarchs and Parliament alike, the substance of her corpus is more varied than is often acknowledged. James offers her opinion on a range of civic matters: taxation, public firework displays and apprenticeship. After her husband's death in 1711, James carried on the printing business. The date of her death is unknown.

☙❧

An Injured Prince Vindicated, or, A Scurrilous and Detracting Pamphlet Answered [1]

What none, that dare in hand to take a pen;
And vindicate the most abused of men!
My once dread lord and sovereign, royal James,
So oft by Whigs reduced to hard extremes. [2]
5　First pluck the beam from thy most cursed eye,
And meddle not with principality: [3]
The mote in his but small, yet big by vogue,
As mountain Alps; cries every rebel rogue.
Valour and conduct his companions were,
10　Nor did he foreign enemies e'er fear.
But when domestics leave their lord forlorn,
And throw him to a mob's contempt and scorn, [4]
Who robbed and stripped from him his very
　　clothes, [5]
As far from all remorse, as some break oaths.
15　Then finds an injured prince the greatest woe,
That ever rightful monarch e'er can know.
A king he was, and from a king he came,
A slaughtered king, to Whigs' eternal shame. [6]
Nor can the poison of their lying lips,
20　His sacred name and harmless life eclipse.
His pious memory will fame outlive;
Justice and truth his character shall give.
Down cursing Shimei and rude Rabshakey,
With false Ahitophel, who would betray
25　So well as him, even his and future all; [7]

---

[1] This broadsheet was issued in 1688, the year in which James II fled from England to France under the threat of invasion by William of Orange, his son-in-law.

[2] *Whigs* a name applied to the Exclusioners of 1679 who opposed the succession of James, Duke of York, to the throne, on the grounds of his being a Roman Catholic (*OED* Whig *sb*[2] A.3a).

[3] *First pluck…cursed eye* "Thou hypocrite, first cast out the beam out of thine own eye; and then shalt thou see clearly to cast out the mote out of thy brother's eye" (Matthew 7:5).

[4] *leave* emended from "leaves"; *throw* emended from "throws."

[5] *stripped from him his very clothes* emended from "Who robbed and stripped him from his very clothes."

[6] *A slaughtered king* Charles I.

[7] *Shimei* the son of Gera and a kinsman of Saul; he cursed and cast stones at King David, who was in flight from his son Absalom's rebellion (II Samuel 16:5–8); *Rabshakey* the field commander of the Assyrian army who derided God and berated King Hezekiah (II Kings 18:17–37; Isaiah 36:22); *Ahitophel* David's counsellor; he conspired with Absalom to usurp his father's throne (II Samuel 16:20–23; 17:1–3). In defences of Charles II and James II, Ahitophel represents

Where Whigs in council sit, there princes fall.
But O you damned rebels, who is it dare,
Assault one single and anointed hair?
The sacred unction by heaven's vicar shed, [1]
30 Preserves each royal consecrated head.
Long strove ye vipers, as ye once have done,
So well as father, to destroy the son.
Mistaken monsters, heaven did only try,
Whether a king could a good martyr die;
35 Else had he never come within your claws;
Ye breakers of divine and human laws.
Since such a thing permitted was to be,
'Twas left to a tribe composed of infamy.
The Almighty their great wickedness foreknew,
40 Had they the King of Heaven, the same they'd do:
Him if they could, they would re-crucify;

And impiously dethrone the deity.
These are the cursed destroying fiends of woe,
These are those thorns, on whom no grapes can
   grow;
45 These are those choking thistles bear no figs; [2]
These are Cain's cursed seed, Furies and Whigs. [3]
These are the murderers of our tranquil rest,
These even are those, we all ought to detest.
—1688

---

the "wicked politician" who schemes to depose the lawful monarch.

[1] *sacred unction* anointing with oil as a symbol of investing with the office of kingship (*OED* unction 2); *heaven's vicar* presumably, in this instance, the Archbishop of Canterbury as God's representative on earth, during the Coronation ceremony; see *OED* vicar 1.

[2] *those thorns…no figs* "Beware of false prophets, which come to you in sheep's clothing, but inwardly they are ravening wolves. Ye shall know them by their fruits. Do men gather grapes of thorns, or figs of thistles?" (Matthew 7:15–16); *bear* emended from "bears."

[3] *Cain's cursed seed* Cain, the firstborn of Adam and Eve, killed his brother Abel because God preferred Abel's offering (Genesis 4:1–17); *Furies* the avenging deities; generally avenging and tormenting spirits (*OED* fury *sb* 5a).

Thomas Wharton
1648 – 1715

In January 1687, James II appointed his friend and fellow Roman Catholic Richard Talbot, Earl and Duke of Tyrconnel (1630–91), to the position of Lord Deputy of Ireland. Tyrconnel was also general of the Irish army, a force with which he was now expected to protect James II and the Catholic cause in England. Thomas Wharton, a staunch Whig and supporter of the Protestant William of Orange, wrote *Lilli Burlero* shortly after the much-opposed appointment, adopting a pseudo-Irish brogue to present a conversation between two Irishmen celebrating Tyrconnel's appointment. Set to a tune by Henry Purcell, the song became popular only after it was revived in October 1688, when Irish troops entered England to bolster James's weakening position. The lyrics fit well in their new context: while the "Protestant wind" of line 18 referred originally to the storms which delayed Tyrconnel's arrival in Ireland, for example, it could now stand for William and his approaching fleet. Wharton later boasted that the song "sung a deluded Prince out of three kingdoms"; Gilbert Burnet wrote that *Lilli Burlero* "Made an impression on the army that cannot be imagined by those who saw it not. The whole army and at last the people, both in city and country, were singing it perpetually." A host of new songs were set to the tune, including one written by the government of James II, hoping to capitalize on the popularity of the original.

Thomas Wharton, later made Marquis of Wharton, corresponded with William of Orange in 1688 and joined him in Exeter; he would go on to an active political career and would himself become Lord-Lieutenant of Ireland in 1708. Lady Mary Wortley Montagu described him as "the most profligate, impious, and shameless of men." Henry Purcell (?1658–1695) began his career as a choirboy in the Chapel Royal, and was made the organist at Westminster Abbey in 1679. One of the greatest of English composers, he wrote for the opera and the theatre as well as composing popular songs, sacred music, and instrumental music.

⁊⁊⁊

Lilli Burlero

Ho, brother Teague, dost hear de decree, [1]
  Lilli burlero, bullen a-la;
Dat we shall have a new debittie,
  Lilli burlero bullen a-la,
5   Lero lero, lero lero, lilli burlero, bullen a-la;
    Lero lero, lero lero, lilli burlero, bullen a-la. [2]

Ho, by my shoul, it is a Talbot,
And he will cut de Englishman's troat.

Though, by my shoul, de English do prat,
10 De law's on dare side, and Chreist knows what.

But if dispense do come from de Pope,
Weel hang Magno Cart and demselves on a rope. [3]

And the good Talbot is made a lord,
And he with brave lads is coming aboard.

15 Who'll all in France have taken a swear,
Dat day will have no Protestant heir.

Oh, but why does he stay behind,
Ho, by my shoul, 'tis a Protestant wind.

---

[1] *Teague* cant nickname for an Irishman (*OED*).

[2] The phrases in the refrain, parodies of Irish, are probably meaningless.

[3] *Magno Cart* Magna Carta, signed in 1215, guaranteed justice and security from illegal interference.

Now Tyrconnel is come a-shore,
20 And we shall have commissions gillore.

And he dat will not go to mass,
Shall turn out and look like an ass.

Now, now, de heretics all go down, [1]
By Chreist and St. Patrick, the nation's our own!
—1687

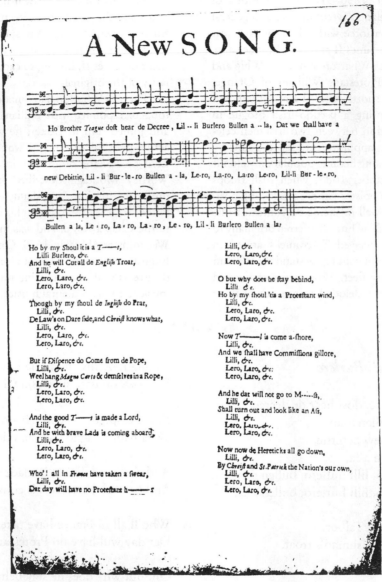

Lilli Burlero, with Purcell's music, as printed in a 1688 broadsheet

[1] *heretics* Protestants.

Jane Barker
1652 – 1732

Jane Barker, who wrote verse, prose fiction and essays, was born in Blatherwicke, Northamptonshire, on May 17, 1652 to Thomas Barker and Anne Connock. Thomas Barker, a Royalist, had served as Secretary to the Great Seal of England in the court of Charles I. By 1662, Barker had moved with her family to Wilsthorpe, Lincolnshire, where her father held a lease on a manor house and sizable agricultural property owned by John Cecil, fourth Earl of Exeter. Barker's "autobiographical novels" suggest that after the death of her father and elder brother, she and her mother left Wilsthorpe for London, where she became intimate with Royalist sympathizers and converted to Roman Catholicism. After the Revolution of 1688, Barker followed the Stuarts into exile in France and lived in St. Germain-en-Laye. In 1688 Barker published *Poetical Recreations,* a collection of her poems followed by the verses of Cambridge students, friends of her late brother Edward. Panegyrics to virginity are scattered throughout this collection; these may reflect a defence of female independence, though they should also be considered within the broader discourse of Catholic polemics. While living in France, Barker wrote several poems in honour of the royal family and in 1700 presented a manuscript book of her poems to the Prince of Wales. Barker returned to England in 1704 to live on her farm at Wilsthorpe, where she resided with her niece Mary Barker and subsequently with Mary's two daughters. Barker paid an annual rent of £47 10s for the land at Wilsthorpe, and because she was a Roman Catholic, her leasehold property was subject to double taxation. Economic straits may have required Barker to write for profit. Between 1713 and 1726, she published five works of prose fiction and a translation of Bishop Fénelon's Lenten meditations. In 1726, Barker was near death and received the last rites. She recovered, however, and traveled to France in May, 1727. Barker attributed her survival to the miraculous curative powers of a cloth dipped in the blood of the dying James II, reporting that a touch of this cloth cured her niece's diseased eye and a cancerous tumor on her breast. There is a record of Barker's death on March 29, 1732 in the parish register of St. Germain-en-Laye.

ഇൗൟ

An Invitation to my Friends at Cambridge

If, friends, you would but now this place accost,
Ere the young spring that epithet has lost,
And of my rural joys participate;
You'd learn to talk at this distracted rate.[1]

5   Hail, solitude, where innocence does shroud
Her unveiled beauties from the cens'ring crowd;
Let me but have her company, and I
Shall never envy this world's gallantry:
We'll find out such inventions to delude
10   And mock all those that mock our solitude,
That they for shame shall fly for their defence
To gentle solitude and innocence:
Then they will find how much they've been
      deceived,
When they the flatt'ries of this world believed.
15   Though to few objects here we are confined,
Yet we have full enlargement of the mind.
From varying modes, which do our lives enslave, [2]
Lo here a full immunity we have.
For here's no pride but in the sun's bright beams,
20   Nor murmuring, but in the crystal streams.

---

[1] *accost* approach (*OED* accost *v* 5); *epithet* an adjective indicating some quality characteristic of the thing described (*OED* epithet *sb* 1a).

[2] *modes* fashions, customs (*OED* mode II.7).

No avarice is here, but in the bees,
Nor is ambition found but in the trees. [1]
No wantonness but in the frisking lambs,
Nor luxury but when they suck their dams.
25   Nor are there here contrivances of states,
Only the birds contrive to please their mates;
Each minute they alternately improve
A thousand harmless ways their artless love.
No cruel nymphs are here to tyrannize,
30   Nor faithless youths their scorn to exercise;
Unless Narcissus be that sullen he
That can despise his am'rous talking she. [2]
No emulation here does interpose,
Unless betwixt the tulip and the rose; [3]
35   But all things do conspire to make us blessed,
(Yet chiefly 'tis contentment makes the feast)
'Tis such a pleasing solitude as yet
Romance ne'er found, where happy lovers met:
Yea such a kind of solitude it is,
40   Not much unlike to that of paradise,
Where all things do their choicest good dispense,
And I too here am placed in innocence.
I should conclude that such it really were,
But that the Tree of Knowledge won't grow here: [4]
45   Though in its culture I have spent some time,
Yet it disdains to grow in our cold clime,
Where it can neither fruit nor leaves produce
Good for its owner, or the public use.

How can we hope our minds then to adorn
50   With anything with which they were not born;
Since we're denied to make this small advance,
To know their nakedness and ignorance? [5]
For in our Maker's laws we've made a breach,
And gathered all that was within our reach,
55   Which since we ne'er could touch; Although our
    eyes
Do serve our longing souls to tantalize,
Whilst kinder fate for you does constitute
Luxurious banquets of this dainty fruit.
Whose tree most fresh and flourishing does grow,
60   E'er since it was transplanted amongst you; [6]
And you in wit grow as its branches high,
Deep as its root too in philosophy;
Large as its spreading arms your reasons grow,
Close as its umbrage does your judgments show;
65   Fresh as its leaves your sprouting fancies are,
Your virtues as its fruits are bright and fair.
—1688

A Virgin Life

Since, O ye powers, ye have bestowed on me
So great a kindness for virginity,
Suffer me not to fall into the powers
Of men's almost omnipotent amours;
5   But in this happy life let me remain,
Fearless of twenty five and all its train,
Of slights or scorns, or being called old maid,
Those goblings which so many have betrayed: [7]
Like harmless kids, that are pursued by men,

---

[1] *ambition*   the ardent desire to rise (*OED* ambition *sb* 1).

[2] *Narcissus*   In classical mythology, a young man who died of self-love after seeing his reflection in water; he was transformed into a flower; *am'rous talking she*   Echo. In love with Narcissus, Echo (who could only repeat what others said) tried to attract Narcissus with fragments of his own speech, but was rejected and wasted away with grief, leaving nothing but her voice.

[3] *emulation*   ambitious rivalry for power or honours (*OED* emulation 2).

[4] *Tree of Knowledge*   The tree of the knowledge of good and evil was planted in the Garden of Eden. Adam and Eve were prohibited from eating its fruit: "But of the tree of the knowledge of good and evil, thou shalt not eat of it: for in the day that thou eatest thereof thou shalt surely die" (Genesis 2:17).

[5] *to know…ignorance*   Before eating fruit from the tree of the knowledge of good and evil, Adam and Eve were innocent in their nakedness and without sin: "And they were both naked, the man and his wife, and were not ashamed" (Genesis 2:25). After eating the fruit, "the eyes of them both were opened, and they knew that they were naked: and they sewed fig leaves together, and made themselves aprons" (Genesis 3:7).

[6] *you*   her friends at Cambridge.

[7] *goblings*   goblins.

10　For safety run into a lion's den.
　　Ah lovely state how strange it is to see,
　　What mad conceptions some have made of thee,
　　As though thy being was all wretchedness,
　　Or foul deformity i'th'ugliest dress;
15　Whereas thy beauty's pure, celestial,
　　Thy thoughts divine, thy words angelical:
　　And such ought all thy votaries to be, [1]
　　Or else they're so, but for necessity.
　　A virgin bears the impress of all good,
20　In that dread name all virtue's understood:
　　So equal all her looks, her mien, her dress, [2]
　　That nought but modesty seems in excess.
　　And when she any treats or visits make,
　　'Tis not for tattle, but for friendship's sake;
25　Her neighb'ring poor she does adopt her heirs,
　　And less she cares for her own good than theirs;
　　And by obedience testifies she can
　　Be's good a subject as the stoutest man.
　　She to her church such filial duty pays,
30　That one would think she'd lived i'th pristine days.
　　Her closet, where she does much time bestow, [3]
　　Is both her library and chapel too,
　　Where she enjoys society alone,
　　I'th'Great Three-One—
35　She drives her whole life's business to these ends,
　　To serve her God, enjoy her books and friends.
　　—1688

The Prospect of a Landscape, Beginning with a Grove [4]

　　Well might the ancients deem a grove to be
　　　The sacred mansion of some deity;
　　For it our souls insensibly does move,
　　At once to humble piety and love,
5　The choicest blessings heaven to us has given,
　　And the best offering we can make to heaven;
　　These only poor mortality make blessed,
　　And to inquietude exhibit rest;
　　By these our rationality is shown,
10　The cognisance by which from brutes we're
　　　known.
　　For who themselves of piety divest,
　　Are surely but a mortal kind of beasts;
　　But those whom gentle laws of love can't bind,
　　Are savages of the most sordid kind.
15　But none like these do in our shades obtrude,
　　Though scornfully some needs will call them rude.
　　Yet Nature's culture is so well expressed,
　　That Art herself would wish to be so dressed:
　　For here the sun conspires with every tree,
20　To deck the earth with landscape-tapestry.
　　Then through some space his brightest beams
　　　appear,
　　Which does erect a golden pillar there.
　　Here a close canopy of bows is made,
　　There a soft grassy cloth of state is spread,
25　With gems and gayest flowers embroidered o'er,
　　Fresh as those beauties honest swains adore.
　　Here plants for health, and for delight are met,
　　The cephalic cowslip, cordial violet.
　　Under the diuretic woodbine grows
30　The splenetic columbine, scorbutic rose; [5]

---

[1]　*votaries*　devout worshippers (*OED* votary *sb* I.1b, 2b).

[2]　*mien*　the air, bearing, carriage, or manner of a person (*OED* mien *sb*[1] a).

[3]　*closet*　a room for privacy or retirement, especially a place of private devotion (*OED* closet *sb* 1a, b).

---

[4]　This belongs to a three-poem series celebrating the natural landscape, taking for their subjects a grove, a rivulet, and a hill. The third poem remained unfinished.

[5]　*cephalic cowslip…scorbutic rose*　Cowslip was believed to relieve disorders of the head (*OED* cephalic *a* 2). Violet was a remedy for invigorating the heart (*OED* cordial *a* 2). Columbine was thought to

The best of which, some gentle nymph doth take,
For faithful Corydon a crown to make; [1]
Whilst on her lap the happy youth's head lies,
Gazing upon the aspects of her eyes,
35 The most unerring, best astronomy,
Whereby to calculate his destiny;
Whilst o'er their heads a pair of turtles coo, [2]
Which with less zeal and constancy do woo;
And birds around, through their extended throats,
40 In careless consort chant their pleasing notes;
Than which, no sweeter music strikes the ear,
Unless when lovers' sighs each other hear;
Which are more soft than austral breezes bring, [3]
Although they say they're harbingers of th'spring.
45   Ah silly town! wil't thou ne'er learn to know,
What happiness in solitude does grow?
But as a hardened sinner for's defence,
Pleads the insipidness of innocence;
Of some whom virtue due respect would grant,
50 But that they feign they're of her ignorant:
Yet blindness is not laudable to plead,
When we're by wilfull ignorance misled.
Should some, who think't a happiness to get
Crowds of acquaintance, to admire their wit;
55 Resolve their sins and follies to discard,
Their cronies quickly would them disregard.
    'Tis hard we must (the world's so wicked grown)
Be complaisant in sin, or live alone:
For those who now with virtue are endued,
60 Do live alone, though in a multitude.
Retire then all, whom fortune don't oblige,
To suffer the distresses of a siege.
Where strong temptation virtue does attack,
'Tis not ignoble an escape to make:

65 But where no conquest can be hoped by fight,
'Tis honourable, sure, to 'scape by flight.
Fly to some calm retreat, where you may spend
Your life in quietude with some kind friend;
In some small village, and adjacent grove,
70 At once your friendship and your wit improve;
Free from those vile, opprobrious, foolish names,
Of Whig or Tory, and from sordid aims
Of wealth, and all its train of luxuries;
From wit sophisticate, with fooleries.
75 From beds of lust, and meals o'ercharged with
        wine,
Here temperately thou may'st on one dish dine:
In wholesome exercise thou may'st delight
Thyself, and make thy rest more sweet at night.
And if thy mind to contemplation leads,
80 Who God and Nature's books has, surely needs
No other object to employ his thought,
Since in each leaf such mysteries are wrought;
That whoso studies most, shall never know
Why the straight elm's so tall, the moss so low.
85 Oh now, I could enlarge upon this theme,
But that I'm unawares come to the stream,
Which at the bottom of this grove does glide;
And here I'll rest me by its flowery side.
—1688

To My Young Lover

Incautious youth, why do'st thou so misplace
Thy fine encomiums on an o'erblown face; [4]
Which after all the varnish of thy quill,
Its pristine wrinkles show apparent still:
5 Nor is it in the power of youth to move
An age-chilled heart to any strokes of love.
Then choose some budding beauty, which in time
May crown thy wishes in thy blooming prime:
For nought can make a more preposterous show,

---

relieve the "spleen," a disorder caused by melancholy or depression of
the spirits (*OED* splenetic *a* A.2b, 5). The rose was believed to cure
scurvy (*OED* scorbutic *a* A.2).

[1] *Corydon* a generic proper name for a rustic in pastoral poetry
(*OED*).

[2] *turtles* turtle doves.

[3] *austral breezes* the south wind, warm and moist (*OED*).

---

[4] *encomiums* formal or high-flown expressions of praise (*OED*
encomium).

10 Than April flowers stuck on St. Michael's brow. [1]
To consecrate thy first-born sighs to me
A superannuated deity; [2]
Makes that idolatry and deadly sin,
Which otherwise had only venial been.
—1688

To My Friends Against Poetry

Dear friends, if you'll be ruled by me,
Beware o'th'charms of poetry;
And meddle with no fawning Muse,
They'll but your harmless loves abuse.
5 Though to Orinda they were tied, [3]
That nought their friendship could divide;
And Cowley's Mistress had a flame [4]
As pure and lasting as his fame:
Yet now they're all grown prostitutes,
10 And wantonly admit the suits
Of any fop, that will pretend
To be their servant or their friend.
Though they to wit no homage pay,
Nor yet the laws of verse obey,
15 But ride poor six-foot out of breath, [5]
And wrack a metaphor to death;
Who make their verse imbibe the crimes;

And the lewd follies too o'th'times; [6]
Who think all wit consists in ranting,
20 And virtuous love in wise gallanting:
And thousand sorts of fools, like these,
Make love and virtue what they please:
And yet as silly as they show,
Are favourites o'th' Muses now,
25 Who then would honour such a she,
Where fools their happier rivals be?
We, surely, may conclude there's none,
Unless they're drunk with Helicon, [7]
Which is a liquor that can make
30 A dunce set up for rhyming quack:
A liquor of so strange a temper,
As can our faculties all hamper;
That whoso drinks thereof is cursed
Unto a constant rhyming thirst;
35 I know not by what spell of witch,
It strikes the mind into an itch;
Which being scrubbed by praise, thereby
Becomes a spreading leprosy;
As hard to cure as dice or whore,
40 And makes the patient too as poor;
For poverty's the certain fate
Which attends a poet's state.
—1688

---

[1] *St. Michael's brow* emended from "bow," which makes no iconographic sense since St. Michael is portrayed with a sword; show/brow is a possible rhyme at this period. Note the rhyme show/now in "To All My Friends Against Poetry." The Feast of St. Michael the Archangel is on September 29; the poet is contrasting the spring of her young lover with her own autumn.

[2] *superannuated* old and infirm (*OED* superannuated *ppl.a* 1).

[3] *Orinda* The poet and translator Katherine Philips (1631–1664) was known as "the matchless Orinda."

[4] *Cowley's Mistress* Cowley's poem *The Mistress* was published in 1647.

[5] *poor six-foot* the hexameter line.

[6] *imbibe* absorb; take into one's mind or moral system (*OED* imbibe *v* II.2. trans.).

[7] *Helicon* the largest mountain in Boeotia, sacred to the Muses. The spring Hippocrene, the inspiration of poets, is a little below the summit.

John Oldham
1653 – 1683

Oldham was born in Gloucestershire, the son and grandson of ministers. He was educated first by his father and then at Tetbury grammar school, where he is also believed to have worked as a private tutor. Oldham then entered St. Edmund Hall, Oxford, and received his B.A. in 1674. Shortly thereafter, he took the position of usher at the Whitgift school at Croydon, a position he held for three years. He composed a number of works at this time, one of which, *Satire Against Virtue*, seems to have attracted the attention of the Earl of Rochester. From 1678 until 1681 he was tutor to the grandsons of Sir Edward Thurland. During this time he began to publish his works. The first of his *Satires upon the Jesuits* and the *Satire against Virtue* were published for the first time in 1679 (perhaps piratically); both were republished in 1681 along with other pieces. Oldham's work exhibits a variety of styles, including odes, and paraphrases of biblical and classical poetry, but much of it is satirical, in imitation of the Roman satirists Juvenal and Horace. At the end of 1681, Oldham became tutor to the son of Sir William Hickes, and through him met Dr. Richard Lower, who apparently encouraged him to study medicine, which he seems to have done for about a year. He made some influential acquaintances during this time, including William Pierrepont, Earl of Kingston, who became his patron, and Dryden. Oldham died of smallpox. Although his life was short, his influence reached forward to Pope and other eighteenth-century satirists.

❦

An Imitation of Horace [1]

BOOK I. SATIRE IX

Ibam fortè viâ sacrâ, &c. [2]

As I was walking in the *Mall* of late, [3]
Alone, and musing on I know not what;
Comes a familiar fop, whom hardly I
Knew by his name, and rudely seizes me: [4]
5 "Dear Sir, I'm mighty glad to meet with you:
And pray, how have you done this Age, or two?"
"Well I thank God" (said I) "as times are now:
I wish the same to you." And so past on
Hoping with this the Coxcomb would be gone. [5]
10 But when I saw I could not thus get free;
I ask'd, what business else he had with me?
"Sir" (answer'd he) "if learning, parts, or sense
Merit your friendship; I have just pretense."
"I honor you" (said I) "upon that score,
15 And shall be glad to serve you to my power."
Mean time, wild to get loose, I try all ways
To shake him off: Sometimes I walk apace,
Sometimes stand still: I frown, I chafe, I fret,
Shrug, turn my back, as in the *Bagnio*, sweat: [6]
20 And show all kind of signs to make him guess
At my impatience and uneasiness.
"Happy the folk in Newgate!" (whisper'd I) [7]
"Who, tho' in chains are from this torment free:

---

[1] *Horace* (65–8 B.C.E.) Roman poet, contemporary of Virgil, known for his Epistles, Odes and Satires.

[2] *Ibam fortè viâ sacrâ, &c* I was walking by chance along the Sacred Way.

[3] *the Mall* a walk bordered by trees in St. James's Park, London, which was a fashionable promenade (*OED* mall [1] 4a).

[4] *fop* a conceited person, a pretender to wit, wisdom or accomplishments (*OED* fop *sb* 2).

[5] *Coxcomb* a foolish, conceited, showy person, vain of his accomplishments, appearance, or dress (*OED* coxcomb 3).

[6] *Bagnio* a bathing house; especially one with hot baths, vapour baths, and appliances for sweating (*OED* bagnio 1).

[7] *Newgate* a London prison.

Would I were like rough Manly in the play,[1]
25 To send impertinents with kicks away!"
    He all the while baits me with tedious chat,
Speaks much about the drought, and how the rate
Of hay is rais'd, and what it now goes at:
Tells me of a new comet at the *Hague*,
30 Portending God knows what, a dearth, or plague:
Names every wench, that passes through the park,
How much she is allow'd, and who the spark
That keeps her: points, who lately got a clap,[2]
And who at the *Groom-Porters* had ill hap[3]
35 Three nights ago in play with such a Lord:
When he observ'd, I minded not a word,
And did no answer to his trash afford;
"Sir, I perceive you stand on thorns" (said he)
"And fain would part: but, faith, it must not be:
40 Come, let us take a bottle." (I cried) "No;
Sir, I am in a course, and dare not now."[4]
"Then tell me whither you design to go:
I'll wait upon you." "Oh! Sir, 'tis too far:
I visit cross the water: therefore spare
45 Your needless trouble." "Trouble! Sir, 'tis none:
'Tis more by half to leave you here alone.
I have no present business to attend,
At least which I'll not quit for such a friend:
Tell me not of the distance: for I vow,
50 I'll cut the Line, double the Cape for you,
Good faith, I will not leave you: make no words:
Go you to Lambeth? Is it to my Lord's?[5]
His steward I most intimately know,
Have often drunk with his Comptroller too."

55 By this I found my wheedle would not pass,
But rather serv'd my suff'rings to increase:
And seeing 'twas in vain to vex, or fret,
I patiently submitted to my fate.
    Strait he begins again: "Sir, if you knew
60 My worth but half so throughly as I do;
I'm sure, you would not value any friend,
You have, like me: but that I won't commend
My self, and my own talents; I might tell
How many ways to wonder I excel.
65 None has a greater gift in Poetry,
Or writes more verses with more ease than I:
I'm grown the envy of the men of wit,
I kill'd ev'n Rochester with grief and spite:[6]
Next for the dancing part I all surpass,
70 St. André never mov'd with such a grace:[7]
And 'tis well known, when e'r I sing, or set,
Humphreys, nor Blow could ever match me yet."[8]
    Here I got room to interrupt: "Have you
A mother, Sir, or kindred living now?"
75 "Not one: they are all dead." "Troth, so I guessed:
The happier they" (said I) "who are at rest.
Poor I am only left unmurder'd yet:
Haste, I beseech you, and dispatch me quite:
For I am well convinc'd, my time is come:
80 When I was young, a gypsy told my doom:"
"This Lad" (saith she, and look'd upon my hand)
"Shall not by sword, or poison come to's end,
Nor by the fever, dropsy, gout, or stone,[9]
But he shall die by an eternal tongue:
85 Therefore, when he's grown up, if he be wise,

---

[1] *Manly* the hero of William Wycherley's play, *The Plain Dealer*.

[2] *clap* gonorrhoea (*OED* clap *sb²*).

[3] *Groom-Porters* officers of the Royal Household, whose principal function was to regulate all matters connected with gaming within the precincts of the court (*OED* groom-porter 1). The reference is to a gaming establishment; see Pepys, *Diary*, January 1, 1668, for a vivid account of his visit; *hap* chance or fortune; luck (*OED* hap *sb*¹1).

[4] *in a course* under a course of treatment by a physician.

[5] *Lambeth* the residence of the Archbishop of Canterbury; the "My Lord" the speaker refers to.

[6] *Rochester* The Earl of Rochester had died shortly before this poem was written.

[7] *St. André* the French choreographer of dance in Thomas Shadwell's tragedy, *Psyche*.

[8] *Humphreys, nor Blow* Pelham Humfrey was Master of the Children at the Chapel Royal. Dr. John Blow, organist and prominent English composer, was his successor.

[9] *dropsy* a morbid condition characterized by the accumulation of watery fluid in the serous cavities or the connective tissue of the body (*OED* dropsy *sb (a.)* 1).

Let him avoid great talkers, I advise."
By this time we were got to *Westminster*, [1]
Where he by chance a Trial had to hear,
And, if he were not there, his cause must fall:
90 "Sir, if you love me, step into the hall
For one half hour." "The Devil take me now,"
(Said I) "if I know any thing of law:
Besides I told you whither I'm to go."
Here at he made a stand, pull'd down his hat
95 Over his eyes, and mus'd in deep debate:
"I'm in a strait" (said he) "what I shall do:"
"Whether forsake my business, Sir, or you."
"Me by all means" (says I). "No" (says my sot) [2]
"I fear you'll take it ill, if I should do't:
100 I'm sure, you will." "Not I, by all that's good.
But I've more breeding, than to be so rude.
Pray, don't neglect your own concerns for me:
Your Cause, good Sir!" "My Cause be damn'd"
    (says he)
"I value't less than your dear company."
105 With this he came up to me, and would lead
The way; I sneaking after hung my head.
    Next he begins to plague me with the plot, [3]
Asks, whether I were known to Oates or not?
"Not I, thank Heaven! I no priest have been:
110 Have never *Douai* nor *St. Omers* seen." [4]
"What think you, Sir? will they Fitz-Harris try? [5]
Will he die, think you?" "Yes, most certainly."

"I mean, be hang'd." "Would thou wert so"
    (wish'd I).
Religion came in next; though he'd no more
115 Than the French King, his punk, or confessor. [6]
"Oh! the sad times, if once the King should die!
Sir, are you not afraid of Popery?" [7]
"No more than my superiors: why should I?
I've no estate in Abbey-lands to lose."
120 "But fire and faggot, Sir, how like you those?"
"Come Inquisition, anything" (thought I)
"So Heav'n would bless me to get rid of thee:
But 'tis some comfort, that my Hell is here:
I need no punishment hereafter fear."
125 Scarce had I thought, but he falls on anew
"How stands it, Sir, betwixt his Grace, and you?" [8]
"Sir, he's a man of sense above the crowd,
And shuns the converse of a multitude."
"Ay, Sir," (says he) "you're happy, who are near
130 His Grace, and have the favour of his ear:
But let me tell you, if you'll recommend
This person here, your point will soon be gain'd.
Gad, Sir, I'll die, if my own single wit
Don't fob his minions, and displace 'em quite, [9]
135 And make your self his only Favourite."
"No, you are out abundantly" (said I)
"We live not, as you think: no family
Throughout the whole three Kingdoms is more free
From those ill customs, which are us'd to swarm
140 In great men's houses; none e'r does me harm,
Because more learned, or more rich, than I:
But each man keeps his place, and his degree."
"'Tis mighty strange" (says he) "what you relate,"
"But nothing truer, take my word for that."
145 "You make me long to be admitted too

---

[1] *Westminster* location of the law courts.

[2] *sot* a foolish or stupid person (*OED* sot *sb*[1] A1).

[3] *the plot* The Popish Plot of 1678 was fabricated by Titus Oates, who claimed that Catholics were planning to assassinate Charles II and place his Catholic brother James, Duke of York, on the throne. Some thirty-five people were executed in the frenzy that followed.

[4] *Douai…St. Omers* seminaries at which priests were trained. Oates was expelled from St. Omers shortly before he perpetrated the Popish Plot.

[5] *Fitz-Harris* a Catholic, arrested for treasonous libel in 1681, who claimed to have extensive information regarding the Popish Plot, and unsuccessfully tried to use this information to avoid execution.

---

[6] *the French King, his punk* the French King is Louis XIV; *punk* prostitute, strumpet, harlot (*OED* punk *sb*[1]).

[7] *the sad times….are you not afraid of Popery* referring to the possibility that the Catholic James would succeed his brother as King.

[8] *his Grace* the Archbishop of Canterbury.

[9] *fob his minions* deceive his favored followers; *fob* cheat, deceive, delude (*OED* fob *v*[1]).

Amongst his creatures: Sir, I beg, that you
Will stand my friend: Your interest is such,
You may prevail, I'm sure, you can do much.
He's one, that may be won upon, I've heard,
150 Though at the first approach access be hard.
I'll spare no trouble of my own, or friends,
No cost in fees and bribes to gain my ends:
I'll seek all opportunities to meet
With him, accost him in the very street:
155 Hang on his coach, and wait upon him home,
Fawn, scrape and cringe to him, nay to his Groom.
Faith, Sir, this must be done, if we'll be great:
Preferment comes not at a cheaper rate." [1]
       While at this savage rate he worried me;
160 By chance a Doctor, my dear friend, came by, [2]
That knew the fellow's humor passing well:
Glad of the sight, I join him; we stand still:
"Whence came you, Sir? and whither go you now?"
And such like questions past betwixt us two:
165 Straight I begin to pull him by the sleeve,
Nod, wink upon him, touch my nose, and give
A thousand hints, to let him know, that I
Needed his help for my delivery:
He, naughty wag, with an arch fleering smile [3]
170 Seems ignorant of what I mean the while:
I grow stark wild with rage. "Sir, said not you,
You'd somewhat to discourse, not long ago,
With me in private? I remember't well:"
"Some other time, be sure, I will not fail:
175 Now I am in great haste upon my word:
A messenger came for me from a Lord,
That's in a bad condition, like to die."
"Oh! Sir, he can't be in a worse, than I:
Therefore for God's sake do not stir from hence."
180 "Sweet Sir! your pardon: 'tis of consequence:

I hope you're kinder than to press my stay,
Which may be Heav'n knows what out of my way."
This said, he left me to my murderer:
Seeing no hopes of my relief appear;
185 "Confounded be the stars" (said I) "that sway'd
This fatal day! would I had kept my bed
With sickness, rather than been visited
With this worse plague! what ill have I e'r done
To pull this curse, this heavy judgment down?"
190   While I was thus lamenting my ill hap,
Comes aid at length: a brace of bailiffs clap [4]
The rascal on the back: "Here take your fees,
Kind gentlemen" (said I) for my release."
He would have had me bail. "Excuse me, Sir,
195 I've made a vow ne're to be surety more: [5]
My father was undone by't heretofore."
       Thus I got off, and blest the fates that he
       Was Pris'ner made, I set at liberty.
—1681

Upon a Bookseller,
that expos'd him by printing a piece of his
grossly mangled, and faulty

CHRISTMAS 1680 REIGATE

Dull and unthinking! had'st thou none but me
To plague and urge to thine own infamy?
Had I some tame and sneaking Author been,
Whose muse to love and softness did incline,
5 Some small adventurer in song, that whines
Phyllis and *Chloris* out in charming lines [6]
Fit to divert mine Hostess, and mislead
The heart of some poor tawdry waiting-maid;
Perhaps I might have then forgiven thee,
10 And thou had'st scap'd from my resentments free.

_____

[1] *Preferment* advancement or promotion in condition, status, or position in life (*OED* preferment I 2).

[2] *a Doctor, my dear friend, came by* Richard Lower, with whom Oldham had studied medicine.

[3] *wag* a mischievous person, a joker (*OED* wag *sb* [2]2); *fleering* grinning, grimacing (*OED* fleering *ppl.a*).

_____

[4] *brace* a pair, a couple of persons (chiefly used with a touch of humour) (*OED* brace *sb* [2] III 15d).

[5] *surety* one who makes himself liable for the default or miscarriage of another (*OED* surety *sb* II. 7).

[6] *Phyllis and Chloris* names common in pastoral verse.

But I, whom spleen, and manly rage inspire, [1]
Brook no affront, at each offence take fire:
Born to chastise the vices of the age,
Which pulpits dare not, nor the very stage,
15 Sworn to lash knaves of all degrees, and spare
None of the kind, however great they are:
Satire's my only province and delight,
For whose dear sake alone I've vow'd to write:
For this I seek occasions, court abuse,
20 To show my parts, and signalize my muse: [2]
Fond of a quarrel as young bullies are
To make their mettle and their skill appear.
And didst thou think, I would a wrong acquit,
That touch'd my tenderst part of honour, wit?
25 No Villain, may my sins ne'r pardon'd be
By Heav'n it self, if e'er I pardon thee.
    Members from breach of privilege deter
By threatning *Topham* and a messenger: [3]
Scroggs and the Brothers of the Coif oppose
30 The force and dint, of statutes and the laws: [4]
Strumpets of *Billingsgate* redress their wrongs
By the sole noise and foulness of their tongues:
And I go always arm'd for my defence,
To punish and revenge an insolence:
35 I wear my Pen, as others do their Sword,

To each affronting sot, I meet, the word
Is satisfaction; straight to thrusts I go
And pointed satire runs him through and through.
    Perhaps thou hop'dst that thy obscurity
40 Should be thy safeguard, and secure thee free:
No, wretch, I mean from thence to fetch thee out,
Like sentenc'd felons to be dragged about.
Torn, mangled, and expos'd to scorn and shame
I mean to hang and gibbet up thy name: [5]
45 If thou to live in satire so much thirst;
Enjoy thy Wish and Fame, till envy burst,
Renown'd as he, whom banish'd *Ovid* cursed, [6]
Or he, whom old *Archilochus* so stung [7]
In verse, that he for shame and madness hung:
50 Deathless in infamy do thou so live,
And let my rage like his to halters drive. [8]
    Thou thoughtst perhaps my gall was spent and
       gone
My venom drain'd, and I a senseless drone:
Thou thoughtst I had no curses left in store,
55 But to thy sorrow know and find, I've more:
More, and more dreadful yet, able to scare
Like Hell, and urge to daggers and despair:
Such, thou shalt feel, are still reserv'd by me
To vex and force thee to thy destiny:
60 Since thou hast brav'd my vengeance thus, prepare
And tremble from my pen thy doom to hear.
    Thou, who with spurious nonsense durst
       profane
The genuine issue of a poet's brain,
May'st thou hereafter never deal in verse,

---

[1] *spleen* hot or proud temper (*OED* spleen *sb* 5).

[2] *signalize* distinguish, render noteworthy (*OED* signalize *v* 1).

[3] *Members from breach of privilege…Topham and a messenger* After passing a bill in a parliamentary session in May 1679 which excluded James from succeeding his brother as King because of his Catholic faith, the Whigs, who favoured exclusion, frequently petitioned Charles II to recall Parliament in order to push the matter further. The Tories, who opposed exclusion, countered these requests with their own positions "abhorring" those of the Whigs. When the Parliament was finally assembled, it determined that abhorring was a breach of parliamentary privilege. Those who committed the offence were arrested by John Topham, the Sergeant at Arms, and his messenger, meaning officer.

[4] *Scroggs and the Brothers of the Coif* Sir William Scroggs, the Lord Chief Justice at the trials of those said to be involved in the Popish Plot, had a reputation of being unfair. *Brothers of the Coif* those who wear the coif, the white cap formerly worn by lawyers, and especially by serjeants-at-law, as a mark of their profession (*OED* coif *sb* 3).

---

[5] *gibbet* to hold up to infamy or public contempt (*OED* gibbet *v* 3).

[6] *he, whom banished Ovid cursed* In his poem, *Ibis*, the exiled Ovid curses an unnamed enemy.

[7] *he, whom old Archilochus so stung* When Lycambes rescinded on a promise to Archilochus to allow him to marry his daughter Neobule, Archilochus took revenge by writing a satire that was so cutting that Lycambes and his daughters committed suicide. See Horace, *Epistles* I.19.23 ff.

[8] *halters* the gallows (*OED* halter *sb*¹ 2b).

But what hoarse Bellmen in their walks rehearse, [1]
Or *Smithfield* audience sung on crickets hears. [2]
Mayst thou print *Howard*, or some duller ass,
Jordan, or him, that wrote *Dutch Hudibras*, [3]
Or next vile scribbler of the house, whose play
70 Will scarce for candles and their snuffing pay.
May you each other curse; thy self undone,
And he the laughing-stock of all the town.

Mayst thou ne'er rise to history, but what
Poor *Grubstreet* penny chronicles relate, [4]
75 Memoirs of *Tyburn* and the mournful state [5]
Of cutpurses in *Holborn* cavalcade, [6]
Till thou thy self be the same subject made.
Compell'd by want, mayst thou print Popery,
For which be the cart's arse and pillory [7]
80 Turnips and rotten eggs thy destiny,

Maul'd worse than *Reading, Christian*, or *Cellier*, [8]
Till thou daubed o'er with loathsome filth appear
Like brat of some vile drab, in privy found,
Which there has lain three months in ordure
    drown'd.
85 The plague of poets, rags and poverty,
Debts, writs, arrests, and serjeants light on thee;
For others bound, mayst thou to durance go, [9]
Condemn'd to scraps and begging with a shoe.
And mayst thou never from the gaol get free,
90 Till thou swear out thy self by perjury.
Forlorn, abandon'd, pitiless, and poor
As a pawn'd cully, or a mortgag'd whore, [10]
Mayst thou an halter want for thy redress, [11]
Forc'd to steal hemp to end thy miseries, [12]
95 And damn thy self to balk the Hangman's fees:
    And may no saucy fool have better fate
    That dares pull down the vengeance of my hate.
—1681

---

[1] *Bellmen*   town criers (*OED* bellman 1).

[2] *Smithfield audience sung on crickets hears*   Bartholomew Fair, which took place in Smithfield, featured crickets singing.

[3] *Mayst thou print Howard...or him, that wrote Dutch Hudibras*   Edward Howard, a much ridiculed playwright; Thomas Jordan, city poet of London, denigrated by Oldham elsewhere; *Dutch Hudibras* was published anonymously.

[4] *Grubstreet penny chronicles*   brief accounts of the crimes and execution of criminals produced by hack writers.

[5] *Tyburn*   where convicted criminals were executed.

[6] *Holborn cavalcade*   Holborn Hill was part of the journey prisoners undertook on their way from imprisonment at Newgate to execution at Tyburn.

[7] *pillory*   a contrivance for the punishment of offenders, consisting of a wooden framework erected on a post or pillar, and formed of two moveable boards, which, when brought together, leave holes through which the head and hands of an offender were thrust, in which state he was exposed to public ridicule, insult, and molestation (*OED* pillory sb).

[8] *Reading, Christian, or Cellier*   Nathanial Reading was a lawyer for Catholic lords implicated in the Popish Plot. He was sent to the pillory for attempting to bribe a witness to change his evidence. Edward Christian was pilloried for a conspiracy against the Duke of Buckingham. Elizabeth Cellier was a Catholic midwife involved in Catholic attempts to discredit Oates's tale of the Popish Plot. She was acquitted of high treason, but after publishing an account of her imprisonment and release, was pilloried for libel.

[9] *durance*   forced confinement, imprisonment, constraint (*OED* durance 5).

[10] *cully*   one who is cheated or imposed upon (*OED* cully sb 1).

[11] *halter*   a rope with a noose for hanging malefactors (*OED* halter sb[1] 2a).

[12] *hemp*   a rope for hanging (*OED* hemp sb 3).

Anne Killigrew
1660 – 1685

The poet and painter Anne Killigrew had a brief but celebrated life. She was born in St. Martin's Lane, London, the daughter of the theologian and dramatist Dr. Henry Killigrew, who served as Chaplain to the Duke of York, later James II. Her father arranged for her service as Maid of Honour to Mary of Modena, Duchess of York. Killigrew's paintings, which included portraits of James II and his Queen, were admired by her contemporaries as was her verse by Dryden himself. Anthony à Wood describes Killigrew as one who had "A Grace for beauty, and a Muse for wit." In 1685, Anne died suddenly of smallpox, and a small volume of her collected poems was published by her father simply under the title *Poems by Mrs. Anne Killigrew* (1686). Dryden's Ode, *To the Pious Memory of the Accomplished Young Lady Mistress Anne Killigrew, Excellent in the Two Sister Arts of Poesy and Painting*, was described by Dr. Johnson as "the noblest Ode that our language ever has produced." Like many young poets, Killigrew experimented with literary genre and theme, writing pastoral verse, sombre meditations, bitter satire, moral epigrams, biblical paraphrase and political panegyric.

❧

A Farewell to Worldly Joys

Farewell ye unsubstantial joys,
  Ye gilded nothings, gaudy toys,
Too long ye have my soul misled,
Too long with airy diet fed:
5 But now my heart ye shall no more
Deceive, as you have heretofore:
For when I hear such Sirens sing,
Like Ithaca's forewarned king, [1]
With prudent resolution I
10 Will so my will and fancy tie,
That stronger to the mast not he, [2]
Than I to reason bound will be:
And though your witchcrafts strike my ear,
Unhurt, like him, your charms I'll hear.
—1686

---

[1] *Like Ithaca's forewarned king* Odysseus had to pass the island of the Sirens, who enchanted unsuspecting sailors with their song, causing them to land and perish. Odysseus, warned by Circe of their powers and following her advice, passed the island safely (*Odyssey*, Book XII).

[2] *That stronger to the mast not he* On Circe's advice Odysseus, who wished to enjoy the Sirens' melody without risk, instructed his men (who plugged their ears with wax) to bind him to the mast of their ship so that he could not compel them to change course to the Sirens' meadow of death (*Odyssey*, Book XII).

The Complaint of a Lover

Seest thou yonder craggy rock,
  Whose head o'erlooks the swelling main,
Where never shepherd fed his flock,
  Or careful peasant sowed his grain.

5 No wholesome herb grows on the same,
  Or bird of day will on it rest;
'Tis barren as the hopeless flame,
  That scorches my tormented breast.

Deep underneath a cave does lie,
10 Th'entrance hid with dismal yew, [3]
Where Phoebus never showed his eye, [4]
  Or cheerful day yet pierced through.

In that dark melancholy cell,
  (Retreat and solace to my woe)

---

[3] *dismal yew* The yew tree, often planted in churchyards, was regarded as symbolic of sadness (*OED* yew *sb* 1)

[4] *Phoebus* a name of Apollo, god of the sun; the sun personified (*OED* Phoebus).

15 Love, sad despair, and I, do dwell,
       The springs from whence my griefs do flow.

Treacherous love that did appear,
    (When he at first approached my heart)
Dressed in a garb far from severe,
20   Or threatening ought of future smart.

So innocent those charms then seemed,
    When Rosalinda first I spied,
Ah! Who would them have deadly deemed?
    But flowers do often serpents hide.

25 Beneath those sweets concealed lay,
       To love the cruel foe, disdain,
With which (alas) she does repay
    My constant and deserving pain.

When I in tears have spent the night,
30   With sighs I usher in the sun,
Who never saw a sadder sight,
    In all the courses he has run.

Sleep, which to others ease does prove,
    Comes unto me, alas, in vain:
35 For in my dreams I am in love,
       And in them too she does disdain.

Some times t'amuse my sorrow, I [1]
    Unto the hollow rocks repair,
And loudly to the echo cry,
40   Ah! gentle nymph come ease my care.

Thou who, times past, a lover wert
    Ah! pity me, who now am so,
And by a sense of thine own smart,
    Alleviate my mighty woe.

45 Come flatter then, or chide my grief;
       Catch my last words, and call me fool;
Or say, she loves, for my relief;
    My passion either soothe, or school.
—1686

On a Picture Painted by Herself, Representing Two Nymphs of Diana's, One in a Posture to Hunt, the Other Bathing

We are Diana's virgin-train, [2]
    Descended of no mortal strain;
Our bows and arrows are our goods,
Our palaces, the lofty woods,
5 The hills and dales, at early morn,
Resound and echo with our horn;
We chase the hind and fallow-deer,
The wolf and boar both dread our spear;
In swiftness we outstrip the wind,
10 An eye and thought we leave behind;
We fawns and shaggy satyrs awe;
To sylvan powers we give the law: [3]
Whatever does provoke our hate,
Our javelins strike, as sure as fate;
15 We bathe in springs, to cleanse the soil,
Contracted by our eager toil;
In which we shine like glittering beams,
Or crystal in the crystal streams;
Though Venus we transcend in form,
20 No wanton flames our bosoms warm!
If you ask where such wights do dwell, [4]

---

[1] *amuse* direct attention away from; beguile (*OED* amuse *v* 4).

[2] *Diana* the moon goddess, patroness of virginity and of hunting.

[3] *sylvan powers* powers belonging to or situated in a wood or woods (*OED* sylvan *adj* B.1). A sylvan was an imaginary being supposed to haunt the woods or groves.

[4] *wights* While the term can denote living beings in general, it is chiefly applied to supernatural, preternatural, or unearthly beings (*OED* wight *sb arch.* 1b).

In what blessed clime, that so excel?
The poets only that can tell.
—1686

Upon the Saying that my Verses
were Made by Another

Next heaven my vows to thee (O sacred
        Muse!)
I offered up, nor didst thou them refuse.

O Queen of Verse, said I, if thou'lt inspire,
And warm my soul with thy poetic fire,
5 No love of gold shall share with thee my heart,
Or yet ambition in my breast have part,
More rich, more noble I will ever hold
The muse's laurel, than a crown of gold.
An undivided sacrifice I'll lay
10 Upon thine altar, soul and body pay;
Thou shalt my pleasure, my employment be,
My all I'll make a holocaust to thee. [1]

The deity that ever does attend
Prayers so sincere, to mine did condescend.
15 I writ, and the judicious praised my pen:
Could any doubt ensuing glory then?
What pleasing raptures filled my ravished sense?
How strong, how sweet, fame, was thy influence?
And thine, false hope, that to my flattered sight
20 Didst glories represent so near, and bright?
By thee deceived, methought, each verdant tree,
Apollo's transformed Daphne seemed to be; [2]
And every fresher branch, and every bough
Appeared as garlands to impale my brow.

25 The learned in love say, thus the winged boy [3]
Does first approach, dressed up in welcome joy;
At first he to the cheated lover's sight
Nought represents, but rapture and delight,
Alluring hopes, soft fears, which stronger bind
30 Their hearts, than when they more assurance find.

Emboldened thus, to fame I did commit,
(By some few hands) my most unlucky wit.
But, ah, the sad effects that from it came!
What ought t'have brought me honour, brought
        me shame!
35 Like Aesop's painted jay I seemed to all, [4]
Adorned in plumes, I not my own could call:
Rifled like her, each one my feathers tore,
And, as they thought, unto the owner bore.
My laurels thus another's brow adorned,
40 My numbers they admired, but me they scorned: [5]
Another's brow, that had so rich a store
Of sacred wreaths, that circled it before;
Where mine quite lost, (like a small stream that
        ran
Into a vast and boundless ocean)
45 Was swallowed up, with what it joined and
        drowned,
And that abyss yet no accession found.

Orinda (Albion's and her sex's grace) [6]
Owed not her glory to a beauteous face,
It was her radiant soul that shone within,
50 Which struck a lustre through her outward skin;

---

[1] *holocaust* a sacrifice wholly consumed by fire; a whole burnt
offering (*OED* holocaust *sb* 1).

[2] *Apollo's transformed Daphne* The nymph Daphne, fleeing the
unwelcome advances of Apollo, prayed for help and was turned into a
laurel tree.

[3] *winged boy* Cupid.

[4] *Aesop's painted jay* The fables of Aesop (d. 564 B.C.E.) were
translated by Roger L'Estrange in 1693. In his translation, we find
written of the jay: he "tricked himself up with all the gay-feathers he
could muster together: and upon the credit of these stolen, or
borrowed ornaments, he valued himself above all the birds in the air
beside."

[5] *numbers* metrical periods or feet; hence, lines, verses (*OED*
numbers *sb* IV.18b).

[6] *Orinda* the pseudonym of the poet and translator Katherine Philips
(1632–1664).

That did her lips and cheeks with roses dye,
Advanced her height, and sparkled in her eye.
Nor did her sex at all obstruct her fame,
But higher 'mong the stars it fixed her name;
55 What she did write, not only all allowed,
But every laurel, to her laurel, bowed!

Th'envious age, only to me alone,
Will not allow, what I do write, my own,
But let 'em rage, and 'gainst a maid conspire,
60 So deathless numbers from my tuneful lyre
Do ever flow; so Phoebus I by thee [1]
Divinely inspired and possessed may be;
I willingly accept Cassandra's fate,
To speak the truth, although believed too late. [2]
—1686

The Discontent

I

Here take no care, take here no care, my
Muse,
Nor ought of art or labour use:
But let thy lines rude and unpolished go,
Nor equal be their feet, nor numerous let them
flow.
5 The ruggeder my measures run when read,
They'll livelier paint th'unequal paths fond
mortals tread.
Who when they're tempted by the smooth
ascents,
Which flattering hope presents,
Briskly they climb, and great things
undertake;
10 But fatal voyages, alas, they make:
For 'tis not long before their feet,

Inextricable mazes meet,
Perplexing doubts obstruct their way,
Mountains withstand them of dismay;
15 Or to the brink of black despair them lead,
Where's nought their ruin to impede,
In vain for aid they then to reason call,
Their senses dazzle, and their heads turn
round,
The sight does all their powers confound,
20 And headlong down the horrid precipice
they fall:
Where storms of sighs forever blow,
Where rapid streams of tears do flow,
Which drown them in a briny flood.
My Muse pronounce aloud, there's
nothing good,
25 Nought that the world can show,
Nought that it can bestow.

II

Not boundless heaps of its admired clay,
Ah, too successful to betray,
When spread in our frail virtue's way:
30 For few do run with so resolved a pace,
That for the golden apple will not lose the race. [3]
And yet not all the gold the vain would spend,
Or greedy avarice would wish to save;
Which on the earth refulgent beams doth
send, [4]
35 Or in the sea has found a grave,
Joined in one mass, can bribe sufficient be,
The body from a stern disease to free,
Or purchase for the mind's relief
One moment's sweet repose, when restless made
by grief,
40 But what may laughter, more than pity, move:

---

[1] *Phoebus* Apollo as the god of poetry and music, presiding over the Muses (*OED* Phoebus b).

[2] *Cassandra's...too late* Cassandra was given the gift of prophecy by Apollo; when she refused his advances, he turned the blessing into a curse by causing her accurate predictions to be disbelieved.

[3] *For few...the race* a reference to Atalanta, who would marry no one who could not beat her in a foot-race; Melanion, or Hippomenes, got three golden apples from Aphrodite and delayed her by throwing them, thus winning the race (*OCD*).

[4] *refulgent* shining with, or reflecting, light (*OED* refulgent a).

When some the price of what they dearest love
Are masters of, and hold it in their hand,
To part with it their hearts they can't command:
But chose to miss, what missed does them
    torment,
45 And that to hug, affords them no content.
Wise fools, to do them right, we these must
    hold,
Who love depose, and homage pay to gold.

III

Nor yet, if rightly understood,
Does grandeur carry more of good;
50 To be o'th'number of the great enrolled,
A scepter o'er a mighty realm to hold.
      For what is this?
      If I judge not amiss.
But all th'afflicted of a land to take,
55 And of one single family to make?
    The wronged, the poor, th'oppressed, the sad,
    The ruined, malcontent, and mad?
    Which a great part of every empire frame,
    And interest in the common father claim.
60   Again what is't, but always to abide
    A gazing crowd? Upon a stage to spend
    A life that's vain, or evil without end?
And which is yet nor safely held, nor laid aside?
And then, if lesser titles carry less of care,
65 Yet none but fools ambitious are to share
Such a mock-good, of which 'tis said, 'tis best,
When of the least of it men are possessed.

IV

But, O, the laurelled fool! that dotes on fame,
Whose hope's applause, whose fear's to want a
    name;
70   Who can accept for pay
    Of what he does, what others say;
Exposes now to hostile arms his breast,
To toilsome study then betrays his rest;
    Now to his soul denies a just content,

75 Then forces on it what it does resent;
And all for praise of fools: for such are those,
Which most of the admiring crowd compose.
O famished soul, which such thin food can
    feed!
O wretched labour crowned with such a
    meed! [1]
80 Too loud, O Fame! thy trumpet is too shrill,
    To lull a mind to rest,
    Or calm a stormy breast,
Which asks a music soft and still.
'Twas not Amalek's vanquished cry,
85 Nor Israel's shout of victory,
That could in Saul the rising passion lay,
'Twas the soft strains of David's lyre the evil spirit
    chased away. [2]

V

But friendship fain would yet itself defend, [3]
    And mighty things it does pretend,
90 To be of this sad journey, life, the bait,
The sweet reflection of our toilsome state.
    But though true friendship a rich cordial be,
    Alas, by most 'tis so allayed, [4]
    Its good so mixed with ill we see,
95   That dross for gold is often paid.
    And for one grain of friendship that is found,
    Falsehood and interest do the mass compound,
Or coldness, worse than steel, the loyal heart doth
    wound.
    Love in no two was ever yet the same,
100   No happy two e'er felt an equal flame.

---

[1] *meed* reward (*OED* meed *sb* 1).

[2] *Twas not Amalek's...chased away* Saul, King of Israel, captured Agag the King of Amalek, and destroyed the Amalekites. He did not, however, despoil their property as instructed by God. As a result, God rent the kingdom of Israel from Saul, and sent an evil spirit to trouble him. Only David, Saul's successor, could refresh his tormented spirit by playing his harp (I Samuel 15 and 16).

[3] *fain* gladly, willingly, with pleasure (*OED* fain *adv B*).

[4] *allayed* debased (*OED* allayed *ppl.a* 1).

VI

Is there that earth by human foot ne'er
    pressed?
That air which never yet by human breast
    Respired, did life supply?   15
      Oh, thither let me fly!
105   Where from the world at such a distance set,
All that's past, present, and to come I may forget:
    The lover's sighs, and the afflicted's tears,
    What e'er may wound my eyes or ears.
      The grating noise of private jars,
110   The horrid sound of public wars,
      Of babbling fame the idle stories,
      The short-lived triumph's noisy glories,
      The curious nets the subtle weave,
      The word, the look that may deceive.
115   No mundane care shall more affect my breast,   25
    My profound peace shake or molest:
But stupor, like to death, my senses bind,
    That so I may anticipate that rest,
    Which only in my grave I hope to find.
—1686?

Cloris' Charms Dissolved by Eudora

I

N ot that thy fair hand
    Should lead me from my deep
      despair,
Or thy love, Cloris, end my care,
    And back my steps command:
5   But if hereafter thou retire,
To quench with tears, thy wandering fire,
    This clue I'll leave behind,
    By which thou may'st untwine
      The saddest way,
10   To shun the day,
    That ever grief did find.

II

First take thy hapless way
   Along the rocky northern shore,
   Infamous for the matchless store
     Of wracks within that bay.
None o'er the cursed beach e'er crossed,
Unless the robbed, the wracked, or lost
    Where on the strand lie spread,
    The skulls of many dead.
      Their mingled bones,   20
      Among the stones,
   Thy wretched feet must tread.

III

    The trees along the coast,
Stretch forth to heaven their blasted arms,
As if they plained the north-wind's harms,
    And youthful verdure lost.
There stands a grove of fatal yew, [1]
Where sun ne'er pierced, nor wind e'er blew.
    In it a brook doth fleet,
    The noise must guide thy feet,   30
      For there's no light,
      But all is night,
    And darkness that you meet.

IV

    Follow th'infernal wave,
Until it spread into a flood,   35
Poisoning the creatures of the wood,
    There twice a day a slave,
I know not for what impious thing,
Bears thence the liquor of that spring.
    It adds to the sad place,   40
    To hear how at each pace,
      He curses God,

---

[1] *fatal yew* The yew was associated with death because it was commonly planted in churchyards; it was doubly fatal as being poisonous and as providing the wood from which long-bows were made; see *OED* yew *sb* 1b. Compare Shakespeare, *Richard II*, III.ii.117 "their bows / of double-fatal yew."

Himself, his load,
For such his forlorn case.

V

45 Next make no noise, nor talk,
Until th'art past a narrow glade,
Where light does only break the shade;
'Tis a murderer's walk.
Observing this thou need'st not fear,
50 He sleeps the day or wakes elsewhere.
Though there's no clock or chime,
The hour he did his crime,
His soul awakes,
His conscience quakes
55 And warns him that's the time.

VI

Thy steps must next advance,
Where horror, sin, and spectres dwell,
Where the wood's shade seems turned hell;
Witches here nightly dance,
60 And sprights join with them when they call, [1]
The murderer dares not view the ball.
For snakes and toads conspire,
To make them up a quire.
And for their light,
65 And torches bright,
The fiends dance all on fire.

VII

Press on till thou descry
Among the trees, sad, ghastly, wan,
Thin as the shadow of a man,
70 One that does ever cry,
She is not; and she ne'er will be,
Despair and death, come swallow me,
Leave him; and keep thy way,
No more thou now canst stray;
75 Thy feet do stand,

In sorrow's land,
Its kingdoms every way.

VIII

Here gloomy light will show
Reared like a castle to the sky,
80 A horrid cliff there standing nigh
Shading a creek below. [2]
In which recess there lies a cave,
Dreadful as hell, still as the grave.
Sea-monsters there abide,
85 The coming of the tide,
No noise is near,
To make them fear,
God-sleep might there reside.

IX

But when the boisterous sea,
90 With roaring waves resumes this cell,
You'd swear the thunders there did dwell.
So loud he makes his plea;
So tempests bellow under ground,
And echoes multiply the sound!
95 This is the place I chose,
Changeable like my woes,
Now calmly sad,
Then raging mad,
As move my bitter throes.

X

100 Such dread besets this part,
That all the horror thou has passed,
Are but degrees to this at last.
The sight must break thy heart:
Here bats and owls that hate the light
105 Fly and enjoy eternal night.
Scales of serpents, fish-bones,
Th'adder's eye, and toad-stones
Are all the light

---

[1] *spright* spirits; supernatural beings, goblins, fairies, etc. (*OED* spright *sb¹* 1b,2).

[2] *horrid* bristling, shaggy, rough (*OED* horrid *a* 1). A secondary meaning (terrible, dreadful, frightful) is also relevant.

Hath blest my sight,
110 Since first began my groans.

XI

When thus I lost the sense
Of all the healthful world calls bliss,
And held it joy, those joys to miss,
When beauty was offence:
115 Celestial strains did rend the air,
Shaking these mansions of despair;
A form divine and bright,
Struck day through all that night,
As when heaven's queen
120 In hell was seen,
With wonder and affright!

XII

The monsters fled for fear,
The terrors of the cursed wood
Dismantled were, and where they stood,
125 No longer did appear.
The gentle power, which wrought this thing,
Eudora was, who thus did sing: [1]
Dissolved is Cloris' spell,
From whence thy evils fell,
130 *Send her this clue,*
'Tis there most due
And thy phantastic hell.

—1686

---

[1] *Eudora* The name "Eudora" means good gift.

John Tutchin
?1661 – 1707

A Whig poet and pamphleteer, Tutchin participated in the Monmouth rebellion (1685), which sought to place a Protestant candidate on the throne instead of James II. He was sentenced to seven years' imprisonment but successfully bribed his way to a pardon. In 1695 he was deprived of a minor post in the navy victualling office, and then subsequently failed to win a post in the customs office; he recorded his resentment in a later autobiographical account in which he complained of his "13 or 14 years in a fruitless attendance upon an ungrateful court."

The power of the foreign-born members of William's court roused considerable resentment in England, a xenophobia exploited for political purposes by both Tories and Jacobites. But while *The Foreigners* does display republican tendencies, Tutchin saw himself as a Whig martyr, so his motivations for attacking the Whig junto and the "upstart foreigners" of William's court differed from those of the political opposition. Tutchin was charged with libel for writing *The Foreigners*, but his use of allegory or "covert names" saved him. Dryden and Swift were using the same technique, and Tutchin seems to have borrowed some of the biblical parallels Dryden used in *Absalom and Achitophel* (e.g., Israel for England, Hebron for Scotland, Sanhedrin for Parliament). *The Foreigners* provoked several answering poems, including Daniel Defoe's *The True-Born Englishman* (1700–01); Tutchin and Defoe would later become allies, though quarrelling frequently.

❧❧❧

The Foreigners

Long time had Israel been disus'd from rest,
   Long had they been by tyrants sore
       oppressed;
Kings of all sorts they ignorantly crav'd,
And grew more stupid as they were enslav'd;
5 Yet want of grace they impiously disown'd,
And still like slaves beneath the burden groan'd:
With languid eyes their race of kings they view,
The bad too many, and the good too few;
Some robb'd their houses, and destroy'd their lives,
10 Ravish'd their daughters, and debauch'd their
       wives;
Profan'd the altars with polluted loves,
And worship'd idols in the woods and groves.
   To foreign nations next they have recourse;
Striving to mend, they made their state much
       worse.
15 They first from Hebron all their plagues did bring,

Cramm'd in the single person of a King; [1]
From whose base loins ten thousand evils flow,
Which by succession they must undergo. [2]
Yet sense of native freedom still remains,
20 They fret and grumble underneath their chains;
Incens'd enrag'd, their passion does arise,
Till at his palace-gate their monarch dies. [3]
This glorious feat was by the fathers done,
Whose children next depos'd his tyrant son, [4]
25 Made him, like Cain, a murd'rous wanderer,
Both of his crimes, and of his fortunes share.
   But still resolv'd to split on foreign shelves,
Rather than venture once to trust themselves,

---

[1] *a King* James VI of Scotland, proclaimed James I of England, Scotland, and Ireland in 1603.

[2] James was the father of Charles I, grandfather of Charles II and James II, and great-grandfather of William III.

[3] Charles I, executed in front of his palace of Whitehall in January 1649.

[4] James II, who left London in December 1688.

To foreign courts and councils do resort,
30 To find a king their freedoms to support: [1]
Of one for mighty actions fam'd they're told,
Profoundly wise, and desperately bold,
Skilful in war, successful still in fight,
Had vanquish'd hosts, and armies put to flight;
35 And when the storms of war and battles cease,
Knew well to steer the ship of state in peace.
Him they approve, approaching to their sight,
Lov'd by the Gods, of mankind the delight.
The numerous tribes resort to see him land,
40 Cover the beach, and blacken all the strand; [2]
With loud huzza's they welcome him on shore,
And for their blessing do the Gods implore.

     The Sanhedrin conven'd, at length debate [3]
The sad condition of their drooping state
45 And sinking Church, just ready now to drown;
And with one shout they do the hero crown.

     Ah Happy Israel! had there never come
Into his councils crafty knaves at home, [4]
In combination with a foreign brood,
50 Sworn foes to Israel's rights and Israel's good;
Who impiously foment intestine jars,
Exhaust our treasure, and prolong our wars;
Make Israel's people to themselves a prey,
Mislead their King, and steal his heart away:
55 United interests thus they do divide,
The State declines by avarice and pride;
Like beasts of prey they ravage all the land,
Acquire preferments, and usurp command:
The foreign inmates the housekeepers spoil,

60 And drain the moisture of our fruitful soil.
If to our Monarch there are honours due,
Yet what with Gibeonites have we to do? [5]
When foreign states employ 'em for their food,
To draw their water, and to hew their wood.
65 What mushroom honours does our soil afford!
One day a beggar, and the next a Lord. [6]
What dastard souls do Jewish nobles wear!
The Commons such affronts would never bear.
Let no historian the sad stories tell
70 Of thy base sons, Oh servile Israel!
But thou, my Muse, more generous and brave,
Shalt their black crimes from dark oblivion save;
To future ages shalt their sins disclose,
And brand with infamy thy Nation's foes.

75   A country lies, due east from Judah's shore, [7]
Where stormy winds and noisy billows roar;
A land much differing from all other soils,
Forc'd from the sea, and buttress'd up with piles.
No marble quarries bind the spongy ground,
80 But loads of sand and cockle-shells are found:
Its natives void of honesty and grace,
A boorish, rude, and an inhumane race;
From nature's excrement their life is drawn,
Are born in bogs, and nourish'd up from spawn.
85 Their hard-smok'd beef is their continual meat,
Which they with rusk, their luscious manna, eat; [8]
Such food with their chill stomachs best agrees,
They sing Hosannah to a mare's milk cheese.
To supplicate no God, their lips will move,
90 Who speaks in thunder like Almighty Jove,
But wat'ry deities they do invoke,
Who from the marshes most divinely croak.
Their land, as if asham'd their crimes to see,
Dives down beneath the surface of the sea.

---

[1] William of Orange (William III), crowned in April 1689.

[2] Since William's landing was witnessed by only a few fishermen, these lines might be ironic.

[3] *Sanhedrin* the supreme council at Jerusalem in New Testament times; here, allegorically the English Parliament.

[4] *crafty knaves* the Whig junto that controlled political affairs under William and Anne; its members included John Somers, Baron Somers; Thomas Wharton, first Baron Wharton; Charles Montagu, first Earl of Halifax; Charles Spencer, third Earl of Sunderland; and Sir Robert Walpole, first Earl of Orford.

[5] *Gibeonites* the Dutch.

[6] William raised a number of foreigners to English peerages.

[7] *A country* the Netherlands.

[8] *rusk* pieces of bread rebaked and sometimes sweetened to form a light biscuit; much used on board ships (*OED*).

95 Neptune, the God who does the seas command,
Ne'er stands on tip-toe to descry their land;
But seated on a billow of the sea,
With ease their humble marshes does survey.
These are the vermin do our state molest;
100 Eclipse our glory, and disturb our rest.
Bentir in the inglorious roll the first, [1]
Bentir to this and future ages cursed,
Of mean descent, yet insolently proud,
Shunn'd by the great, and hated by the crowd;
105 Who neither blood nor parentage can boast,
And what he got the Jewish nation lost:
By lavish grants whose provinces he gains,
Made forfeit by the Jewish people's pains;
Till angry Sanhedrins such grants resume,
110 And from the peacock take each borrow'd plume. [2]
Why should the Gibeonites our land engross,
And aggrandize their fortunes with our loss?
Let them in foreign states proudly command,
They have no portion in the promis'd land,
115 Which immemorially has been decreed
To be the birthright of the Jewish seed.
How ill does Bentir in the head appear
Of warriors, who do Jewish ensigns bear? [3]
By such we're grown e'en scandalous in war.
120 Our fathers' trophies wore, and oft could tell
How by their swords the mighty thousands fell;
What mighty deed our grandfathers had done,
What battles fought, what wreaths of honour won:
Through the extended orb they purchas'd fame,
125 The nations trembling at their awful name:
Such wondrous heroes our fore-fathers were,
When we, base souls! but pygmies are in war:
By foreign chieftains we improve in skill; [4]

We learn how to intrench, not how to kill:
130 For all our charge are good proficients made
In using both the pickax and the spade.
But in what field have we a conquest wrought?
In ten years' war what battle have we fought? [5]
    If we a foreign slave may use in war,
135 Yet why in council should that slave appear? [6]
If we with Jewish treasure make him great,
Must it be done to undermine the state?
Where are the ancient sages of renown?
No Magi left, fit to advise the crown?
140 Must we by foreign councils be undone?
Unhappy Israel, who such measures takes,
And seeks for statesmen in the bogs and lakes;
Who speak the language of most abject slaves,
Under the conduct of our Jewish knaves.
145 Our Hebrew's murder'd in their hoarser throats; [7]
How ill their tongues agree with Jewish notes!
Their untun'd prattle does our sense confound,
Which in our princely palaces does sound;
The self-same language the old serpent spoke,
150 When misbelieving Eve the apple took:
Of our first mother why are we asham'd,
When by the self-same rhetoric we are damn'd?
    But Bentir, not content with such command,
To canton out the Jewish nation's land; [8]
155 He does extend to other coasts his pride,
And other kingdoms into parts divide: [9]

---

[1] *Bentir* Hans Willem Bentinck, first Earl of Portland (1649–1709), William's most trusted advisor on foreign policy.

[2] Parliament revoked William's grants of forfeited Irish lands in 1700.

[3] Bentinck was commissioned Lieutenant-General of the English army in 1690.

[4] *foreign chieftains* William appointed several foreign-born members of his court to high military position.

---

[5] *ten years' war* When William entered England, Louis XIV responded by invading the Palatinate; the ensuing War of the Grand Alliance (1689–97) pitted England, the Netherlands, Spain, Austria, and a number of German states against France.

[6] William's privy council included two naturalized foreigners in 1700.

[7] *Our Hebrew's murdered* referring to the accented English spoken by the Dutch members of William's court.

[8] *To canton out* to subdivide (*OED* canton *v* 1).

[9] Bentinck signed the first and second partition treaties (1698, 1700) that allocated various Spanish territories to England, France, the Netherlands, and the Holy Roman Empire.

Unhappy Hiram! dismal is thy song; [1]
Though born to Empire, thou art ever young!
Ever in nonage, canst no right transfer:
160 But who made Bentir thy executor?
What mighty power does Israel's land afford?
What power has made the famous Bentir Lord?
The people's voice, and Sanhedrin's accord?
Are not the rights of people still the same?
165 Did they e'er differ in or place or name?
Have not mankind on equal terms still stood,
Without distinction, since the mighty flood?
And have not Hiram's subjects a free choice
To choose a king by their united voice?
170 If Israel's people cou'd a monarch choose,
A living king at the same time refuse;
That Hiram's people, shall it e'er be said,
Have not the right of choice when he is dead?
When no successor to the crown's in sight,
175 The crown is certainly the people's right.
If kings are made the people to enthral,
We had much better have no king at all:
But kings, appointed for the common good,
Always as guardians to their people stood.
180 And Heaven allows the people sure a power
To choose such kings as shall not them devour:
They know full well what best will serve themselves,
How to avoid the dang'rous rocks and shelves.
        Unthinking Israel! Ah henceforth beware
185 How you entrust this faithless wanderer!
He who another Kingdom can divide,
May set your Constitution soon aside,
And o'er your liberties in triumph ride.
Support your rightful monarch and his crown,

190 But pull this proud, this croaking mortal down.
        Proceed, my Muse; the story next relate
Of Keppech the imperious chit of state, [2]
Mounted to grandeur by the usual course
Of whoring, pimping, or a crime that's worse; [3]
195 Of foreign birth, and undescended too,
Yet he, like Bentir, mighty feats can do.
He robs our treasure, to augment his state,
And Jewish nobles on his fortunes wait:
Our ravish'd honours on his shoulder wears, [4]
200 And titles from our ancient rolls he tears. [5]
Was e'er a prudent people thus befool'd,
By upstart foreigners thus basely gull'd?
Ye Jewish nobles, boast no more your race,
Or sacred bays that did your Fathers grace!
205 In vain is blood, or parentages, when
Ribbons and garters can ennoble men. [6]
To chivalry you need have no recourse,
The gaudy trappings make the ass a horse.
No more, no more your ancient honours own,
210 By slavish Gibeonites you are outdone:
Or else your ancient courage reassume,
And to assert your honours once presume;
From off their heads your ravish'd laurels tear,
And let them know what Jewish nobles are.
—1700

---

[1] *Hiram* Carlos II of Spain (1661–1700), whose death without an heir sparked the partitioning of Spanish territory that Bentinck helped negotiate.

[2] *Keppech* Arnold Joost van Keppel, first Earl of Albemarle (1669–1718).

[3] *a crime that's worse* likely sodomy.

[4] Knights of the Bath wore their insignia on the left shoulder.

[5] The earldom of Albemarle (or Aumerle) was a thirteenth-century title.

[6] *Ribbons and garters* insignia of Knights of the Bath and Knights of the Garter respectively.

Elizabeth Singer Rowe
"Philomela"
1674 – 1737

Elizabeth Singer Rowe was born in Ilchester, Somersetshire, the eldest of three daughters of Walter Singer, a clothier and dissenting preacher, and Elizabeth Portnell. When her mother died (ca. 1692), the family left Ilchester for Frome. She was tutored in Italian and possibly Latin by Henry Thynne, the son of Lord Weymouth. Her letters reveal that she was well read in poetry, drama, romance, and devotional and philosophical prose. At nineteen, she began a correspondence with John Dunton, the London bookseller, printer, and founder of the "Athenian Society." The Society was comprised of the editors of the *Athenian Mercury,* a weekly journal dedicated to "raise the Soul, as it were, into Daylight, and restore the knowledge of Truth and Happiness, that had wandered so long unknown, and found out by few" (Dunton, *Life and Errors,* 1705).[1] Between 1691 and 1697, Singer Rowe anonymously contributed a series of poems to the *Athenian Mercury.* In 1696, Dunton published a collection of her poems under the title *Poems on Several Occasions. Written by Philomela.*[2] This volume included a selection of pastorals, Pindaric odes, panegyrics, biblical paraphrase, eulogies and songs. Singer Rowe's two Latin translations were included in Tonson's *Poetic Miscellanies* (vol. 5) in 1704. At the age of thirty-six, she married the poet and scholar Thomas Rowe, and established a home in London. After her husband's death of consumption in 1715, she lived a reclusive life with her father in Frome.

Singer Rowe is best known as a representative of eighteenth-century Pietism. In 1728, nine years after her father's death, she published the highly popular prose epistles: *Friendship in Death, or Letters from the Dead to the Living* and *Letters Moral and Entertaining.* Two more books of *Letters Moral and Entertaining, The History of Joseph,* and *Devout Exercises of the Heart* followed in subsequent years. After her death, her brother-in-law, Theophilus Rowe, edited *The Miscellaneous Works in Prose and Verse of Mrs. Singer Rowe,* which was issued in 1739. Her posthumous popularity was such that more than eighty editions of her poetry and prose were issued well into the nineteenth century and her poems, translated into German, were lavishly praised by the German poets Klopstock and Wieland.

❧❧❧

Platonic Love

I

So angels love and all the rest is dross,
Contracted, selfish, sensitive and gross.[3]
Unlike to this, all free and unconfined,
Is that bright flame I bear thy brighter mind.

II

5   No straggling wish, or symptom of desire,
Comes near the limits of this holy fire;
Yet 'tis intense and active, though so fine,
For all my pure immortal part is thine.

III

Why should I then the heav'nly spark control,
10   Since there's no brighter ray in all my soul?
Why should I blush to indulge the noble flame,
For which even friendship's a degrading name?[4]

---

[1] *the Athenian Mercury*   formerly named *The Athenian Gazette.*

[2] Singer Rowe published under the names Philomela ("the nightingale") and the Pindaric Lady.

[3] *dross*   dreggy, impure matter, (*OED* dross *sb* 2).

[4] *indulge*   give oneself up to (*OED* indulge *v* I.3).

IV

Nor is the greatness of my love to thee,
A sacrilege unto the deity.
15 Can I th'enticing stream almost adore,
And not respect its lovely fountain more?
—1696

A Poetical Question concerning the Jacobites, sent to the Athenians [1]

'Twas nobly thought, and worthy-still;
So I resolve t' employ my loyal quill.
Virtue, and our unequalled hero's praise!
What themes more glorious can exact my lays?
5 William! A name my lines grow proud to bear!
A prince as great, and wondrous good, as e'er
The sacred burden of a crown did wear.
Resolve me, then, Athenians, what are those,
(Can there be any such?) you call his foes?
10 His foes, cursed word, and why they'd pierce his
    breast, [2]
Ungrateful vipers! where they warmly rest?
—1696

The Athenians' Answer [3]

Their name is Legion, grinning from afar
Against the throne, who wage unequal war; [4]

Though nearer, on perpetual guard, attends
A far more numerous host of brighter friends:
5 Around our prince, heav'n's care, the sacred band
With fiery arms in firm battalia stand: [5]
To him mild light, and lambent beams they show, [6]
But wrath and terror to his hardened foe.
See the black phalanx melt, they melt away,
10 As guilty ghosts slink from approaching day, [7]
Behold their leaders, decked in horrid state, [8]
Nor wonder why they heaven and Caesar hate.
    First mark their haughty general, armed
        complete
In plates of glowing steel! 'tis Lucifer the great! [9]
15 See his proud standard o'er his tent enlarged!
With bloated toads, an odious bearing, charged. [10]
The ancient arms which once his shield adorned,
Though 'tis of late to Fleur-de-Lis's turned. [11]
    Blasphemous Belial! next thy squadrons stand!
20 Lawless and lewd, a baffled blasted band,
Each holds a kindled pamphlet in his hand.
    These make the gross, the rest we may
        despise, [12]
(Retailers they of treason, and of lies)
Lucifer's friends, and Caesar's enemies.
25 Ah were there none but these, who would not be

---

[1] *Jacobites* adherents of James II of England after his "abdication," or of his son, the Pretender.

[2] *pierce his breast* The enemies of William III are equated with those of Jesus: "But one of the soldiers with a spear pierced his [Jesus's] side and forthwith came there out blood and water" (John 19:34).

[3] This poem cannot be attributed to Singer Rowe with certainty. A longer version of the poem first appeared with *A Poetical Question* in Vol.13, No.3 of the *Athenian Mercury* (May 29, 1694).

[4] *Their name is Legion* "And when he [Jesus] went forth to land, there met him out of the city a certain man, which had devils [a] long time....And Jesus asked him, saying, What is thy name? And he said, Legion: because many devils were entered into him" (Luke 8:27–30; see also Mark 5:9); *grinning* displaying the teeth threateningly as an indication of anger (*OED* grin v^2 1).

[5] *battalia* battle array (*OED* battalia *arch* or *Obs* 1).

[6] *lambent* shining with a soft clear light and without fierce heat (*OED* lambent *a* 1).

[7] *phalanx* a line or array of battle (*OED* phalanx 1).

[8] *horrid state* dreadful pomp (*OED* horrid *a* A.2; *OED* state *sb* II.17a).

[9] Lines 1-21 are indebted to Dryden's *Absalom and Achitophel* and Milton's depiction of Satan and the fallen angels; *haughty general* James II; *Lucifer* Satan, Devil (Latin "light bearer").

[10] *bloated toads* The toad was a type of anything hateful or loathsome (*OED* toad *sb* 1b,3).

[11] *Fleur-de-Lis* the heraldic lily, borne upon the royal arms of France under the old monarchy; hence also the French royal family, flag or nation. James II fled to France for political support after his "abdication."

[12] *gross* the greater part; also the dregs, dross (*OED* gross *sb⁴* B4,B3).

Proud and ambitious of their enmity!
There's one small party, near, too near their line, [1]
Which hover yet, and scarce know which to join.
No black, no ugly marks of sin disgrace
30 Their nobler forms, no malice in their face:
A duskier gleam they wear than ere they fell,
Their plumes just scorched, too near allied to hell.
What mad mistaken bravery draws 'em in,
Where constancy's no virtue but a sin?
35 How can they still their fallen prince esteem?
When false to heaven, why are they true to him?
O! must they sink! a glorious starry race!
They are almost too good, for that sad place
That waits their fall: It must not, cannot be,
40 If err we do, we'll err with charity,
Father! they may be saved! we'll join with Thee!
　　　—1696

A Pindaric, to the Athenian Society

I

I've touched each string, each muse I have
　　invoked, [2]
　　Yet still the mighty theme,
Copes my unequal praise; [3]
Perhaps, the God of Numbers is provoked. [4]
5 I grasp a subject fit for none but him,
Or Dryden's sweeter lays;
Dryden! A name I ne'er could yet rehearse,
But straight my thoughts were all transformed to
　　verse.

II

And now methinks I rise;
10 But still the lofty subject baulks my flight, [5]
And still my muse despairs to do great Athens right;
Yet takes the zealous tribute which I bring,
The early products of a female muse;
Until the God into my breast shall mightier
　　thoughts infuse.
15 When I with more command, and prouder voice
　　shall sing;
But how shall I describe the matchless men?
I'm lost in the bright labyrinth again.

III

When the lewd age, as ignorant as accursed,
Arrived in vice and error to the worst, [6]
20 And like Astrea banished from the stage, [7]
Virtue and truth were ready stretched for flight;
Their numerous foes,
Scarce one of either's champions ventured to
　　oppose;
Scarce one brave mind durst openly engage,
25 To do them right.
Till prompted with a generous rage;
You coped with all th'abuses of the age; [8]
Unmasked and challenged its abhorred crimes,
Nor feared to lash the darling vices of the times.

IV

30 Successfully go on,
T'inform and bless mankind as you've begun,
Till like yourselves they see;
The frantic world's imagined joys to be,
Unmanly, sensual and effeminate,

---

[1] *one small party* either the Tories who remained in contact with James II, or the country Whigs and the Tories who allied to oppose the "new" or "Junto" Whigs who were influential in William III's government.

[2] *each muse* an allusion to the nine Muses, the Greek deities who preside over music, poetry, the arts and sciences.

[3] *Copes* silences; literally to tie or sew up the mouth of (*OED* cope *v*[5]).

[4] *God of Numbers* Apollo, patron of music and poetry; *numbers* metrical periods or feet; hence, lines, verses (*OED* number *sb* IV 18b.)

---

[5] *baulks* hinders (*OED* balk *v*[1] III. 5a).

[6] *worst* worst age.

[7] *And like Astrea…the stage* Astrea, a personification of justice, left the earth at the inception of the Iron Age to live amongst the stars until the reappearance of the Golden Age (Ovid, *Metamorphoses*).

[8] *coped* contended (*OED* cope *v*[2] II.4a). The reference is to the Athenian Society .

35 Till they with such exalted thoughts possessed;
As you've inspired into my willing breast,
Are charmed, like me, from the impending fate.

V

For ah! Forgive me heaven, I blush to say't,
I with the vulgar world thought irreligion great,
40 Though fine my breeding, and my notions high;
Though trained in the bright tracts of strictest
    piety, [1]
I like my splendid tempters soon grew vain,
And laid my slighted innocence aside;
Yet oft my nobler thoughts I have belied,
45 And to be ill was even reduced to feign.

VI

Until by you,
With more heroic sentiments inspired,
I turned and stood the vigorous torrent too,
And at my former weak retreat admired; [2]
50 So much was I by your example fired, [3]
So much the heavenly form did win:
Which to my eyes you'd painted virtue in.

VII

Oh, could my verse;
With equal flights, to after times rehearse,
55 Your fame: It should as bright and deathless be;
As that immortal flame you've raised in me.
A flame which time,
And death itself, wants power to control, [4]
Not more sublime,
60 Is the divine composure of my soul;
A friendship so exalted and immense,
A female breast did ne'er before commence.
—1696

---

[1] *tracts*   possibly books (*OED* tract *sb*[1] I.2); more likely courses, paths (*OED* tract *sb* [3]9).

[2] *stood*   withstood; *admired*   felt surprise (*OED* admire *v* 1).

[3] *fired*   inspired with passion (*OED* fired *v*[1]3a).

[4] *wants*   lacks (*OED* want *v* 2).

To Celinda

I

I can't, Celinda, say I love,
    But rather I adore,
When with transported eyes I view,
Your shining merits o'er. [5]

II

5 A fame so spotless and serene,
A virtue so refined;
And thoughts as great, as e'er was yet
Grasped by a female mind.

III

There love and honour dressed, in all,
10 Their genuine charms appear,
And with a pleasing force at once
They conquer and endear.

IV

Celestial flames are scarce more bright,
Than those your worth inspires,
15 So angels love and so they burn
In just such holy fires.

V

Then let's my dear Celinda thus
Blessed in ourselves contemn
The treacherous and deluding arts,
20 Of those base things called men.
—1696

The Reply to Mr. ——

No: I'm unmoved: nor can thy charming muse
    One tender thought into my breast infuse.
I am from all those sensual motions free;
And you, in vain, speak pretty things to me:
5 For through the splendid gallantries of love,

---

[5] *transported*   enraptured (*OED* transported *ppl.a* 2).

Untouched, and careless, now I wildly rove,
From all th'attacks of those proud darts secure,
Whose trifling force too tamely you endure;
Nor ought, on earth's, so delicate to move
10   My nicer spirit, and exact my love: [1]
Even Theron's lovely and enticing eyes,
Though armed with flames, I can at last despise;
With all the genuine charms and courtly arts,
By which your treacherous sex invade our hearts:
15   No more those little things contract my breast
By a diviner excellence possessed;
And, should I yield again, it dear must cost
My victor ere he shall the conquest boast;
For the mad venom's quite expelled my veins,
20   And calmer reason now triumphant reigns:
      No more the dearest object of my sight
Can move a soft sensation of delight;
Or force my lingering blood a swifter pace,
Or paint new smiles and blushes on my face.
25   I've rent the charming idol from my heart, [2]

And banished all from thence that took his part.
No more the smiling beaux shall tempt me on
To gaze, and sigh, and think myself undone;
Whilst love, like some fierce torrent unconfined,
30   Breaks in, o'er-spreads, and swallows up my mind;
And with its black ungrateful streams control
All the diviner rays within my soul.
No, no: I will, I will no more admire,
And urge the sparks of the now dormant fire:
35   Nor for a wild fantastic ecstasy,
Change the dear joys of this blest liberty;
Free, as a wandering zephyr, through the air,
Methinks I range, and hate my former sphere. [3]
I meet the noblest forms, yet scorn to pay
40   A fond devotion to well-molded clay:
Nor would I even for my late splendid chain
Forgo this charming liberty again;
Which with so sweet a calmness fills my breast
As cannot be in words, no not in thine expressed.
—1696

---

[1] *nicer*   tender; also reluctant (*OED* nice *a* 4c, 5b).

[2] *rent*   torn (*OED* rent *v*[2] 2).

[3] *zephyr*   butterfly (*OED* zephyr *sb* 4).

A Miscellany

Ballads

Tom o' Bedlam

From the hag and hungry goblin
That into rags would rend ye
And the spirit that stan' by the naked man
In the Book of Moons defend ye!
5   That of your five sound senses
You never be forsaken
Nor travel from yourselves with Tom
Abroad to beg your bacon.
     Nor never sing "Any food, any feeding,
10   Money, drink or clothing":
       Come dame or maid, be not afraid,
       Poor Tom will injure nothing.

Of thirty bare years have I
Twice twenty been enraged
15   And of forty been three times fifteen
In durance soundly caged
In the lordly lofts of Bedlam
On stubble soft and dainty,
Brave bracelets strong, sweet whips ding dong,
20   With wholesome hunger plenty.
     And now I sing &c.

With a thought I took for maudlin
With a cruse of cockle pottage [1]
With a thing thus—tall, (sky bless you all),
25   I fell into this dotage.
I slept not since the conquest,
Till then I never wakéd
Till the roguish boy of love where I lay
Me found and stripped me naked.
30   And made me sing &c.

When short I have shorn my sow's face
And swigged my hornéd barrel [2]
In an oaken inn do I pawn my skin
As a suit of gilt apparel.
35   The moon's my constant mistress
And the lonely owl my marrow
The flaming drake and the night-crow make
Me music to my sorrow.
     While there I sing &c.

40   The palsy plague these pounces, [3]
When I prig your pigs or pullen, [4]
Your culvers take, or mateless make [5]
Your chanticlere, and sullen. [6]
When I want provant with Humfrey [7]
45   I sup, and when benighted
To repose in Paul's with waking souls
I never am affrighted.
     But still do I sing &c.

I know more than Apollo,
50   For oft when he lies sleeping
I behold the stars at mortal wars
And the wounded welkin weeping; [8]
The moon embrace her shepherd

---

[1] *cruse* a small pot, jar, or bottle (*OED*); *cockle* a bivalve mollusc, common on sandy coasts and much used for food (*OED* cockle *sb*[2] 1); *pottage* a dish composed of vegetables alone, or along with meat; soup, especially a thick soup (*OED* pottage 1).

[2] *hornéd* provided, fitted, or ornamented with horn (*OED* horned *a* 7).

[3] *pounces* possibly a variant of ponce, which may be derived from the verb "pounce." This in its strict sense means a pimp, but it is used commonly as a term of contempt; or perhaps we should emend to *pouncer*, meaning one who pounces, in this context presumably a gamekeeper.

[4] *prig* steal (*OED* prig *v*[1] 1); *pullen* poultry (*OED* pullen 1).

[5] *culvers* doves or pigeons (*OED* culver 1).

[6] *chanticlere* an appellation applied to a cock (*OED* chanticleer).

[7] *provant* food (*OED* provant); "dining with Duke Humphrey" was a proverbial expression for going hungry.

[8] *welkin* considered the abode of the Deity, or of the gods of heathen mythology: the celestial regions, heaven (*OED* welkin 2 b).

And the queen of love her warrior, [1]
55 While the first doth horn the star of the morn
And the next the heavenly Farrier. [2]
    While I do sing &c.

The Gipsy Snap and Tedro
Are none of Tom's comrados.
60 The punk I scorn and the cutpurse sworn [3]
And the roaring-boys bravadoes.
The sober, white, and gentle,
Me trace, or touch, and spare not;
But those that cross Tom's Rhinoceros
65 Do what the panther dare not.
    Although I sin &c.

With an host of furious fancies
Whereof I am commander
With a burning spear, and a horse of air,
70 To the wilderness I wander.
By a knight of ghosts and shadows
I summoned am to tourney [4]
Ten leagues beyond the wide world's end.
Me thinks it is no journey.
75   All while I sing &c.

---

[1] *The moon…her warrior* Diana, goddess of the moon, having fallen in love with a handsome young shepherd, Endymion, while he was sleeping on Mount Latmos, made him sleep everlastingly so that she could gaze on him forever. Venus is the queen of love, and Mars, the warrior, is her lover.

[2] *horn* to "give horns to": to cuckold (*OED* horn v 2); *farrier* one who shoes horses (*OED* farrier *sb* 1). This is a reference to Vulcan, the god of fire and especially the smithy fire. Vulcan was the husband of Venus, goddess of love, beauty and fertility. Venus is said to have cuckolded her husband with the warrior Mars.

[3] *punk* a prostitute, strumpet, harlot (*OED* punk *sb*[1]).

[4] *tourney* to take part in a tournament (*OED* tourney *v*).

A sweet and pleasant Sonnet, entitled: My mind to me a kingdom is

To the tune of, *In Creet, &c.*

1

My mind to me a Kingdom is,
  such perfect joys therein I find,
It far exceeds all earthly bliss
    that world affords, or grows by kind:
5 Though much I want that most men have,
Yet doth my mind forbid me crave.

2

Content I live, this is my stay,
  I seek no more than may suffice,
I press to bear no haughty sway,
    look what I lack my mind supplies:
10 Lo, thus I triumph like a King,
Content with that my mind doth bring.

3

I see how plenty surfeits oft,
  and hasty climbers oft do fall,
I see how those that sit aloft,
15   mishap doth threaten most of all,
They get, they toil, they spend with care,
Such cares my mind could never bear.

4

I laugh not at another's loss,
20   I grudge not at another's gain,
No worldly way my mind can toss,
    I brook that is another's bane:
I fear no foe, I scorn no friend,
I dread no death, I fear no end.

5

25 Some have too much, yet still they crave,
  I little have, yet seek no more,
They are but poor, though much they have,

And I am rich with little store,
They poor, I rich, they beg, I give,
30 They lack, I lend, they pine, I live.

6

My wealth is health and perfect ease,
    my conscience clear, my chief defence:
I never seek by bribes to please,
    nor by desert to give offence:
35 Lo thus I lie, thus will I die,
Would all did so as well as I.

7

No princely pomp, no wealthy store,
    no force to get the victory,
No wily wit to salve a sore,
40   no shape to win a Lover's eye,
To none of these I yield as thrall,
For why my mind despiseth all.

8

I joy not at an earthly bliss,
    I weigh not Croesus' wealth a straw, [1]
45 For Care, I care not what it is,
    I fear not Fortune's fatal law:
My mind is such as may not move,
For beauty bright or force of love:

9

I wish not what I have at will,
50   I wander not to seek for more,
I like the plain, I climb no hill,
    in greatest storm I sit on shore,
And laugh at those that toil in vain,
To get that must be lost again.

10

55 I kiss not where I wish to kill,
    I fain no love where most I hate,

---

[1] *Croesus* the last king of Lydia, who reigned in the sixth century B.C.E., was renowned for his great wealth.

I break no sleep to win my will,
    I wait not at the mighties' gate,
I scorn no poor, I fear no rich,
60 I feel no want, nor have too much.

11

The Court, ne Cart, I like, ne loath,
    extremes are counted worst of all,
The golden mean betwixt them both,
    doth surest sit, and fears no fall:
65 This is my choice, for why I find,
No wealth is like a quiet mind.

Ditties Lamentation
for the cruelty of this age

To the tune of *Packentons pound.*

1

Well worth Predecessors, and Fathers by name,
That lived in *England* long times ago:
Whose wondrous deeds were done for their fame,
Which now here in *England* breedeth our woe:
5   Then Pity did rest,
    In every man's breast:
    And Cruelty had no place
    To make his nest
Oh happy *England* that lived in that state,
10 When Pity was Porter at every mans gate.

2

But Pity (alack) 'tis quite fled and gone,
True friendship and love is banished away:
Plain dealing now walketh mourning alone,
And no man relieves him by night nor by day:
15   No Pity we see,
    In any degree,
    But fraud and deceit,
    And vile butchery.

Oh happy *England* that lived in that state,
20 When Pity was Porter at every man's gate.

3

Oh what is there now in this wicked age,
That man will not do to accomplish the end,
Which he hath intended in malice and rage,
Though half that he hath in his mischief he spend
25   Man wanting the grace,
  That love to embrace.
  Which in former times,
  Had eminent place:
Oh happy *England* that lived in that state,
30 When Pity was Porter at every man's gate.

4

Now grudging and envy once bred in the heart,
Abates not by reason but still doth increase,
Till it bring into action some tragical part,
By stabbing or poisoning and never will cease,
35   Till he have his due,
  That this is too true,
  Know some that the poison,
  Of enough do rue,
Oh [happy] *England* that lived in that state, &c.

5

40 Now under a color of kindness and love,
In Purges and Potions such cunning is known,
A man unsuspected a murder may prove.
But God will have mischief and villainy shown.
  Tho God for a time,
45   May wink at a crime,
  Yet he can discover,
  When sins in the prime.
Be happy Oh *England* to live in that state,
Let Pity be Porter still at thy gate.

6

50 Look in the Scriptures and there you may read,
That Murder, Adultery had never good end,

I never read yet that well they did speed,
As late hath been seen in this our good land.
  But God turn their hearts,
55   That thus play such parts,
  For Poisons and potions,
  Will turn to their smarts.
O would that good Conscience did live in these days
Then such kind of people would take better ways.

7

60 Poor ragged Conscience, where dost thou live?
Banished (I doubt me) from Town and from City:
Poverty beggeth yet few men will give,
And plenty is sparing the more is the pity,
  For gorgeous array,
65   Now beareth such sway
  That by her continuance,
  All things decay,
O happy *England* that lived in that state, &c.

8

Good house keeping now is quite laid aside,
70 No Butler stands ready to do an alms deed,
And all to maintain fond fashions of pride,
A thousand good fellows do stand in great need,
  Most fair to the eye,
  Are houses built high,
75   Only for pleasure
  Of them that pass by.
But Oh happy *England* to live in that state,
Let Pity be Porter still at thy gate.

THE SECOND PART OF DITTIES COMPLAINT
TO THE SAME TUNE.

9

Since Coaches here flourished so much in this Land,
80 One servant or two now serveth the turn:
Forty good Geldings were else at command,
As many good fellows uprising each morn;

Then Tables were spread,
With good beef and bread,
85 But now this good order,
From England is fled,
Be happy, O *England*, [to live in that state,]
When Pity was Porter at every man's gate.

10

Whole Farms are consumed in pride for the back,
90 In Shoe-strings and Garters of silver or gold:
Which well might suffice to feed them that lack.
And keep the poor widow from hunger and cold.
But hardness of heart,
Hath so played his part,
95 That Pity now weepeth,
To hear of our smart,
Oh happy *England* that lived in that state,
Let Pity be Porter still at thy gate.

11

Yea happy was *England* before it did know,
100 Such pride in apparel as many do wear:
In warm russet clothing our Gallants did go,
And kersies were garments for Ladies most faire: [1]
Then malice and spite,
Did live with no wight, [2]
105 True love and friendship,
Was each man's delight.
Oh happy *England*, &c.

12

A bushel of wheat for six pence was sold,
An Ox for a Mark fat from the stall: [3]
110 A score of fat Lambs for an Angel was told, [4]

---

[1] *kersies* a kind of coarse narrow cloth, woven from long wool and usually ribbed (*OED*).

[2] *wight* a human being, man or woman, person (*OED* wight *sb* 2).

[3] *Mark* 13 shillings and four pence, that is, two-thirds of a pound sterling (*OED* mark *sb²* 2a).

[4] *Angel* an old English gold coin, having as its device the archangel Michael standing upon, and piercing the dragon (*OED* Angel 6).

With heart and good will in payment with all:
And then at each door,
Sat feasting the poor:
The like to that time,
115 Will never come more.
Oh happy *England*, &c.

13

When such a good world was here in this Land,
Neighbor with neighbor did fall at no strife,
Then needless were bonds and bills of their
hands,
120 Men's words were not broken but kept as their
life.
But now in these days,
All credit decays,
Truth is not used,
We see any ways.
125 Oh happy *England*, &c.

14

The time is quite changed we find it by proof,
Poor Conscience a begging now walks in the field:
And Charity blinded, keeps her aloof,
And cannot find where her house for to build,
130 No Pity we see,
In any degree,
But fraud and deceit,
A vile usury.
Oh happy *England*, [&c.]

15

135 If this happy world would once again more,
Return to her former virtue and grace:
All men with bounty would part with their store,
To build up poor Pity a perpetual place:
So Pity will rest,
140 In every man's breast:
And Cruelty find no place,
To make his nest.

Be happy O *England* to live in that state,
When Pity was Porter at every man's gate.

The King's Last Farewell to the World, Or The Dead King's Living Meditations, at the approach of Death denounced against him

1

Through fear of sharp and bitter pain,
    by cutting off my days,
No pleasure in my Crown I take,
    Nor in my Royal Rayes. [1]
5 I shall descend with grieved heart,
    (for none my life can save)
Unto the dismal gates of death,
    to molder in the Grave.

2

Farewell my Wife, and Children all,
10   wipe off my brinish tears.
I am deprived of my Throne,
    and from my future years.
Farewell my people every one,
    for I no more shall see
15 The wonders of the Lord on earth,
    nor with you shall I be.

3

Mine eyes do fail, and to the earth
    to worms I must be hurled:
Henceforth no more shall I behold
20   the people of the world.
My Crown and Scepter I must leave,
    my glory, and my Throne:
Adieu my fellow Princes all,
    I from the earth am gone.

4

25 Mine Age (which did approach to me)
    departed is away;
And as a Shepherd's tent removed,
    and I returned to clay;
And as a Weaver doth cut off
30   his thrum, even so my life, [2]
Must be cut off, from people and
    from Children, and from Wife.

5

In sighs by day, and groans by night
    with bitterness I moan,
35 And do consume away with grief,
    my end to think upon.
Fear in the morning me assails,
    Death lion-like I see,
Even all the day (till night) to roar
40   to make an end of me.

6

I chattered as the shrieking Crane,
    or Swallow that doth fly:
As Dove forlorn, in pensiveness,
    doth mourn, even so do I,
45 I looked up to thee, O Lord,
    but now mine eyes do fail.
Oh ease my sad oppressed soul,
    for death doth now prevail.

7

What shall I say, to God's Decree,
50   if he would speak, I then
should live; it is a work for God,
    I find no help from men.
Yet if my life prolonged was,
    my sins for to repent,
55 Then softly I would go and mourn,
    until my life was spent.

---

[1] *Rayes* form of array, dress (*OED* array *sb* 3).

[2] *thrum* each of the ends of the warp-threads left unwoven and remaining attached to the loom when the web is cut off (*OED*).

8

And all my years, that I should live,
    for mine offences foul,
I would passe o'er in bitterness,
60   of my distressed soul.
O Lord, thou hast discovered
    to me, that by these things
Men live; through thee, Princes do reign,
    thou swayest over Kings.

9

65 In all things here God's Providence,
    and will alone commands,
The life of my poor spirit sad,
    is only in his hands,
Oh, that the Lord would me restore.
70   my strength then I would give,
To serve my God in humbleness
    whilst he would let me live.

10

Behold, O Lord, when I in peace,
    did look to be restored,
75 Then was my soul in bitterness,
    cast off, and I abhorred,
Yet in the love of God most good,
    his righteousness most just
Hath thrown me down into the pit,
80   and to corrupted dust.

11

Because that I have gone astray,
    and cherished war and strife,
My days are now cut off, and I
    am quite bereft of life,
85 Oh cast my sins behind thy back,
    good God, I humbly pray,
And my offences with the blood
    of Christ wash clean away.

12

When my dead body is interred,
90   I cannot praise thee there,
Death cannot celebrate the Lord,
    my God, most good, most dear;
They that go down into the pit
    destructions them devour:
95 For in thy truth they cannot hope.
    but perish by thy power.

13

The living, Lord, the living, they
    shall praise thy holy name.
With all the glorious host above,
100   and I shall do the same.
The father to his children here,
    that are of tender youth,
Shall them forewarn, and unto them
    make known thy glorious truth.

14

105 Forgive my sins, and save my soul
    O Lord, I thee entreat,
And blot out mine offences all,
    for they are very great:
Receive my soul for Christ his sake,
110   my Prophet, Priest, and King,
That I with Saints and Angels may
    eternal praises sing.
—1648

The Royal health to the Rising Sun

To the tune of, *O my pretty little winking, &c.*

1

As I was walking forth one day,
    I heard distressed people say,
Our Peace and Plenty now is gone,

And we poor people quite undone:
5   A Royal Health I then begun
   Unto the rising of the Sun,
Gallant English Spirits
   do not thus complain,
The Sun that sets
10   *may after rise again.*

2

The Tempest hath endured long,
We must not say, we suffer wrong,
The Queen of Love sits all alone.
No man is master of his own.

3

15 We over-whelmed are with grief,
And harbor many a private thief,
Poor house-keepers can hardly live,
Who used in former times to give:

4

The Thistle chokes the Royal Rose,
20 And all our bosom friends turned foes,
The Irish Harp is out of tune,
And we God knows undone too soon.

THE SECOND PART, TO THE SAME TUNE

5

True love and friendship doth now decay,
Poor people's almost starved they say,
25 Our trading's spoiled, and all things dear
We may complain, and ne're the near:

6

Though all be true that here is said,
Kind country-men be not dismayed,
For when the worst of harm is past,
30 We shall have better times at last.

7

When Rulers cast off self-respects,
Then shall our yokes fall from our necks,
Our safeties shall not then depend
On promise of a faithless friend:

8

35 When as the cloud of war is down
The Royal Sun enjoys the crown,
The lamb shall with the lion feed,
'Twill be a happy time indeed:

9

Let us cheer up each other then,
40 And shew our selves true English-men,
And not like bloody wolves and bears,
As we have been these many years.

10

The Father of our Kingdom's dead,
His Royal Son from *England's* fled,
45 God send all well that wars may cease,
And we enjoy a happy peace;
   A Royal Health I then begun
   Unto the rising of the Sun,
Gallant English Spirits,
50   *do not thus complain,*
The Sun that sets
   may after rise again.
—1649

A Looking-Glass for Men and Maids

*Being a brief and true Relation of a sad and
sorrowful mis-chance, which happened to a Young
man and a Maid who both lost their lives, and were
scalded to death in a Brewers Meash-Tun,[1] with
striving about a kiss: this was done upon Twelfth-
day last, near unto Shore-ditch, in the Suburbs of
London; the manner how, shall presently be related.
Here is also set down the time how long they lived
after they were taken out of the scalding Liquor, and
of a very godly speech which the Maid made at the
hour of death, which is worthy to be kept in memory.*

The tune is, *the Bride's Burial*

1

A Sudden sad mischance,
   near *Shore-ditch* late befell.
Which now with grieved heart & mind
   I am prepared to tell:
5 Even on the last *Twelfth-day*,[2]
   being in the afternoon,
Within a Brew-house certainly
   there was this mischief done:

2

The manner how was this,
10   a Maid to the Brew-house came
To fetch hot Liquor for to use,
   and straight upon the same
The Miller being there,
   laid hands upon the Maid,
15 Intending for to kiss her then,
   and would not be denied:

3

The Maid unwilling was
   that he should kiss her there,

---

[1] *Meash-Tun* a tub in which malt is mashed (*OED* mash *sb¹* 5).

[2] *Twelfth-day* the feast of the Epiphany, twelve days after Christmas.

She thrust him back with both her hands
20   as plainly doth appear:
But he poor wretched man
   laid hold on her again,
And swore, before he let her go
   he would a kiss obtain.

4

25 But as they struggled and strived:
   so fiercely one with the other,
Their Feet did slip, and so fell in
   the Meash-Tun both together
Where scalding Liquor was,
30   a grievous tale to tell,
They of each other had fast hold,
   and head-long in they fell.

5

The Liquor was so hot,
   and scalded them so sore,
35 The like I think was never known
   nor heard of here-to-fore:
At last some people came
   and helped them out by strength,
And by that means, they pulled from them
40   their garments off at length.

6

A woeful chance it was,
   as ever could befall,
For as they stripped their clothing off,
   they pulled off skin and all:
45 From bellies, backs and sides,
   and from their private parts,
Which was a sorrowful sight to see,
   and terror to Folks' hearts.

7

The people did their best,
50   the lives of them to save.
But all (alas) it was in vain,

no cure that they could have:
  For why? the woeful man
    did in a short time die,
55 The Maid sore sick upon her bed,
    a longer time did lie.

THE SECOND PART TO THE SAME TUNE

8

But e're she did depart
    she for her True-love sent,
Who being come into her room,
60   she prayed him be content:
You are the man, quoth she,
    which I did dearly love,
And have as faithful been to you,
    as is the Turtle-Dove:

9

65 When you a promise made
    that we should married be,
This ring and bobkin both in love [1]
    you did bestow on me:
The which in courtesy
70   from you I did receive,
And now with willing mind again
    the same to you I give:

10

Still wishing you good days;
    whilst you have breath and life.
75 I do bequeath these things to her
    that you will take to wife:
All that I do request,
    of you this present day,
Is only, whilst I am alive,
80   for my poor soul to pray.

11

And you my Mother dear,
    and all my friends so kind,
I am enforced to leave this world,
    and leave you all behind:
85 I have made my peace with God,
    the mighty Lord of Heaven,
And this I hope through Jesus Christ
    my sins shall be forgiven.

12

My body scalding hot,
90   like fire doth boil and fry.
Sweet Christ I pray receive my soul
    although my body die:
When she these words had spoke,
    her woes were soon released,
95 She died, no doubt, her soul is now
    with them whom God hath blest.

13

The Miller he likewise,
    e're he resigned his breath,
Asked God forgiveness, for his own,
100   and her untimely death:
Advising all young men
    to have a special care
Of rash attempts, and by his fall,
    for ever to beware:

14

105 And to conclude, in brief.
    I wish that all man-kind
What-so-ever they do go about,
    to have God in their mind:
The Book of Common-Prayer,
110   though it be laid aside,
Yet every Christian ought to pray
    that God may be our guide.

---

[1] *bobkin* possibly bodkin, a long pin or pin-shaped ornament used
by women to fasten up the hair (*OED* bodkin 3).

15

From famine, plague, & pestilence,
  preserve us great and small,
115 And from thy wrath, and sudden death
  good Lord deliver us all.

No ring, no Wedding

A merry new Song of the wooing there was,
'Twixt a zealous Young man, and a Cavalier Lass,
He woos (and would wed) she will have no such thing,
Unless she may married be with a King
Have Ribbons, and Globes, Rosemary, and Bays,
And all things that were in her fore-fathers days.

The Tune is, *The Parson of the Parish*

1 YOUNG-MAN

Sweet-Heart I come unto thee,
  hoping thy Love to win,
I mean to try, thy courtesy,
  and thus I do begin:
5 If thou wilt be my Sweeting,
  then I will be thy Dear,
What think'st of me, shall I have thee,
  thou pretty Cavalier.

2 MAID

Good Sir you do but mock me,
10 your mind is nothing so,
You'll speak of Love, my thoughts to prove,
  and then away you'll go:
For if you be a Round-head, [1]
  (as to me it doth appear,)
15 You cannot (yet,) your fancy set,
  upon a Cavalier.

3 YOUNG-MAN

Sweet-Heart I speak in earnest,
  thy beauty hath me ta'en,
And my true-love, to thee (my Dove,)
20 for ever shall remain:
My true affections to thee,
  such zealous thoughts doth bear,
If thou consent, I am content,
  my pretty Cavalier.

4 MAID

25 Your Sect is bent to false-hood,
  and I indeed am jealous,
That this is but, the shell o' th' Nut,
  though your pretense be zealous:
You have no cause to blame me,
30 but I have cause to fear,
'Twould be your sport, to win the Fort,
  and spoil the Cavalier.

5 YOUNG-MAN

My dearest do not doubt me,
  my Heart and Tongue agree,
35 Now *Cupid's* Dart, hath pricked my Heart,
  I love no Lass but thee:
Tomorrow we'll be married,
  then take it for no jeer,
In word and deed, I am agreed,
40 *to wed my Cavalier.*

6 MAID

Sweet Sir you are too hasty,
  to speak of such a thing,
If I should yield, to you the Field,
  where is your Wedding-Ring:
45 Your Bride-Gloves & your Ribbons
  with other things that were,
Fit for a Bride, all things provide,
  I'll be your Cavalier.

---

[1] *Round-head* a member or adherent of the Parliamentary party in
the Civil War, so called from their custom of wearing the hair close cut
(*OED* roundhead 1).

7 YOUNG-MAN

These are but Ceremonies,
50   belong to Popery,
Therefore we will, not use them still
   but all such toys defy,
We'll hand in hand together,
   conjoin (with joyful cheer,)
55 Few words we'll need, I'll do the deed,
   with thee sweet Cavalier.

THE SECOND PART, BEING THE MAIDEN'S ANSWER

8

Sweet-Heart for thy sake,
   I will never make,
Choice of any other,
60 Than by *Cupid's* Mother,
   freely speak,
It's at thy choice my dearest Love,
   Either to leave or take

9

I, thy Mary gold,
65 Wrapped in many fold,
Like the golden client,
To the Sun's suppliant,
   show it's gold:
Display thy beams by glorious Sun,
70   And I'll to thee unfold.

10

Those bright locks of hair,
Spreading o're each ear,
Every crisp and curl,
Far more rich than Pearl,
75   doth appear:
Then be thou constant in thy love,
   And I will be thy Dear.

11

Till I have possessed,
Thee whom I love best,

80 I have vowed for ever,
In thy absence never,
   to take rest:
Deny me not thou pretty little one,
   in whom my hopes are blest.

12

85 If a kiss or two,
Can thee a favor do,
Were it more then twenty,
Love's indued with plenty,
   Lovers know:
90 For thy sweet sake, a thousand take,
   For that's the way to woo.

13

It doth grieve my heart,
From thee for to part,
It is to me more pleasant,
95 Ever to be present,
   where thou art:
Yet in the absence of a Friend,
   My love shall never start.

14

As to me thou art kind,
100 Duty shall me bind,
Ever to obey thee,
Reason so doth sway me,
   to thy mind,
Thou hast my heart, where ere thou art,
105   Although I stay behind.

15

In the Bed or Bark,
I will be thy mark,
Couples yet more loving,
Never had their moving,
110   from the Ark:
Welcome to me my only joy
   All times be it light or dark.

Poems on the Duke of Buckingham

"Never any man, in any age, nor, I believe, in any country or nation, rose, in so short a time, to so much greatness of honour, fame and fortune, upon no other advantage or recommendation than of the beauty and gracefulness and becomingness of his person." With these words the Earl of Clarendon began his character of George Villiers, first Duke of Buckingham (1592–1628), royal favourite to two Kings. The younger son of a Leicestershire knight, Buckingham was sent to France to master the courtly arts of riding, dancing, and duelling. In 1614, shortly after his return, he was introduced to James I, who showered the new favourite with titles and honours over the next few years. Buckingham, who did not lack political talent, soon built up a powerful network based on nepotism and patronage, and he was the leading political figure in the land in the decade before his death. He accompanied Prince Charles on his incognito ride to Spain in hopes of a Spanish bride, and maintained his position after the death of James. In the first two years of Charles' reign Buckingham initiated and then mismanaged scandalously unsuccessful wars against Spain and France, wars which created a great deal of friction between the crown and Parliament. The House of Commons made complaints against the Duke several times in the second half of the 1620s; their animosity toward the favourite probably contributed to Charles's distrust of Parliaments. In August 1628 Buckingham was assassinated in Portsmouth by John Felton, a soldier in Buckingham's expeditions to Cadiz and the Isle of Rhé. Felton had been refused the command of a company and was owed pay; when he read a Parliamentary remonstrance against the Duke he decided to rid the country of him. The murder was cheered in the streets of London, and Felton became a folk hero after he was hanged.

Buckingham had been the target of a great deal of understandably anonymous and surreptitiously circulated manuscript verse throughout the later 1620s. His death brought the expected tributes and complimentary elegies, as well as many satires and mock epitaphs, circulated again in manuscript.

❧❧❧

Upon the Duke of Buckingham

Of British beasts the Buck is king,
His game and fame through Europe ring,
His horn exalted, keeps in awe
The lesser flocks; his will's a law.
5 Our Charlemagne takes much delight [1]
In this great beast so fair in sight,
With his whole heart affects the same,
And loves too well *Buck-King* of *Game*.
When he is chas'd, then 'gins the sport,
10 When nigh his end, who's sorry for't?
And when he falls the hunter's glad,
The hounds are flesh'd, and few are sad:

The foresters say, while he's alive
The tender thickets ne'er can thrive,
15 He doth so bark and pill the trees; [2]
Thus we for game our profit lease.
The huntsmen have pursu'd this deer, [3]
And follow'd him with full career,
But such his craft, and such their lot,
20 They hunt him oft, but take him not.
A *Buck*'s a beast; a *King* is but a man,
A *Game*'s a pleasure shorter than a span;
A beast shall perish; but a man shall die,
As pleasures fade. This be thy destiny.
—1628

---

[1] *Our Charlemagne*   King Charles I.

[2] *pill*   peel or strip (*OED* pill *v*[1] 5).

[3] *huntsmen*   Parliament.

Epitaph on the Duke of Buckingham

This little grave embraces,
One duke and twenty places. [1]

—1628

Epitaph

Fortune's darling, king's content,
Vexation of the parliament,
The flatterer's deity of state,
Advancer of each money-mate,
5 The devil's factor for the purse,
The papist's hope, the common's curse,
The sailor's cross, the soldier's grief,
Commission's blank, and England's thief,
The coward at the Isle of Rhe, [2]
10 The bane of noble chivalry,
The night-work of a painted dame,
Confederate with doctor Lamb. [3]
    All this lies underneath this stone,
    And yet, alas! here lies but one.

—1628

---

[1] *places* income-producing offices or appointments; Buckingham was notorious for the number he held or had in his power to give to others, with his relatives the usual beneficiaries.

[2] Isle of Rhé, off the French coast. Referring to a failed 1627 expedition led by Buckingham to relieve the Huguenots of La Rochelle.

[3] John Lambe, an astrologer indicted for practicing "execrable arts" and protected by Buckingham; he was killed in 1628 by a mob of apprentices who denounced him as "the duke's devil."

Court Satire

Written by and for the members of London's fashionable society, Restoration court satires (contemporaries also used the terms "libels" and "lampoons") targeted the celebrities of the day—court personalities, political, literary, and theatrical figures. Like much coterie poetry of the seventeenth century, these poems customarily circulated in manuscript, passed around first on single sheets of paper and then subsequently copied into manuscript compilations. Most of these satires (hundreds survive of the thousands that were likely written) were not printed at the time. Most also were circulated without an author's name: in addition to the possibility that some courtier might decide to defend his honour by sword or hired thug, a poet could be sued for libel or charged under acts and proclamations that prohibited the circulation of manuscript political poems. While many Restoration satires do have authors' names attached to them in manuscript or print compilations, these attributions are frequently suspect.

The final five or six years of the reign of Charles II were the heyday for personal, as opposed to political, satire. The following anonymous satire on the ladies of the court appeared in the spring of 1682.

৩৩৩

Satire

This way of writing I observed by some
Is introduced by an exordium, [1]
But I will leave to make all that ado,
And in plain English tell you who fucks who.

5 Grafton sets up for ogling and smart answers,
And lies with all her witty set of dancers; [2]
Her crop-eared lord, who is so brisk and airy,
Is managed by the Countess of Orrery. [3]

Lumley has Fox with nose as red as cherry,
10 And when they are alone, they are so merry! [4]

His younger brother, who's so famed for nonsense,
Has fucked, or will fuck, Williams, on my
        conscience. [5]

Poor Nelly all this while has ne'er a runion,
But folks complain that her breath stinks of onion.
15 Though she exposed her poor defunct Sir Carr,
She'd now be glad o'th' brother of Dunbar. [6]

Grey's wife has been so long kept out of town,
I fear she'll lose her so well gained renown;
'Tis a long time since she has had her arse filled,
20 Her husband is so frighted with this Sarsfield. [7]

Arundel, who is in lechery so knowing,
Finding that the earl's other eye was going,

---

[1] *exordium* introductory part, preamble (*OED*); satires ("this way of writing") were often prefaced with high-minded announcements of the poet's reformatory intentions.

[2] *Grafton* Isabella Bennet, Duchess of Grafton; married when still a child (she was still only fifteen the year this poem was written) to Henry Fitzroy, Duke of Grafton, the illegitimate son of Charles II and Barbara Villiers.

[3] *Orrery* Mary Boyle, Countess of Orrery, wife of Richard Boyle, statesman, soldier, and dramatist.

[4] *Lumley* Richard Lumley, at the time Baron Lumley and later first Earl of Scarborough; *Fox* Elizabeth Fox, wife of Charles Fox, Paymaster General of the army.

[5] *younger brother* Henry Lumley, wit and soldier; *Williams* Susannah, Lady Williams, widow of Sir John Williams.

[6] *Nelly* Nell Gwyn (1650–1687), actress and mistress of Charles II; she had dismissed the attentions of Sir Carr Scrope in 1678. William Constable, younger brother of Robert, Viscount Dunbar, was a notorious womaniser—the poet is implying desperation on Gwyn's part; *runion* penis.

[7] *Grey's wife* Mary Berkeley, wife of Ford Grey, Baron Grey of Werke, Whig politician; Captain Patrick Sarsfield challenged Grey to a duel for making an anti-Irish joke; Grey reported the challenge and Sarsfield was taken into custody—but escaped.

Took Hewitt in, who near her cunt did lurk,
On the occasion to fuck journey work,
25 Being told by Mrs. Jennings there's no doubt
That purblind eyes can never be swived out. [1]

Harriet will do the thing whate'er it cost her,
But first intends to get the sneaking Foster. [2]
Kate Villiers, as they say, has got the notion
30 To marry ere she puts her breech in motion. [3]

Vernon, to say the truth, 's a bouncing wench, [4]
She swears and fucks and all the while's so French!
What pity 'tis Wentworth should want a hero.
Oh, Mulgrave, 'twas not done like cavalero
35 To tantalize her with your lobcock tarse,
Then leave her, and but only clap her arse. [5]

Monmouth since Felton's dead is yet in doubt
On whom he shall bestow his single bout. [6]

Jack Gibbons says that Lansdown is the fittest, [7]
40 But Armstrong swears that Lawson is the prettiest,
Who, under the pretense to cure her cough,
Is roaring drunk each night with usquebaugh. [8]

To speak of Scarsdale is but loss of paper;
She's called a stinking whore in every satire; [9]
45 And all the writers have as far as able
Described the lewdness of Hyde's basset table. [10]

Dy tells her Aubrey, believe't who can, [11]
That woman may conceive without a man;
But when alone she gives her lust no check,
50 And Sidney 'tis must get the Lord Bulbeck.

Ogle's returned and will consider further
Who next she'll show her arse to for a murder. [12]
I'll say no more, but only this one thing:
All living creatures fuck, except the King.
—1682

---

[1] *Arundel* Mary Mordaunt, Countess of Arundel; her one-eyed lover was Charles Talbot, Earl of Shrewsbury; his replacement was Sir George ("Beau") Hewitt; *Mrs. Jennings* Frances Jennings, organizer and abetter of court amours.

[2] *Harriet* Lady Henrietta Berkeley, Lord Grey's sister-in-law and mistress. She ran away from home in August 1682, reportedly to marry a man named Forrester.

[3] *ere she puts her breech in motion* before she gave birth. Katherine Villiers was a maid of honour to the Queen.

[4] *Vernon* Mary Kirke, wife of Sir Thomas Vernon. In the mid-1670s, she appears to have been mistress simultaneously to the Duke of York, the Duke of Monmouth, and the Earl of Mulgrave, and had fled to a nunnery in France after a duel was fought over her. She married Vernon, a man twice her age, in Paris in 1677.

[5] *Wentworth* Lady Henrietta Wentworth, maid of honour to the Duchess of York; *Mulgrave* John Sheffield, third Earl of Mulgrave, later first Duke of Buckingham and Normandy, soldier, politician, and writer, patron of Dryden and friend of Pope; *lobcock tarse* a large penis.

[6] *Monmouth* James Scott, Duke of Monmouth and Buccleuch, illegitimate son of Charles II, executed in 1685 for claiming succession to the throne; Lady Betty Felton died in 1681.

[7] *Gibbons* John Gibbons, a gentleman in the service of the Duke of Monmouth; *Lansdowne* Martha Osborne, wife of Charles Granville, Lord Lansdowne.

[8] *Armstrong* Sir Thomas Armstrong, friend of the Duke of Monmouth; *Lawson* probably Elizabeth Lawson, daughter of Sir John Lawson and rumoured to be an aspirant for the post of royal mistress; *usquebaugh* Irish whiskey.

[9] *Scarsdale* Mary Lewis, wife of Robert Leke, Earl of Scarsdale; another manuscript satire from about 1682 features the "famous Scarsdale."

[10] *Hyde* Henrietta Boyle, wife of Lawrence Hyde, son of Clarendon and later made first Earl of Rochester; *basset* a complicated card game, often played for very high stakes.

[11] *Dy* Diana Kirke, wife of Aubrey de Vere, Earl of Oxford; *Sidney* Henry Sidney, son of Robert Sidney, Earl of Leicester. Bulbeck was a barony in the Vere family: the implication is that the Earl's wife has given Sidney the responsibility for begetting an Oxford heir.

[12] *Ogle* Lady Elizabeth Percy (1667–1722), sole heiress to the last Earl of Northumberland, widow (at the age of thirteen) of Henry Cavendish, Earl of Ogle; she married Thomas Thynne in 1681 but fled to Holland before the marriage was consummated. Thynne was murdered by agents employed by a rival suitor in February 1682, and rumours of her complicity persisted for years.

Index of First Lines

Index of Authors and Titles